THE **OFFICIAL**®

STAMP
COLLECTOR'S
BIBLE

STEPHEN R. DATZ

HOUSE OF COLLECTIBLES
THE CROWN PUBLISHING GROUP
NEW YORK

Important Notice: All of the information, including valuations, in this book has been compiled from the most reliable sources, and every effort has been made to eliminate errors and questionable data. Nevertheless, the possibility of error, in a work of such immense scope, always exists. The publisher will not be held responsible for losses that may occur in the purchase, sale, or other transaction of items because of information contained herein. Readers who feel they have discovered errors are invited to *write* and inform us, so they may be corrected in subsequent editions. Those seeking further information on the topics covered in this book are advised to refer to the complete line of *Official Price Guides* published by the House of Collectibles.

HOUSE OF COLLECTIBLES   House of Collectibles is a registered trademark and the colophon is a trademark of Random House, Inc.

Published by House of Collectibles
The Crown Publishing Group
New York, NY

Distributed by the Crown Publishing Group, a division of Random House Inc., New York, and simultaneously in Canada by Random House of Canada Limited, Toronto.

www.houseofcollectibles.com

Printed in the United States of America

ISBN 0-609-80884-2

10 9 8 7 6 5 4 3 2 1

First Edition

ACKNOWLEDGMENTS

I **OWE A DEBT** of gratitude to Louella B. Waldner, Charles Conrad, and James B. Peterson, without whose generosity, enthusiasm, and encouragement philately would never have been so enjoyable and rewarding for me. Special and sincere thanks to publisher Dorothy Harris, without whose unfailing encouragement and guidance this book would never have been a reality. Thanks to Dan Foster, managing editor, and Danielle Foster, book designer and compositor, for their talent and vision in crafting the final draft into an elegant finished product. My appreciation also to assistant editor Roger Generazzo, who is a pleasure to work with. Thanks also to Ken Beiner for his unfailing generosity in furnishing countless stamps and covers, often on short notice, used for illustrations. I am grateful to Cecilia Wertheimer of the Bureau of Engraving and Printing for her kind assistance in researching and making available photographs of stamp printing equipment. Space does not permit individual acknowledgment of the hundreds of private individuals and foreign postal personnel who took the time to respond to requests for information about their organizations. Their courtesy and promptness are appreciated. Last, but not least, thanks to my wife, Susan, for her suggestions and, most of all, her patience during the long months it took to put this book together.

CONTENTS

FOREWORD

WHEN, AS A youngster of 10, I purchased my first packet of stamps for a dime, I didn't know that stamp collecting was the oldest organized hobby in the world, or that it claimed to be the world's largest hobby, or that stamps themselves were a by-product of a revolution in the way fees for the transmission of letters were collected. I bought the packet because the colorful stamps inside fascinated me.

I lived in a small town in rural Colorado in those days, at a time when small towns in the West were, for the most part, blissfully isolated from the outside world. TV had not yet arrived, and aside from ag reports—market prices of beef, corn, and wheat—on Denver radio, no one paid much attention to the goings-on in the larger world.

I discovered the stamp packet, together with a few dozen other packets, tucked away in the toy-and-hobby aisle of the local drugstore-cum-variety store on a shelf stocked with water pistols, toy cars, and model airplanes. It was late summer and I was bored. I pedaled the half dozen blocks to town with a quarter in my pocket, hoping to turn it into something fun at the drugstore. Unfortunately, the toy shelf was just about played out. I already owned several water pistols. I'd built most of the models, at least the ones that interested me. I'd read the latest *Superman*, *Captain Marvel*, and *Strange Tales*. My attention turned once again to the stamp packets. I'd thumbed through them before. I had always found them colorful and intriguing but never had been quite sure what one did with stamps, and, therefore, never bought a packet.

I thumbed through them again that day, arranging them in the order I found most appealing—butterfly stamps, triangle stamps, stamps featuring dogs, and so forth. The more I looked at them, the more I liked them. I didn't know exactly why. Perhaps it was the bright colors or the subjects or the notion of order—the sense of series, grouping, and arrangement. Or perhaps all of those elements. In any case, after a few minutes, I took the butterfly stamps along with a packet of triangle stamps up to the cash register and plunked them, together with a quarter, on the glass countertop.

I opened the packets when I got home and examined my new treasures carefully—again and again—the way a child does, with a mixture of awe and reverence and pleasure. They were exquisite. An album soon followed, a slim affair with spaces for the most common stamps, the kind that come in the packets. It cost a dollar, purchased with money earned mowing lawns. The going rate was a buck a lawn in those days. Before long, armed with some stamp hinges, the slim album, and half a dozen packets of stamps, I became a philatelist. And that was only the beginning.

The incredible thing about stamps is the way in which they broaden one's horizons. My history teacher was amazed when I knew where Bosnia and Herzegovina were, and that together with Serbia, they became part of Yugoslavia following World War I. I knew where Pitcairn Island was long before I ever heard of *Mutiny on the Bounty*. And where Borneo, Sarawak, Bechuanaland, and dozens of other equally far-off and exotic places were. I knew who Louis Pasteur, Copernicus, Edward VII, and Karl Marx were. I knew who William H. Seward was and that he had been instrumental in America's purchase of Alaska. I knew about the founding of Jamestown, and the Pilgrims, and the Huguenots and Walloons. I knew about General Burgoyne and where George Rogers Clark came from. I gained a broad knowledge of the outside world from stamps. I learned that you can get a pretty good idea of what is important to a nation's culture and history by what it chooses to depict on its postage stamps.

As it turned out, stamps would take me on an amazing odyssey. I put them aside when it came time for college. I earned a degree in business administration, married, and began a family. Soon thereafter, stamps once again entered my life. This time as a career, albeit almost by accident. I discovered that as much money could be made buying and selling stamps as working a traditional nine-to-five job. Before long, I was in the stamp business full time. I opened a shop and later an office in Denver. Over the years, I traveled the country buying collections and attending stamp shows. I even staged a few stamp shows of my own. For a time, I held public stamp auctions. And I wrote books. Books about stamps and my experiences in the stamp trade. Stamps bought our home and furnished it, put cars in the garage, allowed us to take family vacations, and eventually put two sons through college.

Stamps have been an integral part of my life for nearly as long as I can remember and enriched it in myriad ways. The purpose of this book is to share some of the knowledge and insights I've gained during nearly five decades of involvement with the hobby. No single volume could come anywhere close to covering all there is to know about stamp collecting, so I've tried to cover the basics, to include information of use to both the novice and the more experienced collector.

I thought the most logical place to start was with the history of mail itself, which eventually necessitated the invention and use of postage stamps. And from there to explore the mind-expanding possibilities of these small works of art. For those new to the hobby, I have included a few introductory chapters, supplemented by chapters on conservation, fakery, faults, and repairs.

I have devoted a chapter to errors on stamps, a subject that has fascinated me for nearly as long as I can remember, and which ends up fascinating most collectors. Errors are odd and often striking in appearance, rarely encountered, and generally worth a considerable amount of money. The famous inverted Jenny airmail is a good example, cataloguing more than $150,000. Every collector dreams of finding an elusive rarity.

I've touched on buying, selling, and investing. Sooner or later, nearly every collector seems to accumulate extra stamps they'd like to turn into cash. I've also tried to provide a glimpse into how stamps are created, from subject selection to production. And no account would be complete without mention of the Universal Postal Union, the oldest and most successful international cooperative effort in history.

Stamp identification frequently proves thorny for both novice and experienced collector alike. I have included an illustrated guide to some of the most frequently encountered difficult-to-identify foreign stamps, as well as a comprehensive inscription identifier. A chapter on foreign terms on postage stamps augments the identifier, as do the foreign philatelic vocabulary and color guide. A glossary of philatelic terms, many accompanied by illustrations, defines the myriad specialized terms that are the lingua franca of the hobby.

The volume is rounded out with chapters listing worldwide philatelic agencies, philatelic societies and clubs, stamp catalogues (both U.S. and foreign), philatelic reference books and periodicals, and a resource section.

Taken together, all should enhance your enjoyment and appreciation of the hobby. It is my hope that you will enjoy stamps and stamp collecting as much as I have.

A BRIEF HISTORY OF MAIL

IF **YOU GO** all the way back to the beginning, there wasn't much in the way of communication—some vocalizations, some gestures, some facial expressions. Over time rudimentary vocalizations gradually evolved into language, an inventory of words to express what was in our minds.

Sometime after the arrival of language came writing, the recording of information in physical form. Among the earliest examples of recorded information are images painted on cave walls dating back about 30,000 years. Of the same approximate age are pieces of ivory and bone with marks etched into them. One contains a series of 29 marks, perhaps phases of the moon recorded by one of our Cro-Magnon predecessors. Even if not representing phases of the moon, the marks are almost certainly counting marks—not yet words, but still the representation of an idea preserved in physical form. Throughout prehistory similar objects, objects containing counting marks or whose purpose it was to count, show up again and again.

Cuneiform writing (left); hieroglyphic writing (right).

Cuneiform is perhaps the earliest form of what we might today recognize as writing. It arose about 3000 B.C. in the region known as Mesopotamia (present-day Iraq). Cuneiform utilized a system of wedge-shaped strokes impressed on tablets of clay. Scribes used a tool known as a stylus to impress the marks. The cuneiform system did not use an alphabet. The marks were, in their earliest form, pictographic in nature, that is, symbols representing objects. Over time the marks took the form of patterns, which represented words rather than objects. Some of the symbols evolved to represent syllables. Eventually, these patterns, or symbols, lost any resemblance to the original pictographs. At its height, the cuneiform system employed about 600 symbols. Egyptian hieroglyphs arose at about the same time as cuneiform writing. They originated as pictographic but over the centuries acquired ideographic and phonetic elements, symbols that represented ideas and spoken sounds. Both the cuneiform and hieroglyphic systems contained a large number of symbols, as do modern Chinese and Japanese systems. By contrast, our Latin alphabet represents individual phonetic sounds (consonants and vowels) and requires only 26 symbols (letters), rather than hundreds, to create writing.

Clay tablets used to record cuneiform were durable but bulky and inconvenient to transport. Ancient Egyptians developed a more lightweight and portable medium, papyrus. Papyrus is made by arranging a series of strips cut lengthwise from the papyrus reed's pithy stem and then adding a second layer crosswise atop it. The arrangement is moistened, pressed, and dried. The adhesive property of the pith bonds the layers together. Once dry, the papyrus is smoothed with a piece of ivory or similar object. Individual sheets of papyrus are then formed into rolls. Egyptians wrote on these rolls, arranging their hieroglyphs in columns, much as we arrange our writing in columns. Although not as durable as clay, papyrus possessed the advantage of portability, an element crucial to the transport of messages of any length or complexity.

Parchment and paper, both of which arrived on the scene somewhat later, likewise possessed the qualities of lightness and portability. Parchment is known from as early as 200 B.C. It is made from animal hides (typically sheep, calf, or goat skin) scraped clean, smoothed, and finished with a pumice rub. The earliest form of paper is attributed to the Chinese, circa the second century A.D. It arrived in Europe via merchants sometime around the eleventh century. We make paper today in much the same fashion that the Chinese made it nearly two millennia ago. Wood (or fabric) is reduced to a pulp, which is poured onto a form that allows the pulp to be shaken into a uniform layer and also allows the water to drain away, leaving a thin layer of fibers. The layer of fibers is turned out onto a cloth, pressed flat and thin, and then dried. Although the modern process is automated, the principle is the same as it was 1,800 years ago.

Symbols representing language and a light, portable medium upon which to record them allowed messages to be written. The evolution of increasingly complex and geographically expansive societies created the means by which messages could be efficiently transmitted—systems of roads. All the ancient empires—Persians, Egyptians, Greeks, and Romans—built and maintained systems of roads.

Although constructed primarily to facilitate the rapid movement of troops, roads also helped support commerce and administer government.

Ancient Persia established one of the best early systems of roads. Nearly 500 years before the birth of Christ, the Greek historian Herodotus wrote of the Persian system, "Nothing mortal travels so fast as the Persian messengers." He noted that along the entire network of roads, men with horses were stationed a day's ride apart, forming a relay system in which dispatches were handed from one rider to the next. He wrote that "these men will not be hindered from accomplishing at their best speed the distance which they have to go, either by snow or rain, or heat, or by darkness of night." Etched in stone above the entrance of the General Post Office in New York appears the motto "Neither snow, nor rain, nor heat, nor gloom of night stays these couriers from the swift completion of their rounds," the creed of modern mail carriers, paraphrased from Herodotus.

Roman messenger on horseback.

Rome created the most extensive network of roads in the ancient world. Roman engineers built roads arrow straight, allowing little to stand in their way. They tunneled through hills and mountains, bridged streams and gorges, connecting city to city. Along these roads, the empire maintained way stations every 5 or 6 miles to house horses. This enabled relay riders to travel 100 miles or more a day. The vast network of roads extended several thousand miles from one end of the empire to the other, each mile along the way marked by a stone post.

Message systems of the early empires were not yet postal systems in the way we think of postal systems, that is, available to the ordinary person. Like its predecessors, the Roman mail was an imperial service used primarily by government. Odd as it might seem today, no formal system existed by which ordinary citizens could send personal communications over any distance. Private individuals were left to their own devices. They relied mostly on travelers, and messages tended to be oral and concise (greetings, news of family, of births and deaths, and of health, and perhaps requests for assistance), so as not to tax the messenger's memory and because in early societies, few were literate.

By the Renaissance, merchants and tradesmen had begun to set up networks utilizing their own couriers. Universities and monasteries also employed messengers who traveled from place to place, often along a circuit, picking up and dropping off messages. In many cases these services would, for a fee, accept messages from individuals who were not members of their group. This message-carrying activity proved to be highly profitable.

Stamp of Thurn and Taxis.

The profitability of carrying messages inevitably attracted entrepreneurs, most notable among them an Italian family of nobles, the Della Torre e Tasso family, better known in philately under the Germanized form of its name, the House of Thurn and Taxis. The Della Torre e Tasso family established a courier service in Italy and later in Germany. Beginning in 1450, Roger Della Torre e Tasso organized a postal service for Frederick the Great, emperor of the Holy Roman Empire, to serve all its imperial possessions in central Europe. Roger's son Francesco (Franz), under a grant of imperial privilege from Emperor Maximilian I in 1516, expanded the area served. The routes extended from Vienna to Brussels, from Brussels to France and Spain, and from Vienna to all the Italian States. During the following century, the family increased its routes and by 1615 had become hereditary postmasters general of the Holy Roman Empire. For their services, they were, in 1695, made princes of the Holy Roman Empire.

Initially, and like its imperial predecessors, the system created by the House of Thurn and Taxis primarily served the needs of administrators of the empire. But early in the sixteenth century, when the imperial treasury found itself unable to pay their stipend, the House of Thurn and Taxis was permitted to accept messages from private citizens, for which they charged fixed fees, fees that today we would call *postage*. Thus was born the first true postal system available to the ordinary individual.

Toward the end of the eighteenth century, the Holy Roman Empire began to disintegrate. Its disintegration, in turn, eroded the postal routes of Thurn and Taxis. At the same time, individual countries began to establish their own postal services, although not necessarily to the complete exclusion of Thurn and Taxis. Still, the trend toward nationally operated systems continued until 1867, when the kingdom of Prussia absorbed what remained of the postal service of Thurn and Taxis.

For its postal routes, buildings, and equipment, Thurn and Taxis received an indemnity of 3 million thalers from the kingdom of Prussia, a fabulous sum at the time. The family enterprise, which had flourished for more than 400 years, had made the Della Torre e Tasso family enormously wealthy.

While the princes of Thurn and Taxis were busy transporting mail throughout Europe, other postal entrepreneurs had less ambitious goals. In 1653 an innovative fellow by the name of Jacques Renouard de Villayer organized a *petit post* in Paris under a royal grant from King Louis XIV. Villayer came up with the novel idea of selling prepaid wrappers to enclose letters, which could then be dropped in collection boxes situated throughout the city. Couriers emptied the boxes three times a day. They took the mail to a central sorting office where the wrappers were removed and the letters dispatched for delivery. Promising as it first seemed, the venture ultimately failed. Parisians, it seems, found the boxes convenient as trash receptacles, and rats, it is reported, found them dry and snug—and perhaps found the letters tasty.

At about the same time, a man named Henry Bishop came up with the idea of marking mail with a circular handstamp that contained the day and month of mailing. Bishop served as master of posts for Charles II of England. *Bishop marks*, as they are known, were applied to mail at the time it was posted in order to prevent postal employees along the way from detaining it, as often happened. And thus was born the postmark.

In Bishop's time, letters were written on sheets of paper, which were then folded and sealed with molten wax. Envelopes had not yet been invented and would not come into general use until well into the nineteenth century. Today the philatelic term for an envelope is *cover*, from its original function to enclose, or cover, a letter.

Not all seventeenth-century Britons used the government postal service. Many residents of London sent letters by private messenger or by servant to addresses located within the city. Labor was cheap, and those who were well-enough educated to write letters usually employed servants or could afford to hire a messenger. It is difficult to imagine, but in those days houses did not have address numbers. Servants or messengers unfamiliar with a recipient's neighborhood found it hard to make deliveries. (Interestingly, and in a similar vein, addresses using rural route box numbers here in the United States were recently assigned road name and number combinations because 911 emergency services found it difficult to locate them by their postal route box designations.)

Folded letter sealed with wax.

In 1680 William Dockwra, a London merchant, and Robert Murray, an upholsterer, established the London Penny Post—and in a big way. They saturated the London area with 450 receiving offices. Mail was processed at 7 sorting offices, and the penny fee included delivery from any part of London directly to a recipient's door in any other part of the city. Astonishingly, at least by today's standards, letters were supposed to be delivered within one hour of receipt. To evidence that letters were expeditiously handled, they were postmarked with the exact time of mailing as well as the date. The Penny Post became an instant success and in no time employed more workers than the government-run General Post Office, whose payroll included only 316 employees in all of Great Britain.

Ironically, the Penny Post turned out to be too successful. As was the custom in those days, revenues from government enterprises often went as perquisites

Eighteenth-century postal carrier (left);
eighteenth-century post rider (right).

either to the royal family or to royal favorites. The Penny Post cut into these revenues. As one can imagine, the royals were not pleased, so in 1682 the government absorbed the Penny Post. The government continued to operate it as a penny post until 1801, when the fee was raised to 2 pence. In 1840, at the time the first postage stamp was introduced, the fee was reduced once again to a penny. In 1855 the Penny Post was discontinued as a separate service and incorporated into the General Post Office as the London District Post.

Penny posts operated in numerous cities, but sending letters any distance remained costly. A separate fee existed for each destination. Postage was based on the distance a letter had to travel, the number of sheets it contained, and a variety of possible surcharges. The high cost of overland postage inevitably encouraged cheating. At the time, it was customary for the recipient of a letter to pay the postage. One of the most common schemes to avoid paying postage involved coding the address. "E. H. Parsons" might mean one thing, "Edward H. Parsons" another, and "Edward Parsons" yet another. Simple messages such as "everyone's fine" could thus be detected at a glance by the recipient, and the letter refused, depriving the post office of its fee. Another ruse involved batching. Letters originating in outlying areas were sometimes batched and carried by traveler to London, where they could be posted in the much cheaper Penny Post.

Despite the chicanery, the mails continued to be highly profitable. Unfortunately, profitable as they were, they remained prohibitively expensive for the consumer. The way in which fees were calculated remained complex and confusing not just in Great Britain but throughout Europe as well. Each jurisdiction had its own rules and rates. In addition to weight and distance, extra fees were often imposed based on the number of post offices through which a letter had to pass. Posting a letter almost always entailed presenting it in person at a post office so that the fees could be calculated.

Creation of the postage stamp was actually the by-product of a proposal to reform the British postal system that Sir Rowland Hill outlined in an 1837 treatise entitled *Post Office Reform: Its Importance and Practicability*. By the 1830s, it became clear that the British postal system was not keeping pace with the needs of a growing population and a burgeoning economy. Innovations in practical technology, such as the railroad and steam-powered manufacturing, had begun to foster an emigration from farms to urban manufacturing centers. Demand for communications services increased as well, driven by the needs of both individuals and commercial enterprises. Economic expansion relied on—indeed, was not possible without—the ability to communicate efficiently and economically. The high cost of postage inhibited that ability to the point where it had begun to be a drag on the British economy. The General Post Office, with its complex and costly method of calculating rates, was clearly out of date.

Sir Rowland Hill and the Penny Black.

Among the reforms Hill suggested was the mandatory prepayment of postage, by use of either a stamped envelope or a small piece of paper that could be affixed to a letter at the time of mailing to evidence payment of postage. Hill also recommended establishing a uniform rate structure, a single fee for a letter sent anywhere in the country, and no charge for extra sheets.

Sensible as they may seem today, Hill's proposals, such as the mandatory prepayment of postage, were considered radical. At the time, postal patrons had the option of prepaying a letter (in which case the postmaster marked the letter "paid" by pen or handstamp) or sending it collect, which many did. Senders felt that since it was the recipient who benefited from a letter, the recipient should pay for it. If a recipient refused a letter, which often happened, the post office was out the cost of transporting it. Prepayment of postage would eliminate losses arising from the inefficient collect system.

In addition, use of postage stamps would tighten accountability, since postmasters would have to account for every stamp sold. Under the previous system of marking letters "paid" by pen stroke, there was little to prevent a postmaster from pocketing postage.

By far the most controversial of Hill's proposals was the single, uniform rate. He suggested a uniform fee (1 penny) for any letter sent anywhere in the kingdom. He reasoned that a uniform rate structure would reduce paperwork, increase efficiency, and encourage people to send more letters. In practice this meant slashing the cost of mailing a letter from an average cost of 9 pence to 1 penny— an 89 percent reduction! Imagine the reaction of the postal bureaucracy today if someone suggested lowering rates to 11 percent of current levels.

The British postal establishment was aghast. Hill's proposals, they insisted, were sheer lunacy, and Hill, surely a madman. They ridiculed him personally and warned that if implemented, his preposterous scheme would lead to the bankruptcy and utter ruination of the postal system. Not everyone, however, greeted the proposed reforms with scorn. Hill found powerful allies in the business community and the press. He refuted the postmaster general's assertion that rate reductions would bankrupt the post office by pointing out the effect tax reduction had had on coffee and tea consumption. Consumption rose so much that tax revenues actually increased.

In the end, Hill's view prevailed, and to the amazement of skeptics, it worked. The volume of mail increased steadily, and the postal system did not collapse as predicted. Hill, the much maligned rogue, turned out to be a brilliant visionary. Queen Victoria knighted Hill for his contribution to creating the modern postal system. Philatelists around the world remember Sir Rowland Hill not for creating the modern postal system, but for inventing the postage stamp.

The medal by William Wyon that inspired the Penny Black (left); the Penny Black (right).

The world's first postage stamp made its debut in May 1840. Printed in black, it became known as the *Penny Black*. It was a simple affair, an engraved profile of the young Queen Victoria together with the words "Postage" and "One Penny." The Penny Black was designed by William Corbould, inspired by a bust of Victoria that appeared on a medal created earlier by William Wyon. Millions of Penny Blacks were sold during the next few years, and many survive. Despite their age, they are still quite affordable and within the reach of any collector who wants to own one.

Benjamin Franklin is regarded as the first postmaster general of the United States, or at least what would become the United States. In 1775, with the American Revolution just under way, the Continental Congress voted to establish its own postal system and selected Franklin to head it. In 1789 Congress formally established the U.S. Postal Service under authority granted by the U.S. Constitution. At the time, the fledgling Postal Service possessed a mere 75 local offices. The cumulative length of its routes in the 13 original states amounted to only about 1,875 miles. And it suffered from many of the inefficiencies that plagued the British post office, including the confusing hodgepodge of rates based loosely on distance and weight, a condition that would persist until the middle of the nineteenth century.

In 1845 Congress, following Britain's lead, established uniform postal rates for the United States. Letters traveling less than 300 miles would cost 5¢ per 1/2 ounce; those traveling farther than 300 miles would cost 10¢ per 1/2 ounce. In 1847 the United States issued its first postage stamps, although prior to that time

The first U.S. postage stamps, 1847.

several postmasters had issued provisionals as the success of the Penny Black became known.

The groundbreaking postal reforms of the early 1840s set in motion a period of improvement and innovation that would continue throughout the second half of the nineteenth century. Many of the services we take for granted today were inaugurated during that time. In 1855 the Postal Service introduced registered mail service, permitting the secure transmittal of letters containing valuables such as stocks and bonds. Letter boxes (mailboxes) were introduced in 1858. Until that time, letters had to be posted at post offices, whether in person or by messenger. In 1863 the Postal Service introduced free mail delivery. It may seem odd now, but before free mail delivery, recipients were expected to pick up their mail at the post office. Delivery was deemed to be a premium service for which an additional fee applied.

By the middle of the nineteenth century, local mail service was very good, even by today's standards. Sending mail over any distance, however, was inexorably slow and costly, especially from the East to the frontier or to the West Coast. The transcontinental railroad had not yet been built. Letters had to be carried overland, usually by freight companies or by stagecoach, or by sea around Cape Horn at the tip of South America, or by rail across the Isthmus of Panama and then once again by ship to their destination. It took a minimum of three weeks—and more often, months—for correspondence to cross the continent.

The Overland Mail, ca. 1858 (left); Pony Express rider (right).

In 1860 the Central Overland California and Pike's Peak Express Company established the Pony Express, which offered expedited mail service between Saint Joseph, Missouri, and Sacramento, California. The Pony Express advertised for "Young, skinny, wiry fellows not over 18. Must be expert riders willing to risk death daily. Orphans preferred. Wages $25 per week." Among those who signed up was 15-year-old William F. Cody, later known as Buffalo Bill. The Pony Express route extended west nearly 2,000 miles across Missouri, Nebraska, Wyoming, Utah, northern Nevada, and California, terminating at Sacramento, along a path similar to that which Interstate 80 follows today.

The Pony Express maintained 100 relay stations, employed 80 riders, and stabled between 400 and 500 horses. Youthful riders galloped from relay station to relay station, which were located about 25 miles apart, mounting a fresh horse at each one, much like post riders in ancient times. Mail was secured in specially designed saddlebags that could be transferred from one horse to another as quickly as a rider could dismount and remount. Each rider was expected to cover 75 miles per day. Even at a gallop, it took 10 days to complete the journey from Saint Joseph to Sacramento. And the service was costly—$5 for a letter up to 1/2 ounce. Proportionately lower rates applied for intermediate destinations along the route.

Despite hefty fees, the Pony Express never really made money. It lasted little more than 18 months, its demise brought about by the completion of the first transcontinental telegraph in October 1861. When the dust had cleared, its founders, William H. Russell, William B. Waddell, and Alexander Majors, found themselves bankrupted by the venture. Still, the Pony Express endures in the popular imagination, part of the legend of the great American West.

Interestingly, today private express companies such Federal Express and Airborne flourish. Most use airbills rather than stamps, although in the early 1980s one short-lived venture, Western Airletter, contemplated the use of service indicators to evidence prepayment of fees and thus eliminate the paperwork involved in airbills. Like the Pony Express, it didn't last long.

Special delivery stamp (left); parcel post stamp (right).

Postal innovation continued throughout the nineteenth and early twentieth centuries. In 1893 the post office began offering special delivery service. In 1896 the Postal Service established rural free delivery. Before rural free delivery, rural patrons had to pick up their mail at a post office, usually in the nearest town. The parcel post system, a service we take for granted today, began operation in the United States in 1913. To publicize it and to keep track of revenues generated by it, the Postal Service issued an attractive set of large stamps featuring the latest modes of transportation and contemporary scenes.

The famous inverted Jenny error (left); Pan Am Clipper, ca. 1930s (right).

In 1918 the Postal Service established the first regular airmail route, which provided service between New York and Washington, D.C. To promote the new service, the Postal Service issued three stamps (8¢, 16¢, and 24¢ denominations) featuring a Curtiss Jenny. The 24¢ value was printed in two colors, red and blue, applied in separate passes through the printing press. When one of the sheets inadvertently passed through the press rotated 180 degrees during the application of its second color, one of the world's most famous and valuable errors was created, the inverted Jenny.

The first regular transcontinental airmail route was inaugurated in 1921, providing service between New York City and San Francisco. Aviation infrastructure (radar, air traffic control, satellite weather data) as we know it today did not exist. Pilots used railroad tracks, roads, and other landmarks to navigate. Pilots, many of them youthful barnstormers, flew mail in open-cockpit biplanes. They flew only during daylight hours. Day-and-night flights would not begin until 1924. Crashes and delays were common. In fact, more airmail pilots lost their lives than did Pony Express riders.

Regular scheduled airmail service between the United States and the Philippines commenced in 1935 utilizing Pan Am clippers. Prior to 1935, dirigibles, such as the *Graf Zeppelin* and the *Hindenburg*, were the only aircraft capable of transoceanic crossings. The *Graf Zeppelin* periodically carried mail to America but did not offer regularly scheduled service. Regular airmail service between America and Europe began in 1939, again using Pan Am clippers. The first route connected New York City and Marseille, France.

For the better part of six decades, airmail remained a premium service. By the mid-1970s, however, most first-class mail was routinely transported by air. As a result, in 1977 the Postal Service discontinued airmail as a separate domestic service. Today virtually all first-class mail traveling any distance is transported by air. Airmail still exists as a separate class of service to foreign destinations.

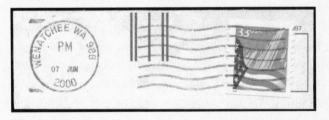

FIM marking.

Beginning in the early 1960s, the Postal Service turned to automation to keep up with the increasing volume of mail. Until the 1960s, each piece of mail was sorted by hand, and each address, read by human eye. As a result of four decades of progress in automation, letters are now sorted and sent on their way by machines, almost never touched or seen by humans until they reach the hands of the route carrier. Modern stamps are coated with (or printed on paper impregnated with) invisible tagging that can be detected by scanners sensitive to the ultraviolet portion of the spectrum. In this fashion, letters are faced (oriented with stamp side out and the stamp in the upper-right corner), addresses read by optical scanning equipment, and a bar code imprinted to facilitate mechanical sorting and routing. Nearly every piece of mail you receive contains a bar code either as part of a printed address or near the bottom of the envelope. Remittance envelopes and business reply envelopes and cards contain facing identification marks (FIMs). FIMs consist of five or six black vertical bars printed near the upper-right corner to the left of the area reserved for postage. FIMs, too, allow envelopes to be faced by automated equipment. Thrifty individuals who use reply envelopes to send correspondence to other than the intended recipient may be surprised to learn that sorting equipment is blind to a written address if a bar code is present. The letter will end up at the utility company or charge card company if the bar code near the bottom of the envelope is not covered or obliterated.

U.S. Postal Service
logo, 1971.

In July 1971, the Postal Reorganization Act of 1970 took effect, and the old Post Office Department became the new U.S. Postal Service. Ostensibly, the rationale behind the reorganization was to remove politics from postal management. Traditionally, the postmaster general was a cabinet-level appointee who served at the pleasure of the president. Postmasters all across the land, too, were appointees, often landing their job as a reward for political support. Perhaps a more pressing motive was Congress's desire to distance itself from burgeoning postal deficits and the politically unpleasant consequences of having to deal with them. In any case, the stated goals and benefits of the postal reorganization were to provide adequate financing authority; establish a postal career service, which would allow collective bargaining between management and employees; and create an independent commission for setting postal rates.

The Postal Service had, for much of its life, been subsidized by Congress, a practice traditionally supported by the view that it was a public necessity of universal benefit—vital to commerce, prosperity, and the well-being of society. By the 1960s, that view began to change. Congress, embarrassed by rising deficits, cut itself loose with the Postal Reorganization Act and put an end to the postal subsidy. Without the subsidy, the cost of postage has continued to rise, driven by the Postal Service's two largest expenses: labor and the cost of fuel. And although the reorganization was meant to depoliticize the service, governors of the postal rate commission, nevertheless, find themselves subject to intense lobbying by large and well-financed bulk mailers, most notably the direct mail industry and periodical publishers.

Still, postage is a bargain. For less than the cost of almost any product, you can send a card or letter across town or across the country, and it usually arrives within a few days. And the colorful bits of paper we use to evidence the payment of postage continue to fascinate us and teach us.

CHAPTER

2

THE WORLD ON STAMPS

EVERYTHING, IT SEEMS, about our world has appeared on postage stamps, from a time before our kind walked the earth to our humble beginning and from those beginnings to our first tentative reach for the stars—and everything one can imagine in between.

Stegosaurus; cave painting, Lascaux, France; astronaut on a space walk.

Stamps parade before us the animals of the world and its fish, birds, and insects.

Spotted hyena; pike; Harlequin duck; Red cicada

Stamps take us to far-off lands and exotic places, revealing landscapes new to our eyes and scenes as familiar as Main Street.

Native Woman, Tahiti; Himalayan Peaks and Glacier; French Foreign Legionnaire; Main Street, western Canada.

They remind us of the familiar, of romance and family, of the things dear and close to the human heart.

Cupid and bow; a stolen kiss; mother and child.

Stamps depict and honor important men and women, pioneers in many fields, individuals who, often against long odds, attain goals that fascinate and inspire us.

Marie Curie; Albert Einstein.

Stamps, too, touch on men of war, on patriots and despots, on battle, on victory and defeat, and on the triumphs and tragedies of the human spirit.

Franklin D. Roosevelt; Adolf Hitler and Benito Mussolini; Winston Churchill.

Women Support the War Effort, World War II; U.S. Marines atop Mount Suribachi, Iwo Jima; Anne Frank.

We can almost feel the exhaustion of the distance runner at the finish line, and we almost experience the giddy, ephemeral moment in midflight before the water below rushes swiftly up at the diver, and we can almost hear the crack of the bat as the home run ball flies toward the far stands.

Olympic runner; diver; baseball player.

We find on stamps the portraits of personalities who capture our imagination, the beautiful, the noble and the charismatic men and women who often remain as indelibly etched in our minds as they are etched on the stamps that portray them.

Eva Peron; John F. Kennedy; Princess Grace of Monaco.

Stamps portray likenesses of men and women who entertain us with their words and stimulate our minds with their ideas.

Robert Frost; Ayn Rand; John Steinbeck.

We find, too, images of the daring and courageous souls eager to test the limits and blaze trails into the record books and our popular imagination.

Amelia Earhart; Charles Lindbergh.

Less pleasant images, too, call attention to matters that concern us all, the condition of our environment and the dangers of drugs and self-destruction.

Stop drug abuse;
prevent suicide;
pollution of
the seas.

And somehow stamps always seem to bring us back to the familiar, to the small joys in life, such as the circus clown or a new puppy.

Rural Home Scene,
Grandma Moses; puppy;
circus clown.

Stamps do all these things—and in revealing the pleasant and the unpleasant, the familiar and the unfamiliar, stamps broaden our understanding of the world, its lands, peoples, and diverse cultures, its historical events, and the individual men and women who have shaped it. Images on stamps come to us from all over our wonderful planet unfiltered by journalist or historian, and they speak volumes. This, then, is the world on stamps. There is much to learn and enjoy.

Youthful stamp collector.

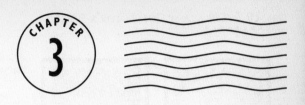

CHAPTER

3

Collecting —
A World of Choices

IN THE EARLY years, stamp collecting meant obtaining a slim album containing spaces for stamps of the world and attempting to fill it. Some collectors used homemade affairs not unlike scrapbooks. Mint stamps were often just licked and stuck to the page. There weren't many stamps in those days. No one knew for sure just how many. Communication across any distance was slow, and information about foreign lands, especially Africa, Asia, and the Pacific, sketchy. Often it was unclear how many authentic jurisdictions existed, let alone which issued stamps. Stamp catalogues did not yet exist. Collectors simply tried to obtain as many different stamps as possible. Much of the thrill lay in discovering something new, something no one else had heard of. Sometimes the discovery arrived on a letter from a faraway place, a letter sent to an acquaintance, or a letter retrieved through the good graces of a friend or contact at a business or missionary service.

The hobby has come a long way since then. We have scores of highly detailed catalogues and thousands of reference works, an abundance of albums and accessories, a wide range of clubs and societies, and communication via the Internet with fellow collectors just about anywhere on the globe. Gone are the slim albums and the single-direction approach to collecting, replaced by myriad possibilities—too many to adequately explore here, although we'll touch on some of the more popular and a few of the peripheral. There's something for every taste and every budget.

MINT OR USED

Newcomers tend to find all stamps appealing, mint and used alike. As they gain experience, most collectors tend to gravitate toward either mint stamps or used stamps. Those who prefer mint stamps feel that a cancellation intrudes on a stamp's design and distracts from its beauty and that soaking a stamp off paper

Mint stamp, (left); used stamp, (right).

diminishes its freshness. Those who prefer used stamps frequently argue that a stamp is not really a stamp until it's gone through the mail, been canceled, and served its intended purpose. You might as well debate which is better, chocolate or vanilla. As a practical matter, country collectors usually obtain mint stamps as far back as they can and then fill in with used stamps. For collectors of U.S. stamps, the dividing line usually falls somewhere between 1890 or 1920.

GENERAL COLLECTING

A generalist collects stamps of all countries of the world. Until about 1940, 1 or 2 albums would accommodate such a collection. Today, however, at least 500,000 different stamps exist, and several thousand new issues appear each year. Between 30 and 40 albums, each 4 to 5 inches thick, are required to accommodate them, and the annual cost just to keep up with new issues typically runs at least $7,500. From a practical standpoint, completing a collection of the world is not possible. For the generalist, however, completion is not what it's about. Generalists enjoy the challenge of acquiring as many different stamps as possible. Although a fair number are costly, tens of thousands are inexpensive. It's possible to build a surprisingly large collection with only a relatively modest outlay. Some generalists approach acquisitions selectively. They work on a country or an album at a time. Others buy in bulk in the form of job lots (large, often disorganized accumulations) and remainders. They search through them, keep what they can use, and then sell or trade the balance.

COUNTRY COLLECTING

Forming a collection devoted to a single country is popular both here and abroad. Collectors tend to collect the stamps of their native land. The British collect British stamps, Russians collect Russian stamps, and Americans collect U.S. stamps. In addition, Americans frequently collect stamps relating to their ethnic heritage, for example, stamps of Great Britain or Germany or Scandinavia. Images of ancestral homelands on stamps invariably evoke a powerful sense of connection. Pondering the images—landscapes, flora and fauna, historical events—puts us in touch with our roots in a way few other tangible objects can.

Czeslaw Slania self-portrait on UN stamp; mail coach engraved by Slania.

TOPICAL COLLECTING

Topical collecting is hugely popular because it's simple and a lot of fun. All one need do is select a topic and begin acquiring stamps. Popular topics include flowers, cats, dogs, animals, birds, Olympic sports, medicine, music, fine art, aircraft, trains, and ships. Rock and roll, film stars, and Walt Disney characters, too, are popular. The list of possible subjects is infinite, limited only by one's imagination.

Some collect according to theme rather than topic. Czeslaw Slania is the world's most prolific stamp engraver and arguably the most talented. He has more than 1,000 stamps to his credit, each superbly engraved and each a miniature masterpiece. He's developed a devoted following who collect just those issues engraved by him.

Some topicalists collect in novel and unorthodox ways, for example, acquiring just those stamps printed in a certain color, such as blue or red, or stamps containing a particular numeral, such as 5 or 10. The notion may sound odd, but the results are often unexpectedly striking.

Some topicalists make their own album pages, either by hand or using computer software. For those who prefer ready-made pages, Washington Press publishes a variety of high-quality pages for topicals under the brand name White Ace. Budding topicalists should check out the American Topical Association (ATA). It is one of the largest philatelic societies in the world. The ATA publishes an excellent journal, the *Topical Time*, in addition to a marvelous variety of useful handbooks, each devoted to a specific topic. Refer to Chapter 31, "Philatelic Societies and Clubs."

POSTAL HISTORY

In the strict technical sense, postal history refers to the study and collection of stamps, covers, or other materials relating to the operation or evolution of a postal system or an element of a postal system. The term, however, is frequently used more loosely, most often to refer to a cover of historical significance or interest (e.g., a piece of concentration camp mail).

The possibilities for postal history collecting are limitless, the choices often esoteric (e.g., Army Post Office service during the Vietnam War, French mail service in treaty ports in China, or the evolution of modern express mail). The undertaking can be as expensive or inexpensive as one chooses to make it.

A postal history collector could unravel the meaning of the various markings on this cover.

It is not uncommon to see valuable and remarkable postal history collections assembled from seemingly unremarkable parts. Finding unrecognized treasures is part of the appeal of postal history. Postal history collectors are fond of telling about the valuable covers found in dealers' bargain boxes, covers passed over because no one recognized their significance. Knowledge derived from study and research makes such finds possible. Every cover, it seems, has a story to tell, if one only takes the time to discover it.

COLLECTING U.S. STAMPS

Collectors of U.S. stamps typically approach the hobby in one of several ways: acquiring general issues, plate blocks, plate number coils, first day covers, or specializing in an individual stamp or series.

GENERAL U.S. COLLECTING

One of the most popular ways to collect U.S. stamps is to begin with current issues and work backward. It's prohibitively expensive to form a complete collection of U.S. stamps, so in most cases, collectors narrow their focus. Some attempt completion back to 1900 and fill spaces for nineteenth-century stamps only if they happen across them and only then if they're not too expensive. Others collect mint stamps back to a threshold date, typically between 1890 and 1920, and then fill in with used stamps, which are generally much less expensive. Still others set a dollar threshold, such as $50 or $100, and work back as far as they can go, bypassing more costly items.

A word of advice: Avoid the temptation to overbuy new issues. Newcomers, especially, tend to purchase unneeded duplicates. Your collecting dollar will go much farther if you limit purchases of new issues to those necessary for your collection. Your collecting dollar will also go farther if you choose to collect singles rather than blocks or multiples.

PLATE BLOCKS

For security purposes, a serial number is assigned to and entered on each plate used to print U.S. stamps, and a record is kept of every impression made from it. That number (or numbers, where multiple plates are used to print a stamp) usually appears in the selvage of the finished pane. A block containing the number or numbers is known as a *plate block*.

Plate blocks vary in size. The correct collectible size and configuration depends on the number of plate numbers, their location, and in the case of se-tenant stamps, the number of stamps required to make a block. Correct collectible size and configuration are important because plate blocks are worth more, often considerably more, than the sum of their individual stamps. Stamp catalogues denote the correct collectible size but in some cases not the correct configuration. The distinction is important. If the correct size for an issue is six stamps, a block of four is not considered a plate block, even though it contains a plate number in its selvage.

In some cases, such as flat plate printed issues of the first half of the twentieth century, location of the number is crucial. These issues call for the plate number to appear on the center selvage tab of a block of six. If, instead, the number is located on either the right or left tab, the block is not considered a plate block. Again the distinction is important because a plate block is worth more than the sum of its individual stamps. One occasionally sees misdescribed plate blocks offered on Internet auctions. Make sure you know the correct size and configuration before buying.

Thousands of impressions are made from the typical plate, resulting in thousands of plate blocks each containing the same number. Print orders usually amount to many millions of stamps. In most cases, it requires several different plates (or in the case of multicolored issues, several different combinations of plates) to fulfill an order. In the case of a first-class definitive stamp with an extended life (e.g., the 3¢ Presidential, in use for more than a decade and a half), hundreds of plates end up being used.

Plate block collecting began to gain popularity in the 1920s and remained popular until the 1970s, when the price of new issues soared. Several factors combined to inflate the cost. The price of postage rose from 6¢ at the beginning of the decade to 15¢ by the end of the decade. The number of new issues increased, and the size of plate blocks ballooned from the traditional 4 stamps to 8, 10, 12, and in some cases, 20 stamps. With the advent of multicolor gravure printing, the Postal Service began spreading plate numbers across the selvage rather than consolidating them in corners. At the beginning of the decade, the typical plate block cost 24¢; by the end of the decade, the cost had risen to anywhere between $1.20 and $3. As

Large se-tenant
plate block typical
of the 1970s.

costs increased, collector enthusiasm diminished. The Postal Service addressed the problem in the 1980s, consolidating the numbers back to corner blocks, which, except in the case of se-tenants, eliminated the large and unwieldy blocks of the 1970s. Plate block collecting is still popular, although not as popular as it was during its heyday, from the 1920s to the 1970s.

Inscription and plate number strip of 3.

With few exceptions, plate blocks of nineteenth-century issues are rare. One would need unlimited resources to even attempt forming a collection of them. In the late nineteenth and early twentieth centuries, those interested in marginal numbers and markings generally saved them in the form of strips rather than blocks. Few plate blocks exist from that era.

In most cases, from the 1920s to the late 1960s, the standard format for plate blocks was either 4 or 6 stamps, depending on whether the issue was printed by rotary press or flat plate. Plate numbers on rotary press issues usually appear in the corner selvage. They are collected in blocks of 4. Plate numbers on flat plate issues appear toward the center of a strip of selvage. They are collected in blocks of 6, except for the infrequent multicolored issue collected in a block of 8, 10, or even 12. Again the location of the number or numbers is critical. Check carefully, especially when purchasing expensive plate blocks.

Typical flat plate
press plate block of
6 (left); typical
rotary press plate
block of 4 (right).

The typical plate block collection consists of an example of each issue as far back as is affordable, which in most cases is the 1920s. Some collectors specialize. They try to obtain an example of every plate number used for a particular issue. Others attempt to assemble a collection of every plate number and every position for a particular issue. Rotary press plate blocks generally exist in four positions, one for each corner of the press sheet: upper right, upper left, lower right, and lower left. Flat plate issues exist as top, bottom, or side plate blocks, although not all issues exist with all positions.

A set of plate blocks, one from each pane position on a press sheet, is known as a *matched set*. Assembling a complete collection of matched sets for some issues is an ambitious project, one that can take years. The 3¢ Presidential stamp is a good example. It was in use more than a decade and a half, and during that time, hundreds of plates were used to print it. A complete collection of matched sets amounts to nearly 1,500 plate blocks.

A compact pane with plate numbers in each of the four corners and diagram of pane position at lower right.

At this writing, press sheets often contain six or more panes. Plate numbers, especially on compact panes, appear on each of the four corners. A plate block, therefore, can no longer be used to establish the position of a pane on a press sheet. Instead, the position of a pane is shown by a diagram appearing in the selvage.

The *Durland Standard Plate Number Catalog* contains the most comprehensive listing of U.S. plate numbers and positions, many of which are rare and valuable. It belongs in every plate block collector's library.

PLATE NUMBER COILS

Since 1981 plate numbers have appeared on coil stamps, giving rise to one of the most popular specialties in U.S. philately—plate number coil (PNC) collecting.

Plate number coil strip of 3. Note plate number under center stamp.

Before 1981 coil plate numbers were trimmed off during the finishing process as stamps were slit apart and rolled into coils.

Coil plate numbers are tiny and sometimes require a little looking to spot. They appear at the bottom of the design and at regular intervals (e.g., every 24 or 48 stamps) that vary according to the type of sleeve and press used to print them. Monocolor issues contain a single number; multicolor issues contain several numbers, one for each color.

PNCs are collected in strips, usually 3 or 5 stamps in length, with the plate number situated on the center stamp. The number must appear on the center stamp or the strip is not considered a collectible strip. Some collectors try to obtain a strip from each issue. Others attempt to obtain every number or combination of numbers for every issue. In some cases, only a few plates or combinations of plates are used to print an issue; in other cases, dozens are used.

PNC collectors prize covers bearing stamps with plate numbers, especially scarce numbers. Each of us receives dozens of pieces of bulk mail per week, some of it mailed with coil stamps. Perhaps today's mail holds a treasure waiting to be discovered.

Anyone serious about collecting PNCs should obtain a copy of *Linn's Plate Number Coil Handbook* by Ken Lawrence, by far the best book on the subject and the essential reference.

FIRST DAY COVERS

Until the early twentieth century, most new issues were placed on sale as needed, where needed, without prior announcement. And until that time, collectors paid no attention to having stamps postmarked on their first day of issue.

Even after the Postal Service began announcing dates of issue, most collectors remained uninterested in obtaining first day covers (FDCs). Consequently, few FDCs made prior to 1920 exist. Those that do are generally worth hundreds or even thousands of dollars. Early FDCs do not bear the slogan cancel "First Day of Issue," and they lack cachets. The date on the postmark is the only clue. More than one lucky collector has discovered a valuable early FDC disguised as an ordinary-looking cover by taking time to check its postmark in a stamp catalogue.

Today almost all new stamps are announced well in advance. In most cases, on its first day, a new stamp is placed on sale in only a single city, known as the

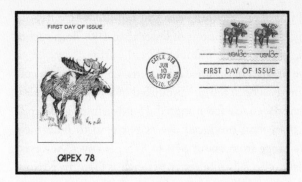

Typical cacheted first day cover.

official city. Release nationwide occurs the following day. In almost all cases, FDCs are serviced (canceled) with a postmark containing the phrase "First Day of Issue" and the name of the official city.

All that is actually required of an FDC is that it contain a stamp postmarked on the first day it became available for public sale. Today, however, most FDCs contain a cachet. A *cachet* consists of text or an illustration usually situated on the left side of the cover, but in some cases occupying the entire front of the cover.

Collectors can send covers to the Postal Service for first day cancellation; however, most prefer to subscribe to a new-issue service. A subscription eliminates the inconvenience of preparing and mailing covers for each of the numerous new issues, ensures that none are inadvertently missed, and avoids the risk of damage or an overstrike (an ordinary cancellation struck atop the first day cancellation) as the cover wends its way through the mail stream on its return journey.

Serious FDC collectors tend to specialize. Some attempt to obtain early, rare FDCs, the rarest of which are worth many thousands of dollars. Others build a collection devoted to a particular cachet maker. Still others focus on a favorite stamp and try to obtain as many different cachets produced for it as possible. In some cases, that means more than 100, some of which are invariably obscure, although not necessarily expensive.

Hand-painted first day cover.

Some prefer to collect hand-painted or hand-colored cachets. Hand-painted cachets are painted entirely by hand in a variety of styles and media: watercolor, acrylic, colored pencil, and just about anything else you can think of. They are produced in limited quantities, usually editions of fewer than 100. Each cachet is a work of art, signed and, in most cases, numbered by the artist.

Hand-colored cachets are printed in outline form on the cover and then colored in by hand. Hand-colored cachets, too, are produced in limited quantities, generally anywhere from a few dozen to a few hundred. Hand-painted and hand-colored cachets cost more than mass-produced covers but tend to hold their value better. Prices typically range from about $10 to $75 per cover; however, the work of well-known artists, especially pioneer artists such as Dorothy Knapp, run anywhere from a few hundred dollars up to a thousand or more.

An *add-on* is a cachet added to an FDC not originally serviced by the artist. Add-ons are usually hand painted, often years after the cover was originally serviced. Purists tend to look down on add-ons, insisting that cachets be contemporaneous to the cover. Those more liberally inclined avidly collect add-ons. It's a matter of personal preference.

In former times, those interested in obtaining a first day cancellation were required to send covers, together with a remittance for the desired number of stamps to be affixed, to the official city in advance of the first day of issue. Postal workers processed the remittances, affixed the stamps, serviced the covers, and returned them, usually through the mailstream. The system was labor intensive, and as the volume grew, it became more and more unwieldy. To streamline the process, the Postal Service instituted a grace period, usually 30 days, during which collectors could submit covers for first day cancellation. Collectors now obtain and affix their own stamps to the covers, a policy that relieves postal personnel from the time-consuming task and eliminates complaints about stamps not being affixed according to instructions.

First day cover canceled with both official and unofficial postmarks.

The grace period means that FDCs are not necessarily canceled on their first day of issue, a fact that doesn't seem to bother most collectors. Purists, however, insist that FDCs contain postmarks applied on the actual first day of issue. To accomplish this, they buy stamps at the official first day city, prepare covers, and then visit branch post offices or post offices in other towns and cities to have them canceled. The grace period applies only to the official first day postmark, that is, the one containing the slogan "First Day of Issue." Covers postmarked with regular business strikes (known as *unofficial cancels*) on the first day are, in fact, FDCs in the true sense of the word. Ironically, covers postmarked with unofficial cancels are indisputably more authentic than those postmarked with the "official" cancel.

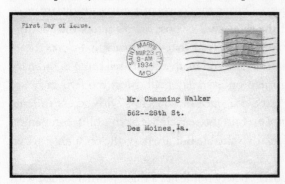

An early first day cover containing only a single typed inscription at upper left.

Today most collectors prefer cacheted covers. In the beginning, it was enough just to obtain a cover postmarked on the first day of issue. Cachets, often consisting of nothing more than a few lines of text, began to appear in the 1920s. Still, they were the exception rather than the rule. They gradually became more popular. Designers began to use illustrations rather than pure text. By the 1930s, most cachets contained illustrations. Today virtually all new FDCs contain cachets, and collectors generally prefer to collect only cacheted cover for stamps issued after 1935.

Addressed means that a cover contains an address. *Unaddressed* means that it does not. Collectors generally prefer unaddressed covers. Prior to 1945, most FDCs were serviced and then returned via the ordinary mail stream, hence the need for an address. After 1945, things began to change. Some cachet makers continued to service covers and deliver them to customers through the mail stream. Others began to service covers in person or have submissions returned in bulk, eliminating the need for an address. Unaddressed FDCs produced before 1945 are prized because of their scarcity. By the same token, addressed FDCs produced after 1945 tend to be shunned because unaddressed FDCs are so readily available.

FDC listings and prices can be found in specialized U.S. stamp catalogues. The voluminous *Planty Photo Encyclopedia of Cacheted First Day Covers* is a must for the serious FDC collector. It lists and illustrates every known cachet from the classic period, 1901 through 1939. Some are exceedingly rare; many are quite valuable. In addition, a variety of other reference works list and price cachets produced later.

FDCs for stamps issued before 1900 are rare, so collectors look for earliest known use (EKU) covers, that is, covers postmarked as near to the first day of issue as possible. Sometimes the earliest known use is only a few days after the actual date of issue; other times it's weeks or months later. Nineteenth-century EKU covers are rare; often no more than a single example per issue exists. Prices generally start in the low thousands and run as high as $100,000 or more.

Today stamps are occasionally inadvertently sold and used before their intended first day of issue. They are known as *early uses*, and covers containing them are known as *early use covers*. During the course of a year, a steady stream of new stamps arrives at each of the thousands of post offices across the country, often well in advance of their announced issue date—so many that clerks sometimes lose track of the official issue date and inadvertently sell some to ordinary customers who end up using them on everyday mail. Most modern early use covers are discovered through the diligence of collectors with access to large numbers of covers, such as empty remittance envelopes from utility companies. Early use covers are not particularly valuable but are nevertheless highly prized by aficionados.

The American First Day Cover Society publishes a thick journal loaded with articles devoted to FDC collecting. It's a must for anyone serious about FDC collecting. Refer to Chapter 31, "Philatelic Societies and Clubs."

Modern definitives offer interesting possibilities for specialization.

SINGLE STAMP OR SERIES

Some collectors become fascinated with a particular series, such as the Washington-Franklin series or the Presidential series, and focus all their attention on it. Others narrow their focus still further, concentrating on a single stamp. Students of single series and single stamps search out and assemble collections of shades, printing and perforation varieties, gum varieties, examples on covers illustrating rates and usages, and even counterfeits.

This form of specializing is nothing new. In the early years, before the proliferation of commemoratives, serious philatelists collected, studied, and documented the definitive stamps of their era, stamps that today are classics. It is beyond the financial resources of most collectors to build a collection of one of the nineteenth-century classic issues, but one can still derive the same sense of challenge and discovery by specializing in a modern issue such as a definitive stamp or series, especially one rife with varieties. Many of the stamps we take for granted will be of interest to future generations of collectors, just as stamps issued years ago fascinate specialists today. A small but growing number of collectors are beginning to study modern definitives because the raw material is readily available and can often be had for the asking. The quest is usually more time intensive than cash intensive.

PERSONAL FAVORITES

Some collect only those sets and singles that catch their eye. The acquisitions often have no logical relationship to one another other than their aesthetic appeal to the individual collecting them. I have such a collection. It's housed on black stock sheets in three-ring binders. New pages are easily added, and individual stamps and sets can be easily rearranged to accommodate acquisitions. I get as much, if not more, enjoyment from viewing this collection as from some of my more traditional collections.

Federal duck stamp (left); state duck stamp (right).

DUCK STAMPS

Waterfowl hunting stamps are a perennial favorite. They're large, colorful, and avidly collected by philatelists, sportsmen, and conservationists alike. The federal government began issuing duck stamps in 1934. States began issuing their own stamps in the early 1970s. Those issued by the federal government are known as *federal issues*; those issued by states, *state issues*.

ERRORS, FREAKS, AND ODDITIES

Errors, freaks, and oddities (EFOs) are avidly collected by those who find their unusual appearance fascinating and appealing. Prices range from a few dollars for more common varieties to thousands for rare varieties. EFOs are covered separately in Chapter 11, "Errors on Stamps." Membership in the Errors, Freaks, and Oddities Collectors' Club (EFOCC) is recommended for anyone interested in EFOs. It publishes an informative newsletter, which contains an auction loaded with every kind of odd-looking stamp you could imagine. Refer to Chapter 31.

These entities no longer issue postage stamps: the Mozambique Company (left); the German Democratic Republic (right).

DEAD COUNTRIES

Some collectors find dead countries intriguing. A dead country is one that no longer issues stamps, most often due to a change in political circumstance, such as former colonies (Belgian Congo, Mozambique Company) or nations absorbed by other countries (East Germany, South Vietnam). Some dead countries come back to life. Estonia, Latvia, and Lithuania issued stamps until they were absorbed by the Soviet Union in 1940. Following the breakup of the Soviet Union in 1991, they again began issuing stamps. The finite, and often limited, scope of a dead country tends to appeal to those who don't care for new issues.

PSEUDOSTAMPS

Some collectors collect stamps that are not really stamps, that is, pseudostamps used in advertising and promotion. With patience it is possible to assemble hundreds of examples, which when displayed together are, indeed, striking and offer evidence of how pervasive, if only subliminally, postage stamps are in our lives and culture.

Back-of-the-book possibilities: U.S. Offices in China (left); parcel post due stamp (center); Navy Department official stamp (right).

BACK-OF-THE-BOOK COLLECTING

Back-of-the-book stamps derive their name from their location in stamp catalogues. Regular postage stamps (e.g., definitives and commemoratives) occupy the front portion of the catalogue. Back-of-the-book material (e.g., special delivery stamps, postage dues, revenues, and so forth) occupies the rear portion of the catalogue, hence its name. Back-of-the-book collecting generally involves fewer stamps, perfect for those who prefer a deep, narrow focus rather than a broad, general approach to collecting.

COLLATERAL MATERIAL

Acquiring collateral material is not a specialty per se, but an adjunct to collecting. Collectors frequently enjoy dressing up their collections with visually interesting items such as FDCs, maximum cards, postcards, exhibition tickets, photographs, proofs, or anything relating to an issue of stamps or events surrounding its issuance. Collateral material (as these stamp-related items are known) adds color to album pages and helps tell the story of the stamps next to which it appears. Some collectors find collateral material as enjoyable as stamps themselves.

PARTING THOUGHTS

Follow your inclinations. Collect what you enjoy, what fits your means and your budget. That's what it's all about. Avoid the temptation to overreach, to collect everything. It usually makes more sense to focus. The narrower your focus, the more resources you can devote to building a coherent and rewarding collection.

TOOLS AND ACCESSORIES

PROPER TOOLS ARE essential to any endeavor, and it is no different with stamp collecting. The basic tools, stamp tongs, perforation gauge, and watermark detector are inexpensive and literally should last a lifetime. Don't skimp; buy the best. Pay attention to quality when shopping for accessories. You'll never regret it. Not all albums, mounts, and cover sleeves are created equal. Invest a little extra time in the beginning to shop for the best. The time spent will pay big dividends in the long run because most accessories, once purchased, end up being used for a lifetime.

TOOLS

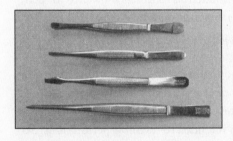

Various styles of stamp tongs.

STAMP TONGS

Stamp tongs are the most basic philatelic tool. Their use quickly becomes second nature, and for good reason. Stamps are much easier to handle with tongs than with fingers. Tongs also reduce the possibility of damage from rough handling, from moisture and oil on fingers, and so forth. Tongs come in a variety of styles: spade tip, round tip, pointed tip, fat tip, and thin tip, as well as long tongs and short tongs. Most collectors end up trying several before finding a pair just right. Many professionals, this author included, regard the Showgard 902 as the Mercedes of tongs. They are slim, light, and well balanced and possess a grip tension as light and subtle as a butterfly's wingbeat.

A word of caution: Don't use manicure tweezers or any other tool not specifically designed for handling stamps. They generally contain sharp edges or ridges for gripping, which can cause damage when used to handle stamps.

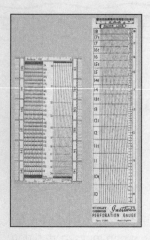

Perforation gauges.

PERFORATION GAUGE

A perforation gauge is used to measure perforations, or more precisely, the spacing of perforations. The majority of stamps exist in only a single perforation variety, so measurement isn't necessary. A few exist in two or more varieties, which is to say they are identical in appearance except for the gauge of their perforations. In some cases, the value of varieties varies significantly, from pennies to thousands of dollars.

Spacing (or gauge) is measured by the number of perforation holes that appear within a space of 2 centimeters. Perforated 12 means that 12 holes appear within 2 centimeters; perforated 8 1/2 means 8 1/2 holes per 2 centimeters, and so forth. When perforations are of the same spacing on all sides of a stamp, the measurement is expressed as "perforated 11," or whatever gauge applies. Sometimes the gauge of horizontal perforations differs from that of vertical perforations. Stamps possessing different horizontal and vertical gauges are described as "compound perforated," and the measurement is expressed as "perforated 10 1/2 x 11," or whatever gauges apply. The first numeral refers to the horizontal gauge, the second to the vertical. In philatelic vernacular, the word "perforated" is routinely shortened to "perf," as in "perf 11" or "perf 10 1/2 x 11." Perforations on opposite parallel sides of a stamp are almost invariably of the same gauge; the rare exception is typically an error, often valuable, and worth keeping an eye open for.

Find a stamp's gauge by aligning the marks on the perforation gauge with either perforation tips or bottoms of perforation holes (many prefer the bottoms) and then referring to the scale on the side of the gauge. Modern self-adhesive stamps often contain serpentine die cuts intended to resemble perforations. Serpentine die cuts can be measured in the same way as perforations. Align the marks with either the peaks or valleys of the die cuts, and then read the gauge. Check both horizontal and vertical edges, as the gauge may differ.

Gauge is expressed either fractionally, usually to the nearest half or quarter hole (e.g., 10 1/2 or 10 1/4), or decimally to the nearest tenth (e.g., 10.1 or 10.4). Serpentine die cuts are usually measured decimally. Traditionally, perforations have been measured in fractions, but the trend is toward decimalization. Obtain a perforation gauge that measures in both fractions and decimals. *Linn's Stamp News* Multi-gauge is one of the best and costs only a few dollars.

Gauge is usually thought of as a measurement of the spacing of holes rather than their size. In most cases, the size (diameter) of holes is of no consequence. Sadly, there are those who fake stamps by adding perforations, either to boost value by eliminating an unwanted straight edge or to simulate a more valuable variety (more about this in Chapter 8, "Forgeries and Fakes"). Fakers usually concentrate on getting the spacing right. They often ignore the size of holes, aware that if a stamp gauges properly, it will pass superficial scrutiny—and often that is the case.

The Kiusalas United States Specialty Gauge is an extremely precise gauge that measures both the spacing and the size of holes for many U.S. stamps and is therefore especially useful in detecting fakes. The Kiusalas gauge has been out of production for a number of years, but at this writing, some dealers still have stocks. It is an indispensable tool for the serious U.S. collector. If you can find one, do not hesitate to buy it.

Watermark tray.

WATERMARK DETECTOR

A *watermark* is a mark impressed on wet pulp during the manufacture of paper. The impressed mark appears lighter than the surrounding paper. Expensive stationery is often watermarked. U.S. currency ($5 bills and larger) is watermarked with busts of presidents. You can see the watermark by holding a bill up to light. The U.S. Postal Service used watermarked paper (reading "USPS") in stamp production between the years 1895 and 1916. A variety of watermark images (including letters, crests, and geometric patterns) have been used by foreign countries on their stamps.

Watermarks on some foreign stamps are visible when held up to light and viewed from the back, but most are not, because of the small size of stamps and the opacity of printing ink. Watermarks on U.S. stamps are almost impossible to see without the aid of a watermark detector.

The time-honored method of detecting watermarks utilizes a small black tray in which the subject stamp is placed facedown and covered with watermark fluid, causing the watermark to become visible. Within the hobby, the word "watermark" is often used as a verb. To watermark a stamp means to check for a watermark. Watermark trays are also used to check for damage (thins, creases, etc.) and repairs.

Most stamp issues are printed on a single kind of paper, be it watermarked or unwatermarked. A few issues exist on both watermarked and unwatermarked paper, which is to say they are outwardly identical, except for type of paper. Still others exist on a variety of watermarked papers. Each is a collectible variety, and each is valued differently. The difference can amount to hundreds, or in some cases thousands, of dollars.

Warning: Do not use water in a watermark detector. You'll ruin the gum on mint stamps and destroy their value. Nor is it practical for used stamps. You'll have to dry and press them, which takes time. Use watermark fluid. It doesn't dissolve stamp gum and it dries almost instantly.

Sooner or later, you'll run across individuals who use lighter fluid to watermark stamps. It works fine and evaporates quickly. Unfortunately, it leaves a slight, almost imperceptible oily residue, one that builds up with repeated dippings, so it's best to avoid it. To be prudent, use only fluid specifically designed for use with stamps. Several brands are available. They can be obtained from most stamp dealers or from any mail-order stamp-supply company.

Be aware that inks used to print some British Commonwealth stamps are soluble in watermark fluid. Consult a stamp catalogue before dipping these stamps.

Here's a tip: A little fluid goes a long way. Place the stamp facedown in the tray. Add only as much fluid as necessary to moisten it and reveal the watermark. It's not necessary to drown the stamp in a tray full of fluid and then have to struggle to pour the excess back into the bottle without spilling it.

Specialists prize inverted watermarks, omitted watermarks, and stamps erroneously printed on watermarked paper, such as the 1938 U.S. $1 Woodrow Wilson postage stamp printed on paper watermarked USIR (United States Internal Revenue) intended for revenue stamps. At this writing, the error stamp is worth about $250 mint and $60 used, compared with only a few dollars mint and a few cents used for the normal, unwatermarked stamp.

Optical watermark detectors eliminate the need for fluid. Some collectors prefer them for that reason. They are more costly (typically $100 and up) and work best on mint, never-hinged stamps and stamps without gum because hinge remnants and disturbed gum tend to obscure watermarks and faults. Those who handle stamps frequently generally prefer the low-tech, tray-and-fluid method because it is inexpensive and portable and invariably gives a reliable result.

MAGNIFYING TOOL

Spend a few dollars to obtain a high-quality magnifying glass. A jeweler's loupe is the best. It should be at least 10-power to adequately view secret marks, type markings, damage, and repairs.

Two styles of 10-power magnifiers.

ULTRAVIOLET LIGHT

Ultraviolet light is used to detect luminescent coatings on stamps. Since the late 1960s, the Postal Service has utilized a variety of luminescent coatings on stamps to trigger automated facing and canceling equipment. All current U.S. stamps, except those of small denomination, contain some form of luminescence, either in the paper or printed atop the design. This invisible coating, referred to by collectors as *tagging*, is visible under ultraviolet light. Untagged varieties of some issues are more valuable than their tagged counterparts. Ultraviolet light is also useful in detecting some kinds of tampering.

Obtain a portable model that fluoresces *both* longwave and shortwave ultraviolet light. Savvy collectors favor the type used by gem and mineral collectors.

Color identification guide.

COLOR IDENTIFICATION GUIDE

A few stamps exist in a confusing variety of similar colors and shades. Two-cent Washington-Franklin issues are known in carmine, carmine rose, red, rose-red, rose, and deep rose. Two-cent First Bureau issues are known in carmine, rose, rose carmine, red, orange red, pink, vermilion, and scarlet. And what is the difference between pink, rose pink, and pigeon blood pink? Valuewise, a few bucks versus thousands. To the untrained eye, the difference is impossible to discern; every shade looks like the elusive and tantalizingly expensive pigeon blood pink. A reliable color guide helps eliminate the confusion. Stanley Gibbons manufactures one of the best.

Those really serious about color varieties on nineteenth-century U.S. stamps—and the field is rife with rare and valuable shades and varieties—own and use the extraordinary and definitive *Encyclopedia of the Colors of United States Postage Stamps*, by R. H. White and W. R. Bower. It is a work without equal, now out of print, yet sometimes available from philatelic literature dealers and occasionally at auction. Expect to pay several hundred dollars for the multivolume set. You should, however, have no trouble recovering your investment should you later decide to sell it.

ACCESSORIES

ALBUMS

Most collectors house their collections in albums. Albums protect stamps, serve as a means of organizing them, and provide a convenient way to view and enjoy them. Most albums feature printed illustrations on each page to indicate placement of stamps. Top-of-the-line hingeless albums come with plastic mounts preinstalled so that all one need do is insert stamps in their appropriate spaces. Albums exist for nearly all countries and for U.S. stamps and U.S. specialties such as plate blocks and plate number coils. Advanced collectors generally prefer loose-leaf albums that accommodate supplement pages, which album companies usually publish annually to enable collectors to keep an album up to date.

Albums for major countries, such the United States, Germany, France, and Great Britain, are available in various styles from various publishers, each catering to a different taste or level of specialization. The most basic contain spaces for each face-different stamp (i.e., without regard to perforation or watermark varieties). More comprehensive versions contain a space for every recognized variety. They range in price from a few dollars up to a thousand.

A word of advice: The array of options can be perplexing. If you're new to the hobby, don't be too hasty or impulsive when choosing an album, especially an expensive one. Network with other collectors and get the benefit of their experience before making a decision. Begin with something basic. It's common for new collectors to want to collect everything. It usually takes a few months for one's collecting focus to narrow. Wait until that happens, until you have some knowledge about the benefits and drawbacks of the various types of albums, to make a decision.

If you decide to collect the whole world and want a set of albums with spaces for every single stamp ever issued, consider acquiring a used set. It's usually much more economical. Auctions frequently offer collections housed in sets of albums. They can often be had at little or no cost above the value of the stamps. A couple of caveats about used albums: If the album or set is long out of date, make sure supplements are still available. Album publishers generally stock supplements for only the most recent prior years. Sometimes the cost of supplements to bring an album up to date is more than the cost of a new album. A good rule of thumb: If a used album is more than five years out of date, it may be more economical to buy a new one. Also, make sure the album paper in a potential purchase is not mildewed, toned, or in any other way impaired. It's false economy to house stamps in a cheap album that is likely to harm them.

Experienced collectors favor album pages printed on one side rather than two sides because stamps on facing pages tend to catch on one another as pages are turned. If you must use double-sided pages, insert glassine interleaves between them to avoid damage. They're available from stamp dealers and album publishers.

Advanced collectors, specialists, and exhibitors often prefer to make their own album pages with as many or as few stamps per page as seems appropriate, and with as much or as little descriptive text as serves their purpose. Most album manufacturers offer quadrille-lined blank pages (a background of faintly imprinted square or rectangular lines), which make designing layouts easy. You can also design album pages using a software program and print them on any paper you desire, including acid-free paper. Several programs are available and mentioned in Chapter 34 under "Electronic Media."

Several firms manufacture albums for covers. The most versatile contain loose-leaf pages that contain clear plastic pockets. The best are made of Mylar. Some types contain polyethylene sleeves. Both are fairly inert. Avoid albums containing pages made of vinyl treated with softening (plasticizing) agents (visible as an oily iridescent film; the more softener, the more iridescence). They are potentially harmful. More about that in Chapter 7, "Conservation."

Stamp hinges (left); plastic mount (right).

MOUNTS

Two basic types of mounts exist: the stamp hinge and the plastic mount. The modern stamp hinge consists of a bit of glassine lightly gummed on one side. The hinge is folded, usually about one-third of the way from the top, and the smaller flap is lightly moistened (too much moisture makes the hinge difficult to remove should the need arise) and attached to the stamp near its top edge. The larger flap is moistened and attached to the album page. Hinges are inexpensive, work well, and remain the mount of choice for low-cost stamps and used stamps.

Hinges have fallen out of favor for use on mint stamps because they leave a mark on gum when removed. Until the mid-twentieth century, no one paid much attention to hinge marks, but during the later half of the century, the hobby became much more condition conscious. Collectors began to prefer stamps with pristine gum. Premiums for never-hinged stamps began to rise, and hinging mint stamps, especially expensive ones, fell out of favor.

Today the mount of choice for mint stamps is the plastic mount. Plastic mounts are easy to use, protect stamps, frame them nicely against an album page, and lend a polished look to the presentation. Plastic mounts come in a variety of sizes to meet any conceivable need. Several different styles and brands exist.

A word of caution: Some types of plastic mounts are slit on the back to allow insertion of the stamp. Do not apply too much moisture to the adhesive on the back of the mount. The excess all too easily seeps into the slit, affecting the stamp's gum, thus defeating the whole purpose of the mount. Another caveat: Don't use cellophane tape to secure the open sides of mounts. It degrades over time, often discoloring the edges of the very stamps it was meant to protect. A properly fitting mount should not require tape to keep a stamp in place.

STOCK BOOKS

Stock book pages consist of horizontal pockets created from manila, glassine, or clear plastic into which stamps can be slipped. Stock books are used to store stamps, such as duplicates or stamps waiting to be mounted in albums. They can be used to house collections as well.

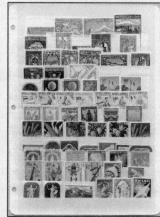

Display-style stock sheet (left); manila stock sheet (right).

STOCK SHEETS

Stock sheets are the loose-leaf version of stock book pages. They come punched for three-ring binders and several other types. Display-style stock sheets are made of card or plastic stock on which as few as 1 or as many as 14 clear plastic pockets have been attached. They are available in either black or white. Many collectors like the flexibility and convenience of stock sheets, and, indeed, there is much to recommend this system, especially if you plan to form a nontraditional collection. Manila stock sheets are less expensive than display-style stock sheets. They are used for storage more than display.

Plastic stock card (left);
manila stock card (right).

STOCK CARDS

Stock cards are small versions of stock sheets and are available in a variety of sizes, the most common of which measures 3 1/4 by 5 1/2 inches. Manila stock cards usually contain three rows or pockets. Plastic stock cards are available in either one- or two-row configurations.

Be careful when handling plastic stock cards. I once placed a handful in an attaché case pocket, only to discover later that the edge of one of the cards had slipped into the pocket of the card underneath it, neatly slitting in two a beautiful mint, never-hinged example of the 1909 Lincoln commemorative on blue paper. That little mistake ruined a $350 stamp.

COVER SLEEVES

One of the most convenient ways to house and protect covers is the cover sleeve, a plastic sleeve sealed on three sides and open on the fourth. Cover sleeves come in a variety of sizes and weights. Some open at the top; others open on the side. The best are made of Mylar or polyethylene, which are generally inert. Mylar sleeves are clear and more rigid than polyethylene sleeves. Poly sleeves are slightly grayish in appearance, are floppy rather than rigid, and weigh less if shipping or traveling is a consideration. Again, avoid any product that contains softeners, especially vinyl.

GLASSINE ENVELOPES

Glassines are ubiquitous. Everyone uses them. They're handy, inexpensive, and available in a variety of sizes.

Glassine envelopes are available in a variety of sizes.

BOOKS AND PERIODICALS

Knowledge is golden, and philately is rich in printed resources. The most basic and essential reference is a stamp catalogue. Scott publishes both a specialized U.S. catalogue and a multivolume set of catalogues that features every postage stamp in the world. Krause-Minkus also publishes a specialized U.S. catalogue as well as a series of foreign catalogues, each devoted to a separate country. A fair number of foreign catalogue publishers publish specialty catalogues covering stamps of their nation. A list appears in Chapter 33, "Foreign Stamp Catalogues." In addition, thousands of books have been published since 1840 covering just about any topic you could think of. A basic reading list appears in Chapter 34, "Philatelic Reference Books."

I would recommend subscribing to at least one philatelic newspaper and the *American Philatelist*, the monthly magazine published by the American Philatelic Society. Refer to Chapter 35, "Philatelic Periodicals," for more information.

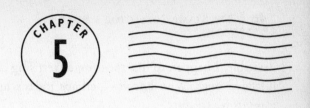

SOURCES FOR STAMPS

MOST LARGE CITIES and some medium and smaller ones maintain philatelic centers. Philatelic centers stock a variety of new issues and recent issues, many of which are not always available at the ordinary postal counter. The Postal Service also maintains a mail-order facility, the USPS Philatelic Fulfillment Service Center in Kansas City. Check Chapter 30, "Worldwide Philatelic Agencies," for the address.

Many nations maintain philatelic bureaus or agencies from which collectors can order new and recent issues by mail at face value. In addition, some foreign postal administrations make issues available at face value through agents in the United States. Most foreign postal services and their U.S. agents offer a standing order service that permits you to receive new issues automatically against a deposit. Some collectors prefer to order directly from foreign postal services; others find their domestic agents more convenient. A list of foreign philatelic agencies appears in Chapter 30.

Interesting items arrive on daily mail.

PERSONAL SOURCES

Start with your daily mail. Check junk mail covers for coil stamps that contain plate numbers. They are tiny and appear at the bottom of the design on those few stamps that possess them. You won't find many, but that's what makes them desirable. I happen to like those on advertising covers, especially colorful, il-lustrated ones. Who knows—perhaps today's junk mail will end up being tomorrow's treasure.

The workplace is an excellent source for material, especially contemporary postal history items. Much incoming mail is franked with postage meters or permits, but keep an eye out for that which is not, such as express mail and priority mail envelopes. They're often franked with scarce high-value denomina-tions, which are sometimes worth nearly as much used as unused. Watch for registered and certified mail covers, too.

A word of caution: Don't remove stamps from covers; leave them intact. They're usually more collectible and valuable that way. As a kid in the late 1950s, I had access to covers from a local bank. Every day after school I picked up a fresh batch of covers: registered covers, certified covers, covers with all kinds of high-denomination Liberty series stamps in nifty combinations. I took them home and stripped off the stamps, which turned out to be a big mistake. Liberty series covers are extremely collectible at present. I ruined hundreds, perhaps thou-sands, of dollars worth of covers at today's prices. The moral: Leave covers intact until you have enough experience to know which stamps can be removed with-out impairing their value.

Keep an eye open for error stamps. Errors are often subtle, so examine stamps carefully. More about errors in Chapter 11, "Errors on Stamps."

Travel agencies are often a good source for foreign stamps. Perhaps an accom-modating agent might be willing to save covers for you. It never hurts to ask.

Friends, neighbors, and relatives are often only too happy to save stamps and covers for you. Ask them to check their attics, trunks, and basements for old letters or stamps. One such request turned up a Civil War correspondence from a prisoner in a POW camp—a postal history bonanza.

Corporations, state agencies, and historical societies, too, are fertile hunting grounds. One fellow was able to obtain dozens of cartons full of old records from an insurance company, some dating back to the nineteenth century. Most contained revenue stamps, including a number of scarce and valuable items. The cartons had been his for the asking.

Be alert for anything unusual: covers with odd markings, runs of correspon-dence from pioneers or from ship captains or crew, early airmail covers, illustrated V-mail from World War II. You get the idea.

STAMP STORES

No two stores are alike, so you never know what you'll find. At minimum, an eclectic variety of singles, sets, covers, mixtures, packets, accumulations, remainders—just about anything philatelic. Don't be afraid to ask questions. Most dealers are generous with their knowledge. It's uncommon to find an advanced collector who did not have a dealer-mentor. Few are more qualified to explain esoteric intricacies and fine shadings. Philately is, after all, a hobby of detail, and an experienced dealer is an invaluable resource.

Stamp stores also afford the opportunity to examine stamps before buying, to compare various types of albums, mounts, and supplies. In addition, many collectors enjoy the social aspect of a stamp store. It's a great place to browse, relax, chat with fellow collectors, and tune in to the local philatelic scene (meetings, clubs, shows, and so forth).

FLEA MARKETS AND GARAGE SALES

Sometimes you run across a find or a great deal at a flea market, an estate sale, or a garage sale, but be careful. Flea-market vendors have been known to purchase cheap remainders and old, intriguing-looking albums from stamp dealers and put them out to tempt treasure hunters, usually at a significant markup. Just because something is old doesn't necessarily mean it's valuable. Lots of old stamps are common and inexpensive, especially the low denominations. In many cases, the same type of material can be obtained more reasonably through a stamp dealer.

That doesn't mean that treasures can't be found, especially among covers and cards. Valuable covers are often innocuous in appearance, their value lying in an esoteric origin, destination, or marking, attributes that require knowledge to recognize and appreciate—knowledge that most flea-market vendors and estate-sale liquidators do not possess. As a rule, the greater your knowledge, the more "luck" you'll have spotting diamonds in the rough.

TRADING

Most philatelic periodicals contain a classified section devoted to parties interested in trading. Trading can be a lot fun, especially with collectors in far-off lands. Sometimes the correspondence ends up becoming a friendship. Many foreigners, especially those in countries formerly behind the Iron Curtain, are eager to make friends with American collectors and obtain U.S. stamps through trade. Inexpensive stamps are usually traded on a stamp-for-stamp basis. New issues are often traded on a face-value-for-face-value basis. Older, more expensive stamps are generally traded on a catalogue-value-for-catalogue-value basis. Any equitable, mutually agreeable basis is okay.

MAIL ORDER

You can obtain just about anything by mail, from individual stamps and sets to mixtures, bulk lots, covers, supplies, books, and new issues, just to name a few. Many dealers publish price lists, some post lists online, and many service want lists.

Another way to obtain stamps is through approvals. *Approvals* are selections of stamps sent by mail for inspection and purchase, subject to the buyer's approval. Approval dealers usually allow 10 days for inspection. At the end of that time, you pay for those you want to keep and return the rest. Buyers are allowed to take as many or as few as they wish, although many approval dealers offer a discount if the entire selection is purchased. Some approval dealers offer rewards, similar to frequent flier miles, that can be used toward future purchases. In most cases, selections automatically continue to be sent until you request that they stop. Approval services span the range from beginner to advanced collector. Advertisements for mail-order dealers and approval dealers can be found in philatelic periodicals.

Most mail-order dealers belong to the American Philatelic Society (APS) or the American Stamp Dealers Association (ASDA). Each has a code of ethics by which member dealers agree to abide.

STAMP SHOWS

Stamp shows are a great place to obtain stamps. Shows range in size from small local affairs with half a dozen dealers to national and international shows featuring hundreds of frames of exhibits and hundreds of dealers. The biggest feature exhibits and dealers from all over the world. Large shows usually feature a section devoted to foreign post office booths that sell recent issues at face value.

Regardless of their size, stamp shows concentrate dealers into a single location, making it easy to shop—and comparison shop. Be sure to take time to check out the exhibits. Nothing gives a better feel for the possibilities of philately than seeing how others have approached it. Large shows often feature

Stamp shows offer browsing opportunities.

informative lectures, programs, and seminars, almost always at no cost, and in many cases followed by a question-and-answer session.

Large metropolitan areas usually host a number of shows during the course of a year, each of three or four days in duration, typically Thursday or Friday through Sunday. In some cities, local dealers get together for a weekend bourse, usually one-day affairs without exhibits. Bourses are often regularly scheduled for a particular weekend each month and sometimes more frequently. Philatelic periodicals contain events calendars that list shows and bourses by locale.

STAMP CLUBS

Most stamp clubs allow members to trade or sell at meetings. In addition to offering the opportunity to acquire stamps, clubs offer access to the knowledge and experience of fellow collectors. It is not unusual for a large metropolitan area to support several clubs. Medium-sized cities often have at least one, as do many smaller towns. In most cases, dues are only a few dollars per year.

Clubs meet in a variety of venues ranging from members' homes to church, school, or other public meeting rooms. The agenda often includes a presentation or slide show by a member or guest speaker. Frequently, the program is followed by a trading session combined with an informal show-and-tell session for those who have brought albums to show and discuss with fellow members.

For information on clubs in your area, check with a local dealer or with the APS, which has names and contacts for more than 750 local clubs across America. The APS address appears in Chapter 36, "Resources."

PHILATELIC SOCIETIES

Some philatelic societies make stamps available to members through sales divisions. Philatelic societies tend to be national in scope, drawing membership from all parts of the country, and they tend to be specialized in nature, catering to those who share a common interest, such as topicals or error stamps. The exception is the APS, which is a general organization worth special mention.

The APS is a nonprofit organization founded in 1886, whose membership stands at about 50,000. The APS sales division offers a circuit book service and an online stamp store. Circuit books contain selections of stamps for sale by other members. Buyers choose as few or as many stamps as they wish from a selection, send payment to the APS, and forward the books to the next name on the enclosed list, hence the name *circuit books*. The last name on the list returns the circuit to the APS. Members can request circuit books from a wide range of countries and specialties. Prices are usually quite reasonable. The service is especially useful to collectors without access to local dealers or stamp clubs.

Anyone can buy from the APS's online stamp store, but only members are allowed to sell. Selections are posted on the store's Web site. Each is described, illustrated, and priced. At this writing, the seller's commission is 20 percent. You can find the APS stamp store at its Web site (www.stamps.org).

American Philatelist magazine.

In addition to sales services, the APS publishes an illustrated, slick-paper monthly journal, the *American Philatelist*, which alone is worth the society's nominal annual dues. Members are entitled to a discount on all of the excellent books published by the APS. Members are also entitled to borrow books from the American Philatelic Research Library (APRL), the largest library in America devoted exclusively to philately. The library building contains 2 linear miles of shelf space housing tens of thousands of books and periodicals on philately. Its card catalogue and article index are truly mind-boggling and almost certainly the most comprehensive resource in existence devoted to philatelic literature. The APRL is open to the public. Check the APS Web site for hours and location. Members may borrow by mail, and many do. In fact, most APRL book loans are made by mail.

The APS also operates the American Philatelic Expertizing Service (APEX). Anyone can submit stamps to APEX for expertizing; however, APS members receive a discount.

Lastly, the APS offers an insurance plan designed specifically for collectors. It is less costly and more comprehensive than those generally available from standard casualty companies.

Dozens of other societies exist, one for nearly every interest. Most publish journals or newsletters. In most cases, dues are nominal and represent an excellent value. Refer to Chapter 31, "Philatelic Societies and Clubs."

INTERNET

The Internet is the new kid on the block, relatively speaking. It's growing and evolving so rapidly that it's almost impossible to write about it without having the information become out of date by publication. The good news is that through the power of search engines and countless links, you'll have no trouble discovering hundreds, even thousands, of philatelic Web sites. Electronic malls, auction sites, classified ads, want list services, online magazines, chatrooms, events calendars—the list is almost endless. At this writing, there's even talk of virtual stamp exhibits. And the opportunities for buying, selling, and trading are virtually limitless. Online auctions are especially popular and are covered in more detail in Chapter 12, "Buying and Selling at Auction."

One site worth mention is that of the Junior Philatelists of America (JPA) (www.jpastamps.org). The JPA is a nonprofit organization devoted to youth philately. Kids will especially enjoy the site's contests and games, all of which are oriented toward philately.

"SUNDAY SUPPLEMENT" COLLECTIBLES

Although a source in the broad sense of the word, mass-marketed or "Sunday supplement" stamps are, as a rule, one of the most costly ways of acquiring stamps. In collectibles mass marketing, the target is to keep the cost of the product under 25 percent of the offering price—under 20 percent is even better. Advertising, not product acquisition, is the largest single cost. It sometimes accounts for as much as 50 percent of the cost of the offering price. The point is, purchase these types of stamps only if you can't live without them. Don't expect them to rise in value, despite all the sweet talk in the advertising presentation. "Officially authorized," "limited edition," and "certificate of authenticity" count for little when it comes time for you to sell. Dealers and fellow collectors simply don't care. They want real stamps, not contrived collectibles.

CONDITION
AND GRADING

CONDITION IS THE sum of a stamp's elements: gum, hinging, centering, margins, color, freshness, perforations, cancellations, and faults. *Grading* is the way in which condition is described. Condition and grading are not so much an issue with common stamps. They are cheap and plentiful, and high-quality examples are rarely difficult to obtain. Condition becomes more of an issue with expensive stamps because it so dramatically affects price. For example, 90 percent of the $3,500 price for a superb, mint $1 Cattle in the Storm represents a premium for condition. The exact same stamp can be had for a few hundred dollars in seriously faulty condition. Any amount above the lowest grade is a premium for condition. When buying any stamp, except the most common, you are buying condition.

The size of margins varies from issue to issue, as these issues illustrate.

MARGINS

At minimum, a stamp should possess margins of at least normal size for its issue. There is no standard size for margins. It varies from issue to issue, so one must judge a stamp's margins against that which is normal for the issue. Nineteenth-century issues tend to have the smallest. Almost no space exists between some, such as the 3¢ issues of 1851 and 1857. Others, such as the U.S. parcel post issues of 1913, are spaced well apart and routinely encountered with large and visually appealing margins. Generally, the larger its margins for issue, the more desirable the stamp.

The stamp at left possesses normal-sized margins for issue; the stamp at right possesses jumbo margins.

Dramatically oversized margins—referred to as *jumbo* or *boardwalk* margins—are especially prized.

CENTERING

Centering is the way in which a stamp's design is situated in relation to its margins. The more balanced the margins, the better the centering and the more visually appealing and desirable the stamp. Nineteenth-century stamps are notoriously poorly centered. Some have almost no room between stamps, which results in perforations touching the design or cutting into it on at least one side. Take this into account when assessing centering. Experienced buyers understand that it is not always possible to find perfectly centered examples for some issues and content themselves with reasonably centered examples.

Familiarize yourself with the characteristic margins and centering of various issues in order to be able to recognize better-than-normal examples. Also bear in mind that modern stamps are usually well centered. Don't try to hold early issues to the same standard. Assess each issue according to its own characteristics. Savvy collectors turn stamps upside down and sideways in order to view centering from every possible angle.

Grades of centering from left to right: average, fine, fine to very fine, very fine, superb.

Standard grades of centering include the following:
- **Superb (S).** Perfectly centered. The highest state of perfection.
- **Extremely Fine (XF).** Very well centered, margins almost perfectly balanced.
- **Very Fine (VF).** Moderately centered.
- **Fine (F).** Poorly centered. Perforations need only be clear of the design.
- **Average (Avg).** Very poorly centered. Perforations often cut into the design.

A variety of split grades, such as fine to very fine (F–VF), describe finer shadings. Catalogues generally list and price stamps in only a single grade of centering, usually a grade in the middle of the spectrum, such as fine to very fine (F–VF). Stamps in higher or lower grades sell for more or less than the listed price. In fact, most stamps sell for a price other than the listed catalogue price. This is especially true of nineteenth-century issues, where only a small fraction (perhaps as few as 10 percent) exist in the grade as high as the one listed and priced by catalogues.

Philatelic terms often have meanings specific to the hobby, while their counterparts in common usage have altogether different meanings. For example, the term "fine," as applied to stamp centering, has come to mean a poorly centered stamp. To be precise, its perforations need only clear the design. In reality, fine stamps are very unattractive. Yet in common usage, "fine" refers to something of higher-than-normal quality. In fact, *Webster's New World Dictionary* defines "fine" as something that is "excellent" or "of superior quality." So take time to familiarize yourself with the nuances of stamp-grading terminology.

GUM AND HINGING

Comments on gum apply to unused stamps. Used stamps are assumed to be without gum, and the lack of gum has no bearing on their value. The terms "mint" and "unused" are frequently used interchangeably, but in many cases "mint" is used to refer to a stamp that has never been hinged, and in some cases "unused" implies uncanceled but without gum. These nuances in usage are by no means universal, so pay attention to the context in which a term is used. Before placing bids at auction, check the "terms" section in the front of the auction catalogue to find out how "mint" and "unused" are used.

Contemporary collectors prefer gum to be in the best possible condition and that means never-hinged (NH) stamps. Until the middle of the twentieth century, stamps were customarily mounted with hinges, which is why so few early stamps survive without hinge marks. Early stamp hinges were often just bits of ordinary paper attached with whatever glue was handy, usually a utilitarian glue made to hold things securely together. As a consequence, old-time hinges are difficult to remove. At best, they disturb a stamp's gum when removed. At worst, they take part of the stamp's paper with them, leaving a thinned area, known as a *thin*. Early commercially produced hinges were little better. They held like iron. More often than not, they leave gum horrendously disturbed when removed.

Frequently, the only way to remove a problem hinge is to soak it off. Dealers sometimes soak hinges off heavily hinged stamps, especially early issues, to improve their appearance. A stamp without gum is generally more appealing and salable than one with gum discolored and disturbed by the presence of an ugly hinge remnant. That's why so few early stamps survive with original gum.

Glassine hinges coated with light adhesive, advertised as peelable, appeared later. Peelable hinges generally cause no damage when carefully removed. They do, however, leave a hinge mark, albeit light. Today collectors of mint stamps prefer never-hinged examples. Although lightly hinged stamps are not considered faulty, most collectors consider them less desirable than never-hinged examples.

Gum on unused stamps is graded according to its presence and on the degree of hinging. Generally, the earlier the stamp, the less perfect the state of its gum. Gum on most nineteenth-century stamps is either partially or completely missing, heavily hinged, or disturbed from hinge removal.

States of gum and hinging are described as follows. Standard abbreviations appear in parentheses.

- **Never Hinged (NH).** Gum to which a stamp hinge has never been applied. The most desirable condition. The term implies original gum. A regummed stamp is never referred to as never hinged.
- **Lightly Hinged (LH).** Gum bearing only the slightest evidence of having been hinged.
- **Heavily Hinged (HH).** A stamp whose hinge or partial hinge (known as a *hinge remnant*) is still in place, so firmly attached that it is impossible to remove without damaging the stamp, or a stamp whose hinge has been removed leaving a distinct and unappealing mark on its gum. Experienced persons, including many stamp dealers, are often reluctant to remove hinges for fear of causing damage or ending up with gum that looks worse than if left alone.
- **Part (or Partial) Original Gum.** Only partial original gum remaining, usually on the lower half of the stamp, the top part most often missing as a result of hinge removal. A condition usually associated with and considered normal for pre-1890 unused stamps.
- **Original Gum (OG).** Gum applied at the time of manufacture. Until late in the twentieth century, usually composed of gum arabic or dextrin, which are smooth and glossy in appearance. Some recent gums (such as polyvinyl alcohol gums) have a dull, mattelike appearance. Original gum is prized. Stamps with full original gum are worth considerably more than stamps with partial gum or no gum.
- **Disturbed Gum (DG).** Generally understood to mean gum disturbed by removal of a stamp hinge, but also any other form of gum damage, such as that arising from a stamp having been partially stuck down to an album page or stuck to another stamp. In some cases, gum initially disturbed by hinge removal is made more unsightly by attempts to smooth or redistribute it, often with a dampened artist's brush. Unfortunately, the attempt often makes more of a mess of the gum and sometimes ends up warping the stamp.
- **Glazed Gum.** A glossy appearance resulting from gum having been partially liquefied and then stuck to a nonporous surface such as the inside of a plastic stamp mount. Glazed gum results from humidity, poor storage, or poor mounting.

- **Tropical Gum.** Gum that has been affected by high humidity, often in a tropical or subtropical climate, causing it to lose its original gloss or texture. Stamps possessing tropicalized gum are often discolored, either uniformly or in spots caused by microorganisms.
- **No Gum (NG).** Lacking gum. The term "no gum" implies that the stamp originally possessed gum that was later removed, hence an inferior state of condition. Stamps issued without gum are referred to as "issued without gum" or "ungummed" rather than "no gum" to make the distinction that they are "as issued" and not impaired. Stamps lacking original gum usually sell for a fraction of those possessing original gum. The absence of gum on stamps issued without gum does not detract from their value.
- **Regummed (RG).** Regumming is a process intended to improve the appearance and salability of a stamp by applying new gum to simulate original gum. Regumming need not be contemporary. It may have been done years or decades earlier. Regummed stamps trade at a substantial discount, typically only 10 to 20 percent of catalogue value.
- **Gum Skips.** Natural gum skips are small areas on the back of a stamp not covered by gum at the time it was laid down during manufacture. Technically not a fault, gum skips generally don't affect a stamp's value unless they are large or unsightly.

The following symbols are often used in advertising and auction catalogues to indicate the state of gum:

★ ★   never hinged

★   hinged

(★)   without original gum, unused

In the early days, gum was made up in batches and applied by hand with brushes, giving uneven results from one job to the next. After aging more than a century and a half, such gum has often cracked, browned, or otherwise degraded and looks nothing like the pristine gum on modern stamps the gum collectors are so accustomed to seeing and associating with premium quality stamps. When first encountering original gum on early stamps, the inexperienced eye often finds it so unappealing, so different from that found on modern issues, that the initial impulse is to refuse to believe it is really original gum. One school of thought holds that original gum used during the first 25 years of stamp manufacture is so ugly that its presence is unimportant anyway. Auctions frequently publish the disclaimer "Original gum is not to be expected on stamps before 1890," and you would do well to bear that in mind. Nineteenth-century stamps possessing original gum are scarce, and those that do have it usually have been heavily hinged. Except for the lowest denominations, never-hinged copies are, indeed, rare. Because only a minuscule percentage of key nineteenth-century stamps (such as the high-value Columbians) are never hinged, certification by a competent expertizing authority is essential for examples purporting to be never hinged.

As with centering, the condition of gum on a stamp must be measured against others of its issue, not against modern issues. One must be forgiving about the condition of gum on early issues. The presence of any reasonably attractive gum, be it hinged or not, on pre-1870 stamps is a bonus. Light hinging is the best one can reasonably expect for most nineteenth-century issues. Twentieth-century stamps are generally available never hinged, although light hinging is sometimes the best one can expect on rarer issues.

Most collectors strive to obtain the best possible examples available. As a general rule, the higher a stamp's overall grade, the greater the premium for never-hinged condition. Don't pay a never-hinged premium for visually unappealing stamps and stamps in lower grades.

PERFORATIONS

Collectors prefer reasonably intact and balanced perforation tips within the limits of an issue. Some U.S. issues, such as the hard-paper banknotes, are prone to irregular perfs because they were printed on brittle paper with poor separation characteristics. The 1875 reprints of the 1857–60 issue usually exhibit ragged, irregular, or short perfs because of the paper on which they were printed. Others, such as perf 8 1/2 or perf 10 Washington-Franklins, are prone to poor separation because of the size or spacing of perforation holes. Occasionally, perforating equipment fails to completely punch out holes, leaving them filled with circular bits of paper known as *chad*. While not technically a fault, chad is, nevertheless, unsightly. Reperforated stamps are held in low esteem and worth only a fraction of catalogue value, typically 10 to 20 percent.

Assess the condition of perforations in context with that which is usual for an issue. Where irregular perfs are the norm, as they are on a majority of nineteenth-century issues, they should not be considered a fault.

Modern issues routinely come with uniform, balanced perforations, and collectors really don't pay much attention to their condition unless it is visually distracting. Nor do they pay much attention to the condition of perfs on inexpensive stamps.

This stamp possesses perforations typical of early issues; note short perforations at midway left and at lower right.

Short or pulled perfs—as opposed to irregular perfs—refer to perforation teeth that are missing, usually all the way to the base of the perforation or below it. Short perfs are considered a fault.

COLOR

The term "color" refers to how vivid or pronounced color is within the range of shades typically encountered on an issue. The more intense the color, the nearer to its issued state, the more appealing the stamp. Fresh, vivid color is especially prized on older stamps because pigments tend to fade over time. Newer stamps tend to be near their issued state, so color is not so much an issue. Some stamps, most notably orange-colored issues, tend to discolor when they come in contact with sulfur compounds, either atmospheric or in album or stock book papers. Others, such as the 30¢ denomination of the 1861 series, are notoriously poorly colored. Assess a stamp's color in comparison to others of its kind, not issues that are routinely boldly colored.

FRESHNESS

Ideally, a stamp possesses "mint bloom" and paper as fresh as the day it was printed. The older the stamp, the less likely it is to be found in a state of pristine freshness. Until the second half of the twentieth century, album manufacturers paid little attention to the quality of paper they used to make albums. Stamps stored for any length of time in albums and stock books made of low-grade paper often exhibit a slight brownish or yellowish cast (referred to as *toning*). Knowledgeable collectors avoid toned stamps. Assess the degree of freshness against that which is typical for the issue.

Light cancel (left); heavy cancel (right).

CANCELS

The ideal cancel is neat and clear and does not distract from or obliterate the underlying design of the stamp. It is legitimate and contemporaneous to the stamp. Serious collectors eschew favor cancels or contrived cancels, especially on expensive stamps. Expensive stamps whose mint and used price is the same or nearly the same are often encountered with bogus cancels because they are more salable than unattractive, heavily hinged mint examples. Hence the emphasis on "legitimate" and "contemporaneous." Be cautious when purchasing used stamps whose value is the same as or more than unused examples.

In many cases, the type of cancel on a nineteenth-century stamp has a bearing on its value. Colored cancels, specialty cancels, and fancy cancels often add

Device-canceled stamp (left); pen-canceled stamp (right).

a considerable premium to the value of a stamp. Device-canceled stamps generally sell for more than pen-canceled examples. Collectors avoid pen cancels on post-nineteenth-century stamps. Revenue cancels and CTOs (canceled to order) are generally worth considerably less than postal cancels. Refer to a specialized catalogue for premiums and discounts for various types of cancels.

FAULTS

Major faults include tears, thins, pinholes, creases, scuffs, abrasions, stains, foxing, discolorations, glazed gum, tropicalized gum, or anything else that might be construed as damage. Minor or trivial faults include things such as perf bends and perf thins. The earlier the issue, the greater the likelihood it will be faulty. The vast majority of nineteenth-century stamps contain faults. Stamps free of faults are referred to as *sound*. Grades of condition that otherwise apply to a sound stamp do not apply to a faulty stamp. Faulty stamps go directly to the lowest price bracket. Stamps with pieces missing are virtually worthless.

Examples of stamps with straight edges.

Other elements, such as straight edges (collectors disdain straight edges on stamps that normally occur with perforations on all sides), heavy cancels, and poor centering, which technically are not faults, nevertheless reduce the value of a stamp to a small fraction of catalogue value.

Natural inclusions (material embedded in paper during its manufacture), unnaturally irregular perfs, gum skips, perf dimples, toned paper, natural gum skips, and natural gum bends (unless severe enough to break the paper fibers), while not technically faults, are elements avoided by many buyers. The absence of these elements generally enhances the value of a stamp.

Unlike other collectible fields (such as fine art or antique automobiles) where restoration is accepted and encouraged, any attempt to improve the appearance of a stamp or repair it is generally regarded as tampering and is held in equally low esteem with outright fakery. Collectors have a strong and historical aversion to "improved" (e.g., regummed or reperforated) and repaired stamps, insisting instead on the best original condition. Repaired and improved stamps are considered faulty nevertheless. The standard for covers is not quite so strict. Erasure of pencil notations (if not evident) and other superficial improvements are generally not deemed improper.

The presence of a major fault or repair generally diminishes the value of a stamp substantially, except in the case of extreme rarities not known (or seldom encountered) without faults or improvements. Many classic rarities do not exist in an unaltered state.

Over the years, a number of attempts have been made to quantify the elements of condition and bring mathematical precision to grading, most often using computer analysis. Grade, however, is largely a matter of subjective taste and in some cases even an acquired taste. It's impossible to reduce visual aesthetics to mathematics. There's just no objective way to measure "eye appeal." You might as well try to create a computer program to measure the physical beauty of human beings. As the old saying goes, "Beauty lies in the eye of the beholder," which is exactly why computer grading will never replace the human eye when it comes to stamp grading. The eye has been and will continue to be the best tool for grading stamps.

In summary, condition is the key factor of value. Sound stamps—those free of faults—are priced according to grade. Faulty stamps are worth only a small percentage of catalogue value, often as little as 5 percent to 20 percent. Grades of condition that might otherwise apply to a sound stamp do not apply to a faulty stamp. Severely impaired stamps, such as those with pieces missing, are virtually worthless.

Experienced buyers look for premium quality stamps—stamps that exhibit the best qualities for their issue. In some cases, such as U.S. Zeppelin airmails of 1930, nicely centered, never-hinged, post-office-fresh examples are easy to obtain. In other cases, such as an unused 10¢ 1847, they are nearly impossible. So maintain a sense of proportion. Strive for quality but never let the quest for quality blind you to the limitations of an issue. Be aware of condition, but don't become obsessed by it. Some buyers become so obsessed with quality that they begin to find something wrong with every stamp, regardless of its general excellence. Avoid unrealistic expectations and never forget the frailties and limitations of nineteenth-century stamps. The rarer the stamp, the more difficult it will be to find in premium condition and the less picky one can afford to be. Some stamps are so rare that a reasonable population of candidates simply does not exist, and selectivity, in the normal sense, is not possible.

CONSERVATION

S TAMPS, ESPECIALLY OLD ones, are fragile objects that must be handled and stored with care. Protect them from hazards, such as light, heat, moisture, and improper storage. House your collection in products made specifically for the hobby or that you know with certainty are safe for stamps and covers. Some hazards, such as moisture, are obvious. Others, such as acidity in paper or the chemical instability of some plastics, are not.

LIGHT

Don't expose stamps and covers to direct light for prolonged periods. Pigments are prone to fading, and paper to yellowing. Sunlight is especially bad; fluorescent light is not much better. Generally, stamps and covers should not be framed for permanent display. Even the use of UV glass to screen out ultraviolet light will not protect against other wavelengths, which too can cause damage over time, although more subtly. Short-term exposure to light, such as exhibiting at a show, is not a danger.

MOISTURE

More stamps are ruined by moisture than any other hazard. Moisture in all forms (water, humidity, dampness) is deadly. Keep stamps as dry as possible. Store stamp albums upright so they can breathe. Never store albums flat, especially piled atop one another, because the weight causes stamps to stick, especially under humid conditions. For the same reason, do not force more albums or stock books on a shelf than comfortably fit. Even stamps in glassines are susceptible to moisture and pressure. Once stuck together, soaking is required to separate them, and gum is lost in the process. Album paper absorbs humidity readily but loses it only slowly. A few humid days are enough to expose stamps to weeks of dampness. Albums exposed to a spell of abnormally high humidity should be opened immediately afterward and allowed to dry. If you live in a damp climate, consider airing stamps out several times a year to avoid glazed gum. Humidity wreaks such havoc on gum that some collectors in places such as Hawaii and the Caribbean collect only used stamps.

Silica gel absorbs moisture. Small pouches of silica gel placed in enclosed spaces such as boxes, drawers, and cabinets reduce humidity. The pouches should be removed occasionally and put in a warm dry place or a drying oven to dry out. Generally, a number of small pouches distributed around the area to be kept dry works better than one large pouch. Silica gel makes sense for safe deposit boxes also.

Talcum powder is sometimes used to prevent mint sheets or blocks from sticking together. Unfortunately, the coating of powder, even a light coating, gives stamps an unappealing appearance and an odd feel. There is no practical way to remove the powder, so it's best to avoid it.

Moisture promotes the growth of mold and mildew, which discolor stamps and attack gum. Even stamps without gum are susceptible to mildew and foxing. Foxing leaves telltale brown or rust-colored spots.

Avoid storing stamps in places prone to dampness or leaks, such as basements, storage sheds, and barns. Don't store stamps near water pipes. Even safe deposit boxes are not 100 percent safe. Stamps in fireproof bank vaults have been ruined by sprinklers set off by a fire in another part of the bank. Occasionally, safe deposit vaults located below ground level are flooded by broken water mains or springtime downpours, perils that do not affect vaults located above ground. In addition, subterranean vaults are more prone to dampness from ground moisture.

HEAT

Keep stamps away from heat. It's harmful in itself, and it compounds the effects of moisture. Avoid storing stamp albums on shelves exposed to direct sunlight. Avoid attics and garages, which, likewise, are prone to overheating. Exposure to heat and moisture causes stamps to curl, often so badly that attempting to uncurl them ruins them. Dry heat is no better. It causes stamps to become brittle and gum to crack. Severely cracked, brittle gum breaks paper fibers along crack lines, ruining stamps as surely as if they had been cut. Prolonged exposure to dramatic temperature swings weakens paper fibers over time as surely as bending a piece of wire again and again weakens it. Avoid temperature extremes and continuous fluctuations.

ABRASIVES AND INSECTS

Keep stamps away from dust and dirt. Windblown grit, the kind that accumulates in garages and sheds, acts like sandpaper, if ever so subtly. Keep stamps away from insects. Even seemingly innocuous ones can be dangerous. Crickets love the flavor of some gums and eagerly nibble away portions of stamps possessing it.

HANDLING

Make sure your hands are clean and dry before working with stamps, and when possible use stamp tongs. Fingers contain moisture, oil, and often small amounts of grime. A fingerprint on otherwise pristine gum stands out like a dirty footprint on a clean floor. When it's not practical to use tongs, as in the case of mint panes, make sure your hands are clean and dry.

Keep food and drink away from stamps. A spilled soda or cup of coffee wreaks havoc on anything nearby. A particle of moist food inadvertently flicked onto a prized stamp or cover usually leaves a stain. Sadly, it happens all too frequently. Save snacks and drinks for time spent watching TV or reading the newspaper.

Always use a stamp mount large enough to comfortably accommodate the stamp. Never force a stamp into a mount too small or too tight fitting. You'll either damage the stamp right then or it will warp over time. Be careful not to use too much saliva on the back of a mount. Excess saliva leaking onto the back of the stamp defeats the whole purpose of the mount.

Don't hinge never-hinged stamps, unless you don't mind reducing their value. It's okay to hinge used stamps, previously hinged stamps, and stamps with no gum.

Don't remove stamps from covers or postcards; they're usually worth more than the stamps by themselves. Don't attempt to separate stamps that are stuck together or stuck down to album pages; you'll only cause damage and reduce their value. Don't attempt to clean stamps. More stamps have been ruined by attempts to clean them than have been salvaged or improved. Remove stamps from mounts carefully to avoid damage.

SUPPLY HAZARDS

Keep tape (adhesive, cellophane, whatever the kind) away from your stamps. Don't use it on album pages, on glassines, or to secure the sides of mounts. Don't use tape on anything stamp related—period. And that goes for so-called archival and low-tack tapes. Archival tape is available from framing supply outlets. It is generally used by picture framers to mount articles on mat board for framing and often touted as harmless. It may be archival and harmless in the sense that it is acid-free, chemically stable, and not prone to discoloration, but it is nevertheless an adhesive, one often difficult to remove. At least one variety of archival tape holds like iron and is almost impossible to peel away without either leaving a residue or taking part of the attached paper with it. To be prudent, avoid tapes of all kinds, even those touted as benign.

Don't mount or store newspaper clippings in proximity to stamps. Newspaper yellows and the yellowing worsens with the passing of time. The chemicals that cause yellowing migrate into any other paper they come in contact with—stamps, covers, album pages. A photocopy on acid-free paper is an excellent alternative.

The jury's still out on recycled paper, which is treated with powerful bleaching agents and other chemicals. In general, avoid any paper with a chemical odor. The stronger the odor, the more chemicals in the paper. It may take years to know what harmful effects, if any, chemicals used in recycling have on paper. In the meantime, avoid taking risks with your stamps.

Avoid using glassine envelopes for long-term storage. They tend to be acidic and contain impurities that cause them to discolor over time. They are fine, however, for short-term storage. Discard old glassines or anything else that has yellowed with the passing of time.

Don't store stamps in variety-store photo albums, especially the kind with waxed or self-adhesive pages, even those advertised as being low-tack. Don't store stamps in kitchen-type waxed paper.

Keep rubber bands away from stamps. They contain a sulfur compound that discolors some pigments. And nothing's worse than a rubber band that has dried out or melted and adhered to whatever it was in contact with.

Don't use paper clips on stamps, on glassines containing stamps, on album pages, or anywhere they might leave a mark. Some paper clips rust, especially in humid climates, leaving spots on anything they've come in contact with.

Periodically, check albums, stock books, and anything else used to house your stamps for any sign of a problem. This may sound like common sense, but you'd be surprised at the number of people who tuck things away in boxes, albums, and stock books and rarely look at them. It's better to catch a problem early than to let it progress. Check mint-sheet files to make sure that pages have not begun to warp. Mint sheets housed within warped mint-sheet file pages retain their warped appearance when removed.

House stamps in materials made specifically for the hobby. If it wasn't made for stamps, think twice about using it. Several companies manufacture high-quality supplies for stamps. Refer to Chapter 36, "Resources."

MICROORGANISMS

Sooner or later most collectors acquire an old album or accumulation that smells musty or contains foxing or discoloration. The musty smell and the discoloration are evidence of microorganisms at work. Mold and mildew require only moisture and a simple nutrient to grow. That nutrient in paper. The last thing you want is harmful microorganisms infecting your stamps and albums. Avoid placing anything that smells of mildew next to stamps or with your collection. Think twice about transplanting mildewed stamps into an otherwise clean and uncontaminated collection. Discard inexpensive mildewed stamps. They are not worth the potential harm they can cause. If you must keep more expensive mildewed items, isolate them or treat them with an anti-fungal agent where practical. Discard mildewed albums and any other mildewed materials as soon as you have removed what you plan to keep from them.

PAPER

Acidity in paper most often arises from aluminum sulfate or alum, which is used as sizing in the manufacture of paper. Over time, acidity destroys paper fiber and affects other paper in close contact with it. The damage is progressive and cumulative.

Acidity is measured on a pH scale, which expresses values numerically ranging from 0 to 14. On the scale, pH 7 is acid neutral. Lower numbers are more acidic; higher numbers more alkaline. The scale is logarithmic, i.e. pH 5 is ten times more acidic than pH 6; pH 4 is 100 times more acidic than pH 6. Small variations in pH, therefore, add up to large variations in actual acidity. Some album manufacturers disclose the pH number for their products, others do not. Generally, the larger the pH number, the more long-lived the paper.

Acid-free or archival paper is best for long-term storage of stamps. Acid-free paper is manufactured with no acidic additives and possesses a pH value of 7.0 or greater. Archival paper likewise is manufactured without acidic additives, possesses a minimum pH value of 7.0 and an alkaline buffer equivalent to a minimum of two percent calcium carbonate.

Even relatively low acidity works mischief on articles exposed to it over long periods of time—articles such as stamps and covers housed for years or decades in the same albums, stock books and glassines.

If you're concerned about your album system's potential acidity, test it with a pH pen. They cost only a few dollars. A excellent report on the acidity of album pages is available from the Arthur Salm Foundation. The report (Report Number 1) includes findings from tests on more than 60 album products. Refer to "Conservation" in Chapter 36, "Resources."

PLASTIC

Plastic is used to manufacture a variety of philatelic products, including stamp mounts, cover sleeves, stock books, and stock pages. Numerous types of plastic exist. The forms most commonly encountered in philately are polyethylene (PE), polyvinyl chloride (PVC), polypropylene (PP), polystyrene (PS), and polyethylene terephthalate (PET, or polyester). PVC is better known as the ubiquitous vinyl. PET is manufactured by DuPont under the trademark Mylar.

PVC, or vinyl, is one of the oldest commercial plastics. It is manufactured in two basic forms: unplasticized, or hard, PVC (uPVC) and plasticized, or softened, PVC (pPVC). Hard PVC is used in products ranging from credit cards to water pipes. Softened PVC is used in products ranging from automobile upholstery to discount-store photo-album pages. The softening agent is visible as an oily iridescent film and smells strongly of "new-car smell." The stronger the odor, the more softener the item contains.

Plasticized (softened) vinyl is not inert. It is highly detrimental to paper and inks—the stuff of stamps. Keep stamps away from anything made of it. The plasticizer or softener has been known to leach the color out of some printing inks and to discolor stamps. Imagine removing a prized first day cover from a "protective" sleeve only to find that the colored image contained in the cachet and postage stamp had migrated into the plastic, leaving only a pale ghostly image where the formerly bright-colored cachet and stamp had been. I've seen it happen—and as they say, it ain't pretty.

Unplasticized vinyl is fairly inert. Archivists generally regard it as safe for storing paper articles. Most manufacturers of unplasticized vinyl hobby products make it a point to advertise that their products contain no softeners. At least one labels its product as being made from "Safety Vinyl." Avoid products not so advertised or labeled. Avoid any vinyl product that displays an oily iridescent film or smells strongly of new car smell.

Of the various plastics, Mylar is preferred by archivists because of its relative chemical stability. It is also widely used in hobby products, especially cover sleeves. For all its virtues, Mylar has one drawback—it yellows under continuous exposure to sunlight or any other ultraviolet source. The yellowing itself does not migrate and is not necessarily detrimental to stamps, but its dingy appearance is unsightly. The problem is easily avoided by keeping Mylar away from direct sunlight or continuous exposure to any other ultraviolet source. A word of caution: Avoid Mylar products that contain ultraviolet inhibitor. It prevents yellowing but is harmful to stamps. I've not encountered any stamp-related Mylar product that contains UV inhibitor but mention it to alert those who might inadvertently use a nonhobby product treated with it, thinking that it might provide added protection.

Polypropylene, too, is fairly inert. It is used to make cover sleeves marketed to the hobby. It is also used to make 8 1/2-by-11-inch sheet holders, the kind punched for three-ring binders and marketed to the general public in office supply stores. Sheet holders are handy for storing letters, documents, and large ancillary items. They are, however, highly flexible and tend to sag in binders stored upright. Once warped, they hold the distorted shape, so be careful how you store them. Some avoid the problem by inserting a rigid backing into the holder; however, avoid using cheap card stock, which is almost always highly acidic. Also, be aware that some brands of sheet holders are made of softened vinyl. They look nearly identical to their polypropylene counterparts, so check the package before you buy to make sure the holders are made of polypropylene.

Polyethylene is primarily used to make cover sleeves. It is lightweight and flexible, even slippery, as anyone who has ever tried to manage a handful can attest. It possesses a slight grayish cast. Polyethylene (or poly) sleeves are favored by dealers who travel because they are lighter than Mylar sleeves and much less expensive. Poly sleeves appear to be fairly inert—at least experience suggests they are. The only drawbacks, if indeed they can be considered drawbacks, are that they are rather floppy and slippery and possess the slight grayish cast. Sometimes sleeves within a batch vary slightly in size. Don't attempt to force a cover into a poly sleeve, even a sleeve only the barest smidgen smaller than the cover. Poly sleeves do not retain the forced stretch for long, and the result is a warped cover.

Polystyrene is most often encountered in stamp mounts. Modern plastic stamp mounts are generally acknowledged to be safe. Some of the earlier mounts, however, have proven to be harmful. Plastics have been used to make stamp mounts since the 1940s. In the early days, not much was known about the long-term stability of plastics. Mounts were produced in a variety of styles using a variety of plastics, some of which proved to be poor choices. By the 1970s, the effects of mounts made from problem plastics became increasingly apparent. Supply manufacturers took note and by the 1980s had begun to produce more thoroughly researched, better engineered, and safer mounts. If your collection contains mounts produced before the 1980s, check for signs of deterioration—cracking, warping, discoloration, melted adhesive, and so forth. Remove stamps in defective mounts and remount them in a new product. Be careful when removing stamps from old mounts, especially those made of heavy gauge plastic that requires cutting. It's all too easy to inadvertently cut or scrape the stamp. Sharp edges on brittle mounts, too, can cause damage.

As a general rule, avoid plastic products not specifically designed for the hobby. Keep stamps and covers away from kitchen wrap (polyvinylidene chloride). It can be detrimental. Don't use heat-sealed shrink-wrap on stamps and covers. That goes for vacuum-freezing systems, too. The Postal Service shrink-wraps some products available from its philatelic mail-order facility. In some cases, products are labeled with a warning that their packaging is not suitable for long-term storage and should be removed; in other cases, products are not so labeled. Take no chances; remove shrink-wrap immediately upon receipt. Plastics are especially vulnerable to heat. Keep them away from heat sources such as furnace vents. Keep plastics as near to room temperature as possible.

Avoid placing different types of plastic next to one another. Not all types chemically interact, but some do. The wrong combination can result in a gooey, melted mess. Don't take chances. Don't interleave album pages containing plastic stamp mounts with plastic sheets. Also, make sure stamps are dry of watermark fluid before inserting them into mounts.

Some plastics are advertised as archival. The term is not a technical term in the sense that plastics so described meet a certain scientific standard. No scientific standard has ever been established for archival plastics. The term "archival" is generally understood to mean that a substance is chemically stable (or relatively chemically stable) over time and does not readily degrade. Perhaps the closest thing to a standard comes from the Preservation Office of the Library of Congress. It uses the following stringent criteria for plastics or "protective films" that come into contact with materials that are archivally stored: "Composition must be clear, colorless (biaxially oriented/stressed/drawn) film such as DuPont Mylar, ICI Melinex 516 or equivalent. The clear and colorless polyester film must not contain plasticizer, surface coatings, UV inhibitors, or adsorbents and be guaranteed to be non-yellowing with natural aging. The material must not contain any coloring agents."

From a practical standpoint, archivists in libraries and museums consider stable plastics—those that are free of harmful additives (the kinds generally advertised as archival)—to be suitable for storage of paper articles. These same kinds of plastics are generally safe for stamps.

INSURANCE

Insure collections of any significant value. Most homeowner's policies cover collectibles, but their limits of liability are low, typically $300 or so, without a special rider. Specialty underwriters offer excellent, low-cost policies that cover most risks, such as fire, theft, and so forth. Their policies' limits of liability are higher and premiums lower than those of most standard casualty policies. In most cases, insurance companies offer discounts for valuables stored in safes and for homes protected by an alarm system monitored by a security firm. Some collectibles policies offer dual coverage, insurance for items kept at home plus, at little or no additional cost, matching coverage for items stored in a bank safe deposit box. Refer to Chapter 36 for more information.

Insurance often makes more sense than paying safe deposit rent, especially for bulky collections and less expensive items. Before spending hundreds of dollars a year on storage, compare the cost with insurance. Be aware that unless the contents of a safe deposit box are insured, they're at risk from loss by fire, theft, natural disaster, and so on. Virtually all banks refuse to accept liability for the contents of a safe deposit box for any reason. Check your box rental agreement.

It pays to have an inventory of your philatelic possessions in case of theft or destruction. Several software companies publish stamp inventory databases. Some permit scans to be imported. A typed or manuscript inventory is okay, too. Be sure to include the country name, the catalogue number, the quantity, mint or used, the condition, the date acquired, and the price paid. Photocopy or make detailed scans of the most expensive items. Detail is vital to identifying stolen property. Snapshots of album pages made under poor lighting or at a distance often fail to reveal usable detail even when enlarged. Take care to make a usable record.

SAFES

Safes fall into three categories: fire resistant, burglar resistant, and resistant to both. Inexpensive safes, such as those available at discount chains, resist fire and tend to deter the amateur thief as well but offer little protection against the experienced pro. Fire-resistant safes are rated according to how long they resist fire. A "one hour" safe is designed to protect contents from an exterior temperature up to 1,700° Fahrenheit for at least one hour; a "two hour" safe, from an exterior temperature up to 1,850° for two hours. In each case, during the rated time, the interior temperature of the safe is not supposed to exceed 350°, well below the temperature at which paper ignites, about 450°. The average house fire burns at about 1,250° Fahrenheit, well below the rated maximum. Bear in mind, however, that fire-resistant safes are designed to protect valuable papers, jewelry, and the like—not stamps. Stamps are vulnerable to warping and gum crazing, hazards caused by exposure to heat as low as 250° to 350°. One final thought: Before buying, check the manufacturer's literature to find out if a safe is water resistant. After all, water is used to extinguish fires. It is an exercise in futility to protect stamps from fire only to have them ruined by water.

Burglar-resistant safes are rated according to how long they resist attack. A TL-15 (short for tool resistant, 15 minutes) resists assault with common tools such as crowbars, picks, drills, and the like for at least 15 minutes; a TL-30 resists for at least 30 minutes. Some safes with higher ratings resist cutting torches as well. Torch-resistant safes contain a layer of composite that rapidly dissipates heat, making it difficult to heat metal behind it sufficiently to cut through. Burglar-resistant safes are much more expensive than simple fire-resistant safes. They range in price from several hundred dollars to several thousand, depending on rating and size.

Safes that are fire and burglar resistant combine the attributes of both but are more expensive yet, ranging in price from about $1,000 and up. Moving and installation may be extra.

SHIPPING

Although not strictly a conservation issue, packing is mentioned here because philatelic shipments often end up damaged due to careless packing. When shipping stamps and covers, pack them with the idea that if something can be damaged, it will be. Mail does not pass from hand to hand nowadays. It is automated. It is collected in bins, dumped into mechanical sorting and canceling equipment, moved along conveyor belts, stuffed into mailbags, piled in cargo containers, and, in short, not necessarily treated with kid gloves or tender loving care. Anticipate how your shipment will handled. Pack accordingly. Don't pack books or albums with their corners tight against the corners of a box. Inevitably, the corners will get dinged somewhere along the line. Pack them in containers large enough to keep their corners safe.

Don't rely on the caution "Do Not Bend" alone to protect something mailed in a large flimsy envelope. Pack it in a container that resists folding. Use plenty of strong tape to secure flaps and edges on cartons. Observe how large, experienced mail-order firms have packed shipments that arrive at your door. They have it down to a science. One need only stand in line at the post office during the holiday season to observe abysmally poor packing jobs. Registered mail offers the best protection for shipments of any value. This is because it is signed for each time it changes hands along its journey. Insured mail offers indemnity, but items are not individually tracked as they make their way through the system.

Private firms, such as Federal Express and UPS, also offer excellent service. Be aware that they will not indemnify certain types of shipments, especially those of "extraordinary value." Do not attempt to circumvent the restriction by declaring the contents to be something such as books. In the event of loss, you'll be out. Shipping companies are under no legal obligation to reimburse for lost or damaged shipments that were misrepresented.

In summary, use common sense in handling and storing stamps. Keep them away from light, heat, moisture, and dirt. Avoid storing stamps in basements, garages, storage sheds, and attics. To the degree possible, store stamps in an area with reasonably constant temperature and humidity. Use high-quality materials, those intended specifically for use with stamps, where possible. Protect valuable stamps and covers with one or a combination of safeguards: bank safe deposit, insurance, home safe, and home alarm system monitored by a security firm. When sending stamps or covers through the mail, pack them carefully to avoid damage.

FORGERIES AND FAKES

STAMPS—COMMON STAMPS and rarities alike—have been forged and faked since the very beginning. Some are crude and obvious, others are clever and fool all but the most practiced eye. Fakes are not much of a problem for the general or casual collector buying moderately priced stamps, but still one should be aware that the problem exists. The most dangerous and deceptive fakes are most often encountered where real money is involved. Not only are stamps themselves faked, but elements of genuine stamps are faked or altered to simulate more valuable varieties. Alterations include such things as overprints, postmarks, and straight edges added to sheet stamps to simulate scarce coil varieties. In addition to forged and faked stamps, elements of condition are altered, especially on early or valuable stamps, to improve value.

FORGERIES

The term "forgery" generally refers to a fabrication created to defraud stamp collectors. Forged stamps simulate authentic stamps.

A Sperati forgery marked as such.

A number of master craftsmen, such as the notorious Jean de Sperati and Francois Fournier, produced dangerously deceptive forgeries, most often of rare and valuable stamps, especially foreign stamps of the nineteenth century.

Plenty of midrange stamps, and even some cheap ones, have been forged over the years. The vast majority, but not all, are forgeries of foreign stamps. In most cases, they do not exhibit the craftsmanship of the master forgers but are, nevertheless, often deceptive. Catalogue footnotes warn of some forgeries. In addition, several excellent reference books exist. *The Serrane*

Guide, published by the American Philatelic Society, covers forgeries up to the year 1926. *Focus on Forgeries*, by Varro E. Tyler, is an illustrated guide that enables collectors to recognize a host of forged stamps from countries all over the world. *Philatelic Forgers: Their Lives and Works*, also by Varro E. Tyler, explores the lives and exploits of the best-known forgers. It's a fascinating read. Refer to Chapter 34, "Philatelic Reference Books," for more information.

Ironically, some collectors specialize in collecting forgeries, especially inexpensive ones. Forgeries of the masters, such as Sperati, are avidly sought, often selling for hundreds of dollars at auction.

This counterfeit is obvious to collectors because the stamp was issued only in booklet format and all genuine examples contain at least one straight edge.

COUNTERFEITS

The term "counterfeit" generally refers to fabrications created to defraud a postal authority rather than stamp collectors. Postal counterfeits are usually ordinary, current definitives. They are prized by specialists and usually worth far more than their genuine counterparts. During World War II, the Allies created counterfeit German stamps for use on propaganda mail dropped inside the Third Reich. These, too, are prized by collectors and worth far more than their genuine counterparts.

ILLEGAL AND UNAUTHORIZED STAMPS

The term "illegal stamps" has recently gained currency with respect to a variety of illicit emissions, such as some recent issues bearing the name of a legitimate country, but created without the permission and knowledge of the postal authority of the country and usually produced outside the country, most often by firms in Europe. The Universal Postal Union issues warnings about illegal stamps based on complaints from member nations in whose names the stamps have been issued.

After the breakup of the Soviet Union, a rash of unauthorized stamps were issued by nominally autonomous territories and regions, whose "sovereignty" in most cases turned out to be fictitious. A listing of them appears in Chapter 22, "Former Soviet Territories Issuing Unrecognized Stamps."

FACSIMILES AND REPRODUCTIONS

A facsimile is a reproduction of a postage stamp. Some facsimiles are marked as such and sold or distributed without intent to deceive. Others are not actually marked but are nevertheless sold or distributed as facsimiles, again without intent to defraud. The term "reproduction" has become more or less synonymous with "facsimile" and tends to be used in place of it in everyday philatelic parlance.

During the early days of the hobby, dealers routinely sold reproductions of rare stamps, which they advertised as such. One dealer went so far as to advertise that collectors ought not waste money on expensive originals when excellent reproductions could be had at little cost and filled album spaces just as nicely. No one seemed to think there was anything wrong with making and selling reproductions so long as no attempt to defraud was involved. Of course, human nature being what it is, some inevitably found it more profitable to sell their handiwork as genuine. The harmless reproduction all too easily became the forgery. By the end of the nineteenth century, the philatelic community began to frown on reproductions, legitimate or otherwise, and they fell into disrepute.

Reproductions still turn up in old-time albums. They're known as *album weeds*, perhaps because of the frequency with which they show up. Among the most notorious and endemic are reproductions of Roman States stamps. Sets of genuine examples are worth thousands; sets of reproductions, worth little. Genuine examples are rarely found in sets; reproductions, invariably, in sets. Genuine examples are rarely in good condition; reproductions, invariably, in excellent condition.

Old stamps usually show their age. Be suspicious of any nineteenth-century stamp in uncharacteristically good condition. And be doubly suspicious of nineteenth-century sets (especially expensive ones) containing stamps of uniform high quality. They're probably reproductions. Pay attention to footnotes in stamp catalogues that warn about bogus issues. They often provide tips on how to identify reproductions.

REPRINTS

Although not fakes, reprints are mentioned here because sooner or later you'll run across the term and should be aware of its meaning. A *reprint* is a stamp printed from original plates, usually at a later date after the original issue is obsolete, or a stamp printed from new plates (often distinguishable from the original plates) and released subsequent to the original issue having become obsolete. Reprints often can be distinguished from originals by virtue of paper, ink, or perforations, which usually vary slightly, and in some cases markedly, from originals. Reprints are not created with intent to deceive. An unauthorized reprint is one made from plates no longer in the possession of or without the permission of the original issuing entity.

FAKE COILS

Valuable U.S. coils are frequently faked by trimming away perforations on parallel sides of an inexpensive sheet stamp of the same design. Fakes are usually narrower than genuine coils; the trimmed sides are often not parallel; and traces of perforations sometimes remain visible on carelessly trimmed edges.

Rare coils of the 1902–03 definitive series are frequently faked and should never be purchased without an expert certificate. Fake coils of the Washington-Franklin series are endemic. *The Expert's Book*, by Paul Schmid, is the best and most authoritative work on Washington-Franklin fakes and how to spot them. Later coil issues are less frequently faked because most are neither rare nor valuable.

Line pairs (lines appear on rotary press coils where curved intaglio printing plates were joined, about every 24 stamps or so) are sometimes faked using a pen and straightedge. Faked lines, which are most often encountered on expensive issues,

This pair contains a natural straight edge at left. Perforations at right could be trimmed away to fake the rare and expensive coil of the same design.

are not generally difficult to detect. Check suspect lines under magnification. Ink of the line and the adjacent stamps should match exactly. The line should be parallel to the edges of adjacent stamps. Genuine intaglio lines rise above the surface of the paper, an effect visible under magnification. Lines added by pen are flat and smooth. Also check for ink inside perforation holes underneath the line. No trace of ink should be present on genuine examples.

Expensive booklet panes are sometimes created by trimming perforations off less expensive sheet stamps. Trimming off perforations usually leaves abnormally small margins, a sure sign of tampering. Make sure booklet panes have large margins on straight-edged sides. Take time to familiarize yourself with the normal size of genuine booklet panes.

FAKE IMPERFORATES

Imperforate singles are easily faked by trimming perforations off perforated copies, especially those with jumbo margins. That's why imperforates are collected in pairs or multiples. The 5¢ definitive of 1902–03 is often trimmed to simulate its valuable regularly issued imperforate counterpart. In general, avoid imperforate singles, especially those that purport to be valuable varieties.

Fake imperforates are often created by trimming perforated examples.

CLEANED STAMPS AND ALTERED CANCELS

"Cleaned" refers to stamps whose cancellations have been removed. Used stamps, especially early issues of the nineteenth century, are cleaned to increase their value, either by making them appear unused or in the case of pen-canceled stamps, by recanceling them with a device cancel, such as a grid or circular date stamp, which are worth more than pen cancels. Pen-canceled stamps are favored candidates for cleaning because writing ink is generally more susceptible to bleaching than inks used for device cancels and because pen-canceled stamps are less valuable than device-canceled stamps.

Some stamps are more prone to cleaning than others because some printing inks are more colorfast than others. Black is among the most colorfast, and the 10¢ 1847, which is black, among the most frequently cleaned. The difference in price between a mint and a used example is several thousand dollars, a strong incentive to remove a cancel.

Device cancels on early nineteenth-century U.S. issues are generally worth double the value of pen cancels. Device cancels in certain colors, such as red, blue, or green, are worth even more. Green cancels are especially scarce and valuable. A heavy, unsightly pen cancel is bleached out, and a light unobtrusive device cancel, perhaps in one of the premium colors, is applied, and voilà—a mediocre stamp is transformed into an attractive, valuable example. Examine device-canceled early stamps for signs of tampering, especially those of significant value. Bleached pen strokes often show up in watermark fluid or under ultraviolet light. Abnormally white or bright paper is a sign of bleaching. Pay attention to the printed image; it should not appear washed out or faded, especially if the paper is unusually white or bright.

FAKE CANCELS AND ALTERED COVERS

Occasionally, a used stamp catalogues either the same as or more than a mint example. A heavily hinged mint stamp (worth only a small fraction of catalogue because of disturbed gum) can be transformed into very fine used copy by soaking off the disturbed gum and applying a light cancel. The resulting "problem-free" used stamp is worth double or triple the impaired mint stamp.

Mint German stamps issued during the runaway inflation of 1922–23 are abundant and inexpensive unused because they were inflated to the point of worthlessness before they could be used. Genuine used examples of some, however, are scarce, and in some cases rare. The disparity in catalogue value often ranges from cents per stamp unused to hundreds of dollars per stamp used, a powerful incentive to add a fraudulent postmark.

These stamps are worth a few dollars mint, but several thousand dollars authentically used.

In late April 1945, the Third Reich lay in ruins, overrun by American and British forces in the west and by the Red Army in the east. In the final days before Berlin collapsed, the Nazis released one last defiant commemorative issue, a pair of bright carmine stamps depicting uniformed storm troopers of the S.A. and S.S. The stamps were on sale in only a few post offices in Berlin and for only a few days before the city fell. Few were purchased and used. Mint examples are fairly common and not particularly expensive, stocks having been "liberated" by occupying forces. Authentically used examples, however, are extremely rare. Faked used examples frequently appear on the market, sometimes canceled by genuine canceling devices also "liberated" at the end of the war. Fortunately, experts can usually spot the fakes because genuine cancellations bear distinct, identifiable characteristics unique to the handful of Berlin post offices operating at the time. Regard used examples of either of these stamps to be fraudulent until proved to be otherwise.

Generally, the greater the disparity between mint and used price—when the used price is more than the mint—the more careful you should be. Always insist on an expert certificate for used stamps of this type. If the item does not have a recent certificate from a recognized service, make purchase contingent on obtaining one.

In some cases, fake cancels and ancillary markings, such as "way" or "steamboat" markings, are added to increase the value of a cover. Examine carefully any cover whose value lies primarily in a scarce postmark or unusual marking. In other cases, stamps are sometimes added to a stampless cover and tied with a fake cancel. In still other cases, a low-denomination stamp is lifted off a common cover and replaced with a high denomination. High denominations are rare on cover and worth much more on cover than off cover. Nineteenth-century covers are the usual targets for this type of fakery, and specialists are the ones most often at risk because they are the primary market for them.

Carefully examine any cover containing stamps that are significantly more valuable on cover than as ordinary used stamps. Check the cancellation. The ink on the stamp and the cover should match exactly, and the cancellation should tie stamp and cover perfectly. Fakers are seldom able to get the alignment exactly right.

Expensive first day covers are sometimes faked with bogus cancels. In many cases, fakes can be detected with a second look and a watchful eye (e.g., a rubber-stamp cancel that mimics a machine cancel on an issue known to exist only with a machine cancel). Rubber-stamp ink is gray; machine-applied ink, black. The type of fakery has shown up on some of the more valuable first day covers for definitive stamps the 1920s and 1930s but is certainly not limited to those issues.

Check cancels carefully on expensive covers. Many fakes are surprisingly obvious if one just pays attention.

FAKE OVERPRINTS AND SURCHARGES

Overprints and surcharges are sometimes faked to create expensive varieties from inexpensive stamps.

In the late 1920s, rural post offices in Kansas and Nebraska suffered a rash of burglaries. In many cases, the thieves fenced the stolen stamps in nearby states. To make it more difficult to fence stolen stamps, the Postal Service overprinted the then-current definitives with either "Kans." or "Nebr." The measure didn't have much impact on thefts and was abandoned after a short time. Relatively few of the overprinted stamps were issued. They became valuable almost right away, and fakes have been turning up ever since.

The Nebraska overprint at left is genuine; the one at right was added by typewriter.

Fake Kansas-Nebraska overprints are most often encountered on used stamps because the raw material (unoverprinted definitives) is abundant and cheap. Most Kansas-Nebraska fakes are laughably amateurish and easy to spot. Genuine overprints were applied by printing press. Fakes are frequently rubber-stamped or typewritten. Stamp pad inks tend to appear grayish when compared to black printer's ink, and the hole often left by a typed period is a dead giveaway. In addition, fakers often overprint the wrong perforation variety. Genuine Kansas-Nebraska overprints always gauge perf 10 1/2 x 11. Those that gauge perf 10 or perf 11 are fakes.

The easiest way to spot fakes of any kind is by comparison with genuine examples. Fakers never quite match the subtleties of an original no matter how hard they try. Also, pay attention to catalogue footnotes that warn of fake overprints.

FAKE ERRORS

Fake errors are covered in detail in Chapter 11, "Errors on Stamps."

Be aware that fakes exist. Remain alert for them, pay attention to catalogue cautions, be diligent in examining nineteenth-century stamps and those prone to fakery, and know when to expertize. Reference books devoted to fakes help identify the most commonly encountered.

CHAPTER

9

FAULTS AND REPAIRS

FAULTS AND REPAIRS are a fact of life. Be aware that they exist, but don't be intimidated by them. They most often escape detection because of complacency, not because they are difficult to detect. Most are reasonably easy to detect if one takes time to look for them and knows what to look for.

The two primary tools for detecting faults and repairs are a watermark detector and a magnifier. A 10-power or 15-power loupe works well. They are inexpensive and fit easily in a pocket or a purse. Don't rely on an ordinary magnifying glass; most are not powerful enough. I use a 10-power loupe for shows and keep a 30-power glass in my office. Nothing escapes notice under 30-power magnification. It reveals even the smallest feature in sharp detail.

I favor the traditional watermark tray and fluid. Watermark fluid is remarkably efficient in all but a few instances. Optical detectors work well, but in my opinion, not as well as tray and fluid. I use an optical detector to supplement tray and fluid. Optical detectors are especially useful for examining stamps printed in light colors. The lack of contrast between paper and ink sometimes makes it difficult to detect either watermarks or faults. Generally, anomalies that show up dark in fluid, show up light when viewed with an optical detector, and vice versa. Keep that in mind to avoid an interpretive error. One last point: Observe the courtesy of asking permission before dipping stamps belonging to someone else. It's good philatelic etiquette.

Few faults and repairs escape detection when examined using these two tools. Now, a few tips.

- It is impossible to return something back to 100 percent original. A telltale sign always exists, even if it takes some looking to discover.
- Inspect before buying. Don't be in a hurry, especially when viewing under pressure, such as at an auction or a stamp show. If viewing conditions do not permit adequate inspection (e.g., a poorly lit show),

ask for the right to return a purchase should it not check out. Don't worry about offending anyone by checking potential purchases. Pros are used to prudent buyers checking things out—and if they're not, they haven't been around long. Improvements and faults are so often encountered on nineteenth-century stamps that it's reflexive for experienced collectors and dealers to hold them up to light or dip them in watermark fluid to check for problems.

- If you think you've spotted a defect, don't allow yourself to be talked out of it. Follow your instinct. After all, when it comes time to sell the item, you'll have to explain it to the next buyer and hope he accepts your explanation. The seller will be long gone.
- Check for the obscure as well as the obvious. More about that in the body of the chapter.
- Ask questions, especially of dealers. What does a filled thin look like? Or a rebacked stamp? They handle stamps day in and day out and have usually seen it all. Ask for a demonstration on how to detect regummed and reperforated stamps. One look is truly worth a thousand of words.
- The more expensive the stamp, the more careful should be your scrutiny. Be suspicious of any stamp, especially an early stamp, that looks too good to be true. Maintain a healthy sense of skepticism, but don't become paranoid.
- Regardless of your degree of proficiency, obtain an expert certificate on any stamp of significant value. Make it a condition of purchase.

REGUMMING

Regumming is the application of new gum to simulate original gum. Regumming is endemic on unused stamps of the nineteenth century and on many stamps of the early twentieth century. As a rule of thumb, the earlier the stamp, the more likely its original gum will be gone. Don't be deceived by the comment that a stamp could not be regummed because it came from an old-time album or collection. Regumming has been going on longer than any of us alive today can remember.

Regumming is done to improve the appearance of a stamp, usually one that has been heavily hinged or lost its original gum. It's also done to cover faults such as thins, ironed-out creases, and closed tears. These kinds of faults can be detected by dipping a stamp in watermark fluid. If they're beneath the gum, the stamp has been regummed.

Regumming jobs vary from crude to nearly undetectable. The majority, especially those on less valuable stamps, are often clumsy, amateurish, and easy to spot with a little practice. However, clever and dangerous regumming jobs exist, especially coming out of Europe, where fakers have learned to apply gum by airbrush and other sophisticated techniques. The most skillful regumming jobs are difficult to detect except by professionals who handle stamps every day, but garden variety jobs are easy to spot if you know what to look for.

Original gum is applied before stamps are perforated. Normally, when stamps are separated, paper fibers at the tips of the perforations feather. During regumming, the liquid glue tends to saturate feathered fibers, binding them together. This effect is readily visible under 10-power magnification. In most cases, the teeth on regummed stamps feel hard and rigid. Pros often gently rub suspect perforation teeth against the skin just at the ridge of their upper lip, an extraordinarily sensitive area. Normal teeth feel soft and pliable. Teeth on regummed stamps usually feel hard and rigid, like a tiny saw blade. The test is useful in catching obvious cases but is not entirely infallible. Occasionally, a block or multiple is regummed and individual stamps separated from it afterward. Perforation tips of stamps thus separated usually display natural feathering. On occasion, regummers use emery boards and other abrasives to try to soften perf tips. Usually, the effort results in little more than the tips appearing to have been filed down.

In most cases, regumming is applied with a brush, so keep an eye open for brush marks. Look for unevenly applied gum, thinly applied gum, or gum speckled with dust or tiny air bubbles. All are indications of regumming. You'd be surprised how sloppy some "stamp mechanics" are. One of the easiest and most useful methods of spotting regumming is to compare suspicious gum with gum on genuine examples of the same set or series. Denominations of 1¢ or 2¢ make good comparison specimens because they are comparatively inexpensive and rarely regummed. Hinged examples are okay, just so long as they contain an area of undisturbed gum large enough for useful comparison.

Bogus gum can be aged and colored to simulate original gum, but it's nearly impossible to duplicate the exact appearance of the original—texture, thickness, gloss, and evenness of application. So take time to familiarize yourself with the look of original gum of various issues. Compare suspect stamps to known genuine examples.

The foregoing notwithstanding, be aware that gum was applied by hand with brushes to the first few issues of U.S. stamps. Gum used on these issues often varied in color and consistency from one batch to the next, and it was frequently applied unevenly, sometimes leaving brush strokes. Original gum on some early stamps looks so bad that those unfamiliar with it often assume that it could not possibly be original.

Ultraviolet light is useful for comparing suspect gum to authentic gum. Be aware that original gum varies from issue to issue and that the various gums do not necessarily fluoresce similarly. Compare suspect gum to genuine gum on stamps of the same issue or series.

A number of years ago, a collector offered me a complete never-hinged set of 1893 Columbians, the first U.S. commemorative issue. Never-hinged examples of the low values are not abundant but are available. Never-hinged examples of the midvalues are scarce but not unobtainable. Never-hinged examples of the five top values, the $1 through $5 denominations, are indeed rare. They appear only infrequently at auction. In fact, I'd never seen a complete never-hinged set nor even heard of one. I was eager to examine the Columbians because a never-hinged set, if such a set existed, would truly be a rare and remarkable thing.

The set was neatly arranged on a black stock sheet, a stunning group—nicely centered, fresh bright colors. I could scarcely believe my eyes. I carefully removed them one by one, turned them over, examined their gum. Except for the two lowest values, no two gums were alike. There were 15 different types of gum on 16 stamps. The Columbians are known to exist with 3 types of gum but not 15. Some had thick gum, some had thin gum, some had yellow gum, some had white gum, some had gray gum. A couple had tiny bubbles, fibers, or brush marks on their gum. They might have been convincing viewed individually, but together they had a patchwork appearance.

I pointed out the variations and advised that most of the stamps were regummed, but the collector was skeptical. So I suggested a look under UV light. Sure enough, each stamp fluoresced differently—grays, violets, yellows, whites. The demonstration left no doubt.

Gum-breaker ridges.

Check rotary press sheet stamps for the presence of gum-breaker ridges. Gum-breaker ridges were applied during manufacture to prevent finished sheets from curling. They disappear when gum is soaked off, as is the case when disturbed gum is removed to prepare the back of a stamp for regumming. Once removed, gum breakers are virtually impossible to duplicate; therefore, it is safe to assume that unused rotary press sheet stamps lacking gum breakers have been regummed.

In some cases, regummed stamps, especially early issues, are lightly hinged to throw off suspicion. After all, a lightly hinged stamp is worth considerably more than one with no gum or severely disturbed gum. Occasionally, disturbed gum is liquefied and carefully redistributed with an artist's watercolor brush to improve its appearance. The result can resemble regumming, although technically it is not.

Examine all unused nineteenth-century stamps for regumming, *especially* if offered as never hinged. Remember, few nineteenth-century stamps, especially scarce ones, exist never hinged and that the earlier the stamp, the more likely it is to have been regummed. Be extremely cautious of expensive stamps, especially high values of the Columbian and Trans-Mississippi series.

REPERFORATING

Reperforating, adding perforations to simulate original perforations, is done either to get rid of a straight edge (frequently) or to improve centering (infrequently). Occasionally, reperforating is performed to transform a less expensive imperforate stamp into a more valuable perforated variety, such as a rare Washington-Franklin series coil. The more expensive the stamp, the greater the incentive to eliminate a straight edge.

The general aversion to straight-edged stamps is long standing, dating back to the nineteenth century. Prevailing sentiment held that a perforated stamp ought to possess perforations on all sides for the sake of balance and aesthetics. Collectors shunned stamps not so endowed. In fact, the reason early coil stamps are so rare is that few collectors bothered to acquire any, regarding them as inferior examples of regular stamps by virtue of their straight edges on parallel sides. Later, of course, the collecting community came to recognize coil stamps and booklet stamps as distinct, collectible varieties and accepted the presence of straight edges on them. That did nothing to alter the ingrained aversion to straight-edged examples of sheet stamps, an aversion that persists to this day—and the reason they are reperforated.

Reperforating is most often encountered on stamps issued in panes containing one or more natural straight edges. That includes most nineteenth-century issues, as well as most twentieth-century flat-plate issues up to the 1930s. Not all twentieth-century flat-plate issues contain natural straight edges. Exceptions include the U.S. Zeppelin issues of 1930 and 1933 and the $5 America definitive of 1922, which are seldom encountered reperforated. A few later issues possess natural straight edges but are of insufficient value to tempt reperforators.

Half the battle is just being aware that reperforating exists and taking time to check for it. Compare suspect perforations with genuine perforations. A row of perforations consists of two elements: the size of the hole and the spacing between holes. Sometimes a stamp will "gauge" right (i.e., the spacing is proper), but the reperforated holes will be either larger or smaller than the genuine holes. In most cases, reperforators do not get both right. Place a suspect stamp atop a known genuine example of the same stamp or a stamp from the same set. Both hole size and spacing should match. If they don't, the stamp's likely been reperforated. An inexpensive 1¢ or 2¢ value from a set, such as the Columbian set, works well to check other values of the set.

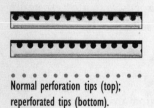

Normal perforation tips (top);
reperforated tips (bottom).
Note differences in tips and holes.

Examine perforations under at least 10-power magnification. Reperforators typically use a razor-sharp metal punch that leaves holes sharp and clean. Production holes appear somewhat ragged in comparison and occasionally less perfectly round.

Be suspicious of a row of perforations with flat tops, the result of punching holes along an otherwise straight edge. Normal teeth tend to be somewhat uneven and fibers at the tips feathered. Reperforated teeth usually lack feathering, instead retaining the clean cut of the straight edge. Reperforators sometimes scrape at tips with a sharp instrument in an attempt to simulate feathering, but the ruse is rarely convincing under 10-power magnification.

Top and bottom rows of perforations should be parallel, as should left and right rows. If they're not, chances are the stamp has been reperforated. By and large, normal rows of perforations form a straight line. Occasionally, a hole strays from the line, but it is the exception rather than the rule. If placement of perforations appears somewhat haphazard, beware.

The foregoing are not entirely infallible but will enable you to spot the majority of problems. It pays to become familiar with the appearance of genuine perforations, especially under magnification. Nothing looks exactly like an original. With experience, you'll develop an instinct for what looks right and what doesn't.

THINS

Thins are most often caused by the careless removal of a stamp hinge. Large, deep thins are readily apparent to the naked eye. Small thins and shallow thins are less obvious. Some are visible when held up to a strong light, where they appear lighter than surrounding paper. Dipping in watermark fluid, however, is much more reliable. In watermark fluid, thins appear darker than surrounding paper. The deeper the thin, the darker its appearance. Thins on used stamps are generally more obvious in watermark fluid because gum is not an issue. Experienced buyers routinely dip potential purchases of any significant value, especially nineteenth-century issues.

In some cases, thins, especially minute ones, are masked by a bit of gum artfully redistributed to hide their presence. Regumming, also, tends to disguise thins. Check by dipping. If a thin shows up underneath otherwise flawless gum, the stamp has been regummed. Occasionally, gum skips are mistaken for thins, but they can be ruled out by dipping or checking under magnification.

A small section of a watermark, most often near the edge of a stamp or on a perforation tooth, is sometimes mistaken for a thin. The translucency of watermarks, however, is less pronounced than that of thins. Occasionally, but rarely, a watermark itself contains a tiny thin. When the stamp is dipped, the thinned portion of the watermark appears darker than the unthinned portion. This type of thin is easily overlooked. Bear that in mind when checking watermarked stamps.

Printing inks differ in opacity and contrast, as do papers. In some cases, the opacity of dark or dense printing ink makes a thin less obvious. Issues printed with yellow or orange ink, such as the 10¢ Washington-Franklins, are notoriously difficult to watermark because of the lack of contrast between paper and ink. The same lack of contrast makes it difficult to detect some thins, especially small, shallow ones. Sometimes they don't show up at all in watermark fluid. Fortunately, they can usually be detected using the dip-and-dry technique, in which a suspect stamp is pulled out of watermark fluid back side up and observed closely as it dries, which occurs in a matter of seconds. As paper dries, it tends to become whiter. Thins dry faster than surrounding paper and "flash white" or "white up" just before the rest of the stamp dries and whitens. The time between the thin whiting up and the rest of the stamp drying is usually only a second or two. Several dips and dryings are often required to accomplish a satisfactory observation. This technique works best on used stamps and stamps without gum. It is less effective on regummed stamps because the gum interferes with the way paper whitens up. Nevertheless, it is extremely useful and well worth the practice to become proficient at it.

Optical watermark detectors, too, are useful for detecting thins. They work best on used stamps and stamps without hinge remnants or disturbed gum. Stamps are viewed against a white background in such devices, and thins show up lighter because they are less opaque than surrounding paper. Filled thins (more about them shortly) show up darker because they are more opaque. An optical detector is a useful adjunct to dipping in fluid, but not a replacement for it.

Examples of heavily hinged stamps. The stamp at far right exhibits severely disturbed gum.

Thins are more difficult to detect under areas of disturbed gum, especially on stamps containing hinge fragments. Coarsely redistributed gum sometimes masks a thin. In such cases, dipping often yields inconclusive results. Optical detectors, likewise, tend to yield confusing results. Severely disturbed gum tends to show up as patches of light and dark, making it difficult to positively identify anomalies, leaving one to wonder if the light areas are due to irregularities in the gum or thins. Occasionally, even the experienced eye is stumped.

Thins, especially small ones, are sometimes filled and sanded smooth. A variety of pastes have been used to fill thins, but none ever seem to quite match the opacity of the subject's paper. Some filled thins are visible with the naked eye. Others require dipping to detect. When dipped in watermark fluid, filled thins appear lighter or brighter than surrounding paper, sometimes amazingly so. The trick is to look for the ones that don't jump right out, the tiny, tiny thins and the expert repairs. Spotting these requires active vigilance, not passively waiting for something to pop out. The presence of gum tends to mask filled thins on regummed stamps; still, they generally are not too difficult to detect if one takes time to look for them. Dip suspects or examine them under UV light. A filled thin usually shows right up.

Check for concealed thins. Some are disguised by a normal cancellation or by black ink applied either to darken an existing cancellation or to augment it with a bit of stray ink. Occasionally, hinges (or hinge remnants) are applied to hide thins or other faults. Many dealers soak hinges off used stamps before adding them to inventory. This bit of detailing allows dealers to check for faults as well as make stock more presentable. Be suspicious of hinges left on expensive stamps, either mint or used. If you're interested in an item, ask the dealer to remove the hinge. Few balk at removing a hinge from a used stamp. It takes only a few moments to soak it free, even at a show. Removing a hinge from a mint stamp is not always so easy, especially a stubborn, old-time hinge. Some dealers decline the request, especially if the hinge is heavily stuck down, for fear of either damaging the stamp or revealing earlier damage they are not aware of. So if you must buy such a stamp, be aware that you are buying "as is" and assuming all risk. Never, never remove a hinge from a stamp that doesn't belong to you. Let the owner remove it.

I once witnessed an episode that drives home the point. Two collectors were attempting to negotiate a deal for a set of Zeppelins owned by one of them. The potential buyer lifted the Zepps from the seller's stock card with his tongs and examined them one by one. The set was hinged, the hinges still neatly in place.

Without warning, the buyer pulled the hinge off the $2.60 value and in the process thinned the stamp. A loud and angry exchange followed. Voices thundered, faces reddened. It looked as if the two might come to blows.

Clearly the buyer was at fault. He should never have pulled the hinge off. The argument escalated, seesawing back and forth. It progressed from the seller insisting that the buyer buy the stamps at the undamaged price to the seller finally refusing to sell the stamps at any price to a such a gosh-darn, irresponsible, ignorant son of a gun (I've toned down the language considerably).

In the end, the seller kept the stamps and the buyer stalked out. I got the impression that the seller kept them because he felt it gave him the right to bad-mouth the buyer in local collecting circles, which he did at every opportunity. The moral: Don't take liberties with stamps that don't belong to you.

CREASES

A *crease* is a bend severe enough to cause individual paper fibers to break. Once broken, nothing can return them to their original condition. Severe creases are usually visible to the naked eye. Less pronounced examples require dipping but are not difficult to detect. They show up as a dark line in watermark fluid. Some appear darker than others, depending on the paper and the severity of the crease.

Creases on unused stamps affect gum and in most cases can be spotted with the naked eye. Creases on used stamps are generally more difficult to detect, especially those that have been pressed or ironed out. Creases are sometimes repaired by soaking the subject stamp to soften its paper fibers and then pressing it dry under pressure to "heal the wound." Done by an accomplished restorer, this technique frequently eliminates the crease to the naked eye, especially if the subject is subsequently regummed. Nothing, however, can completely eliminate a crease. No matter how expertly pressed out, a crease is nevertheless detectable in watermark fluid. A crease visible under otherwise undisturbed gum means the stamp has been regummed.

Creases appear as dark lines in watermark fluid. Note the corner crease at upper right.

Corner creases are quite common, especially on early issues, and are treacherous because they affect such a small part of the stamp that they are easily overlooked. The practiced eye always gravitates to the corners, looking for any sign of a dark line no matter how small or how faint. Perforation creases are similar to corner creases in that they affect only a very small part of the stamp and thus are easily overlooked. Again, be alert.

TEARS

A *tear* is the outright separation of paper fibers. Occasionally, one encounters an internal tear (i.e., one that does not begin at the edge of a stamp). Most tears, however, begin at the edge of a stamp and progress inward. Long tears are usually apparent to the naked eye unless they have been skillfully repaired. Even then, they show up in watermark fluid. Unlike creases, which appear as a straight line in watermark fluid, tears appear irregular and never follow a straight path.

Small incipient tears are the most treacherous because they are so easily overlooked, especially if one is in a hurry or inattentive. So take time to check carefully near the edges of a stamp.

Tears that show up under gum indicate regumming. In some cases, long tears, especially on nineteenth-century stamps, are repaired using an adhesive such as egg white before regumming. They, too, show up in watermark fluid.

Occasionally, one encounters a stamp containing a reattached piece (i.e., a separated piece glued back in place). Sometimes the reattached piece is small and escapes casual inspection, but immersion in watermark fluid invariably reveals it. Occasionally, the reattached piece is borrowed from a second stamp. The repair usually involves cutting the two pieces so that their edges match up. The alignment, however, is seldom perfect and often apparent if one is alert. Frequently, the ink or paper of the two married pieces doesn't quite match due to variations in aging or production. Occasionally, a stamp containing a reattached piece is rebacked, in which case the reattachment may not be evident in watermark fluid. These kinds of reattachments, however, are evident under magnification on the front of the stamp. Tiny spots of color are sometimes applied to hide stray white fibers along the rejoined seam on the front of the stamp. These, too, are evident under magnification.

Note the short perforations along the right side.

Occasionally, but not often, one encounters a repaired perforation. Some short perfs extend below the base of the perforation and significantly detract from the appearance of a stamp. To repair a short perf, a whole new tooth is added. In cases where only part of the tooth is missing, only a tip is added. Perforation repairs show up in watermark fluid but often escape notice because they are so small.

Sometimes a short perf is disguised by reducing adjoining or nearby perforation teeth to make it appear less pronounced. The improvement is usually impossible to detect unless poorly executed. And if undetectable, it's not really anything to worry about.

SEPARATED PERFORATIONS

Perforation bridges on blocks or multiples of older stamps tend to weaken and separate with the passing of time. Separated perforations most often occur on mint blocks possessing gum; used blocks generally are not as susceptible. Separations usually begin at the edge of a row of perforations and progress inward. They are easily detectable with the naked eye.

In some cases, separations are rejoined by liquefying the gum on or near the affected tips to form a bond. Glue, and in some cases sizing, is used to rejoin separations on used stamps. Rejoining is generally visible to the naked eye and always apparent under sufficient magnification.

Sometimes an entire row of perforations is reinforced because most or all perforations have weakened and separation is imminent or inevitable. It's not uncommon to encounter a combination of rejoined perforations and reinforced perforations along the span of the row.

The presence of selvage on an ordinary block is generally extraneous to its value and separations in the selvage of little consequence. Plate blocks, however, are perceived as a unit of which selvage is an integral part. Separations in the selvage of plate blocks are, therefore, undesirable.

Plate block with normal-sized selvage (left); plate block with radically reduced selvage (right).

Separations afflict both flat plate and rotary press plate blocks up to the 1940s. Little can be done to remedy separated perforations on rotary press issues, aside from rejoining them. Flat plate issues, however, possess selvage that can be trimmed to eliminate separations. It's not always possible to detect trimmed selvage, especially if the trim is minimal and the cut, straight and even. In these cases, it doesn't make much difference because the aesthetics of the block are not really affected and the trim, undetectable. In many cases, however, the trim is crooked or sloppy, or the selvage is radically reduced—sure signs of tampering. The reduction is usually most evident on top plate blocks, which tend to have wider selvage than side or bottom blocks. Check to make sure that the edge of the selvage is straight and parallel to the edges of the stamp designs.

Note that the top of the trimmed selvage on this block is not parallel to the edges of the stamps' designs.

Occasionally, one sees someone take a ruler to selvage. Measuring, however, is never a foolproof test for reduced selvage because there is no standard width for selvage. It varies from issue to issue. It varies, too, on blocks within an issue. In some cases, top blocks contain wider selvage than bottom or side blocks. In the case of the National Parks set, stamps with vertical formats contain wider top selvage than those with horizontal formats. All one can do is compare the width of suspect selvage with that which lies in the normal range for the issue. In many cases, it cannot be known with certainty whether or not selvage has been trimmed.

The prejudice against modification of any kind is so ingrained and powerful that collectors often focus more on the absence of separations than on the overall appearance and aesthetics of the block. There comes a time, however, when one must be realistic and forgiving about separations if one wishes to collect early plate blocks.

The same holds true for nineteenth-century multiples. Multiples are scarce and in many cases rare. Separations and reinforcements are the rule rather than the exception. Serious collectors understand the frailties of early blocks and tend to be forgiving because scarcity does not permit selectivity. Besides, it makes sense to preserve early blocks, especially classic and rare items, and if that means sensible reinforcement, then so be it. The phrase "sensibly reinforced," which is now and again encountered in auction descriptions, implies that reinforcement is appropriate because of the rarity of the item. Collectors can afford to be less forgiving of separations on issues from the 1920s onward because the population of blocks is sufficiently large to permit selectivity. It is wise to take into account the age of an item and maintain a sense of balance.

PINHOLES

During the early years of philately, before anyone cared much about condition, dealers sometimes showcased their wares by tacking them to display boards. Stamps so displayed contain pinholes. In many cases, the displaced paper is smoothed back in place and the presence of the hole is not readily apparent from the front. Pinholes usually become apparent when a stamp is held up to a strong light source. All reveal themselves in watermark fluid. Like thins, pinholes are sometimes filled or patched, which, too, shows up when the stamp is dipped.

INCLUSIONS

Natural inclusions are bits of matter embedded in paper during manufacture. Most often, they are unprocessed wood pulp, or infrequently, tiny particles of metal or other small fragments. Wood pulp inclusions occur more frequently on some issues than others. They are not necessarily an issue unless they are large, visually distracting, or in danger of coming free and leaving a hole. Occasionally, one sees an inclusion mentioned in an auction description with the disclaimer "mentioned for accuracy only," which means that in the opinion of the describer, the inclusion is insignificant and mentioned only to forestall return of the lot.

Inclusions, or at least the ones most likely to become an issue, are usually visible to the naked eye. Some regard inclusions of almost any size to be an aesthetic impairment, one to be avoided if possible. Others are more forgiving. It's all a matter of opinion and subjective taste.

Extraneous material, such as fibers, stray perf rounds, even insects, sometimes becomes lodged underneath gum or printing ink during production. Some extraneous inclusions are considered undesirable, such as a perforation round embedded beneath otherwise faultless gum. In other cases, extraneous inclusions, such as the outline of an inked-over insect, are considered an oddity and prized by EFO collectors. In these cases, the more dramatic the inclusion, the more prized the stamp.

SCUFFS AND SCRAPES

When scrutinizing for faults, attention is usually focused on the back of a stamp. Check the front for scuffs and scrapes, especially small, unobtrusive ones. Unretouched scuffs and scrapes are fairly obvious. Retouched scuffs and scrapes are not so obvious, hidden by the careful application of colored ink to the affected areas. Retouched areas are not difficult to spot if one takes time to look. Unfortunately, few but the most experienced take the time, and thus scuffs and scrapes are often overlooked.

STAINS AND DISCOLORATIONS

Stains, such as those caused by ink, tea, coffee, tape, oil, foxing, and water, are readily apparent to the naked eye. Stains are difficult to remove, especially from mint stamps where gum is an issue, so most remain untreated.

Used stamps are easier to treat, still many attempts fail. Bleach is the most common chemical used to treat stains, but many, such as tape stains, do not respond to it. Some treated stains disappear and remain undetectable. Others show in watermark fluid or under UV light. It pays to check. Anyone serious about dealing with stains is advised to obtain a copy of the *Dealers' Guide to the Chemical Restoration of Stamps*, the best reference on the subject. The sad truth is that more stamps and covers are ruined by chemical shenanigans than are saved or improved.

Discoloration and toning, too, are sometimes treated with bleach but are difficult to reverse without detection. As a young fellow, I once immersed a toned nineteenth-century stamp in a Clorox bath in an attempt to rid it of its distracting brownish color. The bath worked like a charm. Away went the toning—and the blue design along with it. Out came a blank, perfectly white piece of perforated paper. Needless to say, I didn't make the same mistake twice.

Chemicals are potent and unpredictable. I offer this advice: Leave bleaches alone. Even diluted solutions are unpredictable. Removing an item from bleach does not in itself stop the chemical reaction. A thorough rinse—a minimum of at least 20 minutes in running tap water—is the only way to ensure that it stops. Otherwise, bleach remains in the paper, still chemically active, albeit subtly. The effectiveness of the rinse depends on the concentration of the bleach and the length of the rinse. I mention this only for those foolhardy enough to ignore the advice against bleaching.

Toned covers are sometimes swabbed with a mild solution of bleach to reverse the discoloration. Check for evidence of this under UV light. Swab marks often leave streaks that resemble brush strokes.

Certain orange inks, such as those on the first U.S. airmail stamp and 6¢ definitive of the 1922 series, possess a tendency to brown when exposed to compounds containing sulfur, and that includes atmospheric sulfur. The discoloration is easily reversed in a mild solution of household hydrogen peroxide. Be sure the solution is mild; too strong a solution will end up bleaching the stamp. Do not leave stamps unattended. You want to be able to pull the stamp out the moment the desired effect is achieved. The treatment works best for used examples where gum is not an issue. Immersing an unused example will result in loss of gum. Swabbing the front of a discolored mint stamp with cotton dampened with peroxide works to reverse the effect but should be approached cautiously. The reversal is not instantaneous. The inclination is to overswab, to apply too much moisture, which ends up warping the stamp. There is no way to quickly stop the reaction when swabbing a mint stamp. Immersing it in water, as one would do with a used stamp, results in loss of gum and reduction of value. Treated by an inexperienced hand, a discolored mint stamp all too often ends up a ruined stamp.

REBACKING

Rebacking is major reconstructive surgery, one that involves several steps. In many cases, the stamp is first cleaned and freshened. Next, its back is sanded down to a fraction of its original thickness, in the process removing or ameliorating problems such as thins and creases. The reduced stamp is carefully glued to a piece of paper thin enough so that their combined thickness approximates that of the original stamp. If the stamp is unused, new gum is applied. If the original was perforated, perforations are added using the stamp's original perforation holes as a template. If the stamp was an imperforate, excess selvage is trimmed away.

Rebacked stamps are treacherous because rebacking is not necessarily the first thing one looks for, checking instead for thins, creases, and that sort of thing. I hate to admit it, but I've been fooled. At one of the old National Stamp Shows in New York during the boom days of the early 1980s, I came across an outstanding example of the 12¢ 1857. Large balanced margins, intact perforations, excellent color. A magnificent, astonishing gem. I was in a hurry, and as it turned out, careless. I gave it a quick dip. No thins, no creases, no tears. A few days later, back in Denver, I dipped it once again. The back was indeed fault-free but seemed a little too white. I examined the stamp's edges under magnification, and sure enough, two layers became apparent. And that was not all. In addition to rebacking it, whoever "reconditioned" the stamp had added margins, hence the wonderfully large, balanced margins. To accomplish this, he had trimmed the stamp net to its design and then nestled it in a cutout. Together, they became the top layer of the rebacked stamp. The trim lines didn't show in watermark fluid, masked by the rebacking. So masterful was the job that the trim lines were not readily apparent to the naked eye. They became apparent only under magnification. I felt like a fool. I'd been had—to the tune of $400, a costly mistake, but one not repeated.

Check for rebacking by floating a suspect stamp facedown atop watermark fluid. The paper should saturate instantly. If it doesn't, suspect rebacking. The adhesive used to bond the two layers inhibits instantaneous saturation of the backing layer. Backs of rebacked stamps, especially backs of used examples, when fully immersed in watermark fluid often appear too opaque, the result of abnormal thickness and the sandwiched adhesive. In some cases, they look brighter than normal.

It's extremely difficult to duplicate the exact thickness of the original. Rebacked stamps often feel stiff or rigid due to the lamination of layers and often appear too thick. Regumming tends to make the deception less obvious, especially in watermark fluid. Careful scrutiny of the edges, however, almost always reveals the deception.

A block of plate proofs. Mint stamps of this design are worth more than 20 times as much as plate proofs.

Proofs of many nineteenth-century stamps are readily available and considerably less expensive than their postage stamp counterparts. In addition, proof impressions are crisp and sharp, their colors vivid and intense, making them candidates for transformation into visually stunning postage stamps. Plate proofs on India paper are occasionally rebacked to simulate stamps. India paper is thin and delicate. Proofs on India paper can be easily attached to backing paper, gummed and perforated.

Plate proofs also exist on card stock. They can be sanded to stamp thickness, perforated, and gummed. Even when sanded down, however, card stock is more rigid than stamp paper. Be suspicious of any stamp, especially a nineteenth-century stamp, in exceptional and atypical condition. Better yet, familiarize yourself with the look of proofs. Proofs of nineteenth-century stamps look much better—light-years better—than their postage stamp counterparts. Once you've seen the difference, stamps faked from proofs are easy to recognize.

Any discussion of faults and repairs makes the situation sound worse than it is. They're really not much of a problem for the worldwide generalist or the collector of low or moderately priced stamps. Still, possessing the skill to recognize faults and repairs is an asset to any collector. Most of the problems mentioned in the foregoing paragraphs are surprisingly obvious if one just takes the time to check for them. So we'll end this chapter with a point worth remembering: The experienced eye is always skeptical—always.

CHAPTER

10

EXPERTIZING

A N EXPERT CERTIFICATE is a written opinion rendered by a recognized expertizing body. Expertizing services verify genuineness, confirm valuable varieties, and report faults, repairs, tampering, and deceptive alterations such as regumming, reperforating, or removal of a cancellation to simulate an unused stamp.

SELECTING A SERVICE

The two oldest and most respected expertizing services in the United States are the Philatelic Foundation (PF) and the American Philatelic Expertizing Service (APEX). Neither deals in stamps; they are impartial and their opinions are highly respected throughout the philatelic community. Both rely on panels of experts to examine submissions and render opinions. Both services issue photographic certificates that illustrate subject stamps with perfect fidelity together with a summary of their findings. And since no two stamps are identical (by virtue of margins, perforations, and centering), the photographs serve as the philatelic equivalent of a fingerprint.

Both services maintain extensive reference collections of stamps, varieties, overprints, covers, and postal markings so that submissions can be compared with authentic examples and known fakes. Both services own sophisticated diagnostic equipment that can reveal almost any sign of tampering. And the expert committees of both services consist of some of the most experienced and widely respected authorities in philately.

Other expertizing services exist. Many are affiliated with stamp societies (such as the American First Day Cover Society) and issue opinions on items within their field of specialty. In many foreign countries, expertizing is performed by recognized individual experts rather than by a panel of experts.

While the practice is widely accepted abroad, collectors in this country feel more comfortable with the consensus approach.

Some services indelibly mark items they consider to be fakes or frauds; however neither the PF nor the APEX does. Avoid using any service that indelibly marks stamps, because on occasion an opinion is wrong and stamps thus marked are ruined. Both of the foregoing services stress that opinions rendered are just that—opinions. However, their opinions are rarely incorrect and their certificates are universally accepted as *bona fides* for stamps.

Fees are based on the value of the stamp (or cover), with a minimum fee applicable for items of nominal value or for items returned as not genuine. Turnaround time is typically four to eight weeks. Obtain a submittal form before sending anything for an opinion. Consult Chapter 36, "Resources."

Experienced buyers resubmit auction purchases accompanied by a certificate older than five years or so. Recent certificates always carry more weight because the opinion backing them is based on the latest information. Most auction firms honor requests for resubmissions. Some disallow the request if the certificate is less than five years old. You can always request that a private purchase be subject to confirmation by expert opinion. If the seller refuses, think twice. And when it comes time to sell, you'll find that dealers usually pay more for stamps, especially expensive varieties, with expert certificates.

Over time, you are likely to run across a variety of types of expert certificates. Remember, to carry any weight, the certificate *must* originate from a *recognized* service, one acknowledged and respected within the philatelic community. One with no financial interest in stamps submitted for opinion. Stamp investment promoters sometimes issue, or cause to be issued by front services under their exclusive control, expert certificates. The certificates may not be intended to deceive, but in terms of an objective impartial opinion, they are not worth the paper they are printed on. The worst tend to overlook or minimize faults and inflate grade. They tend to use puffed-up names intended to sound impressive, such as the National Federal American Independent Expertizing Service (the name is made up, but you get the idea), and emulate the appearance of certificates issued by the PF, the APEX, and other recognized bodies.

Investment firms often issue a guarantee with their stamps. There is nothing wrong with that. A guarantee means that the firm will stand behind its product. A guarantee, however, should not be confused with an expert certificate—which is an independent third-party opinion. To my way of thinking, it is deceptive for a firm to issue, or cause to be issued by a front service, so-called expert certificates on its own products, when the term "expert certificate" implies the opinion of a credible, neutral third party.

BOGUS CERTIFICATES

A final word of caution: Occasionally, an unscrupulous party adds information to or tries to remove information from a genuine certificate to enhance the description of its subject stamp. Recent certificates are almost foolproof; still, it pays to be prudent. When making a purchase accompanied by an expert certificate, especially an earlier one, examine it carefully to make sure that no tampering, such as additional typed information or a substituted photo, has occurred.

ERRORS ON STAMPS

EACH TIME YOU purchase postage, the possibility of discovering a potentially valuable error presents itself. It could be a sheet of stamps with one of the colors omitted or a roll of stamps lacking perforations or die cuts (die cuts are used on self-adhesive stamps). Several years ago while standing in line at my local post office, I witnessed an irate customer demand her money back for what she perceived to be defective merchandise.

"Look," she complained to the window clerk, holding up an opened roll of stamps, "they don't have any holes. They won't tear right." Her tone of voice made it clear that she expected the roll to be replaced and was not about to take no for an answer.

I was about to step forward and offer to buy the roll, but before I could act, the clerk had the stamps in hand. He glanced at them and said, "No problem." He reached into his drawer and handed her a new roll. Mollified, she turned and hurried off, unaware that she had won the post office lottery—and then thrown away her ticket.

I wanted to talk to the clerk, hoping he'd sell me the roll. I waited my turn, got to the head of the line, let several pass ahead of me until he was free. When at last I reached the counter, I said, "I couldn't help overhear about that roll of stamps the lady turned in. I collect stamps and I'd sure appreciate having them."

"Sorry," the clerk said. "Got to turn them in. Post office policy."

I was aware of the policy. I'd hoped that he might not be and would let me have them. But it was not to be. I bought what I needed, turned and left, disappointed that I had come so close to getting my hands on an error and missed. The opportunity seldom presents itself.

It is not uncommon for postal patrons to return defective stamps. To the average consumer, defective stamps are no different than any other defective product, but to collectors they are a treasure.

Post office counters are not the only place errors can be found. I've been writing stamp books for a number of years. In 1991 I got a letter from a reader who had discovered a sheet of error stamps at a coin show—and made $20,000 on it. This is the story he told:

> *I'd gone to a coin show. I'm one of those guys who collects both stamps and coins. While riffling through a stack of modern mint commemorative sheets at a dealer's table, I came across one that didn't look quite right. It was the Energy Conservation commemorative of 1974. It looked like one of the colors was missing—perhaps the green. I couldn't be sure. The omission—if indeed there was an omission—was subtle, perhaps just my imagination. Surely, I kept thinking, the original buyer would have spotted it if, indeed, it were an error. And if not the original buyer, then surely the dealer. I riffled through the stack a second time, pausing at the sheet, studying it without pulling it out. The longer I looked at it, the more sure I was that one of the colors had been omitted. Finally, I pulled it, along with several other sheets, from the stack and handed them to the dealer. The stack was marked "Mint Sheets - Face Value + 10%."*
>
> *He smiled and started adding them up.* Would he notice? *I wondered. He stopped, calculated the face value of each sheet, and then punched it into his calculator. "Fifty times ten cents, five dollars. Fifty times thirteen cents, six-fifty." And so on.*
>
> *He didn't even pause at the Energy Conservation sheet. He just called out its face value, punched it into the calculator, and kept going.*
>
> *"Sixty-two bucks," he said when he'd finished, "plus ten percent. Sixty-four twenty altogether."*
>
> *I handed him three twenties and a five. He made change and then slid the sheets into a paper sack and handed it to me.*
>
> *I skipped the rest of the show and hurried to the parking lot, my heart in my throat. I got into my car and carefully slid the sheet out, eager to check it in daylight. The show had not been particularly well lit, and it was possible that the sheet may have appeared odd because of the poor lighting.*
>
> *I studied it for a long moment. It didn't look right; still, I wasn't completely sure. The error, if indeed it was an error, wasn't the kind of thing that jumps right out at you.*
>
> *All the way home—about an hour's drive—I flip-flopped back and forth, thinking one moment I had a rarity, the next that I was deluding myself.* How much is it worth? *I wondered.* A thousand dollars? Five thousand? *Then I chided myself for getting my hopes up. I'd been disappointed*

more than once over the years, thinking I'd discovered a valuable variety, only to learn I had misidentified the item. I drove on, vacillating between elation and despair, anxious to get home and settle the matter.

Once home, I looked it up in a stamp catalogue, which listed three possible color omissions: green, green and orange, and blue and orange. I checked the sheet under magnification, and sure enough, green appeared to be omitted—a subtle omission, but nevertheless, omitted. The catalogue valued the error at $750 per stamp. The sheet contained 50 stamps, which meant a total of $37,500! I was stunned. I couldn't believe it. It didn't seem possible.

I called one of the error dealers whose ads I'd seen from time to time. Yes, he was interested but wanted me to send the sheet so he could verify both the error and the condition of the sheet. I hesitated.

"No one's going to make an offer without seeing it," he said. "I've been in business more than twenty years." He rattled off a number of references and in the end, I agreed to send the sheet for inspection.

"If it's genuine, how much can you offer?" I asked.

"After I've seen it, we'll talk business," he said.

"Can't you give me some idea?" I pressed.

"Not until I've seen it." Then perhaps sensing my hesitation, he said, "It's a good item. Not a new discovery, but still a good item. Something I can use. I'll call you the minute I've had a chance to look at it. I'm sure we can get together on a price. In the meantime, be thinking about how much you want for it."

I overnighted the sheet per his instructions. The dealer called late the next morning, confirmed it to be genuine, and asked how much I wanted. All night, I'd debated how much to ask. I knew I wouldn't get full catalogue. Judging by what I knew, I figured half catalogue—$18,750—was probably the best I could hope for. I took a deep breath and, allowing a little room for negotiation, said, "Twenty thousand."

He didn't say anything right away. The moment stretched. I braced myself for a counteroffer—a low counteroffer. Then to my surprise, he said, "Okay." A few days later, his check for $20,000 arrived. The face value of the sheet had been $5. I paid $5.50 for it. I'd cleared nearly $20,000 literally overnight. I still have trouble believing my good fortune.

By definition, an *error stamp* is one created unintentionally and by mistake. The terms "unintentionally" and "by mistake" are key. For example, over the years, various stamps have been intentionally issued without perforations. They are not

An original Pan American invert (left); the 2001 commemorative (right), which is distinguishable by the tiny date 2001 in the lower-left corner.

errors. Only when perforations are unintentionally omitted is the item an error. The Pan American inverts contained in the 2001 commemorative sheet were intentionally issued with inverted centers. The original inverts issued in 1901 are errors. The 2001 commemoratives are not. They are normally prepared stamps commemorating the original error stamps. Ironically, if any of the reissue contained a normal, noninverted center, it would be an error!

The error-collecting field has its own set of terminology to describe and classify abnormal stamps. The broad field is often referred to by the umbrella term "EFOs" (errors, freaks, and oddities). Of the three categories, the error category is the most exclusive; the freak and oddity categories tend to be more inclusive, which is to say that any odd-looking stamp that does not fit into the first category ends up by default in one of the other two.

The error category (or major error category, as it is now most often called) can be loosely defined as including errors that merit individual catalogue recognition. Of those types that merit recognition, the big three are imperforate errors, color-omitted errors, and inverts. In addition, catalogues usually, but not in every case, list stamps printed in a color other than the normal color, gutter pairs, double impressions (stamps imprinted with more than one of the same image), grill errors, stamps printed on both sides, and watermark errors.

Freaks can be thought of as children of a lesser god—abnormal stamps that do not merit individual catalogue recognition. The term "freak" refers to stamps with random, individually unique, and nonrepeatable imperfections stemming from freak occurrences during production, such as foldovers, perforation shifts, ink smears, and the like. Thousands of freaks exist—far too many for stamp catalogues to even begin to attempt to list separately.

As a rule, catalogue-listed errors are worth much more than freaks. Generally, listed errors range in price from a few hundred dollars into the thousands, and in some cases such as inverts, five- and six-digit figures. Freaks, on the other hand, usually range in price from a few dollars to the low hundreds. Their moderate value is due in part to the fact that catalogue publishers do not mention them individually and because, although often individually unique, they are, as a class, plentiful.

Sometimes a freak falls just short of the major error mark. For example, if so much as a single perforation hole remains between two stamps, the pair does not qualify as an imperforate error. It is considered a freak. If a pair contains blind perforations (lightly impressed perforations not punched completely through the paper), even if visible only under magnification, it likewise fails to pass muster and is relegated to the freak category. The principle also applies to color-omitted errors. All traces of the omitted color must be absent. If so much as a pixel is present, the item is a freak, not a full-blown major error.

The term "oddities" describes stamps or philatelically related items that are unusual in appearance but not necessarily errors.

With regard to value, stamp catalogues usually assign values to listed errors, values based on retail and auction prices. The value of freaks is a function of appearance and topical appeal. Generally, the more visually striking the item, the greater its value. Freaks on stamps with topical appeal, such as space exploration or Olympics, in most cases sell for more than similar items with no topical appeal.

ERRORS

IMPERFORATE ERRORS

Imperforate errors are stamps on which perforations or die cuts have been unintentionally omitted between two (or more) stamps. Perforations are used for lick-and-stick (water-activated gum) stamps; die cuts are used for self-stick (self-adhesive gum) stamps. Stamps with die cuts omitted are often referred to as *imperforate*, although technically they are die-cut-omitted errors. Except in a strictly technical sense, the distinction is not really important. The fact remains that the element intended to facilitate separation has been omitted.

An imperforate error can occur on any issue that normally contains perforations (or die cuts), including sheet stamps, coil stamps, booklet panes, and souvenir sheets. Of these, coil stamps most often turn up imperforate, perhaps because coil stamp production is highly automated. Modern coil stamps begin as blank paper on a roll at the head of a web press. The press starts and the paper unrolls, speeds through printing cylinders, and is perforated (or die cut), slit into strips, counted, rolled, and sealed in plastic bubbles for retail sale—all faster than the eye can follow. Electronic sensors are supposed to spot defects and errors, and they do catch most, but every once in a while, a few imperforate stamps manage to slip through undetected, often created at the beginning or end of a press run before perforating equipment is engaged or after it is disengaged.

Imperforate sheet stamp errors do not show up as often as imperforate coil errors and therefore tend to be more valuable. Unlike coils, sheet stamps are usually not packaged for retail sale, and thus errors are more easily detected by postal clerks and turned in for destruction.

A variety of terms are used to describe imperforate errors. "Imperforate" means that the item contains no perforations at all. "Imperforate between" means that a pair of stamps lacks perforations between the stamps but contains perforations

Imperforate (left);
imperforate between (right).

Horizontal pair, imperforate vertically (left);
vertical pair, imperforate horizontally (right).

on its exterior sides. "Imperforate vertically" means that the item lacks vertical perforations but contains normal horizontal perforations. "Imperforate horizontally" means that the item lacks horizontal perforations but contains normal vertical perforations.

Medal of Honor commemorative with color
omitted (left); normal (right).

COLOR-OMITTED ERRORS

A color-omitted error occurs when one or more colors are unintentionally omitted from a multicolored stamp. Color-omitted errors usually, but not always, occur as the result of an omission of one or more colors in process-color printing. In process-color printing, the image to be printed is broken down into a series of basic colors—usually black, yellow, cyan (pale blue), and magenta (red)—each of which is printed by a separate plate (or cylinder or sleeve). When printed, the dots mingle and yield a full-color result. Examine a lithographed or gravure-printed stamp under magnification and you will be able to see the dot structure.

An omission most often occurs at the beginning or end of a press run when one or more plates is disengaged. It can also result from a dry ink fountain. An *ink fountain* is a reservoir that supplies ink to the press. Each plate or cylinder is fed by its own ink fountain.

During the intaglio era, each color on multicolored stamps was printed as a pure solid, either in a separate press run (one for each color) or, in the case of

Giori equipment, a single press run in which the various inks were physically separated on the design to avoid contamination by adjacent colors. Few color-omitted errors exist on intaglio-printed issues. One of the rarest is the Red Cross commemorative of 1932, on which the cross was omitted due to a paper fold blocking the application of red ink during the second press run.

Stamps that appear to have a color omitted as the result of shifted perforations are not considered to be color-omitted errors. This, because the imprinted design defines a stamp, not the location of perforations. A stamp otherwise properly prepared and containing all colors does not become a color-omitted error simply because shifted perforations eliminate part of the design.

On rare occasions, a plate number is omitted from selvage. Plate numbers are not part of a stamp, and their omission, therefore, is not considered a color-omitted error. They are nevertheless interesting and collectible curiosities.

The value of color-omitted errors depends on rarity and visual appearance. Generally, the more dramatic and visually striking the error, the more valuable it is.

Some color-omitted errors are visually striking and leap out at you. Others are subtle and can easily be missed even by philatelically experienced persons, as the foregoing anecdote illustrates, so it pays to examine stamp purchases carefully.

INVERTS

Inverts are the superstars of the error field. Only 11 have ever been discovered on U.S. postage stamps (a handful more exist on U.S. revenue stamps). Each is rare and expensive.

The Rush Lamp
flame invert.

An invert occurs when one of the elements of the design on a multicolored stamp is unintentionally inverted. The inverted Jenny is perhaps the best-known example. Most modern stamps are printed during a single pass through a web-fed press, eliminating the possibility of an invert. In earlier times, each color was laid down on a separate pass through a sheet-fed press. Multicolored stamps printed by this method often consisted of a frame printed in one color and a vignette (a scene, an object, or a portrait) printed in a second color. One can only speculate about how a sheet might happen to end up rotated 180 degrees (inverted) from its original position. Perhaps during printing of the first color the pressman pulled a sheet to check for quality, as pressmen periodically do, and inadvertently returned it to the stack rotated 180 degrees.

How did the rotated sheet escape notice on its second pass? Well, operating a printing press is a monotonous task. When the press is humming, pressmen do not scrutinize every individual sheet as it goes by. Imagine for a moment working hour after hour, a never-ending procession of identical sheets marching by.

Imagine the end of your shift approaching. You're tired. Your mind wanders. Perhaps you're thinking about getting home, about making your way through the snow outside, or perhaps you're daydreaming about an impending trip, or any one of a thousand other things. Imagine the unvarying, mind-numbing cadence of the press, the sheets beginning to blur together. One of the many thousands of sheets, the sheet inadvertently rotated during the first printing, slips by unnoticed. Perhaps that's how the inverted Jenny—or any of the other early inverts—came into existence.

Should quality control inspectors have detected the imperfect sheet? Yes. But they, too, are only human. Perhaps most remarkable is that in the long history of stamp production, so few inverts have reached public hands.

COLOR ERRORS

Occasionally, stamps are printed in a color other than intended. This can be caused by introducing the wrong color into an ink fountain. It can also be caused by using the wrong transfer die to enter an image on a printing plate.

In 1917 a technician at the Bureau of Engraving and Printing inadvertently entered impressions from a 5¢ transfer die on plates containing 2¢ Washington-Franklin series stamps. During the heyday of intaglio printing, stamp designs were engraved by hand on a master die of soft steel, which, when completed, was hardened. The image on the hardened die was impressed onto a roller (or transfer die), which in turn was used to impress individual images onto a printing plate. During the process, images were laid down one by one until all rows had been completed. If during the course of a plate's life an individual image became worn or damaged, as sometimes happened, it could be burnished out and replaced by reentry from the transfer die.

Strip of three containing the 5¢ color error at center.

We can only speculate why the technician inadvertently picked up the transfer die for the 5¢ stamp instead of the 2¢ stamp. Perhaps it was because the image on the transfer die was small, was on a curved surface, and, being metallic, lacked the contrast of a printed image. Perhaps he confused the numeral "5" and the numeral "2." Designs for stamps of the Washington-Franklin series are identical up to the 10¢ value; except for denomination, one stamp looks exactly like another, so it is easy to imagine that in haste he might have confused the die with the "5" for the die with the "2." Or perhaps he was just inattentive or preoccupied. We will never know for sure. What we do know is that he used the 5¢ die to enter impressions on a plate otherwise filled with 2¢

stamps. Two 5¢ impressions appear on one pane (one quadrant of the press sheet) and one impression appears on another. Panes containing the errors were printed in rose, the normal color for 2¢ stamps. The rose-colored 5¢ stamps blended in perfectly with other stamps on the pane, and no one noticed them at first. It's amazing how little attention the average person pays to the appearance of postage stamps. But once discovered, the rose 5¢ stamps looked startlingly different than normal 5¢ stamps, which were printed in blue.

Some stamps exist in a variety of shades. Shade varieties and color variations are not considered color errors. Shades often arise from variations in batches of printing ink or variations in the density of ink laid down during printing. They can also result from changes in pigment over time due to exposure to light or atmospheric chemistry. Pigments prone to fading are known as *fugitive*. Stamps printed by the process-color method sometimes display color variations caused by variations in balance between one or more ink fountains, each of which prints a separate color. Shades are interesting and collectible in their own right, but again, they are considered varieties rather than errors. Stamps that have been intentionally exposed to chemicals or light to cause a change in color are known as *changelings* and have no philatelic value.

GUTTER ERRORS

In most cases, stamps are printed in large sheets, known as *press sheets*, from which smaller, individual, finished panes are cut. The number of panes per press sheet varies according to the size and layout of the panes. The space separating one pane from another is known as a *gutter*. During finishing, panes are severed from press sheets by cuts made down the center of interpane gutters.

Sometimes press sheets are miscut so that gutters survive with examples of stamps from adjoining panes on either side of the gutter. Pairs (or multiples) containing complete stamps on both sides of the gutter are referred to as *full gutter pairs*. Those containing a full stamp on one side but only a partial stamp on the other are known as *gutter snipes*. Gutter pairs or multiples from uncut press sheets available to the public are not errors. A gutter pair must have been created unintentionally to qualify as an error.

An error pair containing a gutter and a complete stamp on either side.

To merit catalogue recognition, a gutter pair must contain a complete stamp (including intact perforations) on each side of the gutter. More often than not, only a partial stamp survives on one side. Partial stamps range from as little as the mere hint of a frame line to as much as the complete design just short of perforations. Generally, the greater the size of the incomplete stamp, the more desirable the gutter snipe.

On occasion, rows of perforations intended to fall on either side of a gutter are shifted into a pane of stamps. They are considered freaks, not gutter errors. It is the presence of a gutter between two stamps that determines the error, not the placement of perforations.

DOUBLE OR MULTIPLE IMPRESSIONS

Also known as double (or doubled) prints or stamps printed twice, a double impression, on monocolor stamps, occurs when the design is inadvertently printed two or more times. On multicolor stamps, a double impression occurs when

one or more colors are inadvertently printed two or more times. In most cases, the impressions are slightly out of register and appear slightly blurred.

One of the most startling multiple-impression errors occurred on the 29¢ Christmas Stocking issue of 1994, which received an astonishing seven extra impressions: three black, two yellow, and one each of red and blue.

The 1994 Christmas Stocking issue containing multiple impressions.

To be considered a true multiple impression, the error must have occurred from two or more actual impressions of the printing plate and not be the result of plate stutter or blanket offsetting or ghosting.

GRILL ERRORS

Grills came into use in 1867 as a security measure to prevent the cleaning and reuse of stamps. Grills are wafflelike patterns impressed onto stamps by dies laid out in the same arrangement as stamps. They were designed to break paper fibers so they would more readily absorb ink, making it difficult to remove cancellations. Some stamps are known with grills omitted. Others are known with doubled grills or split grills. Split grills occur on sheets misaligned so that they receive impressions from two (or more, depending on the position of the misalignment) adjacent grill-embossing dies.

WATERMARK ERRORS

Between 1895 and 1916, U.S. postage stamps were printed on paper watermarked "USPS." Between 1878 and 1958, revenue stamps were printed on paper watermarked "USIR." The "IR" stands for Internal Revenue. A few 6¢ and 8¢ postage stamps of the 1895 definitive series were inadvertently printed on paper watermarked "USIR" instead of "USPS." Both errors are rare and valuable.

In 1951 a few $1 Wilson stamps of the 1938 Presidential series were accidentally printed on USIR-watermarked stock, at a time when postage stamps were no longer being printed on watermarked paper. The USIR error is scarce and much more valuable than its normal unwatermarked counterpart.

PERFORATIONS OF OTHER THAN NORMAL GAUGE

Some stamps are known with one or two sides perforated in a gauge other than intended or announced—for example, a stamp normally perforated 11 on four sides containing one side perforated 10. The postal service may not regard the variation as significant since the stamp can be sold and used like any other stamp. Collectors, however, consider aberrant perforation variations significant.

TAGGING OMITTED

Tagging (invisible luminescent coating) is applied in the same fashion as visible ink. Occasionally, tagging is unintentionally omitted. Tagging-omitted errors are not considered to be color-omitted errors for a couple of reasons. Tagging is not part of the graphic design of the stamp, and it is transparent to the naked eye and not a color per se. Tagging is, however, one of the elements of a properly prepared modern stamp, and its unintentional omission constitutes an error. Tagging-omitted errors are avidly collected by specialists.

PRINTED ON BOTH SIDES

Some stamps, usually nineteenth-century issues, exist printed on both sides. This type of error frequently occurs as a result of make readies escaping with usable images printed on one side. "Make readies" is a term for paper used to make trial impressions during press setup. Trial impressions are necessary to adjust the register and pressure of printing plates and to adjust ink fountains. It usually takes a fair number of impressions to get everything adjusted exactly right. Make readies are often printed front and back, sometimes more than once, before being discarded. In some cases, make readies with a usable impression on one side—especially those with a faint impression on the other—may have unintentionally escaped destruction. We can speculate that in other cases, perhaps a frugal nineteenth-century printer saw nothing wrong with using paper containing an imprint on the reverse—especially a faint imprint—to cut costs and increase profits and included some sheets printed on both sides with regularly prepared stamps, hoping no one would notice or object.

OVERPRINT INVERTED

Inverted overprints are most often found on foreign stamps. They occur more frequently than design inverts, perhaps because less care is taken when applying overprints than when producing regular stamps. In most cases, inverted overprints are neither as visually striking nor as valuable as design inverts. Still, they are quite collectible.

OVERPRINT OMITTED

In some cases, an overprint is omitted due to paper-feed misalignment during overprinting. In other cases, spacing of the sheet itself presents the opportunity for a stamp or row of stamps to escape overprinting. Overprint-omitted errors are often collected in pairs or multiples containing both normal and error stamps.

OVERPRINT MISSPELLED

Misspelled overprints arise for any of several reasons, most frequently a typesetting error, and typically affect only one subject on the plate. In other cases, damage to one of the subjects changes the appearance of a letter or letters in a word, for example an "E" altered to resemble an "F." Some overprint spelling errors are catalogue listed, others are not. Misspelled overprints are usually collected as an adjunct to a regular collection rather than a specialty.

GUMMED ON BOTH SIDES

Some stamps exist gummed on both sides. This anomaly harks back to a time when stamps were gummed in a separate operation after printing and when, for reasons unknown, a sheet ended up gummed on both sides.

FREAKS

ALBINOS

Albinos are stamps from which all colors have been omitted. All that remains is blank paper. Albinos of intaglio-printed stamps sometimes contain a "blind" intaglio impression where color otherwise would have appeared. Intaglio albinos can usually be identified by the blind impression. Lithographed and gravure albinos are generally impossible to identify unless a fully or partially printed normal stamp is attached, which is often the case and the way in which they are usually collected.

Ironically, albinos are, by tradition, not considered color-omitted stamps, although all colors have been omitted. Perhaps it is because a blank stamp is not as visually interesting as one that contains part of an image. Some feel that without a printed impression, no stamp existed to begin with. A while back, several booklets were discovered, each containing an imperforate, albino pane. At first blush, it sounds like a spectacular double error—complete omission of both perforations and color. In reality, the error pane was nothing more than a blank piece of paper indistinguishable from any other blank piece of paper. Had the blanks not occurred in booklets together with normal panes, it would have been impossible to tell that they were intended to be stamps. When offered at auction, the booklets sold for little more than $100 apiece.

Albino impressions are relatively common on older (pre-1960s) stamped envelopes, usually caused by two sheets of paper sticking together during printing and embossing, then separating prior to forming (the process of cutting, folding, and gluing printed stock into finished envelopes). Albino stamped envelopes usually contain the blind impression of the embossing die used to impress a three-dimensional image within the printed portion of the design.

A strip containing a dramatic color shift. The honey bee appears to have crawled to the right.

COLOR SHIFTS

Color shifts are misalignments, not unlike misalignments sometimes encountered on full-color newspaper photos or Sunday comic strips, in which one or more printing plates are "out of register" with the others. Some color shifts are slight and barely noticeable; others are severe and dramatic. Generally, the more visually striking and dramatic the shift, the more desirable and valuable the item. Slight color shifts are worth little.

MISPERFORATED STAMPS

Misperforated stamps result from rows of perforations (or die cuts) shifting from their normal position. Misperforated stamps are also referred to as *misperfs, shifted perfs, perf shifts,* or *misplaced perforations.* Perforations shifted just enough to touch the design of an adjacent stamp are regarded as severely off-center and not an error. Misperforated stamps are often collected in blocks or multiples (pairs or strips in the case of coil stamps) in order to more dramatically reveal the

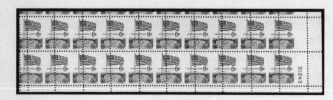

A misperforated block.

nature of the error. Generally, the more visually striking or dramatic the perforation shift, the more valuable the item.

Sometimes misplaced perforations are skewed and run at an angle. In some cases, only one set of rows, either horizontal or vertical, is skewed. In other cases, both horizontal and vertical rows are skewed, yielding a strange and visually dramatic item.

Changed design (left); normal stamp (right).

Sometimes a slight shift in perforations results in a denomination or inscription from an adjacent stamp appearing in a position not inconsistent with that of an intentionally created design. Misperfs containing these kinds of out-of-place elements are known as *changed designs*. Sometimes shifted perforations truncate a portion of the denomination resulting in a changed denomination, such as 4¢ instead of 14¢.

Changed designs or denominations occur infrequently and are more highly prized than garden-variety misperfs.

BLIND PERFORATIONS

Blind perforations (or blind perfs) are perforations (or die cuts) that do not completely penetrate the paper. In some cases, incompletely punched perforations appear as bumps known as *dimples*. In other cases, they are so lightly impressed as to appear to have been omitted. Sometimes rows of blind perforations occur shifted into the design, disguising their presence and adding to the illusion that the affected stamps are imperforate.

IMPERFORATE MARGIN

An imperforate margin occurs when perforations that would normally appear between stamp and selvage are omitted. Stamps with imperforate margins are not considered full-fledged imperforate errors because the

A block possessing an imperforate margin.

omission of perforations does not occur between two

stamps. Some stamps are created with natural straight edges on one or more sides; they are not errors.

MULTIPLE PERFORATIONS

Some stamps contain doubled or tripled rows of perforations. They arise from any of several causes, including a sheet (or pane) accidentally punched twice, a glitch in the perforator, or the edge of a sheet punched with an extra row of perforations when it failed to clear the perforator. Some earlier doubled or tripled perforation varieties are catalogue listed, but recent examples tend not to be. Today they are regarded more as freaks.

A miscut strip.

MISCUT STAMPS

Occasionally during production, press sheets become misaligned as they pass through cutting equipment. The result is a miscut. Coil stamps seem to be more prone to miscuts than other types of stamps, perhaps because their production is so highly automated. As coil stamps come off the press, the web of paper upon which they have been printed is slit into the individual ribbons of stamps that are then coiled into rolls and packaged for retail sale. If the web is out of alignment, even slightly, miscut stamps result. Miscuts are known on both perforated and imperforate coil stamps.

Miscut booklet panes and miscut sheet stamps sometimes show portions of adjoining stamps and, in drastically miscut examples, complete adjoining stamps, gutters, or partial adjoining panes. Occasionally, miscuts occur in combination with misperforated stamps, yielding extraordinarily odd-looking pieces.

In some cases, miscut booklet panes and sheet stamps reveal partial or complete marginal markings that otherwise would have been trimmed away. Before 1981 plate numbers on coil stamp and booklet pane production were trimmed off during finishing. Miscut pre-1981 coil stamps and booklet panes sometimes show a partial and occasionally—but rarely—a complete plate number. Those possessing complete numbers are known as *full plate number miscuts* and are prized.

Miscut coils can be collected as singles or in pairs or multiples. The choice usually hinges on which form shows the error to its best advantage. Miscut sheet stamps are collected in whatever form best demonstrates the error. Again, the more dramatic the miscut, the more desirable the item.

An underinked block.

UNDERINKED STAMPS

Underinking is most commonly encountered on inta-glio-printed stamps. It is sometimes caused by an ink fountain running low or running dry. It can also be caused by ink diluted with cleaning solvent. Severely underinked examples, possessing no more than a ghost-like impression, are known as *dry prints*. Some dry prints result from impressions made to remove solvent-thinned ink from intaglio plates during press cleanup.

A printing offset. Note the image is reversed.

OFFSETS

An offset is usually caused when a printing press skips a sheet of paper, and ink that should have been applied to the paper is instead applied to an underlying roller. The roller, in turn, deposits the impression on the underside of the next and subsequent sheets of paper until the offset has been exhausted. Sheets thus printed receive a normal impression on top and an offset (or negative) impression on the underside. The first impression after the skipped sheet is the most pronounced. Additional impressions grow successively more faint until they disappear altogether, often after fewer than a dozen sheets. The desirability of an offset is usually in proportion to its boldness and intensity.

Occasionally, improperly stored stamps stick together, especially in damp climates. When pulled apart, ink from one stamp sometimes adheres to the gum on the back of the stamp on top of it, simulating a production offset. Offsets from stuck-together stamps have no philatelic value.

An imperforate strip containing a splice.

SPLICES

In the course of production, tape is sometimes used to splice sheets or webs of paper together and to repair tears. Splices are normally trimmed off and discarded, although sometimes they escape. Splices are known in a variety of tapes and colors: masking tape, cellophane tape, red, green, black, and clear tape, to name a few. Splices are known on sheet stamps and booklet panes but are most frequently encountered on coil stamps, especially imperforate coil errors, which themselves have escaped detection and destruction.

Occasionally, stamps are inadvertently printed on a splice made during the manufacture of paper (known as a *mill splice*). Mill splices sometimes cover a relatively large area, resulting in stamps printed on two thicknesses of paper, or doubled paper.

Early in the twentieth century when coil stamp production was still in its infancy, strips cut from sheets of stamps were spliced together to form coils of varying length. These splices are known as *paste ups* and were intentionally released on finished coils. More recently, splices on some issues have been made with small, unobtrusive strips that no attempt is made to cull. These, of course, are not considered errors.

FOLDOVERS

Occasionally during production, part of a sheet—most often a corner—becomes folded over on itself, resulting in an error known as a *foldover*. Foldovers that occur prior to printing sometimes result in part of the design being blocked from where it would normally be printed. The blocked portion ends up printed on the folded flap; the underlying portion remains blank.

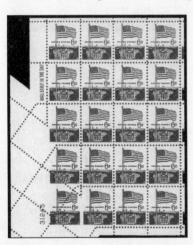

Sometimes the fold occurs after printing but before perforating, allowing perforations to penetrate both the folded flap and underlying paper. When unfolded, the flap reveals an odd arrangement of perforations known as *crazy perfs*. Some foldovers occur after printing and perforating but before trimming and result in odd-shaped pieces of selvage known as *appendages*. If the foldover causes the omission of perforations between two adjacent stamps, an imperforate error occurs.

Foldovers usually involve multiple stamps and are collected that way. Once again, the more striking the appearance, the more desirable the item.

A foldover exhibiting an appendage and crazy perfs.

CREASES

Occasionally during milling or in handling prior to printing, paper acquires a crease. Some creases are slight; others are large enough so that when pulled apart,

A strip revealing an open crease.

they reveal blank, unprinted paper. Creases that can be opened to reveal unprinted paper are known as *open creases*. Open-crease stamps can be collected as singles or multiples. Knowledgeable collectors prefer to collect creases in the largest multiple possible in order to most dramatically display the anomaly. The larger the open space, the more dramatic and desirable the item.

A note of caution: Creased stamps should be opened with care to avoid tearing along crease lines. This is especially true of older stamps. Many collectors mount or store creased stamps with the crease open to reduce weakening caused by repeated openings and closings.

STRAY PERFORATIONS

Occasionally, one or more perforations (usually arising from bent perforation pins) stray into the design area of a stamp. Stamps with stray perforations are unusual but not particularly valuable.

A partially imperforate pair.

PARTIALLY IMPERFORATE

Occasionally, bent or missing perforating pins result in the omission of some, but not all, perforations between stamps. Misalignment of perforating equipment also can cause partially perforated stamps. The most striking examples possess only one or two perforation holes. They are not quite full-blown imperforate errors but are nevertheless unusual in appearance and highly collectible.

UNPRINTED AREAS

Sometimes a bit of extraneous matter, such as lint, fibers, or a piece of paper, lands on an inked plate. It leaves a blank spot or in some cases an oddly inked area on the stamp. The larger the extraneous matter, the larger the unprinted area. The more unusual the shape, the more striking the freak.

PLATE WIPING PATTERN

During intaglio printing, a blade is used to wipe excess ink from the plate before each impression is made. When the plate has been overinked or when solvent contaminates the ink supply, the wiping motion leaves a wavy pattern visible on stamps. The pattern is best revealed on panes or large multiples.

A block containing an ink blotch.

INKING IRREGULARITIES

Smears, blobs, and blotches are inking irregularities commonly caused by either too much ink, congealed ink, thinned or diluted ink, residue from a cleaning solvent, or oil or some other chemical incompletely removed from a plate prior to printing. Solvent smears are especially interesting when found on multiples that reveal the complete smear pattern. The more profound the overinking or chemical contamination, the more dramatic the effect, and the more highly prized and valuable the item.

GHOSTING

Ghosting occurs when an inked image is picked up by the blanket roller and laid down on successive sheets of paper as they pass through the printing press. Unless the blanket roller and plate drum (or cylinder) are exactly the same size, which is usually not the case, the ghosted image drifts slightly from one impression to the next. Ghost images lighten quickly and disappear after a few impressions.

ODDITIES

EARLY RELEASES

In recent years, occasionally and not all that infrequently, some stamps have been inadvertently released, used, and canceled before their official first day of issue. They are known as *early releases*. Although interesting, cancellations on modern early releases are not particularly valuable.

ERRORS ON CANCELING DEVICES

These include misspellings, inverted dates, incorrect ZIP codes, and the like. Although unusual, none are valuable.

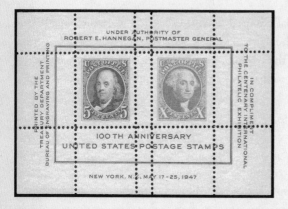

Issued imperforate, this souvenir sheet was later privately perforated.

UNAUTHORIZED PRIVATE PERFORATIONS

Generally, stamp catalogues do not recognize unauthorized private perforation varieties. In some cases, unauthorized private perforations have been applied to imperforate souvenir sheets to create novelties. Occasionally, unauthorized private perforations have been applied to imperforate stamps to facilitate their normal use. Again, although interesting, none are particularly valuable.

OTHER UNUSUAL ITEMS

DESIGN ERRORS

Design errors (such as the wrong number of stars on a flag, a misspelled inscription, or an incorrect date) are generally not considered errors in the philatelic sense (unless a corrected version is released and the term "error" is used to distinguish the two) and have no particular value above and beyond their ordinary value. Design errors are more numerous than one might expect, especially on foreign stamps. Design errors usually go unnoticed until after a stamp has been issued and with rare exception are not recalled.

One exception is the 1994 Legends of the West issue. The Legends of the West commemorative pane contained 20 stamps, each depicting a famous personality from the Old West, such as Buffalo Bill, Annie Oakley, and an African American cowboy named Bill Pickett. After the stamps had been printed, but before they were released, members of the Pickett family notified the Postal Service that the likeness on the Pickett stamp was not Bill Pickett but was, in fact, another man. The Postal Service hastily recalled the entire issue, which had been distributed to post offices but not released. Prior to the recall and in advance of the official release date, a few panes were inadvertently sold. Upon news of the recall, the few examples in collectors' hands became instant rarities potentially worth a great deal of money.

The Postal Service reprinted the Legends of the West pane with the correct likeness of Bill Pickett and released it. In the meantime, the few original Pickett stamps in collectors' hands soared in value to several thousand dollars. Some took advantage of their good fortune and sold. Others held out. Those who sold were lucky, and perhaps wise, because the Postal Service subsequently offered 150,000 "recalled" Pickett panes in a public lottery for face value—$5.80—thus destroying much of the value of the early-release panes. At this writing, the recalled panes trade in the $100 to $150 range.

Setting sun over Tien An Men error.

In another case, the People's Republic of China withdrew an issue after only an hour on sale. The error—if indeed it can be called an error—is subtle. The design depicts the sun rising in a burst of light over Tien An Men in Beijing. The stamp was withdrawn when someone noticed that the sun could not rise from such an angle—it could only set. The sunrise was intended to be an allegory of China's ascendance. A setting sun conveyed the exact opposite meaning. One can only surmise that postal officials withdrew the issue fearing the wrath of Chairman Mao, who was in power at the time, should they allow it to remain on sale. Today the "error" stamp is worth thousands of dollars.

With the exception of those prematurely withdrawn from sale, design errors are generally considered to be curiosities and of no value above and beyond that of the stamp.

PLATE VARIETIES

Plate varieties are small flaws (often tiny and noticeable only upon close inspection) that arise from damage to a printing plate, an irregularity in the surface of a plate, or in some cases, from a worn plate. Damage can occur from mishandling, from metal fatigue (e.g., gripper crack varieties), and from doubled impressions caused by the inexact reentry of a transfer die. Plate varieties are constant from one impression to the next. Collecting plate varieties was more popular in years gone by when fewer stamps were issued and collectors spent more time studying characteristics of each.

ERRORS ON FOREIGN STAMPS

The foreign error field is a mixed bag. Error stamps from some countries are truly scarce, while errors from others are abundant and sometimes intentionally released—and in the most blatant cases, actually marketed. The latter is pure junk, although sometimes spectacular in appearance. Intentionally released "errors" almost never gain catalogue recognition, and those foolish enough to buy them seldom, if ever, get back anywhere near what they've invested.

In the early 1980s, I bought a hoard of several hundred Nicaraguan "errors" from a political refugee who had come to America to escape the Sandinista regime. He had had to leave Nicaragua on short notice with little more than he could carry. Among the possessions he escaped with were the "error" stamps, which dated back to the 1930s. A well-educated and refined gentlemen, he came to me with the stamps—rarities, as he referred to them—hoping to raise a substantial amount of cash.

It was a spectacular group of stamps and souvenir sheets replete with "errors": inverts, items printed in a variety of other-than-issued colors, inverts in other-than-issued colors, imperforates, imperforate inverts, misperfs—just about any kind of "error" you could imagine. From its abundance and variety, I could only assume the group had been intentionally created. I tried to imagine how. The image that came to mind was a couple of guys staying late at the printing plant, throwing back a few beers, and having a ball trying to see how many different combinations and permutations of "errors" they could come up with. They were creative—I have to hand it to them. The array was fantastic. Still, the items would never merit catalogue recognition, and the market for Nicaraguan errors in the United States, even had they been legitimate, was, at best, small. A fatalistic look came across the gentleman's face as I explained this to him. When I'd finished, he sighed and tried to manage a smile. "Just give me what you think they're worth," he said. I wrote him a check for $750. The money wouldn't go far, judging by the kind of lifestyle I suspected he was accustomed to in Nicaragua. But it was a fair price. As he left, I wondered where I would find a buyer. Sometime later, I found a home for the lot with a collector who specialized in Nicaraguan stamps. I priced it at a couple of dollars per item, which in total amounted to somewhat more than a thousand dollars.

PRINTER'S WASTE

Paper used in the production of postage stamps can be divided into two categories: that resulting in properly prepared stamps and printer's waste. "Waste" is the term applied to production that, for whatever reason, is defective, is improperly prepared, or lacks one or more elements that a properly prepared stamp should possess. In the broad sense, all errors are printer's waste because all should have been culled and discarded. In the narrower or philatelic sense, the term "printer's waste" refers to errors that have reached the market through the back door rather than across a post office counter. An error sold across the counter is deemed legitimate. Printer's waste is not. The term "printer's waste" implies that an item was misappropriated from a printing plant or wastepaper destruction facility and illicitly sold into the hobby. The term invariably carries a negative connotation. Many collectors do not consider printer's waste to be errors—and rightly so.

Security printers are supposed to destroy printer's waste. In rare cases, it inadvertently escapes destruction (e.g., a piece blown off a truck on its way to a wastepaper destruction facility or a partially incinerated scrap lifted up through a furnace smokestack). In most cases, however, printer's waste reaches the market illicitly through dishonest employees who sneak it out well aware of the value of error stamps.

Some printer's waste is obvious; that is to say, it exists in a form that could not have been purchased at a post office. An example is the 13¢ Liberty Bell booklet stamp of 1975. Properly finished booklet panes contain a slogan label in the upper-right corner. Some so-called error panes contain the slogan label in the lower-left corner. The switch in position results from so-called error panes being separated from press sheets along rows of perforations that would normally fall between stamps, leaving intact the imperforate interpane space between stamps where a cut would normally occur and thus giving the pane the appearance of an imperforate error. At the time it first appeared on the market, the "error" also showed up in uncut sheets, a form in which it never could have been purchased at a post office. The Secret Service tracked the chain of possession of various of the uncut sheets back to the source—a worker at a destruction facility, whom they arrested and charged with theft of federal property. They recovered what uncut sheets they could, but many had been broken up into individual panes and dispersed.

It is not always possible to tell whether an error is printer's waste. In some cases, printer's waste is indistinguishable from an ordinary error. In other cases, circumstantial evidence suggests printer's waste. Some ostensible errors are so outrageously flawed (e.g., the $14 express mail stamp of 1991 both imperforate and with two colors omitted) that it is difficult to imagine how they could have escaped detection at all of the numerous stages along the way to the retail counter. It would be impossible for a clerk not to notice so spectacular an error. The conclusion is inescapable—the item is printer's waste. It could only have reached the market through the back door.

FAKES

Inverts are most often faked by cutting out the center of a normal stamp and replacing it in an inverted position. This kind of fakery is crude and easy to spot. A few years ago, someone faked a Canada Seaway invert so expertly that it initially fooled everyone. The enterprising faker cut around the center vignette of a normal stamp with such a light touch so as not to penetrate through to the backside of the stamp and disturb the gum. He carefully peeled the image away, inverted it, and glued it back in place. Perfect, intact gum on the invert allayed any suspicion that it might have been faked. It was consigned to and accepted for auction. The tampering only became evident when a dealer happened to examine the front under magnification prior to the auction and noticed the cut lines.

Imperforate pairs (or multiples) are tough to fake. No one has ever come up with a way to fill in perforation holes. At least one faker, however, created fake imperforate pairs by trimming two normal stamps around their frame lines and carefully placing them atop a strip of gummed selvage. At first glance, the faked pair appeared to be imperforate but did not pass close scrutiny.

Imperforate singles are easily faked by trimming off perforations, which is why imperforates are usually collected in pairs or multiples. Many stamps, especially nineteenth-century stamps and twentieth-century booklet pane singles, contain large margins and one or two natural straight edges. Trimming the occasional large-margined example yields an ostensibly credible imperforate single. Large-margined examples of the 5¢ definitive of 1902 are often trimmed to simulate the expensive imperforate of the same design. Countless imperforate singles of this stamp exist, almost all of which are fakes.

Spliced examples of imperforate coil stamps are not uncommon, nor are they difficult to fake. One need only cut an imperforate strip apart and reattach it with tape. One fellow made a collection of different colored splices on an inexpensive imperforate coil issue. His collection included splices made from just about every type of tape imaginable: clear, red, green, white, self-adhesive, masking tape, paper tape (white and manila), electrical tape, duct tape—everything but

Band-Aids and surgical tape. Some of the splices were authentic, but I became suspicious when he enumerated the astounding variety of splices he had accumulated for a single issue and the exorbitant prices he had paid for them. I found it difficult to believe that pressmen at the Bureau of Engraving and Printing just happened to have so many different kinds of tape near at hand. My suspicion deepened when he told me that he had obtained each of the splices from the same source. I suspected some of the unusual splices had been created just to take advantage of the collector's fondness for them and his willingness to pay whatever it took to obtain them.

Color-omitted errors are easily faked, either to simulate an existing error or to create a new and valuable find. Fakers most often attempt to remove colors by chemical bleaching or exposure to light. The most frequent targets are used stamps, which can be exposed to liquid chemicals without fear of disturbing gum. For this reason and because they are so frequently faked, most catalogues refuse to list used color-omitted stamps unless legitimate mint examples are also known.

It's a commonly held belief that some colors are more susceptible to fading or bleaching than others. In reality, susceptibility to fading is a property of pigment, not of color. Some blue pigments are fugitive, others are not. The same holds true for reds, yellows, greens, and every other color. Black pigments tend to be the most colorfast, especially those containing carbon black—but not all black pigments are carbon based. Do not make the mistake of generalizing that certain colors are colorfast and that any stamp lacking such a color must, therefore, be a genuine color-omitted error.

It is difficult to fake mint stamps because most kinds of manipulation disturb either gum or tagging. Some fakers try to apply bleaching agents on a spot basis, using a small brush. Such attempts are almost always detectable under ultraviolet light. Others try chemical fogs or intense light. Still others employ more devious methods.

In 1999 I came across a treacherous fake, a mint, never-hinged 10¢ Benjamin West commemorative described as having intaglio black (the inscription "Benjamin West") omitted. The Benjamin West stamp had been originally issued in 1975. Purportedly, the black-omitted error was the only known example, suddenly appearing on the scene 24 years after it had been issued. What made the fake treacherous is the way in which it was described—intaglio black omitted. Black intaglio pigment is invariably carbon-black based and impossible to bleach or remove without detection. Even if successfully bleached, intaglio ridges remain. It is common knowledge that intaglio black-omitted errors are impossible to fake without detection. So how did the faker accomplish the deception? Not so much by solving the problem of removing the ink as by sleight of hand.

The Benjamin West stamp, you see, contains no intaglio printing. It was printed by gravure, and the inscription "Benjamin West" was printed in light gray, not black. The faker discovered that the inscription could be removed with

Fake Benjamin West error (left); normal stamp (right).

an eraser using a feather-light touch. He presented the omission as "intaglio black omitted," counting on common knowledge that intaglio black is impossible to successfully remove to throw off any suspicion of tampering. And it almost worked. The inscription was gone, no question about it. The error looked legitimate, at least to the naked eye. No one bothered to scrutinize it too closely or question the omission, precisely because it was common knowledge that intaglio black-omitted errors cannot be faked. The faker counted on this and the likelihood that no one would bother to compare the "error" to a normal stamp. And therein lay his genius. No one did.

A collector purchased the stamp for several thousand dollars. Subsequently, he mentioned his new and rare acquisition to me in a letter. I knew immediately even without seeing it that something was amiss because the Benjamin West stamp was gravure printed and contained no black ink. Although it's within the realm of possibility for someone to misdescribe a gravure inscription as "intaglio," it's impossible to mistake light gray for black. The item had not been inadvertently misdescribed. It had been intentionally described as intaglio black omitted, a deception especially treacherous because the faker relied on his knowledge that the hobby views intaglio black-omitted errors as impossible to fake to accomplish the deception. I wrote the collector, warning that he likely had purchased a fake. And sure enough, under high magnification, the inscription could be seen to have been erased. The story has a happy ending. The collector got his money back. And the faker, as far as anyone knows, is still out there. Who knows what he might come up with next.

The moral to the story: Be suspicious of any color-omitted error on a decades-old stamp—even an unused copy—that suddenly turns up and for which only a single example is known. Always have rare and expensive errors expertized, especially color-omitted errors. Refer to Chapter 36, "Resources," for expertizing services.

COLOR CHANGELINGS

A color changeling is a stamp whose original color has been altered, either by chance or as a result of manipulation. Changelings are created by exposure to sunlight or chemicals, including those in the air and in some storage materials, especially cheap ones. Sulfur causes some orange pigments to turn brown.

Color changelings, whatever their origin, have no philatelic value.

BUYING AND SELLING AT AUCTION

UNTIL THE ADVENT of the Internet, stamp auctions generally fell into two categories: floor (or public) auctions and mail bid sales. Floor auctions are called by an auctioneer to a live audience known as the floor. Buyers can also bid by mail (or fax or, in some cases, online) or through an agent. Auctioneers execute absentee bids for mail, fax, and online bidders as if the bidders were present at the sale, a practice called *bidding for the book*, the book being a compilation of absentee bids. Most auctions use an absentee bidder's highest bid only if necessary, buying lots where possible at one increment above the next highest bid. Bidding increments vary according to the level of bidding (e.g., $1 up to $20; $2 up to $40; $5 up to $75; and so forth). A table of increments appears in the front of each auction catalogue. Absentee bids in other than published increments are rounded down to the next lowest increment.

An array of illustrated auction catalogues.

Lots are described and illustrated in catalogues sent to prospective bidders in advance of the auction. In addition, some firms post online versions. Lots are generally available for viewing (inspection) in person prior to the auction. Some firms offer viewing by mail to established customers. They usually require that lots be returned the day after receipt and usually limit the number of lots sent at one time.

Most lot descriptions include a price, such as catalogue price, estimated cash value (ECV), face value (for lots consisting largely of postage), a previous price realized, or a minimum bid. In some cases, such as for odd, esoteric, or difficult-to-value material, the price is left blank or indicated with a dash. Except in the case of minimum bids, lots typically open for less than the listed figure. Often the opening figure is one increment above the second highest absentee bid. Lots with no absentee bids are opened at a figure the auctioneer deems appropriate, in most cases, less than the listed price.

Some auctions are unreserved, which means that lots are sold to the highest bidder without reserve. Others are reserved, which means that lots are subject to a minimum below which they will not be sold. More about that later.

Mail bid sales, as their name suggests, are conducted exclusively by mail (and fax) with no live floor bidding. A recent variation is the online sale, again with no live floor. The majority of mail bid sales differ from live auctions in that lots are sold for the highest bid as opposed to one bid above the second highest bid. For example, in the case of the two best bids being $70 and $100, the lot is sold for $100 rather than $75 ($70 plus one increment of $5). In some cases, lots are sold Dutch-auction style, with the top several bidders each buying an identical item for their top bid.

Most floor auctions add a buyer's premium of 10 or 15 percent to the hammer price. Mail bid sales generally do not. Nearly all floor auctions publish a list of prices realized following a sale; some post prices realized online as well. Mail bid sales generally do not publish prices realized. Both floor auctions and mail bid sales charge for catalogues; however, the fee is invariably waived for regular buyers. Floor auctions accept consignments, although most feature some house lots (lots owned by the firm) as well. The majority of mail bid sales feature house lots.

Some floor auctions allow bids to be made online. In addition to floor sales, some hold separate online-only auctions (analogous to mail bid sales). Still others maintain a regular presence on party-to-party sites such as eBay.

Online auctions hosted by established stamp auction firms differ from party-to-party auctions in one important respect: reputation, or "brand name." They offer buyers peace of mind, confidence that lots are described accurately and that the company will stand behind its product. Bidders are more reluctant to bid on items, especially expensive items, offered by unknown online sellers, regardless of feedback history. Perfectly honest and reliable persons, such as antique dealers or autograph dealers, often get into trouble when they attempt to identify esoteric varieties, especially outwardly similar stamps that, depending on minute differences, vary in value from pennies to tens of thousands of dollars. For the most part, they lack experience in and appreciation for the nuances of grading—usually to the buyer's detriment.

Established stamp auction firms offer sellers exposure to qualified, serious buyers—a clientele built up over years, even decades, buyers more likely to bid aggressively. A traditional, printed catalogue gets potential buyers' attention and holds it. It's nearly impossible not to spend time paging through a thick, well-illustrated catalogue to see what mouthwatering gems cry out to be bought. Printed catalogues tend to remain in a buyer's awareness because they can be—and usually are—picked up and paged through time and again. An advantage in a fast-paced world where consumer attention span seems to shorten as the number of voices clamoring to be heard and noticed increases.

BUYING

If possible, attend an auction in person to get a feel for the action, the ebb and flow of bidding. Pay attention to who's bidding—collector, dealer, agent—and how they go about it. Sometimes the floor is electric with action; other times, lots plod by like fence posts on a long, dull drive. You'll notice that some bidders can't sit still, while others seem bored and only half awake. Make no mistake, all are there to buy. Pay attention. There's more than meets the eye, as you'll see in the following pages.

Determine in advance your maximum bid for each lot and stick to it. It's easy to get caught up in a bidding frenzy—especially at a floor auction—overbid, and regret it later. But how to arrive at a price? Study prices realized for similar material in recent auctions. Compare them to local retail prices and advertised mail-order prices, which tend to be, but are not always, higher than auction prices. This sounds like common sense, but you'd be surprised at the number of auction bidders who pay no attention to the market.

Other factors, such as rarity and opportunity, bear on calculating the "right" price and on bidding strategy. Some items, such as the U.S. Zeppelin set of 1930, show up frequently at auction, despite being expensive. Bid conservatively in such situations. If you miss out, another will be along soon. It may take 2 or 3 or even 10 tries, but sooner or later you will be successful, and you will have bought at your price. In the meantime, apply the strategy to other items on your want list. You'll end up buying bargains and, with the money saved, be able to acquire additional stamps.

A client and friend once asked what I liked in an upcoming auction. He was worried about bidding against me. I told him not to worry, that I was a stingy bidder, that he could easily outbid me. The comment seemed to surprise him. He knew that I bid regularly at auction and no doubt assumed I was an aggressive bidder. I chuckled and said, "I bid every lot based on a price at which I can not afford to say no."

He seemed puzzled. "How do you ever buy anything?" he asked.

"I bid on hundreds of lots. As many as four hundred or five hundred in some sales. I don't end up with many, maybe twenty or thirty if I'm lucky—but the ones I do buy, I buy right. Now you know my secret."

Collectors generally don't bid on as many lots as dealers, but they can approach bidding with the same patience and discipline. It may take 10 auctions, bidding on the same 15 items per sale, to acquire what you're after, but sooner or later success will come. This is the message I was trying to impart to my friend. Until our conversation, his strategy had been to bid according to how much it would take to buy a lot. After our conversation, he changed his focus from "How much will it take to buy it?" to buying it right.

The foregoing strategy is appropriate in many, but not all, cases. Most intermediate and advanced collectors arrive at a point where their collections lack one or more elusive "keys." Elusive keys are not necessarily expensive, just exceedingly difficult to locate. For example, some of the most elusive precancel stamps catalogue as little as $25, $50, or $100 yet seldom appear on the market—often not for decades. Experienced collectors know better than to hesitate when an opportunity presents itself. They buy—and buy regardless of price. Catalogue price in these cases becomes irrelevant.

The following illustrates the approach and the reasoning. A customer of long standing called one day for advice about a rare die proof coming up for auction.

"How much should I bid?" he asked.

"Depends on how badly you want it," I said.

The item in question was a large die proof of one of the 1954 Liberty series definitives. Proofs of all denominations in the series are rare and in most cases, unique. At the time, catalogue value for the proof was $750.

"It's likely unique," I said.

"So, what do you think it'll take to buy it?" he asked.

"Hard to say. I'd feel comfortable bidding up to twenty-five hundred."

"Triple cat . . . I don't know . . . that's a lot." He sounded uncertain.

"Not really. First of all, catalogue value, given its rarity, should probably be in the neighborhood of twenty-five hundred. Secondly, the item is likely unique. You could wait decades for another chance at it. Thirdly, catalogue editors monitor auction prices. I wouldn't be surprised to see the value adjusted to reflect the market after the sale. But the bottom line is, how badly do you want it? And when, if ever, will you have another opportunity to own it?"

He was silent for a moment and then said, "Will twenty-five hundred buy it?"

"I don't know. Depends on who else wants it and how badly. If you're lucky, catalogue value will loom large in their thinking. There's a good chance that they'll strategize in terms of percentages over catalogue—twenty percent, fifty percent, that sort of thing—not in multiples—two or three times catalogue."

He thought for a moment and then said, "Okay. I'll give it a shot."

After the auction, he called back. "You'll never guess," he said, "how much I paid." I could hear the glee in his voice. I knew he had done well.

"One bid over seven hundred and fifty!" he said. "One bid over!"

I was surprised the proof sold so reasonably. My friend was lucky. He got his proof, his elusive key for a song, although he was prepared to spend much more. His experience illustrates another point. In many cases, an item can be obtained for less than your maximum potential bid.

The foregoing approach applies to condition rarities as well. Some nineteenth-century stamps are notoriously faulty and seldom available in decent condition, much less gem quality. Flawless examples tend to be truly rare. Increasingly, sophisticated buyers are willing to stretch to acquire gem quality examples.

So when it comes to the elusive, decide how badly you want the item and consider how long you might have to wait for another opportunity to own it. Don't be overly influenced by catalogue value and be prepared to stretch for the privilege of owning it.

Whenever possible, view lots in advance to verify condition and check for faults. Some auctions grade and describe conservatively; others, more liberally. Viewing eliminates unpleasant surprises. Remember, once the hammer drops, you own the lot.

Be aware that viewers occasionally disparage lots with comments such as "Looks regummed to me," in order to plant seeds of doubt and discourage others from bidding on them. Bidders who doubt their ability to spot regumming (or other problems) usually shy away from such lots. Don't be surprised to see the fellow who knocked the lot bidding on it. It's an old tactic.

Collections, accumulations, balances, and remainders can be especially challenging. Lot descriptions usually begin with the best selling points, highlights such as scarce or valuable items, comments about variety or completeness— points intended to present the lot in the best possible light and pique the interest of bidders. Disclaimers appear at the end of the description, usually in innocuous language. For example, consider this summary of a hypothetical lot: "Tremendous variety, replete with better items, condition mixed, viewing recommended." "Mixed condition" means "contains faulty stamps." "Viewing recommended" means "don't say we didn't warn you to look it over."

The phrase, "viewing may prove useful" indicates that the lot describer didn't have time to thoroughly scrutinize the lot and that careful viewing might reveal hidden goodies that justify bidding more aggressively than the description suggests. Occasionally, a disclaimer is too strongly worded and the lot is actually better than the description makes it sound. Either way, viewers have the advantage. Knowledge is power.

Sometimes a lot is carelessly described. I once paid $200 for an album that contained a rare Washington-Franklin series coil line pair, which I subsequently consigned to another auction where it sold for more than $8,000. The rarity lay hidden in the album, hinged under a pair of common coil stamps of similar design. The album was described as a "remainder," a term applied to albums and collections containing items whose individual value is too small to be lotted separately. It was a beat-up old-time album containing scores of duplicate pairs hinged under one another, as was the custom years ago. The lot describer must have scanned the album, noticed only inexpensive coil pairs, and assumed the ones mounted underneath were duplicates. The rare pair escaped the notice of bidders as well. I bought the lot quietly just at the estimated price, $200. So examine lots carefully. Remember that in all cases, viewers have the edge over nonviewers and careless viewers.

Why don't pros pick up on these opportunities? Often they do. I did. But just as often, they don't have time to view lots as thoroughly as they might like to. Remember, for a dealer, viewing and bidding is a task—a task necessary to obtain inventory—not a pastime. Dealers get dozens and dozens of auction catalogues, each with hundreds or thousands of lots. Before long the lots and descriptions begin to blur together. Stamps begin to look the same. The dealer's edge is sometimes offset by fatigue or inattentiveness.

Why don't collectors pick up on misdescribed lots? Sometimes they do, especially if the lot contains material of interest to them. But collectors tend not to be bargain hunters, at least not in the sense that they'll bid on anything if it's cheap enough. In most cases, they're interested only in material that fits into their collection and tend to ignore everything else. And collectors tend not to be risk takers. They tend to lack confidence in their own expertise, reasoning that the pro—the lot describer—is unlikely to have made a mistake.

Some collectors watch dealers bid, then jump in at the end and buy lots out from under them. The reasoning is that any lot bought for one bid more than a dealer is willing to pay is bound to be a bargain. For this reason, many dealers prefer to sit in the back of the room or use an agent to execute their bids.

Look for material in other than its best venue—for example, a stray high-value Columbian in an auction devoted to specialized German states. Lots like these tend to get lost in the shuffle and ignored by bidders who've come for the main event. They tend to sell for less than they would in a sale devoted to like material. Better still if they appear unobtrusively near the end of a long sale, when most of the enthusiasm and money have been spent and the floor is exhausted.

Look for runs of the same item. Successive lots of identical stamps tend to decrease in hammer price, and the greater the number of lots, the more the price tends to slip. Sometimes as few as three or four identical lots are enough to depress price. Generally, the first and last lots tend to sell for more than those in between.

External factors affect auctions and sometimes present opportunities. The unexpected blizzard that discourages attendance and reduces competition. The bad day on Wall Street or the international crisis that stifles bidding and depresses prices, if only temporarily. During the week after the stock market crash of October 1987, nervous bidders sat on the sidelines and much excellent material went begging. Two weeks later, after everything had settled down, bidders were back in force as if nothing had happened. In the meantime, bargains were to be had.

Summer is usually a good time to buy, and conversely, a poor time to sell. Years ago, the auction trade more or less shut down during the summer months because collectors were busy with vacations and outdoor activities. That changed during the boom years of the 1970s. Auctioneers held auctions as fast as material came in. After the boom ended, they continued to hold summer auctions, despite the fact that they tend not to be as strong as those held during cold-weather months.

I prefer to sit toward the back of an auction gallery. It affords a panoramic view of the action and makes it difficult for competitors to see how I'm bidding. I avoid jumping in at the beginning. When the initial flurry has died down and the auctioneer is poised to drop the hammer, I signal unobtrusively. Usually by that time, the impulse to make a contest of it has waned. The tactic doesn't work every time, but often enough to make it pay.

Another tactic is preemptive bidding, that is, bidding early and aggressively to intimidate potential competitors. This tactic is useful if you intend to buy a lot at any price and have nothing to lose by gambling that you can intimidate the less determined to pull out early. Some preemptive bidders raise their hand high and keep it up—as opposed to flashing a separate and discreet signal each time the bid goes up—a display that announces, "I'm going to buy this lot, forget about challenging me." The tactic is intimidating and it does work. A variation of the tactic involves making a show of aggressively overpaying on a few cheap lots at the beginning of a sale to unnerve competitors and weaken their inclination to bid assertively when the "good stuff" comes up. Another variation involves jumping the bid, raising a $100 bid to $150 instead of the next increment, $110—and sometimes doing it more than once. Floor auctions move with amazing rapidity. It's not unusual for the action to be over in less than 30 seconds. In the heat of the moment, there is little time to analyze or reason. The gut takes over, and more often than not, the faint of heart fade.

Have expensive stamps, especially rare varieties and errors, expertized. Most auctions permit lots to be put "on extension" while an expert opinion is obtained. An extension postpones final consummation of the transaction until an opinion is received. In most cases, the auction firm submits the item to the expertizing service. Expertizing typically takes from four to six weeks, although sometimes longer. Usually, the buyer stands the cost if the opinion comes back positive; the auction or seller absorbs the fee if it comes back negative. Most auctions require full payment for lots put on extension. Payment is refunded in the event of a negative opinion. Occasionally, a verdict comes back marked "no opinion," which means the expertizing service was unable to make a determination one way or the other. Some auctions refuse to accept returns, make refunds, or stand the cost of expertizing in the event of a "no opinion" verdict. Some firms make it a policy not to grant extensions unless notified in advance of the sale date that the bidder intends to request one. Most state their policy under "terms and conditions" in the front of their catalogues. If there's any doubt, raise the point before the auction. Some auctions refuse to accept the opinions of certain expertizing services. The exclusion often stems from a past disagreement or dispute over an opinion and not the integrity of the service. Generally, the greater the number of options open to the bidder, the better. Limitations, if any, are usually mentioned in the terms and conditions section of an auction catalogue.

The majority of purchases do not require expertizing; nevertheless, absentee buyers should check purchases upon receipt to make sure they are as described. You'd be surprised how many collectors don't bother to check purchases, only to discover later, after any possibility of recourse has passed, that the item was not as described.

A reserve is the price below which a lot is not sold. Some auctions reserve every lot. Others reserve none, or in some cases, only the occasional lot. The most straightforward list minimums or reserves with lot descriptions. Others leave you to guess. They knock down lots that fail to meet reserves to the book as if they had actually sold. The deception becomes apparent when the same lots appear in the next auction, and in some cases, two or more subsequent auctions, just waiting for the "right" buyer to come along, one who is unaware of how frequently the material has failed to attract so much as a single bid. Ethical firms—and most are—omit unsold lots from their prices realized. The less principled list unsolds at the minimum bid, as if they had sold—in my opinion, a misleading and unethical practice. As a consequence, I disregard prices realized for all lots listed as sold for the minimum bid in reserved auctions.

The best auctions, in my opinion, are unreserved auctions. I prefer them because they offer the best opportunities. The rationale behind reserves is that they provide guidance, that they help buyers by not encouraging unrealistic (a euphemism for "low") bids. In reality, reserves benefit only the auction, not the buyer. Don't be induced to bid more than your instinct tells you just because a lot is reserved.

It's not uncommon for an auction, especially one that reserves lots, to offer a list of unsolds after a sale, usually under the original terms: minimum bid plus buyer's premium. In most cases, one must request the list. Most auctions insist that minimums are not negotiable, but in some cases they are, especially on high-priced lots.

In the late 1990s, I bid, via an agent, $10,000 for a lot in a West Coast sale. The auction catalogue estimated it to be worth $7,500 to $10,000—a conservative figure, in my opinion. I bid toward the high side of the estimate, hoping it would be enough to buy the lot. Unfortunately, it wasn't. My auction agent reported that it sold to the book for one bid more than my top bid. At least that's what I thought. A couple of days later, however, the auctioneer called me. He wanted to know if I was still interested in the lot.

"Yes," I said. "Did the top bidder back out?"

"No," he said. "The lot was reserved."

"At what price?"

"Twenty thousand."

"Why the low estimate with such a high reserve?"

"A favor to the consignor," the auctioneer said. "He gave me a sizable consignment. I thought a conservative estimate might stimulate bidding." His tone struck me as apologetic.

"The lot's not worth twenty thousand," I said, "if that's what you're asking."

"I know," he sighed. He then asked, "What *is* it worth to you?"

"My original bid. Ten thousand."

"He won't go for that," the auctioneer said, referring to the consignor. "He feels it ought to be worth at least fifteen thousand."

"Pass," I said. Then, "If it were worth fifteen, someone would have bid that much. It was exposed to a large audience of interested buyers. They had every opportunity to bid. Surely you've explained the facts of life to him."

"Yes . . . but on the other hand, we all know it's worth more than ten."

Although I didn't want to admit it, the auctioneer had a point. It was worth more than ten thousand.

"So, make me an offer," he said.

I considered for a moment and then said. "Twelve-five . . . and no buyer's premium."

"How about thirteen-five?" he countered. "And I'll work something out with him on the commission?"

I hesitated. Judged the upside potential of the lot, which consisted of a number of items. Considered how I'd break it down for resale. How long it would take to get my money back. What my downside risk would be. Then, just for the hell of it, said, "Thirteen. Thirteen thousand even."

I bought the lot. It turned out to be quite profitable over time. So inquire about unsolds. It never hurts to make an offer.

I often use an auction agent when I can't attend an auction in person. I use an agent to avoid overpaying and because I need a set of experienced eyes to view lots. Absentee bids, when successful, are supposed to buy lots at one advance over the second highest bid. Unfortunately, not every auction observes this protocol. Those that don't, open a lot using the highest absentee bid and knock it down for that price if there are no bids from the floor. I learned this the hard way early on and as a result, started using an agent. I can't begin to guess how many thousands of dollars it has saved me. The first time out, nearly 30 years ago, I bought a lot for $300, which was $700 less than my maximum bid of $1,000. The agent fee amounted to $15—cheap insurance against overpaying.

A good agent does more than just save a client money. Agents attend auctions week in and week out. They have their hands on the pulse of the market. Feedback after a sale—who did most of the buying (collectors, dealers, or other agents), what was hot, what was not—is valuable intelligence, literally worth its weight in gold. Agents also keep their eyes open for material of interest to their clients, items clients might otherwise overlook.

Agents typically charge from 3 to 5 percent of the total purchase price. Rates vary depending on size of account, frequency of bidding, and whether travel or viewing is involved. Most charge a minimum fee if none of a client's bids are successful. You'll find the names of established auction agents listed in most auction catalogues.

Occasionally, I submit bids by mail or fax without using an agent. I do so when I know from experience that the auction uses top bids only if necessary. Unfortunately, the only way to sort out those who play fair from those who don't is through trial and error or word of mouth.

SELLING

Public auction is a good way to get the best price—if you have the right stamps. Auctions offer sellers direct access to the market, bringing stamps directly to interested, qualified buyers who bid competitively for the right to own them. Presumably when the hammer falls, all parties interested in the consignor's stamps will have bid on them, and they will have sold for the best possible price.

Auction is not right for every stamp. It won't work magic on common, low-priced stamps. It won't turn junk into gold. High-quality stamps do the best at public auction, as do rarities and specialty items. Genuinely rare stamps—the kind that come to market only infrequently—often bring record prices at auction, as do lower-priced stamps of superlative quality.

Some argue that the auction market is a wholesale market, and in many respects it is, but not entirely. In reality, specialty material, elusive material, and material in superlative condition are avidly purchased by the end consumer—the collector.

Most auctions require a minimum consignment, typically $1,000 net yield, although it varies from firm to firm. Narrow profit margins make it uneconomical to handle small consignments. If your consignment doesn't meet the minimum, chances are that it wouldn't do well at public auction anyway.

Sellers usually pay a 10 percent commission, although some auctions have a sliding scale. Generally, the smaller the consignment and the smaller the value of the individual lot, the higher the commission. Some auctions assess a minimum fee for each lot that sells for less than $100. The fee is usually $10 or $15. Some auctions settle (pay) 30 days after a sale, although 45 days is more typical. Typical time from consignment to settlement is four to six months.

The best auctions carefully describe and illustrate lots in eye-appealing catalogues, which are mailed to customer lists containing thousands of names, including many absentee bidders. Consignments are lotted (subdivided into individual lots) according to their merits. Stamps of substantial value or superlative quality are described and illustrated separately. Most auctions apply a threshold, a minimum lot value, often $100 but sometimes $50, when lotting. The costs of lotting, catalogue printing and mailing, and overhead make it uneconomical to lot individual stamps valued at less. Stamps not meeting the individual lot minimum are grouped into lots known as *remainders* or *balances*. Stamps belonging to different consignors, however, are never commingled.

Most auctions offer cash advances, typically 50 percent of the expected net yield, but in some cases more depending on size and desirability of the consignment. Some charge interest on advances, others do not. Some add a percentage point or two to the seller's commission in lieu of interest.

Reputable auction firms give a realistic estimate of the expected net yield. This is important because you don't want an unpleasant surprise at settlement. It's no fun getting a $6,000 settlement check instead of a $10,000 check. Be suspicious of anyone who promises the moon to secure your consignment, especially those who have not been in business long.

Some consignors, especially inexperienced ones, request reserves because they fear that their stamps might sell too cheaply. Some auction firms allow reserves, others do not. Unrealistic reserves generally prove to be a futile exercise; the reserved lots simply fail to attract bids.

A better strategy is to consign sufficient material to ensure that the yield averages out. As long as you're satisfied with the aggregate net yield quoted in the estimate (which is why it is so important to get a *realistic* estimate), don't waste time trying to second-guess the price of each individual lot. Some lots sell for more than expected, others for less, but in the end, they tend to average out. Concern yourself with the estimated aggregate net yield. If you don't like the size of the estimate, don't consign.

Auctions that allow reserves usually charge for them. After all, they put in the same amount of work and incur the same expenses whether or not a lot sells. No one can afford to hold sales and not sell lots. Those that do not permit reserves generally advise consignors to bid on their own lots if they want to protect them, and generally charge either the seller's commission for lots bought back or both the buyer's premium and seller's commission. Occasionally, one hears a horror story about a consignment with unrealistic reserves that ends up almost completely unsold, costing the consignor thousands of dollars in commissions. Unless you don't mind getting stamps back, paying for the privilege, and wasting months going through the consignment pipeline a second time, avoid reserves.

Occasionally—but not often—one comes across an auction that offers consignors a no-fee, blanket reserve. In most cases, they are either new to the business or desperate for material. The reserves, an incentive to attract consignments, often turn out to be an exercise in futility for seller and auction alike. In many cases, the newcomer's customer list is not sufficiently developed to generate the kind of bids necessary for the strategy to succeed. So consignors get back most of their material and the auction is out the cost of offering the lots.

A few years back, an energetic and somewhat arrogant new auctioneer suddenly appeared on the scene. He put out a fantastic catalogue—glossy paper, lavish illustrations, wonderful material. I loved the lots. Unfortunately, all were encumbered by unrealistically high reserves.

I didn't bid. A couple of days after the sale, a fax arrived announcing that unsold lots could be had for the original minimum bid plus a 15 percent buyer's premium. The lengthy fax featured 90 percent of the lots in the auction catalogue. Only 10 percent had sold—nowhere near enough to offset the cost of printing and mailing catalogues, let alone yield a profit. It seemed obvious that the would-be auctioneer had attracted consignments by promising high prices— prices protected by unrealistically high reserves—but underestimated the market consciousness of the buying public. It proved to be a fatal miscalculation.

I studied the list and then called the auctioneer, thinking that he might be open to negotiation in light of the 90 percent no-sale rate. My optimism was short-lived. He was intransigent. The experience seemingly had left him no less arrogant. So I passed.

I can only imagine how irate his consignors were when they got their lots back instead of fat settlement checks. Suffice it to say, that was his first and last auction.

Most established auctions do not encourage reserves because, more often than not, those who insist on them have an unrealistically high opinion of their stamps' value. Besides, if the auction does a good job at presentation and if it has a large, established mailing list, the consignment should do fine.

One last point on the subject of reserves: A few established auctions, a small minority, give consignors no choice. They place reserves on every lot—period. The rationale (touted as a selling point) that reserves yield higher prices and protect lots from selling too cheaply sounds appealing. But anytime reserves are in place, some lots fail to sell—sometimes, more than are sold. Nothing is more irritating than getting lots back instead of a settlement check. And if the settlement amounts to less than the advance, the consignor is faced with refunding the difference, as well as being out the interest. Before consigning to a reserves-only auction, find out what percent of a typical consignment ends up unsold.

Auction firms tend to specialize. Some specialize in U.S. stamps, others in foreign stamps. Some specialize in rarities and top-quality gems, others in everyday, bread-and-butter material. Some are national in reach, others regional or local. Don't expect top dollar for U.S. stamps auctioned by a firm that specializes in British Commonwealth. Seek out an auction with an established clientele for the type of material you have for sale.

In some cases, small specialized firms often get amazing prices for material in their specialty. I was flabbergasted to get $900 for a box Vietnam covers placed at a specialized auction, flabbergasted because the box had languished on a shelf for several years priced at $100. I couldn't even interest other dealers in it. So do your homework; get the best price by finding the right venue.

Advertisements and announcements for public auctions can be found in philatelic periodicals. Obtain sample catalogues and prices realized from several companies for recent sales in order to get an idea of how your stamps will be presented and how much similar stamps have realized. Compare lot descriptions to get a feel for how your stamps will be described. Some firms tend toward descriptive minimalism, mentioning only the bare essentials, while others are more liberal and marketing oriented in their lot descriptions. Ask how your consignment will be broken down. Get at least a general commitment about which items will be lotted individually and which will be bulked together. Individually lotted items usually realize higher prices than grouped items, which tend to sell to dealers. Try to get a commitment that individually lotted items will be illustrated. Illustrated lots attract more bids and fetch higher prices. If possible, speak to former consignors to find out if they were satisfied or dissatisfied.

Consign stamps in a timely fashion. Don't wait until the last minute. Lot describers end up under a great deal of pressure at deadline precisely because consignors tend to procrastinate. Your stamps are likely to get more careful attention if consigned early. Experienced consignors prefer to have their material appear in fall or winter auctions, when the collecting season is in full swing.

Be aware that consignors assume market risk. In the time between consignment and sale, typically three or four months, market prices can rise or fall. Drastic fluctuations rarely occur, but still the element of uncertainty exists. And as mentioned earlier, unforeseen occurrences such as a stock market downturn affect confidence and prices.

Successful bidders often request that expensive lots be put on extension pending an expert opinion. Payments for lots on extension are not dispersed to consignors until the lots have been returned with a satisfactory opinion. Established auctions almost always correctly identify stamps, so the risk of having a lot returned with an adverse opinion is small. Still, the weeks involved in obtaining the opinion delay payment. Savvy consignors obtain expert certificates before consigning for two reasons: faster payment (it eliminates extension) and higher yield (bidders tend to bid more liberally on lots with expert certificates).

Make sure your consignment is insured. Don't hesitate to ask for proof in writing. Established auctions usually state an insured value in their consignment agreement. If the estimate seems low, request that it be increased. Back in the early 1980s, the offices of a two-year-old auction firm were robbed at gunpoint. Employees were bound with duct tape and the safe methodically cleaned out. The thieves were pros who knew exactly what they were looking for. The material was never recovered, and shortly thereafter, the auction declared bankruptcy. Consignments had not been insured. Consignors were left holding the bag.

Foreign auctions can be useful for the right property. It is axiomatic that stamps are most in demand in the nation of their origin. German and Swiss auctions advertise heavily in the United States for consignments. Foreign auctions often get tremendous prices for top-quality, specialized material native to their locale but also tend to be very selective—even picky.

Go in with your eyes open when consigning abroad. Terms and conditions vary from country to country. Some foreign auctions charge lotting and illustration fees; most U.S. auctions don't. You may encounter insurance fees, special taxes, and other types of fees typically not encountered in U.S. auctions. Also, remember that in case of disagreement, stamps outside the country are beyond U.S. jurisdiction and easy legal recourse.

Some foreign auctions have the annoying habit of reserving lots whether you want reserves or not. It's very frustrating to wait six months for your stamps to be sold, only to receive most of them back. It's happened to me and I didn't like it. And one more thing: Don't consign U.S. stamps to foreign auctions. The best market for U.S. stamps is in the United States.

INTERNET AUCTIONS

Internet auctions fall into two categories: party-to-party auctions, such as eBay, and online auctions hosted by traditional stamp auction firms.

Party-to-party auctions are more egalitarian than traditional auctions. Anyone can sell. No minimum consignment is required. Sellers can list as few or as many items as they wish. They can illustrate lots in color. They can write their own descriptions, say as much or as little as they like. They can set reserves and minimum bids at any level that suits their fancy. They can list items on short notice, cancel bids, and even end a sale prematurely if they so desire. Settlements usually arrive within a few days, as opposed to 30 or 45 days for traditional auctions. In fact, the whole process takes days or, at most, a couple of weeks instead of months.

Buyers are treated to a wide range of material, so much, in fact, that skill at making searches is necessary to locate items of interest.

SELLING ONLINE

First and foremost, take time to familiarize yourself with the medium. Browse a few auctions. Check what's being offered, note what kinds of lots attract the most action, compare write-ups and presentations, look at prices realized for completed sales, and pay attention to what kinds of things end up unsold.

You'll notice a glut of some material, so much that it either attracts few bids or goes unsold. Don't expect good results when offering similar items. Avoid the typical, offer the unusual. Online auctions will not work magic on common material. You'll also notice an astonishing quantity and variety of material. So much, that potential bidders invariably use searches to narrow the array. They search using keywords likely to appear either in the title of a lot or in its text. Smart sellers use keywords to lead searchers to their offerings.

Recently, a dealer-friend, new to online auctioning, called to tell me he'd posted his first lots on eBay. He'd chosen several World War II–era covers sent to or posted from Japan. They contained common stamps but unusual censor markings. He'd not been able to find mention of them in any of the reference books he had, which didn't necessarily mean they were rare or valuable, but he thought they might bring a good price to the right buyer.

I logged on to see how they were doing. I searched "Japanese covers." Nothing came up. I searched "censored covers." Again, nothing. I searched "World War II" and "World War 2" and "Second World War." Nothing. I searched using every keyword I could think of, but without luck. I knew the dealer's eBay handle, so I clicked on his "other auctions" and the five covers popped up. He'd described each succinctly in technically correct terms: "Cover with Scott #xxx, postmarked Tokio (I had not thought to search under Tokio—or Tokyo, for that matter). He'd listed the postmark date, mentioned that the covers appeared to be commercial (as opposed to philatelically inspired), and noted that they had been opened by censor and sealed with examiner's tape.

I got on the phone and, not wanting to rain on his parade, said, "You could do yourself a big favor."

"How's that?" he asked.

"Pay more attention to keywords in your titles and descriptions." I reported the lack of results of my search. "Visualize the auction bidder as a walk-in customer,"

I said. "If his interest is World War II Japanese covers, what will he ask to see? Every cover in the store or those specific to his interest? Online auction buyers think in the same way, and in essence, search to pose their requests. Anticipate which keywords will likely first come to mind. Use them in the title. In this case, the words 'Japanese,' 'World War II,' 'censored,' and 'cover.' And load the description with as many others as you can think of."

One can only guess how many potential bidders never saw the Japanese censored covers because neither titles nor descriptions contained the most logical keywords. I'm pleased to report that since that inauspicious beginning, my friend has offered hundreds of lots online, with excellent results. He has paid attention to the use of keywords. He has experimented and learned. He has listened to the market and paid attention to what it had to say.

The following is my approach to Internet auction selling. I've used eBay as an example because I'm familiar with it. A number of other online auctions offer similar features and service.

First the basics. Listings contain three essential elements: One, keywords to enable bidders to locate the lot. Two, the illustration. One picture is worth a thousand words. Three, the description. It should contain essential details including condition or anything remarkable about the item.

When you've readied your listings and logged on to the auction site, a listing screen will guide you through a sequence of steps requiring decisions. Among them are category, title, description, illustration, gallery, quantity, minimum bid, reserve price, duration, escrow, payment methods, and shipping terms. I will only touch on the most crucial.

CATEGORY

Pick "stamps" on the first menu. A number of subcategories will appear. Select the most appropriate. Some items easily fit into two or more categories. The foregoing Japanese covers could be listed under "Japan" or "Postal History." Select the one you consider most logical. A secondary category listing is available at eBay, however listing and optional fees double. Some swear by the two-category method, while others question the expense, reasoning that bidders tend to locate lots more by searching than by browsing. I tend to agree with the latter view and put more emphasis on getting keywords right.

TITLE

Make sure titles contain keywords most likely to come to a bidder's mind. Pack the title with as many as possible. Space is limited (45 characters on eBay at this writing), so don't worry about grammar, just fit the words in. Example: World War II Japanese Censored Cover. The word "commercial" would have been nice to include, but it exceeded the character count. That's okay. Mention it in the description. Some prefer to use capital letters, others use uppercase and lower-case. I've tried both and don't think it makes much difference. Bidders seem to be more interested in content than hype. Avoid cutesy come-ons such as "L@@K!" They're overdone, trite, and downright annoying.

DESCRIPTION

Summarize essential facts in a straightforward manner at the beginning the description. Include any keywords that wouldn't fit in the title, such as "commercial" in the foregoing example. "Commercial" is an important bit of information because commercial covers are generally more desirable than phila-telically inspired covers. Mention other relevant information in whatever detail is appropriate. Wax poetic if the mood strikes you. If you have specialized knowledge or the item would benefit from the telling of a story, don't hesitate to share what you know. Avoid, however, gilding the lily. Don't hype a group of 50¢ first day covers as "rare and valuable." Buyers are not dummies. I find that it helps to write the description in advance. I use the Notepad feature on my computer to write them the day before posting them online. Many times an overlooked detail comes to me overnight.

ILLUSTRATION

One picture is worth a thousand words. Strive for quality scans. If you're new at scanning, practice until you get it right. Nothing turns off buyers like a lousy illustration. As a general rule, scanning works better than digital photography for flat items. Be sure scans are large enough to reveal detail. Include a scan of the back of an item, such as a cover, if it contains anything relevant to value. Also, avoid the temptation to clutter your listing with motion effects and blar-ing color options should you choose to use any of the optional lot listing platforms. They're distracting and don't impress anyone, especially experienced Web surf-ers who have to suffer through them on site after site.

GALLERY

This option provides a thumbnail illustration of an item in the preview gallery as well as with the summary array brought up by searches. The fee is minimal and just might entice a browser to click on your primary listing page for a full description and illustration. In my opinion, the gallery preview option is well worth the money (25¢ at this writing). A second option "features" your item within the gallery, in effect giving it top billing. It's costly ($19.95 at this writ-ing) and, in my opinion, not worth the expense in most cases, especially for modestly priced items.

QUANTITY

Check "one," unless you plan to hold a Dutch auction. A Dutch auction features multiple identical items, each selling to a separate bidder. For example, if you check "three," then the top 3 bidders (whether 4 or 400 participate) each win one of the items.

MINIMUM BID

This is the price at which bidding starts. Keep minimums reasonable. Newcomers (known as *newbies* in Internet jargon) tend to set minimums too high, a practice that discourages bidding. Remember, you incur a listing fee whether or not the lot sells—and unsold lots cut into profits. They cost money rather than creating income. Experienced sellers tend to opt for low minimums precisely because they encourage bidding. Once involved, a bidder is more likely to follow a lot and bid on it later. A bidder, even a low bidder, has more invested in a lot than one who has passed it by. Besides, if a lot is truly worthwhile, it will fetch a good price.

RESERVE PRICE

This feature allows sellers to set a reserve in addition to the minimum bid. Minimum bid is the price at which bidding starts. Reserve is the price below which a lot will not be sold. It is possible, for example, to set a minimum bid of $1 and a reserve of $1,000. Reserves remain hidden from bidders until the reserve has been met. Some bidders feel that a reserve implies an unreasonably high expectation on the part of the seller, an expectation so unreasonable that the seller is embarrassed to come right out and say it in the form of a minimum bid. Still, if you're new, reserves offer an opportunity to test the market by setting low minimums. As you gain experience, you'll probably decide that reserves are not worth the extra fee.

DURATION

Typical choices include 3, 5, 7, or 10 days. Seven days is about right. Some feel that longer exposure is better and opt for 10 days (eBay, for one, charges extra for the 10-day option). Others feel that because the Internet, by nature, is fast paced, active bidders are sure to spot an item regardless of duration. They feel that a short duration imparts a sense of urgency and worry that, faced with too long a duration, some bidders lose interest and the inclination to post follow-up bids. Start out with the 7-day option. Experiment with other durations as you gain experience.

ESCROW

Escrow services guarantee that buyers pay and sellers deliver. As a seller, you have three options: seller pays fees, buyer pays fees, or seller doesn't accept escrow. In most cases, escrow is not necessary. After all, sellers get to hold the goods until payment is in hand. If you're concerned about a buyer's check, hold the shipment until the check clears. More about that in the next section, "Payment Methods." Escrow is primarily intended to protect buyers. It guarantees that goods will be shipped, received, and as described before payment is disbursed. It works fine in principle and for many types of commodities, but be aware that it does not guarantee authenticity or condition for collectibles such as stamps. It will not protect you from an inexperienced seller misdescribing a common stamp as a rare and valuable variety. Escrow only guarantees that you will receive the stamp; it does not guarantee that the stamp will, in fact, be the scarce and valuable variety you expected. I don't accept escrow, and it has never been a problem. Most stamp buyers don't expect it, especially where small sales are concerned. If a buyer absolutely insists on escrow, you can always arrange it after the fact.

PAYMENT METHODS

Select those you feel comfortable with. The listing page offers a variety of options, which, if checked, appear with the listing. The options include money order, cashier's check, personal check, credit cards (Visa, MasterCard, American Express, etc.), COD (collect on delivery), "See Item Description," and other. Cash is not a listed option, but you are welcome to list it in your description. I prefer to check "See Item Description" and reiterate the forms of acceptable payment at the end of the description. Cash, check, or money order work fine if you're an occasional seller offering only a few items at a time. If you sell regularly or overseas, consider adding payment services, such as BillPoint (eBay's in-house service) and PayPal, which allow buyers to pay by credit card. Payment services credit payments, less a small fee, directly to your bank account. Some services offer the option of sending payment to you in the form of a money order. At this writing, PayPal offers the option of withdrawing cash by using a debit card issued to account holders. Some, such as BidPay, assess the transaction fee to buyers rather than sellers. Comparison shop before signing up for a payment service. Some offer a better value than others. All can be accessed by clicking on link icons located on auction sites.

SHIPPING TERMS

Menu options include "Seller Pays Shipping," "Buyer Pays All Shipping," "Buyer Pays Fixed Amount," and "See Item Description." "Buyer Pays All Shipping " is pretty standard. Most sellers charge actual shipping costs, and buyers regard that as fair. If you choose to charge a fixed amount, state it in the description. Large mail-order corporations have come to regard shipping as a profit center, often assessing unnecessarily high fees to offset discounts on merchandise. Consumers are not dummies. Although silently resentful, they tolerate the practice because they have no other choice. They tend not to be so forgiving when dealing with private parties, so think twice about trying to collect $3 to cover 50¢ worth of shipping.

SHIP-TO LOCATIONS

Options include "United States Only," "Internationally (worldwide)," or "United States and the Following Regions." The regions include Canada, Europe, Australasia (Australia and the Pacific), Asia, South America, Africa, Mexico and Central America, Middle East, and Caribbean. Often the strongest bids for foreign stamps and covers come from overseas. Some sellers, however, prefer not to sell overseas because of language, payment, and security issues—shipments to some countries tend to get "lost." Others report favorable, and occasionally amusing, experiences selling overseas. One seller received an e-mail from a successful bidder in Beijing, China, who wanted to trade stamps for the lot rather than send payment. After a series of e-mails spanning several days and complicated by the buyer's minimal English skills, they came to terms.

"When listing terms," the seller chuckled as he related the tale, "it never occurred to me to mention that trades were not acceptable."

Experiment and use what works best for you.

NONMENU ISSUES

State your return policy. Most sellers accept returns for cause, such as inadvertent misdescription. Even the best of us occasionally make mistakes. Some do not permit returns and state clearly with lot descriptions, "All sales are final." If returns are permitted, set a time limit, such as 3, 5, or 7 days from time of receipt. I once had a buyer ask to return a lot 14 months later! I accommodated him but cautioned that future returns would have to be made within 7 days of receipt and for cause. If returns are permitted only under special circumstances, spell them out clearly.

SERVICE AND FEEDBACK

Notify successful bidders promptly by e-mail. Reiterate acceptable forms of payment. Set a due date for payment. Seven days is standard for domestic bidders, 10 or 14 days for international bidders. State the waiting period, if any, that purchases will be held for personal checks to clear. Some sellers waive the waiting period if the buyer has a positive feedback rating of 50 or more and no negative feedback. Others waive the waiting period on small sales, $25 or $50, or selectively impose it in the case of unusually large sales. Calculate shipping and add it to the purchase price. Protect yourself by including the disclaimer that uninsured shipments are sent at the buyer's risk.

Following is a sample e-mail notification form.

```
Congratulations!
You were the high bidder on eBay lot(s):
#100 999 1234 (butterfly topical set) $10.00
#100 999 5678 (state flag first day covers) $21.00

Subtotal: $31.00

Please add shipping as follows:
First-Class Mail: $1.00
Insurance (optional, see below): $1.10

Grand Total: $32.00 (plus insurance, if desired)

Please send payment to:

Auction Seller
P.O. Box 2020
Anytown, USA 00000

Cash, money order, or BidPay (for credit cards) for immediate
shipment. Personal check okay; please allow time to clear. Pay-
ment within 7 days, please.
IMPORTANT: Please include eBay item number(s) with your remittance.
Also, PLEASE NOTE: Uninsured shipments are sent at buyer s risk
(including damage and nondeliver). Please advise us of your mail-
ing address. Thanks.
```

Ship goods promptly upon receipt of payment. Use stamps rather than a postage meter. Fellow collectors appreciate the courtesy. Pack shipments securely to avoid damage in transit. I include an "Invoice/Packing Slip" with each shipment just to be sure the buyer knows who sent the shipment. It helps avoid problems. Believe it or not, some online buyers have so many lots coming in that they have trouble keeping track of who sent what. A sample appears below.

EBAY AUCTION BID WINNER'S INVOICE/PACKING SLIP

Auction Seller, P.O. Box 2020, Anytown, USA 00000   E-Mail: seller@server.net

Enclosed are eBay item Number(s)/Description.   Date: _____

_____

_____

_____

Thank you for your purchase.
Feedback: We will respond to your feedback after you have received your purchase and indicated that everything is fine by posting positive feedback for us.

As the form indicates, I wait for buyers to post positive feedback, then I recip-
rocate. Most buyers pay promptly, either through an online service or by mail.
Now and then, one doesn't. I allow 10 days for payment to arrive (3 days beyond
the 7 stated in the terms and conditions) because some people wait until the 7th
day to mail it. If payment has not arrived by the 10th day, I send an e-mail re-
minder. Most reminders elicit an apology and a promise to send payment right
away. After 20 days, I post a nonpaying bidder alert, a feature specific to eBay
auctions, whereupon eBay immediately notifies the buyer that a nonpaying bidder
alert has been filed. About 99 percent of the time the notice triggers an apology
and payment. In those rare instances in which it does not, I request a final value fee
credit from eBay at the 30-day mark. Within 48 hours of the request, eBay credits
my account for the final value fee (but not the insertion fee) and issues a warning
to the nonresponsive buyer. Three warnings result in a buyer being suspended
indefinitely. Fortunately, most transactions are problem-free. In my own experience, drastic action was necessary in only about 1 of every 500 transactions.

Buyers reward accurate descriptions, prompt shipment, and secure packing with
lavish praise in the comment section of the online feedback form. Positive feedback
is important. It gives bidders confidence and encourages liberal bidding. Respond
immediately to positive feedback. It's both courteous and good business. Post negative feedback only after you have exhausted every other avenue to resolve nonpayment
or a dispute—and then not so much in a spirit of revenge as to warn others.

Some final thoughts about selling via online auction: If you're new to selling,
experiment with expendable material. Think of it as an investment in knowledge, an investment that will enable you to better present important material, as
well as establish a feedback history. Don't expect to attract high bids for expensive varieties that can easily be confused with cheap varieties until you have built
up a track record of positive feedback. Experiment with write-ups and presentation, with various closing times and closing days. Conventional wisdom holds
that better results occur with evening closings, generally around 7:00 P.M. Pacific
time, which is 10:00 P.M. Eastern time, and that Friday and Saturday nights
should be avoided. Experienced sellers report better results during the cold-
weather months. The savviest buy in the summer and sell in the winter. Pay
attention to timeliness. You're likely to get stronger bids for presidential inaugu-
ration covers during a presidential campaign and stronger bids for Olympics-related
material in the weeks prior to Olympic Games.

BUYING ONLINE

Check feedback of party-to-party sellers. Avoid sellers with too much negative
feedback, but keep a sense of proportion. A thousand positives outweigh five

negatives. Volume sellers inevitably pick up a few negatives, from the occasional malcontent, if nothing else. At the same time, beware the seller with three positives and five negatives. Yes, I once encountered such a seller and would not have bid on any of his material, much less sent payment expecting to be satisfied with the goods. More and more established stamp dealers now sell via online auction. They offer the added security of name and reputation.

The most frequently heard complaints about online auctions are misdescribed material and grade inflation. Some misdescriptions are innocent, posted by inept sellers; others are intentional, posted with intent to deceive, so be careful. Beware sellers who display unfamiliarity with philatelic terminology in their write-ups. They almost certainly possess minimal identification skills and minimal awareness of the all-important nuances of condition.

Recently, I spotted a set of U.S. Zeppelins online described as "high grade mint." "High grade" is not a philatelic term. It imparts no objective information, such as hinging, gum condition, freshness, and so forth. Precise standard terminology is important because fine shadings of grade can mean a difference of hundreds of dollars in price for an expensive set such as the Zeppelins. The scan showed two of the three stamps to be poorly centered. The seller's use of the term "high grade" clearly indicated that he possessed no knowledge of stamps or grading. Could I trust such a person to detect regumming, tampering, or anything else that would impair the value of the stamps? The answer is no.

Grade inflation—nudging a stamp into a higher grade—is common and is often, but not always, the result of inexperience. As I was writing this chapter, a dealer-friend of mine related that he had just purchased a never-hinged White Plains souvenir sheet in an online auction. At least the seller represented the sheet as never hinged. Unfortunately, it turned out to be hinged. The hinge marks were barely visible. They had been smoothed over using a dampened artist's brush, eliminating their presence except to those with a practiced eye. My dealer-friend contacted the seller, who professed ignorance about the hinging but offered to make things right by refunding $100 of the purchase price—the premium for never-hinged condition. Remember, anyone can sell online, amateur and professional, the knowledgeable and the unknowledgeable, the ethical and the not-so-ethical.

Check scans carefully. If a scan does not reveal what you need to know in order to feel comfortable bidding, send an e-mail to the seller with your questions. Request the right to return the lot in the event it turns out not to be as represented. Some sellers accommodate such requests, others do not. If the seller declines, bid only if you're willing to buy the lot as is. Inspect purchases as soon as you receive them and contact the seller if they are not as represented. Sellers usually try to correct innocent mistakes. If all else fails, contact the auction host and register a complaint.

Occasionally, a seller's inexperience or lack of philatelic knowledge works to a buyer's benefit, such as an innocuous-looking cover bearing a rare, solo-usage of an odd-value Presidential definitive. Browsing may turn up an overlooked gem. Browsing also adds to one's store of knowledge—knowledge likely to prove useful or profitable later.

Reward satisfactory buying experiences with positive feedback. Send e-mail to sellers, asking what similar material might be available. Occasionally, a great off-line transaction results.

Some experienced buyers report that bargains are to be had during summer months when competition is lighter. Bargains can sometimes be found among lots offered by volume sellers (a high feedback number indicates a volume seller). They tend to be more relaxed about minimums, cognizant that some lots sell for less than expected, while others sell for more than expected, and that in the end, it all balances out.

Auctions allow bidders to post maximum bids, bids executed incrementally as necessary in response to other bids. This feature is useful when bidding on lots that close at an inconvenient time, such as 3:00 A.M. Sad to say, unethical sellers sometimes use shills to run up these kinds of bids. If you feel this has happened, cancel your bids before the auction has closed.

No discussion of online auctions would be complete without mention of sniping. *Sniping* is coming in with a bid at the last moment to preclude other bids, and thus win the lot at the lowest price. Sniping is nothing new, just the online variation of bidding at the last second at a live floor auction. Some bidders prefer to keep an eye on online lots as an auction winds down in order to get sense of the action and gauge their final bid. Others prefer to use sniping software. It's inexpensive and readily available online. It allows a bidder to program the auction, ending time, and bids and then automatically executes them. Of course, in many cases everyone has the same idea, which results in a flurry of bidding in the last few moments and, sometimes, astonishing run-ups. Another tactic is to post an early and aggressive preemptive bid (e.g., bumping a $5 minimum bid to $10 or $15). Strong preemptive bidding sometimes discourages bargain hunters, who may skip the lot rather than add it to their watch list.

In summary, both traditional and online auctions have much to offer buyer and seller alike. Explore the possibilities, comparison shop, pay attention to the market, communicate with fellow collectors and dealers, don't hesitate to ask questions, maintain a sense of balance and proportion, learn, grow, and participate.

CHAPTER 13

STAMP INVESTING

ARE STAMPS A good investment? Yes, if purchased wisely, but to do so requires knowledge and experience. It would take an entire book to adequately cover the subject. Since space here is limited, I will touch on what to avoid.

First, let me point out that most collectors of tangible objects—be it coins, sports cards, comic books, or whatever—like to think of them as good investments. It's human nature; besides, it helps rationalize purchases, especially expensive ones. Nevertheless, in most cases, enjoyment, not profit, is the hobbyist's primary motive for making a purchase. My advice: Consider any profit a bonus. That's probably the best way to look at it. After all, what could be better? You get to enjoy yourself, and when you're finished, recapture part, all, and in some cases, more than what you spent.

Now, what to watch out for.

Stamps are often touted as investments by telemarketing operations and radio infomercial promoters. Sadly, the stamps usually turn out to be low-quality examples sold at grossly inflated prices. Recently, a dealer-friend bought an "investment" portfolio from a woman who had purchased it after hearing stamps touted on a radio broadcast originating in Southern California. The broadcast was presented in an interview format. The host played the naive straight man to his pitchman guest.

"Stamps are one of the best-kept secrets in the investment world," the guest asserted. "They've outperformed inflation by one hundred to two hundred percent during the last hundred years."

"How is that possible?" the host asked.

"Stamps are collector based. Demand seldom diminishes. In fact, it grows all the time, and especially lately. Our index of leading issues shows an average increase of forty percent per year during the last two decades. Selected blue chips have performed even more dramatically. We've been watching one that's tripled during the last six months."

151

"Tripled . . . during the last six months?" the host asked, his tone one of astonishment.

"Absolutely," the pitchman guest replied. "It's actually up one thousand percent in the last five years."

"*One thousand percent?* Sounds like a can't-miss opportunity."

"It is," the pitchman assured him—and unsuspecting listeners.

The pitch went on and on and on. "Rare stamps are very safe. They can easily be converted to cash. And there are no commissions to pay."

In the end, the incredulous host asked, "I'm sure our listeners would like to know more. Can they contact you?"

"Of course," the pitchman replied. "Call our toll-free number." He repeated the number a couple of times. "Call and we'll get an informative kit on its way to you."

The victim related to my dealer-friend that initially she had had reservations about the fantastic claims but was nevertheless intrigued. She called the toll-free number. An "account executive" reiterated the selling points and gushed over the potential for quick profits. She asked if she could visit their offices, thinking if it were a boiler room operation the "account executive" would turn her down.

No problem. Come over anytime, he told her. So she did. The firm's "corporate headquarters" were less than an hour's drive away in a spanking new office park. The office suite itself, spacious, bright, and well appointed. Expensive-looking art on the walls, potted palms in the reception area. The best ill-gotten gains could buy. Forgive me for editorializing, but since the Federal Trade Commission later shut down the operation and indicted the promoters for fraud, I think it's safe to say that the gains were ill-gotten and that investors, including the woman, were fleeced.

The account executive greeted her warmly, ushered her to his desk, and reiterated the merits of rare stamp investing. He gussied up the pitch with buzzwords intended to mimic Wall Street language, and in the end, she signed up.

A certificate of authenticity accompanied each stamp. The certificates were printed on light blue security paper and contained a gold-foil stamped logo, a full-color photo of the stamp, a serial number, the expertizer's opinion that the stamp was genuine, and his signature. The certificates looked impressive; unfortunately, the so-called expertizing service was one no one in organized philately had ever heard of.

To make a long story short, she got back about 20 percent of what she had invested.

"Didn't you think to consult a stamp dealer?" my dealer-friend asked as she sat across the counter from him.

"No," she said. "Everything was so upscale . . . and the man sounded so knowledgeable." She paused. "I feel like a fool."

Her investment portfolio consisted of expensive nineteenth-century stamps, such as off-quality dollar-value Columbians, the kind that sell for a fraction of catalogue value. She had paid full price.

The Face on Mars souvenir sheet.

No account of stamp schemes would be complete without mentioning the notorious Face on Mars souvenir sheet. In 1989 the small African nation of Sierra Leone saluted the exploration of Mars with a set of 36 stamps and a souvenir sheet that depicted the well-known Face on Mars, which is a milewide topographical feature resembling a human face. New Age folklore holds that the face was carved by ancient astronauts and that similar faces exist elsewhere in the solar system, on the moon, and even hidden under the Antarctica ice cap.

Shortly after the set was issued, an American promoter bought up nearly the entire press run for about $40 per set and began touting them in his newsletter as having tremendous appreciation potential—thousands of dollars. "Destined to be a bombshell," the newsletter claimed. "Could well become one of the most valuable sets of stamps ever issued." Investors could get in on the ground floor for $100 a set.

To support his claim, the promoter published the opinion of a "space consultant" in his newsletter. The consultant boasted an impressive list of credentials but made no secret that he possessed no philatelic knowledge or background. He asserted that the Face on Mars was "nothing less than the greatest discovery in the world." It therefore followed, according to his reasoning, that the Sierra Leone set was bound to be the most popular set of stamps in the world, easily worth $10,000 to $25,000. According to his logic, the value of a stamp was directly proportional to the importance of the subject depicted on it. Philatelists who read these assertions must have wondered what planet this fellow was from. No new issue from a small third-world nation such as Sierra Leone had ever been or could ever be worth anywhere near $10,000.

According to the promoter, one need not know anything about stamps to profit from the set. One need only sell it to someone else for more than they paid.

Investors bought the pitch and the sets. Before long, classified ads began popping up in newspapers all across the country offering sets at prices ranging from a few hundred dollars to many thousands. Astonishingly, the ads generated buyers. The promoter featured glowing testimonials from sellers in his newsletter, which further fueled demand. Everyone wanted in on the action.

"I sold my set for $5,000!" one writer boasted. "I sold a set for $7,500," another gloated. "I should have bought more!" "I moved a set for $2,500!" another reported. "Your advice is fantastic!"

Some classified ads offered sets for as much as $15,000 to $20,000. Other ads claimed that the sets were rising in price at the rate of 200 percent *daily*! Of course, it was all happy talk and hogwash.

At the time all this was going on, one could buy the Face on Mars set for about $75 in the philatelic trade. I paid $2 for the illustrated example at a stamp show during the time I was preparing the manuscript for this book. Occasionally, one still sees the Face on Mars sets hyped on the Internet.

Generally, avoid investing in stamps on a portfolio-of-the-month basis. My experience has been that portfolio-of-the-month programs are more often oriented toward selling stamps rather than making investors money. I hate to sound harsh, but portfolio selections are more often a function of what's available in sufficient quantity to service subscribers than a function of what's likely to show the best price appreciation.

Occasionally, one comes across advertisements for stamps in national magazines or Sunday supplements. Although the stamps aren't necessarily sold as investments, the ads imply that the stamps are likely someday to be more valuable—possibly far more valuable—than their "modest" purchase price. "Limited edition . . . incredible demand . . . nearly sold out." The pitch, stitched together in breathless prose punctuated with exclamation points, exhorts you to buy. Unfortunately, implying financial gain is just a sales gimmick. I can't think of one instance over the years where anyone has made a profit from these issues— except, of course, the promoter.

To summarize, in order to make a sound investment in stamps, you must have knowledge and experience. Even if you have knowledge and experience, read up on the subject before considering stamps as a pure investment. Refer to Chapter 34, "Philatelic Reference Books."

Beware stamps offered as investment by direct mail, by infomercial, at investment seminars, and by telephone solicitation. Remain alert for red flags, which include unsolicited calls; high-pressure sales tactics; refusal to take "no" for an answer; a retort to every objection or question; unclear or evasive answers to questions; the promise of unrealistically high returns, especially in a short period of time; exaggerated claims of historical performance; guaranteed rates of return; guaranteed buybacks; investments touted as sure things; inside information or special situations (often far-fetched but oddly plausible); pressure to buy quickly; pressure that only a few remain; pooh-poohing risk factors; and puffed-up credentials and fancy titles. The harder the pitch, the less likely the offer has merit.

Stamp investment seminars are sometimes held in upscale hotel settings, complete with visual aids, refreshments, and high-pressure sales tactics. The moment someone tries to twist your arm, walk away. And don't worry about offending high-pressure pitchmen. Just say "no." It's better for you to have your money and them be upset, than for them to have your money and you be upset.

In general, if something sounds too good to be true, it probably is. Use common sense. Ask yourself, "If this possesses so much potential, why aren't the pitchmen buying it instead hustling others to buy it?" Never allow yourself to be talked into buying stamps—or any other investment—on the spur of the moment. Anything worth buying is worth thinking over.

Be cautious, be skeptical. Always remember the advice first counseled in Rome all those centuries ago: "Caveat emptor." Let the buyer beware.

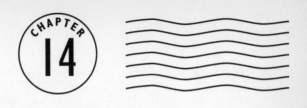

STAMP PRINTING

A LMOST ALL POSTAGE stamps are printed. The few exceptions, such as miniature phonograph records or three-dimensional embossed plastic, are intended more as novelties than for postal duty. Stamp printing is usually done by security printers. Security printing differs from commercial printing in that production is closely monitored and every scrap of printed product is accounted for. Dies, proof impressions, printing plates, make-ready impressions, spoilage (printer's waste), and finished product are all tracked, counted, and logged every step along the way. Each and every printing plate is assigned a number, the *plate number* that appears on the selvage of panes of most stamps and at the bottom of some coil stamps. Finished plates are stored in a secured area vault. A record is made each time a plate leaves the secured area. Another record is made each time it is mounted on press. And every impression made from the plate is counted and accounted for, including spoilage. Finished production is counted and recounted. It is verified when it enters storage, again when it is shipped to regional distribution centers, again when it is distributed to individual post offices, and finally once again when issued to window clerks. And window clerks are periodically audited to ensure that their inventory and cash balance.

The Treasury Department's security printing division is the Bureau of Engraving and Printing (BEP). The BEP is perhaps best known as the printer of our nation's currency, but it has also produced many of our postage stamps. Private security printers, such as the American Bank Note Company, also produce stamps as well as a variety of other accountable paper such as stock and bond certificates, lottery tickets, state revenue stamps, and even currency for some foreign countries.

A BRIEF HISTORY

In 1847, the year the Postal Service began issuing stamps, the Bureau of Engraving and Printing did not yet exist, so the Postal Service contracted out stamp production to the private security printing industry. The private security printing industry got its start printing currency for banks in the decades prior to the Civil War. In those days, banks were permitted to issue banknotes, which were, in essence, receipts for deposits of specie (gold and silver coins). The U.S. Treasury had not yet begun to issue paper currency; at the time, it minted only coins. Private banks proliferated, demand for high-quality banknotes boomed, and with it the security printing industry.

Rawdon, Wright, Hatch & Edson of Philadelphia won the first contract to produce U.S. postage stamps. The initial term ran four years, from 1847 to 1851. Half a dozen firms would hold the contract at one time or another during the nineteenth century. Of these, perhaps the best known are the American Bank Note Company, the Continental Bank Note Company, and the National Bank Note Company, each of which, in its turn, printed stamps of the same basic design during the period 1870 to 1894. Stamps of the series are known as *banknotes* in reference to their origin: banknote companies.

The Bureau of Engraving and Printing—which would print most of our nation's stamps from 1894 to the 1960s—came into existence in August 1862 as a direct result of the Civil War. It arose out of the need for the government to be able print the vast amounts of security paper necessary to finance the war. Before the war, the government obtained most of its revenue for tariffs and customs duties, which were adequate to meet the costs of the minimal services it rendered. But with the coming of war, the government suddenly found itself desperately short of funds. Congress swiftly reacted with a series of revenue measures. It levied taxes on a variety of commodities, such as matches and playing cards—taxes akin to a sales tax except that manufacturers were required to buy revenue stamps and affix them to finished goods to evidence payment of the tax. Revenue stamps were also required on a wide variety of paper documents, including deeds, wills, checks, mortgages, leases, telegrams, life insurance policies, foreign exchange, contracts, conveyances, powers of attorney, bills of lading, warehouse receipts, and tickets of passage. In addition, Congress authorized the Treasury to issue paper money—something it had not done before. Our nation's first federally issued paper money was actually non-interest-bearing notes that circulated like currency, although usually at a discount from specie.

In July 1862, Congress authorized an agency to supervise the collection of taxes—the Internal Revenue Service. The Bureau of Engraving and Printing came into existence a month later. During the Civil War and for many years thereafter, the BEP functioned primarily as a printer of currency. Production of postage stamps and revenue stamps was left to private security printers. When, in 1893, the Postal Service advertised for bids for the next four-year stamp-printing contract, the BEP submitted a bid. It turned out to be the lowest. Private security printers immediately cried foul, claiming that no legal basis existed for allowing the contract to be awarded to a government agency. Upon review, the Justice Department determined that nothing in law prevented the Postal Service from awarding the contract to a government agency. So in 1894 the Bureau of Engraving and Printing began printing stamps and, with rare exception, produced nearly all our postage stamps until the 1960s.

During that time the BEP collaborated with the Postal Service to pioneer a variety of innovations in stamp production and format. It perfected the web-fed rotary press, which was capable of much higher output than sheet-fed, flat plate presses. It perfected mechanical perforating equipment and later automated electric eye perforating equipment guided by marginal markings, again yielding improved efficiency and higher output. It experimented with offset lithography during World War I to meet the burgeoning wartime demand for stamps. It developed a method of printing on pregummed paper, which saved time and streamlined production. The BEP introduced multicolor intaglio printing. It experimented with self-adhesive stamps. And it refined booklet stamp production from a multistep operation involving individual panes stapled into place between covers to a one-press operation, in which paper went in one end and finished booklets emerged from the other, their panes secured into place by adhesive on their own tabs. Later, the BEP pioneered the self-adhesive booklet pane, which could be folded so that its backing paper formed the outer cover of the booklet. Today virtually all U.S. booklet-stamp production is self-adhesive. The BEP's de facto monopoly on stamp production came to an end at about the same time Congress enacted the Postal Service Reorganization Act of 1970.

Congress made it clear that it would no longer subsidize postal deficits. So driven by cost consciousness—the BEP's fee per thousand to print stamps had nearly doubled between 1972 and 1977—the Postal Service once again began to explore subcontracting stamp printing to private industry. They found that private security printers could deliver comparable work for less money. By the 1980s, the Postal Service was once again contracting printing to private industry on a regular basis. Today much U.S. stamp production is done by private security printers. The BEP continues to print some issues but no longer dominates stamp production the way it did during the first three-quarters of the twentieth century.

By some accounts, the BEP has become less competitive in bidding for stamp production for the same reason that forestalled it from printing stamps back in the beginning—lack of capacity. It's busy day and night printing currency, in this case the ubiquitous $1 bill. Public perception of the product, too, has changed over the years. Gone are the days when stamps were supposed to have a certain look to them, the formal look of a government security. Perhaps conditioned by the pervasive use of color in advertising, newspapers, and magazines, the public has come to expect—and perhaps prefer—the realistic look of full-color printing and contemporary scenes on its postage stamps. Still, many collectors regard the BEP's work from the heyday of intaglio printing—the classic subjects, the aesthetics inherent in an engraved design, and the richness of dense intaglio ink—as unsurpassed.

THE PRINTING PROCESS

DESIGN

Design is the first step on the journey to a finished stamp. The artist usually begins by sketching possibilities, experimenting with formats (e.g., horizontal, vertical, triangular, diamond shaped) and various graphics. Should the stamp feature an object or a view or a portrait? How should the inscriptions read? Where should they placed? Where does the denomination best fit?

The most promising are worked up in detail and presented for consideration. The final selection is further refined into a piece of finished artwork. The artwork is usually larger than, but in exact proportion to, the stamp. The artwork can then be photographically reduced to stamp size, either to create the plates for lithographic or gravure printing or to create a model from which an engraver can work to prepare an intaglio die. If the stamp is to be monochromatic, the engraver's model is often rendered in black and white.

Proposed designs are known as *essays*. The term "essay" also is used to refer to any image that differs from the issued stamp, such as a working proof of a partially finished intaglio die. Some essays are nearly identical to issued stamps, varying only in small details.

INTAGLIO

In intaglio (pronounced "in-TAL-yo") printing, the design is recessed below the surface of the plate. Ink is spread across the plate to fill the recesses. An implement known as a *doctor blade* (which works something like a windshield wiper blade) wipes excess ink from the surface of the plate. The plate is then brought into contact with paper. Pressure is exerted against the back of the paper, forcing it against the ink in the recesses, which it picks up and retains. The resulting imprint contains ridges formed by the ink, a feature distinctive of intaglio printing.

If you're unfamiliar with the look and feel of intaglio, examine a piece of U.S. currency, all of which is printed by intaglio. Run your fingertip or fingernail across the printed design. You will be able to feel the ridges. They are also visible under magnification.

Engraving an intaglio die (left); transfer roller (right).

Intaglio printing plates are created either by engraving (hand tooling) or by chemically etching the design on a metal plate. Intaglio-printed stamps are usually hand tooled. Using a set of specialized tools and almost always working with the aid of magnification, the engraver carves a pattern of tiny dots and lines that will make up the design. The block of metal—usually soft steel—upon which the design is engraved is known as a *master die*. The process is slow and takes several weeks to complete. From time to time, the engraver inks the die and pulls (prints) a proof to check the progress and quality of his work. Once the die is completed and approved, it is hardened. The image on the hardened die is impressed onto a soft steel roller (transfer die). The transfer die is hardened and in turn is used to impress, under great pressure, individual images onto a soft steel printing plate. The transfer die lays down the images one by one, until as many rows as are needed have been completed. The printing plate is then hardened and ready for use. If, during the life of the plate, an individual image becomes worn or damaged, it can be burnished out and replaced by reentry from the transfer die.

Before production begins, a series of proofs in various colors (known as *trial color proofs*) is prepared to permit comparison and help determine which color is best suited to the design.

Intaglio was used to print almost all U.S. postage stamps until the 1970s, when gravure, and later lithography, began to come into use. Intaglio is still used to print some monocolor issues, and it is occasionally used to add a denomination, inscription, or accent element to gravure or lithographed issues.

Intaglio equipment is extremely expensive—out of the reach of all but governments and large corporate security printers—and it requires great skill and years of practice to become proficient at engraving dies. In the United States, except for a handful of security printers, no capacity exists for preparing illustrated images on intaglio dies. Although difficult to counterfeit, intaglio has some drawbacks. Engraving a die is time consuming, typically taking six to eight weeks, and sometimes longer—compared to a matter of days for plate preparation for gravure or lithography, an important consideration in the modern, fast-paced world. And unlike gravure and lithography, intaglio does not lend itself well to multicolor printing.

LITHOGRAPHY

The underlying principle of lithography is based on the antipathy of oil and water. Toward the end of the eighteenth century, a German mapmaker discovered that drawings could be faithfully reproduced by applying oil-based ink to an image drawn with a grease pencil on a smooth limestone surface. He found that, when dampened, the stone surface repelled ink everywhere except where the grease pencil had been used. He found that when paper was applied to the inked surface, an exact duplicate of the original was created. And he found that the process could be repeated several hundred times before the image wore out.

By the end of the nineteenth century, the lithographic principle had been adapted to the printing press. Early in the twentieth century, someone discovered that an inked image could be transferred (offset) to an intermediate rubber surface (called a *blanket*) and then to paper. The pliability of the blanket allowed it to conform perfectly to any surface, such as the cylindrical drum of a rotary press.

Modern lithographic printing employs thin metal plates (often aluminum, but also stainless steel). The traditional method of preparing plates involved making a photographic film negative of the image, placing the negative atop a photosensitive printing plate, and then exposing the plate to intense light in the blue and ultraviolet end of the spectrum. The exposed area undergoes a solubility change and, once developed, is receptive to ink. Unexposed areas retain an affinity for water. In addition to the traditional method, advances in computer technology now permit images from digitized files to be burned directly onto a printing plate by means of laser.

The finished plate is mounted on a cylinder (drum). An offset blanket is mounted on a second cylinder. A series of rubber rollers feeds ink and water to the plate. The water keeps the plate damp but does not adhere to the image area. The ink, in turn, adheres only to the image area. The plate transfers the inked image to the offset blanket, which in turn transfers it to the surface to be printed. The image on the plate is positive, the image on the blanket, negative, and the image on the paper, again positive.

Color lithography involves the mingling of areas of dots from several plates, each printing a separate color, in order to achieve the effect of full color. Passes under the various colored plates occur either in several separate press runs or in a single press run through a large press capable of mounting and running multiple plates in series. Stamp production typically involves from four to seven colors.

THE PROCESS-COLOR METHOD

To achieve faithful, full-color reproduction, both lithography and gravure printing use the process-color method. In the process-color method, images are, either by photographic or digital means, broken down into a pattern of dots, which are separated into a series of four basic (or process) colors that, when combined during printing, yield virtually any color of the visible spectrum. The four basic colors are black, magenta (red), cyan (pale blue), and yellow. A separate printing plate is prepared for each color. Each plate lays down a pattern of dots in its assigned color. By itself, the pattern of dots laid down by each plate tends to appear pale and transparent, but together they blend to faithfully reproduce a full-color image. Examine a stamp or color photograph under magnification and you will be able see the dot structure. Commercial printers generally use the basic four colors. Security printers often use more than four colors in order to make their products more difficult to counterfeit. Sometimes one or two of the extra colors (most often, an accent color or a denomination or an inscription) are added by intaglio.

GRAVURE

Also known as *photogravure*, gravure printing shares some aspects of both intaglio and lithography. Like intaglio, ink rests in recesses rather than on the surface of the plate. Like lithography, color and tonal gradations are achieved by mingling patterns of dots, although the dot structure is much finer in gravure. And again like lithography, each color is laid down by a separate cylinder.

Gravure utilizes polished steel cylinders (also known as *sleeves*) upon which a thin layer of copper has been electroplated. Images are either chemically etched or electronically engraved on the copper in the form of minute recesses (as many as 50,000 per square inch) that will accept ink. The array of recesses is analogous to the dot pattern used in lithography. Once the recesses have been etched onto the cylinder, it is chrome plated to produce a hard, durable surface. Each recessed cell transfers a tiny spot of ink to the paper. Recesses vary in depth according to the pattern of the image. The deeper the recess, the darker the dot of ink deposited. The variation permits the wide range of tonal gradation necessary to faithfully reproduce a full-color image.

Cylinders are mounted on a press containing a series of stations, one for each cylinder (color). During printing, the cylinders are partially immersed in a reservoir of ink. As the cylinder rotates, it becomes coated with ink. A wiping blade, which runs the length of the cylinder, removes ink from the polished surface so that it remains only in the recesses. As the cylinder turns, it transfers ink to a moving web of paper. The web of paper passes from cylinder to cylinder with breathtaking speed, up to several thousand feet per minute, picking up ink from each of the thousands of tiny recesses. A finished full-color product emerges from the far end.

LETTERPRESS

Letterpress uses type and cuts (blocks containing images, type, or both) on which the area to printed is in relief and reversed, like the raised area on a rubber stamp. Originally, individual letters of type were set by hand; later, blocks of type were set by machine—such as the Linotype—utilizing hot metal. Type and cuts can be made of wood, metal, or composite. Ink is applied to the raised surface, the surface brought, under pressure, into contact with paper, and the inked image transferred to the paper. Letterpress has not been used to print U.S. stamps, although in some cases it has been used to apply overprints, such as "specimen." Some foreign countries have used letterpress to print stamps, in most cases earlier issues.

Flexography is a type of letterpress printing that utilizes molded, flexible soft rubber or plastic printing plates. It has been used to apply precancel imprints to some U.S. stamps.

FLAT PLATE AND ROTARY PRESSES

This terminology refers to the configuration of a printing press as opposed to the type of printing. A flat plate press uses flat (as opposed to curved) printing plates. Until the twentieth century, most printing was done on flat plate presses. A rotary press uses plates curved in the form of a cylinder or drum to facilitate continuous sheet- or web-fed printing. Some U.S. stamps have been printed in two versions, flat press and rotary press, a distinction important to collectors. Stamps printed by rotary press tend to be either slightly taller or wider—depending on the direction in which the plate was curved—than their identical counterparts printed by flat plate press.

CHAPTER 15

AN ILLUSTRATED TOUR OF BEP PRESSES

STAMP PRINTING PRESSES used by the Bureau of Engraving and Printing are known by various names, sometimes by manufacturer, sometimes by letter designation, occasionally by either. This is not intended to be a definitive study but rather an illustrated glimpse of some of the presses used to create U.S. postage stamps. All photos in this chapter are courtesy of the Bureau of Engraving and Printing.

The Miehle press.

THE MIEHLE PRESS

A four-plate flat-bed intaglio press first used to print postage stamps in 1894. The Miehle press is still operational at the time of this writing.

165

The Stickney press.

THE STICKNEY PRESS

An intaglio web-fed rotary press designed by Benjamin F. Stickney, a BEP mechanical engineer, and built to his specifications. The Stickney press became operational in 1914. It could, in continuous fashion, perform all the steps necessary to turn raw stock into finished stamps. The steps included moistening paper to make it receptive to intaglio ink, applying ink and gum, and then drying and perforating the stamps. Initially, the Stickney press was used to meet the high demand for 1¢ and 2¢ definitives.

THE COTTRELL PRESS

An intaglio web-fed rotary press manufactured by the Cottrell Company of Westerly, Rhode Island. The Cottrell press became operational in the mid-1950s. It was larger and faster than its predecessor, the Stickney press, but functioned in much the same fashion. The BEP owned several Cottrells, which are perhaps best remembered for their prodigious coil stamp production. Cottrells utilized two curved plates locked into place to create a continuous rotary printing surface. Ink accumulated in the recesses where the plates joined and ended up being printed in the same fashion as ink from the intaglio recesses, creating a line every

The Cottrell press.

24 stamps. In 1981 the Postal Service introduced the practice of placing plate numbers on coil stamp production. On Cottrell production, the small plate numbers appear on stamps adjoining lines. Cottrells continued in use until the early 1980s.

The Huck press.

THE HUCK PRESSES

Intaglio web-fed presses manufactured by the Huck firm of New York. The first Huck press was a monocolor model that became operational in 1952 and operated until 1985. The second Huck press, a nine-color model, became operational in 1966 and operated until the late 1970s.

The Giori press.

THE GIORI PRESSES

An intaglio sheet-fed press manufactured by the Giori Company. The first Giori press became operational in 1957. The Giori press was capable of printing up to three intaglio colors at one time. The BEP acquired several models between the late 1950s and mid-1960s. Gioris are best known for the bright multicolored commemoratives of the late 1950s through the 1970s. Gioris were capable of printing on dry (unmoistened) paper, thus eliminating the need to moisten intaglio stock prior to printing and dry it after printing.

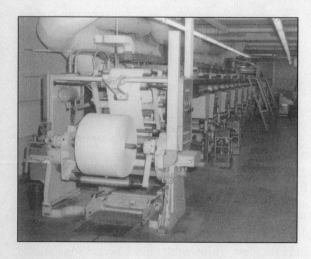

The Andreotti press.

THE ANDREOTTI PRESS

A gravure web-fed press manufactured by the Italian firm Andreotti S.P.A. The Andreotti press became operational in 1971. It is capable of printing color from as many as eight gravure cylinders, including applying one color to the reverse.

The Andreotti press is huge, about the length of five automobiles arranged end to end, and weighs more than 60 tons. The interval between plate numbers on Andreotti coil stamps is usually 38, but in at least one case was 24. The Andreotti press is still in use.

The A (or Combination) press.

THE A (OR COMBINATION) PRESS

An intaglio/gravure web-fed press manufactured by the German firm Koenig and Bauer. The A press became operational in 1976. It was capable of printing up to eight colors, three by intaglio and five by gravure. Gravure impressions occurred first, followed by intaglio. The A press was unusual in two respects. Its gravure cylinders were twice as large as its intaglio cylinders, hence they rotated once for every two intaglio rotations. And instead of the traditional 200- or 400-stamp layout for sheet-format stamps, A-press cylinders contained 230 or 460 stamps. The A-printed web contained an unbroken succession of stamps with no gutters between panes. As a result, plate numbers on the outer selvage appear in various positions from pane to pane, an effect known as *floating*. The interval between plate numbers on A-press coil stamps is usually 38. Toward the end of its life, the A press was used mostly for single-color, intaglio, sheet-format definitive production. The A press was retired in 1993.

THE B PRESS

An intaglio web-fed press manufactured by the German firm Koenig and Bauer. The B press became operational in 1975. It was capable of printing up to three intaglio colors. It could also apply tagging and precanceling. The B press was primarily used to print coil stamps, although occasionally it was used for booklet

The B press.

stamps. B-press cylinders printed 52 stamps during each revolution, hence one plate number every 52 stamps. The B press was retired in 1993.

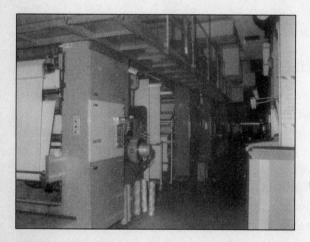

The C press.

THE C PRESS

An intaglio web-fed press manufactured by the German firm Goebel. It became operational in 1982. It was capable of printing up to three intaglio colors. It was used for sheet, coil, and booklet stamps but proved especially well suited for coil and booklet production. The interval between plate numbers on C-press coil stamps is 48. The C press has been idle since 1996, when much of the BEP's former production was shifted to private contractors.

The D press.

THE D PRESS

An intaglio/offset web-fed press manufactured by the German firm Goebel. It became operational in 1984. It was capable of printing up to three intaglio and six offset lithographed colors, as well as applying tagging. The D press was used to print sheet, coil, and booklet stamps. The interval between plate numbers on D-press coil stamps is 48. During its life, it was used to produce both single-color and multicolored issues. The D press has been idle since 1996, when much of the BEP's former production was shifted to private contractors.

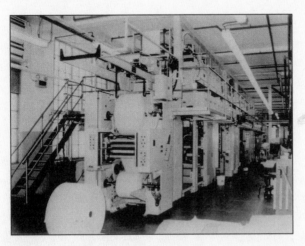

The F press.

THE F PRESS

An intaglio/offset web-fed press manufactured by the German firm Koenig and Bauer. It became operational in 1992 and is still in use.

CHAPTER 16

U.S. POSTAGE STAMP
PRINTING CONTRACTORS

DURING THE NINETEENTH century, the U.S. Postal Service awarded contracts for printing postage stamps on an exclusive basis to the lowest bidder, usually for a four-year term. Modern stamp printing contracts are awarded on nonexclusive basis, often on a project-by-project basis. It is not unusual for several firms to be involved in producing stamps at any one time. In some cases, more than one printer is used to print an issue, especially an issue for which a large quantity is needed on short notice, such as during a rate change. Dates in parentheses for nineteenth-century contractors indicate the term of the contract. Dates for twentieth-century contractors indicate the year in which the firm first printed stamps.

NINETEENTH-CENTURY POSTAGE STAMP PRINTING CONTRACTORS

Rawdon, Wright, Hatch & Edson
(1847–51)

Toppan, Carpenter, Casilear & Company
(1851–57)

Toppan, Carpenter & Company
(1857–61)

National Bank Note Company
(1861–73)

Continental Bank Note Company
(1873–80)

American Bank Note Company
(1880–94)

Bureau of Engraving and Printing
(1894 to present)

TWENTIETH-CENTURY AND LATER POSTAGE STAMP PRINTING CONTRACTORS

Bureau of Engraving and Printing
(1894 to present)

American Bank Note Company
(1943–44, 1979)

Archovure Division of Union Camp, Inc.
(1966)

Photogravure and Color Company (1967)

Guilford Gravure Inc. (1968)

American Bank Note Company (1979)

Banknote Corporation of America (1989)

Avery International (1990)

U.S. Bank Note Company (1990)

KCS Industries (1991)

Stamp Venturers (1991)

Dittler Brothers, Inc. (1992)

3M Corporation (1994)

Ashton-Potter (USA) Ltd. (1995)

Avery Dennison (1995)

Sennett Security Products (1998)

CHAPTER 17

PREFIX LETTERS FOR CONTRACT PRINTERS

THE PRACTICE OF assigning prefix letters to plate numbers on U.S. stamps to denote contract printers began in the 1980s. A single letter is used to denote the printer, except in the case of the Bureau of Engraving and Printing. Plate numbers on issues printed by the Bureau of Engraving and Printer do not contain a prefix letter.

A   American Bank Note Company
B   Banknote Corporation of America
D   Dittler Brothers, Inc.
G   Guilford Gravure Inc.
K   KCS Industries
M   3M Corporation
P   Ashton-Potter (USA) Ltd.
S   Stamp Venturers (until 1998)
S   Sennett Security Products (1998 and later)
U   U.S. Bank Note Company
V   Avery Dennison

Plate single with prefix letter plate number.

THE CITIZENS' STAMP
ADVISORY COMMITTEE

THE CITIZENS' STAMP Advisory Committee (CSAC) was established in 1957 to consider proposals for stamp subjects and recommend those deemed worthy. During the decade before the CSAC was established, a range of questionable subjects found their way onto commemorative stamps, often at the behest of members of Congress seeking to curry favor with certain constituencies.

Commemorative stamps of the late 1940s and early 1950s.

Among the subjects commemorated were the American Banking Association, the American Automobile Association, the trucking industry, the American Bar Association, the American Chemical Society, and the American poultry industry, with its oft-ridiculed chicken stamp. Although there is nothing wrong with any of these organizations, many felt that the commemorative stamp program was being demeaned and cheapened by subjects not in keeping with the previous high standards of the program.

Earlier, more traditional commemorative subjects.

Until the end of World War II, portrayal on a stamp was considered a high honor almost exclusively reserved for important historical subjects (Washington crossing the Delaware), anniversaries (the Declaration of Independence, the adoption of the Constitution), distinguished Americans (presidents, statesmen, inventors, authors, composers), important historical events (anniversaries of battles and victories, anniversaries of statehood), and national landmarks such as national parks. After the war, the Postal Service discovered that it was not immune to acts of Congress, and commemorative pork, as it might be called, began to creep into the stamp program. In addition, the Postal Service found itself bombarded by thousands of proposals for stamps from individual citizens, organizations, and special interest groups. Under precedents set by the often questionable subjects in the years following World War II, a great many appeared to qualify for recognition. At least that's what proponents asserted. Were all to be issued, however, the commemorative program would have been completely overwhelmed. So to screen the subjects and select the most worthy, Postmaster General Arthur E. Summerfield established the Citizens' Stamp Advisory Committee.

The Postal Service and the CSAC established criteria for issuing stamps and postal stationery that precluded the blatantly unworthy from consideration. Over the years, the criteria have been revised and refined. The postmaster general has the final say in all cases, and although the program has been largely depoliticized, occasionally a stamp is issued that appears to have been issued in response to political pressure, such as the Organized Labor commemorative that appeared on short notice, no doubt at the behest of the Carter administration, just before the 1980 presidential election.

The Organized Labor stamp of 1980 (left); Breast Cancer semipostal (right).

In recent years, Congress has largely stayed out of the stamp selection process with the notable exception of semipostals, beginning with the Breast Cancer semipostal of 1998, which it ordered to be issued through legislation, despite resistance by the Postal Service. The Postal Service was not so much opposed to the subject as to the idea of semipostal stamps. The Postal Service feared—and justifiably so—that if it issued a stamp to raise money for one cause, no matter how worthy, it would be deluged with requests and legislative pressure to issue stamps for a potentially limitless number of equally worthy causes. The Postal Service tried to resist but found it hard to deflect the assertion that breast cancer was a far more worthy subject than Bugs Bunny, an argument that harkened back 40 years to the flap over the poultry stamp. In fairness, the Bugs Bunny stamp was issued as an outreach to interest young people in collecting stamps and not necessarily to "honor" Bugs. In the end, Congress mandated the Breast Cancer semipostal but forestalled a flood of semipostals by ordering that new subjects be limited to one every two years. Aside from that intrusion into the stamp program, Congress has largely stayed out of it, leaving the decision for subjects to the Postal Service and the Citizens' Stamp Advisory Committee.

According to the Postal Service, the CSAC's primary goal is to select subjects for recommendation to the postmaster general that are both interesting and educational. It's a difficult task since only a limited number of new commemorative items can be issued annually. The CSAC tries to make selections with all postal customers in mind, not just stamp collectors.

CSAC members are appointed by and serve at the pleasure of the postmaster general. The committee is composed of 15 members whose backgrounds reflect a wide range of educational, artistic, historical, and professional expertise. The committee itself employs no staff. The Postal Service's Stamp Development Group handles CSAC administrative matters, maintains CSAC records, and responds to as many as 50,000 inquiries received annually recommending stamp subjects and designs.

The CSAC meets four times yearly in Washington, D.C. At meetings, the members review all proposals that have been received since the previous meeting. In-person appeals by stamp proponents are not permitted. Members also review and provide suggestions and guidance on artwork and designs for stamp subjects that are scheduled to be issued.

The Postal Service and members of the CSAC have established a protocol of basic criteria used to determine the eligibility of subjects for commemoration on U.S. stamps and stationery. The criteria are intended to ensure that potential subjects have stood the test of time, are consistent with public opinion, and have broad national interest. The criteria are as follows:

- General policy holds that U.S. postage stamps and stationery will primarily feature American or American-related subjects.
- No living person will be honored by portrayal on U.S. postage. Occasionally, living persons appear on U.S. stamps, such as the firemen depicted on the semipostals of the September 11 tragedy, but the persons themselves are not being individually honored; rather, it is the collective spirit of all emergency personnel being honored who were involved in the tragedy and its immediate aftermath.
- Commemorative stamps or postal stationery items honoring individuals usually will be issued on or in conjunction with a significant anniversary of their birth, but no postal item will be issued sooner than 10 years after an individual's death. The only exception to the 10-year rule is stamps honoring deceased U.S. presidents. They may be honored with a memorial stamp on the first birth anniversary following death.
- Events of historical significance will be considered for commemoration only on anniversaries in multiples of 50 years.

- Only events and themes of widespread national appeal and significance will be considered for commemoration. Events or themes of local or regional significance may be recognized by a philatelic or special postal cancellation.
- Stamps or stationery items will not be issued to honor fraternal, political, sectarian, or service/charitable organizations. Stamps or stationery shall not be issued to promote or advertise commercial enterprises or products. Commercial products or enterprises, however, might be used to illustrate more general concepts related to American culture.
- Stamps or stationery items will not be issued to honor cities, towns, municipalities, counties, primary or secondary schools, hospitals, libraries, or similar institutions.
- Requests for observance of statehood anniversaries will be considered for commemorative postage stamps only at intervals of 50 years from the date of the state's first entry into the Union. Requests for observance of other state-related or regional anniversaries will be considered only as subjects for postal stationery, and again only at intervals of 50 years from the date of the event.
- Stamps or stationery items will not be issued to honor religious institutions or individuals whose principal achievements are associated with religious undertakings or beliefs.
- Stamps or postal stationery items with added values (semipostals) will be issued every two years in accordance with Public Law 106253. Semipostals will not be considered as part of the commemorative program and separate criteria will apply.
- Requests for commemoration of universities and other institutions of higher education will be considered only for stamped cards and only in connection with the 200th anniversaries of their founding.
- No stamp will be considered for issuance if one treating the same subject has been issued in the past 50 years. The only exceptions to this rule are traditional themes such as national symbols and holidays.

Ideas for stamp subjects should be submitted in writing and be addressed to the Citizens' Stamp Advisory Committee. The address appears in Chapter 36, "Resources."

The Postal Service recommends that subjects be submitted at least three years in advance of the proposed date of issue to allow sufficient time for consideration and for design and production, if the subject is approved. If submitting a suggestion, be aware that the CSAC does not review or accept unsolicited artwork for designs.

Proposals are screened to make sure they conform to the criteria. Those that do not, receive no further consideration. Subjects that conform to the criteria are further researched to establish merit and listed on the CSAC's agenda for its next meeting. The CSAC considers the new proposals and typically takes one of two actions: it either rejects a proposal or sets it aside for further consideration. Some later make the cut and are approved for issuance, others do not. Most, but not necessarily all, approved subjects end up as stamps. Although the Postal Service relies heavily upon the Citizens' Stamp Advisory Committee, it reserves the exclusive and final authority to determine both subject matter and designs for issued stamps.

POSTAL CLASSIFICATIONS
AND SERVICES

MAIL IS CLASSIFIED according to the level of service required for transmission and delivery. Each classification has its own rate structure. Generally, the more speedy the delivery, the greater the fee. Mailers who perform part of the sortation process prior to depositing large mailings receive a discount from regular single-piece rates since presorting saves the Postal Service the expense of having to sort it. The following touches on the most basic classifications and services.

FIRST-CLASS MAIL

First-class mail includes personal and business correspondence such as letters, postcards, greeting cards, invoices, statements, payments, and just about anything else that weighs less than 13 ounces and can be sealed against inspection. Matter weighing 13 ounces or more, but receiving the same expeditious handling as first-class mail, falls into the priority mail category. Technically, first-class mail comprises three subclasses: letters and small parcels, postcards, and priority mail.

Any item not a postcard weighing less than 1 ounce and not conforming to the following dimensions is subject to a surcharge.

- Height exceeds 6 1/8 inches or
- Length exceeds 11 1/2 inches or
- Thickness exceeds 1/4 inch or
- Length divided by height is less than 1.3 or more than 2.5, which means that it does not meet the aspect ratio.

Aspect ratio is the dimension of a mailpiece expressed as a ratio of length (the direction parallel to the address) divided by height. For example, a postcard 5 1/2 inches long by 3 1/2 inches high has an aspect ratio of 1.57. An aspect ratio between 1.3 and 2.5, inclusive, is required for automation compatibility. For some first-class mail, aspect ratio is used to determine whether a nonstandard surcharge applies.

A stamped card or postcard must be of uniform thickness and not more than 6 inches long, 4 1/4 inches high, or 0.016 inch thick.

Stamped cards (formerly called *postal cards*) are those that contain imprinted postage. Postcards are privately printed cards such as picture postcards. Stamped cards and postcards are supposed to be rectangular in shape and not less than 3 1/2 by 5 inches. Any stamped card or postcard not conforming to the following dimensions is subject to a surcharge.

PRIORITY MAIL

Priority mail is first-class mail that weighs more than 13 ounces and, at the mailer's option, any other mail matter weighing 13 ounces or less. Priority mail provides expedited delivery. Any mailable matter may be sent as priority mail. Both rigid and flexible mailing containers imprinted with priority mail colors and logo are available from the Postal Service at most post offices or by order.

PERIODICALS-CLASS MAIL

Periodicals-class mail (formerly second-class mail) consists of magazines, newspapers, or other periodical publications whose primary purpose is transmitting information to an established list of subscribers or requesters. To qualify, the periodical must be published regularly at a stated frequency and no fewer than four times per year. It must be published from a known office of publication and be formed of printed sheets. The periodical must qualify under one of five categories: general, requester, institutions and societies, foreign, or state departments of agriculture. The periodical must meet standards relating to circulation, documentation, advertising limits, and other conditions that vary by category. For example, general publications must have a minimum 50 percent paid circulation and contain no more than 75 percent advertising in half the issues published during a 12-month period. Requester publications must have a list of requesters and subscribers, with a minimum 50 percent of the circulated copies either requested or paid for by the recipient. Requester publications must have at least 24 pages and advertising may not exceed 75 percent in any one issue.

Preferred rates or discounts are available for publications in other than the requester category that qualify under Nonprofit, Classroom, Science of Agriculture, and In-County categories.

STANDARD MAIL

Standard mail (formerly standard mail (A) and before that, third-class mail) is how most bulk-rate advertising mail is sent. Postage is usually indicated as having been paid by either an imprint in the upper-right corner of the piece or by precancel (or service-inscribed) stamps. Standard mail matter must weigh less than 16 ounces. To qualify for a bulk rate, it must contain at least 200 identical pieces; however, a mailing may contain fewer than 200 pieces if it weighs at least 50 pounds. Mailings under the weight-based rule usually consist of merchandise, such as CDs sent out by a music club. Items often sent by standard mail include circulars, printed matter, pamphlets, catalogs, newsletters, direct mail, and merchandise.

Standard mail consists of two basic categories: regular and nonprofit. Mailings under both categories may qualify for various presort and automation rate discounts. The presort discount varies according to the number of pieces in each mailing that qualify by containing addresses with either the same first three digits or first five digits in their ZIP codes. Automation discounts are available for pieces that contain bar-coded address information. Large mailings bar-coded and sorted into the precise order in which they will be delivered by mail carriers generally receive the most preferential rate. Bulk mailers receive these discounts because presorted and automated mail is the least time-consuming and labor-intensive to handle. Single-piece, hand-addressed mail, such as greeting cards, is the most costly to process. They sometimes go through two or three sorts before being delivered. Bar-coded batches sorted right down to the carrier route sequence speed right through the system and need be broken down only by the carrier just prior to delivery.

Third-class mail used to contain the phrase "Bulk Rate Paid" in the indicia, a tip-off that a piece probably contained junk mail. Now the wording usually reads "Presorted Standard" or "PRSRT STD."

PACKAGE SERVICE

Package service (formerly standard mail (B) and before that, fourth-class mail) consists of matter that generally weighs 16 ounces or more but in no event, more than 70 pounds. The maximum size for package service is 108 inches in combined length and girth, except parcel post, which may measure as much as 130 inches. Package service is composed of four subclasses: Bound Printed Matter, Library Mail, Media Mail, and parcel post.

Bound Printed Matter includes catalogs, directories, books, and other printed material that weighs up to 15 pounds.

Library Mail is intended primarily for use by schools, colleges, universities, museums, public libraries, and nonprofit religious, educational, scientific, philanthropic (charitable) agricultural, labor, veterans, or fraternal organizations or associations. Among the types of materials that qualify as Library Mail are books, printed scholarly material and bibliographies, reading matter containing no advertising matter other than incidental announcements of books, film (16 millimeters or narrower), catalogues of such films of 24 pages or more, printed music in bound or sheet form, printed objective test materials, sound recordings, video recordings, play scripts and manuscripts for books, periodicals, and music.

Media Mail includes books of at least 8 pages, film (16 millimeters or narrower), printed music, printed test materials, sound recordings, play scripts, printed educational charts, loose-leaf pages and binders consisting of medical information, and computer-readable media.

Parcel post includes anything not mailed under any of the other three subclasses for package service.

EXPRESS MAIL

Express mail provides expedited delivery service for mailable matter subject to certain standards. It is available in five basic domestic service offerings: Same Day Airport Service, Next Day Service, and Second Day Service, as well as Custom Designed Service and Military Service. Express mail international service is available between the United States and most foreign countries. Express mail envelopes and labels are available at post offices.

CERTIFIED MAIL

Certified mail provides the sender with a mailing receipt. A record of delivery is kept at the post office of address. Certified mail must be sent at first-class or priority mail rates. Return receipt service and restricted delivery service are available. Certified mail provides no indemnity in case of loss, only proof of delivery. Fees for certified mail are less than those for registered mail.

INSURED MAIL

Insured mail provides indemnity coverage up to $5,000 for a lost, rifled, or damaged article. Although indemnified against loss, insured shipments are not monitored at each point along their journey through the mail stream as is registered mail. Return receipt service is available for shipments valued at more than $50. First-class mail, priority mail, and package service shipments are eligible for insurance. Fees vary according to the value of insurance requested.

REGISTERED MAIL

Registered mail is the most secure service offered by the Postal Service. The Postal Service monitors, through a system of receipts, the movement of each piece of registered mail from the point of acceptance to delivery. The sender receives a receipt at the time of mailing, and a delivery record is maintained at the post office of address. Insurance is available for shipments with values up to $25,000. Return receipt service is available.

RETURN RECEIPT

A return receipt is a mailing card signed by the addressee upon receipt of an article and mailed back to the sender as evidence of delivery. The card shows to whom and at what time the mail was delivered. Return receipts are available for a fee when using recorded delivery, certified mail, collect on delivery, mail insured for more than $50, registered mail, or return receipt for merchandise.

RESTRICTED DELIVERY

Restricted delivery directs that delivery be made only to the addressee or addressee's authorized agent. This service is available for an additional fee when used with certified mail, collect on delivery, insured mail, and registered mail.

DELIVERY CONFIRMATION

Delivery confirmation provides the date and time of delivery or attempted delivery. It is available for an additional fee with priority mail and package service mail. It does not provide proof of mailing, but only a record of delivery. The service is available only at the time of mailing. Delivery information is available through the Postal Service Web site (www.usps.com) or by calling the toll-free number printed on the receipt. A copy of an actual delivery record is available by mail or fax upon request.

SPECIAL HANDLING

Special handling provides preferential handling, but not preferential delivery, to the extent practicable in dispatch and transportation. Special handling is available for an additional fee for first-class mail, priority mail, and package services.

NONMAILABLE ARTICLES AND SUBSTANCES

These are anything that, by statute, "may kill or injure another, or injure the mails or other property." There are some exceptions to this rule that allow otherwise unmailable items to be mailed.

NONMAILABLE WRITTEN, PRINTED, AND GRAPHIC MATTER

This is any matter that would be otherwise mailable if it did not include certain solicitations, lottery and certain advertising matter, and matter using any fictitious name, title, or address in conducting any scheme or device in violation of law. The solicitations may be either in guise of bills, invoices, or statements of account, or they may deceptively imply federal connection, approval, or endorsement.

PROHIBITED ARTICLES

Prohibited articles are any material that is illegal to mail because it can kill or injure an individual or damage other mail. This includes certain poisons and controlled substances and certain flammable or hazardous matter.

RESTRICTED ARTICLES

Restricted articles are any item on which certain mailing restrictions have been imposed for legal reasons other than risk of harm to persons or property involved in moving the mail and that require specific endorsements and markings. Examples include intoxicating liquors, abortive or contraceptive devices, odd-shaped items in envelopes, motor vehicle master keys, locksmithing devices as well as odor-producing materials, certain liquids and powders, and battery-powered devices.

More information on classifications is available at the U.S. Postal Service Web site (www.usps.com).

THE UNIVERSAL
POSTAL UNION

APPROXIMATELY **25 MILLION** pieces of mail cross international borders each day. Without the Universal Postal Union (UPU), the efficient transmission of this mail would be an impossibly complex task encumbered by the rules, regulations, and rates of nearly 200 different countries. That's how it was in the nineteenth century during the tenure of Postmaster General Montgomery Blair. The exchange of mail between countries was governed by myriad bilateral postal agreements. Any but the most direct routing involved a discouraging tangle of rates and carriers. Blair, perhaps inspired by the success of postal reforms to the British postal system initiated by Sir Rowland Hill, conceived the idea of an international postal body that might help streamline the transmission of mail between nations.

In 1863, at Blair's urging, delegates from 15 European and American countries gathered in Paris to discuss how an international postal agreement might take form. Blair hoped some way could be found to do away with the web of bilateral agreements and simplify the transmission of mail. The delegates agreed in principle that something needed to be done but were unable to come to any agreement on a formal arrangement. Eleven years would pass before that would happen.

Montgomery Blair (left);
Heinrich von Stephan (right).

In September 1874, Heinrich von Stephan, head of the North German Confederation, invited representatives of 22 nations to convene in Bern, Switzerland, for an international postal conference. In the space of a few short weeks, the conference, the Universal Postal Convention, as it was known, drafted a comprehensive set of provisions that, in addition to simplifying the way in which rates were calculated, addressed the kinds of correspondence that could be sent internationally; prohibited certain articles, such as narcotics; provided for redirection or return of correspondence that could not be delivered; regulated the division of fees for the mail traveling through the territory of two or more members; and guaranteed freedom of transit through member nations.

On October 9, 1874, the delegates signed the Treaty of Bern, which formalized the provisions that, in effect, established a single postal territory for the reciprocal exchange of letters. The treaty went into effect July 1, 1875, and thus was born the UlÑversal Postal Union, although it would not adopt that name until three years later. In the interim it would be known as the General Postal Union. In 1948 the UPU became a specialized body of the United Nations. It still maintains its headquarters in Bern, Switzerland, its birthplace.

Since its humble beginnings, the UPU has grown into a model of international cooperation. It is a nonpolitical organization that has continued to function even during times of war. Throughout its existence, it has worked to streamline and improve the movement of mail.

In 1897 the UPU adopted an international color code to help postal workers identify rates for stamps arriving on foreign mail. Accordingly, green was to be used for the postal card rate, red for the basic domestic letter rate, and blue for the basic international letter rate. U.S. issues invariably followed the scheme until the 1950s, when it was phased out.

In addition, stamps were to be denominated in numerals rather than script so that postal workers in all countries could identify the value of stamps affixed to mail. The United States began issuing nondenominated stamps in the 1970s. Since then, the practice has become fairly widespread, and with the passing of time, the prohibition relaxed, perhaps because so many nations now issue nondenominated stamps.

The UPU innovated the international reply coupon (IRC). IRCs purchased in one country and sent abroad were originally redeemable for a stamp of the basic international surface rate in any other UPU member country. Today they are redeemable for one airmail stamp equivalent to the minimum postage rate for an airmail letter. This allows correspondents to remit return postage in cases where it is necessary for a reply. Due to variations in the value of currencies, IRCs are worth more in some countries than in others.

In an interesting side note, IRCs gave birth to a type of scheme first promoted by Charles Ponzi, which today is still known by his name. In 1919 Ponzi received an IRC for a man in Spain to pay the cost of a reply. Ponzi was quick to notice that the coupon, which cost 1¢ in Spain, could be redeemed for six cents worth of U.S. stamps. To exploit this disparity, he hastily organized a company, the Security Exchange Company, and began soliciting funds. The premise was

An international reply coupon.

foolproof, he told investors, completely risk-free. He promised a 100 percent profit in 45 short days. Money poured in—millions of dollars, sometimes as much as a million per week. Almost immediately, Ponzi realized that actually buying, transporting, and redeeming coupons, then selling the massive numbers of stamps obtained from redemptions, was infeasible. At the same time, he realized that so long as he paid off earlier investors with funds from new investors, money would continue to roll in. Ponzi had been a clerk only a few months earlier and was in no hurry to give up his new life as a millionaire. Word of mouth kept new dollars pouring in—for a while. Only so long as the pool of fresh investors outnumbered those requiring token payoffs. By August 1920 the fraud began to collapse under its own weight. Ponzi was indicted, tried, and sentenced to prison. He died in 1949, but his name lives on—everyone has heard of Ponzi schemes. Few know that the namesake scheme was first inspired by a lowly 1¢ IRC.

Initially, the UPU focused on streamlining the movement of mail across borders. Lately, it has been assisting less-developed nations improve their postal systems. The UPU's Technical Cooperation Action Group has undertaken field projects in such areas as training, management, and postal operations to help certain countries. The UPU maintains particularly close ties with UN programs such as the United Nations Development Program in the field of postal development, the United Nations Drug Control Program to help impede the shipment of drugs in the mail, and the United Nations Environment Program to increase awareness of the environment among postal services. It also maintains close working relationships with a number of international organizations, such as the International Air Transport Association, the International Organization for Standardization, the World Customs Organization, and Interpol, to help facilitate the flow of international mail.

Through its Postal Security Action Group (PSAG), the UPU helps postal services improve security. It has established a world security network that includes relationships and information sharing among postal services, private courier companies, and a number of international and UN organizations. It strives to combat the use of the mail for illicit drug trafficking and money laundering, mail bombs, and child pornography and promotes the safe transport of diagnostic specimens and potentially infectious substances. PSAG Mail Quality Assurance and Airport Security Reviews have brought postal services, airport authorities, customs, police, airlines, and private courier and cargo services together to address and improve mail handling and security at major airports.

The UPU commemorated on a postage stamp.

Throughout its history, the UPU has been remarkably successful and true to the vision of its founders, which was to promote social, cultural, and commercial communication among the people of the world. And it has been important to philately, too.

Stamp catalogue publishers use UPU membership as one test of a stamp-issuing entity's legitimacy. The UPU recognizes that the issuing, marketing, and selling of postage stamps are up to individual member nations. At the same time, it recognizes that the tremendous potential for profit from philatelic sales has given rise to a number of abuses worldwide. Lately, unauthorized parties have printed and distributed stamps that mimic legitimate issues of certain countries. In a strict sense, this is counterfeiting. The stamps, however, are not intended to defraud the named country's postal service. They are intended to take advantage of unsuspecting collectors. The issues are often printed outside the named country and feature popular topical subjects. They are difficult to police because they are beyond the injured country's jurisdiction. Sometimes the country's authorities are not even aware that the bogus stamps exist until well after sales have commenced.

Unknown parties in certain territories and regions of the former Soviet Union have issued stamps purporting to be legitimate. Legitimate in the sense that the issuing entity has the authority to issue stamps and that stamps bearing the name of the entity have been issued under its authority. The emissions include overprints on genuine stamps of the Soviet Union intended to appear as validating them for use within the ostensibly autonomous territory or region. A list of those known at this writing appears in Chapter 22, "Former Soviet Territories Issuing Unrecognized Stamps."

As a general rule, contemporary issues from countries that are not UPU members or not recognized by stamp catalogues are likely spurious.

The UPU's World Association for the Development of Philately operates as a forum for the philatelic trade, which includes postal services, philatelic agents, collectors, and dealers. It tries to promote awareness of and combat abusive philatelic practices. The UPU also provides guidelines through the Philatelic Code of Ethics and regularly distributes information to the world's postal services regarding unauthorized stamp issues. The UPU has condemned the practice of issuing unnecessarily large numbers of stamps solely for profit, a practice embraced by more than a few countries. It has also worked to promote philately and raise awareness of the hobby, particularly among young people.

The UPU has been honored on countless stamps over the years, and deservedly so. It has contributed to the prosperity and advancement of every nation. Its goal to create a single postal territory for the exchange of mail has endured longer than almost any cooperative venture among nations. It is truly a remarkable organization.

CHAPTER

21

UNIVERSAL POSTAL UNION MEMBER NATIONS

THE LIST OF active Universal Postal Union member nations is arranged alphabetically. The nation's month and year of admission follows in parentheses. Territories administered under the auspices of a member nation are listed below the entry for that nation. Most nations that issue postage stamps belong to the UPU. Several UN members issue postage stamps but were not members of the UPU at this writing. They appear following the main listing under "Other Nations."

MEMBER NATIONS

Afghanistan (April 1928)
Albania (March 1922)
Algeria (October 1907)
Angola (March 1977)
Antigua and Barbuda (January 1994)
Argentina (April 1878)
Armenia (September 1992)
Australia (October 1907)
• Norfolk Island
Austria (January 1875)
Azerbaijan (April 1993)
Bahamas (April 1974)
Bahrain (December 1973)
Bangladesh (February 1973)
Barbados (November 1967)
Belarus (May 1947)
Belgium (July 1875)
Belize (October 1982)
Benin (April 1961)
Bhutan (March 1969)
Bolivia (April 1886)

Bosnia and Herzegovina (January 1993)
Botswana (January 1968)
Brazil (July 1877)
Brunei (January 1985)
Bulgaria (July 1879)
Burkina Faso (March 1963)
Burundi (April 1963)
Cambodia (December 1951)
Cameroon (July 1960)
Canada (July 1878)
Cape Verde (September 1976)
Central African Republic (June 1961)
Chad (June 1961)
Chile (April 1881)
China (People's Republic) (March 1914)
Colombia (July 1881)
Comoros (July 1976)
Congo (Democratic Republic)
   (January 1886)
Congo (Republic) (July 1961)
Costa Rica (January 1881)

Côte d'Ivoire (Ivory Coast; May 1961)
Croatia (July 1992)
Cuba (October 1902)
Cyprus (November 1961)
Czech Republic (March 1993)
Denmark (July 1875)
• Faroe Islands
• Greenland
Djibouti (June 1978)
Dominica (January 1980)
Dominican Republic (October 1880)
Ecuador (July 1880)
Egypt (July 1875)
El Salvador (April 1879)
Equatorial Guinea (July 1970)
Eritrea (August 1993)
Estonia (April 1992)
Ethiopia (November 1908)
Fiji (July 1971)
Finland (February 1918)
• Åland Islands
France (January 1876)
• French Guiana
• French Polynesia
• French Southern and Antarctic
  Territories
• Guadeloupe
• Martinique
• Mayotte
• Réunion
• New Caledonia
• Saint-Pierre and Miquelon
• Wallis and Futuna Islands
Gabon (July 1961)
Gambia (October 1974)
Georgia (April 1993)
Germany (July 1875)
Ghana (October 1957)
Great Britain (July 1875)
• Guernsey
• Isle of Man
• Jersey
Great Britain Overseas Territories
• Anguilla
• Ascension
• Bermuda
• British Indian Ocean Territory

• British Virgin Islands
• Cayman Islands
• Falkland Islands
• Gibraltar
• Montserrat
• Pitcairn Islands
• South Georgia and the South
  Sandwich Islands
• Saint Helena
• Tristan da Cunha
• Turks and Caicos Islands
Greece (July 1875)
Grenada (January 1978)
Guatemala (August 1881)
Guinea (May 1959)
Guinea-Bissau (May 1974)
Guyana (March 1967)
Haiti (July 1881)
Honduras (April 1879)
Hungary (July 1875)
Iceland (November 1919)
India (July 1876)
Indonesia (May 1877)
Iran (September 1877)
Iraq (April 1929)
Ireland (September 1923)
Israel (December 1949)
Italy (July 1875)
Jamaica (August 1963)
Japan (June 1877)
Jordan (May 1947)
Kazakstan (August 1992)
Kenya (October 1964)
Kiribati (August 1984)
Korea (People's Democratic Republic)
  (June 1974)
Korea (Republic) (January 1900)
Kuwait (February 1960)
Kyrgyzstan (January 1993)
Laos (May 1952)
Latvia (June 1992)
Lebanon (May 1946)
Lesotho (September 1967)
Liberia (April 1879)
Libya (June 1952)
Liechtenstein (April 1962)
Lithuania (January 1992)

Luxembourg (July 1875)
Macedonia (July 1993)
Madagascar (November 1961)
Malawi (October 1966)
Malaysia (January 1958)
Maldives (August 1967)
Mali (March 1961)
Malta (May 1965)
Mauritania (March 1967)
Mauritius (August 1969)
Mexico (April 1879)
Moldova (November 1992)
Monaco (October 1955)
Mongolia (August 1963)
Morocco (October 1920)
Mozambique (October 1978)
Myanmar (Burma; October 1949)
Namibia (April 1992)
Nauru (April 1969)
Nepal (October 1956)
Netherlands (July 1875)
• Aruba
• Netherlands Antilles
New Zealand (October 1907)
• Cook Island
• Niue
• Ross Dependency
• Tokelau
Nicaragua (May 1882)
Niger (June 1961)
Nigeria (July 1961)
Norway (July 1875)
Oman (August 1971)
Pakistan (November 1947)
Panama (Republic) (June 1904)
Papua New Guinea (June 1976)
Paraguay (July 1881)
Peru (April 1879)
Philippines (January 1922)
Poland (May 1919)
Portugal (July 1875)
Qatar (January 1969)
Romania (July 1875)
Russia (July 1875)
Rwanda (April 1963)
Saint Christopher (Saint Kitts) and Nevis (January 1988)

Saint Lucia (July 1980)
Saint Vincent and the Grenadines (February 1918)
Samoa (August 1989)
San Marino (July 1915)
São Tomé and Príncipe (Saint Thomas and Prince Islands; August 1977)
Saudi Arabia (January 1927)
Senegal (June 1961)
Seychelles (October 1977)
Sierra Leone (January 1962)
Singapore (August 1966)
Slovakia (March 1993)
Slovenia (August 1992)
Solomon Islands (May 1984)
Somalia (April 1959)
South Africa (August 1994)
Spain (July 1875)
Sri Lanka (July 1949)
Sudan (July 1956)
Suriname (April 1976)
Swaziland (November 1969)
Sweden (July 1875)
Switzerland (July 1875)
Syria (May 1946)
Tajikistan (June 1994)
Tanzania (March 1963)
Thailand (July 1885)
Togo (March 1962)
Tonga (January 1972)
Trinidad and Tobago (June 1963)
Tunisia (July 1888)
Turkey (July 1875)
Turkmenistan (January 1993)
Tuvalu (February 1981)
Uganda (February 1964)
Ukraine (May 1947)
United Arab Emirates (March 1973)
United States of America (July 1875)
• Guam
• Mariana Islands including Saipan and Tinian
• Puerto Rico
• Samoa
• Virgin Islands
Uruguay (July 1880)
Uzbekistan (July 1994)

Vanuatu (July 1982)

Vatican (June 1929)

Venezuela (January 1880)

Vietnam (October 1951)

Yemen (January 1930)

Yugoslavia (June 2001)

Zambia (March 1967)

Zimbabwe (July 1981)

The following member nations have been admitted more than once, their earlier membership or memberships having been terminated or suspended for a variety of reasons including change in sovereignty. Dates of their various admission follow in parentheses.

INTERRUPTED MEMBERSHIPS

Bosnia and Herzegovina
(July 1892; January 1993)

Croatia (December 1921; July 1992)

Czech Republic (May 1920; March 1993)

Estonia (July 1922; April 1992)

Latvia (October 1921; June 1992)

Lebanon (May 1931; May 1946)

Lithuania (January 1922; January 1992)

Slovakia (May 1920; March 1993)

Slovenia (December 1921; August 1992)

South Africa (January 1893; August 1994)

Suriname (April 1877; April 1976)

Syria (May 1931; May 1946)

Yugoslavia (July 1875; December 1921; June 2001)

The following are members of the United Nations and issue postage stamps, but are not members of the UPU.

OTHER NATIONS

Andorra

Marshall Islands

Micronesia (Federated States of)

Palau

CHAPTER 22

FORMER SOVIET TERRITORIES ISSUING UNRECOGNIZED STAMPS

THE FOLLOWING TERRITORIES, autonomous regions, or so-called autonomous regions within states of the former Soviet Union have issued labels that simulate postage stamps but have no post validity, or they have applied overprints to genuine stamps of the Soviet Union (or post-Soviet republics) that ostensibly give them postal validity. The issues originated in the climate of political confusion that followed the breakup of the Soviet Union in 1991. Some issues exist postmarked on cover and for a time may have been tolerated in the local or regional mails but in most cases were not authorized by a central postal authority. Assertions of legitimacy remain cloudy at best and open to interpretation. None are recognized by the Universal Postal Union. Nor are their emissions recognized by major catalogue publishers. Many issues were surely philatelically inspired, intended for sale to collectors. The location of each "entity" follows in parentheses.

Abkhazia (Georgia)
Abruka (Estonia)
Adygea (Russia)
Aegna (Estonia)
Akhal (Turkmenistan)
Aksi (Estonia)
Altai (Russia)
Amur (Russia)
Amurskaya (Russia)
Balkan (Turkmenistan)
Bashkiria (Russia)
Batum, Adjaria (Georgia)
Buriatia (Russia)
Carelia (Russia)
Chechnya (Russia)
Chuvashia (Russia)

Crimea (Ukraine)
Dagestan (Russia)
Dashkhovuz (Turkmenistan)
Evenkia (Russia)
Franz Josef Land (Russia)
Gagauzia (Moldova)
Hiiumaa (Estonia)
Ichkeria (Russia)
Ingoushia (Russia)
Ingushetia (Russia)
Jewish Autonomous Region (Russia)
Jewish Republic (Russia)
Kabarda-Balkaria (Russia)
Kalmykia (Russia)
Kamchatka (Russia)
Karachai-Cherkessia (Russia)

199

Karakalpakia (Uzbekistan)
Khakassia (Russia)
Kolguev Island (Russia)
Komi Republic (Russia)
Komis (Russia)
Koriakia (Russia)
Kunashir Island (Russia)
Kuril Islands (Russia)
Lebap (Turkmenistan)
Manilaid (Estonia)
Mari-El (Russia)
Mary (Turkmenistan)
Mordovia (Russia)
Mountainous Badakhshan (Tajikistan)
Mountainous Karabakh
   (Armenia-Azerbaijan)
Muhu (Estonia)
New Land Island (Russia)
Nlakhichevan (Azerbaijan)
North Ossetia (Russia)

Novaya Zemlya Island (Russia)
Novosibirskiye Islands (Russia)
Osmussaar (Estonia)
Prangli (Estonia)
Ruhnu (Estonia)
Russian Antarctica (Russia)
Saaremaa (Estonia)
Sakhalin Region (Russia)
Sakha-Yakoutia (Russia)
South Ossetia (Georgia)
Spitsbergen (Russia)
Suur-Pakri (Estonia)
Tatarstan (Russia)
Transnistria (Moldova)
Tuva (Russia)
Udmurtia (Russia)
Ukrainian Antarctic (Ukraine)
Ukrainian Arctic Post (Ukraine)
Vaike-Pakri (Estonia)
Vorms (Estonia)

Unauthorized issues are known from the following republics within the Commonwealth of Independent States, republics that have the authority to issue stamps.

Kyrgyzstan
Tajikistan
Turkmenistan

CHAPTER 23

ILLUSTRATED STAMP IDENTIFIER

INSCRIPTIONS USUALLY PROVIDE the best clue to a stamp's origin. Extensive listings of inscriptions appear in Chapter 24, "Foreign Stamp Identifier," and Chapter 26, "Foreign Terms on Postage Stamps." In some cases, stamps either do not contain inscriptions or contain inscriptions in unfamiliar alphabets. Some of the more commonly encountered difficult-to-identify stamps are illustrated in this chapter. They are arranged by the type of alphabetical characters encountered on them, except that the first section is devoted to stamps without country names.

Even when a stamp's country of origin is known, it is sometimes difficult to locate in a stamp catalogue. Pay attention to the following clues. A date or dates may be contained in an inscription. The denomination often places the stamp in a run of stamps with similar denominations. For example, the first-class rate for U.S. mail was 13¢ between 1976 and 1978. That time period is a good place to look for U.S. stamps of 13¢ denominations. Look for visual clues and symbols, such as leaders' portraits and political or national symbols. British stamps can be roughly dated by monarch. Russian stamps displaying the hammer-and-sickle symbol would have been issued during the Communist era, which spanned the years 1918 through 1991. Chinese stamps bearing the portrait of Mao Zedong originate from the People's Republic of China, while stamps bearing the portrait of Chiang Kai-shek originate from the Republic of China, or Taiwan.

STAMPS WITHOUT COUNTRY NAMES

Australia.

Austria.   Austria, postage due.

Austria, newspaper stamp.

Austria (Lombardy-Venetia). Stamps of similar design denominated in kreuzer (Kr.) are from Austria.

Belgium.

Belgium, postage due.

Belgium, railway parcel stamp.

Bosnia and Herzegovina.

Brazil.

Colombia.

Cuba. Some early stamps of Spain and the Philippines have similar designs.

Denmark.

Germany
(East Saxony).

Germany
(Württemberg).

Great Britain.

Hungary.

Italy, postage due.

Italy, official.

Italian States
(Modena).

Italian States (Roman States). Issues
usually contain the Papal Arms crest.

Italian States
(Two Sicilies).

Luxembourg.

Netherlands.

Peru.

Netherlands
(or colonies),
postage due.

Romania.

Spain. Some stamps of Cuba and the Philippines have similar designs.

Switzerland, postage due.

Uruguay.

GREEK INSCRIPTIONS

Crete.

Epirus.

Greece.

Greece,
postage due.

Greece,
postal tax stamp.

Greece,
country name.

Thrace.

CYRILLIC INSCRIPTIONS

In addition to the illusttated examples, other entities that use Cyrillic characters include Kyrgyzstan, Macedonia, Mongolia, Russia (Army of the North, Wenden, and Offices in Turkey), Tajikistan, Transcaucasian Federated Republics, and Western Ukraine.

Batum.

Azerbaijan.

Bulgaria.

БЪЛГАРИЯ

Bulgaria,
country name.

Bulgaria, postal tax stamp.

Far Eastern Republic.

Finland. Some early stamps of Russia have similar designs.

Kazakstan.

Latvia.

ЦРНА ГОРА
Montenegro,
country name.

Montenegro.

Russia. Some early stamps of Finland have similar designs.

Serbia.   South Russia.

Ukraine, semipostal.

УКРАЇНИ

Ukraine,
country name.

Ukraine.

Yugoslavia.   Yugoslavia (Croatia Slovenia).

ARABIC INSCRIPTIONS

In addition to the illustrated examples, other entities that use Arabic inscriptions include Bahrain, India (Jammu and Kashmir, Hyderabad), Iraq, Jordan, Lebanon, Libya, Pakistan, Syria, Thrace, and Yemen.

Iran.   Iran, postal tax stamp.

Egypt.

Saudi Arabia,
national crest.
The national
crest appears
on most
modern issues.

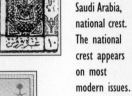

Saudi Arabia.

Turkey.

Turkey in Asia.

ASIAN INSCRIPTIONS

Other entities that use Asian characters include the various Indian states.

Armenia.

Bangladesh,
country name.

Georgia.

India, Bundi State.

Israel.

Israel, revenue.

Nepal.

Tannu Tuva.

Thailand.

ORIENTAL INSCRIPTIONS

In addition to the illustrated examples, other entities that use Oriental characters include Japanese occupations of Korea, Malaya, North Borneo, and the Philippines.

Republic of China, airmail.

Republic of China.

Republic of China
(Shanghai and Nanking).

Republic of
China (Taiwan).
Issues without
overprint were
issued under
Japanese
occupation.

Republic of China
(Northeastern
Provinces).

Republic of
China,
postage due.

Republic of China.
The sunburst symbol
appears on many
issues.

中国人民邮政

People's Republic of
China, country name.

People's Republic of China.

Japan. The
Chrysanthemum
crest appears
on many
issues.

Japan.

 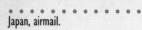 

Japan, airmail.

Burma (Japanese occupation).

Malaya (Japanese occupation).

South Korea. The Yin Yang symbol appears on many issues.

North Korea.

Manchukuo. The Orchid crest appears on many issues.

Manchukuo.

Ryukyu Islands.

Ryukyu Islands, revenue.

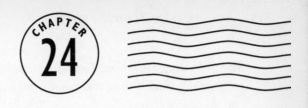

FOREIGN STAMP
IDENTIFIER

IN THE LISTINGS below, locate the name of the stamp-issuing entity as it appears on the stamp. Primary listings contain information about the country and its stamp-issuing history. Secondary (or cross-reference) listings (e.g., **Côte d'Ivoire** - see **Ivory Coast**) direct you to the primary listing.

This chapter deals only with names of stamp-issuing entities. Information about other inscriptions that appear on stamps can be found in Chapter 26, "Foreign Terms on Postage Stamps."

Primary listings are arranged as follows:

- **Name**. The name of the country or stamp-issuing entity as it appears on a stamp. The name may appear either as an inscription (i.e., part of the design) or an overprint (printing or handstamping added later). Primary listings appear under the name of the country in English as it is generally understood in the American stamp-collecting community (e.g., Ivory Coast rather than Côte d'Ivoire) and in the form in which it can usually be located in stamp catalogues. In cases where no primary listing appears, the cross-reference is given in italics and indicates where the stamp can usually be located in a general worldwide stamp catalogue. Variations in spelling appear in parentheses.

- **Location**. Location immediately follows country name in primary listings. Location is given using reference points such as neighboring countries or geographical features.

- **Sovereignty**. Countries are described as independent (regardless of their form of government) if they are not under the direct control of another country. In the case of colonies, possessions, and territories, the identity of the controlling country (such as British, French, or Spanish) is given. Wartime or other temporary occupations are noted together with inscription information.

- **Stamp-Issuing Duration**. Dates in parentheses immediately follow sovereignty information and indicate the span during which the entity issued postage stamps, for example, British (1894–1960). An arrow symbol (→) indicates that an entity has been continuously active from the date given to present. Dates refer only to the time during which the entity has been active issuing stamps. In the case of the United States, Independent (1847→) means that the nation is independent (although it achieved independence in 1776) and that it began issuing stamps in 1847 and has continued to do so until present. Interrupted intervals, as in the case of Latvia, are shown as (1918–40, 1991→). The tilde symbol (~) appears in cases where the span is intermittent or uncertain.

- **Inscriptions**. Inscriptions are given in their chronological order, although in some cases, gaps or overlaps occur. Inscriptions and overprints are shown in bold, as they appear on stamps. Stamps are assumed to be inscribed (i.e., integral to the printed design) unless noted as "overprinted." Overprints are understood to be on stamps of the country listed unless otherwise stated. Names contain diacritical marks if they appear that way on stamps. Country names often appear with additional words such as "Postes," "Correos," or "Republica." Such additional words are included in a listing when they appear consistently as part of the identifying inscription. In cases where they appear elsewhere on the stamp, mention is omitted. In cases where they appear in smaller type or in a subsidiary position, mention is made following the inscription.

- **Period of Use.** The dates during which the inscription was used appear in parentheses immediately following it, along with supplementary information, if any. The period of use in parentheses is not necessarily exclusive.

- **Other Information**. Amplifying information, where appropriate, appears at the end of primary listings.

STAMP-ISSUING ENTITIES AND STAMP INSCRIPTIONS

1 Tical   overprinted on stamps of Siam: Thailand. See **Thailand**.

1.Zone   overprinted on stamps inscribed "Slesvig": Schleswig. See **Schleswig**.

11° Congreso Internacional de Ferrocarriles   inscribed on a commemorative issue (1930): Spain. *Spain*.

15/15   overprinted on stamps of French colonies: Cochin China.

18° Distrito   overprinted on provisional issues of Arequipa: Cuzco, a city in southern Peru and capital of Cuzco Department. *Peru (provisional issues)*.

1901 Antioquia   Antioquia. See **Antioquia**. *Colombia*.

20 Pfg.   surcharged on stamps of Russia: Estonia.

5   surcharged on stamps of French colonies: Cochin China. See **Cochin China**.

5 Pfg.   overprinted together with "China" on stamps of Germany: Kiauchau. See **Kiauchau**.

A & T or **A - T**   Annam and Tonkin. See **Annam and Tonkin**.

Abu Dhabi   on the Arabian shore of the Persian Gulf in the north-central United Arab Emirates. Emirate under British protection (1964–72). Stamps are inscribed **Abu Dhabi**. Abu Dhabi joined the United Arab Emirates in 1971 but continued to use its own stamps until 1972.

Açores   Azores. See **Azores**.

Açores Portugal   Azores. See **Azores**.

Aden   on the southern coast of the Arabian Peninsula, bordered on the north by Saudi Arabia, on the south by the Gulf of Aden, and on the west by the Red Sea. British protectorate (1935–65). Stamps are inscribed **Aden**. Aden also included sultanates that issued stamps inscribed **Aden - Kathiri State of Seiyun** (1942–65), **Aden - Qu'aiti State of Shihr and Mukalla** (1942–55), **Aden - Qu'aiti State of Hadhramaut** (1955–65).

A.E.F.   an abbreviation for "Afrique Équatoriale Française."

A.E.F. - Oubangi-Chari   overprinted on stamps of Middle Congo: Ubangi Shari. See **Ubangi-Shari**.

Afars and Issas   a small territory in northeastern Africa on the Gulf of Aden at the Strait of Bab el Mandeb. French (1967–77). Stamps are inscribed **Territoire Français des Afars et des Issas**. Afars and Issas was formerly the Somali Coast; subsequently, Djibouti Republic.

Afghanistan   in southwestern Asia, bordered on the north by Turkmenistan, Uzbekistan, and Tajikistan, on the east and south by Pakistan, and on the west by Iran. Independent (1871→). Inscriptions include Arabic inscriptions until 1927, **Afghan Postage** or **Postage Afghan** (1927–30), **Postes Afghanes** or **Afghanes Postes** (1928–89), **Postes Afghanistan** (1939–40), **Afghanistan** (1950s), **Afghan Post** (1973, 1989→). Great Britain controlled Afghanistan's foreign affairs between 1880 and 1919.

Afghan Post (or **Postage**)   Afghanistan. See **Afghanistan**.

Africa - Correios   overprinted on stamps of Portuguese colonies: *Portuguese Africa*.

Africa Occidental Española   Spanish West Africa. See **Spanish West Africa**.

Africa Orientale Italiana   Italian East Africa. See **Italian East Africa**.

Afrique Équatoriale Française   French Equatorial Africa. See **French Equatorial Africa**.

Afrique Equatoriale Française   **(1)** overprinted on stamps of French Gabon: Gabon. See **Gabon**. **(2)** overprinted on stamps inscribed "Moyen Congo": Middle Congo. See **Middle Congo**.

Afrique Equatoriale Gabon   Gabon. See **Gabon**.

Afrique Equatorial Française - Oubangi-Chari   overprinted on stamps of Middle Congo: Ubangi-Shari. See **Ubangi-Shari**.

Afrique Française Libre   overprinted on stamps of French Equatorial Africa: French Equatorial Africa. See **French Equatorial Africa**.

Afrique Occidentale Française   French West Africa. See **French West Africa**.

Afrique Occidentale Française - Haut-Senegal-Niger   Upper Senegal and Niger. See **Upper Senegal and Niger**.

Afrique Occidentale Française - Ht Senegal-Niger   Upper Senegal and Niger. See **Upper Senegal and Niger**.

Afrique Occidentale Française - Sénégal   Senegal. See **Senegal**.

Aguera   in western North Africa, in the southwestern corner of Spanish Sahara. Spanish (1920–24). Inscriptions include **La Agüera** overprinted on stamps of Rio de Oro (1920–22), **Sahara Occidental - La Aguera** (1922–24). Aguera was subsequently part of Spanish Sahara.

Aitutaki   in the South Pacific, one of the southern group of Cook Islands. New Zealand (1903–32), independent (1972→). Inscriptions include **Aitutaki** overprinted on stamps of New Zealand (1903–20) or on stamps of Cook Islands (1972), **Aitutaki** inscribed (1920–32), together with "Cook Islands" (1973→). Between 1932 and 1972, Aitutaki used stamps of the Cook Islands.

Ajman   on the Arabian shore of the Persian Gulf between Umm al Qiwain on the northeast and Sharjah on the southwest. Emirate under British protection (1964–71). Stamps are inscribed **Ajman**. Ajman joined the United Arab Emirates in 1971.

Åland   in northern Europe, a group of islands off the southwest coast of Finland, at the mouth of the Gulf of Bothnia, between Sweden and Finland. Finnish (1984→). Stamps are inscribed **Åland**. *Finland.*

Alaouites   a governorate in northwestern Syria that came within the French mandate of Syria and Lebanon following World War I. French (1925–30). Inscriptions include **Alaouites** overprinted on stamps of France (1925), and on stamps of Syria (1925–30). Alaouites subsequently became **Latakia**.

Albania   in southeastern Europe on the northern edge of the Balkan Peninsula, bordered on the north by Montenegro, on the northeast by Serbia, on the east by Macedonia, on the south by Greece, and on the west by the Adriatic Sea. Independent (1913→). Inscriptions include **Postat e Qeverriës së Përkohëshme të Shqiponiës** or **Shqipëniës** (1913), **Shqipënia e Lirë** (1913–14), **Shpiqënia** overprinted on stamps of Turkey (1913), **Commission de Contrôie Provisoire - Korca** (1914), **Shqiperie Korcê Vetqeveritabe** (1917), **Republika Korce Shqipetare** (1917), **Qarku Postes I Korçês** overprinted or inscribed (1918), **Shkodres Shqypnis** overprinted (1919), **Shqiptare** overprinted (1919–20), **Shqipënië** (1920s), **Shqyptare** (1920s), **Mbretnia** (or **Mbre.**) **Shqyptare** or **Shqiptare** (1920s), **Republika** (or **Rep.**) **Shqiptare** overprinted or inscribed (1920s), **Shqipni** (1930s), **Mbretnija** (or **Mbr.**) **Shqiptare** (Italian occupation, 1939–43), **Shqipnija** (German occupation, 1943–44), **Qeverija Demokratike** (or **Dem.** or **Demokrat.**) **e Shqiperise** overprinted or inscribed (1945), **Shqiperija** (occasionally in late 1940s), **Repulika Popullore e Shqiperise** (1946 to late 1970s, often abbreviated **R.P.E. Shqiperise** and sometimes **R.P. Shqiperise** or **R. Popullore e Shqiperise**), **Shqiperia** (1949, mid-1960s and later, and 1995→, and sometimes **Shqipëria**), **Republika Popullore Socialiste e Shqiperise** (late 1970s until 1990, sometimes abbreviated **R.P.S. e Shqiperise**), and **Posta Shqiptare** (1990–95).

Albania   overprinted on stamps of Italy: Italian offices in Albania. *Italy (offices abroad).*

Alderney   one of the British Channel Islands located off the coast of Normandy, France, part of the Bailiwick of Guernsey. British (1983→). Stamps are inscribed **Alderney** together with "Bailiwick of Guernsey." *Great Britain (Guernsey: Alderney).*

Alexandretta   part of the French Mandate in Syria (1938). Alexandretta subsequently became part of Syria. Stamps are overprinted **Sandjak d'Alexandrette** on issues of Syria.

Alexandrie   overprinted on stamps of France or inscribed together with "République Française": French offices in Alexandria, Egypt. *France (offices in Egypt).*

Algeria   western North Africa, bordered on the west by Morocco, on the north by the Mediterranean, on the east by Libya and Tunisia, and on the south by Niger, Mali, and Mauritania. French (1913–58), independent (1962→). Inscriptions include **Algérie** or **Algerie** (both, often with "Postes"). Algeria used stamps of France between 1958 and 1962.

Algérie or **Algerie**   Algeria. See **Algeria.**

Allemagne Duitsland   overprinted on stamps of Belgium: Germany (Belgian occupation, 1919–21). *Germany (occupation issues).*

Allenstein   a city and region in northern Poland, formerly part of East Prussia. Plebescite commission (1920). Inscriptions include **Plébiscite Olsztyn Allenstein** overprinted on stamps of Germany (1920), **Commission d'Administration et de Plebescite** together with "Traité de Versailles" and "Art. 94 et 95" overprinted on stamps of Germany (1920). In 1920, in a plebescite, Allenstein chose to remain with Germany. At the end of World War II, Allenstein was transferred to Poland.

All Guyana Our Heritage   Guyana. See **Guyana**.

Allied Military Postage - Italy   *Italy (occupation issues).*

A.M.G. F.T.T.   (Allied Military Government - Free Territory of Trieste) overprinted on stamps of Italy: Trieste. Also, **A.M.G.-F.T.T.**, **AMG-FTT**, and **AMG FTT**. See **Trieste**. *Italy (Trieste).*

A.M.G. V.G.   (Allied Military Government - Venezia Giulia) overprinted on stamps of Italy: Venezia Giulia. See **Venezia Giulia**. *Italy (occupation issues).*

AM Post - Deutschland   (Allied Military) Post in Germany (1945–46). *Germany (occupation issues).*

Andorra   a tiny principality in the Pyrenees Mountains between France and Spain at one time under the control of France and the Spanish bishop of Urgel, now a parliamentary coprincipality. Stamps have been issued under both French authority (1931→) and Spanish authority (1928→). Inscriptions under French authority include **Andorre** overprinted on stamps of France (1931) and inscribed (1936–75), **Valles d'Andorre** (1932–40s), **Andorre - Andorra** (1975–79), and **Principat d'Andorra** (1979→). Inscriptions under Spanish authority include **Andorra** or **Principat d'Andorra**. Beginning in 1979, stamps of both French and Spanish authority were inscribed **Principat d'Andorra**. Of these, issues under French authority are denominated in francs and centimes and often bear the inscription "Postes" or "La Poste" and the year of issue. Issues under Spanish authority are denominated in pesetas (Pta) and sometimes bear the inscription "Correus Espanyolas."

Andorre   see **Andorra**.

Angola   in central Africa, bordered on the west by the Atlantic Ocean, on the north by the Republic of the Congo, on the east by Zambia, and on the south by the Democratic Republic of the Congo. Portuguese (1870–1975), independent (1975→). Inscriptions include **Angola** (1870–86), **Provincia de Angola** (1886–93), **Correios Angola** overprinted (1894), **Portugal Angola** (1893–1902), **Angola** with "Republica Portuguesa" (at various times between 1912 and 1975), **Angola** with "Correios" and "Portugal" (1914), **Angola** with "Império Colonial Portugués" (1930s), and **Angola** (1975→). Angola was formerly Portuguese West Africa.

Angra   an administrative unit of three Azores islands: Graciosa, São Jorge, and Terciera. Portuguese (1892–1906). Stamps are inscribed **Angra** together with "Correios Portugal."

Anguilla   an island in the Leeward Islands in the West Indies southeast of Puerto Rico. British (1967→). Inscriptions include **Independent Anguilla** overprinted on stamps of Saint Kitts-Nevis (1967), **Anguilla** (1967–71, 1981→) and with "H.M. Commissioner in Anguilla" (1971–81). Anguilla was formerly part of Saint Kitts-Nevis-Anguilla. In 1967 it began issuing stamps of its own.

Anjouan   one of the Comoro Islands. French (1892–1914). Stamps are inscribed **Sultanat d'Anjouan**. Anjouan subsequently became part of Madagascar (1914–46), then one of the Comoro Islands (1950→).

Annam and Tonkin   part of French Indochina. French (1888–92). Stamps are overprinted **A & T** or **A - T** on issues of French colonies. Annam and Tonkin were composed of much of north and central Vietnam.

Antananrivo   an inscription on stamps used by the British in Madagascar (1880s). *Madagascar.*

Antigua and Barbuda   an island nation in the eastern Caribbean Sea southeast of Puerto Rico composed of Antigua and two smaller islands, Barbuda to the north and Redonda, an uninhabited rocky islet, to the southwest. British (1862–1981), independent (1981→). Inscriptions include **Antigua** (1862–1981), **Antigua and Barbuda** (1982→). See also **Barbuda.**

Antioquia   a department (state) located in west-central Colombia. Local issues (1868–1904). Inscriptions include **E. S. de Antioquia** (1868–73), **Estado Sobrano de Antioquia** (1873–75), **E^o S^o de Antioquia** (1873–75), **Correos de Antioquia** (1878–88), **Provisional de Medellin** (1888), **D. de A. Provisional** (1890), **Departmento de Antioquia** (1889–1904), **1901 Antioquia** (1901). *Colombia.*

A.O.   (Afrique Orientale) overprinted on stamps of the Belgian Congo: German East Africa (Belgian occupation). See **German East Africa.**

A.O.F. or AOF   abbreviation for "Afrique Occidentale Française." See **French West Africa.**

A.O.F.   (Africa Orientale Italiana) overprinted on stamps of Italy: Italian East Africa. See **Italian East Africa.**

A.O.F. - Senegal   Senegal. See **Senegal.**

Arabie Saoudite   Saudi Arabia. See **Saudi Arabia**

Arbe   overprinted on stamps of Fiume: Fiume. See **Fiume.** Arbe (Rab) is a small island in the Adriatic Sea near Fiume (Rijeka) and is now part of Croatia.

Archipel des Comores   Comoro Islands. See **Comoro Islands**.

A.R. Egypt   Arab Republic Egypt. See **Egypt**.

Arequipa   overprinted on issues previously overprinted "Provisional 1881–82": Arequipa, a city in southern Peru and capital of Arequipa Department. *Peru (provisional issues).*

Argentina   in southern South America, bordered on the north by Bolivia and Paraguay, on the northeast by Brazil and Uruguay, on the east by the Atlantic Ocean, and on the west by Chile. Independent (1858→). Inscriptions include **Republica Argentina** (1858→) sometimes with "Correos" and sometimes without "Republica." Argentina claims the Islas Malvinas (Falkland Islands) and occupied them briefly in 1982.

Armenia   in the Transcaucus region of western Asia, bordered on the north by Georgia, on the east by Azerbaijan, and on the west and south by Turkey. Independent (1919–23, 1992→). Inscriptions include stylized monogram overprinted on stamps of Russia (1919–21), often a hammer and sickle superimposed on a star (1921–23), **Armenia** (1992→). In 1918 Armenia declared itself independent. By 1923 it had been incorporated into the U.S.S.R. (Union of Soviet Socialist Republics) as one of the Transcaucasian Soviet Federated Socialist Republics. In 1991 Armenia voted to secede from the Soviet Union and the following year became a member of the United Nations.

Arriba España   overprinted on stamps of Spain: Nationalist forces. See **Spain**. *Spain (revolutionary issues).*

Aruba   an island in the West Indies, just north of Venezuela. Netherlands/ autonomous and self-governing (1986→). Stamps are inscribed **Aruba**. Aruba was formerly one of the Netherlands Antilles. It is now a separate, autonomous, self-governing entity of the Netherlands.

Ascension   a small island (34 square miles) in the South Atlantic 900 miles northwest of Saint Helena and midway between Africa and South America. British (1922→). Inscriptions include **Ascension** overprinted on stamps of Saint Helena (1922–24), or inscribed **Ascension** or **Ascension Island** (1924→).

Aunus   (now Olonets) a town located at the extreme south end of Eastern Karelia, northeast of Lake Ladoga. Finnish (1919). Inscriptions include **Aunus** overprinted on stamps of Finland (1919). Finnish forces briefly occupied Aunus during the spring of 1919, at the time of the Russian Civil War, but Russian Bolshevik forces counterattacked and drove them back to Finland within a short time. *Russia.*

Australia   an island continent southeast of Asia. Independent dominion (1913→). Stamps are inscribed **Australia**. Australia is composed of the former British colonial states New South Wales, Queensland, South Australia, Tasmania, Victoria, and Western Australia, each of which issued their own stamps until 1913, when Australia began issuing stamps.

Australian Antarctic Territory in eastern Antarctica south of latitude 60° south and between longitude 45° and 160° east. Australian (1957→). Stamps are inscribed **Australian Antarctic Territory**. *Australia*.

Austria in central Europe, bordered on the north by the Czech Republic, on the northeast by Slovakia, on the east by Hungary, on the south by Slovenia and Italy, and on the west by Switzerland and Germany. Independent (1850–1938, 1945→). Inscriptions include **KK Post Stempel** and denomination in kreuzers (1850–58), bust of emperor or national crest and denomination in kreuzers (1858–83), **Kais. Koenigl. Oesterr. Post** (1883–1908), **Kaiserlich Königlich Österreichische Post** (1908–18), **Deutschösterreich** overprinted or inscribed (1918–20), **Österreich** inscription (1920–38) and overprinted on stamps of Germany (1945), **Republik Österreich** (1945→). Austria was joined with Hungary (Austria-Hungary) until the end of World War I. Austria was incorporated into and used stamps of Germany during the years 1938 to 1945. The first issues of Austria up to 1868 are almost identical to those of Lombardy-Venetia but can be distinguished as follows: issues of Austria are denominated in kreuzers (abbreviated "kr"); issues of Lombardy-Venetia are denominated in centes or soldi.

Azerbaijan in the Transcaucus region of western Asia, bordered on the north by Russia and Georgia, on the east by the Caspian Sea, on the south by Iran, and on the west by Armenia. Independent (1919–22), Soviet Republic (1922–24), Commonwealth of Independent States (1992→). Inscriptions include **Republique d'Azerbaidjan** (1919–22), **АЗЄРБАЙДЖАНСКАЯ** and often with surcharged values (1922–24), **Azärbaycan** (1992), **AzErbaycan** (1992→).

Azärbaycan Azerbaijan. See **Azerbaijan**.

Azδrbaycan Azerbaijan. See **Azerbaijan**.

Azores a group of islands in the Atlantic 800 miles west of Portugal, including nine major islands: Corvo, Faial, Flores, Graciosa, Pico, Santa Maria, São Jorge, São Miguel, and Terciera. Portuguese (1868–1930, 1980→). Inscriptions include **Açores** (or **Açôres**) overprinted on stamps of Portugal or inscribed (1868–1906, 1912–30). *Azores*. Beginning in 1930, the Azores used stamps of Portugal. In 1980 Portugal began issuing stamps inscribed **Portugal Açores** or **Açores Portugal**. *Portugal*.

B overprinted on stamps of Straits Settlements: Bangkok. *Bangkok*.

Baden a state in southwestern Germany. Inscriptions include **(1) Baden** (1851–70), *German States*; **(2) Baden** (French occupation, 1947–49), *Germany (French occupation)*.

B.A. Eritrea   (British Administration) overprinted on stamps of Great Britain: Eritrea (British occupation). *Great Britain (offices abroad).*

Baghdad - In British Occupation   overprinted on stamps of Turkey: Mesopotamia. See **Mesopotamia.**

Bahamas   an archipelago of about 700 islands (only about 40 inhabited) and islets and innumerable cays and rocks, stretching about 750 miles from a point southeast of Palm Beach, Florida, to a point off the eastern tip of Cuba. British (1859–1973), independent (1973→). Stamps are inscribed **Bahamas**.

Bahawalpur   a state within Pakistan (1947–49). Stamps are inscribed **Bahawalpur**. *Pakistan.*

Bahrain   an island nation in the southern Persian Gulf between Saudi Arabia on the west and Qatar Peninsula on the east. British (1933–71), independent (1971→). Inscriptions include **Bahrain** overprinted on stamps of India (1933–48), on stamps of Great Britain (1948–60), or inscribed **Bahrain** (1960–71), **State of Bahrain** (1971→).

Bailiwick   **(1)** of Guernsey: see **Guernsey**; **(2)** of Jersey: see **Jersey**.

Bamra or **Bamra Feudatory State**   Bamra, a native feudatory state in east-central India. *India (native feudatory states).*

Bánát Bácska   overprinted on stamps of Hungary for use in areas occupied by Serbia following World War I: *Hungary.*

Bangladesh   in southeast Asia, bordered on the north, east, and west by India and on the south by the Bay of Bengal, touching Myanmar (**Burma**) on the southeast. Independent (1971→). Stamps are inscribed **Bangladesh**. Prior to independence, Bangladesh was East Pakistan.

Baranya   overprinted on stamps of Hungary for use in areas occupied by Serbia following World War I: *Hungary.*

Barbados   the easternmost island of the West Indies, lying east of Saint Vincent and the Windward Islands of the Lesser Antilles. British (1862–1966), independent (1966→). Stamps are inscribed **Barbados**.

Barbuda   an island in the Antigua group. British Antigua (1922, 1968–81), independent Antigua (1981-). Inscriptions include **Barbuda** overprinted on stamps of the Leeward Islands (1922), on stamps of Antigua (1973-), or inscribed (1968-), **Barbuda Mail** overprinted on stamps of Antigua (1982→). See also **Antigua.**

Barwani State or **Barwani Postage**   Barwani, a native feudatory state in west-central India. *India (native feudatory states).*

B.A. Somalia (British Administration) overprinted on stamps of Great Britain: Somalia (British occupation). *Great Britain (offices abroad)*.

Basutoland in eastern South Africa, surrounded on all sides by South Africa. British (1933–66), independent (1966→). Inscriptions include **Basutoland** overprinted on stamps of South Africa (1945) or inscribed (1933–66). In 1966 Basutoland became independent Lesotho.

B.A. Tripolitania (British Administration) overprinted on stamps of Great Britain: Tripolitania (British occupation). *Great Britain (offices abroad)*.

Batum a port city in southwestern Georgia on the Black Sea. British occupation (1919–20). Inscriptions include **БАТУМ.ОБ.** overprinted on stamps of Russia (1919), **British Occupation** overprinted, together with surcharged value, on stamps of Russia (1919–20).

Bavaria a state in southeastern Germany. Inscriptions include **Bayern** (1849–1920), **Volkstaat Bayern** overprinted on stamps of Bavaria (1919), **Freistaat Bayern** overprinted on stamps of Germany or Bavaria (1919–20), **Deutsches Reich** overprinted on stamps of Bavaria (1920). *German States*.

Bayern Bavaria. See **Bavaria**.

B.C.A. overprinted on stamps of Rhodesia: British Central Africa. See **British Central Africa**.

B.C.O.F. Japan - 1946 (British Commonwealth Occupation Force) overprinted on stamps of Australia: *Australia (occupation forces in Japan)*.

B - Correos overprinted on stamps of Nicaragua: province of Zelaya. *Nicaragua*.

B - Dpto. Zelaya overprinted on stamps of Nicaragua: province of Zelaya. *Nicaragua*.

Bechuanaland Protectorate central South Africa, bordered on the north and west by Namibia, on the northeast by Zambia and Zimbabwe, on the southeast and south by South Africa. British (1888–1966). Inscriptions include **Protectorate** overprinted on stamps of British Bechuanaland (1888–89), **Bechuanaland Protectorate** overprinted on stamps of the Cape of Good Hope (1889), on stamps of Great Britain (1889-1932), on stamps of Transvaal (1910), on stamps of South Africa (1945), **Bechuanaland Protectorate** or **Bechuanaland** inscribed (1932-1966). In 1966 Bechuanaland became independent Botswana.

Belarus in eastern central Europe, bordered on the northwest by Latvia and Lithuania, on the east by Russia, to the south by Ukraine, and on the west by Poland. Commonwealth of Independent States (1992→). Stamps are inscribed **Belarus**. In 1919 Belarus (at the time also known as Byellorussia or White Russia) became a Soviet Socialist Republic, and in 1922, one of the founding republics of the Soviet Union.

Belgian Congo   see **Congo (Belgian)**.

België - Belgique   Belgium. Appears interchangeably as **Belgique-België**. See **Belgium**.

Belgien   overprinted on Belgian stamps during German occupation in World War I: Belgium.

Belgique   Belgium. See **Belgium**.

Belgium   in northwestern Europe, bordered on the northwest by the North Sea, on the north by the Netherlands, on the east by Germany and Luxembourg, and on the south by France. Independent (1849→). Inscriptions include **Postes** with bust of Leopold II or Lion coat of arms (1849–69), **Belgique** (1869–93), **België - Belgique** (1893→).

Belize   in northeastern Central America, bordered on the north and northwest by Mexico, on the east by the Caribbean Sea, and on the south and west by Guatemala. British (1973–81), independent (1981→). Inscriptions include **Belize** overprinted on stamps of British Honduras (1973) or inscribed (1973→). Belize was formerly **British Honduras**.

Benadir   Somalia. See **Somalia**.

Bengasi   overprinted on stamps of Italy: Italian offices in Benghazi, at the time a city in the Ottoman Turkish Empire located in North Africa, in what is now Libya. *Italy (offices abroad)*.

Benin   in western Africa, bordered on the north by Burkina Faso and Niger, on the east by Nigeria, on the south by the Gulf of Guinea, and on the west by Togo. French (1892–95), independent (1975→). Inscriptions include **Bénin** overprinted on stamps of France (1892), **Golfe de Bénin** (1893), **Bénin** (1892–95), **République Populaire du Bénin** (1975–90), **République du Bénin** (1990→). In 1895 Benin became part of Dahomey. Between 1945 and 1958, Dahomey used stamps of French West Africa. In 1960 it became independent Dahomey and issued stamps under that name (see **Dahomey**). In 1975 it changed its name back to Benin.

Bequia   one of the northern group of Grenadine Islands of Saint Vincent, in the Windward chain in the eastern Caribbean Sea. Saint Vincent (1984–97). Inscriptions include **Bequia** overprinted on stamps of Saint Vincent Grenadines (1984), **Bequia - Grenadines of St. Vincent** (1984→). *Saint Vincent Grenadines (Bequia)*.

Bergedorf a city in northern Germany. Stamps are inscribed **Bergedorf** (1861–67). *German States.*

Berlin a city in northeastern Germany, its capital from 1871 to 1945 and again since 1990; occupied by France, Great Britain, the Soviet Union, and the United States following World War II, and in 1949 partitioned into East Berlin and West Berlin. Inscriptions include **Berlin** overprinted on stamps of Germany (U.S. and British zones, 1948–49), **Deutsche Post** (1949–52), **Deutsche Post Berlin** (1952–55), **Deutsche Bundespost Berlin** (1955–90). Berlin discontinued issuing its own stamps after the reunification of Germany in 1990. *Germany (Berlin).*

Bermuda a group of small islands (aggregate area about 20 square miles) in the Atlantic Ocean about 150 miles east of North Carolina, including Bermuda, Somerset, Ireland, Saint George's, Saint Davids, and Boaz. British (1848→). Inscriptions include **Hamilton - Bermuda** (1848–54), **Bermuda** (1865→).

Beyrouth overprinted on stamps of Russia together with surcharge in para(s) or piastre(s): Russian offices in Beirut, at the time part of the Turkish Ottoman Empire. *Russia (offices in the Turkish Empire).*

B. Guiana see **British Guiana**.

Bhopal State Bhopal, a native feudatory state in central India. *India (native feudatory states).*

Bhor State Bhor, a native feudatory state southeast of Bombay, India. *India (native feudatory states).*

Bhutan in south Asia in the eastern Himalayas, bordered by Tibet on the north and India on the west, south, and east. Independent (1962→). Stamps are inscribed **Bhutan**.

Biafra a breakaway republic in the eastern section of Nigeria. Independent (1967–70). Stamps are inscribed **Biafra**. Biafra broke away from Nigeria in May 1967 and was finally subdued in January 1970. Some catalogues do not recognize stamps of Biafra.

B I É overprinted on stamps of Switzerland: International Bureau of Education. *Switzerland (official issues).*

Bijawar State Bijawar, a native feudatory state in central India. *India (native feudatory states).*

B.I.O.T. overprinted on stamps of Seychelles: British Indian Ocean Territory. See **British Indian Ocean Territory**.

BMA (British Military Administration) **(1)** overprinted on stamps of North Borneo: North Borneo; **(2)** overprinted on stamps of Sarawak: Sarawak.

B.M.A. Eritrea (British Military Administration) overprinted on stamps of Great Britain: Eritrea (British occupation). *Great Britain (offices abroad)*.

B M A - Malaya (British Military Administration) overprinted on stamps of the Straits Settlements: Straits Settlements. See **Straits Settlements**.

B.M.A. Somalia (British Military Administration) overprinted on stamps of Great Britain: Somalia (British occupation). *Great Britain (offices abroad)*.

B.M.A. Tripolitania (British Military Administration) overprinted on stamps of Great Britain: Tripolitania (British occupation). *Great Britain (offices abroad)*.

B.N.F. Castellorizo overprinted on stamps of French offices in Turkey: Castellorizo. B.N.F. is an abbreviation for "Base Navale Française." See **Castellorizo**.

Bogota a city in Colombia. Local issues (1889–1903). Stamps are inscribed **Correo Urbano de Bogota**. *Colombia*.

Bohemia and Moravia the western part of Czechoslovakia. German protectorate (1939–45). Inscriptions include **Böhmen und Mähren - Čechy a Morava** overprinted on stamps of Czechoslovakia or inscribed, and in some cases, with "Deutsches Reich" or "Grossdeutsches Reich" (1939–45). *Czechoslovakia*.

Böhmen und Mähren - Čechy a Morava either overprinted on stamps of Czechoslovakia or inscribed: Bohemia and Moravia. See **Bohemia and Moravia**.

Bolivar a department (state) in north-central Colombia. Local issues (1863–1904). Inscriptions include **Estado S. de Bolivar** together with "E^S U^S de Colombia" and "Correos de Estado" (1860s), **Estado Soberano de Bolivar** (1873–82), **Correos de Bolivar** or **Correos del Eo Uo de Bolivar** (1882–1904), **Departmento de Bolivar** (1903). *Colombia*.

Bolivar Sucre Miranda overprinted together with "Decreto de 27 Abril de 1870" or "Decreto de 27 Junio 1870" on stamps of Venezuela: Venezuela. See **Venezuela**.

Bolivia in central South America, bordered on the north and east by Brazil, on the southeast by Paraguay, on the south by Argentina, and on the west by Peru and Chile. Independent (1867→). Inscriptions include **Bolivia** (often with "Correos de").

Bollo Della Posta di Sicilia Sicily (Two Sicilies). See **Two Sicilies**. *Italian States*.

Bollo Della Posta Napoletana Naples (Two Sicilies). See **Two Sicilies**. *Italian States*.

Bophuthatswana a tribal homeland within South Africa. South African (1977–94). Stamps are inscribed **Bophuthatswana**. *South Africa (Bophuthatswana)*.

Bosna I Hercegovina see **Bosnia and Herzegovina (Croat)** or **Bosnia and Herzegovina (Muslim)**.

Bosnia and Herzegovina in southeastern Europe on the Balkan Peninsula, bordered on the north and west by Croatia, on the east by Serbia, on the south by Montenegro, and on the west by the Adriatic Sea. Austro-Hungarian (1879–1918). Inscriptions include **Bosnien Hercegowina** (1906–12), **Bosnien Hercegovina** with "K-u-K Militärpost" (1912–18). Bosnia and Herzegovina was absorbed by Yugoslavia after World War I. It reemerged after the breakup of Yugoslavia but remained in a state of civil conflict until the Dayton Accord of 1995 and the subsequent presence of NATO peacekeeping forces. Croat, Muslim, and Serb factions have each issued postage stamps. See also **Bosnia and Herzegovina (Croat)**, **Bosnia and Herzegovina (Muslim)**, and **Bosnia and Herzegovina (Serb)**.

Bosnia and Herzegovina (Croat) (1993→). Inscriptions include **Republika Bosna I Hercegovina** (1993), **Bosna I Hercegovina** sometimes with "Hrvatska Republika Herceg Bosna" or "HR Herceg Bosna" (1993→).

Bosnia and Herzegovina (Muslim) (1993→). Inscriptions include **Republika Bosna I Hercegovina** (1993–95), **Bosna I Hercegovina** (1995→).

Bosnia and Herzegovina (Serb) (1992→). Inscriptions include **РЕПУБЛИКА СРПСКА** either overprinted on stamps of Yugoslavia or inscribed (1992→).

Bosnien Hercegovina Bosnia and Herzegovina. See **Bosnia and Herzegovina**.

Bosnien Hercegowina Bosnia and Herzegovina. See **Bosnia and Herzegovina**.

Botswana in central South Africa, bordered on the north and northwest by Namibia, on the north and northeast by Zambia and Zimbabwe, and on the south and southeast by South Africa. Independent (1966→). **Botswana** (1966→), **Republic of Botswana** overprinted on stamps of Bechuanaland Protectorate (1966). Prior to independence, Botswana was Bechuanaland Protectorate.

Boyaca a department (state) in central Colombia. Local issues (1902–04). Inscriptions include **Colombia-Boyaca** (1902), **Departmento de Boyaca** (1903), **Dep^{TO} de Boyaca** (1904); all of the preceding with "Colombia" or "Republica de Colombia." *Colombia.*

Brasil Brazil. See **Brazil**.

Braunschweig Brunswick. See **Brunswick**.

Brazil the largest country in South America, bordered on the north by Venezuela, Guyana, Suriname, French Guiana, and the Atlantic Ocean, on the east by the Atlantic, on the south by Uruguay, and on the west by Peru, Bolivia, Paraguay, and Argentina. Independent (1843→). Inscriptions include numeral and scrollwork (1844–66), **Brazil** (1866–90 and occasionally 1890–1910),

Estados Unidos do Brazil or **E.U. do Brazil** (1890–1910), **Brasil** (1918→); and any of the preceding with "Correio."

Bremen   a city in northwestern Germany, capital of the state of Bremen. Inscriptions include **Bremen** (1855–1870), **Franco Marke** together with denomination in "grote" (1859–61). *German States.*

Briefmarke Wendenschen Kreises   Wenden. See **Wenden**.

British Antarctic Territory   a territory consisting of the South Orkney Islands, the South Shetland Islands, and a portion of the Antarctic mainland including the Antarctic Peninsula. British (1963→). Stamps are inscribed **British Antarctic Territory**. The territory is populated only by scientists and staff of British Antarctic Survey stations and bases. British Antarctic Territory was formerly part of the Falkland Islands Dependencies.

British Bechuanaland   in southern central Africa. British (1886–97). Inscriptions include **British Bechuanaland** overprinted on stamps of the Cape of Good Hope (1886–1897), inscribed (1887–97). British Bechuanaland was that part of Bechuanaland Protectorate south of the Molopo River. *Bechuanaland.*

British Central Africa   in central Africa on the west shore of Lake Nyasa (Lake Malawi), bordered on the north by Tanzania, on the south and southeast by Mozambique. British (1891–1907). Inscriptions include **B.C.A.** overprinted on stamps of Rhodesia (1891–95), **British Central Africa** (1895–1903), **British Central Africa Protectorate** (1903–08). In 1908 British Central Africa became the Nyasaland Protectorate, and in 1964, independent Malawi.

British Columbia and Vancouver Island   on the northwest coast of North America just north of the state of Washington. British (1860–71). Inscriptions include **British Columbia - Vancouver Island** (1860–65), **British Columbia** (British Columbia, 1865–71), **Vancouver Island** (Vancouver Island, 1865–71). In 1871 British Columbia and Vancouver Island became part of the Confederation of Canada. *Canadian Provinces.*

British East Africa   in east Africa, composed primarily of Kenya, Uganda, and Tanganyika. British (1890–1904). Inscriptions include **British East Africa Company** overprinted on stamps of Great Britain (1890), **Imperial British East Africa Company** (1890–95), **British East Africa** overprinted on stamps of earlier issues (1895), overprinted on stamps of India (1895–96), or overprinted on stamps of Zanzibar (1897), **British East Africa Protectorate** (1896–1904).

British Guiana   on the northeast coast of South America bordered on the north by the Atlantic Ocean, on the east by Suriname, on the south and west by Brazil, and on the west by Venezuela. British (1850–1966). Stamps are inscribed **British Guiana** and occasionally, **B. Guiana**. In 1966 British Guiana became independent Guyana.

British Honduras   in northeastern Central America, bordered on the north and northwest by Mexico, on the east by the Caribbean Sea, and on the south and west by Guatemala. British (1866–1973). Stamps are inscribed **British Honduras** and occasionally, **Br. Honduras**. In 1973 British Honduras changed its name to Belize. In 1981 it became independent.

British Indian Ocean Territory   a group of small islands in the central Indian Ocean, including Diego Garcia. British (1968→). Inscriptions include **B.I.O.T.** overprinted on stamps of Seychelles (1968), **British Indian Ocean Territory** (1968→).

British New Guinea   see **Papua New Guinea**.

British North Borneo   see **North Borneo**.

British Occupation   overprinted, together with surcharged value, on stamps of Russia: Batum. See **Batum**.

British Protectorate - Oil Rivers   overprinted on stamps of Great Britain: Niger Coast Protectorate. See **Niger Coast Protectorate**.

British Solomon Islands   see **Solomon Islands**.

British Solomon Islands Protectorate   see **Solomon Islands**.

British Somaliland   overprinted on stamps of India: Somaliland Protectorate. See **Somaliland Protectorate**.

British South Africa Company   see **Rhodesia (British)**.

British Virgin Islands   a group of small islands east of Puerto Rico, between the Atlantic Ocean and the Caribbean Sea, forming part of the Lesser Antilles and including the islands of Tortola, Virgin Gorda, Anegada, Jost Van Dyke, Peter Islands, and Salt Island. British (1866→). Inscriptions include **Virgin Islands** (1866–1968), **British Virgin Islands** (1951, 1968→), and occasionally, **Br. Virgin Islands** or **British Virgin Is.** *Virgin Islands*.

Brunei   a small country on the north coast of the island of Borneo, bordered on the north by the South China Sea and on all other sides by Sarawak. British (1888–1983), independent (1983→). Inscriptions include **Brunei** overprinted on stamps of Labuan (1906–07) or inscribed (1907–84), **Brunei Darussalam** (1984→).

Brunswick   a city and state in north-central Germany. Stamps are inscribed **Braunschweig** (1852–68). *German States*.

Br. Virgin Islands   see **British Virgin Islands**. *Virgin Islands*.

Buenos Aires   a city and province in Argentina. Independent (1858–62). Stamps are inscribed **Buenos Aires**. *Argentina*.

Buiten Bezit. (outlying territories) overprinted on stamps of Netherlands Indies: Netherlands Indies. *Netherlands Indies.*

Bulgaria in southeastern Europe in the Balkans, bordered on the north by Romania, on the east by the Black Sea, on the south by Turkey and Greece, and on the west by Serbia, Montenegro, and Macedonia. Independent (1879→). Inscriptions include **БЪЛГАРИЯ** or **БЪЛГАРИЯ** (1879→, sometimes with **Н.Р.** preceding or **пОША** following), **ЦАРСтВО БЪЛГАРИЯ** (occasionally, 1937–45), **Bulgarie** (occasionally, 1930s and 1940s), **Bulgaria** or **N.R. Bulgaria** (1945→), **Republika Bulgaria** (1947).

Bundi State or **Bundi State Postage** Bundi, a native feudatory state in west-central India. *India (native feudatory states).*

Bureau International d'Education overprinted on stamps of Switzerland or inscribed together with "Helvetia": International Bureau of Education. *Switzerland (official issues).*

Bureau International du Travail overprinted on stamps of Switzerland or inscribed together with "Helvetia": International Labor Bureau. *Switzerland (official issues).*

Burkina Faso in western Africa, bordered on the north and west by Mali, on the east by Niger, and on the south by Benin, Togo, Ghana, and the Ivory Coast (Côte d'Ivoire). Independent (1984→). Stamps are inscribed **Burkina Faso.** Burkina Faso was formerly Upper Volta.

Burma in Asia on the Indian subcontinent, bordered on the east by Laos and Thailand, on the northeast by China, and on the west by Bangladesh. British (1937–48), independent (1948→). Inscriptions include **Burma** overprinted on stamps of Burma (1937–38) or inscribed (1938–48), **Union of Burma** (1948–73), **Socialist Republic of the Union of Burma** (1973–89), **Union of Myanmar** (1989→).

Burundi a tiny landlocked country in eastern Africa, bordered on the north by Rwanda, on the east and south by Tanzania, and on the west by the Democratic Republic of the Congo and Lake Tanganyika. Independent (1962→). Prior to independence and together with Rwanda, a UN trusteeship (Ruanda-Urundi). Inscriptions include **Royaume du Burundi** (1962–66), **République du Burundi** or **Burundi** (1966→).

Bushire a port on the Persian Gulf in Iran. British occupation (1915). Inscriptions include **Bushire Under British Occupation** overprinted on stamps of Iran. Great Britain issued stamps for Bushire for a few weeks in 1915.

Bussahir State Bussahir, an Indian feudatory state. *India (native feudatory states).*

B - Vale overprinted on stamps of Nicaragua: province of Zelaya. *Nicaragua.*

C1.H.S.   overprinted on stamps of Germany: Upper Silesia. See **Upper Silesia**.

Cabo   overprinted on stamps of Nicaragua: province of Cabo Gracias a Dios. *Nicaragua*.

Cabo Jubi   overprinted on stamps of Rio de Oro: Cape Juby. See **Cape Juby**.

Cabo Juby   overprinted on stamps of Spain or Spanish Morocco: Cape Juby. See **Cape Juby**.

Cabo Verde   Cape Verde. See **Cape Verde**.

Caicos Islands   see **Turks and Caicos Islands**.

Calimno   overprinted on stamps of Italy. See **Dodecanese Islands**. *Italy (Aegean Islands)*.

Camb Aust Sigillum Nov   New South Wales. See **New South Wales**.

Cambodge   Cambodia. See **Cambodia**.

Cambodia   in southeast Asia, bordered on the north by China and Vietnam, on the east by Vietnam, on the south by Cambodia, and on the west by Thailand. Independent (1951→). Stamps are inscribed **Royaume du Cambodge** or **Cambodge** (1951–70, 1993→), **République Khmere** (1970–82), **République Populaire du Kampuchea** (1982–84), **R.P. Kampuchea** (1984–89), **Etat du Cambodge** (1989–93), **Cambodia** (1993). Cambodia was formerly part of Indochina.

Cameroons   in western Africa, the northern section of the former German colony Kamerun (see **Cameroun**) occupied by Great Britain during World War I and administered by it following the war. British (1915-, 1960). Inscriptions include **C.E.F.** overprinted on stamps of Kamerun (1915-), **Cameroons U.K.T.T.** overprinted on stamps of Nigeria (1960). In 1960 the British held a plebiscite in which the northern section elected to join Nigeria; the southern (French-administered) section became the independent Republic of Cameroun.

Cameroons U.K.T.T.   (Cameroons United Kingdom Trust Territory) overprinted on stamps of Nigeria: Cameroons. See **Cameroons**.

Cameroun (or **Cameroon**)   in western Africa, bordered on the north by Lake Chad, on the east by Chad and the Central African Republic, on the south by the Republic of the Congo, Gabon, and Equatorial Guinea, and on the west by Nigeria. German (1897–1916), French/British (1915–60), independent (1960→). Inscriptions include **Kamerun** overprinted on stamps of Germany (1897–1900) or inscribed (1900–16), **C.E.F.** overprinted on stamps of Kamerun (British occupation, 1915), **Corps Expéditionnarie Franco-Anglais Cameroun** overprinted on stamps of Gabon (French occupation, 1915), **Occupation Francaise du Cameroun** overprinted on stamps of the Middle Congo or French

Congo (French occupation, 1916), **Cameroun - Occupation Française** over-printed on stamps of the Middle Congo (French occupation, 1916–21), **Cameroun** overprinted on stamps of the Middle Congo (1921–24) or inscribed (1924–60), **Etat du Cameroun** (1960), **République Federale du Cameroun** (1961–72), **République Unie du Cameroun** (1972–83), **République du Cameroun** (1984–93), **Republic of Cameroon** (1993→). During World War I, British and French forces occupied Kamerun. Under a League of Nations mandate, the southern section (about 80 percent of the colony) was assigned to the French; the northern section was assigned to Great Britain. In 1960 the French section (Cameroun) achieved independence as the Republic of Cameroun. The British section (the Cameroons) elected to join Nigeria. See also **Cameroons**.

Canada in North America, north of the United States. British (1851–67), confederation (1867→). Inscriptions include **Canada**, often with "Postage" or "Postes" (1867→).

Canal Zone a narrow strip of territory on either side of the Panama Canal, which runs through Panama from the Caribbean Sea to the Pacific Ocean. United States (1904–79). Inscriptions include **Canal Zone - Panama** overprinted on stamps of Panama (1904–06), **Canal Zone** overprinted on stamps of Panama or the United States (1906–28) or inscribed (1928–79). Most of the Canal Zone was turned over to Panama in 1979; the remainder was turned over in 1999.

Canarias overprinted on stamps of Spain: Canary Islands. *Spain.*

Cancelled V-R-I. overprinted on stamps inscribed "Z. Afr. Republiek" or "Zuid Afrikaansche Republiek": Transvaal. See **Transvaal**.

Canouan together with "Saint Vincent of Grenadines": *Saint Vincent Grenadines.*

Canton overprinted on stamps of Indochina: French offices in Canton, China. *France (offices abroad).*

Cape Juby in North Africa, located in Spanish Sahara. Spanish (1926–42). Inscriptions include **Cabo Jubi** overprinted on stamps of Rio de Oro, **Cabo Juby** or **Cabo-Juby** overprinted on stamps of Spain or Spanish Morocco.

Cape of Good Hope (or Cape Colony) occupies the southern part of what is now South Africa. British (1853–1910). Inscriptions include **Cape of Good Hope** (1853–1910). In 1910 the Cape of Good Hope (or Cape Province) became part of the Union of South Africa.

Cape Verde a group of small islands in the Atlantic Ocean about 375 miles west of Mauritania. Portuguese (1877–1975), independent (1975→). Inscriptions include **Cabo Verde** often with "Correio," "Portugal," "Correio Portugal," or "Republica Portuguesa." (1877→), **Provincia de Cabo Verde** (1886–94),

Republica Cabo Verde overprinted (1913).

Carchi overprinted on stamps of Italy. See **Dodecanese Islands**. *Italy (Aegean Islands)*.

Caroline Islands an archipelago in the western Pacific Ocean near the equator, encompassing more than 600 islands, atolls, and islets, spread out over about 450 square miles, and including Palau, Truk, Kosrae, Ponape, and Yap. German (1899–1919). Inscriptions include **Karolinen** either overprinted on stamps of Germany or inscribed (1899–1919). The Caroline Islands were placed under Japanese mandate following World War I, made a U.S. trust territory following World War II, and subsequently became the Federated States of Micronesia and the Republic of Palau. The Caroline Islands used stamps of Japan while under Japanese control and stamps of the United States until it became the Federated States of Micronesia and the Republic of Palau.

Caso overprinted on stamps of Italy. See **Dodecanese Islands**. *Italy (Aegean Islands)*.

Castellorizo a small island (Kastellórizon) in the Mediterranean just off the southwest coast of Turkey near the city of Kas. French (1920–22), Italian (1922–30s). Inscriptions include **B.N.F. Castellorizo** overprinted on stamps of French offices in Turkey (1920), **O.N.F. Castellorizo** overprinted on stamps of French offices in Turkey (1920), **O.F. Castelloriso** overprinted on stamps of France (1920–22), **Castelrosso** overprinted on stamps of Italy (1922–30s), **Occupazione Italiana Castelrosso** (1923).

Castelrosso Castellorizo. See **Castellorizo**.

Cavalle overprinted on stamps of France or inscribed together with "République Française": French offices in Cavalle. *France (offices in Turkey)*.

Cayes of Belize small islands off the coast of Belize. Belize (1984–85). Stamps are inscribed **Cayes of Belize**. *Belize*.

Cayman Islands in the West Indies, in the Caribbean Sea, consisting of three islands: Grand Cayman, located northwest of Jamaica, and Little Cayman and Cayman Brac, located about 80 miles northeast of Grand Cayman. British (1900→). Stamps are inscribed **Cayman Islands**.

CCCP or **CCCP-USSR** Union of Soviet Socialist Republics. See **Russia**.

C. Ch. and **5** overprinted on stamps of French colonies: Cochin China. See **Cochin China**.

C - Dpto. Zelaya overprinted on stamps of Nicaragua: for use in the province of Cabo Gracias a Dios. *Nicaragua*.

Čechy a Morava see **Bohemia and Moravia**.

C.E.F. (Cameroons Expeditionary Force) overprinted on stamps of Kamerun: Cameroun, Cameroons. See **Cameroun**, **Cameroons**.

Centenario de S. Antonio - Inhambane - MDCCCXV overprinted on stamps of Mozambique: Inhambane. See **Inhambane**.

Central African Republic in central Africa, bordered on the north by Chad, on the east by Sudan, on the south by the Republic of the Congo and the Democratic Republic of the Congo, and on the west by Cameroon. Independent (1959→). Inscriptions include **République Centrafricaine** (1959–76, 1979→). **Empire Centrafricaine** (1976–79). Prior to independence, Central Africa was part of French Equatorial Africa.

Česká Republika Czech Republic. See **Czechoslovakia**.

Česko-Slovenska Czechoslovakia. See **Czechoslovakia**.

Česko-Slovensko Czechoslovakia. See **Czechoslovakia**.

Ceylon an island in the Indian Ocean off the southeastern coast of India. British (1857–1972). Stamps are inscribed **Ceylon**. In 1972 Ceylon became independent Sri Lanka.

CFA overprinted on the generic issue for French colonies: Reunion. See **Reunion**.

C.G.H.S. (Commission de Gouvernement - Haute Silesia) overprinted on stamps of Germany: Upper Silesia. See **Upper Silesia**.

CH preceding a string of Korean characters: Korea. *Korea.*

Chad in north-central Africa, bordered on the north by Libya, on the east by Sudan, on the south by the Central African Republic, and on the west by Cameroon, Nigeria, and Niger. French (1922–34), independent (1958→). Inscriptions include **Tchad** overprinted on stamps of Middle Congo (1922), **Tchad** and "Afrique Équatorial Française" overprinted on stamps of Middle Congo (1924–34), **République du Tchad** (1959→). In 1934 Chad became part of French Equatorial Africa and used its stamps until 1958.

Chaimite on stamps inscribed "Portugal" and "Colonia de Moçambique." *Mozambique (postal tax).*

Chala overprinted on stamps of Peru: Chala, a town on the Pacific Coast in the Chala area of southern Peru. *Peru (provisional issues).*

Chamba or **Chamba State** overprinted on stamps of India: Chamba state, a state in northern India. *India (convention states).*

Charkhari State P.O. (or **C.I.**) Charkhari, a native feudatory state in northern India. *India (native feudatory states).*

Chile in southwestern South America, bordered on the north by Peru, on the east by Bolivia and Argentina, and on the west and south by the Pacific Ocean. Independent (1853→). Inscriptions include **Chile** with "Colon" (1853–99) and often with "Correos" (1899→).

China in east Asia, bordered on the northwest by Kyrgyzstan and Kazakstan, on the north by the Republic of Mongolia and Russia, on the northeast by Russia and North Korea, on the east by the Yellow Sea and the East China Sea, on the south by the South China Sea, Vietnam, Laos, Myanmar (Burma), India, Bhutan, and Nepal, and on the west by Pakistan, Afghanistan, and Tajikistan. Independent (1878→). Inscriptions include **China** (1878–97), **Imperial Chinese Post** (1897), **Chinese Imperial Post** (1898–1910), **Chinese Empire** (1909), **Republic of China** (1912→). From about 1923 to 1950, most stamps of the Republic of China are inscribed only with Chinese characters. In addition, overprints from this period, in a wide variety of Chinese characters, are abundant. In 1949 China split into the People's Republic of China, which occupied the mainland, and the Republic of China, which fled to Taiwan. Most stamps of the People's Republic of China are inscribed only with Chinese characters until 1991, when it began adding the inscription **China**. The Republic of China (Taiwan) inscribes its stamps **Republic of China**. A number of foreign nations, among them, France, Germany, Great Britain, Russia, and the United States, maintained post offices in China during the era of the treaty ports, some remaining in operation until the early 1920s.

China (1) overprinted on stamps of Germany: German offices in China, *Germany (offices abroad)*; see **Kiachau**. (2) overprinted on stamps of Germany together with surcharged value "5 Pfg.": Kiachau (Tsingtao).

Chine overprinted on stamps of France or Indochina: French offices in China. *France (offices abroad)*.

Christmas Island an island in the Indian Ocean, south of the western tip of Java. Australian (1958→). Inscriptions include **Christmas Island** (1958–77), **Christmas Island** and "Indian Ocean" (1978–92), **Christmas Island** together with "Australia" (1992→).

Cilicia a small enclave between Syria and Turkey extending along the north and northeast shores of the Gulf of Iskenderun (Gulf of Alexandretta). French occupation (1919–23). Inscriptions include **Cilicie** overprinted on stamps of Turkey (1919), **T.E.O.** overprinted on stamps of Turkey (1920), **T.E.O. Cilicie** overprinted on stamps of Turkey (1919), **Occupation Militaire Française Cilicie** overprinted on stamps of Turkey (1920), **O.M.F. Cilicie - Sand. Est** overprinted on stamps of France (1920), **O.M.F. Cilicie** overprinted on stamps of France (1920–23). Cilicia is now part of Turkey.

Cilicie   Cilicia. See **Cilicia**.

Cirenaica   Cyrenaica. See **Cyrenaica**.

C•I•S   overprinted on stamps inscribed "Slesvig": Schleswig. See **Schleswig**.

Ciskei   a tribal homeland within South Africa. South African (1981–94). Stamps are inscribed **Ciskei**. *South Africa (Ciskei)*.

Città del Vaticano   Vatican City. See **Vatican City**.

Coamo   together with "Correos": Puerto Rico. See **Puerto Rico**.

Cochin or **Cochin Anchal**   Cochin, a native feudatory state located near the southern tip of India. *India (native feudatory states)*.

Cochin China   in southeast Asia, the Mekong Delta area of Vietnam. French (1886–92). Inscriptions include the numeral **5** either by itself or with **C. Ch.** overprinted on stamps of French colonies (1888–92). Cochin China subsequently used stamps of French Indochina.

Co. Ci.   (Commissariato Civile) overprinted on stamps of Yugoslavia: Ljubljana (Italian occupation). See **Ljubljana**. *Yugoslavia (Ljubljana)*.

Cocos (Keeling) Islands   a group of islands in the eastern Indian Ocean. Australian (1963→). Stamps are inscribed **Cocos (Keeling) Islands**.

Colombia   in northwestern South America, bordered on the north by Panama and the Caribbean Sea, on the east by Venezuela and Brazil, on the south by Peru and Ecuador, and on the west by the Pacific Ocean. Independent (1859→). Inscriptions include **Confed. Granadina** (1859–61), **Estados Unidos de Nueva Granada** (1861), **Estados Unidos de Colombia** (1861–80s), **E.U. de Colombia** (1862–85), **E^E U^U de Colombia** (1870s–86), **Republica de Colombia** (1886–1925), **Colombia**, often with "Correos de" until the mid-1960s (1925→).

Colombia   inscribed together with a map of Panama: Panama. See **Panama**.

Colombia-Boyaca   see **Boyaca**. *Colombia*.

Colonia de Moçambique   Mozambique. See **Mozambique**.

Colonia de Rio de Oro   Rio de Oro. See **Rio de Oro**.

Colonia Eritrea   Eritrea. See **Eritrea**.

Colonie Italiane   **(1)** together with the name of the colony: refer to the named colony; **(2)** on stamps with no colony named: general issues for use in any colony *(Italian Colonies)*.

Colonie Italiane - Eritrea   Eritrea. See **Eritrea**.

Colonie Italiane - Poste Somalia   Somalia. See **Somalia**.

Colonies D'Empire Française   an inscription on stamps available for general use in various French colonies (1859–71). *French Colonies.*

Colonies Postes - République Française   inscribed on issues of French colonies from about 1877 to the early 1900s, **(1)** without the name of a specific colony: generic issue for use in any colony: *French Colonies*; **(2)** with the name of specific colony: for use in the named colony.

Colonie Suriname   Suriname. See **Suriname.**

Comité Français de la Libération Nationale   an inscription on some stamps issued by the Free French in overseas colonies during World War II. *French Colonies.*

Commissariato Gen^LE Dell Oltre Giuba   Oltre Giuba. See **Oltre Giuba.**

Commission d'Administration et de Plebescite   overprinted in an oval on stamps of Germany: Allenstein. See **Allenstein.**

Commission de Contrôie Provisoire - Korca   Albania. See **Albania.**

Commission de Gouvernement - Haute Silesie   Upper Silesia. See **Upper Silesia.**

Commission Interallée Marienwerder   either overprinted on stamps of Germany or inscribed: Marienwerder. See **Marienwerder.**

Commonwealth of Dominica   see **Dominica.**

Comoro Islands   a group of islands located in the Mozambique Channel about midway between Mozambique and Madagascar, including Anjouan, Grande Comore, Mayotte, and Mohéli. French (1950–75), independent (1975→). Inscriptions include **Archipel des Comores** (1950–75), **Etat Comorien** (1975–78) and **République Federale Islamique des Comores** (1978–98), **République Islamique des Comores** (1998→). Mayotte opted to remain French at the time the other three islands elected to become independent.

Compa de Moçambique   Mozambique Company. See **Mozambique Company.**

Companhia de Moçambique   Mozambique Company. See **Mozambique Company.**

Companhia do Nyassa   Nyassa Company. See **Nyassa.**

Compañia Colombiana de Navegacion Aerea   a private firm under Colombian government contract to carry airmail during the years 1920 to 1932 and which issued stamps inscribed **Compañia Colombiana de Navegacion Aerea.** *Colombia.*

Comunicaciones   with bust of monarch or coat of arms: Spain. See **Spain.**

Comunicaciones España   Spain. See **Spain.**

Condominium des Nouvelles Hebrides   New Hebrides. See **New Hebrides.**

Confederate States a confederation of 11 Southern states during the American Civil War (1861–65). Inscriptions include **Confederate States of America**, **Confederate States**, **C.S.A. Postage**, and **C.S.** The Confederacy included Alabama, Arkansas, Florida, Georgia, Louisiana, Mississippi, North Carolina, South Carolina, Tennessee, Texas, and Virginia.

Confed. Granadina Grenadine Confederation: Colombia. See **Colombia**.

Confoederatio Helvetica Switzerland. See **Switzerland**.

Congo (1) overprinted on stamps of the Belgian Congo: Democratic Republic of the Congo. See **Congo (Democratic Republic)**; (2) inscribed: Republic of the Congo. See **Congo (Republic of)**.

Congo Belge Belgian Congo. See **Belgian Congo**.

Congo (Belgian) in central Africa, bordered on the northwest by the Republic of the Congo, on the north by the Central African Republic and Sudan, on the east by Uganda, Rwanda, Burundi, and Lake Tanganyika, on the south by Zambia, and on the southwest by Angola. Nominally independent as the Congo Free State under the sovereignty of King Leopold of Belgium (1886–1908), Belgian (1908–60). Inscriptions include **État Independant** (or **Ind.**) **du Congo** (1886–1908), **Congo Belge** either overprinted on the foregoing or inscribed (1908–10), **Congo Belge - Belgisch Congo** (1910–60). In 1960 the Belgian Congo became the Democratic Republic of the Congo, which, for a time, was known as Zaire.

Congo (Democratic Republic) in central Africa, bordered on the northwest by the Republic of the Congo, on the north by the Central African Republic and Sudan, on the east by Uganda, Rwanda, Burundi, and Lake Tanganyika, on the south by Zambia, and on the southwest by Angola. Independent (1960→). Inscriptions include **Congo** overprinted on stamps of the Belgian Congo (1960), **République du Congo** (1960–64), **République Democratique du Congo** (1964–78), **Republique du Zaire** (or **Zaïre**) (1971–79), **Zaire** (1978–97), **République Democratique du Congo** (1997→). The Democratic Republic of the Congo was formerly the Belgian Congo.

Congo (Republic of) in west-central Africa, bordered on the west by Gabon, on the north by Cameroon and the Central African Republic, on the east and south by the Democratic Republic of the Congo, on the southwest by Angola and the Atlantic Ocean. Independent (1960→). Inscriptions include **République du Congo** (1960–70, 1993→), **République Populaire du Congo** (1970–91), **Congo** (1991–93). The Republic of the Congo was formerly the Middle Congo; then later part of French Equatorial Africa.

Congo Belge-Belgisch Congo Belgian Congo. See **Congo (Belgian)**.

Congo Français   overprinted or inscribed: French Congo. See **French Congo**.

Congo Française Gabon   Gabon. See **Gabon**.

Congo Republica   overprinted on stamps of Angola or Portuguese colonies: Portuguese Congo. See **Portuguese Congo**.

Conseil de L'Europe   inscribed together with "République Française" or "France": Council of Europe in Paris. *France (official issues)*.

Consumptives Home   see **New South Wales**.

Contra Sello   overprinted on stamps of El Salvador: El Salvador. *El Salvador*.

Contrasena - Estampillas de Correo   overprinted on stamps of Venezuela: Venezuela. *Venezuela*.

Cook Islands   two groups of widely scattered islands in the southern Pacific Ocean, northeast of New Zealand. The northern group includes Pukapuka, Penrhyn, Manihiki, Palmerston, Rakahanga, Suwarrow, and Nassau; the southern group includes Raratonga, Aitutaki, Atiu, Mangaia, Mauke, Mitiaro, Manuae, and Takutea. New Zealand (1892→). Inscriptions include **Cook Islands Federation** (1892), **Cook Islands** overprinted on stamps of New Zealand (1946) or inscribed (1893–1920, 1932→), **Raratonga** overprinted on stamps of New Zealand (1919–1936), **Cook Is'ds.** overprinted on stamps of New Zealand (1937). In 1965 the Cook Islands became self-governing in free association with New Zealand.

Coolela   on stamps inscribed "Portugal" and "Colonia de Moçambique": *Mozambique (postal tax)*.

Cordoba   a province in central Argentina. Stamps are inscribed **Cordoba**. *Argentina*.

Corean   Korea. See **Korea (South)**.

Corfu   a Greek island in the northern Ionian Sea, separated from Greece by a narrow channel. Italian occupation (1923, 1941–43). Inscriptions include **Corfù** overprinted on stamps of Italy (1923), **Corfu** overprinted on stamps of Greece (1941–43).

Corps Expéditionnarie Franco-Anglais Cameroun   overprinted on stamps of Gabon: Cameroun. See **Cameroun**.

Correio or **Correios**   often accompanying a country's name. Refer to the country name.

Correio de Lourenço Marques overprinted on revenue stamps of Mozambique: Lourenço Marques. See **Lourenço Marques**.

Correio de Portugal   Portugal. See **Portugal**.

Correio de Timor   Timor. See **Timor**.

Correio India   Portuguese India. See **Portuguese India**.

Correio Macau   Macao. See **Macao**.

Correios da Colonia de Moçambique   Mozambique. See **Mozambique**.

Correios Portugal - Congo   Portuguese Congo. See **Portuguese Congo**.

Correios Portugal Continente   Portugal. See **Portugal**.

Correios Portugal - Moçambique   Mozambique. See **Mozambique**.

Correios Portugal - Timor   Timor. See **Timor**.

Correios Portugal - Zambezia   Zambezia. See **Zambezia**.

Correio - Timor   Timor. See **Timor**.

Correo or **Correos**   often accompanying a country's name. Refer to the country name.

Correo de Ayacucho   overprinted on provisional issues of Arequipa: Ayacucho, a city in south-central Peru, west of Cuzco. *Peru (provisional issues)*.

Correo de Venezuela   Venezuela. See **Venezuela**.

Correo Español Marruecos   overprinted on stamps of Spain: Spanish Morocco. See **Spanish Morocco**.

Correo Español Tanger   overprinted on stamps of Spain: Tangier. See **Tangier** *(Spanish Morocco)*.

Correos   overprinted on revenue stamps of Spain together with surcharged value expressed in centavos (or "c." or "cent." often with "de Peso"): Fernando Po. *Fernando Po*.

Correos   together with bust of Simón Bolívar: Venezuela. See **Venezuela**.

Correos de Antioquia   Antioquia. See **Antioquia**. *Colombia*.

Correos de Bolivar   see **Bolivar**. *Colombia*.

Correos de El Salvador   El Salvador. See **El Salvador**.

Correos de España   Spain. See **Spain**.

Correos de Guatemala   Guatemala. See **Guatemala**.

Correos de Honduras   Honduras. See **Honduras**.

Correos del Eº Uº de Bolivar   see **Bolivar**. *Colombia*.

Correo del OSEEUU de Venezuela   Venezuela. See **Venezuela**.

Correos del Paraguay   Paraguay. See **Paraguay**.

Correos del Peru   Peru. See **Peru**.

Correos del Salvador   El Salvador. See **El Salvador**.

Correos del Uruguay   Uruguay. See **Uruguay**.

Correos de Nicaragua   Nicaragua. See **Nicaragua**.

Correos de Venezuela   Venezuela. See **Venezuela**.

Correos E.E.U.U. de Venezuela   Venezuela. See **Venezuela**.

Correos El Salvador or **Correos El Salvador Centro America** (or **C.A.**) El Salvador. See **El Salvador**.

Correos Marruecos - Protectorado Español   Spanish Morocco. See **Spanish Morocco**.

Correos Mexico   Mexico. See **Mexico**.

Correos Mexico - Gobierno Revolucierno   Yucatan. *Mexico (revolutionary issues)*.

Correos Nacionales (or **Nales**)   together with "Estados Unidos de Nueva Granada" or the country name "Colombia": Colombia. See **Colombia**.

Correos Peru   Peru. See **Peru**.

Correos Sonora   Sonora. See **Mexico**.

Correos Transitorio - Estado Libre y Soberano Oaxaca   Oaxaca. See **Mexico**.

Correos Uruguay   Uruguay. See **Uruguay**.

Correos y Teleg^S or **Teleg^{FOS}**   Spain. See **Spain**.

Correo Urbano de Bogota   see **Bogota**. *Colombia*.

Corrientes   a province in northeast Argentina. Stamps are inscribed **Corrientes**. *Argentina*.

Cos   overprinted on stamps of Italy. See **Dodecanese Islands**. *Italy (Aegean Islands)*.

Costa Atlantica - B   overprinted on stamps of Nicaragua: province of Zelaya. *Nicaragua*.

Costa Atlantica - C   overprinted on stamps of Nicaragua: province of Cabo Gracias a Dios. *Nicaragua*.

Costantinopoli   overprinted on stamps of Italy: Italian offices in Constantinople, a city in the Turkish Empire. *Italy (offices abroad)*.

Costa Rica   in southern Central America, bordered on the north by Nicaragua and on the south by Panama. Independent (1863→). Inscriptions include **Costa Rica** often with "Correos" and occasionally with "Republica de" (1863→).

Côte d'Ivoire   Ivory Coast. See **Ivory Coast**.

Côte Française des Somalis   Somali Coast. See **Somali Coast**.

Côte Frse des Somalis   Somali Coast. See **Somali Coast**.

Cour International de Justice   (International Court of Justice) overprinted on stamps of the Netherlands or inscribed. See **Netherlands**. *Netherlands (official issues)*.

Cour Permanente de Justice International   (International Court of Justice) overprinted on stamps of the Netherlands. See **Netherlands**. *Netherlands (official issues)*.

Courrier de la Sociéte des Nations   overprinted on stamps of Switzerland: League of Nations. *Switzerland (official issues)*.

Courrier du Bureau International d'Education   overprinted on stamps of Switzerland: International Bureau of Education. *Switzerland (official issues)*.

Courrier du Bureau International du Travail   overprinted on stamps of Switzerland: International Labor Bureau. *Switzerland (official issues)*.

Courrier du Bureau Internationau d'Education   overprinted on stamps of Switzerland: International Bureau of Education. *Switzerland (official issues)*.

Crete   an island in the Mediterranean, southeast of Greece. Under international administration (1898–1913). Inscriptions include **ΠΡΟΣΩΡΙΝΟΝ ΤΑΧΥΔΡΟΜ ΗΡΑΚΔΕΙΟΝ** (British sector, 1898–99), **ΡΕΘΥΜΝΗΣ ΠΡΟΕΩΡ ΤΑΧΥΔΡ** (Russian sector, 1899), **ΠΡΟΣΩΡΙΝΟΝ ΤΑΧΥΛΙ ΟΜΕΙΟΝ ΡΕΟΥΜΝΗΣ** (Russian sector, 1899), **Retymno Timbre Poste Provisoir** (Russian sector, 1899), **Kphta** either by itself or overprinted "**ΕΛΛΑΣ**" or "**ΕΛΛΑΣ ΠΡΟΣΟΡΙΝΟΝ**" (1900–13). In 1913 Crete became part of Greece. Crete was occupied by Germany from 1941 to 1945.

Crete   inscribed together with "République Française": French offices in Crete. *France (offices in Crete)*.

Croatia   in southeastern Europe, on the Balkan Peninsula, bordered on the north by Slovenia and Hungary, on the east and south by Bosnia and Herzegovina, on the east by Serbia, and on the west by the Adriatic Sea. Nominally independent (1941–45), independent (1991→). Inscriptions include **Nezavisna Država Hrvatska** overprinted on stamps of Yugoslavia (1941) or inscribed (1941–45), **Nez Drž Hrvatska** (1941–45), **N.D. Hrvatska** (1941–45), **Republika Hrvatska** (1991→). Following World War II, Croatia became a constituent republic of Yugoslavia. In 1991 it gained independence following the breakup of Yugoslavia.

Croissant Rouge Turc   inscription on postal tax stamp: Turkey. *Turkey (postal tax)*.

C.S.   Confederate States. See **Confederate States**.

C.S.A.   Confederate States of America. See **Confederate States**.

Cuba an island in the West Indies, south of Florida. Spanish (1855–1989), U.S. occupation (1898–1902), independent (1902→). Inscriptions include **Correos** together with a bust of Isabella and denomination expressed as "R^L Plata" (1855–78), **Ultramar** together with year and denomination in centesimos or pesetas (1868–77), **Cuba** often with "Correos" (1877→), **Isla de Cuba** (1890–97), **Republica de Cuba** (1910–50s).

Cundinamarca a department (state) in west-central Colombia. Local issues (1870–1904). Inscriptions include **Cundinamarca** (1870), **E^O S^O de Cundinamarca** (1877–84), **Estado Sobrano de Cundinamarca** (1884–1904), **Departmento de Cundinamarca** (1904). *Colombia.*

Curaçao see **Netherlands Antilles**.

Cuzco overprinted on provisional issues of Arequipa or on stamps of Peru: Cuzco, a city in southern Peru and capital of Cuzco Department. *Peru (provisional issues).*

Cyprus an island in the western Mediterranean, west of Syria and south of Turkey. British (1880–1960), independent (1960→). Inscriptions include **Cyprus** overprinted on stamps of Great Britain (1880–81) or inscribed (1881–1960), **Kibris Cumhuriyeti** overprinted (1960), **Cyprus** together with "Kibris" and "ΚΥΠΡΟΣ" (1960→).

Cyrenaica in North Africa, a region in northeast Libya. Italian (1923–34), autonomous (1950). Inscriptions include **Cirenaica** overprinted on stamps of Italy (1923–34) or inscribed, often with "Poste" (1926–34), **Cyrenaica** together with "Posts" or "Posts of" (1950). In 1934 Cyrenaica merged with Tripolitania to become the Italian colony of Libya.

Czechoslovakia in central Europe, bordered on the north by Poland, on the east by Ukraine, on the south by Austria and Hungary, and on the northwest and west by Germany. Independent (1918–38, 1945→). Inscriptions include **Česko-Slovenska** (1918–19), **Pošta Československá 1919** overprinted on stamps of Austria (1919), **Československa** (1920–26), **Československo** (1926–93), **Česko-Slovensko** (1939), **Česká Republika** (1993→). In 1938 Czechoslovakia fell under German control. In 1939 Germany split the country into Bohemia and Moravia (a German protectorate) and nominally independent Slovakia. The country was reunified following World War II. In 1993 Czechoslovakia split into the Czech Republic and Slovakia.

Dahomey in western Africa, bordered on the north by Burkina Faso and Niger, on the east by Nigeria, on the south by the Gulf of Guinea, and on the west by Togo. French (1899–1945), independent (1960–75). Inscriptions include **Dahomey et Dependances** together with "République Française - Colonie Postes"

(1899–1905), **Dahomey** together with "Afrique Occidental Française" (1906–40), **Dahomey** (1941–45), **République du Dahomey** (1960–75). Dahomey used stamps of French West Africa between 1945 and 1960. In 1975 Dahomey changed its name to Benin.

Dai Nippon 2602 overprinted on stamps of Kedah: Kedah (Japanese occupation). *Malayan States (Kedah).*

Dai Nippon 2602 Malaya (1) overprinted on stamps of Malaya: Malaya (Japanese occupation, World War II). *Malaya.* (2) the overprint also exists on stamps of Malayan states Negri Sembilan, Pahang, Perak, Selangor, Trengganu for use in those states. *Malayan States.* (3) on stamps of Straits Settlements: Straits Settlements. *Straits Settlements.*

Dai Nippon 2602 Penang overprinted on stamps of Straits Settlements: Penang (Japanese occupation). *Malayan States (Penang).*

Dai Nippon Yubin (1) overprinted on stamps of Malaya (Parak): Parak (Japanese occupation); (2) overprinted on stamps of Malaya (Selangor): Selangor (Japanese occupation). *Malayan States (Parak and Selangor).*

Danish West Indies a group of 3 islands and about 50 islets, east and southeast of Puerto Rico; the 3 islands are Saint Thomas, Saint John, and Saint Croix. Danish (1856–1917). Inscriptions include **KGL Post Fr.M.** with denomination in cents (1856–74), **Dansk-Vestindiske** (1874–1900), **Dansk Vestindien** (1900–17). In 1917 the Danish West Indies became the U.S. Virgin Islands and since, used stamps of the United States. Note: Stamps inscribed "KGL Post Fr.M." and denominated in skillings (abbreviated "s") are issues of Denmark.

Danmark Denmark. See **Denmark**.

Dansk Vestindien see **Danish West Indies**.

Dansk-Vestindiske see **Danish West Indies**.

Danzig a small state of about 750 square miles on the Baltic Sea, at present located in northern Poland. Free state under the League of Nations (1920–39). Inscriptions include **Danzig** overprinted on stamps of Germany (1920), **Freie Stadt Danzig** (1921–39). In 1939 Germany annexed Danzig. Following World War II, Danzig became part of Poland.

Dardanelles overprinted on stamps of Russia together with surcharge in para(s) or piastre(s): *Russia (offices in the Turkish Empire).*

Datia State Postage Duttia, a native feudatory state in north-central India. *India (native feudatory states).*

D. de A. Provisional Antioquia. See **Antioquia**. *Colombia.*

DDR   Deutsche Demokratische Republik. See **Germany (Democratic Republic)**.

Decreto de 27 Junio 1870   overprinted on stamps of Venezuela inscribed "Escuelas - Venezolano": Venezuela. See **Venezuela**.

Dédéagh   overprinted on stamps of France: French offices in Dedeagh. *France (offices in Turkey)*.

Democratic Republic of the Sudan   Sudan. See **Sudan**.

Democratska Federativna Jugoslavija   Yugoslavia. See **Yugoslavia**.

Denmark   in northwestern Europe, occupying most of the Jutland Peninsula and bordered on the west by the North Sea, on the east by straits linking the North Sea and the Baltic Sea, and on the south by Germany. Independent (1851→). Inscriptions include **Frimaerke KGL Post** (1851–54), **Kongeligt Post Frimaerke** (1851–54), **KGL Post Fr.M.** with denomination in shillings (1854–70), **Danmark** (1870→). Note: Stamps inscribed "KGL Post Fr.M." and denominated in cents are issues of Danish West Indies.

Departmento de Antioquia   see **Antioquia**. *Colombia*.

Departmento de Bolivar   see **Bolivar**. *Colombia*.

Departmento de Boyaca   see **Boyaca**. *Colombia*.

Departmento de Cundinamarca   see **Cundinamarca**. *Colombia*.

Departmento del Tolima   see **Tolima**. *Colombia*.

Departmento de Santander   see **Santander**. *Colombia*.

Dep^{TO} de Boyaca   see **Boyaca**. *Colombia*.

Deutsche Bundepost   Germany. See **Germany**.

Deutsche Bundespost Berlin   Berlin. See **Berlin**.

Deutsche Demokratische Republik   German Democratic Republic. See **Germany**.

Deutsche Militaer-Verwaltung Montenegro   overprinted on stamps of Yugoslavia: Montenegro (German occupation). See **Montenegro**.

Deutsche National Versammlung   German National Assembly, an inscription on German stamps (1919–20). *Germany*.

Deutsche Post   an inscription appearing on stamps of (**1**) Germany. See (**1**) **Germany**. (**2**) West Berlin. *Germany*. (**3**) German Democratic Republic. See **Germany (Democratic Republic)**.

Deutsche Post Berlin   Berlin. See **Berlin**. *Germany*.

Deutsche Post Leipzig   West Saxony, an administrative region in Soviet-occupied Germany (1945–46). *German Democratic Republic (Russian occupation)*.

Deutsche Post Osten   overprinted on stamps of Germany: Poland (German occupation). See **Poland**.

Deutsche Reichs Post   Germany. See **Germany**.

Deutsches Reich   (1) by itself: Germany. See **Germany**. (2) with "Böhmen und Mähren - Čechy a Morava": Bohemia and Moravia. See **Bohemia and Moravia**. (3) with "Generalgouvernement": Poland. See **Poland**. (4) overprinted on stamps of Bavaria: Bavaria. See **Bavaria**.

Deutschland   Germany. See **Germany**.

Deutsch-Neu-Guinea   overprinted on stamps of Germany or inscribed: German New Guinea. See **German New Guinea**.

Deutsch-Ostafrica   overprinted on stamps of Germany or inscribed: German East Africa. See **German East Africa**.

Deutschösterreich   Austria. See **Austria**.

Deutsch-Südwestafrika   overprinted on stamps of Germany or inscribed: German Southwest Africa. See **German Southwest Africa**.

Deutsch-Südwest-Afrika   overprinted on stamps of Germany: German Southwest Africa. See **German Southwest Africa**.

Dhar State   Dhar, a native feudatory state in north-central India. *India (native feudatory states)*.

Diego-Suarez   a town in northern Madagascar, which served as a French naval port. French (1890–96). Stamps are inscribed **Diego-Suarez** (1890–96).

Diligencia   inscribed on early issues of Uruguay. See **Uruguay**.

Dios - Patria - Rey - Cataluna   an inscription appearing on some issues of Carlist Spain. *Spain (Carlist issues)*.

Distrito sur de la Baja Cal   Sonora. See **Mexico**.

D J   overprinted on stamps of Obock: Somali Coast. See **Somali Coast**.

Djiboutí   overprinted on stamps of Obock: Somali Coast. See **Somali Coast**.

Djibouti 1893-94   together with "Protectorat de la Côte des Somâlis": Somali Coast. See **Somali Coast**.

Djibouti Republic   a small country in northeastern Africa on the Gulf of Aden at the Strait of Bab el Mandeb, Eritrea lies to the north, Somalia lies to the southeast, Ethiopia to the south and west. Independent (1977→). Stamps are inscribed **Republique de Djibouti**. Djibouti Republic was formerly the French territory of Afars and Issas; before that, it was the Somali Coast.

Dodecanese Islands   a group of islands in the Aegean Sea, located between southeastern Greece and southwestern Turkey. Italian (1912–45). Inscriptions include **Egeo** overprinted on stamps of Italy (1912), **Isole Italiane Dell'Egeo** overprinted on stamps of Italy (1930–40) or inscribed (1932–45). From 1912 to 1932, Italy issued stamps for use on various individual islands. The names of the islands are overprinted on stamps of Italy or inscribed and include **Caso** (Kásos), **Karki** (Khálki), **Carchi** (Khálki), **Calimno** (Kálimnos), **Cos** (Kos), **Leros** (Léros), **Lipso** (Lípsos), **Nisiros** (Nísiros), **Patmos** (Pátmos), **Piscopi** (Tílos), **Rodi** (Rodí, Rhodes), **Scarpanto** (Kárpathos), **Simi** (Sími), and **Stampalia** (Astipálaia). At the end of World War II, the Dodecanese Islands were ceded to Greece. *Italy (Aegean Islands).*

Dominica   the largest island in the Windward group in the Caribbean Sea, southeast of Puerto Rico and approximately midway between the islands of Guadeloupe and Martinique. British (1874–1978), independent (1978→). Inscriptions include **Dominica** (1874–1978), **Commonwealth of Dominica** (1978→).

Dominican Republic   in the Caribbean Sea, occupying the eastern two-thirds of the island of Hispanola, bordered on the west by Haiti. Independent (1865→). Inscriptions include **Correos** with the national coat of arms and denomination "Un Real" or "Medio Real" (1865–79), **Republica Dominicana** (1879→).

D.R. Sudan or **D.R. of Sudan**   Sudan. See **Sudan**.

Drzava SHS   Slovenia. See **Yugoslavia**.

Država S.H.S. - 1918 - Bosna i Hercegovina   overprinted on stamps of Bosnia and Herzegovina: Yugoslavia. See **Yugoslavia**.

Država S.H.S. Bosna i Hercegovina   overprinted on stamps of Bosnia and Herzegovina: Yugoslavia. See **Yugoslavia**.

Državna Posta Hrvatska   Croatia-Slavonia. See **Yugoslavia**.

Drž. Posta Hrvatska - SHS   Croatia-Slavonia. See **Yugoslavia**.

Dubai   on the Arabian shore of the Persian Gulf in the northeastern United Arab Emirates between Sharjah on the northwest and Abu Dhabi far to the southwest. Sheikdom under British protection (1966–71). Stamps are inscribed **Dubai**. Dubai used stamps inscribed **Trucial States** for a time in the early 1960s. In 1971 Dubai joined the United Arab Emirates.

Duc. di Parma   Duchy of Parma. See **Parma**. *Italian States.*

Duitsch Oost Afrika - Belgische Bezetting   overprinted on stamps of the Belgian Congo: German East Africa (Belgian occupation). See **German East Africa**.

Durazzo   overprinted on stamps of Italy: Italian offices in Durazzo (Durrës), a city in western Albania. *Italy (offices abroad).*

Duttia State Postage   Duttia, a native feudatory state in north-central India. *India (native feudatory states)*.

E.A.F.   (East Africa Forces) overprinted on stamps of Great Britain: Somalia (British occupation). *Great Britain (offices abroad)*.

East Africa and Uganda Protectorates   in central Africa on the Indian Ocean, consisting of much of what is now Kenya and Uganda. British (1903–21). Inscriptions include **East Africa and Uganda Protectorates**. The inscription also appears on early issues of *Kenya, Uganda, Tanzania*.

Ecuador   in northwestern South America, bordered on the north by Colombia, on the east and south by Peru, and on the west by the Pacific Ocean; and including the Galapagos Islands about 600 miles off its west coast. Independent (1865→). Inscriptions include **Ecuador** sometimes in combination with "Correos," "Franqueo," or "Republica" (1865→). For a time, Ecuador issued stamps for the Galapagos Islands inscribed **Islas Galapagos**.

E.E.F.   an abbreviation for "Egyptian Expeditionary Force" and the inscription on issues of the British mandate in the Middle East following World War I. The stamps were used as follows: **(1)** without overprint: general use within the mandate (Palestine, Lebanon, Syria, Transjordan, Cilicia, and parts of Egypt); **(2)** overprinted "Palestine" in English, Arabic, and Hebrew: Palestine; **(3)** overprinted in Arabic: Transjordan (Jordan). See **Palestine**, **Jordan**.

Eesti   Estonia. See **Estonia**.

Eesti Vabariik   Estonia. See **Estonia**.

E.E.U.U (or **EE.UU.**) **de Venezuela**   Venezuela. See **Venezuela**.

EFO 1915   (Etablissments Française de l'Océanie) French Polynesia. See **French Polynesia**.

Egeo   overprinted on stamps of Italy: Dodecanese Islands. See **Dodecanese Islands**. *Italy (Aegean Islands)*.

Egypt   in northeastern Africa and southwestern Asia, bordered on the north by the Mediterranean Sea, on the east by Israel and the Red Sea, on the south by Sudan, and on the west by Libya. Ottoman Turkish (1866–1914), British (1914–22), independent (1922→). Inscriptions include Arabic inscriptions (1866–79, 1922–25), **Postes Egyptiennes** (1879–1914), **Egypt Postage** (1914–22), **Royaume d'Egypte** (1922–26), **Egypte** (1926–58), **UAR** or **United Arab Republic** and "Egypt" (1958–59), **UAR** and denomination in milliemes (1959–71), **A.R. Egypt** (1971–75), **Egypt** (1976→).

Egypte   Egypt. See **Egypt**.

Éire or **Eire**   Ireland. See **Ireland**.

Ejercito Renovadar   together with "Estado Unidos Mexicano": Sinaloa. *Mexico (revolutionary issues).*

Elobey, Annobon and Corsico   a group of small islands off the coast of Spanish Guinea. Spanish (1903–10). Inscriptions include **Elobey, Annobon y Corsico** (1903–10). Subsequently, part of Spanish Guinea.

El Parlamento a Cervantes   inscribed on a commemorative issue: Spain (1930). *Spain.*

El Salvador   in Central America, bordered on the north and east by Honduras, on the south by the Pacific Ocean, and on the west by Guatemala. Independent (1867→). Inscriptions include **Correos del Salvador** (1867–79, 1890–96), **Republica del Salvador** and "Union Postal Universal" (1879–87), **Servicio Postale del Salvador** (1887–90), **Union Postale del Salvador** (1889), **Correos de El Salvador** (1896–1912, 1923–25, 1983→), **Estado de El Salvador** (1898), **Republica de El Salvador** (1900–1906, 1928), **Correos El Salvador** (1912–23), **El Salvador, C.A.** (1925, 1930), **Correos El Salvador Centro America** or **C.A.** (1934–83). Many issues of El Salvador contain an additional overprint or surcharge.

El Salvador, C.A.   El Salvador. See **El Salvador**.

Elsas   overprinted on stamps of France: German occupation of Alsace (1940). *France (occupation issues).*

Empire Centrafricaine   Central African Empire. See **Central African Republic**.

Empire d'Ethiopie   Ethiopia. See **Ethiopia**.

Empire Francais   France. See **France**.

Emp. Ottoman   Ottoman Empire (Turkey). See **Turkey**.

Eº Sº de Antioquia   see **Antioquia**. *Colombia.*

Eº Sº de Cundinamarca   see **Cundinamarca**. *Colombia.*

Eº Sº de Panama   Panama. See **Panama**.

Epirus   an area now in southern Albania. Nominally independent (1914–16), Greek (1914–16). Inscriptions include **ΕΛΛ. ΑΥΣΟΝ. ΗΠΕΙΡΟΣ** together with skull and crossbones (1914), **ΑΥΤΟΝΟΝΟΣ ΗΠΕΙΡΟΣ** or **ΗΠΕΙΡΟΣ** (1914), **ΕΛΛΗΝΙΚΗ 1914 ΧΕΙΜΑΡΡΑ** overprinted on stamps of Greece (1914), **Β. ΗΠΕΙΡΟΣ** overprinted on stamps of Greece (1914–16). During the time of the Balkan Wars (1912–13), North Epirus set up a provisional government with the support of Greece. It lasted only until 1916. Epirus is now part of Albania.

Equatorial Guinea   in western Africa, consisting of a mainland section (Río Muni, which is bordered on the north by Cameroon, on the east and south by

Gabon, and the west by the Gulf of Guinea), the islands of Bioko (Fernando Po) and Pagalu (Annobon), and the small coastal islets of Elobey Grande, Elobey Chico, and Corisco. Independent (1968→). Inscriptions include **Republica de Guinea Ecuatorial**. Equatorial Guinea was formerly the Spanish colonies of Fernando Po and Río Muni.

E.R.I.   (Edward Rex Imperator) **(1)** overprinted together with surcharged value on stamps inscribed "Oranje Vrij Staat": Orange River Colony. See **Orange River Colony**. **(2)** overprinted on stamps inscribed "Z. Afr. Republiek": Transvaal. See **Transvaal**.

Eritrea   in northeastern Africa, bordered on the north and northwest by Sudan, on the east by the Red Sea, on the southeast by Djibouti, and on the south and west by Ethiopia. Italian (1892–1936), British (1941–52), Ethiopian (1952–93), independent (1993→). Inscriptions include **Colonia Eritrea** overprinted on stamps of Italy (1892–1910) or inscribed (1910–28), **Eritrea** overprinted on stamps of Italy or inscribed (1921–34), **Eritrea** with "Postes," "Colonie Italiane," or "RR. Poste Coloniali Italiane" (1934–36), **Eritrea** (1993→). In 1936 Eritrea became part of Italian East Africa and used its stamps until the British arrived in 1941.

Escuelas   by itself or with "Venezolano": Venezuela. See **Venezuela**.

E.S. de Antioquia   see **Antioquia**. *Colombia*.

E.S. do Panama   Panama. See **Panama**.

España   Spain. See **Spain**.

España - Rio Muni   Rio Muni. See **Rio Muni**.

España - Sahara   Spanish Sahara. See **Spanish Sahara**.

España Valencia   Carlist Spain. *Spain (Carlist issues)*.

Esposicion de Barcelona 1930   inscribed on a commemorative issue: Spain. *Spain*.

Esposicion General Española   inscribed on a commemorative issue: Spain (1929). *Spain*.

Estado da Guiné-Bissau   Guinea-Bissau. See **Guinea-Bissau**.

Estado da India   sometimes with "Republica Portuguesa": Portuguese India. See **Portuguese India**.

Estado de El Salvador   El Salvador. See **El Salvador**.

Estado del Tolima   see **Tolima**. *Colombia*.

Estado de Nicaragua   Nicaragua. See **Nicaragua**.

Estado Español   Spain. See **Spain**.

Estado Libre y Soberano de Sonora   Sonora. See **Mexico**.

Estado Libre y Soberano Oaxaca   Oaxaca. See **Mexico**.

Estado S. de Bolivar   see **Bolivar**. *Colombia.*

Estado Soberano de Bolivar   see **Bolivar**. *Colombia.*

Estado Soberano de Cundinamarca   see **Cundinamarca**. *Colombia.*

Estado Soberano de Santander   see **Santander**. *Colombia.*

Estado Sobrano de Antioquia   see **Antioquia**. *Colombia.*

Estados Unidos de Colombia   **(1)** Colombia; **(2)** with "E.S. de Panama": Panama. See (1) **Colombia**; (2) **Panama**.

Estados Unidos de Nueva Granada   Colombia. See **Colombia**.

Estados Unidos do Brazil   see **Brazil**.

Est Africain Allemand - Occupation Belge and **Duitsch Oost Afrika - Belgische Bezetting**   overprinted on stamps of the Belgian Congo: German East Africa (Belgian occupation). See **German East Africa**.

Estampillas de Correo - Contrasena   overprinted on stamps of Venezuela: Venezuela. See **Venezuela**.

Estero   overprinted on stamps of Italy: for general use in Italian offices abroad throughout the world during the latter part of the nineteenth century. *Italy.*

Estland   Estonia. See **Estonia**.

Estonia   in northeastern Europe, bordered on the north by the Gulf of Finland, on the east by Russia, on the south by Latvia, and on the west by the Baltic Sea. Independent (1918–40, 1991→). Inscriptions include **Eesti**, **Eesti Post**, and **Eesti Vabariik** (1918–40), **Estland - Eesti** (1941, during German occupation), **Eesti** (1991→). Estonia was occupied by the U.S.S.R. in 1940 and incorporated into the Soviet Union as the Estonian Soviet Socialist Republic. During World War II, it was occupied by German forces. After World War II, it returned to the Soviet Union. In 1991 it regained independence.

Établiss Fr dans l'Inde   French India. See **French India**.

Établiss Fr dans l'Indie   French India. See **French India**.

Établissments de l'Inde   French India. See **French India**.

Etablissments de l'Océanie   French Polynesia. See **French Polynesia**.

Établissments Français dans l'Inde   French India. See **French India**.

Établissments Française de l'Océanie   overprinted on the generic postage-due issue for French colonies: French Polynesia. See **French Polynesia**.

Etat Autonome - Sud Kasai   South Kasai. See **South Kasai**.

État Cameroun   Cameroon. See **Cameroon**.

État Comorien   Comoro. See **Comoro Islands**.

Etat du Cambodge   Cambodia. See **Cambodia**.

Etat du Katanga   Katanga. See **Katanga**.

Etat Francais   France. See **France**.

État Ind. du Congo or **État Independant du Congo**   Belgian Congo. See **Congo (Belgian)**.

Ethiopia   in northeastern Africa, bordered on the west and northwest by Sudan, on the northeast by Eritrea and Djibouti, on the east and southeast by Somalia, and on the southwest by Kenya. Independent (1894–1936, 1942→). Inscriptions include Amharic letter inscriptions, with the occasional **Ethiopie** in Latin letters (1894–1909), **Postes Ethiopiennes**, **Empire d'Ethiopie**, or **Ethiopie** (1909–36), **Etiopia - Posta Coloniali Italiane** (1936), **Ethiopia** (1942–43), **Ethiopie** or **Postes Ethiopie** (1945–50), **Ethiopia** (1950→). Ethiopia was occupied by Italy in 1936 and became part of Italian East Africa. It was administered by Great Britain briefly during World War II.

Ethiopie   Ethiopia. See **Ethiopia**.

Etiopia   Ethiopia. See **Ethiopia**.

E^TS Français de l'Océanie   French Polynesia. See **French Polynesia**.

É^TS Franç dans l'Inde   French India. See **French India**.

E^TS Franç^S de l'Océanie   French Polynesia. See **French Polynesia**.

E.U. de Colombia or **E^E U^U de Colombia**   Colombia. See **Colombia**.

E.U. do Brazil   Brazil. See **Brazil**.

Eupen   overprinted on stamps of Belgium. See **Eupen & Malmédy**.

Eupen & Malmédy   two small districts in eastern Belgium near the German border. The districts were transferred to Belgium after World War I. Inscriptions include **Eupen & Malmédy** overprinted on stamps of Belgium (1920), **Eupen** overprinted on stamps of Belgium (1920–21), **Malmédy** overprinted on stamps of Belgium (1920–21). *Germany (occupation issues)*.

Falkland Islands   a group of islands in the South Atlantic northeast of the southern tip of South America off Argentina, consisting of two main islands, East Falkland Island and West Falkland Island. British (1878→). Stamps are inscribed **Falkland Islands**. In 1982 the Falkland Islands were invaded by Argentina and occupied for about 10 weeks. Argentina refers to the islands as the Islas Malvinas.

Falkland Islands Dependencies   Falkland Islands (1946–80s). Stamps are inscribed **Falkland Islands Dependencies**. Falkland Islands Dependencies includes

South Georgia, South Sandwich, and until 1962, the South Shetland Islands, South Orkneys, and Graham Land, which subsequently became British Antarctic Territory. *Falkland Islands.*

Faridkot State   overprinted on stamps of India: Faridkot state, a state in north-central India. *India (convention states).*

Faroe Islands   a group of islands in the North Atlantic Ocean about midway between the Shetland Islands and Iceland. Danish (1975→). Stamps are inscribed **Føroyar** (1975→).

F^{co} Bollo Postale Italiano   Italy. See **Italy.**

Federacion   Venezuela. See **Venezuela.**

Federated Malay States   see **Malaya (Federated Malay States).**

Federated States of Micronesia   see **Micronesia (Federated States of).**

Federation du Mali   Mali. See **Mali.**

Federation of Malaya   see **Malaya (Federation of).**

Federation of South Arabia   South Arabia. See **South Arabia.**

Fernando Po   an island in the Atlantic Ocean, northwest of Equatorial Guinea. Spanish (1868–1968). Inscriptions include **Fernando Poo** inscribed (1868–1929) or overprinted on revenue stamps (1899), **Fernando Poo** together with "España" (1960–68). Between 1929 and 1960, Fernando Po used stamps of Spanish Guinea. In 1968 Fernando Po (Bioko Island) became part of independent Equatorial Guinea.

Feudatory State of Raj Nandgam   Nandgaon, a native feudatory state in east-central India. *India (native feudatory states).*

Fezzan   see **Fezzan-Ghadames.** *Libya (occupation issues).*

Fezzan-Ghadames   Fezzan is a region located in southwestern Libya in the Sahara Desert; Ghadames is an oasis and city in northwestern Libya near the Tunisian and Algerian borders. French (1943–51). Inscriptions include **R.F. Fezzan** or **Fezzan Occupation Française** overprinted on stamps of Italy (1943), **Territoire Militaire Fezzan Ghadames** (1946–49). And for Fezzan: **Territoire Militaire Fezzan** or **Territoire du Fezzan** (1949–51). And for Ghadames: **Ghadamés - Territoire Militaire** (1949–51). All of the foregoing: *Libya (occupation issues).* In 1912 Fezzan was amalgamated with Cyrenaica and Tripolitania under Italian rule to form what is now known as Libya.

Fezzan Occupation Française   see **Fezzan-Ghadames.** *Libya (occupation issues).*

Fiera Campionaria Tripoli   an inscription on stamps of Libya as an Italian colony. See **Libya.**

Fiera di Trieste (Trieste Fair) overprinted on stamps of Italy: Trieste. *Italy (Trieste)*.

Fiji a group of islands in the southern Pacific Ocean, 3,100 miles southwest of Hawaii and 1,900 miles northeast of Sydney, Australia. Independent (1870–74), British (1874–1970), independent (1970→). Stamps are inscribed **Fiji** (1870→), **V.R.** overprinted on earlier issues (1874–78).

Filipinas Philippines. See **Philippines**.

Finland in northern Europe, bordered on the north by Norway, on the east by Russia, on the south by Russia and the Gulf of Finland, on the southwest by the Baltic Sea, and on the west by Sweden and the Gulf of Bothnia. Russian (1856–1917), independent (1917→). Inscriptions include coat of arms, crown and denomination in "Kop," "Pen," or "Mark" (1856–75), **ПОУТОВАЯ МАРКА** and denomination in "Pen," "Penni," "Markka," or "Markkaa" (1891–1917), **Suomi Finland** (1875–91, 1917→). Stamps of Finland and Russia from the period 1891 to 1917 are nearly identical. Those of Finland are denominated as above; those of Russia, with Cyrillic characters.

Fiume a city, now in northwestern Croatia, on the Gulf of Kvarner, an inlet of the Adriatic Sea. Italy (1918–24). Inscriptions include **Fiume** overprinted on stamps of Hungary (1918–19), **Fiume**, sometimes with "Posta" or "Poste di" (1919–24). In 1919 Gabriele D'Annunzio, leading a band of Italian legionaries, seized Fiume. The legion occupied the city until November 1920, when Fiume was made a free state by treaty between Italy and Yugoslavia. In 1924, following Benito Mussolini's rise to power, a second treaty awarded the city and district to Italy. Fiume used stamps of Italy thereafter. In addition to Fiume, D'Annunzio occupied Arbe and Veglia, small islands near Fiume in the Gulf of Carnaro. Stamps of Fiume exist overprinted **Reggenzia Italiane del Carnaro** (Italian Regency of Carnaro), **Arbe**, or **Veglia**.

F.N.F.L. Forces Navales Française Libre (Free French Naval Forces): Saint-Pierre and Miquelon. See **Saint-Pierre and Miquelon**.

F.N.R. Jugoslavija Yugoslavia. See **Yugoslavia**.

Forces Française Libres - Levant overprinted on stamps of Syria: military stamps (Free French): Syria. *Syria*.

Føroyar Faroe Islands. See **Faroe Islands**.

France in western Europe, bordered on the north by the English Channel, on the northeast by Belgium, Luxembourg, and Germany, on the east by Germany, Switzerland, and Italy, on the southeast by Monaco and the Mediterranean Sea, on the south by Spain and Andorra, and on the west the Atlantic Ocean. Independent (1849→). Inscriptions include **Repub. Franc.** (1849–53, 1870–76),

Empire Francais (1853–71), **République Française** (1876→), **RF** (1924→), **Postes Françaises** (1941–44), **Etat Francais** (1944), **France**, often with "Postes" (occasionally, 1924→).

France Libre or **France Libré**   Free France. An inscription or overprint on stamps issued in many French colonies and possessions not under German control during World War II. Refer to the named colony or possession.

France Libré Cameroun   Cameroun under control of the Free French during World War II.

France Libre F.N.F.L.   overprinted on stamps of Saint-Pierre and Miquelon: Saint-Pierre and Miquelon. See **Saint-Pierre and Miquelon**.

France Libré - Océanie   French Polynesia. See **French Polynesia**.

Franco   together with allegorical Helvetia and a shield with a white cross: Switzerland. See **Switzerland**.

Franco Bollo Postale   with Papal crest and denomination in baj. (bajocchi), scudo, or cent. (centesimi): Roman States. See **Roman States**. *Italian States.*

Franco Bollo Postale Italiano   Italy. See **Italy**.

Francobollo Postale Italiano   Italy. See **Italy**.

Franco Bollo Postale Romagne   Romagna. See **Romagna**. *Italian States.*

Franco Bollo Postale Toscano   Tuscany. See **Tuscany**. *Italian States.*

Franco Cuzco   overprinted on stamps of Peru: Cuzco, a city in southern Peru and capital of Cuzco Department. *Peru (provisional issues).*

Franco Fiume   overprinted on stamps of Hungary: Fiume.

Franco Helvetia   Switzerland. See **Switzerland**.

Franco Marke   together with denomination in "grote": Bremen. *German States.*

Franco Poste Bollo   together with embossed bust of Victor Emmanuel II and denomination in "grana": Two Sicilies. See **Two Sicilies**. *Italian States.*

Franco Scrisorei   Moldavia-Walachia (Romania). See **Romania**.

Franqueo Ecuador   Ecuador. See **Ecuador**.

Franqueo España   Spain. See **Spain**.

Freimarke   together with denomination in "pfenninge" or "silbergr": Prussia. *German States.*

Freistaat Bayern   overprinted on stamps of Germany or Bavaria: Bavaria. See **Bavaria**.

French Congo in west-central Africa, bordered on the north by Cameroon and Ubangi-Chari, on the east and south by the Belgian Congo, on the south by Angola, and on the west by Gabon and the Atlantic Ocean. French (1891–1906). Inscriptions include **Congo Français** overprinted on generic issues for French colonies (1891–92) or inscribed (1892–1906). In 1906 the French Congo became part of French Equatorial Africa.

French Equatorial Africa a federation of four French territories in central Africa, including Chad, Gabon, Middle Congo (Republic of the Congo), and Ubangi-Chari (Central African Republic). French (1936–58). Inscriptions include **Afrique Équatorial Française** overprinted on stamps of Gabon (1936) or inscribed (1937–58), **AEF** (1937), **Afrique Equatorial** (1941), **Afrique Française Libre** overprinted (1940–41). In 1958 the constituent territories became independent nations.

French Guiana on the northeastern coast of South America, bordered on the north by the Atlantic Ocean, on the east and south by Brazil, and on the west by Suriname. French (1886–1946). Inscriptions include **Guy. Franç.** overprinted, together with date and surcharged numeral of value, on the generic issue for French colonies (1886–92), **Guyane** overprinted on the generic issue for French colonies (1892–1905), **Guyane Française** (1905–46). In 1946 French Guiana became an overseas department of France and since has used stamps of France.

French Guinea in western Africa, bordered on the north by Guinea-Bissau, Senegal, and Mali, on the east and southeast by the Ivory Coast (Côte d'Ivoire), on the south by Liberia and Sierra Leone, and on the west by the Atlantic Ocean. French (1892–1945). Inscriptions include **Guinée Française** (1892–1906), **Guinée** together with "Afrique Occidentale Française" or "AOF" and/or "RF" (1906–45). French Guinea used stamps of French West Africa between 1945 and 1958. In 1958 it became the independent Republic of Guinea.

French India four enclaves on the Indian subcontinent, in descending order of size they were Pondicherry, Karaikal, and Yanam, all on the southeast coast, and Mahé, on the southwest coast. French (1892–1956). Inscriptions include **Établissments de l'Inde** (1892–1914), **Inde F^{ÇAISE}** (1903), **Établissments Français dans l'Inde** (1914–1956), **Inde Française** (1929–), **Établis^{TS} Franç dans l'Inde** (1941), **É^{TS} Franç dans l'Inde** (1941), **Établiss Fr dans l'Indie** (1948–56). In 1956, the enclaves were ceded to India.

French Indochina see **Indochina**.

French Morocco in North Africa, bordered on the north by Spanish Morocco and the Mediterranean Sea, on the east and southeast by Algeria, on the south by Western Sahara, and on the west by the Atlantic Ocean. French offices (1891–1912), protectorate (1912–56). Inscriptions include **Centimos** or **Pesetas** overprinted, together with numeral of value, on stamps of France (1891–1902), **Maroc** inscribed (1902–56), and with surcharged value (1902–14), **Protectorat Français** overprinted on stamps of French Morocco (1914–17), **Tanger** overprinted on stamps of French Morocco or on postage-due stamps of France (1918–24). In 1956 Morocco became independent.

French Polynesia   several groups of small islands widely scattered over the eastern South Pacific Ocean, consisting of five archipelagoes: the Society Islands (including Tahiti, Moorea, Mehetia, and Bora-Bora), the Tuamotu Archipelago, the Gambier Islands, the Austral Islands, and the Marquesas Islands. French (1892→). Inscriptions include **Etablissments de l'Oceanie** (1892–1934, 1941), **EFO 1915** overprinted (1915), **Établissments Française de l'Océanie** overprinted on the generic postage-due issue for French colonies (1926–29), **E^{TS} Franç^S de l'Océanie** (1934–41), **E^{TS} Français de l'Océanie** (1934–58), **Océanie** together with "France Libre" (1942), **Polynesie Française** (1958→).

French Southern and Antarctic Territories   comprising the Kerguelen and Crozet archipelagoes and the islands of Saint-Paul and Amsterdam, all located in the southern Indian Ocean, and Adélie Coast, a narrow segment of the Antarctic continent and populated only by scientific personnel numbering about 200. French (1955→). Inscriptions include **Terres Australes et Antarctiques Française** overprinted on stamps of Madagascar (1955) or inscribed (1956→).

French Sudan   in northwestern Africa, bordered on the north by Algeria, on the east by Niger, on the south by the Ivory Coast (Côte d'Ivoire) and French Guinea, and on the west by Senegal and Mauritania. French (1894–1906, 1921–43). Inscriptions include **Soudan Française** inscribed (1894–1906, 1931–43) or overprinted on stamps of Upper Senegal and Niger (1921–31). In 1943 French Sudan became part of French West Africa. In 1958 French Sudan and Senegal merged to form the Federation of Mali. In 1960 Senegal withdrew from the federation.

French West Africa   French colonies in western Africa including Dahomey (Benin), Guinea, the Ivory Coast (Côte d'Ivoire), French Sudan (Mali), Mauritania, Niger, Senegal, and Upper Volta (Burkina Faso). French (1943–58). Stamps are inscribed **Afrique Occidentale Française** or **AOF**. In 1958 the constituent territories became independent nations.

Frimaerke KGL Post   Denmark. See **Denmark**.

Fuerstentum Liechtenstein   Liechtenstein. See **Liechtenstein**.

Fujeira   on the Gulf of Oman in the northeast United Arab Emirates, with Oman lying to the south. Emirate under British protection (1964–71). Stamps are inscribed **Fujeira**. Fujeira joined the United Arab Emirates in 1971.

Funafuti   an island in the Tuvalu group. Tuvalu (1984→). Stamps are inscribed **Funafuti - Tuvalu**. *Tuvalu (Funafuti)*.

Funchal   the capital city of the Madeira Islands, an autonomous region of Portugal. Portuguese (1892–1905). Stamps are inscribed **Funchal** together with "Correios Portugal" (1892–1905). Funchal now uses stamps of Portugal.

Fürstentum Liechtenstein   Liechtenstein. See **Liechtenstein**.

G.   overprinted on stamps of the Cape of Good Hope: Griqualand. See **Griqualand West**.

G & D   overprinted on stamps of Guadeloupe: Guadeloupe. See **Guadeloupe**.

GAB   overprinted, together with numeral of value, on the generic issue for French colonies: Gabon. See **Gabon**.

Gabon   in west-central Africa, bordered on the northwest by Equatorial Guinea, on the north by Cameroon, on the east and south by the Republic of the Congo, and on the west by the Atlantic Ocean. French (1886–1934), independent (1958→). Inscriptions include **GAB** overprinted, together with numeral of value, on the generic issue for French colonies (1886–89), **Gabon Timbre** overprinted, together with numeral of value, on the generic postage-due issue for French colonies (1889), **Gabon-Congo** together with "GAB" (1889), **Gabon** (1904–10, 1931–34), **Congo Française Gabon** (1910–12), **Afrique Equatorial Gabon** (1910–24), **Afrique Equatoriale Française** overprinted on stamps of the two foregoing issues (1924–31), **Gabon A.E.F.** overprinted on the generic postage-due issue for French colonies (1928), **République Gabonaise** (1958→). Between 1934 and 1959, Gabon used stamps of French Equatorial Africa.

Gabon A.E.F.   overprinted on the generic postage-due issue for French colonies: Gabon. See **Gabon**.

Gabon-Congo   Gabon. See **Gabon**.

Gabon Timbre   overprinted, together with numeral of value, on the generic postage-due issue for French colonies: Gabon. See **Gabon**.

Gambia   on the west coast of Africa, a long narrow country surrounded by Senegal except on the west, where it fronts the Atlantic Ocean. British (1869–1965), independent (1965→). Stamps are inscribed **Gambia** or **The Gambia**.

G.D. de Luxembourg   Luxembourg. See **Luxembourg**.

Gᴰ Duche de Luxembourg   Luxembourg. See **Luxembourg**.

G^D Liban   Lebanon. See **Lebanon**.

G.E.A.   (German East Africa) overprinted: **(1)** on stamps of East Africa and Uganda: German East Africa (British occupation). See **German East Africa**. **(2)** on stamps of Kenya, Uganda, and Tanganyika: Tanganyika. See **Tanganyika**.

General Gouvernement   German occupation of Poland during World War II. Sometimes, **Generalgouvernement**. *Poland.*

Gen. Gouv. Warschau   overprinted on stamps of Germany: Poland (German occupation). See **Poland**.

Georgia   in the Transcaucas region of western Asia, bordered on the north by Russia, on the south by Azerbaijan, Armenia, and Turkey, and on the west by the Black Sea. Independent (1919–22, 1991→), Soviet (1922–23). Inscriptions include **La Georgie** (1919), **Republique Georgienne** (1920–22), **Georgia** (1993→). Georgia was formerly a republic in the Soviet Union.

German East Africa   in east-central Africa, bordered on the north by Lake Victoria, Uganda, and British East Africa, on the east by the Atlantic Ocean, on the south by Mozambique, Nyasaland, and Northern Rhodesia, and on the west by Lake Tanganyika and the Belgian Congo. German (1893–1918). Inscriptions include **Pesa** and numeral of value overprinted on stamps of Germany (1893–96), **Deutsch-Ostafrica** overprinted on stamps of Germany (1896–1900) or inscribed (1900–18). Fighting occurred in German East Africa throughout World War I. After the war, the colony was divided among Great Britain (the greatest part of the territory, which would be known as Tanganyika), Belgium (Ruanda and Urundi), and Portugal (the Kionga triangle via annexation by Mozambique). During and after the war, some occupation forces used stamps in their respective areas with various inscriptions: **N.F.** overprinted on stamps of Nyasaland Protectorate (British occupation), **G.E.A.** overprinted on stamps of East Africa and Uganda (British occupation), **Est Africain Allemand - Occupation Belge** and **Duitsch Oost Afrika - Belgische Bezetting** (Belgian occupation), **A.O.** (Belgian occupation).

German New Guinea   in the Pacific Ocean, the northeastern quarter of the island of New Guinea. German (1897–1919). Inscriptions include **Deutsch-Neu-Guinea** overprinted on stamps of Germany (1897–1901) or inscribed (1901–19). Most of German New Guinea was occupied by Australia during World War I. Following the war, it was mandated to Australia under the League of Nations.

German Southwest Africa   in southern Africa, bordered on the north by Angola, on the east by Bechuanaland, on the east and south by South Africa, and on the west by the Atlantic Ocean. German (1897–1915). Inscriptions include **Deutsch-Südwest-Afrika** overprinted on stamps of Germany (1897–98),

Deutsch-Südwestafrika overprinted on stamps of Germany (1899) or inscribed (1900–15). German Southwest Africa was occupied by South Africa during World War I and mandated to it under the League of Nations following the war. The area is now Namibia.

German States   a term used to refer to German cities and states that issued postage stamps prior to German unification in 1871, and in some cases retaining postal autonomy until after World War I. They include Baden, Bavaria, Bergedorf, Bremen, Brunswick, Hamburg, Hannover, Lubeck, Mecklenburg-Schwerin, Mecklenburg-Strelitz, Oldenburg, Prussia, Saxony, Schleswig-Holstein, and Württemberg. Thurn and Taxis and the North German Confederation are often included with the group. *German States.*

Germany   in north-central Europe, bordered on the north by the North Sea, Denmark, and the Baltic Sea, on the east by Poland and the Czech Republic, on the south by Austria and Switzerland, and on the west by France, Luxembourg, Belgium, and the Netherlands, and at various times in its history, consisting of more territory or less territory. Independent (1872→). Inscriptions for Germany and the Federal Republic include **Deutsche Reichs Post** (1872–89), **Reichpost** (1889–1902), **Deutsches Reich** (1902–44), **Grossdeutsches Reich** (1944–45), **Deutsche Post** (1946–51), **Deutsche Bundepost** (1951–95), **Deutschland** (1995→). Following World War II, Germany was divided into British, French, Soviet, and U.S. zones of occupation, and in 1949, into the Federal Republic of Germany (West Germany, consisting of the British, French, and U.S. zones) and German Democratic Republic (East Germany, consisting of the Soviet zone). In 1990 the country was reunified.

Germany (Democratic Republic)   a nominally independent portion of Germany consisting of the area occupied by the Soviet Union following World War II. Soviet occupation (1945–49), German Democratic Republic (1949–90). Inscriptions include **Sowjetische Besatzungs Zone** overprinted on stamps of Germany (1948), **Deutsche Post** (1948–49), **Deutsche Demokratische Republik** (1950–80s) or **DDR** (1960s–90). In 1990 the German Democratic Republic reunited with the Federal Republic of Germany. Several states in the Soviet zone issued stamps during the period 1945 to 1949. Inscriptions include **Deutsche Post Leipzig** (West Saxony), **Mecklenburg Vorpommern** or **Mecklbg-Vorpomm** (Mecklenburg-Vorpommern), **Provinz Sachsen** (Saxony), **Stadt Berlin** (Berlin-Brandenburg), **Thüringen** (Thuringia).

Gerusalemme   overprinted on stamps of Italy: Italian offices in Jerusalem, at the time, a city in the Ottoman Turkish Empire. *Italy (offices abroad).*

Ghadames   see **Fezzan-Ghadames**. *Libya (occupation issues).*

Ghadamés - Territoire Militaire   Ghadames. See **Fezzan-Ghadames**. *Libya (occupation issues)*.

Ghana   in western Africa, bordered on the north and northwest by Burkina Faso, on the east by Togo, on the south by the Atlantic Ocean, and on the west by the Ivory Coast (Côte d'Ivoire). Independent (1957→). Inscriptions include **Ghana Independence 6th March, 1957.** overprinted on stamps of the Gold Coast (1957), **Ghana** (1957→). Ghana was formerly the British colony Gold Coast.

Gibraltar   on the southeast coast of Spain at the entrance to the Mediterranean Sea. British (1886→). Inscriptions include **Gibraltar** overprinted on stamps of Bermuda (1886), or inscribed (1886→).

Gilbert and Ellice Islands   a group of widely scattered islands in the west-central Pacific northeast of Australia, consisting of the Gilbert Islands (33 coral islands and atolls) and the Ellice Islands (9 atolls). British (1911–75). Inscriptions include **Gilbert & Ellice Protectorate** overprinted on stamps of Fiji (1911), **Gilbert & Ellice Islands Protectorate** (1911), **Gilbert & Ellice Islands** (1912–75). In 1976 the Gilbert and Ellice Islands divided and became the Gilbert Islands (later, Kiribati) and Tuvalu.

Gilbert Islands   a group of 33 widely scattered islands and atolls in the west-central Pacific Ocean northeast of Australia. British (1975–79). Inscriptions include **The Gilbert Islands** overprinted on stamps of Gilbert & Ellis Islands (1976), **Gilbert Islands** (1976–79). The Gilbert Islands were formerly the Gilbert and Ellice Islands; subsequently, the Republic of Kiribati.

Gobierno Constitutionalista   overprinted on stamps of Mexico: Mexico. See **Mexico**.

Gobierno Provisorio del Paraguay   Paraguay. See **Paraguay**.

Gobierno Revolucierno   together with "Correos Mexico": Yucatan. *Mexico (revolutionary issues)*.

Gold Coast   in western Africa bordered on the west by the Ivory Coast (Côte d'Ivoire), on the north and northwest by Burkina Faso, on the east by Togo, and on the south by the Atlantic Ocean. British (1875–1957). Stamps are inscribed **Gold Coast**. In 1975 the Gold Coast became Ghana.

Golfe de Bénin   Benin. See **Benin**.

Governatorato de Montenegro   overprinted on stamps of Italy or Yugoslavia: Montenegro (Italian occupation). See **Montenegro**.

Governo Militare Alleato   overprinted on stamps of Italy: allied occupation of Italy. *Italy*.

G P E   overprinted, together with numeral of value, on the generic issue for French colonies: Guadeloupe. See **Guadeloupe**.

Graham Land   the northernmost tip of Antarctica, a peninsula directly south of South America. British (1944). Inscriptions include **Graham Land - Dependency of** overprinted on stamps of the Falkland Islands (1944). *Falkland Islands (dependencies: Graham Land)*.

Grand Comoro   one of the Comoro Islands. French (1897–1914). Stamps are inscribed **Grande Comore** (1897–1914). Between 1914 and 1946, Grand Comoro was part of Madagascar, then one of the independent Comoro Islands.

Grand Duche Luxembourg or **Grand Duche de Luxembourg**   Luxembourg. See **Luxembourg**.

Gran Liban   Lebanon. See **Lebanon**.

Great Britain   an island nation off northeastern Europe composed of England, Scotland, Wales, and Northern Ireland. Independent (1840→). Stamps of Great Britain traditionally carry the portrait of the reigning monarch rather than an inscription.

Greece   in southeastern Europe, at the southernmost region of the Balkan Peninsula and including numerous islands, the mainland portion is bordered on the north by Macedonia and Bulgaria, on the northeast by Turkey, on the east by the Aegean Sea, on the south by the Mediterranean Sea, on the west by the Ionian Sea, on the northwest by Albania. Independent (1861→). Inscriptions include **ΕΛΛΑΣ** or occasionally **ΕΛΛΑC** (1861–1966), **Hellas** (1966→).

During the Balkan Wars (1912–13) and their aftermath, Greece occupied and issued stamps for various Aegean Islands and for Cavalla and Dedeagatch, all of which are now part of Greece. Inscriptions and overprints for the occupied Aegean Islands include **Σ.Δ** overprinted on stamps of Greece for Chios (Khíos), **ΕΛΛΗΝΙΚΗ ΔΙΟΙΥΗΣΙΣ** overprinted on stamps of Greece or inscribed **ΙΚΑΡΙΑΣ** for Icaria (Ikaría), **ΛΗΜΝΟΣ** overprinted on stamps of Greece for Lemnos (Límnos), **Ἑλληνικὴ Κατιοχὴ Μυτλήνης** overprinted on stamps of Greece for Lesbos (Lésvos), **ΠΡΟΣΩΡΙΝΟΝ ΤΑΧΥΔΡΟΜΕΙΟΝ - ΣΑΜΟΥ** or **ΣΑΜΟΥ** for Samos (Sámos), **Σ.Δ.Δ.** overprinted on stamps of Greece for the Dodecanese Islands. Inscriptions for other occupied territories include **ΕΛΛΗΝΙΚΗ ΔΙΟΙΚΗΣΙΣ** overprinted on stamps of Greece for occupied Turkey and overprinted on stamps of Bulgaria for Cavalla (Kaválla), **ΕΛΛΗΝΙΚΗ ΔΙΟΙΚΗΣΙΣ ΔΕΔΕΑΓΑΤΣ ΔΕΚΑ ΛΕΠΤΑ** or **ΕΛΛΗΝΙΚΗ ΔΙΟΙΚΗΣΙΣ ΔΕΔΕΑΓΑΤΣ 10 ΛΕΠΤΑ** overprinted on stamps of Greece or Bulgaria for Dedeagatch (Alexandroúpolus). In 1940 Greece occupied North Epirus, which was in Italian-occupied Albania, and issued stamps overprinted ελλΗΝΙΚΗ ΔΙΟΙΚΗCΙC for use there.

Greenland an island located in the North Atlantic, bordered on the north by the Arctic Ocean, and lying mostly north of the Arctic Circle. Danish (1938→). Inscriptions include **Grønland** (1938–69), **Kalåtdlit Nunåt Grønland** (1969–79), **Kalaallit Nunaat Grønland** (1979→).

Grenada a group of islands in the West Indies, in the southeastern Caribbean Sea, including Grenada, the southernmost of the Windward Islands, and some of the southern Grenadines, the most important of which is Carriacou, to the northeast. British (1861–1974), independent (1974→). Stamps are inscribed **Grenada**.

Grenada - Carriacou & Petite Martinique see **Grenada Grenadines**.

Grenada Grenadines a group of small islands north of Grenada, including the main island of Carriacou. Grenada (1973→) Inscriptions include **Grenadines** overprinted on stamps of Grenada (1973–75), **Grenada Grenadines** (1975–99), **Grenada - Carriacou & Petite Martinique** (1999→).

Grenadines overprinted on stamps of Grenada: Grenada Grenadines. See **Grenada Grenadines**.

Grenadines of Saint Vincent see **Saint Vincent Grenadines**.

G.R.I. (Georgius Rex Imperator) **(1)** overprinted on stamps of German Samoa: Samoa. See (1) **Samoa.** **(2)** overprinted, together with surcharged value in pence or shillings, on stamps inscribed "Deutsch Neu-Guinea" or "Marshall Inseln," or overprinted on registry labels inscribed "Deutsch Neu-Guinea" together with a town name: New Britain. See **New Britain**.

Griqualand West in southern Africa, in what is now South Africa, bordered on the north by British Bechuanaland, on the east by Orange River Colony, and on the south and west by Cape Colony. British (1874–80). Griqualand West became part of the Cape of Good Hope in 1880. Inscriptions include **G** overprinted on stamps of Cape of Good Hope.

Grossdeutsches Reich **(1)** by itself: Germany.; See **Germany. (2)** with "Böhmen und Mähren - Čechy a Morava": Bohemia and Moravia. See **Bohemia and Moravia. (3)** with "Generalgouvernement": Poland. See **Poland**.

Guadeloupe a group of islands in the West Indies, off the northwestern coast of South America, including two principal islands, Basse-Terre and Grande-Terre, and several smaller islands, Marie-Galante, La Desirade, Les Saintes, Saint-Barthelemy, and Saint Martin. French (1884–1947). Inscriptions include **G P E** overprinted, together with numeral of value, on the generic issue for French colonies (1884–91), **Guadeloupe** overprinted on the generic issue for French colonies, either with or without numeral of value (1889–91) or inscribed, either with "Republique Française" or "RF" (1905–47), **Guadeloupe et Dependances** (1892–1905), **G & D** overprinted, together with numeral, of value (1903–04). In 1947

Guadeloupe became an overseas department of France and since has used stamps of France.

Guadeloupe et Dependances   Guadeloupe. See **Guadeloupe**.

Guam   an island in the western North Pacific Ocean, the largest and southernmost of the Mariana Islands. United States (1899–1901). Inscriptions include **Guam**, overprinted on stamps of the United States (1899–1901). Since 1901 Guam has used U.S. stamps.

Guanacaste   a province of Costa Rica. Inscriptions include **Guanacaste** overprinted on stamps of Costa Rica. *Costa Rica.*

Guatemala   in Central America, bordered on the west and north by Mexico, on the east by Belize and the Caribbean Sea, on the southwest by Honduras and El Salvador, and on the south by the Pacific Ocean. Independent (1871→). Stamps are inscribed **Guatemala**, often together with "Correos de" or "Republica de."

Guernsey   a British bailiwick in the English channel off Normandy, France. German occupation (1941–45), British (1969→). Inscriptions include **Guernsey** (1941–45), **Bailiwick of Guernsey**, **Guernsey**, or **Guernsey Bailiwick** (1969→). The Bailiwick of Guernsey includes the islands of Alderney, Guernsey, Herm, Jethou, Lithou, and Sark. Alderney also has issued postage stamps. Some of the other islands have issued stamps, which are generally regarded as local issues.

Guiné   overprinted on stamps of Cape Verde: Portuguese Guinea. See **Portuguese Guinea**.

Guinea (Republic of)   in western Africa, bordered on the north by Guinea-Bissau, Senegal, and Mali, on the east and southeast by the Ivory Coast (Côte d'Ivoire), on the south by Liberia and Sierra Leone, and on the west by the Atlantic Ocean. Independent (1959→). Inscriptions include **Republique de Guinee** overprinted on stamps of French West Africa (1959), **République de Guinée** (1959→). Formerly, French Guinea.

Guinea 1911   overprinted on stamps of Spanish Guinea: Spanish Guinea. See **Spanish Guinea**.

Guinea-Bissau   in northwestern Africa, bordered on the west by the Atlantic Ocean, and wedged between Senegal on the north and Guinea on the east and south. Independent (1974→). Inscriptions include **Estado da Guiné-Bissau** (1974–77), **Republica da Guiné-Bissau** (1977–86), **Guiné-Bissau** (1986→). Guinea-Bissau was formerly Portuguese Guinea.

Guinea Conti[AL] **Española**   Spanish Guinea. See **Spanish Guinea**.

Guinea Continental   overprinted on stamps of Elobey, Annobon, and Corisco: Spanish Guinea. See **Spanish Guinea**.

Guinea Español (or **Española**)   Spanish Guinea. See **Spanish Guinea**.

Guiné-Bissau   Guinea-Bissau. See **Guinea-Bissau**.

Guinée   French Guinea. See **French Guinea**.

Guinée Française   French Guinea. See **French Guinea**.

Guine Portugueza   Portuguese Guinea. See **Portuguese Guinea**.

Gultig 9. Armee   overprinted on stamps of Germany: Romania (German occupation). See **Romania**.

Guyana   on the northeast coast of South America bordered on the north by the Atlantic Ocean, on the east by Suriname, on the south and west by Brazil, and on the west by Venezuela. Independent (1966→). Inscriptions include **Guyana** and "South America" (1966–75), **Guyana** (1975→), **All Guyana Our Heritage** (occasionally, 1980s). In terms of numbers of stamps issued, Guyana is immensely prolific, including many with commemorative overprints. Guyana was formerly British Guiana.

Guyane   overprinted on the generic issue for French colonies: French Guiana. See **French Guiana**.

Guyane Française   French Guiana. See **French Guiana**.

Guy. Franç.   overprinted, together with date and surcharged numeral of value, on the generic issue for French colonies: French Guiana. See **French Guiana**.

Gwalior   overprinted on stamps of India: Gwalior state, a state in central India. *India (convention states).*

Habilitado por la Junta Revolucionaria   overprinted on stamps of Spain: Spain. See **Spain**.

Habilitado por la Nacion   overprinted on stamps of Spain: Spain. See **Spain**.

Haiti   in the Caribbean just east of Cuba, occupying the western one-third of the island of Hispanola, bordered on the east by the Dominican Republic. Independent (1881→). Stamps are inscribed **Republique d'Haiti** or **Haiti**.

Hamburg   a city in north-central Germany. Stamps are inscribed **Hamburg** (1859–70). *German States.*

Hannover   a state in northwest Germany. Stamps are inscribed **Hannover** (1850–66). *German States.*

Hashemite Kingdom of Jordan   Jordan. See **Jordan**.

Hatay   a district in southern Turkey, including the city of Alexandretta (Iskenderun). Turkish (1939). Inscriptions include **Hatay Devleti** overprinted on stamps of Turkey or inscribed (1939). Hatay, part of the French mandate in the Middle East following World War I, was incorporated into Turkey in 1939.

Hatay Devleti   Hatay. See **Hatay**.

Haute-Volta   Upper Volta. See **Upper Volta**.

Haut-Senegal-Niger   Upper Senegal and Niger. See **Upper Senegal and Niger**.

Hawaii   located in the Pacific Ocean about 2,400 miles west of the United States, and including 8 main islands and more than 120 islets, reefs, and shoals. Independent (1851–98). Inscriptions include **Hawaiian Postage** (1851–53), **H.I. & U.S. Postage** (1851–53), **Honolulu Hawaiian I**ˢ (1853–61), **Hawaiian Postage** together with "Inter Island" and sometimes "Uka Leta" (1859–64), **Uka Leta** together with "Elua Keneta" (1861–63), **Hawaii** (1864–99). Beginning in 1898, Hawaii used stamps of the United States. *United States*.

H.E.H. the Nizam's Gov Postage or **Silver Jubilee**   Hyderabad, a native feudatory state in south-central India. *India (native feudatory states)*.

Hejaz & Nedj   see **Saudi Arabia**.

Heligoland   a small island in the North Sea off the northeast coast of Germany. British (1867–90). Stamps are inscribed **Heligoland**. In 1890 Great Britain ceded Heligoland to Germany.

Hellas   Greece. See **Greece**.

Helvetia   (1) Switzerland. See **Switzerland**. (2) with additional inscription such as "Bureau International du Travail": offices of the League of Nations or the United Nations. *Switzerland*.

Herzgoth Holstein   Holstein. *German States (Schleswig-Holstein)*.

Herzgoth-Schleswig   Schleswig. *German States (Schleswig-Holstein)*.

Herzgothum Holstein   Holstein. *German States (Schleswig-Holstein)*.

H.H. Nawabshah Jahanbegam   Bhopal, a native feudatory state in central India. *India (native feudatory states)*.

H.I. & U.S. Postage   Hawaiian Islands and U.S. Postage: Hawaii. See **Hawaii**.

H.K. Jordan or **H.K. of Jordan**   Jordan. See **Jordan**.

Hoi Hao   overprinted on stamps of Indochina: French offices in Hoi Hao (Hai-k'ou), China. *France (offices abroad)*.

Holkar State Postage   Indore, an Indian feudatory state. *India (native feudatory states)*.

Honduras   in Central America, bordered on the north and east by the Caribbean Sea, on the south by Nicaragua, on the southwest by the Pacific Ocean and El Salvador, and on the west by Guatemala. Independent (1865–→). Stamps are inscribed **Honduras**, often together with "Correos de," "Republica de," or abbreviated "Rep. de Honduras" or "Rep. de Honduras, C.A."

Hong Kong in southeast China at the mouth of the Canton River. British (1862–1999), Chinese (1999→). Inscriptions include **Hong Kong** (1862–1999), **Hong Kong, China** (1999→). Hong Kong was occupied by the Japanese during World War II. In 1999 Hong Kong reverted to China.

Honolulu Hawaiian I^s Hawaii. See **Hawaii**.

Horta the chief town on the island of Faial in the Azores Islands and for a time, administrative center for several of the islands. Portuguese (1892–1900s). Stamps are inscribed **Horta**.

H P N overprinted on stamps of Spain: Spain. See **Spain**.

HR Herceg Bosna see **Bosnia and Herzegovina (Croat)**.

Hrvatska Croatia.

Hrvatska Republika Herceg Bosna see **Bosnia and Herzegovina (Croat)**.

Hrvatska SHS overprinted on stamps of Hungary: Croatia-Slavonia. See **Yugoslavia**.

Hrzgl Post Frm (or **Frmke**) Holstein. *German States (Schleswig-Holstein)*.

H^T Senegal-Niger Upper Senegal and Niger. See **Upper Senegal and Niger**.

Hungary in central Europe, bordered on the north by Slovakia, on the northeast by Ukraine, on the east by Romania, on the south by Serbia, Croatia, and Slovenia, and on the west by Austria. Independent (1871→). Inscriptions include bust of Franz Josef I together with denomination and "Kr" (1871–74), **Magyar Kir. Posta** (1874–1918, 1921–25, 1937–45), **Magyar Kiralyi Posta** (occasionally), **Köztársaság** (1918–19), **Magyar Tanács-Koztársaság** or **Magyar Tanácskoztársaság** overprinted or inscribed (1919), **Magyar Posta** (1919–21, 1945–90), **Republica Hungarica** (1946), **Magyarország** (1925–37, 1990→), **Magyar Népköztársaság** (1949).

Hyderabad Hyderabad, a native feudatory state in south-central India. *India (native feudatory states)*.

Ibrahimo on stamps inscribed "Portugal" and "Colonia de Moçambique": *Mozambique (postal tax)*.

Iceland an island in the North Atlantic 185 miles east of Greenland. Danish (1873–1944), independent (1944→). Stamps are inscribed **Island** or **Ísland** (1873→).

Idar State Postage Idar, a native feudatory state in east-central India. *India (native feudatory states)*.

I.E.F. (India Expeditionary Force) overprinted on stamps of India: *India (military stamps)*.

I.E.F. 'D' (India Expeditionary Force) overprinted on stamps of Turkey: *Mesopotamia (British occupation)*.

Ierusalem overprinted on stamps of Russia together with surcharge in para(s) or piastre(s): Russian offices in Jerusalem, at the time, part of the Turkish Ottoman Empire. *Russia (offices in the Turkish Empire)*.

Ifni in southwestern Morocco, largely desert, an enclave of about 580 square miles, with only one city, Sidi Ifni, which has a lighthouse and an airport. Spanish (1941–69). Inscriptions include **Territorio de Ifni** overprinted on stamps of Spain (1941–42, 1948–51) or inscribed (1943–48), **Ifni** (1951–69) often with "Correos" and "España" (1951–69). In 1969 Spain returned Ifni, which had originally been part of Morocco, to Morocco.

Ile de la Réunion Reunion Island. See **Reunion**.

Ile Rouad (or Ruad) an island in the Mediterranean Sea off the coast of southern Syria. French (1916). Inscriptions include **Ile Rouad** overprinted on stamps of French offices in Levant (1916).

Iles Wallis et (or **&**) **Futuna** Wallis and Futuna. See **Wallis and Futuna**.

IM Fürstentum Liechtenstein Liechtenstein. See **Liechtenstein**.

Imperial British East Africa Company see **British East Africa**.

Imperial Japanese Post Japan. See **Japan**.

Império Colonial Portugués inscribed (**1**) on stamps used in Portuguese colonies, accompanied by the name of the colony: refer to the named colony; (**2**) on postage-due stamps without the name of any colony: *Portuguese Africa*.

Imperio Mexicano Correos Mexico. See **Mexico**.

In British Occupation - Baghdad overprinted on stamps of Turkey: Mesopotamia. See **Mesopotamia**.

In British Occupation - Iraq overprinted on stamps of Turkey: Mesopotamia. See **Mesopotamia**.

Inchi ya Katanga Katanga. See **Katanga**.

Inde F^{ÇAISE} French India. See **French India**.

Inde Française French India. See **French India**.

India in south-central Asia, occupying most of the subcontinent of India. British (1854–1947), independent (1947→). Inscriptions include **India** (1854–1955, 1882→), **East India Postage** (1865–82). In 1947 British India was divided into the independent nations of India and Pakistan (East and West). In 1971 East Pakistan broke away to become Bangladesh. Numerous issues exist for the various Native Indian states and feudatory states.

India   with "Correios Portugal" or "Republica Portuguesa": Portuguese India. See **Portuguese India**.

India   and "Comemorativo da Exposiçao de S. Françisco Xavier": Portuguese India. See **Portuguese India**.

India Port.   with "Servicio Postal": Portuguese India. See **Portuguese India**.

India Portugueza   Portuguese India. See **Portuguese India**.

Indochina   also known as French Indochina, in southeast Asia, consisting of and later split into Cambodia, Laos, and Vietnam. French (1889–1949). Inscriptions include **Indo-Chine** (1889–1904, 1907–27), **Indochine Française** (1904–07, 1942, 1944), **Indochine**, often with "Postes" (1927–45).

Indochine or **Indo-Chine**   Indochina. See **Indochina**.

Indochine Française   Indochina. See **Indochina**.

Indonesia   located south and east of mainland Asia and north and west of Australia and composed of more than 13,000 islands (about half of which are inhabited) stretching across 3,000 miles in the Pacific and Indian Oceans near the equator. Its main islands are Java, Sumatra, and Celebes, about three-quarters of the island of Borneo, the western half of the island of New Guinea (known as Irian Jaya or West Irian), and the smaller islands of Madura, Lombok, Sumbawa, Flores, and Bali. Independent (1950→). Inscriptions include **Republik Indonesia Serinat** (1950), **R I S** overprinted on stamps of Netherlands Indies (1950), **Republik Indonesia** (1950→). Indonesia was occupied by Japan during World War II. Much of Indonesia was part of the Netherlands Indies until after World War II. Issues of Netherlands Indies overprinted **Indonesia** or inscribed **Indonesia** without "Republik" were issued in 1948 and 1949 by Netherlands Indies while the country was still formally under control of the Netherlands. For the latter, see *Netherlands Indies*.

Indore State Postage   Indore, a native feudatory state in east-central India. *India (native feudatory states).*

Industrielle Kriegs-wirtshaft   overprinted on stamps of Switzerland: Industrial Board of Trade. *Switzerland (official issues).*

Inhambane   a province in southeastern Mozambique bordering Inhambane Bay on the Mozambique Channel. Portuguese (1895–1919). Inscriptions include **Centenario de S. Antonio - Inhambane - MDCCCXV** overprinted on stamps of Mozambique (1895), **Inhambane** with "Correios" and "Portugal" or "Republica Portuguesa (1903–19). Issues between 1911 and 1919 are often overprinted with "Republica." Subsequently, Inhambane used stamps of Mozambique.

Inini except for a coastal strip, the interior of French Guiana. French (1932–47). Inscriptions include **Territoire de l'Inini** or **Inini** overprinted on the generic issue for French Guiana (1932–47) or inscribed (1937, 1939).

Instruccion together with bust of Simón Bolívar: Venezuela. See **Venezuela**.

International Court of Justice International Court of Justice. *Netherlands (official issues)*.

Ionian Islands a group of islands in the Mediterranean Sea off western Greece, including Kefallinía (Cephalonia, Cefalonia), Kérkira (Corfu), Zákinthos (Zante), Levkás, and Itháki (Ithaca, Itaca). British (1859–64). Inscriptions include **ΙΟΝΙΚΟΝ ΚΡΑΤΟΣ** (1859–64), ITALIA - **Occupazione Militare Italiana Isole Cefalonia e Itaca** overprinted on stamps of Greece (Italian occupation, 1941), **Isole Jonie** overprinted on stamps of Italy (Italian occupation, 1941), **ΕΛΛΑΣ 2·X·43** overprinted on the foregoing stamps of Isole Jonie (German occupation, 1943). The Ionian Islands were a British protectorate until 1864, when they became part of Greece. They were occupied by Italy and Germany during World War II.

Iran in southwestern Asia, bordered on the north by Armenia, Azerbaijan, Turkmenistan, and the Caspian Sea, on the east by Afghanistan and Pakistan, on the south by the Gulf of Oman, the Strait of Hormuz, and the Persian Gulf, and on the west by Iraq and Turkey. Independent (1868→). Inscriptions include **Poste Persane** (1880–94, 1898), **Postes Persanes** (1894–1935), **Postes Iraniennes** overprinted or inscribed (1935–39), **Iran** (1949–79), **Republique Islamique de l'Iran** (1979–80), **Islamic Republic of Iran** (1979–80, 1986→), **R.I. Iran** (1980–84), **I.R. Iran** (1984–86). Some stamps of Iran bear inscriptions only in Arabic.

Iraq in southwest Asia, bordered on the north by Turkey, on the east by Iran, on the south by Saudi Arabia, Kuwait, and the Persian Gulf, and on the west by Jordan and Syria. British mandate (1923–32), independent (1932→). Inscriptions include **Iraq**, often with "postage" (1923–48), **Republic of Iraq** (1958→).

Iraq - In British Occupation overprinted on stamps of Turkey inscribed "Postes Ottomanes": Mesopotamia. See **Mesopotamia**.

Ireland an island just west of Great Britain. Independent (1922→). Inscriptions include **Rialtar Sealadaċ na Héireann 1922** overprinted on stamps of Great Britain (1922), **Saorstát Éireann 1922** overprinted on stamps of Great Britain (1925–29), **Éire** or **Eire** (1922→).

Irian Barat either overprinted on stamps of Indonesia or inscribed together with "Republik Indonesia": West Irian. See **West Irian**.

I.R. Iran Islamic Republic of Iran. See **Iran**.

Islamic Republic of Iran   Iran. See **Iran**.

Island or **Ísland**   Iceland. See **Iceland**.

Islas Galapagos   Galapagos Islands. See **Ecuador**.

Isle of Man   an island in the Irish Sea midway between Northern Ireland and Great Britain. British (1971→). Stamps are inscribed **Isle of Man**.

Isole Italiane Dell'Egeo   overprinted on stamps of Italy: Dodecanese Islands. See **Dodecanese Islands**. *Italy (Aegean Islands)*.

Isole Jonie   overprinted on stamps of Italy: Ionian Islands. See **Ionian Islands**.

Israel   on the eastern shore of the Mediterranean Sea, bordered on the north by Lebanon, on the northwest by Syria, on the east by Jordan, and on the southwest by Egypt. Independent (1948→). Inscriptions include **Israel** (1948→). Israel was part of the British Palestine mandate following World War I.

Istra - Slovensko-Primopje   Istria and the Slovene Coast. See **Yugoslavia**.

Istria - Littorale-Sloveno   Istria and the Slovene Coast. See **Yugoslavia**.

Itä-Karjala sot ballinto   either overprinted on stamps of Finland or inscribed together with "Suomi Finland": Karelia. See **Karelia**.

Italia   Italy. See **Italy**.

Italian Colonies   stamps not containing the name of a specific colony, issued for use in any African colony. Inscriptions include **Colonie Italiane** overprinted on stamps of Italy (1932), **Poste Coloniali Italiane** (1932), **R.R. Poste Coloniali Italiane** or **RR. Poste Coloniali Italiane** (1930s).

Italian East Africa   an area in east Africa consisting of the colonies of Ethiopia, Eritrea, and Italian Somaliland, bordered on the north and west by Sudan, on the east by the Red Sea, Somali Coast, and British Somaliland, and on the south by Kenya. Italian (1938–41). Inscriptions include **Africa Orientale Italiana** (1938–41), **A.O.F.** overprinted on stamps of Italy (1941).

ITALIA - **Occupazione Militare Italiana Isole Cefalonia e Itaca**   overprinted on stamps of Greece: Ionian Islands. See **Ionian Islands**.

Italy   in southern Europe, bordered on the west by the Tyrrhenian Sea, the Ligurian Sea, and the Mediterranean Sea, on the northwest by France, on the north by Switzerland and Austria, on the east by Slovenia and the Adriatic Sea, on the south by the Ionian Sea and the Mediterranean Sea, and including the Mediterranean islands of Elba, Sardinia, and Sicily. Independent (1862→). Inscriptions include **Franco Bollo** with embossed bust of Victor Emmanuel I and denomination (1862), **Franco Bollo Postale Italiano** (1863), **Poste Italiane** (1863–1952, 1955–59), **F**^{CO} **Bollo Postale Italiano** (1866–77), **Francobollo Postale Italiano** (1910),

Italia (1923, 1930s, 1969→), **Regno d'Italia** (1926–30), **Republica Italiana** or **Rep. Italiana** (1952–55).

Italy (Italian Social Republic) portions of fascist Italy under German occupation (1944–45). Inscriptions include **Repubblica Sociale Italiana** overprinted on stamps of Italy (1944), **Repub. Sociale Italiana Poste** (1944), **Poste Repubblica Sociale Italiana** (1944).

Ivory Coast (Côte d'Ivoire) in western Africa, bordered on the north by Mali and Burkina Faso, on the east by Ghana, on the south by the Gulf of Guinea, and on the west by Liberia and Guinea. French (1892–1945), independent (1960→). Inscriptions include **Côte d'Ivoire** inscribed, often with "RF" and "AOF" or "Afrique Occidentale Française" (1892–1945) or overprinted on stamps of Upper Volta (1933–36), **Republique de Côte d'Ivoire** (1959→). Between 1945 and 1958, the Ivory Coast was part of French West Africa and used its stamps.

Izmir Himayei Etfal Cemiyeti inscription on postal tax stamp: Turkey. *Turkey (postal tax)*.

Jaffa overprinted on stamps of Russia together with surcharge in para(s) or piastre(s): Jaffa, then a city in the Ottoman Turkish Empire. *Russia (offices in the Turkish Empire)*.

Jaipur State or **Jaipur Postage** Jaipur, a native feudatory state in north-central India. *India (native feudatory states)*.

Jamahuri Ya Tanganyika Tanganyika. See **Tanganyika**.

Jamaica an island nation in the Caribbean, located south of Cuba. British (1860–1962), independent (1962→). Stamps are inscribed **Jamaica**, the early issues often with "Postage" (1860→).

Jam. Dim. Soomaaliya Somalia. See **Somalia**.

Jamhuri Zanzibar or **Jamhuri Zanzibar Tanzania** Zanzibar. See **Zanzibar**.

Janina overprinted on stamps of Italy: Italian offices in Janina (Ioánnina), a city in northwestern Greece. *Italy (offices abroad)*.

Japan in east Asia, an island nation consisting of four main islands (Honshu, the largest, Hokkaido to the north of it, and Shikoku and Kyushu to the south), the Ryukyu Islands, and numerous smaller islands. The main island is west of the Korean Peninsula across the Sea of Japan and the Korea Strait, to the east lies the Pacific Ocean, and to the south, the Pacific Ocean and the East China Sea. Independent (1871→). Inscriptions include Japanese characters often with chrysanthemum symbol and word "sen" (1871–76), **Imperial Japanese Post** (1876–99), Japanese characters with "sen," "sn," "yen," or "en" (1899–1938), Japanese characters with or without chrysanthemum symbol (1938–66), **Nippon** (1966→).

Java   overprinted on stamps of Netherlands Indies: Netherlands Indies. *Netherlands Indies.*

J.D. Soomaaliya (or **Soomaaliyeed**)   Somalia. See **Somalia**.

Jeend State   overprinted on stamps of India: Jind state, a state in northern India. *India (convention states).*

Jersey   a British bailiwick in the English Channel off the coast of Normandy, France. German occupation (1941–45), British (1969→). Stamps are inscribed **Jersey**.

Jhind State   overprinted on stamps of India: Jind state, a state in northern India. *India (convention states).*

Jind or **Jhind State**   overprinted on stamps of India: Jind state, a state in northern India. *India (convention states).*

Johor or **Johore**   a Malayan (and later, Malaysian) state. **(1) Johor** or **Johore** overprinted on stamps of Straits Settlements: *Malaya (Johore)*; **(2) Johore** inscribed, sometimes with "Malaya" or "Persekutuan Tanah Melayu": *Malaya (Johore)*; **(3) Johore** together with "Malaysia": *Malaysia (Johore).*

Jordan   in southwestern Asia, bordered on the north by Syria, on the east by Iraq and Saudi Arabia, on the south by Saudi Arabia and the Gulf of Aqaba, on the west by Israel. British occupation/mandate (1920–46), independent (1946→). Inscriptions include Arabic inscription overprinted on stamps of British mandate (E.E.F. issue) or on stamps of Hejaz (1918–27), **Transjordan** (1927–49), **Hashemite Kingdom of the Jordan** (1949–53), **Hashemite Kingdom of Jordan**, **H.K. Jordan**, or **H.K. of Jordan** (1953→). Jordan was under the control of the Ottoman Turkish Empire until the end of World War I.

J. Soomaaliya   Somalia. See **Somalia**.

Jugoslavija   Yugoslavia. See **Yugoslavia**.

Jum. Dim. Somaliya   Somalia. See **Somalia**.

Kaiserlich Königlich Österreichische Post   Austria. See **Austria**.

Kais. Koenigl. Oesterr. Post   Austria. See **Austria**.

Kalaallit Nunaat Grønland   Greenland. See **Greenland**.

Kalåtdlit Nunåt Grønland   Greenland. See **Greenland**.

Kalayaan Nang Pilipinas   Philippines during Japanese occupation. See **Philippines**.

Kamerun   see **Cameroun** and **Cameroons**.

Karelia   in northwestern Russia, bordered on the north, east, and south by Russia and on the west by Lake Ladoga and Finland. Independent (1920–23), Finnish (1941–43). Inscriptions include **Karjala** (1922), **Itä-Karjala - sot.**

ballinto overprinted on stamps of Finland (1941–42) or inscribed together with "Suomi Finland" (1943). For several years following the Russian Revolution, Finland and Russia fought over Karelia, which had been part of Russia. In 1922 Karelia briefly asserted its independence. In 1923 it became a republic in the Soviet Union. For a time during World War II, Finland occupied part of Karelia. In 1991 after the breakup of the Soviet Union, Karelia became a republic within independent Russia. It uses Russian stamps.

Karjala   Karelia. See **Karelia**.

Karki   overprinted on stamps of Italy. See **Dodecanese Islands**. *Italy (Aegean Islands)*.

Karolinen   Caroline Islands. See **Caroline Islands**.

Katanga   in west-central Africa, bordered on the north by the Democratic Republic of the Congo, on the east by Tanzania, on the east and south by Zambia, and on the west by Angola. Independent (1960–63). Inscriptions include **Katanga** overprinted on stamps of the Belgian Congo (1960–61) or inscribed, sometimes with "Etat du" or "Inchi ya" (1961–63). In 1960 Katanga Province seceded from the newly independent Democratic Republic of the Congo. After several years of civil war, it was reunited with the DRC in 1963.

Kathiri State of Seiyun   see **Aden**.

Kazahstan   Kazakstan. See **Kazakstan**.

Kazakhstan   Kazakstan. See **Kazakstan**.

Kazakstan   in central Asia, bordered on the north by Russia, on the east by China, on the south by Kyrgyzstan, Uzbekistan, and Turkmenistan, and on the west by Russia and the Caspian Sea. Independent (1992→). Inscriptions include **Kazahstan** (1992), **КАЗАКСТАН** (1992–95), **Kazakstan** (1995–97), **Kazakhstan** (1997→). Kazakstan was formerly a republic in the Soviet Union.

Kedah   a Malayan (and later, Malaysian) state. **(1) Kedah** either by itself or with "Malaya" or "Persekutuan Tanah Melayu": *Malaya (Kedah)*; **(2) Kedah** together with "Malaysia": *Malaysia (Kedah)*.

Kelantan   a Malayan (and later, Malaysian) state. **(1) Kelantan** either with "Postage and Revenue," "Malaya," or "Persekutuan Tanah Melayu": *Malaya (Kelantan)*; **(2) Kelantan** together with "Malaysia": *Malaysia (Kelantan)*.

Kenya   in east Africa bordered on the north by Sudan and Ethiopia, on the east by Somalia and the Indian Ocean, on the south by Tanzania, and on the west by Lake Victoria and Uganda. Independent (1963→). Inscriptions include **Kenya** (1963→), **Republic of Kenya** (1964).

Kenya and Uganda see **Kenya, Uganda, Tanzania**.

Kenya, Uganda, Tanganyika see **Kenya, Uganda, Tanzania**.

Kenya, Uganda, Tanzania in east Africa, bordering the Indian Ocean and consisting of Kenya, Uganda, and Tanganyika. British (1935–60s). Inscriptions include **East Africa and Uganda Protectorates** (1921–27), **Kenya and Uganda** (1927–35), **Kenya, Uganda, Tanganyika** (arranged in various orders, 1935–63), **Kenya, Uganda, Tanganyika, Zanzibar** (1964), **Kenya, Uganda, Tanzania** (1965–76). Tanganyika achieved independence in 1961; Uganda, in 1962; Kenya, in 1963. Tanganyika merged with Zanzibar in 1964 to form Tanzania. Following independence, each nation issued its own stamps.

Kerassunde overprinted on stamps of Russia together with surcharge in para(s) or piastre(s): *Russia (offices in the Turkish Empire)*.

KGC - 19A20 overprinted on stamps of Slovenia: Slovenia. *Yugoslavia (Slovenia)*.

KGL Post Fr.M. **(1)** denominated in skillings (abbreviated "s"): Denmark. See **Denmark**. **(2)** denominated in cents: Danish West Indies. See **Danish West Indies**.

Kiatschou Kiauchau. See **Kiauchau**.

Kiauchau (Tsingtao) a city and surrounding territory in Shantung Province in eastern China leased to Germany in the late nineteenth century. German (1900–15). Inscriptions include **5 Pfg.** overprinted together with "China" on stamps of Germany (1900–01), **Kiatschou** (1901–15).

Kibris Cumhuriyeti overprinted on stamps of Cyprus: Cyprus. See **Cyprus**.

Kibris - Cyprus see **Cyprus**.

Kibris Türk Federe Devleti Postalari Turkish Republic of Northern Cyprus. See **Turkish Republic of Northern Cyprus**.

Kingdom of Lesotho see **Lesotho**.

Kingdom of Saudi Arabia Saudi Arabia. See **Saudi Arabia**.

Kionga a small wedge territory of approximately 245 square miles in southeast Africa, in extreme northeastern Mozambique, just south of the Rio Rovuma, and sometimes referred to as the Kionga triangle. Portuguese (1916). Inscriptions include **Republica Kionga** overprinted, together with surcharged value, on stamps of Lourenço Marques (1916). In 1894 German East Africa seized the Kionga triangle from Portuguese Mozambique. Portugal retook the territory in World War I and retained it after war as part of Mozambique.

Kiribati a widely scattered group of 33 coral islands and atolls in the west-central Pacific Ocean northeast of Australia, of which only about 20 are permanently inhabited. Independent (1979→). Stamps are inscribed **Kiribati**. Kiribati was formerly the Gilbert Islands.

Kishengarh or **Kishengarh State**   Kishengarh, a feudatory state in west-central India. *India (native feudatory states)*. Stamps of Kishengarh handstamped with Urdu script and rectangle are issues of Rajasthan.

KK Post Stempel   **(1)** denominated in kreuzers: Austria. See **Austria**. **(2)** denominated in centes: Lombardy-Venetia. See **Lombardy-Venetia**. *Austria (Lombardy-Venetia)*.

Klaipeda   overprinted together with "(Memel)" on stamps of Lithuania or inscribed together with "Memel": Memel. See **Memel**.

Kongeligt Post Frimaerke   Denmark. See **Denmark**.

Korea (South)   in northeastern Asia, on the southern part of the Korean Peninsula, bordered on the north by China (North Korea, after 1945), on the east by the Sea of Japan, on the southeast and south by the Korea Strait, and on the west by the Yellow Sea. Independent (1884–1910, 1946→). Inscriptions include **Corean** (1884–95), **Korea** (1895–1900, 1948–53), **Imperial Korean Post** (1900–04), **Postes de Corée** (1902), **Postes Imperiales de Coree** (1903), **Republic of Korea** or **Korea** (1961→). Most stamps issued between 1946 and 1961 contain inscriptions only in Korean, but usually with the Yin Yang symbol and often with the letters "CH" preceding the Korean letters. Japan annexed Korea in 1910, and it used stamps of Japan until 1946. In 1945 Korea was divided along the 38th parallel into North Korea and South Korea.

Kouang Tchéou   overprinted on stamps of Indochina: French offices in Kwangchow, China. *France (offices abroad)*.

Kouang Tchéou-wan   overprinted on stamps of Indochina: French offices in Kwangchow, China. *France (offices abroad)*.

Köztársaság   (republic) overprinted on stamps of Hungary: Hungary. See **Hungary**.

Κρhτα   either by itself or overprinted "ΕΛΛΑΣ" or "ΕΛΛΑΣ ΠΡΟΣΟΡΙΝΟΝ": Crete. See **Crete**.

Kr.1.98   overprinted on stamps of Sweden: parcel post. *Sweden*.

Kraljevina Jugoslavija   Yugoslavia. See **Yugoslavia**.

Kraljevina SHS   Slovenia. See **Yugoslavia**.

Kraljevstvo SHS   Slovenia. See **Yugoslavia**.

Kraljevstvo S.H.S.   overprinted on stamps of Bosnia and Herzegovina: Yugoslavia. See **Yugoslavia**.

Kraljevstvo Srba, Hrvata i Slovenaca   overprinted on stamps of Bosnia and Herzegovina or inscribed: Yugoslavia. See **Yugoslavia**.

K.S.A.   Kingdom of Saudi Arabia. See **Saudi Arabia**.

K-u-K (or K-und-K) Feldpost   (**1**) overprinted on stamps of Bosnia: *Austria (military stamps)*; (**2**) with denomination as numeral only or with numeral and "k": *Austria (military stamps)*; (**3**) with denomination in bani or lei: *Romania (Austrian occupation)*; (**4**) overprinted with denomination in lira or centesimi: *Italy (Austrian occupation)*.

K-u-K Militärpost   see **Bosnia and Herzegovina**.

K.U.K. Milit.-Verwaltung Montenegro   overprinted on military stamps of Austria: Montenegro (Austrian occupation). See **Montenegro**.

Kurland   a region on the Baltic coast in Latvia. German occupation (1945). Inscriptions include **Kurland** overprinted on stamps of Germany (1945). *Latvia*.

Kuwait   on the northeastern coast of the Persian Gulf, bordered on the north and west by Iraq, on the south and west by Saudi Arabia, and on the east by the Persian Gulf. British (1923–61), independent (1961→) Inscriptions include **Kuwait** overprinted on stamps of India (1923–49), on stamps of Great Britain (1949–59), **Kuwait** or **State of Kuwait** (1959→).

Kuzey Kirbris Türk Cümhuriyeti   Turkish Republic of Northern Cyprus. See **Turkish Republic of Northern Cyprus**.

K. Wurtt. Post   Württemberg. See **Württemberg**.

Kyrgyzstan   in central Asia, bordered on the north by Kazakstan, on the east by China, on the south by China and Tajikistan, and on the west by Uzbekistan. Kyrgyzstan was formerly a republic in the Soviet Union. Independent (1992→). Inscriptions include **Kyrgyzstan** and/or **КЫРГЫЗСТАН** (1992→).

La Agüera   Aguera. See **Aguera**.

Labuan   an island in the East Indies just off the northwest coast of Borneo. British (1879–1906). Inscriptions include **Labuan** together with "Postage" (1879–94, 1902–03), overprinted on stamps of North Borneo (1894–1906). In 1906 Labuan was incorporated into the Straits Settlements.

La Canea   overprinted on stamps of Italy: Italian offices in Canea (Khaniá), a city in Crete. *Italy (offices abroad)*.

La Georgie   Georgia. See **Georgia**.

Lagos   in western Africa, in southwestern Nigeria, bordered on the west by Dahomey. British (1879–1906). Stamps are inscribed **Lagos**. Lagos was subsequently part of Nigeria.

Land-Post Porto-Marken Baden. *German States.*

Laos in southeast Asia, bordered on the north by China and Vietnam, on the east by Vietnam, on the south by Cambodia, on the west by Thailand, and on the northwest by Myanmar (Burma). Independent (1951→). Inscriptions include **Royaume du Laos** (1951–75), **Postes Lao** (1976, 1981→), **Republique Democratique Populaire Lao** or **Rep. Dem. Pop. Lao** (1977–82). Prior to independence, Laos was part of French Indochina.

L.A.R. or **LAR** Libyan Arab Republic. See **Libya**.

Las Bela State Las Bela, a native feudatory state in northwest India, in part of what is now Pakistan. *India (native feudatory states).*

Latakia a city and governorate in northwestern Syria that came within the French mandate of Syria and Lebanon. French (1931–37). Inscriptions include **Lattaquie** overprinted on stamps of Syria (1931–37). Beginning in 1937, Latakia used stamps of Syria. Latakia was formerly known as Alaouites. It is now situated in Syria.

Lattiquie overprinted on stamps of Syria: Latakia. See **Latakia**.

Latvia in northeastern Europe, bordered on the north by Estonia and the Gulf of Rìga, an inlet of the Baltic Sea, on the east by Russia, on the south by Belarus and Lithuania, and on the west by the Baltic Sea. Independent (1918–40, 1991→). Inscriptions include **Latvija** (1918–40, 1991→), **Libau** overprinted on stamps of Germany (German occupation, 1919), **Latwija** (1919–20), **Latwijas Pasts** (1920), **Latvijas PSR** (Russian occupation, 1940), **Latvija** and "1941 1. VII" overprinted on stamps of Russia (German occupation, 1941). In 1940 the Soviet Union invaded Latvia and absorbed it. In 1941 Germany invaded Latvia and occupied it. At the end of World War II, Latvia returned to the Soviet Union. In 1991, at the time of the breakup of the Soviet Union, Latvia regained independence.

Latvija Latvia. See **Latvia**.

Latvija - 1941 1. VII overprinted on stamps of Russia: Latvia. See **Latvia**.

Latvijas PSR Latvia. See **Latvia**.

Latwija Latvia. See **Latvia**.

Latwijas Pasts Latvia. See **Latvia**.

Lebanon on the eastern Mediterranean Sea, bordered on the north and east by Syria and on the south by Israel. French mandate (1924–41), independent (1941→). Inscriptions include **Gran Liban** (1924–27), **G^D Liban** (1924–25), **Republique Libanaise** (1927–50), **Liban** (1947→). Lebanon was under Ottoman Turkish control until World War I.

Leeward Islands   a chain of islands in the West Indies southeast of Puerto Rico, at the northern end of the Lesser Antilles, between the Atlantic Ocean and Caribbean Sea, including Antigua, Montserrat, Saint Christopher (Saint Kitts) with Nevis and Anguilla, the British Virgin Islands, and, until 1940, Dominica. British (1890–1956). Inscriptions include **Leeward Islands** (1890–1956). Each of the group issued its own stamps during the same time.

Leros   overprinted on stamps of Italy. See **Dodecanese Islands**. *Italy (Aegean Islands).*

Lesotho   in eastern South Africa, an enclave within South Africa. Independent (1966→). Inscriptions include **Lesotho** (1966→) and occasionally, **Kingdom of Lesotho** (1980s). Lesotho was formerly Basutoland.

Levant   overprinted on stamps of Great Britain: British offices in the Ottoman Empire. *Great Britain (offices abroad: Levant).*

Levant   overprinted on Polish stamps: Polish offices in Levant. *Poland (offices abroad).*

Levante   overprinted on stamps of Italy: Italian offices in Levant, an area in the Ottoman Turkish Empire bordering the eastern Mediterranean Sea. *Italy (offices abroad).*

Liban   Lebanon. See **Lebanon**.

Libau   overprinted on stamps of Germany: Latvia. See **Latvia**.

Liberia   in western Africa, bordered on the north by Sierra Leone and Guinea, on the east by the Ivory Coast (Côte d'Ivoire), and on the west and south by the Atlantic Ocean. Independent (1860→). Inscriptions include **Liberia**, **Republic Liberia**, or **Republic of Liberia** (1960→).

Libia   Libya. See **Libya**.

Libya   in northern Africa, bordered on the north by the Mediterranean Sea, on the east by Egypt, on the southeast by the Republic of Sudan, on the south by Chad and Niger, on the west by Algeria, and on the northwest by Tunisia. Italian (1912–43), independent (1952→). Inscriptions include **Libia** overprinted on stamps of Italy (1912–21) or inscribed (1921–43), **Tripoli** together with a Roman numeral and "Fiera Campionaria" (1927–38), **Libya** overprinted on stamps of Cyrenaica (1951) or inscribed (1961), **Kingdom of Libya** (1952–55), **Libye** (1955), **United Kingdom of Libya** (1958–61, 1968–69), **L.A.R.** or **LAR** (1969–77), **Socialist People's Libyan Arab Jamahiriya** (1977→). Libya is composed of the former Italian colonies of Tripolitania, Cyrenaica, and Fezzan. Allied forces occupied Libya during World War II. Following World War II, Great Britain and France shared control of the country until its independence. See also **Fezzan-Ghadames**.

Libye   Libya. See **Libya**.

Liechtenstein   in central Europe, bordered on the west, north, and south by Switzerland and on the east by Austria and amounting to only 62 square miles. Independent (1912→). Inscriptions include **IM Fürstentum Liechtenstein** (1912–20), **Fürstentum** (or **Fuerstentum**) **Liechtenstein** or **Liechtenstein** (1920→).

Lietuva   Lithuania. See **Lithuania**.

Lietuvos Pašta or **Paštas**   Lithuania. See **Lithuania**.

Lietuvos Pasto Zenklas   Lithuania. See **Lithuania**.

Lignes Aeriennnes de la France Libre   military stamps (Free French): Syria. *Syria*.

Lignes Aeriennnes F.A.F.L.   overprinted on stamps of Syria: military stamps (Free French) in Syria. *Syria*.

Lima   overprinted or inscribed: Peru. See **Peru**.

Lipso   overprinted on stamps of Italy. See **Dodecanese Islands**. *Italy (Aegean Islands)*.

Lithuania   in northeastern Europe, bordered on the north by Latvia, on the east and south by Belarus, on the southwest by Poland and Russia, and on the west by the Baltic Sea. Independent (1920–40, 1991→). Inscriptions include **Lietuvos** and "Pašta" or "Paštas" (1918–19), **Lietuvos Pasto Zenklas** (1919–20), **Lietuva** (1921–40, 1991→), **Postgebiet ob. Ost** overprinted on stamps of Germany (German occupation, 1916–18), **LTSR** overprinted together with "1940 VII 12" (Russian occupation, 1940). In 1940 the Soviet Union invaded Lithuania and absorbed it. In 1941 Germany invaded Lithuania and occupied it. At the end of World War II, Lithuania returned to the Soviet Union. In 1991, at the time of the breakup of the Soviet Union, it regained independence.

Litwa Środkowa (or **Srodkowej**)   Central Lithuania.

Ljubljana   (also Lubiana or Liabach) a province (at the time, consisting of the western portion of Slovenia) and city (its capital) in central Slovenia. Italian/German (1941–45). Inscriptions include **Co. Ci.** overprinted on stamps of Yugoslavia (Italian occupation, 1941), **R. Commissariato Civile Territori Sloveni occupati Lubiana** overprinted on stamps of Yugoslavia (Italian occupation, 1941), **Provinz Laibach - Ljubljanska Pokrajina** overprinted on stamps of Italy (German occupation, 1944), **Provinz Laibach** (German occupation, 1945). *Yugoslavia (Ljubljana)*.

L. Marques   overprinted on stamps of Mozambique: Lourenço Marques. See **Lourenço Marques**.

Local Post - Shanghai Municipality   see **Shanghai**.

Lombardy-Venetia   in southern Europe, consisting of two provinces at present in north and northeast Italy (Lombardy and Venetia), which for a time were part of Austria. Austrian (1850–68). Inscriptions include **KK Post Stempel** and denomination in centes (1850–54), bust of emperor or national crest and denomination in soldi (1854–68). The foregoing are almost identical to issues of Austria during the same period but can be distinguished as follows: issues of Austria are denominated in kreuzers (abbreviated "kr"); issues of Lombardy-Venetia are denominated in centes or soldi. *Austria (Lombardy-Venetia).*

Lothringen   overprinted on stamps of France: German occupation of Lorraine (1940). *France (occupation issues).*

Lourenço Marques   a city (now Maputo) and district in far southeastern Mozambique. Portuguese (1895–1920). Inscriptions include **Lourenço Marques** (1895–98), **L. Marques** overprinted on stamps of Mozambique (1895), **Correio de Lourenço Marques** overprinted on revenue stamps of Mozambique (1899), **Lourenço Marques** often with "Correio," "Portugal," or "Republica Portuguesa" (1895–1920). Issues between 1911 and 1920 are often overprinted "Republica."

LTSR - 1940 VII 12   overprinted on stamps of Lithuania: Lithuania. See **Lithuania**.

Lubeck   a city and small state in north-central Germany. Stamps are inscribed **Lübeck** (1859–63), **Luebeck** (1863–70). *German States.*

Luebeck   Lubeck. See **Lubeck**.

Luxembourg   in western Europe, bordered by Belgium on the north and west, Germany on the east, and France on the south. Independent (1852→). Inscriptions include bust of Grand Duke William III together with "Postes" and denomination (1852–59), **G.D. de Luxembourg** (1859–82), **G^D Duche de Luxembourg** (1882–91), **Grand Duche de Luxembourg** (1891–1906), **Luxembourg** (1906→), **Grand Duche Luxembourg** or **Luxembourg** (1914–39), **Luxemburg** overprinted on stamps of Germany (German occupation, 1940–41).

Macao   a territory located on the southeast coast of mainland China. Portuguese (1884–1999), Chinese (1999→). Inscriptions include **Macau** sometimes with "Correios," or "Portugal" and often with "Republica Portuguesa" (1884–1999), **Provincia de Macau** (1888–94), **Macau, China** (1999→). Macao reverted to China in 1999. Issues between 1911 and 1920 are often overprinted with "Republica."

Macau, China   see **Macao**.

Macau - Correios Portugal   Macao. See **Macao**.

Macedonia   in southeastern Europe on the Balkan Peninsula, bordered on the north by Serbia, on the east by Bulgaria, on the south by Greece, and on the west by Albania. Independent (1992→). Inscriptions include **Macedonia** or **Republic of Macedonia** (1992–93), **Makedonija**, often with "PTT" (1994–95),

Republica Makedonija (1998), **ПТТ МАКЕДОНИЈА** or **МАКЕДОНИЈА** (1993-98), **ПОШТИ МАКЕДОНСКИ** (1997), **РЕПУБЛИКА МАКЕДОНИЈА** (1998→). Macedonia was formerly a constituent republic of Yugoslavia.

Macontene on stamps inscribed "Portugal" and "Colonia de Moçambique": *Mozambique (postal tax).*

Madagascar in the Indian Ocean, separated from the southeastern coast of Africa by the Mozambique Channel and composed of the island of Madagascar and several small islands. French (1889–1958). Inscriptions include **Madagascar** and "Postes Française" (1891), **Postes Française Madagascar** overprinted on stamps of France (1895), **Madagascar et Dependances** together with "Republique Française" or "RF" (1896–1930), **Madagascar** (1930–58) and overprinted "France Libre" (1942). In 1958 Madagascar became Malagasy Republic. *Malagasy Republic.*

Madiera an archipelago in the Atlantic Ocean, located about 700 miles southwest of Portugal, consisting of two inhabited islands, Madeira and Porto Santo, and two uninhabited island groups, the Desertas and the Selvagens. Portuguese (1868–98, 1928–29, 1980→). Inscriptions include **Madiera** overprinted on stamps of Portugal (1868–98), **Madiera** inscribed together with "Portugal Correio" (1928–29). In 1898 Madiera began using stamps of Portugal and except for a brief period in the late 1920s continued to do so until 1980. Beginning in 1980, Portugal issued stamps inscribed **Madiera** together with "Portugal" (1980→). For the latter, see *Portugal.*

Madiera (1) overprinted on stamps of Portugal: Madiera. See **Madiera**. (2) inscribed together with "Portugal": Portugal. See **Portugal**.

Madrid - 1920 inscribed on a commemorative issue: Spain. *Spain.*

Madrid - 1930 inscribed on a commemorative issue: Spain. *Spain.*

Mafeking Besieged overprinted on stamps of the Cape of Good Hope or Bechuanaland: Mafeking. Mafeking is a town in northern South Africa that was besieged by the Boers in 1900 during the Boer War. *Cape of Good Hope (Mafeking).*

Magyar Kir. (or **Kiralyi**) **Posta** Hungary. See **Hungary**.

Magyar Nemzeti Kormany - Szeged, 1919 overprinted on stamps of Hungary by the anti-Bolshevik, nationalist government in Szeged: *Hungary.*

Magyar Népköztársaság Hungary. See **Hungary**.

Magyarország Hungary. See **Hungary**.

Magyar Posta Hungary. See **Hungary**.

Magyar Tanács-Koztársaság or **Magyar Tanácskoztársaság** Hungary. See **Hungary**.

Makedonija Macedonia. See **Macedonia**.

Malacca a Malayan (and later, Malaysian) state. **(1) Malacca** with "Malaya": *Malaya (Malacca)*; **(2) Malacca** together with "Malaysia": *Malaysia (Malacca)*.

Malagasy Republic in the Indian Ocean, separated from the southeastern coast of Africa by the Mozambique Channel and composed of the island of Madagascar and several small islands. Independent (1958→). Inscriptions include **Republique Malgache** (1959–61), **Repoblika Malagasy** (1961–76), **Repoblika Demokratika Malagasy** (1976–93), **Repoblikan'i Madagasikara** (1993→). Malagasy Republic was formerly Madagascar.

Malawi in central Africa on the west shore of Lake Nyasa (Lake Malawi), bordered on the north by Tanzania, on the southeast and south by Mozambique. Independent (1964→). Stamps are inscribed **Malawi** and occasionally **Republic of Malawi**. Malawi was formerly British Nyasaland.

Malaya (Federated Malay States) occupying the Malay Peninsula south of Thailand. British (1900–35). Stamps are inscribed **Federated Malay States**. Beginning in 1935, individual states within the federation issued their own stamps. They are inscribed **Malaya** together with the name of the state and include Johore (Johor), Kedah, Kelantan, Malacca (Melaka), Negri Sembilan, Pahang, Penang (Pinang), Perak, Perlis, Selangor, and Trengganu. In addition, some states issued stamps prior to 1900, before the general Federated States issues came into use. In 1957 the states formed the independent Federation of Malaya.

Malaya (Federation of) occupying the Malay Peninsula south of Thailand. Independent (1957–63). Inscriptions include **Malaya - Federation of Malaya** (1957-60), **Malaya - Persekutuan Tanah Melayu** (1957-60), **Persekutuan Tanah Melayu** (1960–63). In 1963 the Federation of Malaya (together with Singapore, Sarawak, and Sabah) became Malaysia.

Malayan Postal Union inscribed on postage-due stamps: Federated Malay States. See **Malaya (Federated Malay States)**.

Malaysia occupying the Malay Peninsula south of Thailand and the northwest part of the island of Borneo. Independent (1963→). Stamps are inscribed **Malaysia**. Malaysia is composed of 13 states: Johore (Johor), Kedah, Kelantan, Melaka (Malacca), Negri Sembilan, Pahang, Perak, Perlis, Pinang (Penang), Sabah (North Borneo), Sarawak, Selangor, and Trengganu, plus two federal districts: Kuala Lampur and Labuan. Singapore joined the federation in 1963 and then withdrew in 1965. Malaysia (excluding Singapore, Sarawak, and Sabah) was formerly the Federation of Malaya. In addition to the general issues, some individual states have, from time to time, issued their own stamps. They contain the state's name together with the inscription "Malaysia."

Maldive Islands   a chain of nearly 2,000 coral atolls in the Indian Ocean southwest of India. British (1906–65), independent (1965→). Inscriptions include **Maldives** overprinted on stamps of Ceylon (1906–09) or inscribed (1909–50, 1986→), **Maldive Islands** (1950–68), **Republic of Maldives** (1968–86).

Mali   in northwestern Africa, bordered on the northeast by Algeria, on the east by Niger, on the south by Burkina Faso, the Ivory Coast (Côte d'Ivoire), and Guinea, and on the west by Senegal and Mauritania. Federation (1959–60), republic (1960→). Inscriptions include **Federation du Mali** (1959–60), **Republique du Mali** overprinted on stamps of the federation (1960–61) or inscribed (1960→), **Mali** (occasionally). In June 1960, the Sudanese Republic (the former French Sudan) and Senegal merged to form the Federation of Mali. In August 1960, Senegal withdrew from the federation.

Malmédy   overprinted on stamps of Belgium. See **Eupen & Malmédy**.

Malta   a small group of islands in the Mediterranean south of Sicily, including Malta, Gozo, Kemmuna, Kemmunett, and Filfla. British (1860–1964), independent (1964→). Stamps are inscribed **Malta**.

Manchukuo   in northeast China, a puppet state set up by the Japanese and including Manchuria and the Chinese province of Jehol. Nominally independent (1932–45). Stamps are inscribed in Chinese or Japanese characters and an orchid crest symbol and are often denominated in "Fen" or "Fn." The bulk of Manchukuo reverted to China following World War II.

Mandated Territory of Tanganyika   Tanganyika. See **Tanganyika**.

Mariana Islands   (also known as the Northern Mariana Islands) in the Pacific Ocean, east of the Philippines and south of Japan and including approximately 16 coral and volcanic islands. Spanish (1899), German (1899–1918). Inscriptions include **Marianas Espanolas** overprinted on stamps of the Spanish Philippines (1899), **Marianen** overprinted on stamps of Germany (1899–1900) or inscribed (1901–18). In 1899 Germany purchased the Marianas. Following World War I, they became a League of Nations mandate under control of Japan. During World War II, they were captured by the United States, and following the war, they were administered by the United States.

Marianas Espanolas   overprinted on stamps of the Spanish Philippines: Mariana Islands. See **Mariana Islands**.

Marianen   overprinted on stamps of Germany or inscribed: Mariana Islands. See **Mariana Islands**.

Marienwerder   a regency centered in the city of Marienwerder, East Prussia (now Kwidzyn, Poland), located just east of the Vistula River and about 45 miles southeast of Danzig (Gdansk). International Commission (1920). Inscriptions include **Commission Interallie Marienwerder** (1920), **Commission Interallée Marienwerder** overprinted on stamps of Germany (1920), **Plebiscite Marienwerder** (1920). In 1920 Marienwerder held a plebiscite to determine whether it should become part of Germany or Poland. It voted to remain part of Germany.

Maroc   (1) Morocco. See **Morocco**. (2) French Morocco. See **French Morocco**.

Marocco   overprinted, together with surcharged value, on stamps of Germany: German offices in Morocco. *Germany (offices abroad)*.

Marruecos   (1) either overprinted on stamps of Spain or inscribed together with "Protectarado Español": Spanish Morocco. See **Spanish Morocco**. (2) without "Protectarado Español": Morocco, northern zone. See **Morocco**.

Marschall Inseln   Marshall Islands. See **Marshall Islands**.

Marshall Inseln   Marshall Islands. See **Marshall Islands**.

Marshall Islands   a widely dispersed group of atolls in the central North Pacific Ocean including Bikini, Eniwitok, and Kwajalein. German (1897–1914), U.S. (1984–90), independent (1990→). Inscriptions included: **Marschall Inseln** (1897–98), **Marshall Inseln** (1897–1914), **Marshall Islands** (1984→). The Marshall Islands were a German possession until World War I, became a League of Nations mandate under control of Japan until World War II, a U.S. Trust Territory in 1947, a self-governing entity in 1979, a sovereign state in free association with the United States in 1986, and a member of the United Nations in 1991.

Martinique   in the West Indies, in the eastern Caribbean Sea, off the northwestern coast of South America. French (1886–1947). Inscriptions include **MQE** overprinted on the generic issue for French colonies (1886–92), **Martinique** overprinted on the generic issue for French colonies or on stamps of France (1886–92, 1927) or inscribed, often together with "RF" or "Republique Française." Martinique became an overseas department of France in 1947 and has used stamps of France since.

Mauritania   in northwestern Africa, bordered on the north by Western Sahara and Algeria, on the east by Mali, on the south by Mali and Senegal, and on the west by the Atlantic Ocean. French (1906–43), independent (1960→). Inscriptions include **Mauritanie** together with "RF" or "Afrique Occidentale Française" (1906–43), **Republique Islamique de Mauritanie** (1960→). Between 1943 and 1960, Mauritania used stamps of French West Africa. In 1944 some issues of Mauritania were surcharged and used in French West Africa *(French West Africa)*.

Mauritanie   Mauritania. See **Mauritania**.

Mauritius   a group of islands in the Indian Ocean east of Madagascar, including Mauritius, Rodrigues, the Agalega Islands, and Cagados Carajos Shoals. British (1849–1968), independent (1968→). Inscriptions include **Mauritius** together with "Post Office" (1847), **Mauritius** together with "Post Paid" (1848), **Mauritius** (1949→). The island of Mauritius contains about 90 percent of the area of the country.

Mayotte   one of the four main islands of the Comoros archipelago, lying at the northern end of the Mozambique Channel about 200 miles from Madagascar. French (1892–1912, 1992→). Inscriptions include **Mayotte** (1892–1912), **Mayotte** together with "Republique Française" (1992→). Between 1912 and 1992, Mayotte used stamps of France, French Comoros, or French Madagascar.

M.B.D.   overprinted on stamps inscribed "Feudatory State of Raj Nandgam": Nandgaon, a native feudatory state in east-central India. *India (native feudatory states)*.

Mbre. Shqiptare   overprinted on stamps of Albania. See **Albania**.

Mbretnia Shqyptare (or **Shqiptare**)   Albania. See **Albania**.

Mbretnija Shqiptare   Albania. See **Albania**.

Mecklenburg-Schwerin   a state in northeastern Germany. Stamps are inscribed **Mecklenb. Schwerin** (1856–70). *German States*.

Mecklenburg-Strelitz   a state in northeastern Germany. Stamps are inscribed **Mecklenb. Strelitz** (1864–70). *German States*.

Mecklenburg Vorpommern or **Mecklbg-Vorpomm**   Mecklenburg-Vorpommern, an administrative region in Soviet occupied Germany (1945–46). *German Democratic Republic (Russian occupation)*.

M.E.F.   (Middle East Forces) overprinted on stamps of Great Britain: British forces in the Middle East and northern Africa. *Great Britain (offices abroad)*.

Memel   a former German territory on the eastern coast of the Baltic Sea, now part of Lithuania. Allied Powers Commission (1920–23). Inscriptions include **Memel=Gebiet** overprinted on stamps of Germany (1920), **Memelgebiet** overprinted on stamps of Germany (1920), **Memel** overprinted on stamps of France together with surcharged value (1920–23), **Klaipeda (Memel)** overprinted on stamps of Lithuania (Lithuanian occupation, 1923), **Klaipeda** inscribed together with "Memel" (1923). Early in 1923, Lithuania seized the region, and the following year, the League of Nations made it a Lithuanian autonomous district. The city of Memel (now Klaipêda) was the capital of the territory.

Memelgebiet or **Memel=Gebiet**   overprinted on stamps of Germany: Memel. See **Memel**.

Mesopotamia   in the Middle East, a part of the former Ottoman Empire encompassing parts of what are now Iraq and Syria. Occupied by the British in World War I, and following the war, split by the League of Nations into mandates administered by the British (Iraq) and French (Syria). Inscriptions include **Baghdad - In British Occupation** overprinted on stamps of Turkey (1917), **Iraq - In British Occupation** (1918–23), **Postage - I.E.F. 'D'** overprinted on stamps of Turkey (1919–).

Metelin   overprinted on stamps of Russia together with surcharge in para(s) or piastre(s): *Russia (offices in the Turkish Empire)*.

Mexico   in North America, bordered on the north by the United States, on the west by the Pacific Ocean, on the east by the Gulf of Mexico and the Caribbean Sea, and on the south by Guatemala and Belize. Independent (1856→). Inscriptions include **Mexico** often with "Correos" (1856–1980), **Imperio Mexicano Correos** (1866–68), **Servicio Postale Mexicano** (1884–95), **Gobierno Constitutionalista** overprinted (1914), **S.P. Mexico** (1916), **Mexico** or **México** (1980→). During the Mexican Revolutionary War, Oaxaca, a state in southeastern Mexico on the Yucatan Peninsula, and Sonora, a state in northwestern Mexico, issued provisional stamps. Inscriptions include **Correos Transitorio - Estado Libre y Soberano Oaxaca** (Oaxaca, 1915), **Estado Libre y Soberano de Sonora** (Sonora, 1913–14), **Transitorio** together with "Mexico" and in some cases "Correos" (Sonora, 1913–14), **Sonora** together with "Correos" and "Mexico" (Sonora, 1913–15), **Distrito sur de la Baja Cal** (Sonora, 1914).

Micronesia (Federated States of)   a group of about 600 islands in the western Pacific Ocean, located north of the equator more than 2,500 miles southwest of Honolulu, Hawaii. U.S. (1984–86), independent (1986→). Stamps are inscribed **Federated States of Micronesia** (1984→). Micronesia was part of the German possession of Caroline Islands (which at the time included **Palau**) until World War I, became a League of Nations mandate under control of Japan until World War II, was captured by the United States during World War II, became a U.S. Trust Territory in 1947, and has been a sovereign state in free association with the United States since 1986.

Middle Congo   in west-central Africa, bordered on the north by Cameroon and the Central African Republic, on the east and south by the Democratic Republic of the Congo, on the southwest by Angola and the Atlantic Ocean, and on the west by Gabon. French (1907–34). Inscriptions include **Moyen Congo** together with "RF" or "Republique Française" (1907–30) and overprinted "Afrique Equatoriale Française" (1924–31), **Moyen-Congo A.E.F.** overprinted on stamps of France (1928), **Moyen-Congo** (1931–34). The Middle Congo used stamps of French Equatorial Africa between 1934 and 1958. In 1958 the Middle Congo became the independent Republic of the Congo.

Moçambique Mozambique. See **Mozambique**.

Modena a province in northern Italy, just to the west of Parma. Duchy (1852–60). Inscriptions include **Poste Estensi** (1852–59), **Provincie Modenes** (1859–60). Modena became part of united Italy in 1861. *Italian States*.

Moheli one of the Comoro Islands, which are located in the Mozambique Channel about midway between Mozambique and Madagascar. French (1906–08). Stamps are inscribed **Mohéli** together with "Republique Française."

Moldova in southeastern Europe, bordered on the north, east, and south by Ukraine and on the west by Romania. Independent (1992→). Stamps are inscribed **Moldova**. Moldova was formerly a republic in the Soviet Union.

Monaco an enclave on the southeastern coast of France, fronting the Mediterranean Sea, with an area of approximately 480 acres. Independent (1885→). Inscriptions include **Principaute de Monaco** (1885–1938), **Monaco** (1939→).

Mongolia (or Outer Mongolia) in east Asia, bordered on the north by Russia and on the east, south, and west by China. Independent (1924→). Inscriptions include **Mongolia** (1926–45, 1959–97), **МОНГОЛ ШУУДАН** or variations (1945–59), **БАМАУ ШУУДАН** or variations (1945–59), **Mongol Post** (1997→).

Mongol Post see **Mongolia**.

Mong-Tseu overprinted on stamps of Indochina: French offices in Mongtseu (Mongtze), China. *France (offices abroad)*.

Mongtze overprinted on stamps of Indochina: French offices in Mongtseu, China. *France (offices abroad)*.

Mont Athos (or **Atho**) overprinted on stamps of Russia together with surcharge in para(s) or piastre(s): *Russia (offices in the Turkish Empire)*.

Montenegro in the Balkans, bordered on the north by Bosnia and Herzegovina, on the east by Serbia, on the south by Albania, and on the southwest by the Adriatic Sea. Turkish (1874–1918). Inscriptions include **ПОШТЕ ЦР. ГОРЕ** (1874–96, 1902–10), **ЦРНА ГОРА** (1896–1902), **ПОШТЕ ЦРНЕ ГОРЕ** (1910–13), **КРАЛ ЦРНАГОРЕ** (1913), **ПОРТОМАРКА** (1913), **K.U.K. Milit.-Verwaltung Montenegro** overprinted on military stamps of Austria (Austrian occupation, 1917), **Governatorato del Montenegro** overprinted on stamps of Italy or Yugoslavia (Italian occupation, 1941–42), **Montenegro - ЦРНА ГОРА -17-IV-41-XIX** overprinted on stamps of Yugoslavia (Italian occupation, 1941), **ЦРНА ГОРА** overprinted on stamps of Italy (1941) or inscribed (1943), **Deutsche Militaer-Verwaltung Montenegro** overprinted on stamps of

Yugoslavia (German occupation, 1943–44), **Nationalier Verwaltungsausschuss 10.IX.1943** overprinted on stamps of Montenegro (German occupation, 1943). In 1918 Montenegro joined the fledgling nation that would become Yugoslavia. During World War II, Montenegro was occupied at various times by either Italian or German forces.

Montenegro - ЦРНА ГОРА - 17-IV-41-XIX   overprinted on stamps of Yugoslavia: Montenegro (Italian occupation). See **Montenegro**.

Montevideo   either with "Correo" or "Republica del Uruguay": Uruguay. See **Uruguay**.

Montserrat   one of the Leeward Islands in the Caribbean, southwest of Antigua and northwest of Guadeloupe. British (1876–90, 1903→). Inscriptions include **Montserrat** overprinted on stamps of Antigua (1876-80s) or inscribed (1876–90, 1903→).

Moquea   overprinted on provisional issues of Arequipa or on stamps of Peru: Moquegua, a city in the southernmost part of Peru. *Peru (provisional issues).*

Moquegua   overprinted on provisional issues of Arequipa or on stamps of Peru: Moquegua, a city in the southernmost part of Peru. *Peru (provisional issues).*

Morocco   in northwest Africa, bordered on the north by the Mediterranean Sea, on the east and southeast by Algeria, on the south by Western Sahara, and on the west by the Atlantic Ocean. Independent (1956→). Inscriptions include **Maroc** (1956–58), **Royaume du Maroc** (1958→); and for the northern (former Spanish) zone, **Marruecos** (1956–57). Prior to independence, Morocco consisted of French and Spanish protectorates.

Morocco Agencies   overprinted on stamps of Great Britain: British offices in Morocco and Tangier. *Great Britain (offices abroad).*

Morvi State Postage   Morvi, a feudatory state in west-central India. *India (native feudatory states).*

Moutawakilite Kingdom of Yemen   Yemen. See **Yemen (Republic of)**.

Moyen Congo or **Moyen-Congo**   Middle Congo. See **Middle Congo**.

Moyen-Congo A.E.F.   overprinted on stamps of France: Middle Congo. See **Middle Congo**.

Mozambique   in southeastern Africa, bordered on the north by Tanzania, on the east by the Mozambique Channel of the Indian Ocean, on the south and southwest by South Africa and Swaziland, and on the west by Zimbabwe, Zambia, and Malawi. Portuguese (1877–1975), independent (1975→). Inscriptions include **Mocambique** or **Moçambique** either by itself or with "Portugal,"

"Correios," "Portugal Correio," or "Republica Portuguesa" (1877–1975), **Provincia de Moçambique** (1886–94 and later), **Republica Moçambique** overprinted on stamps of Portuguese Africa, Macao, or Timor (1913), **Colonia de Moçambique** (1930–31 and later), **Moçambique** with "Imperio Colonial Portugués" (1939, 1949), **Correios da Colonia de Moçambique** (1946–49), **Moçambique** (1975→). Issues between 1911 and 1918 are often overprinted "Republica."

Mozambique Company   a company chartered by Portugal, granted the concession of exploiting resources in Mozambique in exchange for the obligation to develop agriculture, communications, social services, and trade. Inscriptions include **Comp^A de Moçambique** (1892–95), **Companhia de Moçambique** (1895–1941). Mozambique Company's charter ran from 1891 to 1941.

MQE   overprinted, together with numeral, on the generic issue for French colonies: Martinique. See **Martinique**.

Mucuto-Muno   on stamps inscribed "Portugal" and "Colonia de Moçambique": *Mozambique (postal tax)*.

Mujenga   on stamps inscribed "Portugal" and "Colonia de Moçambique": *Mozambique (postal tax)*.

Muscat & Oman   see **Oman**.

Mustique   together with "Saint Vincent of Grenadines": *Saint Vincent Grenadines*.

M.V.i.R.   overprinted on stamps of Germany: Romania (German occupation). See **Romania**.

Nabha or **Nabha State**   overprinted on stamps of India: Nabha state, a state in north-central India. *India (convention states)*.

Naciones Unidas   United Nations, Spanish inscription. See **United Nations**.

Naguema   on stamps inscribed "Portugal" and "Colonia de Moçambique": *Mozambique (postal tax)*.

Namibia   in southwest Africa bordered on the north by Angola, on the south by South Africa, on the east by Botswana, and on the west by the Atlantic Ocean. Independent (1990→). Stamps are inscribed **Namibia**. Prior to independence, Namibia was Southwest Africa.

Nanumaga   an island in the Tuvalu group. Tuvalu (1984→). Stamps are inscribed **Nanumaga - Tuvalu**. *Tuvalu (Nanumaga)*.

Nanumea   an island in the Tuvalu group. Tuvalu (1984→). Stamps are inscribed **Nanumea - Tuvalu**. *Tuvalu (Nanumea)*.

Natal   a province in eastern South Africa bordered on the east by the Indian Ocean. British (1857–1910). Inscriptions include **Natal** blind embossed

(1857–60), **Natal**, often with "Postage" or "Postage and Revenue." In 1910 Natal joined the Union of South Africa.

Nationalier Verwaltungsausschuss 10.X.1943 overprinted on stamps of Montenegro: Montenegro (German occupation). See **Montenegro**.

Nations Unies (1) as part of a multilingual inscription: United Nations. See **United Nations**. (2) together with "Helvetia": UN offices in Geneva. *Switzerland.*

Nations Unies Office Européen overprinted on stamps of Switzerland: United Nations European office. *Switzerland (official issues).*

Nauru a small island (about 8 square miles) just south of the equator in the Pacific Ocean. Australian (1916–47), under joint British/Australian/New Zealand trusteeship (1947–68), independent (1968→). Inscriptions include **Nauru** overprinted on stamps of Great Britain (1916–24), or inscribed (1924–68, 1976→), **Republic of Nauru** (1968–76). During World War II, the Japanese occupied Nauru.

N. Caledonie et Dependances New Caledonia. See **New Caledonia**.

N.C.E., NCE, N.-C.E., or **N-C-E** overprinted, together with numeral of value, on the generic issue for French colonies: New Caledonia. See **New Caledonia**.

N.D. Hrvatska abbreviation for "Nezavisna Država Hrvatska." See **Croatia**.

Ned. Antillen Netherlands Antilles. See **Netherlands Antilles**.

Nederland Netherlands. See **Netherlands**.

Nederlandsch Indie Netherlands Indies. See **Netherlands Indies**.

Nederlandse Antillen Netherlands Antilles. See **Netherlands Antilles**.

Nederlands Nieuw Guinea Netherlands New Guinea. See **Netherlands New Guinea**.

Nederl. Indie Netherlands Indies. See **Netherlands Indies**.

Ned. Indie overprinted on stamps of the Netherlands or inscribed: Netherlands Indies. See **Netherlands Indies**.

Ned. Nieuw Guinea Netherlands New Guinea. See **Netherlands New Guinea**.

Negri Sembilan a Malayan (and later, Malaysian) state. (1) **N. Sembilan** or **Negri Sembilan**, sometimes with "Malaya" or "Persekutuan Tanah Melayu": *Malaya (Negri Sembilan)*; (2) **Negri Sembilan** together with "Malaysia": *Malaysia (Negri Sembilan)*.

Nepal in the Himalayas between India and Tibet. Kingdom (1881→). Inscriptions include Urdu script (1881–1949), **Nepal** (1949→).

Netherlands in northwestern Europe bordered on the north and west by the North Sea, on the east by Germany, and on the south by Belgium. Independent

(1852→). Inscriptions include **Postzegel** and portrait of King William III (1852–67), **Nederland** (1867→). Additionally, at various times, the Netherlands issued special stamps for use by the International Court of Justice. Inscriptions include **Cour Permanente de Justice International** overprinted on stamps of the Netherlands (1930s), **Cour International de Justice** overprinted on stamps of the Netherlands (1940s) or inscribed, sometimes with "International Court of Justice" (1950→).

Netherlands Antilles two island groups of three islands each, the Netherlands Leeward and the Netherlands Windward Islands, in the Caribbean Sea; the Leeward group consisting of Curaçao, Bonaire, and until 1986, Aruba, is situated just north of Venezuela; the Windward group, consisting of the southern half of Saint Martin (Sint Maarten) and all of Saint Eustatius and Saba, is situated at the northern end of the Lesser Antilles chain and to the east of Puerto Rico. Netherlands (1873→). Inscriptions include **Curaçao** (1873–1949), **Nederlandse Antillen** or **Ned. Antillen** (1949→). In 1986 Aruba seceded from Netherlands Antilles and became self-governing.

Netherlands Indies composed of much of what is today Indonesia. Netherlands (1864–1948). Inscriptions include **Nederl. Indie** (1864~), **Ned. Indie** overprinted on stamps of the Netherlands (1900–02) or inscribed (1870~), **Nederlandsch Indie** (1902~), **Indonesia** overprinted on stamps of Netherlands Indies (1948–49) or inscribed (1949). Stamps inscribed **Indonesia** were issued in 1948 and 1949 during which time the country was still formally under control of the Netherlands. The Dutch formally relinquished control of the country at the end of 1949. The Netherlands Indies were also known as the Dutch East Indies.

Netherlands New Guinea the western half of the island of New Guinea, now the Indonesian province of Irian Jaya (West Irian). Netherlands (1950–62). Inscriptions include **Nieuw Guinea** (1950–54), **Nederlands Nieuw Guinea** or **Ned. Nieuw Guinea** (1954–62).

Nevis one of the Leeward Islands in the West Indies. British (1861→). Stamps are inscribed **Nevis** (1861–90, 1980→). Nevis used stamps of the Leeward Islands and/or Saint Kitts-Nevis between 1890 and 1980.

New Britain an island in the western Pacific Ocean northeast of New Guinea. Australian occupation (1914–15). Inscriptions include **G.R.I.** overprinted, together with surcharged value in pence or shillings, on stamps of German New Guinea (Deutsch Neu-Guinea) or Marshall Islands (Marshall Inseln) or on registry labels inscribed "Deutsch Neu-Guinea" together with a town name (1914–15). Prior to 1914, New Britain (then known as Neu-Pommern) was part of the German-controlled Bismarck Archipelago. At the outbreak of World

War I, Australia occupied it. Following the war, it was mandated to Australia by the League of Nations as part of the Territory of New Guinea. New Britain is now part of Papua New Guinea.

New Brunswick   in eastern Canada, bordered on the north by Quebec, on the northeast by Chaleur Bay, on the southeast by Nova Scotia, and on the west by Maine. British (1861–67). Stamps are inscribed **New Brunswick**. In 1867 New Brunswick joined the Confederation of Canada. *Canadian Provinces*.

New Caledonia   in the southwestern Pacific Ocean, east of Australia, consisting of the island of New Caledonia and various smaller islands, including the Loyalty Islands, the Isle of Pines, the Chesterfield Islands, and the Huon Islands. French (1859→). Inscriptions include N^{LE} **Caledonie** (1859), **N.C.E.**, **NCE**, **N.-C.E.**, or **N-C-E** overprinted, together with numeral of value, on the generic issue for French colonies (1881–1903), N^{LLE} **Calédonie** overprinted together with numeral of value (1892), **N. Caledonie et Dependances** (1892–1904), **Nouvelle Caledonie et Dependances** (1905–88) and overprinted "France Libre" (1941), **Nouv^{LLE}-Caledonie et Dependances** (1948), **Nouvelle-Calédonie** (1988→).

Newfoundland   a province in northeastern Canada composed of two sections: Newfoundland, which is an island, and Labrador, which is on the mainland. Newfoundland is bordered on the north by the Strait of Belle Isle, on the east and south by the Atlantic Ocean, and on the west by the Gulf of Saint Lawrence. Labrador is bordered on the north, south, and west by Quebec and on the east by the Atlantic. British (1857–1949). Inscriptions include **St. John's-Newfoundland** (1857–68), **Newfoundland** (1868–1949). In 1949 Newfoundland became a province of Canada. *Canadian Provinces*.

New Guinea   the northeastern part of the island of New Guinea in the South Pacific Ocean north of Australia. Australian (1925–30s). Inscriptions include **Territory of New Guinea** (1925–30s). In 1914 at the beginning of World War I, New Guinea was occupied by Australia. Following the war, it was mandated to Australia by the League of Nations. In 1952 New Guinea merged with the southeastern part of the island, Papua, to form Papua New Guinea. See also **Papua New Guinea**.

New Hebrides   a group of islands in the southwestern Pacific Ocean northeast of New Caledonia. British/French (1908–80). Inscriptions in English include **New Hebrides Condominium** overprinted on stamps of Fiji (1908–11), **New Hebrides** inscribed and denominated in pence or shillings (1911–25), or denominated in dual British and French currencies (1925–38), **New Hebrides** and "Condominium" (1938–80). Inscriptions in French include **Nouvelles Hebrides** overprinted on stamps of New Caledonia (1908–10), **Nouvelles**

Hebrides Condominium overprinted on stamps of New Caledonia (1910), **Nouvelles Hebrides** denominated in centimes or francs (1911–25), or denominated in dual British and French currencies (1925–38), **Nouvelles Hebrides** and "Condominium" (1938–67), **Condominium des Nouvelles Hebrides** (1963–80). From 1911 to 1938, stamps were dually denominated in British and French currencies. Beginning in 1938, issues of both jurisdictions were denominated in gold centimes. Each country (Britain and France) exercised jurisdiction over its own citizens. In 1980 New Hebrides became independent Vanuatu. *New Hebrides, British* and *New Hebrides, French*.

New South Wales   located in southeast Australia. British (1850–1901), Australian (1901–13). Inscriptions include **Camb Aust Sigillum Nov** (1850–51), **New South Wales** (1851–1913), **N.S.W.** (1891–). The inscription **Consumptives Home** appears on 1897 semipostal stamps of New South Wales. New South Wales continued to use its own stamps until Australia began issuing stamps in 1913. *Australian States (New South Wales)*.

New Zealand   an island nation southeast of Australia consisting of two main islands plus dependencies, which include Ross Dependency, Cook Islands, Niue, and Tokelau. British (1855–1907), independent dominion (1907→). Inscriptions include **New Zealand** (1855→).

Nezavisna Država Hrvatska   Croatia. See **Croatia**.

Nez Drž Hrvatska   abbreviation for "Nezavisna Država Hrvatska." See **Croatia**.

N.F.   (Nyasaland Force) overprinted on stamps of Nyasaland Protectorate: German East Africa (British occupation). See **German East Africa**.

Nicaragua   in Central America, bordered on the north by Honduras, on the east by the Caribbean Sea, on the south by Costa Rica, and on the west by the Pacific Ocean. Independent (1869→). Inscriptions include **Nicaragua**, sometimes with "Correos de" or "Republica de" (1869→), **Estado de Nicaragua** (1921). Earlier issues of Nicaragua are often surcharged.

Nieuwe Republiek   in southern Africa, largely composed of Zululand, and now part of South Africa. Independent (1886–88). Stamps are inscribed **Nieuwe Republiek**.

Nieuw Guinea   Netherlands New Guinea. See **Netherlands New Guinea**.

Niger   in western Africa, bordered on the north by Algeria and Libya, on the east by Chad, on the south by Nigeria and Benin, and on the west by Burkina Faso and Mali. French (1921–43), independent (1960→). Inscriptions include **Territoire du Niger** overprinted on stamps of Upper Senegal and Niger (1921–26), **Niger** together with "Afrique Occidentale Française" (1926–41), **Republique du Niger** (1959→). Between 1943 and 1959, Niger used stamps of French West Africa.

Niger Coast Protectorate   on the west coast of Africa on the Gulf of Guinea, the Niger Delta region (then known as the Oil Rivers) of what is now Nigeria. British (1892–1900). Inscriptions include **British Protectorate - Oil Rivers** overprinted on stamps of Great Britain (1892–93), **Niger Coast Protectorate** (1893–1900). In 1900 Niger Coast Protectorate was incorporated into the Protectorate of Southern Nigeria. The protectorate was a center for palm oil production, hence the name, Oil Rivers.

Nigeria   on the west coast of Africa bordered on the north by Niger, on the east by Chad and Cameroon, on the south by the Gulf of Guinea, and on the west by Benin. British (1914–60), independent (1960→). Stamps are inscribed **Nigeria**. In 1914 Northern Nigeria and Southern Nigeria merged to form Nigeria.

Nippon   Japan. See **Japan**.

Nisiros   overprinted on stamps of Italy. See **Dodecanese Islands**. *Italy (Aegean Islands)*.

Niuafo'ou   one of the Tonga islands, also known as Tin Can Island. Tongan (1983→). Inscriptions include **Niuafo'ou - Tin Can Island** (1983–84), **Niuafo'ou** (1984→). *Tonga (Niuafo'ou)*.

Niue   a small coral island in the South Pacific Ocean northeast of New Zealand. New Zealand (1901–74), self-governing (1974→). Inscriptions include **Niue** overprinted on stamps of New Zealand (1902–20, 1946) or inscribed (1920→). Niue is self-governing in free association with New Zealand.

Niutao   an island in the Tuvalu group. Tuvalu (1984→). Stamps are inscribed **Niutao - Tuvalu**. *Tuvalu* (Niutao).

N^{LE} Caledonie   New Caledonia. See **New Caledonia**.

N^{LLE} Calédonie   New Caledonia. See **New Caledonia**.

Nord-Deutsche-Post   North German Confederation. See **North German Confederation**.

Norddeutscher Postbezirk   North German Confederation. See **North German Confederation**.

Noreg   Norway. See **Norway**.

Norfolk Island   a small island (approximately 13 square miles) in the South Pacific Ocean 930 miles east of Australia. Australian (1947→). Stamps are inscribed **Norfolk Island**.

Norge   Norway. See **Norway**.

North Borneo   the northeast part of the island of Borneo. British (1883–1963). Inscriptions include **North Borneo** (1883–86), **British North Borneo** (1886–94),

State of North Borneo occasionally with the additional inscription "British Protectorate" (1884–1963). In 1967 North Borneo (as Sabah) became part of independent Malaysia.

Northern Nigeria in western Africa on the Gulf of Guinea. British (1900–14). Stamps are inscribed **Northern Nigeria**. In 1914 Northern Nigeria merged with Southern Nigeria to become Nigeria.

Northern Rhodesia in southern Africa bordered on the north by the Democratic Republic of the Congo and Tanganyika (Tanzania), on the east by Nyasaland (Malawi), on the south by Southern Rhodesia (Zimbabwe), and on the west by Angola. British (1925–64). Stamps are inscribed **Northern Rhodesia** (1925–53, 1963–64). From 1953 to 1963, Northern Rhodesia belonged to the Federation of Rhodesia and Nyasaland. In 1964 Northern Rhodesia became independent Zambia.

North German Confederation a union of independent German states north of the Main River formed under the leadership of Prussia and a precursor to the unification of Germany, which occurred after the conclusion of the Franco-Prussian War (1868–72). Inscriptions include **Norddeutscher Postbezirk** (1868–72), **Nord-Deutsche-Post** (1870–72). *German States (North German Confederation).*

North Ingermanland a small region, now in Russia, situated between Lake Ladoga and the Gulf of Finland. Provisional government (1920). Inscriptions include **Pohjois Inkeri**. In 1920, following World War I, North Ingermanland, which at the time was on the Russian-Finnish border, staged a unsuccessful, short-lived revolt against Russian rule.

Norway in northern Europe, on the Scandinavian Peninsula, bordered on the north by the Barents Sea, an arm of the Arctic Ocean, on the northeast by Finland and Russia, on the east by Sweden, on the south by Skagerrak Strait and the North Sea, and on the west by the Atlantic Ocean. Independent (1855→). Stamps are inscribed **Norge** or **Noreg**.

Nossi-Be an island of about 120 square miles lying about 5 miles off the northwestern coast of Madagascar. French (1889–96). Inscriptions include **NSB** overprinted on the generic issue for French colonies (1890–93), **Nossi-Be** or **Nossi-Bé** overprinted on the generic issue for French colonies (1893–94) or inscribed (1894–96). Nossi-Be became part of Madagascar in 1896.

Nouvelle-Calédonie New Caledonia. See **New Caledonia**.

Nouvelle Caledonie et Dependances New Caledonia. See **New Caledonia**.

Nouvelles Hebrides New Hebrides. See **New Hebrides**.

Nouvelles Hebrides Condominium New Hebrides. See **New Hebrides**.

Nouv^LLE**-Caledonie et Dependances**   New Caledonia. See **New Caledonia**.

Nova Scotia   in eastern Canada, east of New Brunswick, consisting of a mainland peninsula nearly surrounded by the Atlantic, and Cape Breton Island and numerous small islands. British (1851–67). Stamps are inscribed **Nova Scotia**. In 1867 Nova Scotia joined the Confederation of Canada. *Canadian Provinces*.

Nowanuggur   Nowanuggur, a native feudatory state on the west coast of central India. *India (native feudatory states)*.

NSB   overprinted on the generic issue for French colonies: Nossi-Be. See **Nossi-Be**.

N. Sembilan   Negri Sembilan, a Malayan state. *Malaya (Negri Sembilan)*.

N.S.W.   (New South Wales) on postage-due stamps: New South Wales. *Australian States*.

Nui   an island in the Tuvalu group. Tuvalu (1984→). Stamps are inscribed **Nui - Tuvalu**. *Tuvalu (Nui)*.

Nukufetau   an island in the Tuvalu group. Tuvalu (1984→). Stamps are inscribed **Nukufetau - Tuvalu**. *Tuvalu (Nukufetau)*.

Nukulealea   an island in the Tuvalu group. Tuvalu (1984→). Stamps are inscribed **Nukulealea - Tuvalu**. *Tuvalu (Nukulealea)*.

N.W. Pacific Islands   a group of islands in the western Pacific Ocean, formerly German possessions, including Nauru and German New Guinea. Australian (1915–23). Inscriptions include **N.W. Pacific Islands** overprinted on stamps of Australia.

Nyasaland Protectorate   a small country in southern Africa, bordered on the east by Lake Nyasa (Lake Malawi), on the south by Mozambique, and on the west by Northern Rhodesia (Zambia). British (1908–53). Inscriptions include **Nyasaland Protectorate** (1908–34), **Nyasaland** (1934–53, 1963–64). From 1953 to 1963, Nyasaland Protectorate belonged to the federation Rhodesia and Nyasaland. In 1964 Nyasaland Protectorate became independent Malawi.

Nyassa   a region now in northern Mozambique, situated east of Lake Nyassa. Portuguese (1898–1920s). Inscriptions include **Nyassa** overprinted on stamps of Mozambique (1898–1901) or inscribed (1901–21), **Companhia do Nyassa** (1921~). For a time, Nyassa was administered by the Portuguese Nyassa Company. Subsequently, it was part of Mozambique. Issues between 1903 and 1910 are often overprinted "Provisorio." Issues between 1911 and 1920 are often overprinted "Republica."

N.Z.   (New Zealand) on postage-due stamps: New Zealand. *New Zealand*.

N.Z. Government Life Insurance Department   New Zealand. *New Zealand (Life Insurance)*.

N.Z. Government Life Insurance Office   New Zealand. *New Zealand (Life Insurance).*

Obock   a French coaling station on the Afar (Somali) Coast in northeast Africa in what is now the Djibouti Republic. French (1892–1902). Inscriptions include **Obock** overprinted on the generic issue for French colonies (1892), **Obock** together with "RF" or "Republique Française" and "Colonies Postes" (1892–1902).

Occupation Française   overprinted on stamps of Hungary for use in areas occupied by France following World War I: *Hungary.*

Occupation Francaise du Cameroun   overprinted on stamps of the Middle Congo or French Congo: Cameroun. See **Cameroun.**

Occupation Militaire Française - Cilicie   overprinted on stamps of Turkey: Cilicia. See **Cilicia.**

Occupazione Italiana Castelrosso   Castellorizo. See **Castellorizo.**

Océanie   French Polynesia. See **French Polynesia.**

Œuvres de Solidarité Française   an inscription on some stamps issued by the Free French in overseas colonies during World War II. *French Colonies.*

O.F. Castellorizo   overprinted on stamps of France: Castellorizo. O.F. is an abbreviation for "Occupation Française." See **Castellorizo.**

OKCA   Russian Army of the North. *Russia (Army of the North).*

Oldenburg   a state in northwestern Germany. Stamps are inscribed **Oldenburg** (1852–70). *German States.*

Oltre Giuba   a territory bordered on the north by Ethiopia, on the west by Italian Somaliland (Somalia), on the southwest by the Indian Ocean, and on the west by Kenya. Italian (1925–26). Inscriptions include **Oltre Giuba** overprinted on stamps of Italy (1925–26) or inscribed (1926), **Commissariato Gen**^{LE} **Dell Oltre Giuba** (1926). In 1926 Oltre Giuba became part of Italian Somaliland. It is now part of Somalia.

Oman   on the southeastern corner of the Arabian Peninsula, bordered on the northwest by United Arab Emirates and on the west by Saudi Arabia and Yemen. Independent sultanate (1966→). Inscriptions include Arabic overprinted on stamps of India (1944–48), surcharged values on stamps of Great Britain (1948–66), **Muscat & Oman** (1966–70), **Sultanate of Oman** (1971→). In 1970 the Sultanate of Muscat and Oman changed its name to the Sultanate of Oman.

O.M.F. Cilicie (by itself or with **Sand. Est**)   overprinted on stamps of France: Cilicia. O.M.F. is an abbreviation for "Occupation Militaire Française." See **Cilicia.**

O.M.F. - Syrie (Occupation Militaire Française) overprinted on stamps of France or the Syrian Arabian government: Syria. See **Syria**.

O.N.F. Castellorizo overprinted on stamps of French offices in Turkey: Castellorizo. O.N.F. is an abbreviation for "Occupation Navale Française." See **Castellorizo**.

Olsztyn Allenstein overprinted on stamps of Germany: Allenstein. See **Allenstein**.

Orange River Colony in east-central South Africa. Independent Afrikaner republic (1868–1900), British (1900–10). Inscriptions include **Oranje Vrij Staat** (1868–1900), **V.R.I.** overprinted together with surcharged value (1900–01), **E.R.I.** overprinted together with surcharged value (1902), **Orange River Colony** overprinted on stamps of the Cape of Good Hope (1900) or inscribed (1903–10). The Orange River Colony (then the Orange Free State) fought Britain in the Boer War (1899–1902). In 1910 it joined the Union of South Africa.

Oranje Vrij Staat Orange Free State. See **Orange River Colony**.

Orchha State or **Orchha Postage** Orchha, an Indian feudatory state. *India (native feudatory states)*.

Organisation International Pour les Réfugiés overprinted on stamps of Switzerland: International Organization for Refugees. *Switzerland (official issues)*.

Organisation Météorologique Mondiale inscribed together with "Helvetia": World Meterological Organization. *Switzerland (official issues)*.

Organisation Mondiale de la Propriete Intellectuelle inscribed together with "Helvetia": World Intellectual Property Organization. *Switzerland (official issues)*.

Organisation Mondiale de la Sante overprinted on stamps of Switzerland or inscribed together with "Helvetia": World Health Organization. *Switzerland (official issues)*.

Orts-Post with post horn and white cross: Switzerland. See **Switzerland**.

Österreich Austria. See **Austria**.

Österreichische Post Austria. See **Austria**.

Ostland overprinted on stamps of Germany: an area that included German-occupied territories of Estonia, Latvia, Lithuania, and western Russia (excluding Ukraine) during World War II. *Russia (occupation issues)*.

Oubangi-Chari overprinted on stamps of Middle Congo: Ubangi-Shari. See **Ubangi-Shari**.

Oubangui-Chari-Tchad overprinted on stamps of Middle Congo: Ubangi-Shari. See **Ubangi-Shari**.

Outer Mongolia   see **Mongolia**.

O'ZBEKISTON   Uzbekistan. See **Uzbekistan**.

P   overprinted, together with crescent and star, on stamps of Straits Settlements: Perak. *Malaya (Perak)*.

Packenmarke Wenden Kreises   Wenden. See **Wenden**.

Packhoi   overprinted on stamps of Indochina: French offices Packhoi (Peihai). *France (offices abroad)*.

Pahang   a Malayan (and later, Malaysian) state. **(1) Pahang** overprinted on stamps of Straits Settlements or stamps of Perak, or inscribed, sometimes with "Malaya": *Malaya (Pahang)*; **(2) Pahang** together with "Malaysia": *Malaysia (Pahang)*.

Paita   overprinted on stamps of Peru: Paita, a city on the Pacific coast in northern Peru. *Peru (provisional issues)*.

Pak-Hoi   overprinted on stamps of Indochina: French offices in Packhoi (Peihai), China. *France (offices abroad)*.

Pakistan   in Asia, bordered on the north and northwest by Afghanistan, on the northeast, east, and southeast by India, on the south by the Arabian Sea, and on the west by Iran. Independent (1947→). Inscriptions include **Pakistan** overprinted on stamps of India (1947) or inscribed (1947→). Prior to independence, Pakistan was part of British India. At the time of independence, it consisted of East and West Pakistan. In 1971 East Pakistan broke away to become Bangladesh.

Palau   an archipelago of about 200 islands near the equator in the western Pacific Ocean, about 850 miles east of the Philippines, and consisting of the western section of the Caroline Islands. U.S. (1984–94), independent (1994→). Palau was part of the German possession of the Caroline Islands (which at the time included **Micronesia**) until World War I and became a League of Nations mandate under control of Japan until World War II, a U.S. Trust Territory in 1947, and a sovereign state in free association with the United States in 1994.

Palestine   in the Middle East, on the east coast of the Mediterranean, originally a region under British mandate that included present-day Israel and contemporary Palestine. British occupation, then mandate (1918–48), various (1948–93). Inscriptions include **E.E.F.** (British occupation, 1918–20), **Palestine** overprinted on the foregoing (1920–27) or inscribed (1927–48), **Palestine** overprinted on stamps of Jordan (for use in areas occupied by Jordan, 1948–50; *Jordan*), **Palestine** overprinted on stamps of Egypt (for use in areas occupied by Egypt, 1948–60s; *Egypt*). In 1948 the bulk of the British mandate became Israel; the balance, modern Palestine. Since 1948 Palestine has varied in size and sovereignty as a result of a series of wars and conflicts. See also **Palestinian Authority**.

Palestinian Authority   areas of the West Bank and Gaza Strip under Palestinian administrative authority by virtue of the 1993 peace accord. Stamps are inscribed **Palestinian Authority** (1994→).

Panama   in Central America, bordered on the north by the Caribbean Sea, on the east by Colombia, on the south by the Pacific Ocean, and on the west by Costa Rica. Colombian (1878–1903), independent (1903→). Inscriptions include **E° S° de Panama** together with "Estados Unidos de Colombia" (1878–87), **E.S. de Panama** together with "Estados Unidos de Colombia" (1878–87), **Colombia** and a map of Panama (1887–1903), **Republica de Panama** overprinted on earlier issues (1903–06), **Panama** overprinted on earlier issues (1903–66), **R. de Panama** overprinted on earlier issues (1903–04), **Republica de Panama** or **Panama** (1906→). Panama was a department of Colombia until 1903. The Panama Canal, which bisects the country, was controlled by the United States until 1999, when it was returned to Panama under terms of a treaty that took effect in 1979.

Papua   see **Papua New Guinea**.

Papua New Guinea   consisting of the eastern half of the island of New Guinea plus the Bismarck Archipelago, the Louisiade Archipelago, the Trobriand Islands, the D'Entrecasteaux Islands, and Muyua Island. British/Australian (1901–06), Australian (1906–74), independent (1975→). Inscriptions include **British New Guinea** (1901–06), **Papua** overprinted on previous issues (1906–07) or inscribed (1902–52), **Papua and New Guinea** (1952–72), **Papua New Guinea** (1972→).

Paraguay   in central South America, bordered on the northwest and north by Bolivia, on the east by Brazil, and on the south and southwest by Argentina. Independent (1870→). Inscriptions include **Paraguay** often with "Republica del" or "Correos del" (1870–1970s), **Gobierno Provisorio del Paraguay** (1905–1910), **Paraguay** (1970s→).

Parma   a province in northern Italy, just to the east of Modena. Duchy (1852–61). Inscriptions include **Stati Parm** (1852), **Duc. di Parma** (1857–59), **Stati Parmensi** (1859). Parma became part of united Italy in 1861. *Italian States.*

Pasco   overprinted on stamps of Peru: Pasco, a city in central Peru northeast of Lima and capital of Pasco Department. *Peru (provisional issues).*

Patiala or **Patiala State**   overprinted on stamps of India: Patiala state, a state in north-central India. *India (convention states).*

Patmos   overprinted on stamps of Italy. See **Dodecanese Islands**. *Italy (Aegean Islands).*

P.D.R. (or **PDR**) **Yemen**   People's Democratic Republic of Yemen. See **Yemen (People's Democratic Republic).**

Pechino   overprinted on stamps of Italy: Italian offices in Peking (Beijing), China. *Italy (offices abroad).*

Penang   a Malayan (and later, Malaysian) state. **(1) Penang** either by itself or with "Malaya": *Malaya (Penang);* **(2) Penang** together with "Malaysia": *Malaysia (Penang).*

Penrhyn Island or **Penrhyn**   one of the Cook Islands in the South Pacific. New Zealand (1902–32), Cook Islands (1973→). Inscriptions include **Penrhyn Island** overprinted on stamps of New Zealand (1902–20), **Penrhyn** (1920–32), **Penrhyn - Northern** overprinted on stamps of Cook Islands (1973), **Penrhyn - Northern Cook Islands** (1974→). From 1932 to 1973, Penrhyn used stamps of the Cook Islands.

Penrhyn - Northern   overprinted on stamps of Cook Islands: Penrhyn Island. See **Penrhyn Island.**

Penrhyn - Northern Cook Islands   Penrhyn Island. See **Penrhyn Island.**

People's Democratic Republic of Yemen   see **Yemen (People's Democratic Republic).**

People's Republic of Southern Yemen   overprinted on stamps of Saudi Arabia or inscribed: Yemen. See **Yemen (People's Democratic Republic).**

Perak   a Malayan (and later, Malaysian) state. **(1) P** overprinted, together with crescent and star, on stamps of Straits Settlements: *Malaya (Perak);* **(2) Perak** overprinted on stamps of Straits Settlements, or inscribed, sometimes with "Malaya": *Malaya (Perak);* **(3) Perak** together with "Malaysia": *Malaysia (Perak).*

Perlis   a Malayan (and later, Malaysian) state. **(1) Perlis** together with "Malaya": *Malaya (Perlis);* **(2) Perlis** together with "Malaysia": *Malaysia (Perlis).*

Persekutuan Tanah Melayu   either with "Malaya" or with certain individual state names including "Johore," "Kedah," "Kelantan," "Negri Sembilan," and "Selangor." *Malaya.*

Peru   in west-central South America, bordered on the north by Ecuador and Colombia, on the east by Brazil and Bolivia, on the south by Chile, and on the west by the Pacific Ocean. Independent (1857→). Inscriptions include **P.S.N.C.** with each letter in one of the stamp's four corners and a sailing ship in the center (1957), **Porte Franco** with "Correos" and Peruvian coat of arms (1858–70s), **Peru** or **Perú**, often with "Correos del" (1866→), **Lima** (1871–73), **Union Postal Universal - Peru** overprinted in an oval or a horseshoe (1880s), **Union Postal Universal - Lima** overprinted in an oval (1880s), **Republica Peruana** (1921, 1941).

Pesa   and numeral of surcharged value overprinted on stamps of Germany: German East Africa. See **German East Africa**.

Philippines   part of the Malay Archipelago, located north of Borneo and about 750 miles east of Vietnam and composed of more than 7,000 islands, of which 11 contain the bulk of the population: Luzon, Mindanao, Samar, Negros, Palawan, Panay, Mindoro, Leyte, Cebu, Bohol, and Masbate. Spanish (1854–98), U.S. (1899–1946), independent (1946→). Inscriptions include bust of Queen Isabella and "Correos" or "Correos Interior" and "Franco" (1854–72), **Filipinas** (1872–98), **Philippines** overprinted on stamps of the United States (1899–1906) or inscribed (1946, 1948–62), **Philippine Islands** and "United States of America" (1906–35), **Commonwealth of the Philippines** and "United States of America" (1935–46), **Kalayaan Nang Pilipinas** (Japanese occupation, 1943), **Republika Ng Pilipinas** overprinted or inscribed (Japanese occupation, 1944–45), **Pilipinas Republika** (Japanese occupation, 1944), **Republic of the Philippines** (1947–62), **Pilipinas** (1962→). Japan occupied the Philippines during World War II.

Pilipinas   Philippines. See **Philippines**.

Pilipinas Republika   Philippines under Japanese occupation. See **Philippines**.

Pisco   overprinted on stamps of Peru: Pisco, a city on the Pacific coast in southern Peru. *Peru (provisional issues)*.

Piscopi   overprinted on stamps of Italy. See **Dodecanese Islands**. *Italy (Aegean Islands)*.

Pitcairn Islands   a group of small islands in the central South Pacific Ocean about midway between Australia and South America. British (1940→). Stamps are inscribed **Pitcairn Islands**.

Piura   overprinted on stamps of Peru: Piura, a city in northern Peru and capital of Piura Department. *Peru (provisional issues)*.

Piura Vapor   overprinted on stamps of Peru: Piura, a city in northern Peru and capital of Piura Department. *Peru (provisional issues)*.

Plebiscite Marienwerder   see **Marienwerder**.

Plébiscite Olsztyn Allenstein   overprinted on stamps of Germany: Allenstein. See **Allenstein**.

Plebiscit Slesvig   Schleswig. See **Schleswig**.

P.L. Teheran   (Poste Locale Teheran) overprinted on stamps of Iran: *Iran*.

Poczta Polska   Poland. See **Poland**.

Pohjois Inkeri   see **North Ingermanland**.

Poland   in central Europe, bordered on the north by the Baltic Sea and Russia, on the east by Lithuania, Belarus, and Ukraine, on the south by the Czech Republic and Slovakia, and on the west by Germany. Independent (1918→). Inscriptions include **ZATOTEOP** inscribed on stamps similar to those of imperial Russia (1860–65); **Poczta Polska** overprinted on Warsaw local issues or on stamps of Austria (1918–19) or inscribed (1919–50s), **Polska Poczta** overprinted on stamps of Austria (1919), **Russisch-Polen** overprinted on stamps of Germany (German occupation, 1915), **Gen. Gouv. Warschau** (German occupation, 1916–18), **Polska** (1930s→), **Deutsche Post Osten** overprinted on stamps of Germany (German occupation, 1939), **General Gouvernement** overprinted on stamps of Germany (German occupation, 1940), **Generalgouvernement** often with "Deutsches Reich" or "Grossdeutsches Reich" (German occupation, 1941–45). Poland was occupied by Germany during both World War I and World War II.

Polska   Poland. See **Poland**.

Polska Poczta   Poland. See **Poland**.

Polynesie Française   French Polynesia. See **French Polynesia**.

Ponta Delgada   a city located on the island of Sao Miguel in the Azores and center for the administrative district that included the islands of Sao Miguel and Santa Maria. Portuguese (1892–1905). Inscriptions include **Ponta Delgada** together with "Correios" and "Portugal."

Port Gdańsk   overprinted on stamps of Poland or inscribed together with "Poczta Poland": Polish offices in Danzig (1925–38). *Poland (offices abroad)*.

Port Lagos   overprinted on stamps of France: French offices in Port Lagos. *France (offices in Turkey)*.

Porto   together with surcharged value overprinted on postage-due stamps of Bosnia and Herzegovina: Yugoslavia. *Yugoslavia (Slovenia)*.

Porto Rico   overprinted on stamps of the United States: Puerto Rico. See **Puerto Rico**. Also *United States*.

Port-Said   overprinted on stamps of France or French offices in Turkey, or inscribed together with "République Française": French offices in Port Said, Egypt. *France (offices in Egypt)*.

Portugal   in southwestern Europe, situated in the western portion of the Iberian Peninsula, bordered on the north and east by Spain and on the south and west by the Atlantic Ocean, and including the insular regions of the Azores and the Madeira Islands. Independent (1853→). Inscriptions include **Correio** and bust of monarch (1853–66), **Portugal** together with "Correios" (1866–80, 1895–1912), **Portugal Continente** (1880–82), **Portugal** often with "Correios e Telegraphos"

(1882–92), **Portugal** together with "Correios" and "Continente" (1892–1910), **Republica Portuguesa** often with "Correios" or "Correio" (1912–41), **Correio de Portugal** (1940–45), **Portugal** (1940→). In 1892 and 1893, some earlier issues were overprinted "Provisorio." In 1911 and 1912, some earlier issues were overprinted "Republica."

Portugal - Açores - (1) Açores overprinted on stamps of Portugal: Azores. See **Azores**. **(2) Açores** inscribed together with "Portugal": Portugal. See **Portugal**.

Portugal - Congo   Portuguese Congo. See **Portuguese Congo**.

Portugal Continente   Portugal. See **Portugal**.

Portugal Correio - Guiné   Portuguese Guinea. See **Portuguese Guinea**.

Portugal Correio - Moçambique   Mozambique. See **Mozambique**.

Portugal - Guiné   Portuguese Guinea. See **Portuguese Guinea**.

Portugal India   Portuguese India. See **Portuguese India**.

Portugal - Madiera   (1) Madiera overprinted on stamps of Portugal: Madiera. See **Madiera**. **(2) Madiera** inscribed together with "Portugal": Portugal. See **Portugal**.

Portugal - S. Thome e Principe   Saint Thomas and Prince Islands. See **Saint Thomas and Prince Islands**.

Portugal Timor   Timor. See **Timor**.

Portugal - Zambezia   Zambezia. See **Zambezia**.

Portuguese Congo   in central Africa, an exclave (Cabinda) north of Angola, bordered on the north by the Republic of the Congo, on the east and south by the Democratic Republic of the Congo, and on the west by the Atlantic Ocean. Portuguese (1894–1920). Inscriptions include **Congo** together with "Portugal" (1894–1905), **Congo** together with "Correios" and "Portugal" (1898–1914), **Congo Republica** overprinted on stamps of Angola or other Portuguese colonies (1911–14), **Congo** and "Republica Portuguesa" (1914–20).

Portuguese Guinea   in northwestern Africa, bordered on the west by the Atlantic Ocean and wedged between Senegal on the north and Guinea on the east and south. Portuguese (1881–1973). Inscriptions include **Guiné** overprinted on stamps of Cape Verde (1881–86) or inscribed (1948), **Guine Portugueza** (1886–93), **Guiné** with "Portugal" (1893–98), **Guiné** with "Correos Portugal" (1898–1914), **Republica Guiné** overprinted on stamps of Portuguese Africa, Macao, or Timor (1913), **Guiné** with "Republica Portuguesa" (1914–33), **Guiné** with "Portugal Correio" (1933–48, 1955–73), **Guinea Portuguesa** (1948–55). In 1973 Portuguese Guinea became **Guinea-Bissau**. Issues between 1911 and 1931 are often overprinted "Republica."

Portuguese India   five districts on the Indian subcontinent, of which three are coastal, Goa and adjacent islands Daman (formerly Damao) and Diu (an island south of the Kathiawar Peninsula), and two are inland, Dadra and Nagar Aveli. Portuguese (1871–1961). Inscriptions include **India Port.** with "Servicio Postal" (1871–86), **India Portugueza** (1877–95), **Portugal - India** (1895–98), **India** with "Correios" and "Portugal" (1898–1913), **India** with "Republica Portuguesa" (1913–33), **Correio India** (1933–46), **Estado da India** (1946–49) and with "Republica Portuguesa" (1953–61), **India Portuguesa** (1949–53). Issues between 1911 and 1920 are often overprinted "Republica." India seized the inland districts in 1954 and occupied the three coastal districts in 1961.

Posesiones Españolas del Sahara Occidental   Spanish Sahara. See **Spanish Sahara**.

Posta   often accompanying a country's name. Refer to the country name.

Post and Receipt   together with Urdu script and denomination in annas: Hyderabad, a native feudatory state in south-central India. *India (native feudatory states).*

Pošta Československá 1919   overprinted on stamps of Austria: Czechoslovakia. See **Czechoslovakia**.

Posta Coloniali Italiane   Ethiopia. See **Ethiopia**.

Posta Gazetei   Moldavia (Romania). See **Romania**.

Postage   together with Urdu script and denomination in annas: Hyderabad, a native feudatory state in south-central India. *India (native feudatory states).*

Postage - I.E.F. 'D'   overprinted on stamps of Turkey: Mesopotamia. See **Mesopotamia**.

Posta Romana or **Poşta Română**   Romania. See **Romania**.

Posta Romana - Constantinopol   overprinted on stamps of Romania: Romanian offices in the Ottoman Turkish Empire. *Romania (offices in the Turkish Empire).*

Posta Romania   Romania. See **Romania**.

Posta Romina   Romania. See **Romania**.

Posta Shqiptare   Albania. See **Albania**.

Postat e Qeverriës së Përkohështme të Shqiponiës (or **Shqipëniës**)   Albania. See **Albania**.

Poste Cirenaica   Cyrenaica. See **Cyrenaica**.

Poste Coloniali Italiane   **(1)** together with the name of the colony: refer to the named colony; **(2)** on stamps with no colony named: general issues for use in any colony *(Italian Colonies).*

Poste de Genève   cantonal issue for Geneva. See **Switzerland**.

Poste Estensi   inscription on stamps of Modena. See **Modena**. *Italian States*.

Poste Italiane   **(1)** inscription on stamps of Italy. See **Italy**. **(2)** together with "Prima Esposizione Fiera Campionaria di Tripoli" or "Fiera Campionaria Tripoli": Libya. See **Libya**, *Libya*.

Poste Italiane - Somalia   Somalia. See **Somalia**.

Poste Locale   with post horn and white cross: Switzerland. See **Switzerland**.

Poste Persane   Iran. See **Iran**.

Poste Rep. San Marino   San Marino. See **San Marino**.

Poste Repubblica Sociale Italiana   Italian Social Republic. See **Italy (Italian Social Republic)**.

Postes   often accompanying a country's name. Refer to the country name.

Postes Afghanes   Afghanistan. See **Afghanistan**.

Postes Algerie   Algeria. See **Algeria**.

Postes de Corée   Korea. See **Korea (South)**.

Postes Egyptiennes   Egypt. See **Egypt**.

Postes Ethiopie   Ethiopia. See **Ethiopia**.

Postes Ethiopiennes   Ethiopia. See **Ethiopia**.

Postes Françaises   France. See **France**.

Postes Française - Etablissments de l'Océanie   French Polynesia. See **French Polynesia**.

Postes Française - ÉTS Franç dans l'Inde   French India. See **French India**.

Postes Française Madagascar   overprinted on stamps of France: Madagascar. See **Madagascar**. *Malagasy Republic*.

Postes Hediaz & Nedje   see **Saudi Arabia**.

Postes Hedjaz & Nedjde   see **Saudi Arabia**.

Postes Imperiales de Coree   Korea. See **Korea (South)**.

Postes Iraniennes   Iran. See **Iran**.

Postes Lao   Laos. See **Laos**.

Poste Somalia   Somalia. See **Somalia**.

Postes Ottomanes   Ottoman Empire (Turkey). See **Turkey**.

Postes Persanes   Iran. See **Iran**.

Postes RF   RF is an abbreviation for "République Française." See **France**.

Postes Serbes   overprinted on stamps on stamps of France: for use in Corfu. See **Serbia**.

Postes Syrie   Syria. See **Syria**.

Poste Tripolitania   Tripolitania. See **Tripolitania**.

Poste Vaticane   Vatican City. See **Vatican City**.

Postgebiet ob. Ost   overprinted on stamps of Germany: Lithuania. See **Lithuania**.

Post Stamp   together with Urdu script and denomination in annas: Hyderabad, a native feudatory state in south-central India. *India (native feudatory states)*.

P.P.   overprinted, together with numeral of value and "centimos" on postage-due stamps of French Morocco: French Morocco. *French Morocco*.

P.P.C.   (Poste Polonaise Constantinople) overprinted on stamps of Poland: Poland (consular offices in Levant). *Poland*.

Preussen   Prussia. See **Prussia**.

Prima Esposizione Fiera Campionaria di Tripoli   together with "Poste Italiane": Libya. *Libya*.

Prince Edward Island   an island off eastern Canada just north of Nova Scotia and just east of New Brunswick. British (1861–73). Stamps are inscribed **Prince Edward Island**. In 1873 Prince Edward Island joined the Confederation of Canada. *Canadian Provinces*.

Principat d'Andorra   Andorra. See **Andorra**.

Principaute de Monaco   Principality of Monaco. See **Monaco**.

Protectorado Español en Marruecos   overprinted on stamps of Spain: Spanish Morocco. See **Spanish Morocco**.

Protectorado Marruecos   overprinted on stamps of Spain: Spanish Morocco. See **Spanish Morocco**.

Protectorat de la Côte des Somâlis   Somali Coast. See **Somali Coast**.

Protectorate   overprinted on stamps of British Bechuanaland: Bechuanaland Protectorate. See **Bechuanaland Protectorate**.

Protectorat Français   overprinted on stamps of French Morocco: French Morocco. See **French Morocco**.

Provincia de Angola   Angola. See **Angola**.

Provincia de Cabo Verde   Cape Verde. See **Cape Verde**.

Provincia de Macau   Macao. See **Macao**.

Provincia de Moçambique   Mozambique. See **Mozambique**.

Provincie Modenes   Modena. See **Modena**. *Italian States*.

Provinz Laibach   Ljubljana. See **Ljubljana**. *Yugoslavia (Ljubljana)*.

Provinz Laibach - Ljubljanska Pokrajina   overprinted on stamps of Italy: Ljubljana (German occupation). See **Ljubljana**. *Yugoslavia (Ljubljana)*.

Provinz Sachsen   Saxony, an administrative region in Soviet-occupied Germany (1945–46). *German Democratic Republic (Russian occupation)*.

Provisional 1881–1882   overprinted on stamps of Peru: Arequipa, a city in southern Peru and capital of Arequipa Department. *Peru (provisional issues)*.

Provisional de Medellin   Antioquia. See **Antioquia**.

Provisoire or **Provi Soire**   overprinted in a semicircle or an octagonal device on stamps of Iran: *Iran*.

Prussia   a state and kingdom in northern Germany. Stamps are inscribed **Preussen** (1861–68). *German States*.

P.S.N.C.   each letter in one of the four corners of a stamp and a sailing ship in the center: Peru. See **Peru**.

P^{TO} Rico   Puerto Rico. See **Puerto Rico**.

PTT Makedonija   Macedonia. See **Macedonia**.

Puerto Rico   an island in the West Indies east of the Dominican Republic. Spanish (1873–98), U.S. (1898–1900). Inscriptions include **P^{TO} Rico** (1877–80, 1898), **Puerto Rico** (1880–98), **Correos Coamo** (1898), **Porto Rico** overprinted on U.S. stamps (1899), **Puerto Rico** overprinted on U.S. stamps (1900). Since the early twentieth century, Puerto Rico has used U.S. stamps.

Puno   overprinted on provisional issues of Arequipa or on stamps of Peru: Puno, a city in southern Peru on Lake Titicaca. *Peru (provisional issues)*.

Puttialla State   overprinted on stamps of India: Patiala state, a state in north-central India. *India (convention states)*.

Qarku Postes I Korçês   Albania. See **Albania**.

Qatar   occupying a small peninsula jutting into the Persian Gulf, bordered on the west and south by Saudi Arabia and the United Arab Emirates. Independent (1957→). Stamps are inscribed **Qatar** or **State of Qatar**.

Qeverija Demokratike (or **Dem.** or **Demokrat.**) **e Shqiperise**   Albania. See **Albania**.

Qu'aiti State of Hadhramaut   see **Aden**.

Qu'aiti State of Shihr and Mukalla   see **Aden**.

Queensland a state in northeastern Australia. British (1860–1901), Australian (1901–13). Stamps are inscribed **Queensland**. Queensland joined the Commonwealth of Australia in 1901 but continued to use its own stamps until Australia began issuing stamps in 1913. *Australian States (Queensland).*

Quelimane a province (and city) in central Mozambique on the Gulf of Mozambique. Portuguese (1913–). Inscriptions include **Republica Quelimane** overprinted on stamps of Portuguese Africa, Macao, or Timor (1913), **Quelimane** together with "Republica Portuguesa" (1914–). Quelimane subsequently used stamps of Mozambique.

R enclosed at the apex of an inverted valentine-style heart: Jind, a native feudatory state in northern India. *India (native feudatory states).*

Rah Nandgam State Postage Nandgaon, a native feudatory state in east-central India. *India (native feudatory states).*

Rajasthan overprinted on stamps of Jaipur: Rajasthan, a union of 14 native feudatory states in central India. *India (native feudatory states).*

Raratonga overprinted on stamps of New Zealand or inscribed: Cook Islands. See **Cook Islands**.

Ras al Khaima on the Arabian coast of the Persian Gulf at the very northeast tip of the United Arab Emirates. Emirate under British protection (1964–72). Stamps are inscribed **Ras al Khaima**. In 1972 Ras al Khaima joined the United Arab Emirates.

RAU (Republique Arabie Syrie) Syria. See **Syria**.

Rayon either by itself or with Roman numeral "I," "II," or "III": Switzerland. See **Switzerland**.

R. Commissariato Civile Territori Sloveni occupati Lubiana overprinted on stamps of Yugoslavia: Ljubljana (Italian occupation). See **Ljubljana**. *Yugoslavia (Ljubljana).*

R. de Panama Panama. See **Panama**.

Regatul Romaniei overprinted in a circular device on stamps of Hungary for use in areas occupied by Romania following World War I: *Hungary.*

Regence de Tunis Tunisia. See **Tunisia**.

Reggenza Italiane del Carnaro overprinted on stamps of Fiume: Fiume. See **Fiume**.

Regno d'Italia Italy. See **Italy**.

Regno d'Italia Trentino overprinted on stamps of Austria: Trentino (Italian occupation). See **Trentino**. *Austria (occupation stamps).*

Regno d'Italia Venezia Giulia   overprinted on stamps of Austria: Venezia Giulia (Italian occupation). See **Venezia Giulia**. *Austria (occupation stamps)*.

Reichpost   Germany. See **Germany**.

Rep. de Honduras or **Rep. de Honduras C.A.**   Honduras. See **Honduras**.

Rep. Dem. Pop. Lao   Laos. See **Laos**.

Rep. di San Marino   San Marino. See **San Marino**.

Rep. Italiana   Italy. See **Italy**.

Repoblika Demokratika Malagasy   Malagasy Republic. See **Malagasy Republic**.

Repoblika Malagasy   Malagasy Republic. See **Malagasy Republic**.

Repoblikan'i Madagasikara   Malagasy Republic. See **Malagasy Republic**.

Rep. O. del Uruguay   Uruguay. See **Uruguay**.

Rep. S. Marino or **Rep. San Marino**   San Marino. See **San Marino**.

Rep. Syriénne   Syria. See **Syria**.

Repubblica di San Marino or **Repubblica di S. Marino**   San Marino. See **San Marino**.

Repubblica Sociale Italiana   Italian Social Republic. See **Italy (Italian Social Republic)**.

Repub. di S. Marino   San Marino. See **San Marino**.

Repub. Franc.   abbreviation for République Française. See **France**.

Republica   often accompanying a country's name. Refer to the country name.

Republica   **(1)** overprinted on stamps of Portugal: Portugal; **(2)** overprinted on stamps of Portuguese colonies: refer to the named colony.

Republica Argentina   Argentina. See **Argentina**.

Republica Cabo Verde   overprinted on stamps of various Portuguese colonies: Cape Verde. See **Cape Verde**.

Republica da Guiné-Bissau   Guinea-Bissau. See **Guinea-Bissau**.

Republica de Colombia   Colombia. See **Colombia**.

Republica de Costa Rica   Costa Rica. See **Costa Rica**.

Republica de El Salvador   El Salvador. See **El Salvador**.

Republica de Guatemala   Guatemala. See **Guatemala**.

Republica de Guinea Ecuatorial   Equatorial Guinea. See **Equatorial Guinea**.

Republica de Honduras   Honduras. See **Honduras.**

Republica del Ecuador   Ecuador. See **Ecuador**.

Republica del Paraguay   Paraguay. See **Paraguay**.

Republica del Uruguay   Uruguay. See **Uruguay**.

Republica Democratica de S. (or **São**) **Tomé e Principe**   Saint Thomas and Prince Islands. See **Saint Thomas and Prince Islands**.

Republica de Nicaragua   Nicaragua. See **Nicaragua**.

Republica de Panama   overprinted or inscribed: Panama. See **Panama**.

Republica de Venezuela   Venezuela. See **Venezuela**.

Republica Dominicana   Dominican Republic. See **Dominican Republic**.

Republica Español   overprinted on stamps inscribed "Territorios Españoles del Golfo de Guinea": Spanish Guinea. *Spanish Guinea*.

Republica Española   Spain. See **Spain**.

República Española   overprinted on stamps inscribed "Posesiones Españolas del Sahara Occidental": Spanish Sahara. See **Spanish Sahara**.

Republica Guiné   overprinted on stamps of Portuguese Africa, Macao, or Timor: Portuguese Guinea. See **Portuguese Guinea**.

Republica Hungarica   Hungary. See **Hungary**.

Republica Italiana   Italy. See **Italy**.

Republica - Lourenço Marques   Lourenco Marques. See **Lourenço Marques**.

Republica Makedonija   Macedonia. See **Macedonia**.

Republica Moçambique   overprinted on stamps of Portuguese Africa, Macao, or Timor: Mozambique. See **Mozambique**.

Republica O. del Uruguay   Uruguay. See **Uruguay**.

Republica Oriental   Uruguay. See **Uruguay**.

Republica Oriental Uruguay or **Republica Oriental del Uruguay**   Uruguay. See **Uruguay**.

Republica Peruana   Peru. See **Peru**.

Republica Populara Romana (or **Romina**)   Romania. See **Romania**.

Republica Portugal - Guiné   Portuguese Guinea. See **Portuguese Guinea**.

Republica Portuguesa   Republic of Portugal. See **Portugal**.

Republica Portuguesa - Congo   Portuguese Congo. See **Portuguese Congo**.

Republica Portuguesa Correio   Portugal. See **Portugal**.

Republica Portuguesa - Inhambane   Inhambane. See **Inhambane**.

Republica Portuguesa - Macau   Macao. See **Macao**.

Republica Portuguesa - Moçambique   Mozambique. See **Mozambique**.

Republica Portuguesa - Quelamine   Quelimane. See **Quelimane**.

Republica Portuguesa - S. Tomé e Principe   Saint Thomas and Prince Islands. See **Saint Thomas and Prince Islands**.

Republica Portuguesa - Tete   Tete. See **Tete**.

Republica Portuguesa - Timor   Timor. See **Timor**.

Republica Quelimane   overprinted on stamps of Portuguese Africa, Macao, or Timor: Quelimane. See **Quelimane**.

Republica Tete   overprinted on stamps of Portuguese Africa, Macao, or Timor: Tete. See **Tete**.

Republic Indonesia Serinat   see **Indonesia**.

Republic Maluku Selatan   Republic of South Moluccas. See **South Moluccas**.

Republic of Yemen   Yemen. See **Yemen (Republic of)**.

Republiek Stellaland   see **Stellaland**.

Republiek van Suid-Afrika   South Africa. See **South Africa**.

Republika   often accompanying a country's name. Refer to the country name.

Republika Bosna I Hercegovina   Bosnia and Herzegovina. See **Bosnia and Herzegovina**.

Republika Hrvatska   Croatia. See **Croatia**.

Republika Korce Shqipetare   Albania. See **Albania**.

Repúbliká Ng Pilipinas   Philippines. See **Philippines**.

Republika Popullore e Shqiperise   Albania. See **Albania**.

Republika Shqiptare   Albania. See **Albania**.

Republik Österreich   Austria. See **Austria**.

Republique   often accompanying a country's name. Refer to the country name.

Republique Arabie Unie - Syrie   Syria. See **Syria**.

Republique Autonome du Togo   Togo. See **Togo**.

République Centrafricaine   Central African Republic. See **Central African Republic**.

Republique d'Azerbaidjan   Azerbaijan. See **Azerbaijan**.

Republique de Côte d'Ivoire   Ivory Coast. See **Ivory Coast**.

République de Djibouti   Djibouti. See **Djibouti**.

République de Guinée or **Republique de Guinee**   Republic of Guinea. See **Guinea (Republic of)**.

République de Haute-Volta   Upper Volta. See **Upper Volta**.

République Democratique du Congo   Democratic Republic of the Congo. See **Congo (Democratic Republic)**.

Republique Democratique Populaire Lao   Laos. See **Laos**.

République des Comores   Comoro Islands. See **Comoro Islands.**

Republique d'Haiti   Haiti. See **Haiti**.

République du Bénin   Benin. See **Benin**.

République du Congo   appears at various times on issues of both the Democratic Republic of the Congo and the Republic of the Congo. See **Congo (Democratic Republic)** and **Congo (Republic of)**.

Republique du Mali   Mali. See **Mali**.

Republique du Niger   Niger. See **Niger**.

Republique du Senegal   Republic of Senegal. See **Senegal**.

République du Tchad   Chad. See **Chad**.

Republique du Togo   Togo. See **Togo**.

Republique du Zaire (or **Zaïre**)   Zaire. See **Congo (Democratic Republic)**.

République Federale du Cameroun   Cameroon. See **Cameroon**.

République Federale Islamique des Comores   Comoro Islands. See **Comoro Islands**.

République Française   France. Often abbreviated **R.F.** See **France**. With "Colonies Postes," *French Colonies*.

Republique Française Colonies Postes   (1) by itself: French colonies; (2) with the name of a colony at bottom of stamp: see named colony.

Republique Française - Mayotte   Mayotte. See **Mayotte**.

Republique Française - Senegal et Dependances   Senegal. See **Senegal**.

République Gabonaise   Gabon. See **Gabon**.

Republique Georgienne   Georgia. See **Georgia**.

Republique Islamique de l'Iran   Iran. See **Iran**.

Republique Islamique de Mauritanie   Mauritania. See **Mauritania**.

République Islamique des Comores   Comoro Islands. See **Comoro Islands**.

République Khmere   Khmer Republic. See **Cambodia**.

Republique Libanaise   Lebanon. See **Lebanon**.

Republique Malgache   Malagasy Republic. See **Malagasy Republic**.

République Populaire du Bénin   Benin. See **Benin**.

République Populaire du Congo   see **Congo (Republic of)**.

République Populaire du Kampuchea   see **Cambodia**.

Republique Syriénne   Syria. See **Syria**.

Republique Togolaise   Togo. See **Togo**.

Republique Tunisienne   Tunisia. See **Tunisia**.

République Unie du Cameroun   Cameroun. See **Cameroun**.

Repub. Sociale Italiana Poste   Italian Social Republic. See **Italy (Italian Social Republic)**.

Retymno   together with "Timbre Poste Provisoir": Crete, Russian sector of Rethymnon (or Réthimnon) during international administration in 1899 following the Turkish-Greek War. See **Crete**.

Reunion   an island in the Indian Ocean southeast of Madagascar. French (1852–1975). Inscriptions include **Ile de la Réunion** (1852), **Réunion** or **Reunion** overprinted on the generic issue for French colonies (1885–92) or inscribed (1892–1947), and overprinted "France Libre" (1943), **CFA** overprinted, together with surcharged numeral of value, on the stamps of France (1949–75) or inscribed (1963-72). Reunion used generic stamps of French colonies from the 1850s to 1885. In 1974 Reunion became an administrative region of France and since has used stamps of France. The term "CFA" (Colonies Française d'Afrique) refers to the currency, the French African franc, used in Reunion.

R.F. or **RF**   abbreviation for **République Française**. Often appears on issues of France and on stamps of French colonies, territories, and possessions.

R.F. Fezzan   see **Fezzan-Ghadames**. *Libya (occupation issues)*.

Rheinland-Pflaz   Rhineland Palatinate (French occupation, 1947–49): *Germany (French occupation)*.

Rhodesia (British)   in southeastern Africa, bordered on the north by Zambia, on the east by Mozambique, on the south by South Africa, and on the west by Botswana. British (1890–1923). Inscriptions include **British South Africa Company** (1890–1909), **Rhodesia** overprinted stamps of British South Africa Company (1909), **British South Africa Company - Rhodesia** (1910–23). In 1923 Rhodesia was split into Northern Rhodesia and Southern Rhodesia.

Rhodesia (independent)   in southeastern Africa, formerly Southern Rhodesia, bordered on the southwest and west by Botswana, on the north by Zambia and Mozambique, on the east by Mozambique, and on the south by South Africa. Independent (1965–78). Stamps are inscribed **Rhodesia**. In 1978 Rhodesia became Zimbabwe.

Rhodesia and Nyasaland   in southern Africa. British (1953–63). Stamps are inscribed **Rhodesia and Nyasaland**. Rhodesia and Nyasaland was a federation of Northern Rhodesia, Southern Rhodesia, and Nyasaland.

Rialtar Sealadaċ na Héireann   provisional government of Ireland. See **Ireland**.

Rialtar Sealadaċ na Héireann 1922   overprinted on stamps of Great Britain: Ireland. See **Ireland**.

Riau   an archipelago in western Indonesia, lying southeast of the Malay Peninsula and east of the island of Sumatra, and extending northwest to southeast from the Straits of Singapore to the Straits of Berhala. Indonesian (1954–60s). Inscriptions include **Riau** overprinted on stamps of Netherlands Indies or Indonesia. *Indonesia*.

R.I. Iran   Republique Islamique de l'Iran. See **Iran**.

Rio de Oro   in northwest Africa, bordered on the north by Saguia el Hamra, on the west and south by Mauritania, and on the west by the Atlantic Ocean and consisting of the southern section of what would later become Spanish Sahara. Spanish (1905–24). Inscriptions include **Colonia de Rio de Oro** (1905–22), **Rio de Oro** overprinted on stamps inscribed "Territorios Espanoles de Africa Occidental" (1908), **Sahara Occidental Rio de Oro** (1922–24). Rio de Oro subsequently became part of Spanish Sahara.

Rio Muni   in western Africa, bordered on the north by Cameroon, on the east and south by Gabon, and on the west by the Gulf of Guinea. Spanish (1960–68). Inscriptions include **Rio Muni**, usually with "España." Rio Muni was formerly part of Spanish Guinea; subsequently, independent Equatorial Guinea.

R I S   (Republik Indonesia Serinat) overprinted on stamps of Netherlands Indies: Indonesia. See **Indonesia**.

Rizeh   overprinted on stamps of Russia together with surcharge in para(s) or piastre(s): *Russia (offices in the Turkish Empire)*.

R.O.   overprinted together with "Roumelle Orientale" on stamps of Turkey: *Eastern Rumalia*.

R.O. del Uruguay   Uruguay. See **Uruguay**.

Rodi   overprinted on stamps of Italy or inscribed. See **Dodecanese Islands**. *Italy (Aegean Islands)*.

Romagna   in north-central Italy consisting of the eastern portion of what is today the region of Emilia-Romagna. Independent (1859). Inscriptions include **Franco Bollo Postale Romagne** (1859). *Italian States*.

Romagne   Romagna. See **Romagna**. *Italian States.*

Romania   in southeastern Europe, bordered on the north by Ukraine, on the east by Moldova, on the southeast by the Black Sea, on the south by Bulgaria, on the southwest by Serbia, and on the west by Hungary. Kingdoms of Moldavia and Walachia (1858–64), independent (1865→). Inscriptions include **ЦОРТО СКРИСОРН** (Moldavia, 1858), **Porto Gazetei** (Moldavia, 1858–59), **Franco Scrisorei** (Moldavia-Walachia, 1862–65), **Posta Romana** (1865–90), **Romania** often with "Posta" (1890–1948), **Пощавъ Ромжния 1916–1917** overprinted on stamps of Bulgaria (Bulgarian occupation, 1916–17), **M.V.i.R.** overprinted on stamps of Germany (German occupation, 1917–18), **Rumänien** overprinted on stamps of Germany (German occupation, 1918), **Gultig 9. Armee** overprinted on stamps of Germany (German occupation, 1918), **Republica Populara Romana** (1948–54), **Republica Populara Romina** or **R.P. Romina** (1954–63), **Posta Romina** (1963–64), **Posta Romana** or **Poşta Română** (1964–96), **România** (1996→).

Roman States   also known as the Papal States, a territory that, excluding Tuscany, included nearly all of central Italy, was under direct sovereignty of the pope, and was dissolved in 1870, when nearly all the territory was annexed by the newly united Italy. Under Papal authority (1851–70). Stamps are inscribed **Franco Bollo Postale** together with the Papal crest and denomination in baj. (bajocchi), scudo, or cent. (centesimi). *Italian States.*

Ross Dependency   an area of land and sea extending from the South Pole to latitude 60° South, and bounded by longitude 160° East and 150° West; the Antarctic territory of New Zealand. New Zealand (1957→). Stamps are inscribed **Ross Dependency**.

Rossija   Russia. See **Russia**.

Rouad   see **Ile Rouad**.

Roumelle Orientale   either inscribed or overprinted on stamps of Turkey: *Eastern Rumalia.*

Royaume al Moutawakkiliyyah du Yemen   Yemen. See **Yemen (Republic of)**.

Royaume Arabie Soudite   Kingdom of Saudi Arabia. See **Saudi Arabia**.

Royaume d'Egypte   Egypt. See **Egypt**.

Royaume de l'Arabie Soudite   Kingdom of Saudi Arabia. See **Saudi Arabia**.

Royaume de Yemen   Yemen. See **Yemen (Republic of)**.

Royaume du Burundi   Burundi. See **Burundi**.

Royaume du Cambodge   Cambodia. See **Cambodia**.

Royaume du Laos   Laos. See **Laos**.

Royaume du Maroc   kingdom of Morocco. See **Morocco**.

R.P.E. Shqiperia   Albania. See **Albania**.

R.P. Kampuchea   Cambodia. See **Cambodia**.

R. Popullore e Shqiperise   Albania. See **Albania**.

R. Poste Italiane - Benadir   Somalia. See **Somalia**.

R.P. Romina   Romania. See **Romania**.

R.P.S. e Shqiperise   Albania. See **Albania**.

R.P. Shqiperia   Albania. See **Albania**.

R.R. (or RR.) Poste Coloniali Italiane   (1) together with the name of the colony: refer to the named colony; (2) on stamps with no colony named: general issues for use in any colony (*Italian Colonies*).

RSA   South Africa. See **South Africa**.

R.S.M.   Republic of San Marino. See **San Marino**.

R. Syriénne   Syria. See **Syria**.

Ruanda-Urundi   in east-central Africa, bordered on the north by Uganda, on the east and south by Tanzania, and on the west by Lake Tanganyika and the Democratic Republic of the Congo. Belgian (1924–61). Inscriptions include **Ruanda Urundi** overprinted on stamps of the Belgian Congo (1924-61), **Ruanda-Urundi** inscribed (1931-61). Before World War I, Ruanda-Urundi was part of German East Africa. In 1923 Belgium received Ruanda-Urundi as a mandate territory from the League of Nations and after 1946 administered it under UN jurisdiction. In 1962 the trusteeship ended and the territory was divided into the independent states of Rwanda and Burundi.

Rumänien   overprinted on stamps of Germany: Romania (German occupation). See **Romania**.

Russia   in eastern Europe and Asia, stretching about 6,000 miles from east to west and more than 2,000 miles north to south. Independent (1857→). Inscriptions include **ПОЧТОВАЯ МАРКА** (1857–1913), **ПОЧТА** (1913–22), **РОССІЯ** (1918), **РСФСР** (1922–23), **СССР**, occasionally with "USSR" (1923–91), **Rossija** (1991→). Russia was a monarchy until the revolution of 1917. During the civil war that followed (1918–21), it consisted of various political entities, the most dominant of which was the Bolshevik R.S.F.S.R. (Russian Soviet Federated Socialist Republic), which became the core for the formation of the U.S.S.R. in late 1922. In 1991 the U.S.S.R. collapsed and Russia became an independent republic. It then coordinated the formation of a political alliance with many of the former republics of the U.S.S.R., which is known as the Commonwealth of Independent States (CIS).

Russisch-Polen   overprinted on stamps of Germany: Poland (German occupation). See **Poland.**

Rwanda   in east-central Africa, bordered on the north by Uganda, on the east by Tanzania, on the south by Burundi, and on the west by Lake Kivu and the Democratic Republic of the Congo. Independent (1962→). Inscriptions include **Republique Rwanda** (1962–75), **Rwanda** (1975→). Prior to 1962, Rwanda was part of the Belgian-administered territory of Ruanda-Urundi. In 1962 the territory was divided into the independent nations of Rwanda and Burundi.

Ryukyu Islands   a group of 63 islands between southwestern Japan and Taiwan. U.S. (1947–72). Inscriptions include **Ryukyus** (1949–51, 1961–72), inscriptions in Japanese characters (1951–61). The United States occupied the Ryukyus in 1945; the islands were returned to Japan in 1972. *United States.*

S   overprinted, together with crescent and star, on stamps of Straits Settlements: Selangor. *Malaya (Selangor).*

S.   overprinted on stamps of Straits Settlements: Selangor. *Malaya (Selangor).*

S.A.   Saudi Arabia. See **Saudi Arabia.**

Saar   a state in southwestern Germany, bordered on the north and east by Rhineland-Palatinate, on the south by France, and on the west by France and Luxembourg. League of Nations (1920–35), French (1947–57), German (1957–59). Inscriptions include **Sarre** overprinted on stamps of Germany or Bavaria (1920), **Saargebiet** overprinted on stamps of Germany (1920–21) or inscribed (1921–35), **Saar** (1947–57), **Saarpost** (1948), **Saarland** and "Deutsches Bundespost" (1957–59). Following World War I and under terms of the Treaty of Versailles, France retained control of Saar for 15 years. In 1935 Saar chose to rejoin Germany. In 1945, at the end of World War II, Saar was made part of the French Zone of Occupation and in 1946, a separate zone. In 1956 Saar requested incorporation into Germany, and on January 1, 1957, under the name Saarland, became a state in the Federal Republic of Germany. In 1959 it discontinued issuing its own stamps.

Saargebiet   overprinted on stamps of Germany: Saar. See **Saar.**

Saarland   Saar. See **Saar.**

Saarpost   Saar. See **Saar.**

Sabah   a Malaysian state. Inscriptions include **Sabah** overprinted on stamps of North Borneo or inscribed together with "Malaysia": *Malaysia (Sabah).* Before joining Malaysia, Sabah was North Borneo.

Sachsen   Saxony. See **Saxony**.

Sahara   overprinted on stamps of Spain: Spanish Sahara. See **Spanish Sahara**.

Sahara - España   Spanish Sahara. See **Spanish Sahara**.

Sahara - Español   either inscribed or overprinted on stamps of Spain: Spanish Sahara. See **Spanish Sahara**.

Sahara Occidental Rio de Oro   Rio de Oro. See **Rio de Oro**.

Saint Christopher   one of the Leeward Islands, southeast of Puerto Rico. British (1870–90). Stamps are inscribed **Saint Christopher**. Between 1890 and 1903, Saint Christopher used stamps of the Leeward Islands. In 1903 it began using stamps of Saint Kitts-Nevis.

Saint Christopher-Nevis-Anguilla   see **Saint Kitts-Nevis**.

Saint Helena   a small island in the Atlantic Ocean about 1,200 miles west of Africa. British (1856→). Stamps are inscribed **St. Helena**.

St. John's-Newfoundland   see **Newfoundland**.

Saint Kitts   (Saint Christopher) one of the Leeward Islands in the West Indies. British (1980→). Stamps are inscribed **St. Kitts**.

Saint Kitts-Nevis   Saint Kitts (Saint Christopher), Nevis, and Anguilla, three of the Leeward Islands in the West Indies southeast of Puerto Rico. British (1903–80). Inscriptions include **St. Kitts-Nevis** (1903–52), **St.** (or **Saint**) **Christopher-Nevis-Anguilla** (1952–80). In 1967 Anguilla began issuing stamps of its own. In 1980 Saint Kitts and Nevis each began issuing stamps of their own.

Saint Lucia   one of the Windward Islands in the West Indies, lying between Martinique on the north and Saint Vincent on the south. British (1860–1979), independent (1979→). Stamps are inscribed **St. Lucia** or **Saint Lucia**.

Saint-Pierre and Miquelon   in the North Atlantic Ocean south of Newfoundland, Canada, consisting of two small groups of islands, with a total area of 93 square miles, of which the main islands are Saint-Pierre, Miquelon, and Langlade. French (1885→). Inscriptions include **SPM** or **S P M** overprinted, together with surcharged value, on the generic issue for French colonies (1885–91), **St-Pierre M-on** overprinted, together with surcharged value, on the generic issue for French colonies (1891–92), **S^T Pierre et Miquelon** (1892–1909, and occasionally thereafter), **Saint-Pierre et Miquelon** (1909–38), **St. Pierre et Miquelon** inscribed (1938), or overprinted on stamps of France (1990–98), **France Libre F.N.F.L.** overprinted (1941–42), **Saint Pierre et Miquelon** (1947→).

Saint Thomas and Prince Islands   the islands of Sao Tomé, Príncipe, and several small islets, located off the western coast of Africa, in the Gulf of Guinea. Portuguese (1869–1975), independent (1975→). Inscriptions include **S. Thome**

e Principe (1869–95), **S. Thome** (or **Thomé) e Principe** together with "Portugal" (1895–1913), **Republica S. Tomé e Principe** overprinted on stamps of Macao, Timor, or Portuguese Africa (1913), **S. Tomé e Principe** usually with "Republica" or "Republica Portuguesa" (1913–75), **Republica Democratica de S. Tomé e Principe** (1975–77), **Republica Democratica de São Tomé e Principe** (1977), **São Tomé e Príncipe** or **S. Tomé e Príncipe** (1977→). Issues between the years 1912 and 1931 are often overprinted "Republica."

Saint Trsta Vuja   Trieste. See **Trieste**. *Yugoslavia (Trieste).*

Saint Vincent   in the West Indies Windward Islands chain in the southeastern Caribbean, situated between Saint Lucia on the north and Grenada on the south, including the island of Saint Vincent and the northern islands of the Grenadines group, the largest of which include Bequia, Canouan, Mustique, Mayreau, and Union. British (1861–1979), independent (1979→). Inscriptions include **St. Vincent** (1861–1993), **St. Vincent and the Grenadines** (1992→). See also **Saint Vincent Grenadines**, which has issued stamps concurrent with those of Saint Vincent.

Saint Vincent Grenadines   in the West Indies Windward Islands chain in the southeastern Caribbean, situated between Saint Lucia on the north and Grenada on the south, including the northern islands of the Grenadines group belonging to Saint Vincent, the largest of which include Bequia, Canouan, Mustique, Mayreau, Prune, Petit Saint Vincent, and Union. Saint Vincent (1974–97). Inscriptions include **Grenadines of** overprinted on stamps of **Grenadines of St. Vincent** (1973–97), Saint Vincent (1974). In addition, Bequia Island and Union Island each have issued stamps of their own.

S.A.K.   Saudi Arabian Kingdom. See **Saudi Arabia**.

Salonique   overprinted on stamps of Russia together with surcharge in para(s) or piastre(s): Russian offices in Salonika (Thessaloníki), a city in northern Greece. *Russia (offices in the Turkish Empire).*

Samoa   an island nation in the central South Pacific Ocean 1,800 miles northeast of New Zealand, primarily composed of two large islands, Sava'i and Upola. Kingdom (1877–99), German (1900–14), New Zealand (1914–62), independent (1962→). Inscriptions include **Samoa Express** (1877–81), **Samoa** together with "Post" or "Postage" (1895–1900), **Samoa** overprinted on stamps of Germany (1900) or inscribed (1900–15), **G.R.I.** overprinted on stamps of German Samoa (1914), **Samoa** overprinted on stamps of New Zealand (1914–35), **Western Samoa** overprinted on stamps of New Zealand (1935–58) or inscribed (1935–58), **Samoa i Sisifo** (1958–81), **Samoa** (1981→). In 1900 Germany and the United States divided Samoa. Germany took the western part, which came to be known as Western Samoa; the United States occupied the eastern part, which is known as American Samoa.

Samoa Express   see **Samoa**.

Samoa i Sisifo   see **Samoa**.

Sandjak d'Alexandrette   overprinted on stamps of Syria: Alexandretta. See **Alexandretta**.

San Marino   an enclave in northern Italy of about 24 square miles. Independent (1877→). Inscriptions include **Repub. di S. Marino** (1877–94), **Repubblica di San Marino** (1894–99, 1937–42), **Rep. S. Marino** (1899–1970, 1935–37), **Rep. di San Marino** (1903–70), **Repubblica di S. Marino** (1932–60s), **San Marino** (1942, 1960s→), **Poste Rep. San Marino** (1943–46), **R.S.M.** (1949), **Rep. San Marino** (1960s–).

Santander   a department (state) in north-central Colombia. Local issues (1884–1907). Inscriptions include **Estado Sobrano de Santander** (1884–86), **E. S. de Santander** (1886), **Departmento de Santander** (1887–1903), **Depto.** or **Dep. de Santander** (1904). *Colombia*.

Saorstát Éireann   Free State of Ireland. See **Ireland**.

Saorstát Éireann 1922   overprinted on stamps of Great Britain: Ireland. See **Ireland**.

São Tome e Principe or **São Tomé e Príncipe**   Saint Thomas and Prince Islands. See **Saint Thomas and Prince Islands**.

Sarawak   the northeastern portion of the island of Borneo bordering Sabah. British (1869–1963), Malaysian (1963–80s). Inscriptions include **Sarawak** (1869–1964), **BMA** overprinted on earlier issues (1945), **Sarawak - Malaysia** (1964–80s). In 1841 Sir James Brooke, with the approval of Great Britain, obtained Sarawak from the Sultan of Brunei. In 1888 Sarawak became a formal British protectorate. In 1963 Sarawak joined the Federation of Malaysia.

Sarawak - Malaysia   see **Sarawak**.

Sarre   overprinted on stamps of Germany or Bavaria: Saar. See **Saar**.

Saseno   (or Sazan) an island in the Adriatic Sea off the entrance to Valona Bay in southwestern Albania, used by Italy as a fortress. Italian (1923). Inscriptions include **Saseno** overprinted on stamps of Italy (1923).

Saurashtra or **Saurashtra Postage**   overprinted or inscribed: Soruth, a native feudatory state in west-central India. *India (native feudatory states)*.

Saudi Arabia   in southwestern Asia, occupying most of the Arabian Peninsula, bordered on the north by Jordan, Iraq, and Kuwait, on the east by the Persian Gulf and Qatar, on the southeast by the United Arab Emirates and Oman, on the south by the Republic of Yemen, and on the west by the Red Sea and the Gulf of Aqaba. Independent (1916→). Inscriptions include **Hejaz & Nedj**

(1929), **Postes Hediaz & Nedje** (1930), **Postes Hedjaz & Nedjde** (1931–34), and from 1934 onward, used somewhat interchangeably, **Royaume Arabie Soudite** (1934~), **Royaume de l'Arabie Soudite** (1934~), **Kingdom of Saudi Arabia** (1952~), **S.A.K.** (1960~), **Saudi Arabia** (1961~), **Arabie Saoudite** (1963~), **Saudi Arabian Kingdom** (1965~), **S.A.** (1966~), **K.S.A.** (1975~). Issues before 1929 and many issues after 1983 contain only Arabic inscriptions. In 1932, after having unified various territories conquered since 1901 (including the kingdoms of Hejaz and Nedj), Abdul Aziz ibn Saud, renamed his realm Saudi Arabia and proclaimed himself king.

Saudi Arabian Kingdom   see **Saudi Arabia**.

Saxony   a state in northwestern Germany. Stamps are inscribed **Sachsen** (1850–68). *German States.*

SCADTA   see **Sociedad Colombo-Alemania de Transportes Aereo**.

Scarpanto   overprinted on stamps of Italy. See **Dodecanese Islands**. *Italy (Aegean Islands).*

Schleswig   region in northern Germany just south of Denmark. Allied Commission (1920). Inscriptions include **Slesvig** together with "Plebiscit" (1920), **1.Zone** overprinted (1920), **C•I•S** overprinted (1920). In 1920, in the aftermath of World War I, plebiscites were held in the northern and southern portions of North Schleswig so inhabitants could choose between Denmark and Germany. The northern part (Zone 1) voted to join Denmark, while the southern part (Zone 2) voted to remain within Germany, becoming part of the state of Schleswig-Holstein.

Schleswig-Holstein   a state in northern Germany just south of Denmark. Inscriptions include **Schleswig-Holstein** (1865), **Herzgoth-Schleswig** (Schleswig, 1864–65), **Herzgoth Holstein** (Holstein, 1865–66), **Herzgothum Holstein** (Holstein, 1865–66), **Hrzgl Post Frm** (Holstein, 1864), **Hrzgl Post Frmke** (1864). *German States.*

Scutari di Albania   overprinted on stamps of Italy: Italian offices in Scutari (Shkodër), a city in northwestern Albania. *Italy (offices abroad).*

S.d.N. Bureau international du Travail   overprinted on stamps of Switzerland: International Labor Bureau. *Switzerland (official issues).*

Selangor   a Malayan (and later, Malaysian) state. **(1) S.** either by itself or together with crescent and star, overprinted on stamps of Straits Settlements: *Malaya (Selangor)*; **(2) Selangor** overprinted on stamps of Straits Settlements, or inscribed either by itself or "Malaya" or "Persekutuan Tanah Melayu": *Malaya (Selangor)*; (3) **Selangor** together with "Malaysia": *Malaysia (Selangor).*

Senegal   in western Africa, bordered on the north by Mauritania, on the east by Mali, on the south by Guinea and Guinea-Bissau, and on the west by the Atlantic Ocean. French (1887–1941), independent (1960→). Inscriptions include generic issues of French colonies surcharged with numeral of value ("5," "10," or "15," 1887–92), **Senegal** or **Sénégal** overprinted on the generic issue for French colonies (1892), **Senegal et Dependances** and "Republique Française" or "RF" (1892–1906), **Sénégal** and "Afrique Occidentale Française" or "A.O.F." (1906–41), **Republique du Senegal** or **Senegal** (1960→). Senegal was briefly part of the Mali Federation between June and August 1960. In August 1960, it withdrew to become a separate independent state.

Senegal et Dependances   Senegal. See **Senegal**.

Serbia   in south-central Europe, bordered on the north by Hungary, on the east by Romania and Bulgaria, on the south by Macedonia, on the southwest by Albania, and on the west by Montenegro, Bosnia and Herzegovina, and Croatia. Inscriptions include **К.С. ПОШТА** (1866–68), **К. СГБСКА ПОШТА** (1866–68), **ПОШТА** (1869–80), **КЊСРП ПОШТА** (1872–80), **СГБИJA** (1880–1920), **КРАЛЕВИНА СГБИJA** (1904, 1918–20), **Serbien** overprinted on stamps of Bosnia and Herzegovina (Austrian occupation, 1916); overprinted on stamps of Yugoslavia (German occupation, 1941), **Postes Serbes** overprinted on stamps of France (for use in Corfu, 1916–18). Serbia is now the larger of the two remaining Yugoslav republics, the smaller being Montenegro.

Serbien   (1) overprinted on stamps of Bosnia and Herzegovina: Serbia (Austrian occupation); (2) overprinted on stamps of Yugoslavia: Serbia (German occupation). See **Serbia**.

Service de Bureau International du Travail   overprinted on stamps of Switzerland: International Labor Bureau. *Switzerland (official issues)*.

Service de la Societe des Nations   overprinted on stamps of Switzerland: League of Nations. *Switzerland (official issues)*.

Servicio Postale del Salvador   El Salvador. See **El Salvador**.

Servicio Postale Mexicano   Mexico. See **Mexico**.

Servicio Postal - India Port.   Portuguese India. See **Portuguese India**.

Seychelles   an archipelago of about 115 islands scattered across the Indian Ocean north of Madagascar and consisting of three main groups, the Aldabra group, the Farquhar group, and in the north, the Amirante group, which includes the main islands, Mahé, Praslin, Silhouette, and La Digue. British (1890–1976), independent (1976→). Stamps are inscribed **Seychelles**. During the 1980s and 1990s, the Aldabra and Farquhar island groups issued stamps inscribed **Zil Elwannyen Sesel**, **Zil Elwagne Sesel**, or **Zil Eloigne Sesel** together with "Seychelles."

Shanghai   a city in eastern China, on the Huangpu River, a tributary of the Yangtze River, near the Yangtze's mouth to the East China Sea. British (1865–98). Inscriptions include **Shanghai L.P.O.** (1865–90), **Shanghai Local Post** (1890–93), **Local Post - Shanghai Municipality** (1893–98). In the nineteenth century, Great Britain, France, and the United States maintained small territorial zones near the city. The Shanghai Local Post served as a reliable alternative to the Chinese postal system.

Sharjah   on the Arabian shore of the Persian Gulf in the northeastern United Arab Emirates, between Ajman on the north and Dubai on the south. Emirate under British protection (1963–71). Inscriptions include **Sharjah & Dependencies** and **Sharjah & Dependencies - Trucial States**. Sharjah joined the United Arab Emirates in 1971.

Shqipënia   Albania. See **Albania**.

Shqipënia e Lirë   Albania. See **Albania**.

Shqipënië   Albania. See **Albania**.

Shqiperia   Albania. See **Albania**.

Shqiperie Korcê Vetqeveritabe   Albania. See **Albania**.

Shqiperija   Albania. See **Albania**.

Shqipni   Albania. See **Albania**.

Shqipnija   Albania. See **Albania**.

Shqypnis   Albania. See **Albania**.

Shqyptare   Albania. See **Albania**.

Siam   see **Thailand**.

Siege of Mafeking   inscribed together with "V.R." and "Local Post": Mafeking. Mafeking is a town in northern South Africa that was besieged by the Boers in 1900 during the Boer War. *Cape of Good Hope (Mafeking)*.

Sierra Leone   a small nation in western Africa bordered on the north and east by Guinea, on the southeast by Liberia, and on the southwest by the Atlantic Ocean. British (1859–1961), independent (1961→). Stamps are inscribed **Sierra Leone**.

Simi   overprinted on stamps of Italy. See **Dodecanese Islands**. *Italy (Aegean Islands)*.

Singapore   includes a main island just off the southern tip of the Malay Peninsula and about 50 smaller islands. British (1948–59), independent (1959–63, 1965→), Malaysian (1963–65). Inscriptions include **Singapore** together with "Malaya" (1948–59), **State of Singapore** (1959–63), **Singapore** (1963→), **Republic of Singapore** (1966). Until 1946 Singapore was part of the Straits Settlements, and then until 1959, part of the Federation of Malaya. In 1963 Singapore joined the Federation of Malaysia. In 1965 it withdrew.

Sirmoor State Postage Stamp   Sirmur, a native feudatory state in north-central. *India (native feudatory states).*

Slesvig   Schleswig. See **Schleswig**.

Slovakia   in central Europe, bordered on the north by Poland, on the east by Ukraine, on the south by Hungary, on the southwest by Austria, and on the northwest by the Czech Republic. Nominally independent (1939–45), independent (1993→). Inscriptions include **Slovenský Štát** and "1939" overprinted on stamps of Czechoslovakia (1939), **Slovenska Posta** (1939), **Slovensko** (1939–45, 1993→) In 1939 Slovakia, the eastern section of Czechoslovakia, declared itself independent at the urging of Nazi Germany. At the same time, Germany seized the western section, Bohemia and Moravia, making it a German protectorate. After World War II, Slovakia again became part of Czechoslovakia. In 1993 it became an independent country.

Slovenia   in southeastern Europe, on the Balkan Peninsula, bordered on the north by Austria, on the northeast by Hungary, on the southeast and south by Croatia, and on the west by Italy and the Adriatic Sea. Independent (1991→). Stamps are inscribed **Slovenija**. Slovenia was formerly a Yugoslav republic.

Slovenija   Slovenia. See **Slovenia**.

Slovenska Posta   Slovakia. See **Slovakia**.

Slovensko   Slovakia. See **Slovakia**.

Slovenský Štát   and "1939" overprinted on stamps of Czechoslovakia: Slovakia. See **Slovakia**.

Smirne   overprinted on stamps of Italy: Italian offices in Smyrna (Izmir), a city in the Turkish Ottoman Empire, now located in western Turkey. *Italy (offices abroad).*

Smyrne or **Smyrn**   overprinted on stamps of Russia together with surcharge in para(s) or piastre(s): Russian offices in Smyrna (Izmir), a city in the Turkish Ottoman Empire, now located in western Turkey. *Russia (offices in the Turkish Empire).*

S O   overprinted on stamps of Czechoslovakia: *Eastern Silesia.*

Socialist People's Libyan Arab Jamahiriya   Libya. See **Libya**.

Socialist Republic of the Union of Burma   Burma. See **Burma**.

Sociedad Colombo-Alemania de Transportes Aereo (SCADTA)   a private firm under Colombian government contract to carry airmail during the years 1920–32. *Colombia.*

Sociéte des Nations   overprinted on stamps of Switzerland: League of Nations. *Switzerland (official issues).*

Solidarité Française   an inscription on some stamps issued by the Free French in overseas colonies during World War II. *French Colonies.*

Solomon Islands   a group of about 30 islands plus numerous atolls in the western South Pacific east of New Guinea; the main islands include Guadalcanal, New Georgia, Santa Isabel, Malaita, Choisell, San Cristobal, and Vella Lavella. British (1907–78), independent (1978→). Inscriptions include **British Solomon Islands Protectorate** (1907–13), **British Solomon Islands** (1913–75), **Solomon Islands** (1975→).

Solonicco   overprinted on stamps of Italy: Italian offices in Salonika (Thessaloníki), a city in northern Greece. *Italy (offices abroad).*

Somalia   in eastern Africa, bordered on the north by the Gulf of Aden, on the east and south by the Indian Ocean, on the southwest by Kenya, on the west by Ethiopia, and on the northwest by Djibouti. Italian (1903–36), independent (1960→). Inscriptions include **Benadir** and "R. Poste Italiane" (1903–22), **Somalia Italiana** overprinted on stamps of Italy (1922–30) or inscribed (1936), **Poste Somalia** and "Colonie Italiane" (1924–25), **Somalia Ital.** (1926), **Somalia** overprinted on stamps of Italy (1926, 1930–31) or inscribed (1950–52), **Poste Somalia Italiana** (1928), **Somalia** and "Poste Italiane" (1932–36), **Somalia** with "RR. Poste Coloniali Italiane" (1932–36), **Somalia**, occasionally with "Poste" or "Posta," (1950–70), **Somali Democratic Republic** or **Somali Democratic Rep.** (1970–73), **Jum. Dim. Somaliya** (1973–74), **Jam. Dim. Soomaaliya** (1974–79), **Soomaaliya** (1975), **J.D. Soomaaliya** (1975–89), **J.D. Soomaaliyeed** (1978–89), **J. Soomaaliya** (1992–). In 1936 Somalia became part of Italian East Africa. In 1941 Great Britain invaded Somalia and occupied it until 1950. In 1950 it was made an Italian trust under UN supervision. In 1960 it joined with British Somaliland Protectorate to become independent Somalia.

Somalia Italiana   overprinted on stamps of Italy: Somalia. See **Somalia.**

Somalia Posta   Somalia. See **Somalia.**

Somali Coast   in northeastern Africa, bordered on the north by Eritrea, on the east by the Gulf of Aden, on the southeast by Somalia, and on the south and west by Ethiopia. French (1894–1967). **D J** overprinted on stamps of Obock (1894), **Djibouti** overprinted on stamps of Obock (1894–1902), **Protectorat de la Côte des Somâlis** together with "Djibouti 1893–94" (1894–1902), **Côte Française des Somalis** (1902–67), overprinted "France Libre" (1943), **Côte Fr^{SE} des Somalis** (1947). In 1967 Somali Coast became Afars and Issas, and in 1977, Republic of Djibouti.

Somali Democratic Republic (or **Rep.**)   Somalia. See **Somalia.**

Somaliland Protectorate   in east Africa (the northern part of present-day Somalia), south of the Gulf of Aden. British (1903–60). Inscriptions include **British Somaliland** overprinted on stamps of India (1903), **Somaliland Protectorate** (1904–60). In 1960 the Somaliland Protectorate joined Italian Somaliland to become independent Somalia.

Soomaaliya   Somalia. See **Somalia**.

Soruth Postage   Soruth, a native feudatory state in west-central India. *India (native feudatory states).*

Soudan   Sudan. See **Sudan**.

Soudan Française   French Sudan. See **French Sudan**.

Sourashtra Postage   Soruth, a native feudatory state in west-central India. *India (native feudatory states).*

South Africa   the southernmost country in Africa. British dominion (1910–61), independent (1961→). Many issues contain bilingual English/Afrikaans inscriptions. In some cases, English and Afrikaans appear individually on alternating se-tenant stamps. Inscriptions include **Union of South Africa** and **Unie van Zuid Afrika** (1910–26), **South Africa** or **Suidafrika** alternating on se-tenant stamps (1926–33), **South Africa** and **Suid-Afrika** either together or alternating on se-tenant stamps (1933–61), **Republic of South Africa** and **Republiek van Suid-Afrika** (1961–67), **RSA** (1967–97), **South Africa** (1997→). In the 1970s, South Africa set aside several nominally independent tribal homelands, which operated until 1994. They include **Bophuthatswana, Ciskei, Transkei**, and **Venda**.

South Arabia   on the Arabian Peninsula south of Saudi Arabia consisting largely of the Aden and the Aden Protectorate. British (1963–67). Stamps are inscribed **Federation of South Arabia**. In 1967 South Arabia became the People's Democratic Republic of Yemen (Southern Yemen).

South Australia   in central southern Australia. British colony (1855–1901). Stamps are inscribed **South Australia**. South Australia joined the Commonwealth of Australia in 1901 but continued to use its own stamps until Australia began issuing stamps in 1913. *Australian States (South Australia).*

Southern Nigeria   in western Africa bordering the Gulf of Guinea. British (1901–14). Stamps are inscribed **Southern Nigeria**. In 1914 Southern Nigeria became part of Nigeria.

Southern Rhodesia   in southeastern Africa, bordered on the north by Zambia and Mozambique, on the east by Mozambique, on the south by South Africa, and on the west and southwest by Botswana. British (1924–53, 1963–65). Stamps are inscribed **Southern Rhodesia**. Southern Rhodesia belonged to and used stamps of the Federation of Rhodesia and Nyasaland from 1953 to 1963. In 1965 Southern Rhodesia declared itself independent under the name Rhodesia. In 1978 it became Zimbabwe.

South Georgia   an island in the South Atlantic southeast of the Falkland Islands. British (1944, 1963→). Inscriptions include **South Georgia - Dependency of** overprinted on stamps of the Falkland Islands (1944, see *Falkland Islands*), **South Georgia** (1963–86), **South Georgia and the South Sandwich Islands or Is.** (1986→).

South Kasai   a secessionist area located north of and bordering Katanga Province in the south-central region of the Republic of the Congo, nominally independent during the civil war of 1960 to 1961. Stamps are inscribed **Etat Autonome - Sud Kasai**. South Kasai seceded from the Republic of the Congo in August 1960; by December 1961 the central government had reestablished control over it.

South Moluccas   a group of islands, including Ambon, Buru, and Ceram, that lies north of Australia, east of Celebes Island, and west of New Guinea. Secessionist state (1950). Stamps are inscribed **Republik Maluku Selatan**. In 1949 South Moluccas declared independence from Indonesia, an act not generally recognized by other nations. In 1951 Indonesia recaptured and occupied it. Secessionists fled and established a government-in-exile in the Netherlands.

South Orkneys   an island group in the South Atlantic, southeast of Tierra del Fuego. Laurie and Coronation are the largest islands of the group, which also consists of two smaller islands and several rocky islets. British (1944). Inscriptions include **South Orkneys - Dependency of** overprinted on stamps of Falkland Islands (1944). *Falkland Islands (dependencies: South Orkneys).*

South Russia   a loosely defined region in southern Russia under the control of White Russian (anti-Bolshevik) forces, generally from the Ukraine south and east to Caucasus region between the Black Sea and Caspian Sea. Independent (1918–21). Inscriptions include **ЕРМАКЪ** (1919), **КРЫМСЂАГО КРАЕВОТО ПРАВКТЕДЬСТБА** (1919), **ЮГЪ РОССІИ** overprinted, together with surcharge, on stamps of Russia (1919), **ПЯТЬ** overprinted, together with surcharge, on stamps of Russia (1919), **ЕДИНАЯ РОССІЯ** (1919).

South Shetlands   an archipelago in the South Atlantic, southeast of Cape Horn, the southernmost point of South America, and off the tip of the Antarctic Peninsula. Among the larger islands are Deception, Elephant, and King George. British (1944). Inscriptions include **South Shetlands - Dependency of** overprinted on stamps of Falkland Islands (1944). *Falkland Islands (dependencies: South Shetlands).*

South West Africa in southwest Africa, bordered on the north by Angola, on the east by Botswana, on the south by South Africa, and on the west by the Atlantic Ocean. Many issues contain bilingual English-Afrikaans inscriptions. In some cases, English and Afrikaans appear individually on alternating se-tenant stamps. Inscriptions include **South West Africa** or **Zuid-West Afrika** overprinted on stamps of South Africa (1923–26), **South West Africa**, **Suidwes Afrika**, or **Suidwes-Afrika** overprinted on stamps of South Africa (1926–41), **SWA** overprinted on stamps of South Africa (1941–53) or inscribed (1968–90), **South West Africa** and **Suidwes-Afrika** inscribed, either together or alternating se-tenant stamps (1953–68). Until World War I, South West Africa was German Southwest Africa. Following the war, it was mandated to South Africa under the Treaty of Versailles. In 1990 it became independent Namibia.

Sowjetische Besatzungs Zone overprinted on stamps of Germany or Berlin-Brandenburg: German Democratic Republic. See **Germany (Democratic Republic)**.

Spain in southwestern Europe, occupying most of the Iberian Peninsula, and bordered on the north by the Bay of Biscay, France, and Andorra, on the east by the Mediterranean Sea, on the south by the Mediterranean Sea and the Atlantic Ocean, and on the west by Portugal and the Atlantic Ocean; and including two insular provinces, the Canary Islands in the Atlantic Ocean off the coast of Africa and the Balearic Islands in the Mediterranean. Independent (1850→). Inscriptions include **Correos** and **Franco** with bust of Isabella II, denomination in cuartos or reales, and date (1850–54), or with coat of arms (1854), **Correos Certificado** with bust of Isabella II (1850), **Correo Interior - Franco** (1853), **Correos** with bust of Isabella (1856–67), **España** often with "Correos" (1860–70s, 1900–31, 1936→), **Correos de España** (1867–69), **Habilitado por la Junta Revolucionaria** overprinted (1868–69), **Habilitado por la Nacion** overprinted (1868–70), **H P N** overprinted (1868–70), **Comunicaciones** (1870–79, 1889–99), **Comunicaciones España** (1872–74), **Franqueo España** (Carlist forces, 1873), **Correos y Teleg^S** or **Correos y Teleg^FOS** with bust of Alfonso XII (1879–89), **Republica Española** overprinted or inscribed (1931–38), **Estado Español** (1936–40). During the Spanish Civil War (1936–39), both sides issued stamps. The Nationalists overprinted many stamps of Spain with **Viva España** or **Arriba España**.

Spanish Guinea in western Africa, initially consisting of Rio Muni and later including Fernando Po, Elobey, Annobon, and Corsico. Spanish (1902–59). Inscriptions include **Guinea Espanola** (1902), **Guinea Conti^AL Española** (1903–09), **Guinea Continental** overprinted on stamps of Elobey, Annobon, and Corisco (1906), **Territorios Españoles del Golfo de Guinea** (1909–51) or overprinted on stamps of Spain (1938, 1943), **Guinea 1911** overprinted on stamps of Spanish Guinea (1911), **Terrs Españoles del Golfo de Guinea** (1914–19), **Guinea Español** (1949–59). In 1960 Spanish Guinea was split into separate colonies of Rio Muni and Fernando Po. In 1968 they rejoined to form independent Equatorial Guinea.

Spanish Morocco   in northwest Africa, just across the Strait of Gibraltar from Spain, bordered on the north by the Mediterranean Sea, on the east and south by French Morocco, and on the west by the Atlantic Ocean. Spanish (1903–56). Inscriptions include **Correo Español Marruecos** overprinted on stamps of Spain (1903–14, 1920s–30s), **Marruecos** overprinted on stamps of Spain (1914, 1930s), **Protectorado Español en Marruecos** overprinted on stamps of Spain (1915), **Zona de Protectorado Español en Marruecos** overprinted on stamps of Spain (1916–30s) or inscribed (1928–30s), **Zona Protectorado Español** (1926), **Protectorado Marruecos** overprinted on stamps of Spain (1929–33), **Marruecos** together with "Protectorado Español" (1933–44), **Correos Marruecos** together with "Protectorado Español" (1944–56). In 1956 Spanish Morocco joined with French Morocco to become independent Morocco.

Spanish Sahara   in northwestern Africa, bordered on the north by Morocco, on the northeast by Algeria, on the east and south by Mauritania, and on the west by the Atlantic Ocean. Spanish (1924–76). Inscriptions include **Posesiones Españolas del Sahara Occidental** (1924–29) and overprinted "República Española" (1931–41), **Sahara** overprinted on stamps of Spain (1929–31), **Sahara Español** overprinted on stamps of Spain (1941–46) or inscribed (1946–61), **Sahara** together with "España" (1961–76). Spanish Sahara included the possessions of Cape Juby, Rio de Oro, and La Aguera. In 1976 Spanish Sahara was divided between Mauritania and Morocco. Since 1979 it has been entirely occupied by Morocco.

Spanish West Africa   an administrative area encompassing various Spanish possessions in North Africa, including Spanish Sahara and Ifni. Spanish (1949–51). Inscriptions include **Africa Occidental Española** (1949), **Territorios del Africa Occidental Española** (1950–51).

SPM   overprinted, together with surcharged value, on the generic issue for French colonies: Saint-Pierre and Miquelon. See **Saint-Pierre and Miquelon**.

S.P. Mexico   Mexico. See **Mexico**.

Sri Lanka   an island nation in the Indian Ocean off the southeastern of India. Independent (1972→). Stamps are inscribed **Sri Lanka**. Sri Lanka was formerly Ceylon.

Srodkowa Litwa   *Central Lithuania.*

Stadt Berlin   Berlin-Brandenburg, an administrative region in Soviet-occupied Germany (1945–46). *German Democratic Republic (Russian occupation).*

Stadt Post Amt - Bremen   Bremen. *German States*.

Stadt Post Basel   cantonal issue for Basel. See **Switzerland**.

Stampalia   overprinted on stamps of Italy. See **Dodecanese Islands**. *Italy (Aegean Islands)*.

State of Bahrain   see **Bahrain**.

State of North Borneo   see **North Borneo**.

State of Qatar   Qatar. See **Qatar**.

State of Travancore-Cochin   Travancore-Cochin, an Indian feudatory state. *India (native feudatory states)*.

Stati Parm   Parma. See **Parma**. *Italian States*.

Stati Parmensi   Parma. See **Parma**. *Italian States*.

Stellaland   a Boer enclave in South Africa (1884–85). Stamps are inscribed **Republiek Stellaland**.

S^{TE} Marie de Madagascar   Saint Marie de Madagascar. See **Saint Marie de Madagascar**.

S. Thome (or Thomé) e Principe   Saint Thomas and Prince Islands. See **Saint Thomas and Prince Islands**.

S. Tomé e Principe   Saint Thomas and Prince Islands. See **Saint Thomas and Prince Islands**.

St-Pierre M-on   overprinted, together with surcharged value, on the generic issue for French colonies: Saint-Pierre and Miquelon. See **Saint-Pierre and Miquelon**.

Straits Settlements   includes the Malay states of Malacca and Penang, and Singapore. British (1867–1946). Inscriptions include **Straits Settlements** overprinted on stamps of Labuan (1907) or inscribed (1867–1935), **Straits Settlements** together with "Malaya" (1935–41), **Dai Nippon 2602 Malaya** overprinted (Japanese occupation, 1943), **B M A - Malaya** overprinted (1945–48). In 1946 Malacca and Penang joined the Federation of Malaya; Singapore became separate colony.

STT-VUJA   (Yugoslav Military Government - Free Territory of Trieste) either overprinted on stamps of Yugoslavia or inscribed. See **Trieste**. *Yugoslavia (Trieste)*.

STT Vujna   (Yugoslav Military Government - Free Territory of Trieste) either overprinted on stamps of Yugoslavia or inscribed. See **Trieste**. *Yugoslavia (Trieste)*.

SU   overprinted, together with crescent and star, on stamps of Straits Settlements: Sungei Ujong. *Malaya (Sungei Ujong)*.

S.U. overprinted on stamps of Straits Settlements: Sungei Ujong. *Malaya (Sungei Ujong).*

Sudan in northeastern Africa, bordered on the north by Egypt, on the east by Eritrea and Ethiopia, on the south by Kenya, Uganda, and the Democratic Republic of the Congo, and on the west by the Central African Republic and Chad. Anglo/Egyptian (1897–1955), independent (1956→). Inscriptions include **Soudan** overprinted, together with Arabic characters, on stamps of Egypt (1897), **Sudan** sometimes together with "Postage" (1898–1969), **Democratic Republic of the Sudan** or **D.R. Sudan** (1969–84), **Sudan** (1978→).

Suidafrika South Africa. See **South Africa**.

Suid-Afrika South Africa. See **South Africa**.

Suidwes Afrika or **Suidwes-Afrika** see **South West Africa**.

S. Ujong Sungei Ujong, a Malayan state. *Malaya (Sungei Ujong).*

Sultanat d'Anjouan Anjouan. See **Anjouan**.

Sultanate of Oman see **Oman**.

Sungei Ujong a Malayan state. Inscriptions include **SU** overprinted, either by itself or with crescent and star, on stamps of Straits Settlements or **S. Ujong** inscribed. *Malaya (Sungei Ujong).*

Suomi Finland Finland. See **Finland**.

Suriname in northeastern South America, bordered on the north by the Atlantic Ocean, on the east by French Guiana, on the south by Brazil, and on the west by Guyana. Netherlands (1873–1975), independent (1975→). Inscriptions include **Suriname** (1873→), **Colonie Suriname** (1902–13).

Sverige Sweden. See **Sweden**.

SWA South West Africa. See **South West Africa**.

Swazieland see **Swaziland**.

Swaziland a tiny country in southern Africa bordered by South Africa on the north, south, and west and by Mozambique on the east. Transvaal (1889–1906), British (1933–68), independent (1968→). Inscriptions include **Swazieland** overprinted on stamps of Transvaal (1889–1906), **Swaziland Protectorate** (1933–38), **Swaziland** overprinted on stamps of South Africa (1945) or inscribed (1938→). Between 1906 and 1933, Swaziland used stamps of Transvaal or British colonies.

Sweden in northern Europe, on the Scandinavian Peninsula, bordered on the north and west by Norway, on the east by the Gulf of Bothnia and the Baltic Sea, and on the southwest by the Skagerrak, Kattegat, and Öresund straits. Independent (1855→). Stamps are inscribed **Sverige**.

Switzerland in west-central Europe, bordered on the north by France and Germany, on the east by Austria and Liechtenstein, on the south by Italy, and on the west by France. Independent (1843→). Inscriptions include **Zürich** and either "Local-Taxe" or "Cantonal-Taxe" (cantonal issue, 1843–50), **Stadt Post Basel** (cantonal issue, 1845), **Poste de Genève** (cantonal issue, 1845–48), **Orts-Post** with post horn and white cross (1850), **Poste Locale** with post horn and white cross (1850), **Rayon** by itself or with Roman numeral "I," "II," or "III" (1850–54), **Franco** together with allegorical seated Helvetia and a shield with a white cross (1854–62), **Helvetia** (1862→), **Confoederatio Helvetica** (occasionally). Various bureaus of the League of Nations and organizations of the United Nations have maintained offices in Switzerland. Some stamps of Switzerland have been overprinted or inscribed for use by them, for example: **Industrielle Kriegs-wirtshaft** (Industrial Board of Trade) and **Organisation Mondial de la Sante** (World Health Organization). They are considered to be Swiss official stamps.

Syria in the Middle East, bordered on the north by Turkey, on the east by Iraq, on the south by Jordan and Israel, and on the west by Lebanon and the Mediterranean Sea. French (1919–46), independent (1946→), Inscriptions include **T.E.O.** overprinted on stamps of France or French offices (1919), **O.M.F. Syrie** overprinted on stamps of France or the Syrian Arabian government (1920–23), **Syrie-Grand Liban** overprinted on stamps of France (1923–24), **Syrie** overprinted on stamps of France (1924–25) or inscribed (1925–34), **Republique Syriénne** (1934–55), **Postes Syrie** (1946), **Rep. Syriénne** (1953), **R. Syriénne** (1954), **United Arab Republic - Syria** (1958), **U.A.R.-Syria** (1958), **UAR** or **U.A.R.** with denomination in piasters, abbreviated "p" (1958–61) or overprinted on stamps of Syria (1959), **Republique Arabie Unie - Syrie** (1958), **RAU** (1958), **Syrian Arab Republic** (1961–76), **Syrian A.R.** (1976–84), **Syrian Arab R.** (1983–84), **Syria** (1984→). Syria was part of the Ottoman Turkish Empire until the end of World War I and then part of the French mandate in the Middle East until the end of World War II, when it achieved independence. In 1958 it joined with Egypt to form the United Arab Republic, which dissolved in 1961.

Syrian Arab Republic or **Syrian Arab R.** or **Syrian A.R.** Syria. See **Syria**.

Syrie Syria. See **Syria**.

Syrie overprinted on stamps of France or inscribed: Syria. See **Syria**.

Syrie-Grand Liban overprinted on stamps of France: Syria. See **Syria**.

Tadžikistan Tajikistan. See **Tajikistan**.

Tahiti an island in French Polynesia in the South Pacific. French (1882–1915). Inscriptions include **Tahiti** overprinted on the generic issue for French colonies or on stamps of French Oceania, sometimes with surcharged numeral of value (1882–1915). Subsequently, Tahiti used stamps of French Oceania (French Polynesia).

Tajikistan in central Asia, bordered on the north by Uzbekistan and Kyrgyzstan, on the east by China, on the south by Afghanistan, and on the west by Uzbekistan. Independent (1992→). Inscriptions include **Tadžikistan** (1992–95), **Tajikistan** (1995→).

Tanganyika in southeastern Africa bordered on the north by Kenya and Uganda, on the east by the Indian Ocean, on the south by Mozambique, Malawi, and Zambia, and on the west by Rwanda, Burundi, and the Democratic Republic of the Congo. British (1921–61), independent (1961–64). Inscriptions include **G.E.A.** overprinted on stamps of Kenya, Uganda, and Tanganyika (1921–22), **Tanganyika** (1922–27), **Mandated Territory of Tanganyika** (1927–35), **Tanganyika** (1961–64), **Jamahuri Ya Tanganyika** (1962). Between 1935 and 1961, Tanganyika used stamps of Kenya, Uganda, Tanganyika. In 1964 Tanganyika merged with Zanzibar to form Tanzania.

Tanger **(1)** overprinted on stamps of French Morocco or on postage-due stamps of France: French Morocco. See **French Morocco**. **(2)** overprinted on stamps of Spain or inscribed: Spanish Morocco (Tangier). See **Tangier** *(Spanish Morocco)*.

Tanger Correo or **Tanger Correos Español** Tangier. See **Tangier** *(Spanish Morocco)*.

Tangier overprinted on stamps of Great Britain: Tangier. *Great Britain (offices abroad)*.

Tangier a city in northern Morocco, together with a surrounding zone of about 140 square miles. Inscriptions include **Correo Español Tanger** overprinted on stamps of Spain (1926), **Tanger** overprinted on stamps of Spain (1929), **Tanger Correo** or **Tanger Correos Español** (1948–56). In 1911 and 1912 Tangier was temporarily internationalized. In 1925 Great Britain, France, and Spain signed a protocol providing for permanent security of the city. In 1929 an international legislative body was established to rule and Spain was given responsibility for police. During the years 1940 to 1945, Spain had full control of the zone. In 1945 international control was resumed. In 1956 Tangier was incorporated into Morocco. *Spanish Morocco (Tangier)*.

Tannu Tuva in south-central Siberia, a Russian republic, bordered on the south by Mongolia. Semi-independent state under Russian authority (1926–30s). Inscriptions include **Tovva Postage** overprinted (1927), **Touva** (1927–30s). In 1944 Tannu Tuva was incorporated into the Soviet Union.

Tanzania in southeastern Africa bordered on the north by Kenya and Uganda, on the east by the Indian Ocean, on the south by Mozambique, Malawi, and Zambia, and on the west by Rwanda, Burundi, and the Democratic Republic of the Congo. Independent (1964→). Inscriptions include **United Republic of Tanganyika & Zanzibar** (1964), **Tanzania** (1965→).

Tasmania   an island about 150 miles south of southeastern Australia. British (1855–1901), Australian (1901–13). Inscriptions include **Van Dieman's Land** (1855–58), **Tasmania** (1858–1913). Tasmania joined the Commonwealth of Australia in 1901 but continued to use its own stamps until Australia began issuing stamps in 1913. *Australian States (Tasmania).*

Tassa Gazzette   together with eagle and crown: Modena (newspaper tax stamp). *Italian States.*

T.-C.   (Travancore-Cochin) overprinted on stamps of Cochin: Travancore-Cochin, a native feudatory state in India. *India (native feudatory states).*

Tchad   Chad. See **Chad**.

Tchongking   overprinted on stamps of Indochina: French offices in Chungking, China. *France (offices abroad).*

Tch'ong K'ing   overprinted on stamps of Indochina: French offices in Chungking, China. *France (offices abroad).*

T.C. Postalari   Turkey. See **Turkey**.

Te Betalen - Port   inscription on postage-due stamps without country name, **(1)** various shades of blue: Netherlands; **(2)** green or blue green: Netherlands Antilles; **(3)** shades of red: Netherlands Indies; **(4)** lilac or purple: Suriname.

T.E.O.   (Territoires Ennemis Occupés) overprinted on stamps of France or French offices: Syria. See **Syria**.

T.E.O. or **T.E.O. Cilicia**   overprinted on stamps of Turkey: Cilicia. T.E.O. is an abbreviation for "Territoires Ennemis Occupés." See **Cilicia**.

Terres Australes et Antarctiques Française   French Southern and Antarctic Territories. See **French Southern and Antarctic Territories**.

Territoire de l'Inini   overprinted on stamps of French Guiana: Inini. See **Inini**.

Territoire du Fezzan   Fezzan. See **Fezzan-Ghadames**. *Libya (occupation issues).*

Territoire du Niger   overprinted on stamps of Upper Senegal and Niger: Niger. See **Niger**.

Territoire Française des Afars et des Issas   Afars and Issas. See **Afars and Issas**.

Territoire Militaire Fezzan   Fezzan. See **Fezzan-Ghadames**. *Libya (occupation issues).*

Territoire Militaire Fezzan Ghadames   Fezzan-Ghadames. See **Fezzan-Ghadames**. *Libya (occupation issues).*

Territorio de Ifni   Ifni. See **Ifni**.

Territorios del Africa Occidental Española   Spanish West Africa. See **Spanish West Africa**.

Territorios Españoles del Golfo de Guinea   overprinted on stamps of Spain or inscribed: Spanish Guinea. See **Spanish Guinea**.

Territory of New Guinea   see **New Guinea**.

Terrs Españoles del Golfo de Guinea   Spanish Guinea. See **Spanish Guinea**.

Tete   a province (and town) in western Mozambique, bordered on the west and north by Zambia, on the north and east by Malawi, and on the south by Zimbabwe. Portuguese (1913–20). Inscriptions include **Republica Tete** overprinted on stamps of Portuguese Africa, Macao, or Timor (1913–), **Tete** together with "Republica Portuguesa" (1914–20). Subsequently, Tete used stamps of Mozambique.

Tetuan   a city in northern Morocco on the Mediterranean Sea, the capital of Spanish Morocco. Inscriptions include **Tetuan** overprinted on issues of Spain or Spanish Offices in Morocco. *Spanish Morocco (Tetuan)*.

Thai   Thailand. See **Thailand**.

Thailand   in southeast Asia, bordered on the west and north by Myanmar (Burma), on the northeast by Laos, on the southeast by Cambodia and the Gulf of Thailand, on the south by Malaysia, and on the southwest by the Andaman Sea and Myanmar. Independent (1883→). Inscriptions include **1 Tical** overprinted (1880s), **Siam** (1887–1949), **Thai** (1940s), **Thailand** (1940s→). Some issues of the 1880s, 1920s, and 1930s are inscribed only in Thai characters. Thailand was formerly known as Siam.

Thrace   a region in southeast Europe, portions of which were acquired by, or occupied by, various powers at various times, including Bulgaria, Greece, and Turkey. Inscriptions include ΕΛΛΔΙΟΙΚ ΓΚΙΟΥΜΟΥ ΛΤΖΙΝΑΣ overprinted on stamps of Greece (1913), **Thrace Interalliée** overprinted on stamps of Bulgaria (Allied occupation, 1919–20), **Thrace Occidentale** overprinted on stamps of Bulgaria (Allied occupation, 1920), Διοίκησις Αντικής Θπάκης overprinted on stamps of Greece (Greek occupation, 1920), Διοίκησις Θπάκης overprinted on stamps of Greece (Greek occupation, 1920), Υπάτη Απμοστεία Θπακης overprinted on stamps of Turkey (Greek occupation, 1920), ΔΙΟΙΚΗΣΙΣ ΔΥΤΙΚΗΣ ΘΡΑΚΗΣ overprinted on stamps of Greece (Greek occupation, 1920). At present, Thrace forms part of Bulgaria, Greece, and Turkey. ΕΛΛΔΙΟΙΚ. ΓΚΙΟΥΜΟΥ ΛΤΖΙΝΑΣ overprinted on stamps of Greece: Thrace. See **Thrace**.

Thüringen   Thuringia, an administrative region in Soviet-occupied Germany (1945–46). *German Democratic Republic (Russian occupation)*.

Thurn and Taxis   a private postal enterprise of several hundred years' standing operating in Europe. By the time it issued postage stamps in the mid-nineteenth century (1852–67), most of its routes lay within Germany. Inscriptions include **Thurn und Taxis** or **Thurn u. Taxis**. *German States.*

Tibet   in southern Asia, bordered on the north and east by China, on the south by Myanmar (Burma), India, Bhutan, and Nepal, and on the west by India. Independent (1912–50). Stamps are inscribed **Tibet Postage** or **Tibet**. In 1950 China invaded Tibet and took control of it. It is now known as Xizang Autonomous Region.

Tientsin   overprinted on stamps of Italy: Italian offices in Tientsin, China, a port city near Beijing. *Italy (offices abroad).*

Timor   a large island in southeast Asia, in the Malay Archipelago, west of New Guinea and north of Australia. Portuguese (1885–1976). Inscriptions include **Timor** overprinted on stamps of Macao (1885–87, 1893) or inscribed (1946–48), **Correio de Timor** (1887–94), **Timor** and "Portugal" (1894–98), **Timor** with "Correios" and "Portugal" (1898–1914), **Correio - Timor** (1935–48), **Timor Portugués** (1948–56), **Timor** with "Republica Portuguesa" (1914–35, 1956–76). Issues between 1911 and 1930 are often overprinted "Republica." Timor became part of Indonesia in 1976. However, the eastern half remains a disputed region, which Indonesia claims as the province of East Timor, a claim not recognized by the United Nations or many countries of the world.

Timor Portugués   Timor. See **Timor**.

Tin Can Island   see **Niuafo'ou**.

Tobago   an island in the Caribbean off the coast of Venezuela and about 20 miles northeast of Trinidad. British (1879–89). Stamps are inscribed **Tobago**. In 1889 Tobago merged with Trinidad and used its stamps until 1913, when the united colony began issuing stamps under the name "Trinidad and Tobago."

Toga   Tonga. See **Tonga**.

Togo   in western Africa, bordered on the north by Burkina Faso, on the east by Benin, on the south by the Gulf of Guinea, and on the west by Ghana. German (1897–1914), Anglo/French (1914–21), French (1921–57), independent (1957→). Inscriptions include **Togo** overprinted on stamps of Germany (1897–1900) or inscribed (1900–14), **Togo - Anglo-French Occupation** overprinted on stamps of German Togo or on stamps of the Gold Coast (British occupation, 1914-), **Togo - Occupation franco-anglaise** overprinted on stamps of German Togo or on stamps of Dahomey (French occupation, 1914–21), **Togo** overprinted on stamps of Dahomey (1921–24) or inscribed (1924–57), **Republique Autonome du Togo** (1957–58), **Republique du Togo** (1958–61, 1997), **Republique Togolaise** (1961→).

Togo - Anglo-French Occupation overprinted on stamps of German Togo or on stamps of the Gold Coast: Togo. See **Togo**.

Togo - Occupation franco-anglaise overprinted on stamps of German Togo or Dahomey: Togo. See **Togo**.

Tokelau Islands a group of atolls in the southwestern Pacific Ocean, including Atafu, Fakaofo, and Nukunonu. An overseas territory of New Zealand (1948→). Inscriptions include **Tokelau Islands** inscribed (1948–76) or overprinted on stamps of New Zealand (1966–67), **Tokelau** (1976→).

Tolima a department (state) in west-central Colombia. Local issues (1870–1904). Inscriptions include **E.S. del Tolima** (1871–79), **Estado S. del Tolima** (1871–79), **Correos Eo. So. del Tolima** (1879–86), **Correos del Estado del Tolima** (1886–88), **Departmento del Tolima** (1888–1904). *Colombia*.

Tonga a group of islands in the southern Pacific about 400 miles southeast of Fiji and 1,150 miles northeast of New Zealand. Independent (1886–90, 1970→), British protectorate (1890–1970). Inscriptions include **Tonga** together with "Postage & Revenue" (1886–92), **Tonga** (1882–97, 1949→), **Toga** (1897–1949).

Toscano Tuscany. See **Tuscany**. *Italian States*.

Touva Tannu Tuva. See **Tannu Tuva**.

Tovva Postage overprinted: Tannu Tuva. See **Tannu Tuva**.

Traité de Versailles overprinted on stamps of Germany together with "Art. 94 et 95": Allenstein. See **Allenstein**.

Transcaucasian Federated Republics in western Asia, bordered on the north by Russia, on the east by the Caspian Sea, on the south by Iran, and on the west by Turkey and consisting of Armenian, Georgian, and Azerbaijan Republics. Soviet Republic (1923). Stamps are inscribed **ЗСФСР** The Transcaucasian Soviet Federated Socialist Republic became one of the four original republics of the Soviet Union.

Transitorio together with "Mexico" and in some cases "Correos": Sonora, Mexico. See **Mexico**.

Transkei a tribal homeland within South Africa. South African (1976–94). Stamps are inscribed **Transkei**. *South Africa (Transkei)*.

Transvaal a province in northeastern South Africa. Afrikaner republic (1869–77), British (1877–84), autonomous Afrikaner republic under British authority (1884–99), British (1900–10). Inscriptions include **Z. Afr. Republiek** (1869–71), **Z. Afr. Republiex** (1871–77), **V.R. Transvaal** overprinted (1877–80), **Transvaal** together with "Postage" (1878–84), **Z. Afr. Republiek** (1888–95), **Zuid Afrikaanshe Republiek** (1895–1900), **V.R.I.** overprinted (1900–01), **V.R.**

overprinted on stamps of Transvaal or Cape of Good Hope (1900), **Cancelled V-R-I.** overprinted (1900), **Z. Afr. Rep.** (1901), **E.R.I.** overprinted (1901–02), **Transvaal** (1902–10). During the Boer War, Transvaal was contested, with each side issuing its own stamps. In 1910 Transvaal joined the Union of South Africa.

Travancore Anchel   Travancore, a native feudatory state on the southeast tip of India. *India (native feudatory states)*.

Trebizonde   overprinted on stamps of Russia together with surcharge in para(s) or piastre(s): *Russia (offices in the Turkish Empire)*.

Trengganu   a Malayan (and later, Malaysian) state. **(1) Trengganu** either with "Postage and Revenue" or "Malaya": *Malaya (Trengganu)*; **(2) Trengganu** together with "Malaysia": *Malaysia (Trengganu)*.

Trentino   a province (capital, Trento) in northern Italy, bordered on the north and northeast by Austria, on the southeast by the Italian province Venetia, and on the west by the Italian province Lombardy and by Switzerland. Italian occupation (1918–19). Inscriptions include **Regno d'Italia Trentino** overprinted on stamps of Austria (1918), **Venezia Tridentina** overprinted on stamps of Italy (1918–19). Italy occupied Trentino at the end of World War I and remains part of Italy today. *Austria (Trentino)*.

Trieste   city and port (and capital of the Friuli-Venezia Giulia region) in northeastern Italy on the Gulf of Trieste, at the northeastern extremity of the Adriatic Sea. Zone A - Allied Military Government (1947–54), Zone B - Yugoslav Military Government (1947–54). Inscriptions for Zone A include **A.M.G.-F.T.T.**, **AMG-FTT**, or **AMG FTT** overprinted on stamps of Italy (1947–54). For Zone B: **V.U.J.A. S.T.T.** (1948–49), **VUJA-STT** overprinted on stamps of Yugoslavia (1949–51), **St. Trsta Vuja** (1949–50), **STT-VUJA** overprinted on stamps of Yugoslavia (1949–52) or inscribed, sometimes with "Jugoslavia" (1950–53), **STT Vujna** overprinted on stamps of Yugoslavia (1952–54) or inscribed together with "Jugoslavija" (1953–54). Yugoslavia occupied Trieste late in World War II and until 1947. Beginning in 1947, the Free Territory of Trieste came under the protection of the United Nations. The territory was divided into Zone A (Northern Zone, under Allied control), which included the city of Trieste, and Zone B (Southern Zone, under Yugoslav control), which included territory in Istria and along the Slovene coast. In 1954 most of Zone A, including the city of Trieste, was returned to Italian control under the provisions of an agreement between Italy and Yugoslavia that allowed it to remain a free port. The rest of the territory was incorporated into Yugoslavia and since 1991 has been part of Croatia and Slovenia. Zone A, *Italy (Trieste)*; Zone B, *Yugoslavia (Trieste)*.

Trinidad   an island just off the coast of Venezuela opposite the mouth of the Orinoco River. British (1851–1913). Stamps are inscribed **Trinidad**. In 1913 Trinidad began using stamps inscribed "Trinidad and Tobago."

Trinidad and Tobago   the southernmost of the Caribbean islands, located just off the coast of Venezuela, Trinidad, opposite the mouth of the Orinoco River, and Tobago, about 20 miles northeast of Trinidad. British (1913–62), independent (1962→). Stamps are inscribed **Trinidad & Tobago**. Trinidad merged with Tobago in 1889. Both islands used stamps of Trinidad until 1913, when stamps inscribed "Trinidad and Tobago" came into use.

Tripoli di Barberia   overprinted on stamps of Italy: Italian offices in Tripoli, a city in the Ottoman Turkish Empire located in North Africa, in what is now Libya. *Italy (offices abroad)*.

Tripolitania   a region in northwestern Libya, including the city of Tripoli. Italian (1923–34). Inscriptions include **Tripolitania** overprinted on stamps of Italy (1923–34) or inscribed (1934), **Poste Tripolitania** (1926–30). In 1934 Tripolitania became part of the Italian colony of Libia.

Tristan da Cunha   a group of small islands in the South Atlantic 1,200 miles west of Africa. Administered under the British dependency of Saint Helena (1952→). Inscriptions include **Tristan Da Cunha** overprinted on stamps of Saint Helena (1952) or inscribed (1953→).

Trucial States   in the southeastern corner of the Arabian Peninsula, bordered on the north by the Persian Gulf, on the east by Oman and the Gulf of Oman, and on the south and west by Saudi Arabia and consisting of the emirates that would, in 1971 and 1972, form the United Arab Emirates. The emirates are Abu Dhabi, Ajman, Dubai, Fujeira, Ras al Khaima, Sharjah, and Umm al Qiwain. Stamps inscribed **Trucial States** were available for use, however, only in Dubai.

T. ta. C.   inscription on air postal tax stamp: Turkey. *Turkey (postal tax)*.

Tunisia   a small country in North Africa, bordered on the north and east by the Mediterranean, on the southwest by Libya, and on the west by Algeria. French (1888–1956), independent (1956→). Inscriptions include **Regence de Tunis** (1888–1906), **Tunisie** or **Tunisie Poste** (1906–57), **Republique Tunisienne** (1957→).

Tunisie   Tunisia. See **Tunisia**.

Tunisie Poste   Tunisia. See **Tunisia**.

Turkey   in southeastern Europe and southwestern Asia, bordered on the northwest by Bulgaria and Greece, on the north by the Black Sea, on the northeast by Georgia and Armenia, on the east by Iran and the Azerbaijani exclave of Naxcivan, on the south by Iraq, Syria, and the Mediterranean Sea, and on the west by the

Aegean Sea. Independent (1863→). Inscriptions include inscribed in Arabic, often with star and crescent (1863–76, 1902–26), **Emp. Ottoman** (1876–92), **Postes Ottomanes** (1913–22), **Turk Postalari** (1926–29), **Türkiye Cümhuriyeti** (1929–37, 1967→), **T.C. Postalari** (1931), **Türkiye Postalari** (1937–50), **Türkiye Cümhuriyeti Postalari** (1941, 1950–56, 1959–67), **Türkiye** (1956–59). Turkey was at the heart of the Ottoman Empire until its breakup following World War I. Many stamps of Turkey, especially during the periods 1863 to 1876 and 1892 to 1926, contain only Arabic inscriptions.

Turkish Republic of Northern Cyprus   approximately the northern third of the island of Cyprus. Turkish (1974→). Inscriptions include **Kibris Türk Federe Devleti Postalari** (1974–83), **Kuzey Kirbris Türk Cümhuriyeti** (1983→). In 1974 Turkey invaded northern Cyprus and in 1975 proclaimed the Turkish Cypriot State in that area which they controlled. Most nations have not recognized the so-called republic.

Türkiye   Turkey. See **Turkey**.

Türkiye Cümhuriyeti   Turkey. See **Turkey**.

Türkiye Cümhuriyeti Postalari   Turkey. See **Turkey**.

Türkiye Postalari   Turkey. See **Turkey**.

Turkmenistan   in central Asia, bordered on the north by Kazakstan and Uzbekistan, on the east by Uzbekistan and Afghanistan, on the south by Afghanistan and Iran, and on the west by the Caspian Sea. Independent (1992→). Stamps are inscribed **Türkmenistan** or **Turkmenistan**. Turkmenistan was formerly a republic in the Soviet Union.

Turk Postalari   Turkey. See **Turkey**.

Turks and Caicos Islands   a group of small islands in the West Indies, southeast of the Bahamas, in two groups: the Turks Islands include two inhabited islands (Grand Turk and Salt Cay) and a large number of small rocky islands, and the Caicos Islands include six principal islands (Grand Caicos is the largest) and a number of islets. British (1867–1959), independent (1959→). Inscriptions include **Turks Islands** (1867–1900, see *Turks Islands*), **Turks and Caicos Islands** or **Is.** (1900–84), sometimes shortened to **Turks & Caicos** beginning in 1980. For a time in the 1980s, the Caicos Islands issued their own stamps. They are inscribed **Caicos Islands** or occasionally, **Caicos Islands - Turks and Caicos Islands**.

Turks Islands   see **Turks and Caicos Islands**.

Tuscany   a region in northwest Italy. Grand duchy (1851–61). Inscriptions include **Franco Bollo Postale - Toscano** (1851–61). In 1860 Tuscany voted to join newly united Italy. *Italian States*.

Tuvalu   a group of small islands (total area about 10 square miles) in the South Pacific northeast of Australia. Funafuti is the main island. Independent (1976→). Inscriptions include **Tuvalu** overprinted on stamps of Gilbert and Ellice Islands (1976) or inscribed (1976→). During the 1980s, some islands in Tuvalu issued their own postage stamps. They are inscribed **Tuvalu** together with the name of the island. The islands include Funafuti, Nanumaga, Nanumea, Niutao, Nui, Nukufetau, Nukulealea, and Viatupu. Prior to independence, Tuvalu was the Ellice Islands.

Two Sicilies   a kingdom in Italy consisting of the Kingdom of Sicily and the Kingdom of Naples, which included most of the lower half of the Italian Peninsula, including the present-day regions of Abruzzi, Molise, Campania, Calambria, Basilicata, and Apulia. Kingdom (1858–61). Inscriptions include **Bollo Della Posta Napoletana** (Naples, 1858–61), **Bollo Della Posta di Sicilia** (Sicily, 1859–61), **Franco Poste Bollo** together with embossed bust of Victor Emmanuel II and denomination in grana (1861). In 1861 the Kingdom of Two Sicilies became part of newly united Italy. *Italian States*.

UAE   United Arab Emirates. See **United Arab Emirates**.

UAR or **U.A.R.**   (United Arab Republic) a short-lived union of Egypt and Syria (1958–61); **(1)** issues denominated in milliemes (abbreviated "m"): Egypt. See **Egypt**. **(2)** issues denominated in piasters (abbreviated "p"): Syria. See **Syria**.

U.A.R.-Syria   (United Arab Republic) Syria. See **Syria**.

Ubangi-Shari   (or Ubangi-Chari) in west-central Africa, bordered on the north by Chad (which was part of the territory until 1920, at which time it was split into a separate colony), on the east by Sudan, on the south by the Belgian Congo (Democratic Republic of the Congo), and on the west by Kamerun (Cameroon). French (1915–36). Inscriptions include **Oubangui-Chari-Tchad** overprinted on stamps of Middle Congo (1915–22), **Oubangi-Chari** overprinted on stamps of Middle Congo (1922–24) and with additional overprint "Afrique Equatoriale Française" or "A.E.F." (1924–36). Beginning in 1936 Ubangi-Shari used stamps of French Equatorial Africa. In 1958 it became the independent Central African Republic.

U G   typewritten in the upper corners of a rectangle: Uganda. See **Uganda**.

Uganda   in eastern Africa bordered on the north by Sudan, on the east by Kenya, on the south by Tanzania, and on the west by the Democratic Republic of the Congo. British protectorate (1895–1962), independent (1962→). Inscriptions include **U G** typewritten in the upper corners of a rectangle (1895), **V.96.R - Uganda** typewritten (1896), **Uganda Protectorate** (1896–1902), **Uganda** (1962→). Between 1903 and 1961, Uganda used stamps of the East Africa and Uganda Protectorates or Kenya, Uganda, and Tanganyika (or Tanzania).

Uka Leta   see **Hawaii**.

Ukraine in eastern Europe, bordered on the north by Belarus, on the east and northeast by Russia, on the south by the Black Sea and Sea of Azov, on the southwest by Romania and Moldova, and on the west by Poland, Slovakia, and Hungary. Independent (1918–19, 1923, 1992→). Inscriptions include **УКРАЇНСЬКА** (1918–19), **У.С.Р.Р.** (1923), **Ukraine** overprinted on stamps of Germany (German occupation, 1941–43, *Russia*), **ПОШТА УКРАЇНИ** (1992–95), **Ukrania** (1995→).

Ukrania Ukraine. See **Ukraine**.

Ultramar on stamps **(1)** denominated in centesimos or pesetas: Cuba or Puerto Rico; **(2)** denominated in avos or reis: Guinea or Macao.

Ultramar Português inscription on some issues of some Portuguese colonies together with the name of the colony. Refer to the named colony.

Umm al Qiwain on the Arabian shore of the Persian Gulf in the northeastern United Arab Emirates, between Ras al Khaima on the north and Ajman on the south. Emirate under British protection (1964–72). Stamps are inscribed **Umm al Qiwain**. In December 1971, Umm al Qiwain joined the independent United Arab Emirates but continued to use its own stamps for some months thereafter.

UNESCO inscribed together with "République Française" or "France": United Nations UNESCO office in Paris. *France (official issues)*.

Unie van Zuid Afrika Union of South Africa. See **South Africa**.

Union Internationale de Telécommunications inscribed together with "Helvetia": International Telecommunications Union. *Switzerland (official issues)*.

Union Island one of the northern group of Grenadine Islands of Saint Vincent, in the Windward chain in the eastern Caribbean Sea. Saint Vincent (1984→). Inscriptions include **Union Island** overprinted on stamps of Saint Vincent Grenadines (1984), **Union Island - Grenadines of St. Vincent** (1984→). *Saint Vincent Grenadines (Union Island)*.

Union of Myanmar Burma. See **Burma**.

Union of South Africa see **South Africa**.

Union Postale del Salvador El Salvador. See **El Salvador**.

Union Postale Universelle - Helvetia inscribed together with "Helvetia": Universal Postal Union. *Switzerland (official issues)*.

Union Postal Universal - Lima overprinted in an oval: Peru. See **Peru**.

Union Postal Universal - Peru overprinted in an oval or a horseshoe on stamps of Peru or inscribed: Peru. See **Peru**.

Union Postal Universal - Republica del Salvador El Salvador. See **El Salvador**.

United Arab Emirates   in the southeastern corner of the Arabian Peninsula, bordered on the north by the Persian Gulf, on the east by Oman and the Gulf of Oman, and on the south and west by Saudi Arabia. Independent (1972→). Stamps are inscribed **United Arab Emirates** or **UAE**. The United Arab Emirates is a federation of seven emirates. It was formed in December 1971 by Abu Dhabi, Ajman, Dubai, Fujeira, Sharjah, and Umm al Qiwain. Ras al Khaima joined in early 1972. The seven emirates are also known as the Trucial States.

United Arab Republic   a short-lived union of Syria and Egypt (1958–61). Each nation continued to issue its own postage stamps. Egyptian issues are denominated in milliemes, abbreviated "m." Syrian issues are denominated in piasters, abbreviated "p." See **Egypt** or **Syria**.

United Kingdom of Libya   Libya. See **Libya**.

United Nations   an organization with headquarters in New York and offices in Geneva, Switzerland, and Vienna, Austria. New York (1951→), Geneva (1969→), Vienna (1979→). Issues from New York are denominated in dollars and cents and inscribed in English "United Nations" and/or French "Nations Unies," Spanish "Naciones Unidas," Russian "**ОБЪЕДИНЕННЫЕ НАЦИИ,**" and Chinese in Chinese characters. Issues from Geneva are denominated in Swiss francs and centimes and inscribed in French "Nations Unies"; issues from Vienna are denominated in Austrian schillings and groschen and inscribed in German "Vereinte Nationen."

United Republic of Tanganyika & Zanzibar   see **Tanzania**.

United States of America   located in North America, bordered on the north by Canada and on the south by Mexico. Independent (1847→). Inscriptions include **Post Office** (1847–51), **United States Postage, United States, U.S., U.S. Postage, United States Postal Service** (1851–1985), **USA** (1985→).

UNTEA   (United Nations Temporary Executive Authority) overprinted on stamps of Netherlands New Guinea: West Irian. See **West Irian**.

Upper Senegal and Niger   in western Africa, bordered on the north and west by French Sudan (Mali), on the east by Niger, and on the south by Dahomey (Benin), Togo, the Gold Coast (Ghana), and the Ivory Coast (Côte d'Ivoire). French (1906–21). Inscriptions include **H^T Senegal-Niger** together with "Afrique Occidentale Française" (1906–14), **Haut-Senegal-Niger** together with "Afrique Occidentale Française" (1914–21). Beginning in 1921 the colony used stamps of French West Africa. In the 1930s it was divided between the Ivory Coast and French Sudan. In 1947 the divided territory was reconstituted as Upper Volta.

Upper Silesia   the southeastern portion of Silesia, a region in the arm of south-central Germany that, at the time, extended between Poland on the north and

Czechoslovakia on the south. Allied commission (1920–23). Inscriptions include **Commission de Gouvernement - Haute Silesie** (1920–23), **C1.H.S.** overprinted on stamps of Germany (1920), **C.G.H.S.** overprinted on stamps of Germany (1920–23). Following World War I, unrest between the German and Polish populations of Upper Silesia at one point erupted in an armed uprising by Poles. The uprising ended only when the Allied powers agreed to include the eastern section in the newly formed nation of Poland. The western section remained in Germany.

Upper Volta in western Africa, bordered on the north and west by Mali, on the east by Niger, and on the south by Benin, Togo, Ghana, and the Ivory Coast (Côte d'Ivoire). French (1920–33), independent (1958–84). Inscriptions include **Haute-Volta** overprinted on stamps of Upper Senegal and Niger (1920–28) or inscribed (1928–33), **Republique de Haute-Volta** (1959–84). In 1984 Upper Volta changed its name to Burkina Faso. See **Burkina Faso**.

Uruguay in east-central South America, bordered on the north by Brazil, on the east by Brazil and the Atlantic Ocean, on the south by the Atlantic Ocean and the Río de la Plata, and on the west by Argentina. Independent (1856→). Inscriptions include **Diligencia** (1856–57), **Montevideo** and "Correo" (1858–64), **Republica Oriental** (1864–66), **Republica del Uruguay** together with "Montevideo" (1866–77), **Republica Oriental Uruguay** (1877–81), **Republica Oriental del Uruguay** (1877–1948), **Rep. O. del Uruguay** (1880s), **Republica O. del Uruguay** (1882–94, 1922–50), **Correos del Uruguay** (1920–35), **Correos Uruguay** (1932–33, 1943), **R.O. del Uruguay** (1950), **Uruguay** often with "Correos" (1910–24, 1956→).

U.S.T.C. (United State of Travancore-Cochin) overprinted on stamps of Cochin: Travancore-Cochin, a native feudatory state in India. *India (native feudatory states).*

Uzbekistan in central Asia, bordered on the west and north by Kazakstan, on the east by Kyrgyzstan, on the southeast by Tajikistan, and on the south by Afghanistan and Turkmenistan. Independent (1992→). Inscriptions include **Uzbekistan** (1992–97), **УЗБЕКИСТОН** overprinted on stamps of Russia (1993, 1995), **O'ZBEKISTON** (1997→). Uzbekistan was formerly a republic in the Soviet Union.

V.96.R - Uganda typewritten in the upper corners of a rectangle: Uganda. See **Uganda**.

Vale - Postale B overprinted on stamps of Nicaragua: province of Zelaya. *Nicaragua.*

Valles d'Andorre Andorra, French administration. See **Andorra**.

Valona overprinted on stamps of Italy: Italian offices in Valona (Vlorë), city and port in southwestern Albania. *Italy (offices abroad).*

Vancouver Island   see **British Columbia and Vancouver Island**.

Van Dieman's Land   Tasmania. See **Tasmania**.

Vanuatu   a group of about 70 islands in the southwestern Pacific Ocean northeast of New Caledonia, among the islands are Espiritu Santo, Malakula, Efate, Erromango, and Ambrym. Independent (1980→). Stamps are inscribed **Vanuatu**. Prior to independence, Vanuatu was the British-French condominium of New Hebrides.

Vathy   overprinted on stamps of France: French offices in Samos. *France (offices in Turkey)*.

Vatican City   a sovereign enclave of approximately 109 acres within the city of Rome. Independent (1929→). Inscriptions include **Poste Vaticane** (1929–92), **Città del Vaticano** (1992→).

Veglia   overprinted on stamps of Fiume: Fiume. See **Fiume**. Veglia (Krk) is an island in the Adriatic Sea near Fiume (Rijeka) and is now part of Croatia. See **Fiume**.

Venda   a tribal homeland within South Africa. South African (1979–94). Stamps are inscribed **Venda**. *South Africa (Venda)*.

Venezia Giulia   a province in northeastern Italy (capital, Trieste), bordered on the north by Austria, on the east by Croatia, on the south by the Adriatic Sea, and on the west and southwest by the Italian province Venetia. Italian occupation (1918–19), Allied Military Government (1945–47). Inscriptions include **(1) Regno d'Italia Venezia Giulia** overprinted on stamps of Austria (Italian occupation, 1918), **Venezia Giulia** overprinted on stamps of Italy (Italian occupation, 1919). *Austria (occupation issues)*. **(2) A.M.G. V.G.** (Allied Military Government - Venezia Giulia) overprinted on stamps of Italy (Allied occupation, 1945–47). Italy occupied Venezia Giulia at the end of World War I, and it is part of Italy today. *Italy (occupation issues)*.

Venezia Giulia   overprinted on stamps of Italy: Italian occupation. See **Venezia Giulia**. *Austria (occupation issues)*.

Venezia Tridentina   overprinted on stamps of Italy: Trentino. See **Trentino**. *Austria (Trentino)*.

Venezolano   and "Escuelas": Venezuela. See **Venezuela**.

Venezuela   in northern South America, bordered on the north by the Caribbean Sea and Atlantic Ocean, on the east by Guyana, on the south by Brazil, and on the west and southwest by Colombia. Independent (1859→). Inscriptions include **Correo de Venezuela** (1859–62, 1902–), **Federacion** (1860s), **Correo del** OSEEUU **de Venezuela** inscribed (1865–71) and overprinted "Estampillas de Correo - Contrasena" (1870s), **Escuelas** overprinted "Bolivar Sucre Miranda" and decree date (1870–80s), **Escuelas - Venezolano** overprinted "Decreto de 27 Junio 1870"

(1879), **Venezuela** (1880–82), **Correos de Venezuela** (1882–1910, 1924–30, 1949), **Correos** together with bust of Simón Bolívar (1893–95), **Instruccion** together with bust of Simón Bolívar (1893–95), **E.E.U.U** (or **EE.UU.**) **de Venezuela** (1905, 1914–55), **Correos E.E.U.U. de Venezuela** (1914–55), **E.E.U.U. de Venezuela Correos** (1914–55), **Republica de Venezuela** often with "Correos" (1955–63), **Venezuela** sometimes with "Correos" (1963→).

Vereinte Nationen   (United Nations) an inscription on stamps issued by the UN office in Vienna, Austria. See **United Nations**.

Viatupu   an island in the Tuvalu group. Tuvalu (1984→). Stamps are inscribed **Viatupu - Tuvalu**. *Tuvalu (Viatupu).*

Victoria   southeastern Australia. British (1850–1901), Australia (1901–13). Stamps are inscribed **Victoria** (1850–1912). Victoria joined the Commonwealth of Australia in 1901 but continued using its own stamps until Australia began issuing stamps in 1913. *Australian States (Victoria).*

Vietnam   (or Viet Nam) in southeast Asia, bordered on the north by China, on the east and south by the South China Sea, and on the west by Cambodia and Laos. Independent (1951–54). Stamps are inscribed **Viet-Nam**, often with "Búu Chính." In 1954 Communist forces secured control over the northern part of the country. The southern part continued to exist as a separate country (South Vietnam) until 1975, when North Vietnam overran it and absorbed it.

Vietnam (North)   (or Socialist Republic of Vietnam) in southeast Asia, bordered on the north by China, on the east and south by the South China Sea (and during the years 1954 to 1975, on the south by South Vietnam), and on the west by Cambodia and Laos. Independent (1954→). Inscriptions include **Viet-Nam Dan-Chu Cong-Hoa** (1951–76), **Viet-Nam** or **Viet Nam** often with "Búu Chính" (1976→). Before 1951 North Vietnam was part of French Indochina.

Vietnam (South)   in southeast Asia, Vietnam south of the 17th parallel. Independent (1954–75). Inscriptions include **Viet-Nam Cong-Hoa** often with "Búu Chính" (1954–75). Before 1951 South Vietnam was part of French Indochina. In 1975 South Vietnam was overrun by North Vietnam and absorbed by it.

Viet-Nam Cong-Hoa   South Vietnam. See **Vietnam (South)**.

Viet-Nam Dan-Chu Cong-Hoa   North Vietnam. See **Vietnam (North)**.

Virgin Islands   see **British Virgin Islands**. *Virgin Islands.*

Viva España   overprinted on stamps of Spain: Nationalist forces. See **Spain**. *Spain (revolutionary issues).*

Vojna Uprava Jugoslavenske Armije   overprinted on stamps of Yugoslavia: Istria and the Slovene Coast. See **Yugoslavia**.

Volkstaat Bayern   overprinted on stamps of Bavaria: Bavaria. See **Bavaria**.

Volkstaat Wuerttemberg   Württemberg. See **Württemberg**.

Volkstaat Württemberg   overprinted on official stamps: Württemberg. See **Württemberg**.

V.R.   (Victoria Regina) **(1)** overprinted on stamps of Fiji: Fiji. See **Fiji**. **(2)** overprinted on stamps inscribed "Z. Afr. Republiek" or "Cape of Good Hope": Transvaal. See **Transvaal**.

V.R. Transvaal   overprinted on stamps inscribed "Z. Afr. Republiek" or "Z. Afr. Republiex": Transvaal. See **Transvaal**.

V.R.I.   (Victoria Regina Imperatrix) **(1)** overprinted, together with surcharged value, on stamps inscribed "Oranje Vrij Staat": Orange River Colony. See **Orange River Colony**; **(2)** overprinted on stamps inscribed "Z. Afr. Republiek": Transvaal. See **Transvaal**.

V.U.J.A. S.T.T. or **VUJA-STT**   (Yugoslav Military Government - Free Territory of Trieste) either overprinted on stamps of Yugoslavia or inscribed. See **Trieste**. *Yugoslavia (Trieste)*.

Wadhwan State   Wadhwan, a native feudatory state in west-central India. *India (native feudatory states)*.

Wallis and Futuna   in the southwestern Pacific Ocean, consisting of two groups of volcanic islands approximately 125 miles apart, the Wallis Archipelago consisting of a main island, Wallis (Uvéa) and about 20 smaller islands and islets, and the Futuna Archipelago consisting of two mountainous islands, Futuna (Hooru) and Alofi. French (1920→). Inscriptions include **Iles Wallis et Futuna** overprinted on stamps of New Caledonia (1920–44), **Iles Wallis & Futuna** together with "France Libre" overprinted or inscribed (1941–44), **Wallis et** (or **&**) **Futuna** (1957→).

Wallis et Futuna   Wallis and Futuna. See **Wallis and Futuna**.

Wenden   an area in Livonia, which is on the eastern coast of the Baltic Sea, in what is now the southern part of Estonia and the northern part of Latvia, and at the time the stamps were issued, a province within the Russian Empire. Inscriptions include **Wendensche Kreises Briefpost** (1863), **Briefmarke Wendenschen Kreises** (1863–1900), **Packenmarke Wenden Kreises** (1863), **ВЕНДЕНСКАЯ УѢЗДНАЯ ПОЧТА** (1901-). *Russia (Wenden)*.

Wendensche Kreises Briefpost   Wenden. See **Wenden**.

Western Australia   occupying the western third of Australia. British (1850–1901). Stamps are inscribed **Western Australia** (1854–1913). Western Australia joined the Commonwealth of Australia in 1901 but continued using its own stamps until Australia began issuing stamps in 1913. *Australian States (Western Australia)*.

Western Samoa   see **Samoa**.

West Irian   (or Irian Barat, and after 1973, Irian Jaya) the western half of the island of New Guinea. United Nations (1962–63), Indonesian (1963–70s). Inscriptions include **UNTEA** (United Nations Temporary Executive Authority) overprinted on stamps of Netherlands New Guinea (1962–63), **Irian Barat** overprinted on stamps of Indonesia (1963) or inscribed together with "Republik Indonesia" (1963–70). West Irian was formerly Netherlands New Guinea. In 1962 the Netherlands turned over West Irian to UN authority. From 1963 to 1969, Indonesia administered West Irian under UN mandate. In 1969 it voted to join Indonesia.

Württemberg   a state in southern Germany (1851–1923). Inscriptions include (1) **Württemberg** (1851–75), **K. Wurtt. Post** (1875–1919), **Volkstaat Württemberg** overprinted on official stamps (1919–20), **Volkstaat Wuerttemberg** (1920–23). *German States (Württemberg).* (2) **Württemberg** (French occupation, 1947–49). *Germany (French occupation).*

Y.A.R.   Yemen Arab Republic. See **Yemen (Republic of)**.

Yca   overprinted on stamps of Peru: Ica, a city in southern Peru located about 30 miles from the Pacific Ocean and capital of Ica Department. *Peru (provisional issues).*

Yca Vapor   overprinted on stamps of Peru: Ica, a city in southern Peru located about 30 miles from the Pacific Ocean and capital of Ica Department. *Peru (provisional issues).*

Yemen (People's Democratic Republic of)   (or Southern Yemen) on the southwest Arabian Peninsula, bordered on the north by Saudi Arabia, on the east by Oman, on the south by the Gulf of Aden, and on the west by North Yemen (Republic of Yemen). Independent (1968–90). Inscriptions include **People's Republic of Southern Yemen** overprinted on stamps of Saudi Arabia (1968) or inscribed (1968–70), **People's Democratic Republic of Yemen** (1971–90), **Yemen** with "P.D.R." or "PDR" (late 1970s–1990). In 1990 the People's Democratic Republic of Yemen merged with the Republic of Yemen. Formerly, Aden.

Yemen (Republic of)   (or North Yemen) on the southwestern corner of the Arabian Peninsula, bordered on the north and northeast by Saudi Arabia and to the east by Oman, on the south by the Gulf of Aden, and on the west by the Red Sea. Independent (1926–→). Inscriptions include Arabic script (1926–30), **Yemen** (1930–39, 1947–62), **Postes du Royaume de Yemen** (1940–45), **Royaume de Yemen** (1946, 1963–70s), **Royaume al Moutawakkiliyyah du Yemen** (1951–57), **The Moutawakilite Kingdom of Yemen** (1952), **Post Yemen** (1954), **Y.A.R.** (1962), **Yemen Arab Republic** (1964–90), **Yemen Republic** (1990),

Republic of Yemen (1990→). In 1990 the Republic of Yemen merged with the People's Democratic Republic of Yemen.

Yemen Arab Republic   Yemen. See **Yemen (Republic of)**.

Yemen P.D.R. (or PDR)   People's Democratic Republic of Yemen. See **Yemen (People's Democratic Republic of)**.

Yemen Republic   Yemen. See **Yemen (Republic of)**.

Yugoslavia   in southeastern Europe on the Balkan Peninsula, bordered on the north by Austria and Hungary, on the east by Romania and Bulgaria, on the south by Albania and Greece, and on the west by Italy and the Adriatic Sea. Independent (1918→). In 1918 Bosnia and Herzegovina, Croatia, Dalmatia, Montenegro, Serbia, and Slovenia came together to form a new country. Initially, and until 1921, the fledgling country was known as the Kingdom of Serbs, Croats, and Slovenes. Later it became known as Yugoslavia. Inscriptions for stamps valid in Bosnia and Herzegovina include **Država S.H.S. - 1918 - Bosna i Hercegovina** overprinted on stamps of Bosnia and Herzegovina (1918), **ДРЖАВА С.Х.С. - 1918 - БОСНА И ХЕРЦЕГОВНИНА** overprinted on stamps of Bosnia and Herzegovina (1918), **Kraljevstvo S.H.S.** overprinted on stamps of Bosnia and Herzegovina (1919), **КРАЉЕВСТВО С.Х.С.** overprinted on stamps of Bosnia and Herzegovina (1919), **КРАЉЕВСТВО - СРБА, ХРВАТА И СЈIОВЕНАЦА** overprinted on stamps of Bosnia and Herzegovina (1918–19), **Kraljevstvo Srba, Hrvata i Slovenaca** overprinted on stamps of Bosnia and Herzegovina (1918–19), **Država S.H.S. Bosna i Hercegovina** overprinted on stamps of Bosnia and Herzegovina (1918–19).

Inscriptions for stamps valid in Croatia-Slavonia include **Hrvatska SHS** overprinted on stamps of Hungary (1918–19), **Hrvatska** inscribed together with "SHS" (1918), **Hrvatska** and "Državna Posta" (1919), **Hrvatska** with "Drž. Posta" and "SHS" (1919).

Inscriptions for stamps valid in Slovenia include **Drzava SHS** (1919), **Kraljevina SHS** (1919–20), **Kraljevstvo SHS** (1920).

Inscriptions for stamps valid throughout Yugoslavia include **Kraljevstvo Srba, Hravata i Slovenaca** (1921–24), **Kraljevina Srba, Hravata i Slovenaca** (1924–31), **Kraljevina Jugoslavija** (1931), **ЈУГОСЛАВИЈА** and **Jugoslavija** overprinted (1933–34), **ЈУГОСЛАВИЈА** and/or **Jugoslavija** inscribed (1931–48), with "**ФНР**" or "**F.N.R.**" (1948–55), often with "**ПТТ**" or "**РТТ**" (1955→), **Democratska Federativna Jugoslavija** (1945–46), **ДЕМОКРАТСКА ФЕДЕРАТИВНА ЈУГОСЛАВИЈА** overprinted on stamps of Serbia (1944). Toward the end of World War II, Yugoslavia occupied the Istrian Peninsula, which formerly had been part of Italy. **Istra - Slovensko-Primopje** and **Istria - Littorale-Sloveno** (1945–46), **Vojna Uprava Jugoslavenske Armije** overprinted on stamps of Yugoslavia (1947). In 1991 four of the Yugoslav republics—Bosnia and Herzegovina, Croatia, Macedonia, and Slovenia—broke away and declared independence, leaving only Serbia and Montenegro in the Federal Republic of Yugoslavia.

Yunnan-Fou   overprinted on stamps of Indochina: French offices in Yunnan, China. *France (offices abroad).*

Yunnansen   overprinted on stamps of Indochina: French offices in Yunnan, China. *France (offices abroad).*

Z. Afr. Republiek or **Republiex** or **Rep.**   Transvaal. See **Transvaal**.

Zaire   a name used by the Democratic Republic of the Congo between 1971 and 1997. See **Congo (Democratic Republic)**. *Zaire.*

Zambezia   a region in central Mozambique that included the provinces (and towns) of Quelimane and Tete. Portuguese (1894–1910s). Inscriptions include **Zambezia** with "Portugal" (1894–98), **Zambezia** together with "Correios Portugal" (1898–1910s), both of the foregoing often additionally overprinted "Republica." Subsequently, Zambezia was divided into the provinces of Quelimane and Tete.

Zambia   in southern Africa, bordered on the north by the Democratic Republic of the Congo and Tanzania, on the east by Malawi, on the southeast by Mozambique, on the south by Zimbabwe, Botswana, and a fingerlike strip of Namibia, and on the west by Angola. Independent (1964→). Stamps are inscribed **Zambia**.

Zanzibar   a group of islands off the coast of Africa 20 miles from mainland Tanzania. British (1895–1963), independent (1963–64), Zanzibar/Tanzania (1964–67). Inscriptions include **Zanzibar** overprinted on stamps of India (1895–96) or British East Africa (1896), or inscribed (1896–1964), **Jamhuri Zanzibar** (1964–65), **Jamhuri Zanzibar Tanzania** (1965–66), **Zanzibar-Tanzania** (1966–67). In 1964 Zanzibar merged with Tanganyika to become Tanzania. From 1967 onward, they used stamps of Tanzania.

Zanzibar   overprinted on stamps of France or inscribed together with "République Française": French offices in Zanzibar. *France (offices in Zanzibar).*

Zanzibar-Tanzania   see **Zanzibar**.

Z.A.R.   (Zuid Afrikaansche Republiek) overprinted on stamps during the Boer occupation of Vryburg in South Africa (1899). *Cape of Good Hope (Vryburg).*

ZATOTEOP   inscribed on issues similar to those of imperial Russia: Poland. See **Poland**.

Zil Eloigne Sesel   see **Seychelles**.

Zil Elwagne Sesel   see **Seychelles**.

Zil Elwannyen Sesel   see **Seychelles**.

Zimbabwe   in southeastern Africa, bordered on the north by Zambia and Mozambique, on the east by Mozambique, on the south by South Africa, and on the west and southwest by Botswana. Independent (1980→). Stamps are inscribed **Zimbabwe**. Zimbabwe was formerly Rhodesia.

Zona de Ocupatie - Romana   overprinted in an oval on stamps of Hungary for use in areas occupied by Romania following World War I: *Hungary*.

Zona de Protectorado Español en Maruecos   overprinted on stamps of Spain or inscribed: Spanish Morocco. See **Spanish Morocco**.

Zona Protectorado Español   overprinted on stamps of Spain: Spanish Morocco. See **Spanish Morocco**.

Zone Francaise Briefpost   French zone of occupation in Germany (1945–46). *Germany (occupation issues)*.

Zuid Afrikaanshe Republiek   Transvaal. See **Transvaal**.

Zuid-West Afrika   South West Africa. See **South West Africa**.

Zuid-West Afrika   overprinted on stamps of South Africa: South West Africa. See **South West Africa**.

Zululand   the northeastern part of Natal, South Africa. British (1888–97). Inscriptions include **Zululand** overprinted on stamps of Great Britain or Natal (1888–94) or inscribed (1894–97). In 1897 Zululand was incorporated into Natal.

Zürich   and "Local-Taxe" or "Cantonal-Taxe": cantonal issue for Zurich. See **Switzerland**.

CYRILLIC ALPHABET INSCRIPTIONS

АЗЄРБАЙДЖАНСКАЯ   with or without surcharged values: Azerbaijan. See **Azerbaijan**.

БАТУМ.ОБ.   overprinted on stamps of Russia: Batum. See **Batum**.

БАНДЕРОЛЬНОЕ ОТЦРАВЛЕНІЕ   Russian offices in Turkey. *Russia*.

БАМАУ ШУУДАН   Mongolia. See **Mongolia**.

БЪЛГ̌АРИЯ or БЪЛГ̌АРИЯ   sometimes with **Н.Р.** preceding or **пОША** following: Bulgaria. See **Bulgaria**.

ВЕНДЕНСКАЯ УѢЗДНАЯ ПОЧТА   Wenden. See **Wenden**.

ВОСТОЧНАЯ КОРРЕСПОНДЕНЦІЯ   Russian offices in the Turkish Empire. *Russia (offices in Turkey).*

ДРЖАВА С.Х.С. - 1918 - БОСНА И ХЕРЦЕГОВНИНА   overprinted on stamps of Bosnia and Herzegovina: Yugoslavia. See **Yugoslavia.**

ДЕМОКРАТСКА ФЕДЕРАТИВНА ЈУГОСЛАВИЈА   overprinted on stamps of Serbia: Yugoslavia. See **Yugoslavia.**

ЕДИНАЯ РОССІЯ   South Russia. See **South Russia.**

ЕРМАКЪ   South Russia. See **South Russia.**

КАЗАКСТАН   Kazakstan. See **Kazakstan.**

К.С. ПОШІТА   Serbia. See **Serbia.**

К. СГБСКА ПОШТА   Serbia. See **Serbia.**

КИТАИ   overprinted on stamps of Russia: Russian offices in China. *Russia (offices in China).*

КРАЛ ЦРНАГОРЕ   Montenegro. See **Montenegro.**

КРАЛЕВСТВО С.Х.С.   overprinted on stamps of Bosnia and Herzegovina: Yugoslavia. See **Yugoslavia.**

КРАЉЕВСТВО - СРБА, ХРВАТА И СЈІОВЕНАЦА   overprinted on stamps of Bosnia and Herzegovina: Yugoslavia. See **Yugoslavia.**

КРАЛЕВИНА СГБИЈА   Serbia. See **Serbia.**

КРЫМСЂАГО КРАЕВОТО ПРАВКТЕДЬСТБА   South Russia. See **South Russia.**

КЫРГЫЗСТАН   Kyrgyzstan. See **Kyrgyzstan.**

КЊСРП ПОШТА   Serbia. See **Serbia.**

МАКЕДОНСКИ   Macedonia. See **Macedonia.**

МОНГОЛ ШУУДАН   Mongolia. See **Mongolia.**

Н.Р. БЪЛГАРИЯ   Bulgaria. See **Bulgaria.**

ОБЪЕДИНЕННЫЕ НАЦИИ   United Nations, Russian inscription.

ПОРТОМАРКА   Montenegro. See **Montenegro.**

ПОЧТОВАЯ МАРКА   **(1)** denomination in "Pen," "Penni," "Markka" or "Markkaa": Finland; **(2)** denomination in Cyrillic characters: Russia.

ПОЧТА   see **Russia.**

ПОЧТА РУССКОИ АРМЇИ   overprinted, together with surcharged value, on stamps of Russia, Russian offices in the Turkish Empire, or South Russia: Wrangel issue. *Russia (offices in Turkey, Wrangel issue).*

ПОШТА УКРАЇНИ   Ukraine. See **Ukraine**.

ПОШТА   Serbia. See **Serbia**.

ПОШТЕ ЦР. ГОРЕ   Montenegro. See **Montenegro**.

ПОШТЕ ЦРНЕ ГОРЕ   Montenegro. See **Montenegro**.

ПОШТИ МАКЕДОНСКИ   Macedonia. See **Macedonia**.

Пощавъ Ромжния 1916–1917   overprinted on stamps of Bulgaria: Romania (Bulgarian occupation). See **Romania**.

ПТТ МАКЕДОНИЈА or МАКЕДОНИЈА   Macedonia. See **Macedonia**.

ПТТ ЈУГОСЛАВИЈА   Yugoslavia. See **Yugoslavia**.

ПЯТЬ   overprinted, together with surcharge, on stamps of Russia: South Russia. See **South Russia**.

РЕПУБЛИКА СРПСКА   see **Bosnia and Herzegovina (Serb)**.

РЕПУБЛИКА МАКЕДОНИЈА   Macedonia. See **Macedonia**.

Р.О. П.иТ.   Russian offices in the Turkish Empire. *Russia (offices in Turkey)*.

РОССІЯ   see **Russia**.

РСФСР   see **Russia**.

РУССКАЯ ПОЧТА   overprinted, together with surcharged value, on stamps of Russia, Russian offices in the Turkish Empire, South Russia, or Ukraine: Wrangel issue. *Russia (offices in Turkey, Wrangel issue)*.

УКРАЇНСЬКА   Ukraine. See **Ukraine**.

У.С.Р.Р.   Ukraine. See **Ukraine**.

УЗБЕКИСТОН   overprinted on stamps of Russia: Uzbekistan. See **Uzbekistan**.

ФНР ЈУГОСЛАВИЈА   Yugoslavia. See **Yugoslavia**.

ЦАРСтВО БЪЛГАРИЯ   Bulgaria. See **Bulgaria**.

ЦОРТО СКРИСОРН   Moldavia (Romania). See **Romania**.

ЦР. ГОРЕ   Montenegro. See **Montenegro**.

ЦРНА ГОРА   either overprinted on stamps of Italy or inscribed: Montenegro (Italian occupation). See **Montenegro**.

ЗСФСР   Transcaucasian Federated Republic. See **Transcaucasian Federated Republic**.

ЈУГОСЛАВИЈА   Yugoslavia. See **Yugoslavia**.

ЮГЪ РОССIИ   overprinted, together with surcharge, on stamps of Russia: South Russia. See **South Russia**.

GREEK ALPHABET INSCRIPTIONS

ΑΥΤΟΝΟΝΟΣ ΗΠΕΙΡΟΣ   Epirus. See **Epirus**.

B. ΗΠΕΙΡΟΣ   overprinted on stamps of Greece: Epirus. See **Epirus**.

Διοίκησις Θράκης   overprinted on stamps of Greece: Thrace (Greek occupation). See **Thrace**.

ΔΙΟΙΚΗΣΙΣ ΔΥΤΙΚΗΣ ΘΡΑΚΗΣ   overprinted on stamps of Greece: Thrace (Greek occupation). See **Thrace**.

Διοίκησις Δντικής Θράκης   overprinted on stamps of Greece: Thrace (Greek occupation). See **Thrace**.

Ε*Δ   overprinted on stamps of Greece: Chios (Khíos). See **Greece**.

ΕΛΛΑΣ   Greece. See **Greece**.

ΕΛΛΑΣ or ΕΛΛΑΣ ΠΡΟΣΟΡΙΝΟΝ   overprinted on stamps inscribed "Κρhta": **Crete**.

ΕΛΛΑΣ 2·X·43   overprinted on stamps of Italy together with "Isole Jonie": Ionian Islands. See **Ionian Islands**.

ΕΛΛ. ΑΥΤΟΝ. ΗΠΕΙΡΟΣ   together with skull and crossbones: Epirus. See **Epirus**. See **Crete**.

ΕΛΛΗΝΙΚΗ 1914 ΧΕΙΜΑΡΡΑ   overprinted on stamps of Greece: Epirus. See **Epirus**.

ελλΗΝΙΚΗ ΔΙΟΙΚΗCΙC   overprinted on stamps of Greece: North Epirus. See **Greece**.

ΕΛΛΗΝΙΚΗ ΔΙΟΙΚΗΣΙΣ   (1) overprinted on stamps of Greece: Greek-occupied Turkey; (2) overprinted on stamps of Bulgaria: Cavalla (Kaválla). See **Greece**.

ΕΛΛΗΝΙΚΗ ΔΙΟΙΥΗΣΙΣ   overprinted on stamps of Greece: Icaria (Ikaría). See **Greece**.

ΕΛΛΗΝΙΚΗ ΔΙΟΙΚΗΣΙΣ ΔΕΔΕΑΓΑΤΣ ΔΕΚΑ ΛΕΠΤΑ or ΕΛΛΗΝΙΚΗ ΔΙΟΙΚΗΣΙΣ ΔΕΔΕΑΓΑΤΣ 10 ΛΕΠΤΑ   overprinted on stamps of Greece or Bulgaria: Dedeagatch. See **Greece**.

ΗΠΕΙΡΟΣ   Epirus. See **Epirus**.

ΙΚΑΡΙΑΣ   Icaria (Ikaría). See **Greece**.

ΙΟΝΙΚΟΝ ΚΡΑΤΟΣ   overprinted on stamps of Greece: Ionian Islands. See **Ionian Islands**.

ΛΗΜΝΟΣ   overprinted on stamps of Greece: Lemnos (Límnos). See **Greece**.

ΠΡΟΣΩΡΙΝΟΝ ΤΑΧΥΔΡΟΜΕΙΟΝ - ΣΑΜΟΥ   Samos (Sámos). See **Greece**.

ΠΡΟΣΩΡΙΝΟΝ ΤΑΧΥΛΙ ΟΜΕΙΟΝ ΡΕΟΥΜΝΗΣ   Crete. See **Crete**.

ΠΡΟΣΩΡΙΝΟΝ ΤΑΧΥΔΡΟΜ ΗΡΑΚΔΕΙΟΝ   Crete. See **Crete**.

ΡΕΘΥΜΝΗΣ ΠΡΟΕΩΡ ΤΑΧΥΔΡ   Crete. See **Crete**.

ΣΑΜΟΥ   Samos (Sámos). See **Greece**.

Σ.Δ.Δ.   overprinted on stamps of Greece: Dodecanese Islands. See **Greece**.

Υπάτη Απμοστεία Θπακης   overprinted on stamps of Turkey (Greek occupation). See **Thrace**.

Ἑλληνικὴ Κατιοχὴ Μυτλήνης   overprinted on stamps of Greece: Lesbos (Lésvos). See **Greece**.

CHAPTER 25

CURRENT AND FORMER
COUNTRY NAMES

L OCATE A NAME in the left column; its current, former, or alternate name appears in the right column.

Aden .... now part of **People's Democratic Republic of Yemen**

Afars and Issas .... now **Djibouti Republic**

Bangladesh .... formerly **East Pakistan**

Basutoland .... now **Lesotho**

Bechuanaland Protectorate .... now **Botswana**

Belgian Congo .... subsequently **Democratic Republic of the Congo**; then **Zaire**

Belize .... formerly **British Honduras**

Benin .... formerly **Dahomey**

Botswana .... formerly **Bechuanaland Protectorate**

British Guiana .... now **Guyana**

British Honduras .... now **Belize**

Burkina Faso .... formerly **Upper Volta**

Burma .... now **Myanmar**

Burundi .... formerly part of **Ruanda (Rwanda-Urundi)**

Cambodia .... formerly **Khmer Republic** (1970–82); then **Kampuchea** (1982–89)

Central African Empire .... formerly **Central African Republic**; subsequently **Central African Republic**

Central African Republic .... subsequently **Central African Empire** (1976–79); then again **Central African Republic**

Ceylon .... now **Sri Lanka**

Côte d'Ivoire .... also **Ivory Coast**

Czech Republic .... formerly part of **Czechoslovakia**

Dahomey .... now **Benin**

361

Democratic Republic of the Congo .... formerly **Belgian Congo**; then **Congo Democratic Republic** (1960–71); then **Zaire** (1971–97)

Djibouti Republic .... formerly **Somali Coast**; then **Afars and Issas**

East Pakistan .... now **Bangladesh**

Equatorial Guinea .... formerly **Fernando Po** and **Rio Muni**; then **Spanish Guinea**

Ellice Islands .... now **Tuvalu**

Fernando Po .... subsequently part of **Spanish Guinea**

French Congo .... now **Republic of the Congo**

French Guinea .... now **Republic of Guinea**

French Sudan .... now **Mali**

German Democratic Republic .... (East Germany) now part of **Germany**

Ghana .... formerly the **Gold Coast**

Gilbert Islands .... now **Kiribati**

Gold Coast .... now **Ghana**

Guinea-Bissau .... formerly **Portuguese Guinea**

Guyana .... formerly **British Guiana**

Indonesia .... formerly **Netherlands Indies**

Ivory Coast .... also **Côte d'Ivoire**

Jordan .... formerly **Transjordan**

Kampuchea .... now **Cambodia**

Kenya .... formerly part of **Kenya, Uganda, Tanganyika** (later **Tanzania**)

Kenya, Uganda, Tanganyika .... subsequently **Kenya, Uganda, Tanzania**; then split into the respective countries

Khmer Republic .... formerly **Cambodia**; then **Kampuchea** (1982–89); now **Cambodia**

Kiribati .... formerly the **Gilbert Islands**

Lesotho .... formerly **Basutoland**

Madagascar .... subsequently **Malagasy Republic**

Malagasy Republic .... formerly **Madagascar**

Malawi .... formerly **Nyasaland Protectorate**

Mali .... formerly **French Sudan**

Myanmar .... formerly **Burma**

Namibia .... formerly **South West Africa**

Netherlands Indies .... now **Indonesia**

Netherlands New Guinea .... now part of **Indonesia** (West Irian)

New Hebrides .... now **Vanuatu**

Northern Rhodesia .... now **Zambia**

Nyasaland Protectorate .... now **Malawi**

Portuguese Guinea .... now **Guinea-Bissau**

Rhodesia .... now **Zimbabwe**

Republic of Guinea .... formerly **French Guinea**

Rio Muni .... subsequently part of **Spanish Guinea**

Ruanda .... formerly part of **Rwanda-Urundi**

Rwanda-Urundi .... split into **Ruanda** and **Burundi**

St. Christopher, Nevis, Anguilla .... formerly **St. Kitts and Nevis**

St. Kitts and Nevis .... now **St. Christopher, Nevis, Anguilla**

Slovakia .... formerly part of **Czechoslovakia**

Somali Coast .... became **Afars and Issas**; then **Djibouti Republic**

Spanish Guinea .... now **Equatorial Guinea**

Sri Lanka .... formerly **Ceylon**

South West Africa .... now **Namibia**

Tanzania .... formed by merger of **Tanganyika** and **Zanzibar** and part of **Kenya, Uganda, Tanzania** until independence

Transjordan .... now **Jordan**

Tuvalu .... formerly the **Ellice Islands**

Uganda .... formerly part of **Kenya, Uganda, Tanganyika** (later **Tanzania**)

Upper Volta .... now **Burkina Faso**

Vanuatu .... formerly **New Hebrides**

Zaire .... formerly the **Belgian Congo**; subsequently the **Democratic Republic of the Congo**

Zambia .... formerly **Northern Rhodesia**

Zimbabwe .... formerly **Rhodesia**

CHAPTER 26

FOREIGN TERMS ON POSTAGE STAMPS

THE FOLLOWING TERMS and abbreviations are commonly encountered on foreign postage stamps, most often denoting a class of service (such as airmail or parcel post) or currency. The terms are often useful in either identifying the country of origin or providing a clue as to a stamp's location within a country's listing in a stamp catalogue.

Terms as they appear on foreign stamps are followed by their English equivalent. The English equivalent is not intended to be a precise translation, but rather to indicate the type of stamp on which the inscription appears. Also included are some English terms whose meaning may not be clear to American English speakers. Country information is given when a term is specific to a country and may aid in identifying a stamp. Entries are arranged in alphabetical order.

Letters in parentheses indicate plurals. Abbreviations are punctuated only where they appear that way on a stamp. Terms appearing in bold within a definition indicate a cross-reference elsewhere in this chapter. An arrow symbol (→) indicates that an entity has been continuously active from the date given to present. Dates refer only to the time during which the entity has been active issuing stamps. In the case of the United States, Independent (1847→) means that the nation is independent (although it achieved independence in 1776) and that it began issuing stamps in 1847 and has continued to do so until present. Interrupted intervals, for example, are shown as (1918–40, 1991→).

Currency abbreviations on stamps of some countries vary from issue to issue and can appear as uppercase letters, lowercase letters, or a combination of the two.

TERMS

A or **a**   abbreviation for currency: (1) **Anna**, various countries; (2) **Aurar**, Iceland; (3) **Avo**, Macao, Timor.

A   abbreviation for "anotacion," or registered mail, Colombia.

A Cobrar   postage due.

Admiralty Official   overprinted on stamps of Great Britain: official mail (Admiralty).

Aereo or **Aéreo**   airmail.

Aereo Espresso   airmail special delivery. Somalia.

Aereo Exterior   international airmail. Guatemala.

Aereo Interior   domestic airmail. Guatemala, Honduras.

Aereo Internacional   international airmail. Guatemala.

Aerienne   airmail. France, French colonies, territories, and possessions, and French-speaking countries.

Aerne   abbreviation for **Aerienne**.

Af(s)   abbreviation for **Afghani(s)**.

Afghani(s)   unit of currency. Afghanistan. Subdivided into **Pouls**.

Ag(s)   abbreviation for **Angolar(s)**.

Agorot   subunit of the **Pound** or **Shekel**. Israel.

Ajánlás   registered mail. Hungary. Abbreviated **Ajl**.

Ajl.   abbreviation for **Ajánlás**.

Amtlicher Verkehr   official mail. Württemberg.

Angolar   unit of currency. Angola (1932–77). Abbreviated **Ag(s)**.

Anna(s)   subunit of the **Rupee**. Abu Dhabi, Aden, Bahrain, British East Africa, Burma, India, Iraq, Kuwait, Mesopotamia, Muscat, Pakistan, Somalia, Somaliland Protectorate, Uganda, Zanzibar. Abbreviated **As**.

Annas   overprinted, together with surcharged value, on stamps of France or on stamps of Zanzibar: France (offices in Zanzibar).

Anotacion   registered mail. Colombia.

Any.   overprinted, together with a numeral, on stamps of Hungary: printed matter.

A.O.I.   overprinted on postage due stamps of Italy. Italian East Africa.

A Payer - Te Betalen   postage due. Belgium, Belgian Congo, Ruanda-Urundi.

A Percevoir   postage due. France, French colonies, territories, and possessions, and French-speaking countries. Also, Belgium, Canada, Egypt.

A.R. or **AR**   abbreviation for "aviso recepcion," or acknowledgment of receipt. Panama and other Spanish-speaking countries.

Ariary   unit of currency. Malagasy/Republic of Madagascar.

Armenwet   official mail. Netherlands.

Army Official   overprinted on stamps of Great Britain: official mail (Army).

Army Post   military stamp. Egypt.

Army Service   official mail. Sudan.

As   abbreviation for **Annas**.

Asistenta Sociala   inscription on some postal tax stamps. Romania.

Assistencia   inscription on some postal tax stamps. Portuguese colonies, territories, and possessions.

Assistencia Nacional dos Tuberculosos   Tuberculosis Aid Society (franchise stamps). Portugal.

At Betale - Portomærk   postage due. Norway.

Att(s)   subunit of the **Sio** or **Salung**. Thailand.

Auks   abbreviation for **Auksinas**.

Auksinai   plural of **Auksinas**.

Auksinas   unit of currency. Lithuania. Plural, **Auksinai** or **Auksinu**. Abbreviated **Auks**.

Auksinu   plural of **Auksinas**.

Aur.   abbreviation for **Aurar**.

Aurar   subunit of the **Krona**. Iceland. Singular of **Eyrir**. Abbreviated **A** or **Aur.**

Austral   unit of currency. Argentina.

Autopaketti   parcel post. Finland.

Avião   airmail. Macao.

Avion   airmail.

Avion Messri Tafari   airmail. Ethiopia.

Avionska Posta   airmail. Yugoslavia.

Aviso de Recepcion   acknowledgement of receipt. El Salvador.

Avisporto Mærke   newspaper stamp. Denmark.

Avo(s)   subunit of the **Rupee** or **Pataca**. Macao, Timor. Abbreviated **A**.

B or b   abbreviation for currency: (1) **Balboa**, Panama; (2) **Bani**, Moldova; (3) **Bogaches**, **Bogchah**, and **Bogsha**, Yemen; (4) **Butut**, Gambia.

Baht   unit of currency. Thailand.

Bai   abbreviation for **Bajocchi**.

Baiza   subunit of the **Rupee** and later the **Rial Saidi**. Oman.

Baj   abbreviation for **Bajocchi**.

Bajar Porto   postage due. Indonesia.

Bajocchi   subunit of the **Scudo**. Romagna, Roman States. Abbreviated **Bai** or **Baj**.

Balboa   unit of currency. Panama. Abbreviated **B**.

Ban(i)   subunit of the **Leu**. Moldova, Romania. Abbreviated **B** or **b**.

Banica   subunit of the **Kuna**. Croatia (1940s).

Bayar porto   postage due. Indonesia.

Besa   genuine. Overprinted to validate certain stamps of the early 1920s. Albania.

Besa(s)   subunit of the **Anna** or **Rupee**. Somalia.

Bijzondere Vlucthen   special flight. Netherlands.

Bipkwele   plural of **Ekuele**, a unit of currency. Equatorial Guinea.

Birr   unit of currency. Eritrea, Ethiopia.

Bit   subunit of the **Franc**. Danish West Indies.

Bk   abbreviation for **Bipkwele**. Equatorial Guinea.

BMA   abbreviation for "British Military Administration," overprinted on stamps of North Borneo: North Borneo.

Board of Education   overprinted on stamps of Great Britain: official mail (Board of Education).

Bogaches   plural for **Bogchah**, a subunit of the **Imadi**. Yemen.

Bogchah   subunit of the **Imadi**. Yemen. Abbreviated **B**.

Bogsha(s)   subunit of the **Imadi**. Yemen. Variant spelling of **Bogchah**. Abbreviated **B**.

Bolivar(s)   unit of currency. Venezuela. Abbreviated **Bs**.

Boliviano(s)   unit of currency. Revalued in 1963 to the **Peso Boliviano**, revalued in 1987 to the **boliviano**. Bolivia. Abbreviated **Bs** or symbols **$b** and **B$**.

Bollo Straordinario per le Poste   newspaper tax stamp. Tuscany.

Briefmarke   postage stamp.

Bs   abbreviation for (1) **Bolivars**, Venezuela; (2) **Bolivianos**, Bolivia.

Bultos Postales   parcel post. Mexico.

Butut(s)   subunit of the **Dalasi**. Gambia. Abbreviated **B** or **b**.

C or **c**   abbreviation for currency: (1) **Cedi** or **New Cedi**, Ghana; (2) **Cent**; (3) **Centai**, **Centas**, or **Centu**, Lithuania; (4) **Centavo**; (5) **Centesimo**; (6) **Centime**; (7) **Centimo**; (8) **Som**, Kyrgyzstan.

Ca   abbreviation for **Cache**. French India.

Cache(s)   subunit of the **Fanon**. French India. Abbreviated **ca**.

Candarin or **Candareen**   subunit of the **Mace**. China (nineteenth century). Abbreviated **cn**.

Cash   subunit of the **Chukram**. Travancore (India).

Caury   subunit of the **Syli**. Republic of Guinea.

C.d. (or **de**) **Peseta**   abbreviation for "centimos de peseta." Cuba, Puerto Rico, Spain.

C.d. Peso   abbreviation for "centavos de peso." Cuba, Fernando Po, Philippines.

Cedi   unit of currency. Ghana. Abbreviated **c**.

C.E.F.   abbreviation for (1) "Cameroon Expeditionary Force": Great Britain; (2) "China Expeditionary Force": India.

Cen de Esc   abbreviation for "centimos de escudo." Fernando Po.

Cent   abbreviation for currency: (1) **Centavo**; (2) **Centesimo**; (3) **Centimo**; (4) **Centu**, Memel.

Cent(s)   subunit of many currencies, including: (1) **Birr** and **Nakfa**, Eritrea; (2) **Dobra**, Saint Thomas and Prince Islands; (3) **Dollar**; (4) **Emalangeni**, Swaziland; (5) **Gulden**, Netherlands and colonies; (6) **Leone**, Sierra Leone; (7) **Piaster** or **Riel**, Cambodia; (8) **Pound**, Cyprus; (9) **Rand**, Basutoland, Bechuanaland Protectorate, Namibia, South Africa, and others; (10) **Ringgit**, Malaysia; (11) **Rupee**, Ceylon, Seychelles, Zanzibar, and others; (12) **Shilling**; (13) **Tael**, China (late nineteenth century onward). Abbreviated **c**, **cs**, **ct**, or **cts**.

Centai   plural for **Centas**. Iceland.

Centas   subunit of the **Litas**. Lithuania (early 1920s). Plural, **Centai** or **Centu**. Abbreviated **c**, **ct**, or **cnt**.

Centavo(s)   subunit of many currencies, including: (1) **Angolar**, Angola; (2) **Boliviano**, Bolivia; (3) **Colón**, El Salvador; (4) **Cordoba**, Nicaragua; (5) **Cruzado** and **Cruzeiro**, Brazil; (6) **Escudo**, many Portuguese colonies; (7) **Lempira**, Honduras; (8) **Metical**, Mozambique; (9) **Peso**, many Central and South American countries; (10) **Quetzal**, Guatemala; (11) **Real**, Guatemala, Uruguay, Venezuela; (12) **Sol**, Peru. Abbreviated **c**, **cs**, **ct**, **cos**, **cts**, **ctvs**, **cent**, **cents**, **ctvos**, or **ctvs**.

Centesimo(s) or **Centésimo(s)**   subunit of several currencies, including: (1) **Balboa**, Panama; (2) **Corona**, Fiume; (3) **Escudo**, Chile, Cuba; (4) **Lira**, Fiume, Italy, Italian colonies, territories, and possessions, also San Marino, Vatican City; (5) **Peso**, Uruguay; (6) **Somalo** or **Somali Shilling**, Somalia; (7) **Venezolano**, Venezuela. Abbreviated **c**, **cs**, **cmi**, **cts**, **cent**, or **centes**.

Centime(s)   subunit of several currencies, including: (1) **Franc**, France, French colonies, territories, and possessions, and French-speaking countries; Belgium, Belgian Congo, Haiti, Luxembourg, Switzerland, and others; (2) **Thaler**, Ethiopia; (3) **Piastre**, Syria. Abbreviated **c**, **cts**, or **cmes**.

Centimes   overprinted, together with surcharged value, (1) on stamps of Germany: German offices in the Ottoman Empire; (2) on stamps of Great Britain: British offices in Morocco.

Centimes Or   gold centimes. New Hebrides.

Centimo(s) or **Céntimo(s)**   subunit of several currencies, including: (1) **Bolivar**, Venezuela; (2) **Colon**, Costa Rica; (3) **Ekuele**, Equatorial Guinea; (4) **Escudo**, Spain and Spanish colonies, territories, and possessions; (5) **Guarani**, Paraguay; (6) **Peseta**, Spain and Spanish colonies, territories, and possessions; (7) **Peso**, Philippines; (8) **Sol** or **Inti**, Peru. Abbreviated **c**, **co** or **cs**, **cent**, **cents**, **cmos**, **ctms**, **cto**, **cts**, or **ctos**.

Centimos   overprinted, together with numeral of surcharged value, (1) on stamps of Great Britain: Great Britain (offices in Morocco); (2) on stamps of France: French Morocco.

Cent. Peseta   abbreviation for "centimos de peseta." Cuba, Fernando Po, Spain.

Cents   overprinted, together with surcharged value, on stamps of Russia: Russia (offices in China).

Cent^s Peseta   abbreviation for "centimos de peseta." Cuba, Spain.

Centu or **Centų**   plural for **Centas**, a subunit of the **Litas**. Memel.

Certificada   registered mail.

Certificado   registered mail. Venezuela.

C.F.   abbreviation for "Communauté Française." Nations belonging to the French Community of Nations.

CFA   abbreviation for (1) "Colonies Française d'Afrique"; (2) "Communauté Française d'Afrique." Also refers to the CFA franc, used by nations belonging to the French Community in Africa.

Ch   abbreviation for **Cheun** or **Chun**. Korea.

ch   abbreviation for **Chai** and **Chahis**. Iran.

ch   abbreviation for currency: (1) **Chetrum**, Bhutan; (2) **Chun**, Korea.

Chahi or **Chahis**   subunit of the **Kran**. Iran.

Chai   subunit of the **Kran**. Iran. Spelling variants and plurals include **Chain**, **Chahi**, or **Chahis**. Abbreviated **ch**.

Chain variant of **Chai**. Iran.

Chemins de Fer - Spoorwegen railway parcel post. Belgium.

Chetrum subunit of the **Ngultrum**. Bhutan. Abbreviated **ch**.

Cheun unit of currency. Korea. Abbreviated **Cn**.

Chiffre Taxe - A Percevoir postage due. France, French colonies, territories, and possessions, and French-speaking countries.

Chukram(s) unit of currency. Travancore (India).

Chun unit of currency. Korea. Abbreviated **Ch**.

C•I•S overprinted on stamps of Schleswig: official mail. Schleswig.

cm abbreviation for **Stotinki**, plural for **Stotinka**. Bulgaria.

Cmi abbreviation for **Centesimos**.

C^MOS abbreviation for **Centimos**. Spain.

C.M.T. overprinted on stamps of Austria: Romanian occupation of Pokutia. Western Ukraine.

cn abbreviation for currency: (1) **Candarin** and **Candareen**, China; (2) **Cheun**, Korea.

cnt abbreviation for **Centai**, **Centas**, and **Centu**.

co abbreviation for **Centimo**.

Çocuk Esirgeme inscription on certain postal tax stamps. Turkey.

Çocuk Esirgeme Kurumu inscription on certain postal tax stamps. Turkey.

Colis Postaux parcel post stamp. Belgium, Benin, Dahomey, Morocco.

Colon(es) or **Colón(es)** unit of currency. Costa Rica, El Salvador.

cop abbreviation for **Kopeck**. Azerbaijan.

Cordoba unit of currency. Nicaragua.

Corona unit of currency. Fiume. Sometimes spelled **Korona**.

Correio(s) mail. Brazil, Portugal, and Portuguese colonies, territories, and possessions.

Correio Aereo or **Correio Aéreo** airmail. Brazil, Portugal, and Portuguese colonies, territories, and possessions.

Correios e Telegraphos newspaper stamp. Azores, Portugal.

Correo or **Correos** mail. Spain and Spanish-speaking countries.

Correo Aereo or **Correos Aéreo** airmail. Spain and Spanish-speaking countries.

Correo Aereo Interior   domestic airmail. Dominican Republic, Nicaragua.

Correo Aereo Interno   airmail postal tax stamp. Dominican Republic.

Correo Aéreo Oficial   official airmail. Nicaragua.

Correo Oficial   official mail. Spain and Spanish-speaking countries.

Correos de Oficio   official mail. El Salvador.

Correos Departmentales   department (state) official mail. Colombia.

Correos Depmentales   official mail. Colombia.

Correos Expreso   special delivery. Ecuador.

Correos y Telegrafos   mail and telegraph. Argentina.

Correo Urgente   special delivery. Spain and Spanish-speaking countries.

Correspondencia a Debe   postage due. Panama.

Correspondencia Oficial   official. Dominican Republic, Ecuador, Mexico.

Correspondencia Urgente   special delivery. Spain.

Courrier Officiel   official mail. Ivory Coast.

Cr   abbreviation for **Cruzeiro**. Brazil.

Cr$ abbreviation for **Cruzeiro**, **New Cruzeiro**, and **Cruzeiro Real**. Brazil.

Croissant Rouge   Red Crescent. Analogous to the Red Cross, Muslim countries.

Crown   a generic term for the primary unit of currency for many countries. Variations include corona, korona, koruna, krone, etc.

Crs   abbreviation for **Cruzeiro**. Brazil.

Cruzado   unit of currency. Brazil. Abbreviated **Cz** or **Cz$**.

Cruzeiro   unit of currency. Brazil. Abbreviated **Cr** or **Cr$**. Also, **New Cruzeiro** (early 1990s). Abbreviated **Cz$**, **Cr$**, or **NCz$**. Also, **Cruzeiro Real** (1993→). Abbreviated **R$** or **Cr$**.

Cruz Roja   Red Cross.

Cruz Vermehla - Porto Franco   Red Cross franchise mail. Also, **Cruz Vermehla Portuguesa - Porto Franco**. Portugal.

Cs   abbreviation for (1) **Centesimos**; (2) **Centimos**; (3) **Cuartos**.

Cs.   abbreviation for **Csomag**, overprinted, together with numerals, on stamps of Hungary: parcel post. Hungary.

Cˢ de Eº   abbreviation for "centimos de escudo." Philippines.

Cˢ de Peseta   abbreviation for "centimos de peseta." Philippines.

C^S de Peso   abbreviation for "centimos de peso." Philippines.

Csomag   overprinted, together with kilogram weight, on stamps of Hungary: parcel post. Hungary.

C^S Peseta   abbreviation for "centimos de peseta." Cuba, Puerto Rico, Spain.

Ct   abbreviation for (1) **Cent**; (2) **Centai**, **Centas**, and **Centu**, Lithuania; (3) **Centavo**; (4) **Stotinki**, Bulgaria.

Cto   abbreviation for (1) **Centesimo**; (2) **Centimo**.

ctos or **CTOS**   abbreviation for (1) **Centimos**; (2) **Cuartos**.

Ctot   abbreviation for **Stotinka** or **Stotinki**. Bulgaria.

ctovs   abbreviation for **Centavos**.

cts   abbreviation for (1) **Centavos**; (2) **Centesimos**; (3) **Centimes**; (4) **Centimos**; (5) **Cents**.

Cuarto(s)   subunit of the **Real**. Spain and Spanish colonies, territories, and possessions (nineteenth century). Abbreviated **Cs** or **C^{TOS}**.

Cz   abbreviation for **Cruzado**. Brazil

Cz$ abbreviation for **Cruzado** or **New Cruzeiro**. Brazil.

D or **d**   abbreviation for currency: (1) **Dalasi**, Gambia; (2) **Dinar**; (3) **Dong**, Vietnam; (4) **Penny** or **Pence**, Great Britain, British colonies, territories, and possessions, before decimalization.

Dalasi   unit of currency. Gambia. Abbreviated **D**.

Db   abbreviation for **Dobra**.

Deficiento de Franqueo   postage due. El Salvador.

Deficit or **Déficit**   postage due. Peru.

Dencito Franqueo   postage due. Peru.

Denda   postage due. Malaysia.

Derecho de Entrega   delivery tax stamp. Spain.

Dh   abbreviation for **Dirham**.

Dienst   official mail. Netherlands.

Dienstmarke   official stamp. Germany and German-speaking countries. With numeral "21" in corners, Prussia.

Dienst Sache   official stamp. Württemberg, North German Confederation.

Di   abbreviation for **Dinar**. Iran.

Din   abbreviation for **Dinar**.

Dinar (1) unit of currency; Croatia (abbreviated **HDR**); Algeria (abbreviated **Da**); Sudan (abbreviated **D** or **S.D.**); Algeria, Jordan, Iran, Iraq, Kuwait, Serbia, Tunisia, Umm al Qiwain, Yemen PDR, and Yugoslavia (abbreviated **D**, **Din**, or **Drs**); (2) subunit of the **Rial**, Iran (abbreviated **Di**).

Dinero unit of currency. Peru (nineteenth century).

Dirham subunit of the **Riyal**. Dubai, Qatar, Libya, Umm al Qiwain, United Arab Emirates. Abbreviated **Dh**.

D M abbreviation for (1) **Dienstmarke**, Danzig; (2) **Deutsche Mark**, Germany.

Dobra unit of currency. Saint Thomas and Prince Islands. Abbreviated **Db**.

Dollar a unit of currency of many nations at various times, usually with no connection to the U.S. dollar, and often with cents as the subunit. Among them, Australia, Canada, China, Danish West Indies, Ethiopia, Malaya, New Zealand, North Borneo, Singapore, United States, Zimbabwe.

Dollar(i) overprinted on stamps of Italy: Italy (offices in China).

Dollar(s) overprinted on stamps of Russia: Russia (offices in China).

Dong unit of currency. Vietnam. Abbreviated **d**.

Doplata postage due. Central Lithuania, Poland.

Doplatit postage due. Czechoslovakia.

Doplatne or **Doplatné** postage due. Czechoslovakia, Slovakia.

Drachma unit of currency. Greece.

Drijvende Brandkast marine insurance. Netherlands.

Drs abbreviation for **Dinars**.

E abbreviation for **Emalangeni**.

E. Especial abbreviation for "entrega especial," or special delivery. Cuba.

Efterporto postage due. Danish West Indies.

Eilmarke special handling. Bosnia and Herzegovina during the Austro-Hungarian Empire.

Ekuele unit of currency. Equatorial Guinea.

Emalangeni unit of currency. Swaziland.

Encomendas Postais parcel post. Portugal.

Encomienda or **Encomiendas** parcel post. Uruguay.

Entrega Especial special delivery.

Entrega Inmediata special delivery. Colombia, Costa Rica.

E⁰ abbreviation for **Escudo**. Chile, Spain.

Esc. abbreviation for **Escudo**.

Eˢᶜᵒ. abbreviation for **Escudo**. Spain.

Escudo unit of currency. Portugal and Portuguese colonies, territories, and possessions; Spain and Spanish colonies, territories, and possessions; Chile (1960–75). Abbreviated **E, E⁰, Eos, E**ˢᶜᵒ, or **Esc**.

Espresso special delivery. Italy, Italian colonies, territories, and possessions, and Italian-speaking countries.

Expres special delivery. Egypt, Italy.

Expreso special delivery. Some Central and South American countries including Colombia, Dominican Republic, Guatemala, and Venezuela.

Express special delivery. Belgium, Costa Rica.

Express Delivery special delivery. Mauritius.

Expresso special delivery. Brazil.

Eyrir subunit of the **Krona**. Iceland.

F or **f** abbreviation for currency: (1) **Fenigi**, Poland; (2) **Fennigi**, Central Lithuania; (3) **Filler**; (4) **Fils**, Republic of Yemen; (5) **Florin**, Surinam; (6) **Franc**.

Fa abbreviation for **Fanon**. French India.

Factaj parcel post. Romania.

Fanon unit of currency. French India. Abbreviated **Fa**.

Fardos Postales parcel post. El Salvador.

Farthing subunit of the penny. British Commonwealth.

F CFA abbreviation for the CFA (Communauté Française d'Afrique) franc, a currency used by some nations in the French Community of Nations in Africa.

Feldpost field post. Military mail. Germany.

Fen (1) subunit of the **Yuan**, Manchukuo; abbreviated **Fn**; (2) abbreviation for **Fenigi**, a subunit of currency, Poland.

Fenigi subunit of the **Marka**. Poland. Abbreviated **f** or **fen**.

Fennigi subunit of the **Markka**. Central Lithuania. Abbreviated **f**.

Fil(s) or **Fill(s)** subunit of various currencies, including: (1) **Dinar**, Abu Dhabi, Bahrain, Iraq, Jordan, Kuwait, Palestine Authority, Umm al Qiwain; (2) **Dirham**, PDR Yemen; (3) **Rupee**; (4) **Shekel**, Palestinian Authority.

Filler subunit of the (1) **Korona**, Fiume (1919), Hungary (until 1926); (2) **Forint**, Hungary (1946 and later). Abbreviated **f**.

Florin   (1) unit of currency, Italy (nineteenth century), Lombardy-Venetia; (2) subunit of the **Gulden**, Surinam.

Flugfrimerki   airmail. Iceland.

Flugpost   airmail.

F.M.   abbreviation for "Franchise Militaire." Military stamp. France, French Cameroun.

FMG   abbreviation for Malagasy **franc**.

Fn   abbreviation for **fen**. Manchukuo.

FNH   abbreviation for the New Hebrides franc. New Hebrides, Vanatu.

Fomento Aero Comunicaciones   airmail tax stamp. Ecuador.

Fondul Aviatiei   postal tax for aviation. Romania.

Forces Française Libres - Levant   French military in Syria (World War II).

Forint   unit of currency. Hungary. Abbreviated **Ft**.

Franc(s)   unit of currency. France and French colonies, territories, and possessions, including many after independence. Also, Belgium, Belgian Congo, Danish West Indies, Liechtenstein, Malagasy, Monaco, Ruanda-Urundi, Switzerland. Abbreviated **F**, **f**, **F^{CS}**, or **Fr**.

Franca   an overprint on validating provisional issues. Peru.

France Libre or **France Libré**   Free France. Inscription on stamps issued in French areas not under German control during World War II.

Franco   official mail when used on stamps of Uruguay.

Franco Bollo di Stato   official mail. Italy.

Francobollo Postale per Giornali   newspaper stamp. Fiume.

Franco Marke   postage due. Bremen.

Franken   plural of **Franc**. Liechtenstein.

Franqueo Deficiente   postage due. Nicaragua, El Salvador.

Franqueo Deficiento   postage due. Ecuador.

Franqueo Oficial   official. Dominican Republic, Ecuador, Guatemala.

Franquicia Postal   franchise stamp. Spain.

Frei Durch Ablösung   official mail. With numeral "16," Baden; with numeral "21," Prussia.

Frimärke Lokabref.   city post local delivery. Sweden.

Fs   abbreviation for **Francs**.

Ft   abbreviation for **Forint**. Hungary.

G or **g**   abbreviation for currency: (1) **Giapik**, Azerbaijan; (2) **Gourde**, Haiti; (3) abbreviation for government, official stamps, Canada; (4) **Groschen**; (5) **Guarani**, Paraguay; (6) **Gulden**.

Gebyr   late fee. Denmark.

Gebyrmarke   late fee stamp. Denmark.

G.F.B.   abbreviation for "Gaue Faka Buleaga," or official mail. Tonga.

Giapik   subunit of the **Manat**. Azerbaijan. Abbreviated **g**.

Giornali Stampe   newspaper tax stamp. Italy, Sardinia.

Gld   abbreviation for **Gulden**.

Gobierno   official mail. Peru.

Gold Centime   subunit of the **Gold Franc**. New Hebrides.

Gold Franc   unit of currency. New Hebrides.

Gourde   unit of currency. Haiti. Abbreviated **G**.

Govt Parcels   overprinted on stamps of Great Britain: official mail.

Gr.   abbreviation for (1) **Grana**, Two Sicilies; (2) **Groschen**; (3) **Groszy**, Poland.

Grana   subunit of the **Ducat**. Two Sicilies. Abbreviated **G**, **Gr**, or **Gra**.

Groschen   subunit of the (1) **Schilling**, Austria; (2) **Thaler**, Brunswick, Germany, Hannover, North German Confederation, Saxony. Abbreviated **g** or **Gr**.

Grosz(e) or **Groszy**   subunit of the **Zloty**. Abbreviated **Gr**.

Grote   subunit of the silver groschen. Bremen.

Gs   abbreviation for **Guaranies**. Paraguay.

Guarani(es)   unit of currency. Paraguay. Abbreviated **G**, **Gs**, or **G**.

Guerche(s)   subunit of the (1) **Dollar**, Ethiopia; (2) Garch, Qirsh, **Riyal**, or Sovereign, Saudi Arabia and abbreviated **P**.

Gulden   unit of currency. Austria (nineteenth century), Danzig, Netherlands, and Netherlands colonies, territories, and possessions. Abbreviated **G** or **Gld**.

Gutegr.   abbreviation for **Gutegroschen**. Brunswick.

Gutegroschen   subunit of the **Thaler**. Brunswick, Hannover.

H or **h**   abbreviation for currency: (1) **Halalas**, Saudi Arabia; (2) **Halerzy**, Poland; (3) **Halierov**, Slovakia; (4) **Halérü**, Czechoslovakia.

Habilitado   validated. Overprint appearing on some stamps of Spanish-speaking countries, often in Central or South America.

hal abbreviation for **Halérü**. Czechoslovakia.

Halalas subunit of the **Riyal**. Saudi Arabia. Abbreviated **H**.

Halérü subunit of the **Koruna**. Czechoslovakia. Abbreviated **hal** or **h**.

Halerzy subunit of the **Korona**. Poland.

Halierov subunit of the **Koruna**. Slovakia. Abbreviated **h**.

HDR abbreviation for "Hrvatska dinar." Croatia.

Heller subunit of the **Krone**. Austria (early twentieth century), Bosnia and Herzegovina (early twentieth century), German East Africa (early twentieth century), Liechtenstein (until 1921).

Helyi levél overprinted on stamps of Hungary: local matter. Hungary.

Helyi lev.-lap. overprinted on stamps of Hungary: local postcard. Hungary.

Hirlap Belyec newspaper tax. Hungary.

Hirlapjecy newspaper stamp. Hungary.

Hivatalos official mail. Hungary.

Hl. abbreviation for "Helyi levél," overprinted, together with a numeral, on stamps of Hungary: local matter. Hungary.

Hlp. abbreviation for "Helyi lev.-lap.," overprinted, together with a numeral, on stamps of Hungary: local postcard. Hungary.

Hryvnia unit of currency. Ukraine.

Htado abbreviation for **Habilitado** or validated.

I abbreviation for **Inti**. Peru.

I/ or **I/m** abbreviation for **Inti**. Peru.

I.C.C. abbreviation for "International Control Commission." India military stamp.

Idrovolante hydroplane. Overprinted on some stamps for airmail service by hydroplane. Italy.

Í Gildi valid. Iceland.

Imadi unit of currency. Yemen.

Impresos newspaper stamp. Cuba, Philippines.

Imprime newspaper stamp. Turkey.

Imprimés newspaper stamp. Iran.

Imp^TO de Guerra war tax. Spain.

Impuesto a Encomiendas   parcel post. Uruguay.

Impuesto de Encomiendas   parcel post. Uruguay.

Impuesto de Guerra   war tax. Puerto Rico, Spain.

Impuesto Encomiendas   parcel post. Uruguay.

Inselpost   (island post) overprinted on feldpost (field post) stamps of Germany: Greek islands, including Crete, Leros, Milos, and various Dodecanese islands occupied by Germany during World War II.

Instrução D.L. n.° 7 de 3 2-1934   postal tax issue. Timor.

Insufficiently Paid - Postage Due   postage due. Zanzibar.

Inti   unit of currency. Peru. Abbreviated **I, I/**, or **I/m**.

I.R. Official   abbreviation for "Inland Revenue Official," overprinted on stamps of Great Britain: official mail.

Jornaes   newspaper stamp. Brazil, Portugal, and Portuguese colonies, territories, and possessions.

Journaux   newspaper stamps. France.

Journeaux Dagbladen   newspaper stamp. Belgium.

K or **k**   abbreviation for currency: (1) **Kina**, Papua New Guinea; (2) **Kip**, Laos; (3) **Kobo**, Nigeria; (4) **Kopeck**; (5) **Kopiyok**, Ukraine; (6) **Korona**, Hungary, Poland; (7) **Koruna**, Czechoslovakia, Slovakia; (8) **Kran**, Iran; (9) **Kuna**, Croatia; (10) **Makuta**, Zaire; (11) **Kwacha**, Macao, Malawi, Zambia; (12) **Kyat**, Burma.

Kan   subunit of the **Rubli**. Latvia.

Kap   abbreviation for **Kapeikas**.

Kapeikas   subunit of the **Rubli**. Latvia (until 1923). Abbreviated **Kap**.

Karbovanets   unit of currency. Ukraine. Abbreviated **K**.

Kč(s)   abbreviation for **Koruna**.

Kenttäpostia   military post. Finland.

Kenttä-Posti Fältpost   military post. Finland.

Kina   unit of currency. Papua New Guinea. Abbreviated **K**.

Kip   unit of currency. Laos. Abbreviated **K**.

Kizilay Cemiyetí   inscription on certain postal tax stamps. Turkey.

Kizilay Dernegí   inscription on certain postal tax stamps. Turkey.

Kn   abbreviation for **Kuna**. Croatia.

Kobo subunit of the **Naira**. Nigeria. Abbreviated **K**.

Kopeck(s) subunit of the (1) **Manat**, Turkmenistan; (2) **Ruble**, Russia and Russian-speaking areas or areas under or formerly under Russian influence, such as Azerbaijan, Belarus, Estonia, Moldova, Tannu Tuva, Turkmenistan, and Ukraine. Abbreviated **K** or **Cop**.

Kopiyok subunit of the **Hryvnia** or **Karbovanets**. Ukraine. Abbreviated **K**.

Koreo alternate spelling of **Correo**. Philippines.

Korona unit of currency. Hungary, Poland (1918–24). Abbreviated **K** or **Kr**.

Koruna unit of currency. Czechoslovakia, Slovakia. Plural, **Koruny**. Abbreviated **K**, **Kč(s)** or **korun**, Czechoslovakia; **Ks** or **Sk**, Slovakia.

Koruny plural of **Koruna**.

(K.P.) abbreviation for "Kagamitang Pampamahalaan" (official business): official mail. Philippines (Japanese occupation, World War II).

Kr abbreviation for currency: (1) **Korona**, Hungary, Poland; (2) **Kran**, Iran; (3) **Kreuzer**; (4) **Krone**; (5) **Kronor(i)**, Sweden; (6) **Kroon**, Estonia; (7) **Kurus**, Turkey.

Kran(s) unit of currency. Iran (nineteenth century). Abbreviated **K** or **Kr**.

Kreuzer subunit of the (1) **Gulden**, Austria-Hungary (nineteenth century), Baden, Bavaria, Bosnia and Herzegovina (during the Austro-Hungarian Empire), Germany, North German Confederation, Prussia, Thurn and Taxis, Württemberg; (2) **Forint**, Hungary (nineteenth century). Abbreviated **Kr**.

Krona unit of currency. Iceland (nineteenth century), Sweden (nineteenth century).

Krone unit of currency. Austria (early twentieth century), Bosnia and Herzegovina (early twentieth century), Denmark, Faroe Islands, Greenland, Iceland, Liechtenstein (until 1921), Norway. Abbreviated **Kr**.

Kronor(i) unit of currency. Sweden. Abbreviated **Kr**.

Kroon(i) unit of currency. Estonia. Abbreviated **Kr**.

Krs or **Krş** abbreviation for (1) **Kurus**, Turkey; (2) **Kurush**, Hatay.

Kruna unit of currency. Yugoslavia (Croatia-Slovenia, early twentieth century).

Ks abbreviation for **Koruna**. Slovakia.

K.u.K. Feldpost field post, military mail. Austrian territories (World War I).

K.u.K. Militärpost military mail. Bosnia and Herzegovina (World War I).

Kuna or **Kune** unit of currency. Croatia. Abbreviated **K** or **Kn**.

Kurus or **Kuruş** unit of currency. Turkey. Also, a subunit of the **Lira**. Turkey, Turkish Republic of Northern Cyprus. Abbreviated **Krs** or **Krş**.

Kurush   unit of currency. Hatay. Abbreviated **Krs**.

Kwacha   unit of currency. Malawi, Zambia. Abbreviated **K**.

Kwanza   unit of currency. Angola. Abbreviated **Kz**.

Kyat   unit of currency. Burma. Abbreviated **K**.

Kz   abbreviation for **Kwanza**.

L   abbreviation for currency: (1) **Laree**, Maldive Islands; (2) **Lei** or **Leu**, Romania, Moldova; (3) **Lempira**, Honduras; (4) **Lev**, Bulgaria; (5) **Lira**; (6) **Litai**, **Litas**, and **Litu**, Lithuania, Memel.

Land-Post Porto-Marke   postage due. Baden.

Laree(s)   subunit of the **Rifiyaa**. Maldives. Abbreviated **L**.

Le   abbreviation for **Leone**. Sierra Leone.

Legi Posta or **Legiposta**   airmail. Hungary.

Lei   unit of currency. Singular, **Leu**. Romania. Abbreviated **L**.

Lek   unit of currency. Albania. Also, **Lekë**.

Lempira   unit of currency. Honduras. Abbreviated **L**.

Leone   unit of currency. Sierra Leone (since 1964). Abbreviated **Le** or **LE**.

Lepta   subunit of the **Drachma**. Greece.

Leu   unit of currency. Plural, **Lei**. Romania, Moldova. Abbreviated **L**.

Lev   unit of currency. Bulgaria. Abbreviated **L** or **Lv**.

Lignes Aeriennes de la France Libre   French military forces in Syria (World War II).

Lignes Aeriennes - F.A.F.L.   French military forces in Syria (World War II).

Likuta or **Li-kuta**   unit of currency. Zaire.

Lipa - subunit of the **Kuna**. Croatia.

Lira or **Lire**   unit of currency: (1) Italy and Italian colonies, territories, and possessions, San Marino, Vatican City. Abbreviated **L**, **l**, or **Lre**. (2) Turkey and Turkish Republic of Northern Cyprus. Abbreviated **TL**.

Lisente(s)   subunit of the **Maloti**. Lesotho. Abbreviated **s**.

Litas   unit of currency. Lithuania, Memel. Plural **Litai** or **Litu**. Abbreviated **L** or **Lt**.

Livre   unit of currency (pound). Egypt. Abbreviated **L.E.**

L.L.   abbreviation for Lebanese pound.

Losen   postage due. Sweden.

Lotnicza   airmail. Poland.

Lt   abbreviation for **Litai**, **Litas** and **Litu**.

Luchpost   airmail. Belgium, Netherlands and Netherlands possessions.

Luftfeldpost   military airmail. Germany (World War II).

Luftpost   airmail. Austria, Germany, Denmark.

Lugpost   airmail. Southwest Africa.

Lweys   subunit of the **Kwanza**. Angola.

M or **m**   abbreviation for currency: (1) **Maloti**, Lesotho; (2) **Manat**, Azerbaijan; (3) **Mark**; (4) **Markka**, Central Lithuania, Finland; (5) **Markkaa**, Finland; (6) **Marka**, Estonia, Poland; (7) **Markes**, Memel; (8) **Mil**, Malta; (9) **Milliemes**.

M.A.   overprinted on stamps of Argentina: official mail, Ministry of Agriculture.

Mace   subunit of the **Tael**. China (nineteenth century).

Makuta or **Ma-kuta**   subunit of the **Zaire**. Democratic Republic of the Congo, Zaire. Abbreviated **K**.

Maloti   unit of currency. Lesotho (1979→). Abbreviated **M**.

Manat   unit of currency. Azerbaijan, Turkmenistan. Abbreviated **M** or **Man**.

Mar   abbreviation for **Markka**.

Mark   unit of currency. Germany, German states and German colonies, territories, and possessions, and areas under German influence such as Danzig, Saar.

Mark.   abbreviation for **Markes**. Memel.

Marka   unit of currency. Estonia, Poland. Abbreviated **M** or **Mk**.

Markes   unit of currency. Also, **Markių**. Memel. Abbreviated **M** or **Mark.**

Markių   unit of currency. Spelling variant of **Markes**. Memel.

Markka   unit of currency. Central Lithuania, Finland. Abbreviated **Mar**.

Markkaa   unit of currency. Finland. Also, **Markka**.

Mehalek   subunit of the **Talari**. Ethiopia (1928–36).

Mensajerias   special delivery. Uruguay.

Metical   unit of currency. Mozambique (1980s). Abbreviated **Mt**.

M.G.   overprinted on stamps of Argentina: official mail, Ministry of War.

M.H.   overprinted on stamps of Argentina: official mail, Ministry of Finance.

M.I.   overprinted on stamps of Argentina: official mail, Ministry of Interior.

Mil   subunit of the cent. Ten mils = one cent. Abbreviated **M**.

Mil(ls)   abbreviation for **Milliemes**.

Mil^A de E^O   abbreviation for "Milesima de Escudo." Spain.

Mil^A de Peso   abbreviation for "Milesima de Peso." Puerto Rico.

Milesima(s)   subunit of the (1) **Peseta**, Fernando Po; (2) **Peso**, Cuba.

Milesimo(s)   subunit of the **Peso**. Uruguay.

Milliemes   subunit of the (1) **Dinar**, Tunisia; (2) **Piastre**, Egypt, Jordan, Sudan, Syria; (3) **Pound**, Cyprus, Egypt, Libya. Abbreviated **M**, **Mil**, **Mils**, **Mills**, or **Mill^{MES}**.

Milreis   unit of currency. Brazil (until 1942), Portuguese colonies, territories, and possessions.

Mil^S de Esc or **Mil^S de Esc^S**   abbreviation for "Milesimas de Escudo." Spain.

Mil^S de Peso   abbreviation for "Milesimas de Peso." Puerto Rico.

M.J.I.   Ministry of Justice and Information. Overprinted on stamps of Argentina: official mail. Argentina.

Mk   abbreviation for (1) **Mark**; (2) **Marka**, Estonia, Poland.

M.M.   overprinted on stamps of Argentina: official mail, Ministry of Marine.

Mms   abbreviation for **Milliemes**. Sudan.

Mn   abbreviation for **Mon**.

Mon   subunit of the **Tempo**. Korea. Abbreviated **Mn**.

M.O.P.   overprinted on stamps of Argentina: official mail, Ministry of Public Works.

M.R.C   overprinted on stamps of Argentina: official mail, Ministry of Foreign Affairs and Religion.

Mt   abbreviation for **Metical**. Mozambique.

Muestra   specimen.

Multa or **Multas**   postage due. Portugal, Spanish-speaking countries of Central and South America, including Bolivia, Chile, Costa Rica, Dominican Republic, Ecuador.

Multada   postage due. Chile.

Mung   a subunit of the **Tugrik**. Mongolia.

₦   symbol for **Naira**. Nigeria.

n   abbreviation for (1) **Naira**, Nigeria; (2) **Ngwee**, Zambia.

N$ symbol for (1) dollar, Namibia; (2) revalued peso, Uruguay.

Nach Porto   postage due. Liechtenstein.

Naira   unit of currency. Nigeria. Abbreviated **N, ₦.**

Nakfa   unit of currency. Eritrea. Abbreviated **Nfa**.

Naye Paise   subunit of the **Rupee**. Ajman, Fujeira, India (1957–64), Qatar. Abbreviated **NP**.

NCz$ abbreviation for **New Cruzeiro**. Brazil.

Neu-Grosch.   abbreviation for **Neu Groschen**. Saxony.

New Cedi   unit of currency. Ghana.

New Pesewa   subunit of the **New Cedi**. Ghana. Abbreviated **NP**.

Nfa   abbreviation for **Nakfa**. Eritrea.

Ngultrum   unit of currency. Bhutan. Abbreviated **Nu**.

Ngwee   subunit of the **Kwacha**. Zambia. Abbreviated **N**.

Noviny   newspaper stamp. Czechoslovakia.

NP   abbreviation for **Naye Paise**. Abu Dhabi, Bahrain, Dubai, Fujeira, India, Kuwait, Qatar, Ras al Khaima, Sharjah, Trucial States, Umm al Qiwain.

NP   abbreviation for **New Pesewas**. Ghana.

Nu   abbreviation for **Ngultrum**. Bhutan.

Nyomtatv   overprinted, together with denomination, on stamps of Hungary: printed matter. Hungary.

NZ   abbreviation for **New Zaire**. Zaire.

O.B.   abbreviation for "Official Business." Philippines (U.S. administration).

Offentlig Sak   official mail. Norway. Abbreviated **Off. Sak.** or **O.S.**

Official Paid Mainland   official mail. Cocos (Keeling) Islands.

Official Service   official mail. Australia.

Officiel   (1) official mail; (2) overprinted on stamps of Iran: indicates that a surcharge was officially authorized (1880s).

Off. Sak.   abbreviation for "Offentlig Sak." Norway.

Oficial   official mail.

Oficiel   official mail. Chad. French-speaking countries.

Offisieel   official mail. South Africa, South West Africa.

O.H.E.M.S.   official mail. Egypt.

O.H.H.S.   abbreviation for "On His (Her) Highness's Service." Official mail. Egypt.

O.H.M.S.   abbreviation for "On His (Her) Majesty's Service." Official mail. Great Britain and some countries with British ties.

Ohupost   airmail. Estonia.

On C.G.S.   abbreviation for "On Cochin Government Service." Official mail. Cochin State (India).

On H.M.S.   abbreviation for "On His (Her) Majesty's Service." Official mail. India.

On Service   official mail. Ceylon.

On S.S.   abbreviation for "On State Service." Official mail. Travancore (India).

On S.S.S.   abbreviation for "On Sirmoor State Service." Official mail. Sirmoor State (India).

On State Service   official mail. Iraq (British occupation).

OPS   official mail. Guyana.

Øre   subunit of the **Krone**. Denmark, Faroe Islands, Greenland, Norway.

Öre   subunit of the **Krona** or **Riksdaler**. Sweden.

Oro Paštas   airmail. Lithuania.

O.S.   abbreviation for (1) **Offentlig Sak**, Norway; (2) **Official Service**, Australia.

O.S.G.S.   abbreviation for "On Sudan Government Service." Official mail. Sudan.

Ouguiya   unit of currency. Mauritania. Abbreviated **Um**.

O.W. Official   abbreviation for "Office of Works Official," overprinted on stamps of Great Britain: official mail.

P or p   abbreviation for currency: (1) **Paisa**; (2) **Paise**, India; (3) **Pengö**, Hungary; (4) **Penni**, Finland; (5) **Penny** or **Pence**, Great Britain, British colonies, territories, and possessions, after decimalization; (6) **Pesewa**, Ghana; (7) **Peso**; (8) **Pfennig**; (9) **Piaster** or **Piastre**; (10) **Pice**, Nepal; (11) **Poul**, Afghanistan; (12) **Pula**, Botswana; (13) **Pyas**, Burma; (14) **Ruble** (in Cyrillic).

Pa   abbreviation for **Para**.

Pa'anga   unit of currency. Tonga. Symbol **T$**.

Pacchi Postali   parcel post. Italy and areas under Italian influence.

Pahlavi   unit of currency. Iran.

Paisa(s)   subunit of the (1) **Rupee**, Bangladesh (from 1972), Pakistan (from 1951), Nepal (from 1958); (2) **Taka**, Bangladesh. Abbreviated **P** or **Ps**.

Paise   subunit of the **Rupee**. India. Abbreviated **P**.

Pakke-Porto   parcel post. Greenland.

Par   abbreviation for **Parale**. Romania.

Para   overprinted, together with surcharged value, (1) on stamps of France: France (offices in Turkey); (2) on stamps of Germany: Germany (offices in Turkey); (3) on stamps of Great Britain: Great Britain (offices in Turkey); (4) on stamps of Italy: Italy (offices in Turkey); (5) on stamps of Romania: Romania (offices in Turkey); (6) on stamps of Russia: Russia (offices in Turkey).

Para(s)   subunit of the (1) **Dinar**, Croatia, Serbia, Yugoslavia; (2) **Kurus**, Turkey; (3) **Piaster** or **Piastre**, many nations including Albania, Cilicia, Egypt, Syria, Turkey.

Parale   subunit of the **Piaster**. Romania.

Par Avion   airmail.

Pataca(s)   unit of currency. Macao, Timor. Abbreviated **Ptcs**.

Pen.   abbreviation for **Penni** or **Pennia**.

Pence   subunit of the **Shilling**. Plural of penny. Great Britain and British Commonwealth.

Pengö   unit of currency. Hungary (mid-1920s to mid-1940s). Abbreviated **P**.

Penni   subunit of the **Mark** or **Markka(a)**. Estonia (1920s), Finland, Karelia, North Ingermanland. Abbreviated **P** or **Pen**. Plural **Pennia**.

Pesa   subunit of the **Rupee**. German East Africa.

Peseta(s)   unit of currency: (1) Spain, Spanish colonies, territories, and possessions, Costa Rica (nineteenth century), Gibraltar (nineteenth century). Abbreviated **Ps**, **Pta**, **Pts**, or **Ptas**. (2) subunit of the **Peso**. Peru.

Pesetas   overprinted, together with numeral of surcharged value, on stamps of France: French Morocco.

Pesewa   subunit of the **Cedi**. Ghana. Abbreviated **P** or **p**.

Peso   unit of currency. Argentina, Chile, Colombia, Cuba, Ecuador, El Salvador, Fernando Po, Guinea-Bissau Honduras, Mexico, Nicaragua, Paraguay, Philippines (variant spelling, **piso**). Abbreviated **P** or **PG** (Guinea-Bissau). Also, symbols **$** (many countries) or **$a** (Argentina).

Pfennig(e) or **(s)**   subunit of the (1) **Gulden**, Danzig; (2) **Groschen**, Hannover, Prussia, Saxony; (3) **Mark**, Germany, German States, German colonies, territories, and possessions, including Danzig, Marienwerder, Saar, Upper Silesia. Abbreviated **p**.

PG   abbreviation for **Guinea-Bissau Peso**.

P.G.S.   abbreviation for "Perak Government Service." Official mail. Perak (Malaysia).

Piaster   overprinted, together with surcharged value, (1) or inscribed on stamps of Austria: Austria (offices abroad, Turkey); (2) on stamps of Germany: Germany (offices abroad, Turkey).

Piaster(s)   unit of currency. Cambodia (1950s), Romania (nineteenth century). Variant spelling of **Piastre**.

Piastra   overprinted, together with surcharged value, on stamps of Italy: Italy (offices abroad, Crete, North Africa, and Turkey).

Piastre(s)   (1) unit of currency. Alaouites, Cyprus, Egypt, Haiti, Lebanon, Sudan, Syria, Turkey. Abbreviated **P**. (2) subunit of the **Pound**. Egypt, Syria. (3) subunit of the **Riyal**. Saudi Arabia.

Piastre(s)   overprinted, together with surcharged value, (1) on stamps of France: France (offices in the Turkish Empire); (2) on stamps of Great Britain: Great Britain (offices abroad, Turkey); (3) on stamps of Italy: Italy (offices abroad, Turkey); (4) on stamps of Russia: Russia (offices abroad, Turkey).

Pice   subunit of the **Anna** and **Rupee**. Nepal.

Pie(s)   subunit of the **Anna**. Burma, India, Pakistan.

Piso   unit of currency. Philippines.

Pjon. Frim.   official mail. Iceland.

Pjonusta or **Pjonustu**   official mail. Iceland.

Pjónustumerki   official mail. Iceland.

Pjonustu Post Frim   official mail. Iceland.

P.M.   Posta Militare. Military post. Italy.

Poçtu   postage, post. Azerbaijan.

Poctza   postage, post. Central Lithuania, Poland.

Poczta Lotnicza   airmail. Poland.

Poskilai   special delivery. Indonesia.

Pol   spelling variant of **Poul**. Afghanistan.

Polecona   inscription on official mail (registered mail).

Ponustu   official mail. Iceland.

Ponustu Frimerke   official mail. Iceland.

Poon   subunit of the **Cheun**. Korea.

Por Aviao   airmail. Angola.

Porteado   postage due. Portugal and Portuguese colonies, territories, and possessions.

Porteado a Receber postage due. Angola, Cape Verde, Macao, Mozambique, Portugal, Portuguese Guinea, Portuguese India.

Porte de Conduccion parcel post. Peru.

Porte de Mar carriage fee for dispatch by ship. Mexico.

Porte Franco (1) inscription on early stamps of Peru; (2) inscription on some franchise stamps of Portugal.

Porto or **Portó** postage due. Austria, Denmark, Hungary, Romania, Yugoslavia.

Portomærke postage due. Danish West Indies, Norway.

Porto Marka postage due. Croatia.

Portomarke postage due. Bosnia and Herzegovina during the Austro-Hungarian Empire.

Portzegel postage due. Netherlands.

Posseel (or **Posseël**) **Inkomste** postage and revenue (Afrikaans).

Posta Aerea airmail. Italy and Italian-speaking areas.

Posta Aeriana airmail. Romania.

Posta Aerieo airmail. Iran.

Posta Aerore airmail. Albania.

Posta(t) Ajrore airmail. Albania.

Posta Porto postage due. Moldova.

Postat Ekspres special delivery. Albania.

Postcolli parcel post. Belgium.

Posta Estensi newspaper stamp. Madeira.

Postage and Revenue inscription on some issues of Great Britain and areas under British influence.

Postal Charges postage due. Papua New Guinea.

Posta Pneumatica pneumatic post. Italy.

Postas le híoc postage due. Ireland.

Postat Ekspres special delivery. Albania.

Poste Aérienne airmail.

Poste Par Avion airmail. Syria.

Postes Oficiel official mail. Central African Republic.

Postfærge parcel post stamp. Denmark.

Postluchdienst   airmail. Belgian Congo.

Post Par Avion   airmail. Lebanon.

Postzegel   postage stamp. Inscription of some early stamps of the Netherlands.

Poul(s)   subunit of the **Afghani**. Afghanistan (from 1927). Spelling variants, **Pool**, **Puls**. Abbreviated **P** or **Pol**.

Poulususvoimat Kenttäpostia   military post. Finland.

Pound   unit of currency in many countries at various times, often with no direct connection to the British pound. Great Britain, Cyprus, Egypt, Ireland, Israel, Lebanon, Malta, Sudan, Syria.

Prensa   newspaper stamp. Uruguay.

P.R.G.   abbreviation for "People's Revolutionary Government." Grenada and Grenadines, official mail (1982).

Prima Valores Declarados   insured letter stamp. Dominican Republic.

Primer Vuelo   first flight.

Pro Desocupados   unemployment tax. Peru.

Provicional   provisional. Colombia.

Provisorio   overprint on stamps Portugal and its colonies (1892 to early 1900s).

Przesylka Urzedowa   official mail. Poland.

Ps   abbreviation for (1) **Paisa**; (2) **Pies**, Burma.

P.T.   abbreviation for **Piastres**.

Pta or **Ptas**   abbreviation for **Peseta**.

Ptcs   abbreviation for **Patacas**.

Pts   abbreviation for **Pesetas**.

Pula   a unit of currency. Botswana. Abbreviated **P**.

Puls   spelling variant of **Poul**.

Pya(s)   subunit of the **Kyat**. Burma (from 1953). Abbreviated **P**.

Q or **q**   abbreviation for currency: (1) **Qindar**, Albania; (2) **Quetzal**, Guatemala.

Qindar or **Qintar**   subunit of the **Lek** or **Franc**. Albania. Abbreviated **Q**, **Qd**, **Qind**, or **Qint**.

Qintar   see **Qindar**.

Quàn-Buu   on some military stamps of South Vietnam.

Quetzal   unit of currency. Guatemala. Abbreviated **Q**.

R abbreviation for "registered" or "recomendado," often on a registry label or rubber-stamped on cover.

R or r abbreviation for currency: (1) **Rand**; (2) **Rial**; (3) **Riel**; (4) **Rupee**, India, Nepal, Seychelles, Somaliland Protectorate.

Rafiyaa unit of currency. Maldive Islands. Abbreviated **Rp**.

Rand a unit of currency. Basutoland, Bechuanaland Protectorate, Botswana, South Africa, South West Africa, Swaziland. Abbreviated **R**.

Rappen subunit of the **Franc**. Liechtenstein, Switzerland (now obsolete). Abbreviated **Rp**.

Rbl abbreviation for (1) **Ruble**, Azerbaijan; (2) **Rublis**, Latvia.

R.B.S. Rigsbank Skilling. Denmark.

Re abbreviation for **Rial Saidi**. Plural. Oman.

Re or Ri subunit of the **Cheun**. Korea.

Real(es) (1) unit of currency and subunit of the **Peseta**, Spain; (2) subunit of the **Centavo**, El Salvador, Paraguay; (3) subunit of the **Peso**, often in the nineteenth century. Buenos Aires, Costa Rica, Ecuador, Guatemala, Honduras, Mexico, Peru, Uruguay, Venezuela; (4) subunit of the **Tanga**, Portuguese India. Abbreviated **Rl**.

Real(es) Plata subunit of the **Peso**, often in the nineteenth century. Cuba Dominican Republic, Philippines. Abbreviated **RL Plata** or **RL Pta**.

Recapito Autorizzato authorized delivery. Italy and Italian territories.

Recomendada or **recomendado** registered mail. Colombia.

Recouvrements Tax a Percevoir postage due. French Andorra.

Recouvrements Valeurs Impayées postage due. France, Monaco.

Regierungs Dienstsache official mail. Liechtenstein.

Registro registered mail. Antioquia (Colombia).

Reil unit of currency. Cambodia, Khmer Republic.

Reis or **Réis** subunit of the (1) **Milreis**, Brazil, Portugal, Portuguese colonies, territories, and possessions, including Angola, Angra, Azores, Cape Verde, Funchal, Horta, Inhambane, Lorenço Marques, Macao, Madeira, Mozambique, Mozambique Company, Ponta Delgada, Portuguese Congo, Portuguese Guinea, Portuguese India, Saint Thomas and Prince Islands, Timor, and Zambezia; (2) **Tanga**, Portuguese India. Abbreviated **Rs**.

Rejistro registered mail. Colombia.

Republica overprinted on stamps of the Portuguese monarchy after the inception of the republic in 1910 to indicate that they were issues of the republic. Portugal and Portuguese colonies (1910–20s).

Repülö Posta airmail. Hungary.

Résistance overprint, French military in Syria during World War II.

Resmî official mail. Turkey.

Resello revalidated.

Retardo late fee. Colombia, Panama.

Revalidado revalidated. Portugal.

Revalorizado revalued. Argentina.

Rf abbreviation for **Rifiyaa**.

R.H. Official overprinted on stamps of Great Britain: official mail ("Royal Household").

Ri abbreviation for **Rial**.

Rial(s) (1) subunit of the **Pahlavi** or **Toman**, Iran; (2) variant spelling of **Riyal**. Abbreviated **R, Rl, Ri**, or **Rls**.

Rial Saidi unit of currency. Oman (since 1970).

Riel unit of currency. Cambodia.

Rifiyaa unit of currency. Maldive Islands.

Rigsbank Skilling unit of currency. Denmark (nineteenth century). Abbreviated **R.B.S.**

Riksdaler Banco unit of currency. Sweden (until 1858).

Ringgit unit of currency. Malaysia. Abbreviated **RM**.

Riyal unit of currency. Dubai (since 1966), Qatar (since 1967), Saudi Arabia (since 1960), Umm al Qiwain (since 1967). Abbreviated **R** or **S.R.** (**Saudi Riyal**, Saudi Arabia).

Rl or **R^L** abbreviation for (1) **Rial**; (2) **Real**.

R^L Plata or **R^L Pta** abbreviation for **Real Plata**. Cuba, Dominican Republic, Philippines.

Rls abbreviation for **Riyals** or **Rials**.

RM abbreviation for (1) Reichsmark, Germany; (2) **Ringgit**, Malaysia.

Roupie(s) variant spelling of **Rupee**. French India. Abbreviated **Ro**.

Rp abbreviation for (1) **Rappen**, Liechtenstein; (2) **Rupia**, Portuguese India; (3) **Rupiah**, Indonesia.

Rpf abbreviation for Reichspfennig, (1) overprinted on stamps of Germany: Luxembourg; (2) overprinted on stamps of Danzig: Danzig.

R$ abbreviation for **Cruzeiro Real**. Brazil.

Rs abbreviation for (1) **Reis**; (2) **Rial Saidi** (singular), Oman.

Rub abbreviation for **Rublis**. Latvia.

Ruble unit of currency. Azerbaijan, Belarus, Russia, Tannu Tuva, Uzbekistan. Abbreviated **P** or **Rbl**.

Rublis unit of currency. Latvia. Plural, **Rubli**. Abbreviated **Rbl** or **Rub**.

Rupee(s) unit of currency, at one time or another, for many countries, especially in the Middle East, South Asia, and parts of Africa, including Abu Dhabi, Aden, Afghanistan, Ajman, Bahrain, Bangladesh, British Indian Ocean Territory, Burma, Ceylon, Dubai, East Africa and Uganda Protectorate, Fujeira, German East Africa, India, Iraq, Kuwait, Maldive Islands, Mauritius, Mesopotamia, Muscat, Nepal, Pakistan, Qatar, Ras al Khaima, Seychelles, Sharjah, Somaliland Protectorate, Somalia, Sri Lanka, Trucial States, Uganda, Umm al Qiwain, Zanzibar. Abbreviated **R**, **Re**, or **Rs**.

Rupia unit of currency. Portuguese India. Abbreviated **Rp**.

Rupiah unit of currency. Indonesia. Abbreviated **Rp**.

R.Y. abbreviation for **Riyal Yemen**. Yemen.

S or **s** abbreviation for currency: (1) **Cents**, Tokelau (early 1980s); (2) **Lisente**, Lesotho; (3) **Satang**, Thailand; (4) **Schilling**, German States; (5) **Sene**, Somoa; (6) **Sengi**, Democratic Republic of the Congo, Zaire; (7) **Seniti**, Tonga; (8) **Senti**, Estonia; (9) **Sentimo**, Philippines; (10) **Shilling**, Great Britain, British Commonwealth; (11) **Skilling**, Denmark, Iceland; (12) **Sol**, Peru; (13) **Syli**, Republic of Guinea.

S/. symbol for (1) **Shilling**; (2) **Sucre**, Ecuador.

Salung subunit of the **Tical**. Thailand.

Sant. abbreviation for (1) **Satang**, Thailand; (2) **Santim**, Hatay; (3) **Santimi**, Latvia.

Santim subunit of the **Kurush**. Hatay. Abbreviated **Sant**.

Santimi subunit of the **Lat**. Latvia. Abbreviated **Sant**.

Santimu spelling variation of **Santimi**.

Satang(s) subunit of the **Tical**. Thailand. Abbreviated **St.** or **Sant**.

Schilling(e) or **(s)** (1) unit of currency, Austria (1925 and later); (2) subunit of the **Mark**, Bergedorf, Hamburg, Lubeck, North German Confederation, Schleswig-Holstein; (3) subunit of the **Thaler**, Mecklenburg-Schwerin. Abbreviated **S**.

Scudo unit of currency. Romagna, Roman states.

S.D. abbreviation for "Sudan dinar." Sudan.

Seatiku subunit of the **Auksinas**. Lithuania (early 1920s).

Segnatassa postage due. Italy, Italian-speaking areas, San Marino, Vatican City.

Segnatasse postage due. Fiume, Italy, Italian-speaking areas.

Seguro Postal insured letter. Mexico, Panama.

Sen subunit of the (1) **Dollar**, Brunei, Malaya (variant of cents), Malaysia, West Irian; (2) **Rupiah**, Indonesia; (3) **Yen**, Japan, Ryukyus. Abbreviated **Sn**.

Sene subunit of the Samoan dollar (tala). Samoa. Abbreviated **S**.

Sengi subunit of the **Likuta**. Democratic Republic of the Congo, Zaire. Abbreviated **S**.

Seniti subunit of the **Pa'anga**. Tonga. Abbreviated **S**.

Senti subunit of the **Kroon**. Estonia. Abbreviated **S**.

Sentimo alternate spelling of centavo. Philippines. Abbreviated **S**.

Service official mail. British Commonwealth. Also, Indochina, Iran.

Service de L'Etat or **Service de LEtat** official mail. Egypt.

Service Postal Aerien airmail. Belgian Congo, Morocco.

Servicio Aereo airmail. Ecuador, Honduras.

Serviço Aereo airmail. Brazil.

Servicio Aereo Exterior international airmail. Honduras.

Servicio Aereo Interior domestic airmail. Guatemala.

Servicio Aereo Internacional international airmail. Honduras.

Servicio del Estado official mail. Chile.

Servicio Oficial official mail. Argentina.

Servicio Ordinario surface mail (as opposed to airmail). Nicaragua.

Servicio Postal Aereo airmail. Colombia, Guatemala, Uruguay.

Servizio di Stato official mail. Italy and Italian colonies.

S F abbreviation for "Soldater Freimaerke" or soldier's mail. Denmark.

S.G. abbreviation for "Sudan Government." Official mail. Sudan.

Sgr.   abbreviation for **Silbergroschen**. German states.

sh   abbreviation for **Shilling**. Uganda.

Shekel   unit of currency. Israel. Subdivided into **Agorot**.

Shilling   subunit of the **Pound**. Great Britain and British Commonwealth, primarily prior to decimalization. Abbreviated **S** or **Sh**. Symbol **/**.

Sh. So.   abbreviation for **Somali Shilling**.

Silberg.   abbreviation for **Silbergroschen**. Prussia.

Silbergroschen   unit of currency, the silver groschen. Bremen, Brunswick, Hannover, Mecklenburg-Strelitz, Oldenburg, Prussia, Schleswig-Holstein, Thurn and Taxis. Also Luxembourg. Abbreviated **Sgr.** or **Silb. Gr.**

Silb. Gr.   abbreviation for **Silbergroschen**. German states.

Silb Grosch   abbreviation for **Silbergroschen**. Thurn and Taxis (northern district).

Sk   abbreviation for (1) **Koruna**, Slovakia; (2) **Skatiku**, Lithuania.

Skatiku   subunit of the **Auksinas**. Lithuania. Abbreviated **Sk**.

Skilling   (1) unit of currency, Denmark, Iceland; (2) subunit of the **specie daler**, Norway. Abbreviated **S** or **Skill**.

Skilling Banco   subunit of the **Riksdaler Banco**. Sweden. Abbreviated **Skill B**^{CO}.

Skilling B^{CO}.   abbreviation for **Skilling Banco**. Sweden.

Sl   abbreviation for **Sol**.

Sn   abbreviation for **Sen**.

So.   abbreviation for **Somalo**.

Sobre Clota Para Multos Postales   parcel post. Mexico.

Sobreporte   postage due. Colombia.

Sobreporte Aereo   airmail fee. Colombia.

Sobretasa Aerea   airmail fee. Colombia.

Sobretasa Obligatoria   postal tax. Spanish Morocco.

Sociedade de Geographia de Lisboa   Geographic Society of Lisbon. Portugal. Inscription on franchise stamps used by the organization.

Sociedade Portugueza da Cruz Vermehla   Red Cross Society of Portugal. Inscription on franchise stamps used by the organization.

S. Oficial   abbreviation for "Servicio Oficial." Argentina.

Sol(es)   unit of currency. Peru. Abbreviated **S**, **Sl**, or **S/**.

Soldi   subunit of the (1) **Florin**, Italy, Lombardy-Venetia; (2) **Lira**, Tuscany.

Som   unit of currency. Kyrgyzstan. Abbreviated **C.**

Somali Shilling   unit of currency. Somalia. Abbreviated **Sh. So.**

Somalo   unit of currency. Somalia. Abbreviated **So.**

S.P.   abbreviation for "Service Publique." Official mail. Luxembourg, Zaire.

Spoorwegen   parcel post. Belgium.

S.R.   abbreviation for **Saudi Riyal.**

St   abbreviation for (1) **Satang**, Thailand; (2) **Stotinka** or **Stotinki**, Bulgaria.

staatsmarke   official mail. Württemberg.

Steuermarke - 2 Berlin   postal tax stamp. Germany.

Stotinka   subunit of the **Lev**. Plural, **Stotinki**. Bulgaria. Abbreviated **St, Cm, Ct,** or **Ctot.**

Sucre(s)   unit of currency. Ecuador. Symbols **S/.** or **$.**

Sum   unit of currency. Uzbekistan.

Sürgös   special delivery. Hungary.

Su Vu   official mail. Vietnam.

Sy   abbreviation for **Syli.** Republic of Guinea.

Syli   unit of currency. Republic of Guinea. Abbreviated **S** or **Sy.**

T or t   abbreviation for currency: (1) **Tambala**, Macao, Malawi; (2) **Tanga**, Portuguese India; (3) **Theba**, Botswana; (4) **Tiyin**, Uzbekistan; (5) **Toea**, Papua New Guinea; (6) **Tyiyn**, Kyrgyzstan.

T$ abbreviation for **Pa'anga.** Tonga.

Tael   unit of currency. China (nineteenth century).

Taka   unit of currency. Bangladesh.

Takca   postage due. Bulgaria.

Taksë   postage due. Albania.

Takse Pulu   postage due. Hatay, Turkey.

Tala   unit of currency. Samoa.

Talari (or **Thaler**)   unit of currency. Ethiopia.

Tambala(s)   subunit of the **Kwacha**. Macao, Malawi. Abbreviated **T.**

Tanga(s)   subunit of the **Rupia**. Portuguese India. Abbreviated **T** or **Tgs.**

Tasa   postage due. Uruguay.

Tasa Por Cobrar   postage due. Cuba.

Tassa Gazzette   newspaper tax stamp. Modena.

Távolsági levél   overprinted on stamps of Hungary: domestic letter. Hungary.

Távolsági lev.-lap.   overprinted on stamps of Hungary: domestic postcard. Hungary.

Taxa de Factagiu   parcel post. Romania.

Taxa de Guerra   war tax. Macao, Portugal, Portuguese Africa, Portuguese India.

Taxa de Plata   postage due. Romania.

Taxa Devida   postage due. Brazil.

Taxa Recibida   airmail (fee for airmail service). Mozambique.

Taxe   postage due. Albania, Luxembourg.

Taxe a Percevoir   postage due. Algeria, France.

Taxe Perçue   airmail (fee for airmail service). Mozambique.

Taxxa Postali   postage due. Malta.

Tcl   abbreviation for **Tical**.

Te Betaal   postage due. South Africa.

Te Betalen   postage due. Belgium, Netherlands.

Te Betalen Port   postage due. Netherlands and Netherlands colonies, territories, and possessions.

Tempo   unit of currency. Korea.

Thaler   unit of currency in German-speaking areas (mostly nineteenth century) including, Brunswick, Hannover, Mecklenburg-Strelitz, North German Confederation, Oldenburg, Saxony, and Thurn and Taxis. Also, Ethiopia (from 1936). Variant spellings include "daler" and "taler." It is also the root word for "dollar."

Theba   a subunit of the **Pula**. Botswana. Abbreviated **T**.

Thieu Cuoc   postage due. Vietnam.

Tical   unit of currency. Thailand. Abbreviated **Tcl**.

Timbre - Colis Postaux   parcel post. Indochina.

Timbre Complementario   postage due. Mexico.

Timbre Fiscal   revenue stamp.

Timbre Taxe   postage due. France, French colonies, territories, and possessions, and French-speaking countries.

Timbru de Ajutor   inscription on postal tax stamps and on postal tax due stamps. Romania.

Timbrul de Aviatiei   postal tax for aviation. Inscription on postal tax stamps and on postal tax due stamps for aviation. Romania.

Timbru Oficial   official mail. Romania.

Tiyin   subunit of the **Sum**. Uzbekistan.

Tjänste Frimärke   official mail. Sweden.

Tjeneste Frimærke   official mail. Denmark.

Tjenste Frimärke   official mail. Sweden.

Tjenestefrimerke   official mail. Norway.

TL   abbreviation for "Turkish Lira."

Tl.   abbreviation for "Távolsági levél," overprinted, together with a numeral, on stamps of Hungary: domestic letter. Hungary.

Tlp.   abbreviation for "Távolsági lev.-lap.," overprinted, together with a numeral, on stamps of Hungary: domestic postcard. Hungary.

Toea   subunit of the **Kina**. Papua New Guinea. Abbreviated **T**.

Toman   unit of currency. Iran (nineteenth century).

To Pay   postage due. Great Britain and British Commonwealth nations.

Tornese   subunit of the **Grana**. Two Sicilies.

Transporto Pacchi in Concessione   parcel post, private delivery. Italy.

T.Ta.C.   airmail postal tax. Turkey.

Tug   abbreviation for **Tugrik**.

Tugrik   unit of currency. Mongolia. Abbreviated **Tug**.

Tyiyn   subunit of the **Som**. Kyrgyzstan. Abbreviated **T**.

Uçak   airmail. Turkey.

Ultramar Portugués   overseas province. Portugal.

Um   abbreviation for **Ouguiya**. Mauritania.

UNEF   abbreviation for "United Nations Emergency Force." Overprinted on stamps of India for use in Gaza. India.

U.N. Force   abbreviation for "United Nations" Force. Overprinted on stamps of India for use in the Congo. India.

Uniao Dos Atiradores Civis   Civilian rifle clubs. Portugal. Inscription on franchise stamps used by the organizations.

Urgente   special delivery. Colombia, on department (state) stamps. Spain.

Valor   value. Colombia.

Venezolano   unit of currency. Venezuela.

Vom Empfänger Einzuziehen   postage due. Danzig.

Vom Empfänger Zahlbar   postage due. Bavaria.

Voor Het Kind   for the children. Inscription on some semipostal stamps of the Netherlands.

V.R.   abbreviation for "Victoria Regina" (Queen Victoria).

War   war tax stamp. British Honduras, World War I.

War Stamp   war tax stamp. British Commonwealth countries, most often during World War I.

War Tax   war tax stamp. British Commonwealth countries, most often during World War I and occasionally, World War II.

Weihnachten 1944   overprinted on stamps of Rhodes: German occupation of Rhodes, World War II.

Weun   spelling variant of **Won**. Korea.

Winterhilf   winter relief. Germany.

Winterhilfe   winter relief. Austria.

Winterhilfswerk   winter relief. General Government (German occupation of Poland in World War II).

Wir Sind Frei   We Are Free. Czechoslovakia (1938). An ironic overprint on Czech stamps at the time the Nazis arrived.

Wn   abbreviation for **Won**.

Won   unit of currency. Korea. Abbreviated **Wn** or **Ws**.

Ws   abbreviation for **Won**.

Xu   subunit of the **Dong**. Vietnam.

Yen   unit of currency. Japan, Ryukyus. Symbol ¥.

YKp H.P. (or **Peu.**)   overprinted on stamps of Austria. Western Ukraine.

Yuan   unit of currency. China, Manchukuo.

Z   abbreviation for the **Zaire**.

Zł   abbreviation for **Zloty**.

Zaire   unit of currency. Congo Democratic Republic, Zaire. Abbreviated **Z**, **NZ** for **New Zaire**.

Zeitungs Marke   newspaper stamp. Austria, Germany.

Zeitungs Stampel (or **Stempel** or **Stæmpel**)   newspaper tax stamp. Austria.

Zentraler Kurierdienst   official stamp. German Democratic Republic.

Zloty   unit of currency. Poland. Abbreviated **Zł**.

Zracna Posta   airmail. Yugoslavia.

Zulassungsmarke   military parcel post. Germany (World War II).

Zurno   special delivery. Croatia-Slovenia (Yugoslavia).

Zwyczajna   official mail. Poland.

Zwykła   official mail. Poland.

SYMBOL INSCRIPTIONS

¢   symbol for **cents**, **centavos**, preceding the numeral, abbreviation for **New Cedi**. Ghana.

£   symbol for **Pound**.

£M   abbreviation for **Pound**. Malta.

$ symbol for the **Dollar** and many other currencies such as the **Dong**, **Escudo**, **Peso**, and **Sucre**. It often appears together with the initial of the currency, either preceding it or following it.

$a   New Peso, Argentina (1983).

$b and **B$**   symbol for **Boliviano**.

/   symbol for **Shilling**, such as 3/6 or three shillings, six pence.

CYRILLIC ALPHABET INSCRIPTIONS

КОП   abbreviation for **Kopeck**.

РУБ   abbreviation for **Ruble**.

РУБЛЕЙ   **Ruble**.

ПАРЕ   **Para**.

ДОПЛАТА   postage due. Russia.

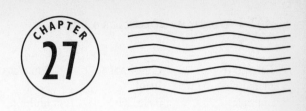

FOREIGN VOCABULARY — PHILATELIC TERMS

ENGLISH	GERMAN	FRENCH	SPANISH
airmail	Flugpost	poste aerienne	correo aereo
bar	Balken	barre	barra
block	Block	bloc	bloque
block of four	Viererblock	bloc de quatre	bloque de cuarto
booklet	Heftchen	carnet	cuadernillo
bottom	Unten	bas	abajo
canceled	entwertet	oblitere	usado, matasellado
cancellation	Abstempelung	obliteration	matasello
coil	Markenrolle	rouleau de timbres	rollo de sellos
color	Farbe	couleur	color
color shade	Farbton	nuance	variacion de color
common	gewonlich	commun	comun
condition	Erhaltung	condition	estado (de conserv.)
cover	Briefumschlag	envelope	sobre
dash	Strich	trait	linea
definitive	Endgultig	definitif	definitivo
design	Zeichnung	dessin	diseno
error	Fehler	erreur	error
essay	Probedruck	essais	ensayo
expertized	gepruft	expertise	expertizado
fake	Falschung	faux	falsificacion
faulty	Mangelhaft	defautueux	defectuoso
genuine	echt	authentique	autentico
gravure	Rastertiefdruck	heliogravure	huecograbado
gum	Gummi	gomme	goma
hinge	Falz	charniere	fijasello
horizontal	liegand	couche	acostado
imperforate	ungezahnt	non dentele	sin dental
intaglio	Stichtiefdruck	grave	grabado
inverted	kopfstehend	renverse	invertido
left	links	gauche	izquierda
letterpress	Buchdruck	typographie	tipografia

ENGLISH	GERMAN	FRENCH	SPANISH
margin	Rand	bord	carta
multiple	mehrfach	multiple	multiple
not regularly issued	nicht ausgege	ben non emis	no emitto
number	Nummer	numero	numero
numeral	Ziffer	chiffre	cifra
official	Dienstmarke	timbre de service	sello de servicio
offset lithography	Steindruck, Offsetdruck	lithographie	litografia
overprint	Aufdruck	surcharge	sobrecarga
pair	Paar	paire	pareja
perforated	gezahnt	dentele	dentado
photogravure	Rastertiefdruck	heliogravure	huecograbado
postage due	Portomarke	timbre taxe	sello de tasa
postmark	Poststempel	cachet postale	matasello
price	Preis	prix	precio
proof	Probe	epreuve	prueba
rare	selten	rare	raro
reprint	Neudruck	reimpression	reimpresion
reverse	Ruckseite	verso	reverso
set	Satz	serie	serie
se-tenant	zusammendruck	se tenant	combinacion
sheet	Bogen	feuille	hoja
souvenir sheet	Kleinbogen	bloc-feuillet	hoja bloca
special delivery	Eilmarke	expres	urgente
strip	Streifen	bande	tira
strip of three	Dreierstreifen	bande de quatre	tira de tres
tete-beche	Kehrdruck	tete-beche	capicua
thick	dick	epais	grueso
thin	dunn	mince	delgado
top	Oben	haut	arriba
type	type	type	tipo
unused	ungebraucht	neuf	nuevo
used	gebraucht	oblitere	usado, matasellado
variety	Abart	variete	variedad
vertical	hochstehend	vertical	vertical
watermark	Wasserzeichen	filigrane	filigrana
without	ohne	sans	sin
without gum	ohne Gummi	san gomme	sin goma

FOREIGN VOCABULARY — COLORS

ENGLISH	GERMAN	FRENCH	SPANISH
bistre	gelbraun	bistre	sepia
black	schwarz	noir	negro
blue	blau	bleu	azul
bright	lebhaft	vif	vivo
brown	braun	brun	castano
buff	samisch	chamois	anteado
carmine	karmin	carmin	carmin
chocolate	schokoladen	chocolat	chocolate
claret	weinrot	lie de vin	rojo vinoso
dark	dunkel	fonce	oscuro
deep	tief	fonce	subido
dull	trub	terne	color apagado
flesh	fleischfarben	chair	carne
gray	grau	gris	gris
green	grun	vert	verde
indigo	indigo	indigo	azul indigo
lake	lackfarbe	lie de vin	laca
light	hell	clair	claro
lilac	lila	lilas	lila
magenta	magentarot	magenta	magenta
multicolored	mehrfarbig	polychrome	multicolores
ochre	ocker	ocre	ocre
olive	oliv	olive	aceintuna
orange	orange	orange	naranja
pale	blass	pale	palido
pink	rosa	rose	rosa
Prussian blue	preussisch blau	bleu de Presse	azul de Prusia
purple	purpur	pourpre	purpura
red	rot	rouge	rojo
rose	rosa	rose	rosa
scarlet	scharlach	ecarlate	escarlata
ultramarine	ultramarin	outremer	ultramar

ENGLISH	GERMAN	FRENCH	SPANISH
vermilion	zinnober	vermillon	bermellon
violet	violett	violet	violetta
white	weiss	blanc	blanco
yellow	gelb	juane	Amarillo

GLOSSARY OF
PHILATELIC TERMS

AAMS   abbreviation for American Air Mail Society.

accountable mail   mail that requires the signature of the addressee or addressee's agent upon receipt to provide proof of delivery or indemnification for loss or damage. Accountable mail includes registered mail, certified mail, insured mail, and so forth.

accountable materials   certain items possessing monetary value, such as stamps, postal stationery, money order forms, international reply coupons, and so forth.

additional entry office   a post office other than the office of original entry where a publisher is authorized to mail periodicals.

add-on   a cachet, usually hand painted, added to a first day cover not originally serviced by the artist, and often years after the cover was originally serviced.

addressed   a first day cover that contains an address as opposed to one that does not, which is referred to as *unaddressed*.

addressee   the person or entity to whom a piece of mail addressed.

à découvert   a Universal Postal Union term for open transit mail (mail that crosses U.S. borders while en route from one foreign country to another) that is in unsealed containers.

adherence   any unwanted bit of paper or other material that adheres to the gum of a mint stamp. An adherence often results from a stuck-down stamp being pulled up and taking a bit of album paper with it.

adhesive   (1) the guhm used to attach a stamp to mail. Traditional adhesives required moistening and are often referred to as *lick-and-stick*, although the technical term is *water-activated*. Self-adhesives do not require moistening. They are often called *self-stick* stamps; (2) a synonym for any stamp that can be affixed by means of adhesive to an envelope, card, or other item.

advertised letter   a letter (typically in the nineteenth century), which when after a period of time remains unclaimed at a post office, was advertised in the local newspaper, usually in a special section for such notices. Such mail was marked "advertised" at the time the notice was placed.

advertising collar   advertising printed in the form of a frame or "collar" and positioned in the upper-right corner of a cover so that, when affixed, a postage stamp would occupy the center space and be surrounded by the advertisement.

advertising cover   a cover containing a printed advertisement, especially those created during the nineteenth and early twentieth centuries.

aerogramme   (also aerogram or airmail lettersheet) a lightweight type of postal stationery, letter sized with gummed flaps that can be folded and sealed for mailing, and often imprinted with an indicia to evidence the prepayment of postage. Aerogrammes are intended primarily for international airmail correspondence.

aerophilately   the collecting of airmail stamps, covers, and related items.

AFDCS   abbreviation for American First Day Cover Society.

affixing machine   a mechanical device used for affixing stamps to covers or cards. Early affixing machines were handheld and operated and were used to facilitate mailings of statements and advertisements; later, most models were powered and capable of high-speed performance, affixing thousands of stamps per hour to mass mailings. Clipped perforations are a telltale sign of machine-affixed stamps.

agency   **(1)** a private firm that acts as an official representative for a foreign postal administration, usually for the purpose of selling postage stamps, often at face value, to collectors; **(2)** a post office operated abroad, such as the U.S. Postal Agency in China during the early part of the twentieth century.

airmail   **(1)** a stamp issued or intended primarily for use on airmail, although in the United States, airmail stamps can be used on any class of mail; **(2)** mail carried by air.

albino   a printed impression that lacks ink, usually occurring on a stamped envelope, and the result of the inked portion of the design failing to print, leaving only an impression of the uncolored embossed portion of the design. Also a postage stamp from which all ink has been omitted during printing.

album   a book in which a collection of stamps or covers is housed.

album weeds   nongenuine stamps, such as fakes, forgeries, reproductions, and so on.

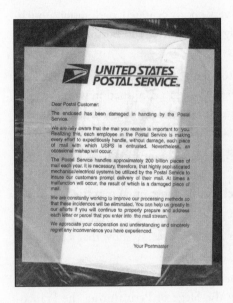

ambulance bag   a bag, most often made of plastic, used to contain and forward an individual piece of mail damaged in transit, in modern times most often by postal machinery.

ancillary service endorsement a marking used to request the new address of an addressee and to provide the Postal Service with instructions on how to handle mail that is undeliverable as addressed.

aniline ink   inks containing pigment derived from coal tar. Aniline inks are water soluble and were, for a time, used to print some stamps of the British Commonwealth.

APEX   abbreviation for American Philatelic Expertizing Service.

APO   abbreviation for Army Post Office.

approvals   selections of stamps sent by mail, usually consisting of inexpensive singles or sets for the beginning or general collector. The collector purchases those that he likes and returns the balance.

APS   abbreviation for American Philatelic Society.

arrow block   a block of stamps on whose selvage appears an arrowlike marking whose purpose is to aid in plate registration or to guide cutting or perforating equipment.

ASDA   abbreviation for American Stamp Dealers Association.

ATA   abbreviation for American Topical Association.

automation-compatible mail   mail that can be scanned and processed by automated mail-processing equipment such as a bar-code sorter.

automation discount   a postage reduction offered to mailers who bar-code their mailpieces and meet addressing, readability, and other requirements for processing on automated equipment.

auxiliary marking   a mark placed on a cover explaining why it was handled in a certain way (e.g., "Return to Sender," "Postage Due," and the like).

average   the lowest grade of condition; very poorly centered, perforations touching or cutting into the design, visually unattractive, the bottom end of the condition spectrum.

Baby Zeppelin   (or Baby Zepp) nickname for the U.S. 50¢ Zeppelin of 1933 issued in conjunction with the Chicago World's Fair, in the sense of it being a junior sibling to the U.S. Zeppelin set of three first issued in 1930.

back of the book   (abbreviated B-O-B) includes stamps such as postage dues, special deliveries, parcel posts, officials, revenues, and so forth; anything listed in the rear of the catalogue following definitives and commemoratives.

backstamp   a postmark placed on the reverse of a cover to indicate its arrival date or time at a receiving post office, or in some cases, to show that a piece was dispatched or missent.

Ballon Monte   mail carried by manned balloon, but in the philatelic sense, usually referring to mail carried during the Siege of Paris during the Franco-Prussian War (1870–71).

bank mixture   mixture of stamps on paper, so called because it traditionally originated from bank correspondence. Bank mixtures are regarded as premium mixtures because they contain a large number of high denomination and seldom encountered stamps.

banknotes   (or bank notes) U.S. definitive stamps issued between 1870 and 1894, so called because they were, in their turn, printed by various private banknote companies, including the National Bank Note Company, Continental Bank Note Company, and the American Bank Note Company.

bar code   a series of vertical bars and spaces that represent a series of number such as a ZIP code on the address of a piece of mail. The bar code enables the address to be read by automated-processing equipment.

bargain box   a box containing inexpensive covers. When breaking down collections, dealers put covers they perceive to be of minimal value in boxes not unlike shoe boxes. The price of the cover is usually penciled in on the back. Prices for individual covers in bargain boxes typically range from 10¢ to a few dollars.

bar tagging   luminescent tagging applied in the form of a rectangle either to a stamp or to postal stationery. In some cases, the bar of tagging is applied to postal stationery to one side of the imprinted indicia for postage rather than atop it.

beaver   a nickname for Canada's first stamp, whose vignette featured a beaver.

BEP   abbreviation for Bureau of Engraving and Printing.

BIA   abbreviation for Bureau Issues Association, now the United States Stamp Society.

bicolor   (or bicolored) a stamp printed in two colors.

bisect   a stamp cut in half (often diagonally) and used as one-half the face value of the uncut stamp.

Bishop mark   a marking devised by Henry Bishop in England in the 1660s that contained the day and month of mailing, and generally regarded as the forerunner of the modern postmark. Bishop created the mark to discourage mail carriers from delaying the transmission of items entrusted to their care.

Black Jack   a nickname for the 2¢ stamp of 1863, which featured a portrait of Andrew Jackson printed in black.

black print   the high-quality impression of a stamp, printed in black, of the type made by the Austrian Postal Service for distribution with press releases for new stamps.

blind perforations   lightly impressed perforations that often give stamps the appearance of being imperforate. Stamps with blind perforations are not considered to be imperforate errors. Some modern perforations are ground into paper rather than punched. The term "blind perforations" also applies to stamps with incomplete perforations due to a problem during the grinding process. The term is also used in connection with incompletely impressed die cuts, which occasionally occur on self-adhesive stamps.

block four or more unseparated stamps arranged in a rectangle. Unless described otherwise, the term is understood to mean a block of four.

block tagging tagging applied to cover only the printed design of the stamp rather than the entire area of the stamp.

blue paper (or bluish paper) refers to U.S. stamps of the Washington-Franklin issue and the Lincoln Memorial issue printed on experimental paper, which because of its high rag content, possessed a faint bluish or grayish cast in comparison to the white paper normally used.

BNA abbreviation for British North America.

boardwalk margins abnormally oversized margins, which by virtue of their aesthetic appeal and scarcity are highly prized by collectors. Also known as **jumbo margins**.

B-O-B abbreviation for **back of the book**.

bogus items that are intended to resemble stamps or pass for stamps, including imitations, unauthorized issues, emissions from fictional places, and so forth, but that are not real stamps.

booklet pane a small sheetlet of stamps bound between card stock covers by staples, thread, or glue. Also, modern self-adhesive stamps sold in small panes that can be folded for carrying in a purse or wallet.

booklet stamp a stamp from a booklet pane. Booklet stamps often, but not always, have one or more straight-edged sides.

bourse a show or portion of a show in which dealers offer their wares from booths or tables to the stamp-collecting public. Bourses are often held in conjunction with stamp shows or exhibitions.

boxed postmark a postmark in which the name of the mailing office and date are contained in a rectangle or box rather than a circular device.

BPA   abbreviation for British Philatelic Association.

branch   a substation of a main post office, usually in a city but sometimes a rural station of a nearby post office.

bridge   the narrow band of paper lying between perforation holes and connecting unseparated stamps.

broken set   a set of stamps missing some values; an incomplete set.

bulkie   an informal postal term for a regular-size envelope that contains an object making the mailpiece nonmachinable (such as a pen, film roll, or thermometer).

bulk mail   mail qualifying for reduced rates by having been sorted in ZIP code sequence and bundled for routing by the mailer for dispatch directly to certain types of destinations, such as state, city, section, or even individual carrier route. Bulk mail is also known as *junk mail*, because it is used heavily by mailers sending unsolicited advertisements and offers.

bulk rate   the postage rate available for mail that is part of a large volume mailing and that meets volume and preparation requirements.

bull's-eye   nickname for the first issues of Brazil.

bull's-eye cancel   (or bullseye cancel) a cancellation, usually a circular date stamp, struck squarely on the center of the stamp; also known as *socked on the nose*.

Bureau of Engraving and Printing   (abbreviated BEP) a branch of the U.S. Treasury established in 1862 to print government securities including currency and postage stamps.

bureau precancel   (or bureau print) a precancel whose overprint was applied at the Bureau of Engraving and Printing. Precancels not prepared at the BEP are known as *local precancels*. See also **local precancel**.

burelage   a faint background network printed on some stamps as a security measure.

business reply mail   mail from customers on which postage and fees are paid by the business to whom it is sent. Postage is collected only on the pieces actually returned.

business strike   an ordinary, everyday postmark as opposed to a philatelic postmark such as a first day cancellation or event cancellation.

BWI   abbreviation for British West Indies.

bypass mail   a postal term for metered mail, permit imprint mail, and official mail that does not require preparation, such as canceling, before outgoing distribution.

CA   (**Crown Agents**) a watermark appearing on some issues of the British area that were produced by the **Crown Agents**.

cachet   (pronounced "ka-SHAY") a decorative illustration on a cover, usually on the left side and most often in connection with the first day of issue of a new stamp or some other special event. Cachets have been applied by a variety of means, including printing, rubber stamping, hand painting, laser or ink-jet printing, and pasted illustration.

cage   a postal term for a secure, enclosed area in a post office, where registered mail and other accountable mail is kept.

calendared paper   paper possessing a smooth finish, not unlike that found in slick magazines.

cancel   (or cancellation) an obliterating mark applied to a stamp rendering it invalid for future use. Cancellations may be applied by handstamp, machine, or pen. See also **postmark**.

canceled to order   (abbreviated CTO) a term used to describe the bulk cancellation (typically applied to full sheets by printing press but in some cases by canceling equipment) of sheets of mint stamps, which are then usually sold at a discount from face value packet makers, approval dealers, and the like. Canceled-to-order stamps do not see postal duty. The U.S. Postal Service does not sell CTOs. Some foreign postal administrations do. CTOs most often appear in inexpensive mixtures, packets, and approvals. CTOs are generally easy to spot. A neatly applied, nonobliterative, printed cancel on a stamp with full original gum is a dead giveaway. Note the exact, identical wording and placement of cancellations in the illustration.

carrier route   the addresses to which a carrier delivers mail. In common usage, carrier route includes city routes, rural routes, highway contract routes, post office box sections, and general delivery units.

carrier stamp in the mid-nineteenth century, regular U.S. postage stamps paid only the cost of transmitting mail from one post office to another. Carrier stamps evidenced the payment of fees for delivery by a carrier from a post office to an addressee or delivery of a letter from one local address to another.

catalogue a reference work that lists, illustrates, and prices postage stamps. Stamp catalogues can be general or specialized.

catalogue number each stamp listed in a stamp catalogue is assigned a unique number, which is known as its catalogue number.

catalogue value the value assigned to a stamp in a stamp catalogue. Market value (the value for which a stamp can be purchased on the open market) often varies from catalogue value. It is sometimes more, but most often less, than catalogue value. When a stamp is routinely priced at catalogue value, it is said to be worth "full catalogue."

catapult mail mail carried by ship most of the way on transatlantic routes and then by a ship-based, catapult-launched airplane on the final leg of the journey. Catapult mail saved a day or two in transit time in the era before nonstop transatlantic flights were possible. Catapult mail flourished from the late 1920s to the late 1930s.

CDS (circular date stamp) a circular postmark showing place of mailing together with date and, in some cases, time.

censored mail mail opened by examiners, most often during time of war, and resealed, usually with tape, and often, but not always, marked with a censor's handstamp. World War II spawned a wide variety of censored mail as many nations inspected both incoming and outgoing mail.

centering the position of a stamp's design in relation to its perforations or, in the case of imperforate issues, to its edges. Well-centered stamps possess even margins all around.

center line block a block of stamps on which guidelines or color registration marks meet and cross. Center line blocks are most commonly encountered on twentieth-century U.S. issues up to the dollar values of the Presidential issue of 1938.

CEPT abbreviation for Conference Europienne des Adminstrations des Postes et des Telecommunications, or Conference of European Postal and Telecommunication Administrations.

ceremony program   see **first day ceremony program**.

certificate of mailing   a service that provides a receipt prepared by the mailer as proof of mailing.

certified mail   a service that provides for proof of mailing and delivery without indemnity for contents.

chalky paper   paper manufactured with a thin coating of chalk on its surface, a coating easily disturbed, hence its suitability for security printing. Stamps printed on chalky paper tend to be extremely fragile when soaked. A number of British issues were printed on chalky paper.

changeling   a stamp whose normal color has been altered or eliminated by exposure to light or chemicals. Color changelings have no philatelic value.

charity stamp   a semipostal. See **semipostal**.

check letters   letters appearing in the corners of some nineteenth-century British issues. One letter represented the vertical row from which the stamp originated; the second letter, the horizontal row. Each stamp on a pane possessed its own unique pair of letters, for example AA or GL.

checklist   an inventory list generally encompassing the scope of a collection to which a collector can refer to see which items it contains and which are yet to be acquired.

chop mark   a mark consisting of Chinese or Japanese characters, often, but not always, within a border. Japanese authorities often used chop marks to create provisional occupation issues for territories they overran during World War II.

Christmas casual   a postal term for a temporary employee hired during the Christmas holiday period.

Christmas seal   a stamplike seal sold to raise money for charitable purposes. Christmas seals have been produced and sold in a number of countries. Their use on holiday mail helps publicize the charitable cause.

cinderella   a general, all-encompassing term applied to any stamplike item not valid for postage, such as exhibition labels, Christmas seals, parodies, imitations, modern advertising fantasy issues, and the like. Anything that looks like a postage stamp but is not, including fantasy labels, phantoms, modern local post labels, and so on.

classic   an early or particularly notable issue, usually, but not always, a nineteenth-century issue. The Penny Black is a classic, as is the inverted Jenny issued in 1918.

cleaned   a stamp whose cancellation has been removed in order to make it appear uncanceled.

cliché   a philatelic term for an individual image or "cut," which when locked together with other units forms a plate from which stamps are printed. The term dates back to the time when stamps were often printed by typography and plates were assembled from individual cuts or clichés. Images impressed on single plate, such as those used in intaglio, gravure, or lithography, are known as *subjects* rather than clichés.

closed transit dispatches   a postal term for sealed bags of international mail that travel through the postal service on their way from one country to another country, and which are not opened for redistribution.

coil stamps   stamps issued in rolls. U.S. coil stamps contain straight edges on opposite parallel sides; some, but not many, foreign coil stamps do not contain straight edges. U.S. coil stamps are often collected in pairs.

coil waste   odd-sized remnants left over from coil stamp production, which rather than discard, the Bureau of Engraving and Printing perforated along the straight-edged sides and shipped to the Postal Service for sale as regular stamps. The perforation combinations of coil waste issues vary from those of regularly produced sheet stamps, and because coil waste was produced in relatively small quantities, many of the stamps are now extremely rare and expensive. Coil waste was produced between the years 1919 and 1924 as a cost-saving measure.

collateral material   material—often nonphilatelic—related to stamps, covers, or postal history that provides additional insight or background about the items or the area collected. For example, maps, photos, railway timetables, brochures, and so on.

collection box   a box in which postal patrons may deposit mail.

color changeling   a stamp whose normal color has been altered or eliminated by exposure to light or chemicals. Color changelings have no philatelic value.

color shade   the variation of a given color, often slight, but occasionally pronounced.

color shift   the misregistration of one or more individual colors on a multicolor stamp. Some shifts are slight and barely noticeable; others are pronounced and visually striking.

combination cover   most often a cover containing stamps of more than one country, usually the country of origin and the destination country. Also a first day cover that contains additional stamps related to the stamp being issued or to a first day cover bearing both official and unofficial first day cancellations.

comb perforation   perforations applied by a device that punches one row of stamps at a time, the pattern consisting of a single top line of perforations and as many lines of side perforations as there are stamps in the row. The top line of perforations doubles as the bottom line for each row as the sequence progresses. See also **harrow perforation** and **line perforation**.

commemorative   a stamp issued to honor a special event, personality, anniversary, or topic; typically larger and more colorful than a definitive stamp and usually available for a only limited time.

commercial cover   a cover used for business correspondence without any philatelic intent (although more recently any cover of a nonphilatelic nature), as distinct from one created for a philatelic purpose. See also **philatelic cover**.

compact sheet. A pane of modern U.S. postage stamps containing fewer than the traditional 50 or 100 stamps—often only 15 or 20 stamps—and in some cases with a marginal inscription, decoration, or illustration. Most modern U.S. sheet stamps are issued in compact sheet format.

complete set   a set containing all of the stamps that constitute the set.

compound perforations   perforations of two different gauges on the same stamp, for example, perforated 10 on top and bottom and perforated 11 on either side.

computer vended postage   stamps dispensed by vending machines that imprint the denomination at the time the stamp is vended, usually on security paper containing a preprinted background.

condition crank   one obsessively, and often unrealistically, fussy about even the most trivial detail of condition; one possessing unreasonably high standards for stamps.

constant variety   a variety usually occurring on one subject within a printing plate and therefore constant on every impression printed from that plate.

consular fee stamp   a stamp used by the U.S. foreign service to evidence payment of fees. Consular fee stamps are usually attached to documents or receipts.

contract station   a postal station usually located in a store or place of business and operated by a contractor who accepts mail from the public, sells postage and supplies, and provides selected services such as postal money orders or registered mail. Also called a *contract branch* or *community post office*.

controlled mail   an arrangement with a recipient to save stamps or covers from the sender and return them to him.

cork cancel   a cancellation carved on a piece of cork such as the end of a bottle stopper. Cork cancellations were used during the nineteenth century, especially by small-town postmasters who were required to provide their own canceling devices and did not wish to buy a commercially produced device. Some designs are plain and utilitarian; others are complex and ornate.

corner block   a block of stamps from the corner of a pane or sheet and containing selvage, either with or without marginal markings, plate numbers, or inscriptions.

corner card   a printed return address located on the upper-left corner of a cover or card.

counterfeit   a stamp fabricated to defraud a postal authority.

counterfoil   the receipt portion of a two-part stamp, such as those on parcel stamps of Italy.

counting number   **(1)** a number imprinted, often by jet spray, at regular intervals on the back side of coil stamps to facilitate counting; **(2)** a small number printed on selvage of Cottrell-printed coil stamps, much smaller than and not to be confused with a plate number, and which, except in the case of a misaligned cut, was trimmed away during finishing.

cover   an envelope or a folded letter, usually implying that the item has gone through the mail or at least received a cancellation, as in the case of a first day cover or an event cover. A stamp attached to a cover is referred to as being *on cover*. A cover without stamps, usually from the era before the introduction of postage stamps, is referred to as a *stampless cover*.

cpl or **cpt**   abbreviation for complete, as in complete set.

crash cover   a cover salvaged from a wreck, such as an airplane crash or a train wreck, and forwarded to the addressee. Crash covers are usually marked by the postal service to explain the delay in delivery.

crease   a crease occurs when paper is bent sufficiently to break its fibers. Once the fibers break, the paper can never be returned to its original condition. Creases, especially on early or expensive stamps, can be ironed out, often so expertly that their presence can be detected only by immersion in watermark fluid. Creases are regarded as a fault, and stamps possessing them are worth less than those without them.

Crown Agents   originally an agency of the British government, but from 1980, a corporation. The Crown Agents was created to provide services, including stamp production, to colonies, territories, and possessions under British control. The Crown Agents first became involved in stamp production in 1848. In 1906 it began making philatelic sales. Today the Crown Agents Stamp Bureau Ltd. produces, distributes, and publicizes stamps for various client states, many of which are former British colonies.

CTO   abbreviation for **canceled to order**.

cull   a postal term meaning to remove nonletter mail (such as small parcels, rolls, and odd-shaped material) from letter mail by hand or machine. During culling, items such as certified mail and flats are separated from ordinary letters.

cut cancel   a cancellation that cuts into the stamp, thus defacing it. Cut cancels are most often encountered on documentary stamps. Stamps with cut cancels are generally worth less than those canceled with ink.

cut close   **(1)** refers to a margin on an imperforate stamp that has been cut close to the design; **(2)** refers to how stamps in bulk mixtures are trimmed. Those clipped very close to the stamp are said to be "cut close." Mixtures of stamps cut close generally contain more stamp per pound than those cut more liberally and are, therefore, considered to be a better value.

cut square   a piece containing the postage imprint or indicia cut from postal stationery, usually to facilitate mounting in an album. Once popular, collecting cut squares has fallen out of favor; most collectors prefer entires. See **entire**.

cut to shape   an item, often an indicia from a stamped envelope, that is trimmed precisely to the contour of its design. Cut to shape items are generally worth little, unless the item happens to be a rarity.

cylinder number   technical term for plate numbers printed on gravure issues.

dated   a U.S. precancel with an imprinted date, usually appearing above the top line. Dates, consisting of the month and year, were applied by individual precancel permit holders to denominations of 10¢ and higher to conform to a requirement designed to prevent their reuse.

dead country   a country that no longer issues postage stamps, most often due to a change in political circumstance, such as former colonies (Belgian Congo, Mozambique Company) or nations absorbed by other countries (East Germany, South Vietnam).

dead letter   a letter or piece of mail that can neither be delivered because of a problem with the address nor returned, often because of a lack of return address. Dead letters are forwarded to the dead letter office, where they are opened in an attempt to locate either the address of the addressee or sender. If neither can be found, the letter is destroyed.

dead post office   (or **discontinued post office**) a post office no longer in operation.

decimal issue   a British stamp issued after the conversion of the monetary system to decimal currency.

definitive   a stamp, usually part of a series of various denominations, available over an extended period of time for use on everyday mail. Definitives are also known as *regular issues*.

delivery-sequenced mail   a postal term for mail that is arranged by a mailer in delivery order for a particular carrier route.

demonetized   (or invalidated) no longer valid for the payment of postage. U.S. stamps were demonetized at the outbreak of the Civil War and replaced by stamps with new designs in order to prevent stocks in Southern post offices from being used by the Confederacy.

denomination   the value imprinted on a stamp or item of postal stationery, for example, 1¢ or $1. Also known as **face value**.

departmental stamp   refers to U.S. official stamps of the nineteenth century that were issued for use by the various departments, for example, the Post Office Department or the State Department.

DG (disturbed gum) gum disturbed by removal of a stamp hinge, but also any other form of gum damage, such as that arising from a stamp having been partially stuck down to an album page or stuck to another stamp.

die a piece of metal upon which a single example of a stamp is engraved or etched. Intaglio dies are engraved by hand. The resulting master die is then used to impress an image on a transfer roll, which in turn impresses images on a printing plate.

die cut cutting applied between self-adhesive stamps to permit separation. Some die cuts are straight; others are serpentine (wavy) in appearance to simulate perforations. A few issues are die cut to shape.

die cut omitted lacking die cutting, implies unintentional omission, analogous to the term "imperforate."

die proof a proof pulled (printed) from a master die. Proofs are pulled to check the quality and progress of the work. See also **large die proof** and **small die proof**.

diplomatic pouch mail mail carried by diplomatic pouch from one country to another and deposited in that country's mail stream. Pouch mail often contains stamps of the country of origin and a postmark of the destination country.

directory marking a marking applied to undeliverable mail giving the reason, such as "Moved—No Forwarding Address" or "Deceased." Directory markings can be applied by handstamp, by manuscript notation, or now increasingly by computer-generated labels.

discontinued post office (or **dead post office**) a post office no longer in operation.

discount postage postage sold for less than its face value. A term applied to common mint stamps whose only value is as postage, and for which dealers are willing only to offer less than face value.

disinfected mail mail treated, usually by fumigation, to prevent transmission of disease, such as cholera, during an outbreak or epidemic such as occurred during the nineteenth and early twentieth centuries. Disinfected mail was sometimes opened to achieve complete fumigation, but more often perforated or slit to achieve the result. Disinfected mail was frequently marked as such.

distribution a postal term for the sorting of mail into pigeonhole cases, trays, sacks, machine bins, or pouches in order to group pieces with a common destination for transportation to the post office of address. It may be done by manual, mechanized, or automated means.

docketing (also docketed) notations, usually handwritten but occasionally rubber stamped, added to a cover by the recipient, noting contents, action taken, date answered, and the like. Docketing sometimes helps date or place a cover.

doctor blade in intaglio and gravure printing, ink is deposited in recessed areas of the plate. Excess ink is wiped away from high-relief areas (which are not intended to print) by the pass of a doctor blade. The remaining ink (in the recesses) prints the image.

documentary stamp a revenue stamp used to evidence payment of tax on documents such as mortgages and wills, and usually attached to the documents.

domestic mail mail transmitted within, among, and between the United States, its territories and possessions, Army Post Offices (APOs), Fleet Post Offices (FPOs), and mail for delivery to the United Nations in New York.

domestic mail manual the Postal Service manual that contains the basic standards governing domestic mail services; descriptions of the mail classes and services and conditions governing their uses; and standards for rate eligibility and mail preparation.

double impression an impression caused by paper coming into contact with a printing plate more than once. Often the resulting impressions are slightly misregistered and, therefore, appear blurred.

double transfer inadvertent, and usually minor, doubling of some parts of an intaglio design created during the transfer die process. Double transfers usually result from a replacement impression made atop an incompletely removed worn or defective earlier impression. More about the transfer die process appears in the chapter on printing.

DPO abbreviation for **discontinued post office**.

drop box a receptacle where city carriers leave mail on the line of travel for later pickup and delivery by another carrier. It is also called a *relay box*. U.S. Postal Service drop boxes are similar to collection boxes but are typically painted olive green.

drop letter (1) a letter posted at the same post office at which it was delivered. Before 1863 postage paid only for transmission from post office to post office. Home and business delivery did not yet exist. Letters not requiring transportation from one post office to another qualified for a reduced rate and became known as drop letters; (2) a postal term for a letter mailed for local delivery at a post office that has neither city delivery nor collection and delivery by a rural carrier or highway contract route carrier, and therefore, must be picked up by the addressee.

dry gum nonglossy gum that is flat in appearance, as opposed to "wet" gum, which is glossy or shiny in appearance. Dry gum is also referred to as *matte gum* or *dull gum*. See also **wet gum**.

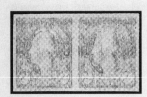

dry print   a stamp, especially from intaglio production, that lacks most of its ink and possesses only a ghostlike image. In the early days of intaglio printing, paper had to be fairly damp in order to accept ink. If a run of paper was not sufficiently damp, it would not accept ink, and the result was a faint impression or dry print.

Dry printing (left); wet printing (right).

dry printing   an intaglio printing process utilizing low-moisture content paper. Most U.S. stamps prior to the mid-1950s were printed on paper with high moisture content, which was necessary to ensure receptivity to intaglio ink. The wet-print process was phased out in the 1950s after the appearance of dry-print presses capable of handling low-moisture content paper. Dry-printed stamps usually display a sharper, more crisp appearance than wet-printed stamps. See also **wet printing**.

dual address   mail containing both a street address and a post office box number. Delivery is made to the address on the line immediately above the city, state, and ZIP code line.

duck stamp   a waterfowl-hunting stamp. The federal government began issuing duck stamps in 1934. Duck stamps are intended to be attached to hunting licenses. Hunters are supposed to cancel the stamps by signing their name across the front. Some do not, hoping to salvage the unsigned stamp as a collectible once the hunting season is over; however, unsigned stamps that lack gum from being soaked off licenses are nevertheless regarded as used stamps. Many states also issue duck stamps. They are known as *state duck stamps*.

dummy booklet   a booklet-sized dummy used to set up or test booklet vending machines.

duplex cancel   a postmark containing two elements: one giving the name of the location and date; the second an obliterating mark intended to cancel the stamp.

duplicates   extra copies; copies in addition to the one that occupies a place in a collection.

duty plate   see **key type**.

earliest known use   (abbreviated EKU) the earliest date a stamp is known to have been used as evidenced by a postmark, either on the stamp itself or tying the stamp to a cover or piece. In some cases, especially during the nineteenth century, the Postal Service placed stamps on sale without prior announcement. EKUs are often the only clue to approximate dates these stamps were first placed on sale.

early use a stamp used before its official first day of sale.

ECV (estimated cash value) a term used in auction catalogues representing the auctioneer's opinion of the value of the lot.

EE bars see **electric eye bars**.

EFO abbreviation for errors, freaks, and oddities.

EFOCC abbreviation for Errors, Freaks, and Oddities Collectors' Club.

EKU (earliest known use) the earliest date a stamp is known to have been used.

elbow and eyeball an informal term used by postal employees that means to open and examine the interior of a presumably empty sack to ensure that it does not contain mail trapped inside.

electric eye bars (or EE bars) bars printed in the selvage of some issues to guide them into position to be perforated. In most cases, EE bars are trimmed off coil stamps and booklet pane production during finishing. They are not always trimmed off sheet stamp production and appear on the selvage of some issues.

embossing a raised design impressed onto paper by an embossing die, most commonly on stamped envelopes.

encased postage a postage stamp encased in coinlike metal token, with one side covered by a transparent material, such as mica, in order to reveal the stamp. Encased postage tokens were popular in the United States during the Civil War, when a coin shortage dried up most small change. Encased postage had been used from time to time in other countries.

endorsement a marking on a mailpiece that shows handling instructions, a special service, or a request for an ancillary service.

engraved see **intaglio**.

entire a complete, intact item of postal stationery, either used or unused.

error a stamp with a production error. The field is usually divided into major errors and minor errors (or freaks). Major errors include a stamp lacking perforations or die cuts, a stamp with a design element inverted, a stamp with a color or colors omitted, or a stamp printed in the wrong color. Minor errors (or freaks) result from production irregularities such as perforation shifts, ink blotches and smears, misregistration of color, and the like. Stamps with design errors (such as the wrong number of stars on a flag) are generally not considered "errors" in the philatelic vernacular.

essay   an unadopted stamp design, either an entire design not used or a design very similar to the issued design except for small differences. The term includes sketched ideas and proposals, preliminary artwork, and die and plate proofs that differ from the final issued design and any other images during the creative process. In order to be considered a legitimate essay, an image usually must have been officially requested, authorized, or produced.

etiquette   a label used to indicate a special service, most often airmail. Some etiquettes are plain and utilitarian; others, especially those distributed by airlines, are more elaborate and eye-catching.

event cover   a cover postmarked to commemorate an event or anniversary, often with cachet; similar to a first day cover, but not marking the issuance of a stamp.

exceptional address   a postal term for an alternative addressing format that indicates that the mailpiece should be delivered to the current resident if the addressee has moved.

exhibition label   a label created to promote and publicize an exhibition, either philatelic or nonphilatelic, such as a world's fair or national philatelic exhibition.

expert certificate   a certificate issued by an acknowledged expert or expertizing body attesting to the genuineness or nongenuineness of a stamp or cover.

expertize   to have a stamp examined by an acknowledged expert or expertizing body and have an opinion given.

expert mark   a mark of authentication placed on the reverse of a stamp or cover by a recognized expert.

exploded   a booklet that has been dissembled into individual panes.

face   the side of a piece of mail with the delivery address. Also to arrange mail with the delivery address facing forward and the postage stamp, meter stamp, or permit imprint positioned in the upper-right corner.

face different   stamps different solely by virtue of their outward appearance and not taking into account watermark, perforation, or other differences. A face different collection of Washington-Franklin definitives consists of one example of each denomination regardless of watermark and perforation varieties.

facer-canceler   mail-processing equipment that automatically faces letter-size mail in a uniform orientation and cancels the postage stamps.

face value   a stamp's denomination.

facing identification mark   (abbreviated FIM) a series of five or six vertical bars used by automated postal equipment to identify, orient, and separate reply mail.

facing slip   a postal term for a paper label attached to the top of a bundle that shows where the mail is to be distributed, the class and type of mail, and the country or military post office.

facsimile   a reproduction, most often a rare stamp, and usually offered or marked as such.

fake   an outright forgery; also a stamp (or cover) that has been modified to improve its value or desirability with the intent to defraud a buyer.

false franking   a stamp that ostensibly underpays the proper rate of postage. Most often seen on bulk mailings where the difference between the face value of the false franking and the actual rate has been paid by the mailer at the time of mailing.

FAM   (foreign airmail [route]) routes served by U.S. airlines to foreign destinations. The term "FAM" is most often used in conjunction with first flight covers (FAM covers) inaugurating one of these routes.

fancy cancel   a cancellation featuring a pictorial device or geometric design.

fantasy   an ostensible stamp that is, in reality, from a fanciful or imaginary entity.

Farley's Follies   a derisive nickname given to a series of special printings made available to collectors in response to outrage over Postmaster General James A. Farley's habit of presenting similar items, that is ungummed press sheets unavailable to the public, to President Roosevelt and other favored friends. The imperforate National Parks set is perhaps the best known of the group.

fault   any defect affecting the appearance or integrity of a stamp, such as a tear, cut, crease, thin, scrape, stain, scuff, fold, pinhole, foxing, and so on.

favor cancel   a cancellation applied to a stamp or cover as a favor by a postal employee, often on an item that might not normally have been used on mail or have gone through the mail, or with a postmarking device not normally used for the issue.

FDC   abbreviation for **first day cover**.

FDOI   abbreviation for first day of issue.

field post office   a military post office operating in the field and capable of moving with troops and often using their own distinct postmarks.

FIM   abbreviation for **facing identification mark**.

fingering the mail   an informal postal term for checking the addresses on mail between delivery stops on a carrier route before selecting mailpieces for the next stop.

FIP   Federation Internationale de Philatelie (or International Federation of Philately) an international organization established to promote philately and set regulations for judging, standards for exhibiting, and so forth at international exhibitions held under its patronage. Membership is composed of national philatelic organizations, each country permitted to be represented by only one organization, usually the primary organization, within the country.

first day ceremony program   (also ceremony program) a program distributed to guests attending a first day of issue ceremony. The programs usually contain an example of the newly released stamp together with a first day cancellation. Some programs are produced by the Postal Service, others by private sponsoring organizations. Some are scarce, having been distributed to VIPs and invited guests; others are made available to the general public and are not scarce.

first day cover   (abbreviated FDC) a cover, usually cacheted, postmarked on the first day a stamp is officially available for sale. An official first day cover is one postmarked in the city (or one of the cities) where the stamp was officially first placed on sale. An unofficial first day cover is one postmarked in any city other than one designated as "official."

first flight cover   a cover, usually cacheted, carried on the first flight of a new airmail route.

fiscal   a revenue stamp. Postage stamps used for revenue purposes are called **postal-fiscals**.

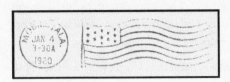

flag cancel a cancellation that features a flag as part of its design, most often a machine cancellation, on which the wavy lives of the killer portion have been made to resemble part of a flag.

flat a postal term for larger than letter-size mail, so called because it is sorted without bending it.

flat plate printing printing accomplished by a flat, as opposed to curved or rotary, plate. Most U.S. stamps produced before the 1920s were printed on flat plate presses.

flaw a minor imperfection, the term is usually used to refer to an imperfection in a printing plate, but also, if less frequently, to refer to a condition fault on a stamp.

fleet post office (abbreviated FPO) a branch of the civilian post office that falls under the jurisdiction of the postmaster of either New York City or San Francisco and that serves Coast Guard, Navy, or Marine Corps personnel.

flexography a form of relief printing accomplished by use of a flexible rubber or plastic plate suitable for use on rotary press drums. Flexographic plates are much more economical and easily constructed than intaglio plates. Flexographic plates have been used to overprint precancel stamps and produce postal stationery.

floating plate number a plate number whose position on the selvage varies from pane to pane. Plate numbers on most U.S. stamps are nonfloating and appear in the same position on every pane.

floor bidder someone who attends an auction and bids in person from the "floor," as opposed to an absentee bidder.

flown cover a cover (or card) flown aboard an aircraft, either in the normal course of business or on a special flight. Flown covers for special events are usually, but not always, marked as flown, often with details of the flight appearing in a cachet, although some are not.

flyspecking   the study of minute variations. The term "flyspecking" is often used in a pejorative sense, implying that the variations, often visible only under magnification, are not worth bothering with.

folded letter   before envelopes came into general use, letters were folded blank side out, sealed, and addressed.

foot route   a postal term for a city route on which the letter carrier walks to deliver the mail rather than driving a vehicle.

foreign stamp   any stamp issued by a country other than that of the collector. For example, in the United States, any stamp not issued by the United States or under its authority.

forwarding agent   an agent, usually in a foreign port or city, who could expedite the transmission of letters deposited with him. Prior to the establishment of the Universal Postal Union, letters might have had to travel through several jurisdictions in order to reach their destination. Senders relied upon forwarding agents in distant places to dispatch letters by the most efficient means to get them to their destination.

four-bar cancel   a hand cancel containing a circular dating device at left and four killer bars at right. Some four-bar type devices contain a slogan or message between some of the bars or in place of some of the bars.

foxing   discoloration, often brown, orange-brown, or rust colored, on paper, usually caused by microorganisms but sometimes resulting from other forms of deterioration.

FPO   abbreviation for **(1)** fleet post office, a military post office maintained aboard ship or at a shore station for Coast Guard, Navy, or Marine Corps personnel; **(2)** [British] field post office.

Frama   a form of vended postage utilizing security paper on which the denomination is printed at the time the stamp is vended. The denomination is selected by the customer. The name is taken from the Frama firm, which manufactures automated postage vending machines.

frame   the outer border surrounding the central design of a stamp. See also **vignette**.

franchise stamp   a postage stamp used by an organization under privilege granted by the issuing government. Franchise stamps are generally provided at no cost to the authorized organization.

frank   a mark indicating that postage has been paid, or in the case of those granted the privilege (known as the *franking privilege*), that postage is free. Presidents and members of Congress have the franking privilege, as often do members of the military during time of war.

franking a term used to describe the type of stamps used to pay postage (e.g., franked with 10¢ stamps) or way in which postage was paid.

freak a production variety including such anomalies as shifted perforations, ink blotches, paper folds, miscuts, or other minor production mistakes.

free frank a privilege extended to some, such as presidents and members of Congress, that permits them to send mail without paying postage. The privilege is usually evidenced by signature, either handwritten, printed, or applied by machine, appearing where postage would normally be affixed.

front the front part of an envelope from which the back or back flaps have been trimmed away.

fugitive ink ink susceptible to fading or change of color with exposure to light or chemicals. Also inks—especially aniline inks—that run or bleed when wetted, to discourage reuse.

general delivery general delivery is primarily provided at offices without letter carrier delivery or for transients and customers who do not have a permanent address or who prefer not to use post office boxes.

generalist one who collects stamps without specializing in an area or era.

general post office (abbreviated GPO) usually the main post office in a city. See also **main post office**.

ghosting the inadvertent placement of a "ghost" impression, often as the result of the tagging roller or blanket picking up a faint impression of the stamp design or plate number from damp printing ink on the sheet and depositing it along with tagging on the next one or more sheets.

ghost town a discontinued post office that was located in a town that no longer exists.

glassine a translucent material (cellulose acetate) from which envelopes (known as glassines), stamp hinges, and in some cases stock book pockets are made.

granite paper a type of security paper milled with countless minute colored fibers of various hues and intended to discourage counterfeiting.

grill a wafflelike pattern impressed into some nineteenth-century stamps to break their paper fibers and make them more receptive to postmarking ink. Used to prevent the removal of cancellations and reuse of stamps.

gripper crack   a minute fracture on an intaglio printing plate caused by stress from the grippers that hold the plate in place at top and bottom. The stress fractures, or cracks, collect ink in the same way that recessed stamp subjects on the intaglio plate accept ink, and they deposit it on paper in the same fashion. The resulting imprint appears as a narrow irregular line.

guillotine perforator   a perforator utilizing a single row of perforations applied in a stroke reminiscent of a guillotine stroke.

gum   the adhesive on the back of a stamp. Modern collectors prefer gum to be in the best condition possible.

gum breakers   ridges impressed by special rollers on sheets of stamps to counteract their tendency to curl, especially when exposed to humidity. They are visible on the backs of most rotary press stamps issued between the 1920s and 1960s.

gum crease   a natural crease often found on flat plate printed stamps of the first half of the twentieth century and usually caused by handling during production or by the uneven rate of shrinkage between damp paper and gum.

gum skip   a space, often small, on which gum was omitted during its original application. Most often encountered on flat plate printed U.S. stamps from the 1910s to the 1930s.

gutter   the space between two adjacent panes of stamps on a sheet.

gutter pair   a pair of stamps possessing an interpane gutter between them.

hand back   a cover, such as a first day cover or an event cover, presented in person for cancellation and then handed back as opposed to being returned through the mail.

hand canceled   canceled with a handheld device as opposed to canceled by machine. Also called *handstamped*.

hand colored   a cachet, usually in outline form, that has been printed on a cover and then finished by coloring in by hand.

hand drawn   a cachet that has been individually drawn by an artist.

hand painted   a cachet that has been individually painted by an artist. Hand-colored cachets are similar but differ in that the basic design is first printed, then the blank areas are painted in by hand.

handstamp   a cancellation that has been applied by a handheld device.

harrow perforation   perforations made by a device that perforates an entire sheet of stamps at one stroke. See also **comb perforation** and **line perforation**.

HCR   abbreviation for **highway contract route**.

heavily hinged   (abbreviated HH) hinged with strong glue that has disturbed gum or will disturb it when removed, or containing a stubborn hinge remnant.

herringbone cancellation   a punched cancellation in a herringbone pattern, most often encountered on revenue stamps.

highway contract route   (abbreviated HCR) a postal term for a route served by a postal contractor to carry mail over highways between designated points. Some HCRs include mail delivery to addresses along the line of travel. Formerly called a **star route**.

hinge   a stamp hinge. A small piece of paper or glassine used to attach a stamp to an album page. Hinges are folded about one third of the way from the top. The smaller flap is attached to the stamp, the larger flap to the album page.

hinge remnant   part of a stamp hinge remaining on the back of a stamp, usually one resistant to removal.

hologram   a thin film containing an image that when viewed at an angle appears three-dimensional. Holograms have been used on some stamps and postal stationery.

holograph   a document written entirely by hand and signed by the person who wrote it.

house lot   an auction lot owned by the auction firm as opposed to one owned by a consignor.

HPO   (highway post office) for a time, the Postal Service used specially equipped motor vehicles to process mail en route from one post office to another, much as mail was processed in railway post offices. The system is no longer in use.

hunting stamp   see **duck stamp**.

hybrid proof   a proof printed on India paper and then mounted on card stock to resemble a large die proof.

illegal use   any stamp, such as a revenue stamp or savings stamp, or stamplike item improperly used to pay postage. Some illegal uses are intentional, others are unintentional. Usually, and especially in isolated cases, postage due is collected rather than any action being taken against the sender.

imperforate   lacking perforations. The term has become generic and is often used to refer to stamps with die cuts, roulettes, or other means of separation omitted. Perforated stamps unintentionally issued without perforations are *errors*.

Naturally occurring edges lacking perforations on coil stamps and booklet stamps are referred to as *straight edges* rather than imperforate.

imperforate margin   a margin copy from which perforations have been unintentionally omitted between the edge of the stamp and the selvage. Use of the term implies erroneous omission. Margin copies that normally possess a straight edge are referred to as having a straight edge rather than in imperforate margin.

imprint   information imprinted on the selvage of a pane of stamps, such as the name of the printer, value of the stamps, and so forth.

imprint block   a block analogous to a plate block, but instead of numbers, containing an inscription.

inconstant variety   a random, rather than constant, variety.

India paper   a tissuelike paper, delicate but tough, not unlike Bible paper, and most often used for proofs by virtue of its ability to pick up and hold fine detail.

indicia   although technically plural for "indicium," the term is used in the sense of being singular to refer to the stamplike imprint on postal stationery, the imprint of a postage meter device, or the printed imprint in the corner of bulk mail items.

inflation issue   foreign stamps issued during inflationary times, often with extraordinarily high face values, such as those issued in Germany during the inflation of 1921 to 1923, many of which carried face values in the millions of marks.

ink-jet cancel   (also known as a sprayed or sprayed-on cancel) a cancellation applied by ink-jet printer, often as a single straight line, and in the United States, most often in addition to a traditional cancellation.

inscription   words or phrases that appear as part of a stamp design; also words or phrases printed on selvage or in the margins of sheets or panes.

inscription block   a block of stamps on whose selvage appears a printed inscription.

Inspection Service   the federal law enforcement agency of the U.S. Postal Service that investigates criminal acts against the mails and misuse of the postal system. The Inspection Service protects mail, postal funds, and postal property, and it conducts internal audits. Agents of the Inspection Service are known as *postal inspectors.*

intaglio   a method of printing in which the design is engraved (recessed) into a metal plate. Ink fills the recesses and when printed forms small ridges, which can be detected by magnifying glass or by running a finger over the design and feeling the ridges. Sometimes referred to as *engraved printing* or *line-engraved printing.*

interleaves   sheets, often glassine, inserted between pages of an album or a stock book to prevent stamps on facing pages from catching on one another or rubbing against each other.

international mail   mail originating in one country whose destination is in another.

international reply coupon   (abbreviated IRC) a coupon exchangeable for postage (representing the minimum postage on an unregistered airmail letter) at post offices in member countries of the Universal Postal Union. The coupon is sold by post offices worldwide. Used to enable an individual in one country to send postage for a reply to an individual in another country.

interrupted mail   mail delayed in transit by the intervention of an external event, such as a train wreck, a post office fire, or war.

invalidated   see **demonetized**.

invert   a stamp with an element of its design printed upside down in relation to the other elements of the design.

IRC   abbreviation for **international reply coupon**.

IWOG   abbreviation for issued without gum.

job lot   a mishmash consisting of just about anything—loose stamps, stamps on album pages, covers, mixtures, mint sets, remainders, etc.—often sold by the carton. Dealers often dispose of surplus, disorganized material in the form of job lots. Sometimes called a *mystery lot.*

joint issue stamps of two (or more) countries featuring a similar design, issued in collaboration with one another specifically to commemorate something important to both.

joint line pair see **line pair**.

JPA (Junior Philatelists of America) an organization serving youth philately.

jumbo margins margins significantly larger than normal. Also known as **boardwalk margins**.

key type an identical design used by a number of different entities, such as colonies, differing only in the name of the entity and in some cases, currency and/or color. Key types are often printed from the same (or key) plate. Elements specific to each various entity are printed by a second (or duty) plate.

killer cancel a heavy mark, typically covering most of a stamp's design, rendering it nearly unrecognizable, hence "killing" it. Killer cancels do not contain information about mailing, such as date or location.

kiloware mixture of stamps on paper sold by the pound or kilogram, hence the name "kiloware." See also **mixture**.

label in the philatelic sense, anything that resembles a stamp but is not. See also **cinderella**.

laid paper paper containing rows of subtle parallel lines impressed during manufacture. The rows are often visible to the naked eye if held up to light and are invariably visible when immersed in watermark fluid.

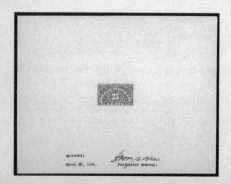

large die proof a die proof printed on card stock. The size of the card can vary, but in almost all cases it is larger than 4 by 6 inches. Small die proofs are often printed on India paper and possess margins, which although are larger than those encountered on issued stamps, are quite small in comparison to those encountered on large die proofs. See also **die proof** and **small die proof**.

last day cancel   (1) a cancellation applied on the last day of operation of a local post office or branch; (2) a cancellation applied to a stamp on its last day of availability. See also **last day cover**.

last day cover   (1) a cover or card bearing the postmark of the last day of operation of a local post office or branch; (2) a cover bearing a stamp postmarked on its putative last day of availability. The U.S. Postal Service created and sold last day covers for a brief period in the late 1990s. They never caught on because, although technically stamps were removed from sale at the Philatelic Fulfillment Center on an announced date, in practice they often remained available at various post offices across the nation.

late fee stamp   a stamp used to evidence payment of a fee charged to accept an item after the normal closing of the mails, such as to convey mail to a ship after the regular mail had closed. In the nineteenth century, ships sailed from some ports only infrequently. If a letter arrived at a port post office after the mail had been dispatched to the ship, it would be held for the next ship, which might not sail for days or weeks—unless the sender was willing to pay the late fee for a messenger to get it to the ship before it sailed.

letterpress   (also relief printing or typography [archaic]) the oldest form of printing, a method in which the ink sits atop raised type and is transferred directly to paper. Some stamp catalogues list stamps printed by letterpress as "typographed."

letter sheet   (or lettersheet) a self-contained sheet with gummed flaps that can be folded and sealed for mailing after a message has been written on its interior. Similar to an aerogramme, but for surface transmission.

lightly hinged   (abbreviated LH) hinged so that the hinge mark is barely noticeable.

line engraved   see **intaglio**.

line pair   (or joint line pair) a pair of coil stamps on which a line appears between stamps. On engraved, rotary press coil stamps, lines are created by ink that fills the space where the curved plates join and is then printed in the same fashion as ink from recesses in an intaglio stamp design.

line perforation   perforations made one row at a time. See also **harrow perforation** and **comb perforation**.

lithography   a printing process using photographically etched plates. In some cases, the image from the metal plate is offset onto a rubberlike blanket before being impressed onto the paper, hence the term "offset printing." In lithography, images are broken up into a series of dots to achieve tonal gradation. Color lithography involves mingling areas of dots from several plates, each printing a separate color, in order to achieve the effect of full color. The dot structure is visible under magnification.

local post stamps   stamps issued by private individuals or firms to evidence the payment of fees for the transport of mail. In the nineteenth century, many private local posts carried mail in the United States, most often between patrons within a city (hence the name "local post"). By the twentieth century, these firms had died out. Modern local posts began to spring up in the twentieth century, such as those on Lundy Island and Rattlesnake Island, which lacked postal service and whose local entrepreneurs offered to transport mail to and from the mainland for a fee. In addition to those that actually provided a service, others sprang up purely as a creative outlet, issuing stamps only for collectors or their proprietors' own amusement.

local precancel   a precancel applied locally rather than at the Bureau of Engraving and Printing. See also **bureau precancel**.

local stamp   (or locals) a stamp issued by a private firm to evidence payment of a fee for conveyance of mail to or from a nearby post office. Prior to the mid-1840s, the Postal Service did not offer delivery to customers. Postage paid only for transport between post offices. Local posts, each unique to its own locality, provided pickup and delivery.

L perforator   a perforating machine configured in the shape of an "L" on which sheets of stamps travel, receiving horizontal rows of perforations on one leg and vertical perforations on the other.

luminescence   a property of paper or tagging that causes it to fluoresce when exposed to ultraviolet light.

luminescent indicia detector   a postal term for a device on the facer-canceler that detects luminescent material in the ink on postage stamps and meter stamps. This allows automated facing and canceling of mail.

luminescent ink   a technical postal term for indicia or stamp ink that contains light-reflecting additives (such as phosphor) that allow a facer-canceler machine to face and cancel letter-size mail. Also known as **tagging**.

machinable   a postal term for the capacity of a mailpiece to be sorted by mail-processing equipment.

machine cancel   a cancellation applied by machine, as opposed to one applied by hand.

machine readable   a postal term for the capability of a delivery address being interpreted electronically by automated mail-processing equipment.

Machin heads   British stamps bearing the bust of Queen Elizabeth II, designed by Arnold Machin and first introduced in 1968. The long-running series has lasted more than 30 years

mail bidder   someone who bids by mail to an auction or mail bid sale.

mail bid sale   similar to an auction, except that bids are accepted by mail only (or by fax or e-mail).

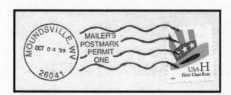

mailer's postmark   (or mailer's permit postmark) a postmark issued to mailers upon completion and acceptance of an application. Individuals and firms holding mailer's postmark permits can cancel their own mail prior to delivery at a post office.

mail stop order   a postal term for an order issued by the postal service judicial officer that directs the post office of delivery to return to the sender any mail responding to a false representation or lottery scheme.

mail stream   (1) a postal term for the total live mail at any time in the postal service mail collecting, processing, and delivery function; (2) a mailing industry term that describes the assembly line production of mailpieces in a highly automated plant.

main post office   the primary postal facility in a city where the post office uses subordinate post office stations or post office branches. It provides complete postal services to a specified geographic area. Formerly called **general post office**.

main stock   a postal term for all postage stamps and postal stationery, nonpostal stamps, and philatelic products received by a post office but not yet consigned to the main office window unit or to window clerks.

make-up rate stamp   a nondenominated stamp prepared in advance for release on short notice during a rate change and intended to be used with first-class stamps of the former rate to "make up" the difference with the new rate.

manual distribution   a postal term for the sorting of mail into cases by hand as opposed to mechanized means, such as a letter sorting machine, or automated means, such as an optical character reader.

manuscript cancel (abbreviated MS) a handwritten cancellation, usually including the date and location of mailing.

margin the unprinted area surrounding a stamp design. Stamps whose margins are balanced on all sides are known as *well centered*. Stamps whose margins are not balanced are said to be *off center* or *off centered*. Margins that are significantly larger than normal are known as *jumbo*, or *boardwalk*, margins.

margin copy usually referring to a stamp with sheet margin or selvage attached, but technically any stamp, with or without selvage, that occupies a position at the edge of a pane or sheet.

market value see **catalogue value**.

master die the original die from which intaglio production dies are made.

match and medicine stamps see **private die proprietary stamp**.

matched set a set of plate blocks each with the same plate number (or numbers) and containing one from each of the possible pane positions on the press sheet. Sometimes referred to as *round robin*.

maximum card an illustrated postcard with a stamp of the same design affixed to its picture side and canceled with a postmark relating to the subject.

meter stamp (or postage meter stamp) a stamp imprinted by a postage metering machine such as those made by the Pitney-Bowes Company.

meter tape tape on which metered postage is imprinted.

microprinting tiny, invisible, or nearly invisible, letters or numerals incorporated into a stamp design.

military mail a postal term for domestic mail and international mail that bears a U.S. military delivery address or return address and that, in some stage of its transmission, is in the possession of the Department of Defense.

military stamp a postage stamp used exclusively by military personnel, often provided at no cost.

miniature sheet (1) a smaller than normal sheet, often similar to a souvenir sheet but lacking any special marginal inscription; (2) a British term for souvenir sheet.

mint a stamp that has not been used (canceled). Often used in a stricter sense to mean a never-hinged, post-office-fresh stamp; however, there is no hard and fast rule. See also **unused**.

missionaries nickname for the first stamps of Hawaii, which were often used by missionaries on correspondence back home.

mission mixture an on-paper mixture of stamps so called because its traditional source was religious or charitable organizations, and usually containing a wide variety of foreign stamps.

mixed franking bearing stamps of more than one country.

mixture an assortment of stamps, most often on paper and unsorted, containing a variety of stamps including duplicates, most often sold in bulk by the ounce, pound, or kilogram. See also **kiloware**.

monochrome consisting of one color only.

monocolor consisting of one color only.

motorized carrier a postal term for a letter carrier who uses a vehicle to deliver mail. The route is called a *motorized route*, or a *mounted route*.

mount a clear plastic pouch or sleeve used to protect a stamp and attach it to an album page.

mounted [British] hinged.

mounted route a postal term for a city route on which the letter carrier drives a vehicle to deliver the mail rather than walk as done on a foot route.

mourning cover a cover imprinted with a black border, popular in former times.

mourning stamp a stamp imprinted with a black border.

MS abbreviation for **manuscript cancel**.

multicolored containing more than one color.

multiple a group of two or more unseparated stamps, such as a block, pair, strip, or pane.

mute cancel a postmark that lacks the name of the place of cancellation and in some cases, the date (e.g., double oval registry postmarks and some military field post postmarks).

mystery lot see **job lot**.

negative postmark a postmark on which light and dark areas are reversed as on a photographic negative.

never hinged (abbreviated NH) a stamp that has never been hinged.

new issue a newly issued stamp or set, often received by subscription either directly from a postal administration or from a stamp dealer.

newspaper stamp a stamp used to pay postage for newspapers and periodicals.

NGAI (no gum as issued) used to denote a lack of gum, but to advise that the omission is normal for the issue.

nibbed perforation a perforation tooth whose tip is somewhat short and ragged looking, the result of careless separation.

nixie a mailpiece that cannot be sorted or delivered because of an incorrect, illegible, or insufficient delivery address. A nixie clerk specializes in handling this mail.

no gum without gum. Implies that the stamp once possessed gum. See also **ungummed**.

nondenominated a stamp that does not contain a numerical denomination. The denomination is often represented by a letter, such as A, B, or C, or by some other inscription. In most cases, nondenominated stamps are transitional issues readied when a rate increase is anticipated but before the actual new rate is known.

nonmachinable a postal term for a piece of mail that cannot be sorted on mail-processing equipment because of size, shape, content, or address legibility. Such mail must be processed manually.

nonstandard size mail a postal term for any piece of first-class mail weighing 1 ounce or less that exceeds certain size limits. This type of mail incurs a surcharge.

NSDA abbreviation for National Stamp Dealers Association.

obliterator a postal term for a cancellation device, which includes the validator, registry, or round-dater stamp; the parcel post canceler; the rubber oval stamp; and the all-purpose dating stamp.

obsolete a stamp no longer available at the post office.

occupant address a postal term for an addressing format that uses one of four designations (postal customer, occupant, householder, or resident) rather than an addressee name.

occupation stamp a stamp issued for use in a country or territory overrun by another power; for example, after World War II, the Allies issued stamps for use in occupied Germany.

OCR abbreviation for **optical character reader**.

off center a stamp whose design is poorly centered in relation to its margins.

offices abroad post offices maintained in foreign nations, such as the U.S. agency in Shanghai, China.

official first day cover   see **first day cover**.

official mail   a postal designation for mail authorized by federal law to be sent by government officials without postage prepayment. It includes franked mail sent by members of Congress and penalty mail sent by U.S. government agencies.

official seal   a post office seal affixed to mail opened either intentionally or by accident. The seal is affixed across the opening.

official stamp   a stamp intended for use by a government agency, intended for use only on official mail, and typically valid only when used for that purpose.

off paper   used stamps that have been soaked off paper. Most often in reference to mixtures, which are sold either "on paper" or "off paper." See also **on paper**.

offset printing   see **lithography**.

OG   abbreviation for **original gum**.

omnibus issue   taken together, a group of stamps issued by a number of postal administrations to mark or commemorate a single theme or event (e.g., those issued by nations of the British Commonwealth to commemorate the coronation of Queen Elizabeth II).

on cover   a stamp attached to a cover, card, or mailing piece.

on paper   refers to mixtures of used stamps still attached to pieces of paper. See also **off paper**.

on piece   a stamp attached to a piece of paper torn or cut from an envelope or a wrapper to which it was originally affixed.

optical character reader   (abbreviated OCR) an automated mail-sorting machine that interprets the address information on letter-size mail and sprays the corresponding ZIP code information below the address as a bar code.

original gum   (abbreviated OG) gum applied to a stamp at the time of manufacture.

overall tagging   tagging applied to the entire area of the stamp as opposed to just a portion of it.

overprint   (abbreviated ovpt.) printing applied to a stamp subsequent to regular production, typically to denote a special purpose (such as airmail), to commemorate something, or as a control measure. An overprint intended to change the face value of a stamp is known as a *surcharge*. Overprints are not cancellations.

packet   typically a printed window envelope containing an assortment of stamps for the beginner or general collector.

packet material   common, inexpensive stamps.

pair   two unseparated stamps.

PAL   abbreviation for **parcel airlift**.

pane   a finished "sheet" of stamps as sold in post offices, as distinct from a press or production sheet, which usually contains multiple panes of stamps.

paquebot   a marking applied to mail posted aboard ships at sea to be deposited upon making port and bearing stamps of the ship's country of origin. The rate for paquebot mail is that of the country's prevailing domestic rate. The paquebot marking is to make the port post office aware that no additional postage is due.

parcel airlift   (abbreviated PAL) a service that provides air transportation for parcels on a space-available basis to or from military post offices outside the contiguous 48 states.

parcel post stamp   a stamp intended for use on parcel post; however, some countries allow their use on ordinary mail as well.

part perforate   containing perforations on fewer than all sides, the term implying intentionally so. Some U.S. revenue stamps of the nineteenth century were perforated either vertically or horizontally but not both directions.

paste-up pair   the term "paste up" arose in the early twentieth century when coils of stamps were created by gluing strips of stamps together to achieve the desired length. The glued splice was referred to as a paste up. Pairs that possessed the splice were known as *paste-up pairs*.

patriotic cover   a cover bearing a patriotic cachet or slogan, most often produced during time of war, especially during the Civil War and World War II.

penalty envelope   an envelope intended for official use by government agencies with a printed indicia that often contained the warning "Penalty for Private Use" or similar wording. The penalty applied to anyone using the envelope for private use, whether they were government employees or private citizens.

pen cancel   a cancellation applied by hand, usually an "X" or other mark to deface a stamp.

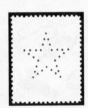

perfin   short for perforated initials. Refers to a stamp with initials or a design punched in it by a perforating device. Perfins are utilized by firms (most frequently) and governments (occasionally) as a control measure to prevent pilferage or unauthorized use.

perforations   rows of holes punched between stamps to facilitate their separation. The size of the holes and spacing vary from issue to issue. Perforations are measured by a perforation gauge. Holes not completely punched through are known as **blind perforations**.

perforation tooth   one of the toothlike tips of paper that protrude along the tear line after perforated stamps have been separated. While still joined, the paper lying between perforation holes and connecting unseparated stamps is known as a **bridge**.

perishable matter   a postal designation for an item (such as produce, a live animal, or a live plant) that can deteriorate in the mail and thereby lose value, create a health hazard, or cause a nuisance or disturbance under ordinary mailing conditions. Such matter usually requires special packaging.

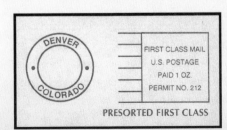

permit imprint   printed indicia used by permit-holding bulk mailers to evidence payment of postage.

Persian rug (or Persian carpet) a nickname for the $500 denomination of the second U.S. revenue issue by virtue of its large size, intricate pattern, and coloration.

PF abbreviation for the Philatelic Foundation.

phantom a fantasy issue, an ostensible stamp that is, in reality, from a fanciful or imaginary entity.

philatelic agency (or bureau) an official outlet established to sell stamps and other philatelic items to collectors.

philatelic cover a cover prepared and sent by or for a stamp collector, often with stamps or combinations of stamps not normally encountered on mail, such as complete sets of semipostals. See also **commercial cover**.

photogravure also known as gravure printing. Photogravure uses photographically etched printing plates. In photogravure, ink lies in small recesses and is very thinly applied. Tones are achieved by varying the depth of the recesses and thickness of the ink. The image is broken up into a series of fine points that keep the paper from being pressed into the recesses. The dot structure in photogravure is usually much finer than that of lithography. The difference is apparent under 10-power magnification.

pictorial cancel a cancellation, usually a handstamp and commemorative in nature, that incorporates an illustration.

pictorial stamp (or pictorial) a stamp featuring a scene or topic rather than the portrait of an individual, a numeral, a coat of arms, or the like. Pictorials are generally large and colorful.

piece part of an envelope or mailing piece containing postage stamps and in most cases, a cancellation.

pigeonhole a postal term for one opening or section for sorting mail into a distribution case.

pinhole a small hole. Pinholes are sometimes encountered on nineteenth-century stamps, often the result of the practice of pinning them up for display on sale boards in the early days of philately. Pinholes are not necessarily obvious, especially those that have been closed and ironed out; however, they can usually be spotted by holding a stamp up to light or immersing it in watermark fluid.

plate block   a block of stamps, often a block of four, on whose selvage appears the printing plate number(s). Plate blocks vary in size according to the number and placement of plate numbers appearing on the selvage. In addition, plate blocks of se-tenant stamps vary according to the number of different se-tenant designs necessary to form a block containing one of each design.

plate flaw   a defect or damage, usually small, on an individual subject on a printing plate and appearing as a constant variety on all impressions made by the plate.

plate number   a security number assigned to a printing plate by the printer for inventory and control purposes and most often seen on U.S. issues. All sheets of stamps in a print run made from the same plate will share the same plate number. Occasionally, some countries have placed serial numbers on selvage for inventory control. The serial numbers, which are consecutive and vary from pane to pane, should not be confused with plate numbers.

plate number coil   (abbreviated PNC) a coil stamp on which a small plate number appears at the bottom of the design. Plate numbers appear at predetermined intervals (e.g., every 24th or 52nd stamp). PNCs are usually collected in strips of three, five, or seven, with the numbered stamp occupying the center position in the strip.

plate proof   a proof impression taken from a printing plate, usually an intaglio plate, typically to check that all stamps are positioned properly and entered in good condition. Plate proofs of U.S. stamps are usually printed either on India paper or card stock and are known for their sharp impressions and solid colors. They are collected as individual images or multiples but rarely as intact sheets. The practice of releasing plate proofs of U.S. stamps was discontinued toward the end of the nineteenth century. Plate proofs are known for some issues of some foreign countries.

plate single   a single stamp with selvage tab attached containing a plate number.

plating   the reconstruction of a pane of stamps by sleuthing the position of each stamp within the pane. Great Britain's Penny Black can be easily plated because each subject on the printing plate contained a different two-letter combination, such as AA, AB, AC, and so on. Plating stamps without intentional position markers is more challenging and can take years to complete. Plating became popular in the nineteenth century, when philatelic scholars discovered they could identify each subject on a printing plate because each possessed slight differences unique to it. The location of each stamp on the plate could be deduced by studying the position of individual subjects in blocks and multiples. One enthusiast described plating as an intellectual jigsaw puzzle.

PMG   abbreviation for postmaster general.

PMS   (Pantone Matching System) a standardized system of color identification used throughout the printing industry, featuring an identification number for each of thousands of individual shades. Each shade is created by mixing inks according to a standard formula, permitting a press technician to print the precise shade specified by the designer, ensuring that the finished stamp will look exactly like the original design.

PNC   abbreviation for **plate number coil**.

points down   grilling applied from the front of a stamp resulting in raised points pushed up on the back side. See also **grill**.

points up   grilling applied from the back of a stamp resulting in raised points pushed up on the front side. See also **grill**.

position block   a block that contains printed markings on its selvage specific to a certain position on a sheet of stamps, such as a center line block or arrow block.

postage   payment for delivery of a piece of mail that is affixed or imprinted to a mailpiece, usually in the form of a postage stamp, permit imprint, or meter impression.

postage and revenue   an inscription on many British and British-area stamps used to indicate that the stamps could be used either to pay postage or revenue fees.

postage-due stamp   a stamp affixed to underpaid mail to indicate that postage is due from the addressee. The United States discontinued postage-due stamps in 1986. Postage-due stamps were used on ordinary single-piece underpaid mail and on receipts for postage due from business reply mail, bulk mail address correction fees, and so forth.

postage meter   a mechanical or electromechanical device that can print one or more denominations of an authorized postage indicia.

postage stamp   a stamp used to evidence prepayment of postage. The term "postage stamp" distinguishes it from other types of stamps such as revenue stamps or savings stamps.

postage validation imprinter   (abbreviated PVI) a computerized printing device that attaches to an integrated retail terminal to produce a postage label similar to a meter stamp strip. The label may contain a bar-coded destination ZIP code that is compatible with automated mail-processing equipment.

postal cancel   a cancellation showing that a stamp has been used to pay postage rather than for revenue purposes.

postal card   a card upon which postage has been printed. The U.S. Postal Service now refers to them as **stamped cards**.

postal code   a delivery code, analogous to a ZIP code, used by a foreign country.

postal counterfeit   a stamp that has been counterfeited to defraud the postal service.

postal-fiscal   a postage stamp used for revenue purposes.

postal history   the study of postal systems and the collecting of stamps, covers, markings, and other materials, such as rate information, relating to their evolution and operation.

postally used   a stamp actually used for postage rather than canceled to order or used for some other purpose such as revenue service. Serious collectors generally prefer postally used stamps to CTOs or those bearing revenue cancels. They feel postally used stamps are more legitimate, having performed the duty for which they were intended. Postally used stamps are generally worth more than CTOs or revenue-canceled examples of the same stamp.

postal note stamp   a stamp used to evidence payment of fractions of a dollar on postal money orders. The stamps were affixed to the money order. The use of postal note stamps was discontinued in 1951.

postal savings stamp   a stamp issued to evidence a deposit in the postal savings system, which was established in the early part of the twentieth century. Beginning in 1941, postal savings stamps could be redeemed for savings bonds. The postal savings system was discontinued in 1966. See also **savings stamp**.

postal stationery stationery sold by a postal service usually, but not always, with imprinted postage. The imprint is known as an *indicia*. Postal stationery includes stamped cards (postal cards), stamped envelopes, letter sheets, and aerogrammes (air letters).

postcard a privately produced card without imprinted postage and usually containing a printed greeting or an illustration on the reverse. See also **viewcard.**

poste restante international mail sent to general delivery.

postmark an official marking (usually circular but can be any shape or in manuscript or, most recently, sprayed-on dot-matrix style characters) applied to a piece of mail, most often indicating date and place of mailing.

postmaster's provisional (or postmaster provisional) a stamp issued by a postmaster to meet a local need. Generally refers to those issued during the period between the enactment of uniform postal rates by Congress in 1845 and the first U.S. postage stamps in 1847.

post office seal an adhesive seal used to reseal letters opened in transit, either intentionally or inadvertently, such as an item damaged by sorting machinery.

Bureau precancel; local precancel; bars only precancel; service inscribed precancel.

precancel a stamp canceled prior to being sold and affixed to a mailing piece. Precancels are most often used by bulk mailers. Traditionally, precancels contained the name of the mailer's city and state between two parallel bars. In the 1970s the style evolved into a pair of black bars. Later, even the bars were omitted, and most precancels today contain no apparent cancellation. Instead, they are "service inscribed" according to their intended use (e.g., "bulk rate" or "presorted standard").

Service-inscribed stamps are commonly used on junk mail because marketing surveys have shown that recipients open a higher percentage of mail when it bears a stamp (as opposed to a printed indicia or postage meter). Collectors of traditional (city and state inscribed) precancels generally don't expect gum on their stamps. However, collectors of mint service-inscribed precancels prefer that they possess full original gum. Mail bearing precanceled stamps does not go through canceling equipment.

presorted mail a form of mail preparation, required to bypass certain postal operations, in which the mailer groups pieces in a mailing by ZIP code, carrier route, carrier walk sequence, or other separations. Presorted mail is sorted by the mailer to the finest extent required by the standards for the rate claimed. Generally, presort is performed sequentially, from the lowest (finest) level to the highest level, to those destinations specified by standard, and is completed at each level before the next level is prepared.

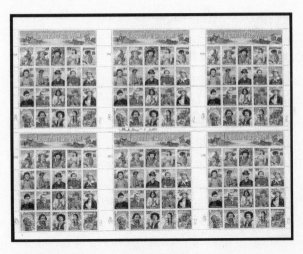

press sheet (or uncut press sheet) a sheet containing multiple panes of stamps in the form in which they were printed and before being separated into individual panes.

pressure sensitive a synonym for self-adhesive.

printer's waste (1) paper used in the production of postage stamps that, for whatever reason, is defective, is improperly prepared, or lacks one or more elements that a properly prepared stamp should possess; (2) a philatelic term for errors that have been, or are thought to have been, misappropriated from a printing plant or wastepaper destruction facility and illicitly sold into the hobby. The term invariably carries a negative connotation. Many collectors do not consider printer's waste to be errors—and rightly so.

private die proprietary stamp a revenue stamp used to evidence payment of tax on proprietary items such as patent medicine, playing cards, and matches. Firms were permitted to design and print stamps of their own design, which usually advertised or promoted their products. They received a small discount for saving the government the cost of printing the stamps. Of course, they still were responsible for paying the taxes the stamps represented. Private die proprietary stamps are also known as *match and medicine stamps*.

Private Express Statutes laws that give the U.S. Postal Service the exclusive right, with certain exceptions, to carry letters for compensation. Regulations under these statutes are published in title 39 of the Code of Federal Regulations parts 310 and 320, as amended by final rules published in the Federal Register.

private perforations see **vending and affixing machine perforations**.

private treaty an arrangement in which a stamp dealer acts in the capacity of agent for a seller, receiving a commission for his services.

proof a trial impression made from a die or plate before regular production in order to check engraving, color, and so forth. See also **large die proof** and **small die proof**.

propaganda forgery an imitation of a genuine stamp of an enemy nation, either nearly identical to the original or with slight variations intended to mock, taunt, or ridicule the nation, its culture, or its leadership. The forgeries are sometimes used on mailings containing propaganda, mailings usually entered illicitly into the enemy nation's mail stream.

proprietary stamp a revenue stamp used to evidence payment of tax on certain commodities such as matches, medicines, playing cards, and so forth.

provisional a stamp issued to meet an immediate need, often under local authority and often as the result of a stamp shortage, and usually for a limited time until regular supplies become available.

PSS abbreviation for Precancel Stamp Society.

PTS abbreviation for (1) Philatelic Traders Society, a British trade association for professional stamp dealers; (2) Postal Transport Service, the successor appellation for Railway Mail Service.

PTT (posts, telephone, and telegraph) in some foreign countries, postal, telephone, and telegraph services are government controlled, usually under the authority of a single ministry, often known by the initials "PTT."

pulled perforation   (or pulled perf) a perforation tooth missing all the way to the base of the tooth or, in some cases, below the base, having taken with it a small bit of paper of the stamp itself. See also **short perforation**.

punch cancel   generally a small hole punched to invalidate a stamp, most often a revenue stamp, but also sometimes proofs of foreign stamps.

PVA gum   (polyvinyl alcohol gum) polyvinyl alcohol (or dry) gum is flat in appearance, unlike glossy (or wet) gum.

quadrille paper   paper printed with a background of horizontal and vertical lines forming a grid of small squares, usually faintly imprinted. Blank quadrille pages are used by collectors who design their own album pages. The grid makes it easy to lay out a geometric arrangement and does not distract.

R   abbreviation for **regummed**.

railroad cancel   (or RPO cancel) a cancellation applied aboard a railway post office.

railway post office   (abbreviated RPO) a post office located aboard a railway mail car in which mail is processed while in transit.

receiving mark   a postmark applied, normally to the back of an item of mail, showing the name of the receiving city, the date, and frequently the time. Receiving marks were routinely used on first-class mail until the early twentieth century, and for a few decades thereafter, on special delivery, registered mail, and certain items of airmail. At present, receiving marks are primarily used on registered mail.

recess printing   see **intaglio**.

recut   an intaglio image that has been reworked, touched up, or repaired on plate.

red   an informal postal term for a piece of registered mail. The term originated when registered mail was dispatched in red-striped pouches.

redrawn a design nearly identical to the original design except for some small modification.

reentry the subsequent impression of a subject by a transfer roller. Reentries are made to replace worn or imperfect subjects within a printing plate. In some cases, the reentry causes a subtle doubling of the image.

refused mail mail that is not accepted by the addressee and is returned to the sender.

registration the alignment of colors imprinted by the various individual plates involved in multicolor printing. Each lays down a separate color. When out of alignment, the colors are said to be *misregistered*.

regummed a stamp that has had new gum applied to simulate its original gum.

reissue an obsolete issue once again placed on sale, sometimes from remainders of the original release. See also **reprint**.

relief printing see **letterpress**.

remainder (1) the balance of a collection that has been stripped of better stamps; (2) a quantity of obsolete stamps, often canceled to order, sold to the philatelic market by a postal service.

repaired refers to a stamp or cover possessing faults, such as a tear or a pinhole, repaired. Repaired stamps are generally held in low esteem by the philatelic community, especially when the repairs were intended to enhance value by deception.

reperforated a stamp that has had perforations added either to a straight edge or to a perforated edge that has been trimmed in order to improve centering.

reprint (1) a stamp printed from new plates (often distinguishable from the original plates) and released subsequent to the original issues having become obsolete; (2) a stamp printed from original plates subsequent to becoming obsolete, often for sale to stamp collectors. See also **reissue**.

restricted delivery a service that generally limits who may receive an item. This service is available for a fee when used with certified mail, collect on delivery, insured mail, and registered mail.

return receipt a mailing card signed by the addressee of an article and mailed back to the sender as evidence of delivery.

  **revenue** a stamp used to evidence payment of a tax or fee. Postage stamps are occasionally used as revenue stamps, most often abroad. Examples of revenues include waterfowl hunting stamps, documentary stamps, playing card stamps, and cigarette

stamps. Revenues are often referred to as *fiscals* in other countries. Postage stamps are sometimes used to evidence payment of revenue fees, especially in countries of the British Commonwealth.

revenue assurance   a postal term for an ongoing policy to prevent the loss of revenue by identifying uncanceled postage stamps and misclassified mail and collecting postage and fees for unpaid or short-paid mail.

revenue stamped paper   items, such as nineteenth-century bank checks, upon which revenue stamps were imprinted prior to their use.

RFD   (rural free delivery) RFD was inaugurated October 1, 1896. Before that time, rural customers had to pick up their mail at the post office.

RMS   (railway mail service) "RMS" often appeared on cancellations applied aboard railway mail cars, on which mail was processed en route from one city to the next.

roller cancel   a self-inking, handheld device that can apply a continuous cancellation from its cylindrical roller.

rough perforations   (or rough perfs) perforations resulting from careless separation, usually ragged or uneven in appearance. Also, poor-quality perforations applied by worn or defective equipment.

roulette   a philatelic term referring to a series of small slits applied between stamps to facilitate separation. The slits may appear in a straight line or in other configurations, such as serpentine or sawtooth patterns.

round robin   see **matched set**.

RPO   (railway post office) "RPO" often appeared on cancellations applied aboard railway mail cars, on which mail was processed en route from one city to the next.

RPSC   abbreviation for Royal Philatelic Society of Canada.

rural carrier   in rural communities lacking convenient postal facilities, a USPS employee assigned to deliver and collect all mail classes, thus providing most services available at a small post office.

SAE   abbreviation for stamped addressed envelope.

sample   an overprint applied to samples, often distributed by salesmen representing nineteenth-century U.S. banknote companies. In many cases, samples were overprinted with the word "specimen" rather than "sample."

Sand Dunes a pejorative term referring to the small desert states on the Persian Gulf that, before joining the United Arab Emirates in the early 1970s, generated a constant flow of large, gaudy stamps far in excess of legitimate postal need. The so-called "sand dunes" were Abu Dhabi, Ajman, Dubai, Fujiera, Ras al Khaima, Sharjah, and Umm al Qiwain.

sanitary fair stamps stamps issued in conjunction with fairs sponsored by the U.S. Sanitary Commission to raise money to provide for medical and nursing care for wounded Union soldiers during and shortly after the Civil War. The commission also promoted awareness for sanitary conditions in the field and in hospitals.

SASE abbreviation for self-addressed stamped envelope.

satchel cart a small, portable handcart used by city carriers to transport satchels of mail on their routes.

savings stamp similar to and replacing postal savings stamps. Savings stamps were issued by the Postal Service and could be redeemed for savings bonds. The stamps were discontinued in 1970. See also **postal savings stamp**.

seal in the philatelic sense, a stamplike item not valid for postage, and often sold for charitable purposes, such as Christmas seals or Easter seals.

secret mark a small, difficult-to-detect engraver's mark applied to a design so that stamps printed by one source (such as the Continental Bank Note Company) can be distinguished from identical stamps printed by another source (such as the National Bank Note Company). Occasionally, secret marks have appeared on later U.S. issues and on a variety of foreign issues.

sectional center facility (abbreviated SCF) a processing and distribution center for post offices in a designated geographic area as defined by the first three digits of the ZIP codes of those offices. Some SCFs serve more than one three-digit ZIP code range.

Seebecks a pejorative term for any of the several issues printed by the Hamilton Banknote Company during the 1890s for Ecuador, El Salvador, Honduras, and Nicaragua under an arrangement formulated by Nicolas F. Seebeck. Under the arrangement, Hamilton supplied the governments with new postage stamps each year or two at no cost in exchange for their unused remnants and the right to reprint obsolete issues, which they sold to collectors. This arrangement outraged collectors of the time, who felt they were being exploited and who, as a result, scorned "Seebecks."

selective block tagging a form of block tagging in which tagging is intentionally omitted from part of the block, most often to allow the omitted or untagged areas to more readily accept canceling ink.

self-adhesive (1) a stamp whose gum does not require moisture to become adhesive; (2) gum that does not require moisture to become adhesive.

selvage (or selvedge) the marginal area or border surrounding a sheet or pane of stamps.

semiofficial airmail stamp a stamp issued by a private carrier to evidence payment of fees for mail transported on the carrier's airline. The fee for private carriage was above and beyond that applicable for transport through the normal mails. In the early part of the twentieth century, residents of remote Canadian mining camps often made use of the service offered by small airlines to transport mail to the nearest venue served by the Canadian post office. Semiofficial airmail stamps were usually affixed to the back of envelopes.

semipostal a postage stamp for which only part of the purchase price is valid for postage; the balance is collected for some other purpose, often a charitable cause, such as child welfare, flood reconstruction, a building fund, or medical research. Semipostals are usually, but not always, denominated by two figures: the first is valid for postage, the second (or surtax) is the amount allocated for the other purpose (e.g., 50¢ plus 20¢). In some cases, such as the U.S. Breast Cancer Research stamp of 1998, the denominations do not appear on the stamp. Also called *charity stamps*.

series a group of stamps, usually definitives, sharing a theme or motif, and often issued over a period of time ranging from months to years, and usually in use for a number of years.

serpentine roulette rouletting in a wavy pattern, reminiscent of the pattern displayed by a moving serpent.

service inscribed a type of stamp used by bulk mailers on which the class of service is inscribed (printed) at the time of production. Referred to as *precancels* by some; however, the printed inscription usually appears to be the part of the design rather than a cancellation.

sesquicentennial   150th anniversary.

set   two or more stamps sharing a similar theme, motif, or appearance, usually commemoratives, usually issued within a short period time, and usually, but not always, of different denominations.

se-tenant   two or more different stamp designs printed next to one another on a pane of stamps, a souvenir sheet, a booklet, or a coil.

sewing machine perforations   perforations applied by sewing machine.

shade   a variation in color, often slight or subtle, from the color normally encountered on an issue.

sheet   **(1)** short for press sheet or uncut press sheet; **(2)** vernacular for a pane of stamps. See **press sheet** and **pane**.

sheet-fed   a printing press that is fed individual sheets of paper as opposed to being fed by a web or roll of paper.

sheet stamp   a stamp issued in sheet form. Sheet stamps generally have perforations on all four sides, unless issued imperforate or unless one or more edges of the pane contain a straight edge.

short paid   a marking, most often seen on nineteenth-century covers, indicating that insufficient postage was affixed and that postage due should be collected.

short-paid mail   mail on which additional postage is collectable on final delivery.

short perforation   (or short perf) a perforation that is shorter than nearby perforations, and if sufficiently short to be visually distracting, considered a fault.

short set   an incomplete set of stamps, usually comprising only the lower denominations.

siderography   refers to the process by which intaglio printing plates are created by impressing individual images, one at a time, from a transfer roll.

silk paper   paper containing colored silk fibers. Silk paper was used to print some U.S. revenue stamps.

skip   a stamp or piece of mail that has gone through the mail without being canceled.

sleeper (1) a stamp perceived to be worth much more than its current value once its rarity or special qualities become fully appreciated. The term is an informal one, often nothing more than speculative opinion; (2) an informal postal term for a letter that is lodged in the back of a case instead of lying flat in the pigeonhole or bin.

slogan cancel the killer portion of a cancel, usually a machine cancel, that contains a slogan, such as "Pray for Peace," a slogan often seen during the 1950s and 1960s.

small die proof a die proof often printed on India paper and possessing margins, which although larger than those on issued stamps, are quite small in comparison to those on large die proofs. See also **die proof** and **large die proof**.

small packet a class of international mail that can be used to send disks and tapes, computer materials, commercial samples or other lightweight merchandise items or business documents that do not have the character of personal correspondence.

smiles, frowns, and upside downs a postal term for accidental deviations from the uniform alignment of envelopes on a facer-canceler or letter-sorting machine. When the back of the envelope faces the machine or operator, it is either a smile (flap makes a V) or a frown (flap is inverted); when the address side faces the machine but is inverted, the envelope is called an upside down.

snorkel collection box a collection box that is placed at the curbside, fitted with a chute to receive mail deposited by motorists.

soaking removing stamps from paper by soaking in water.

socked on the nose see **bull's-eye cancel**.

SON abbreviation for **socked on the nose**.

sound free of faults.

souvenir card a card containing printed examples of stamps (or currency). Souvenir cards are usually issued in connection with a stamp show or philatelic event. Souvenir cards are produced by both the government and private entities. Stamps appearing on souvenir cards are not valid for postage.

souvenir panel a souvenir product sold by the U.S. Postal Service that features one or more engravings relating to a stamp and contains a block of four of the stamp.

souvenir sheet a sheet, usually small, containing one or more stamps, usually bearing a commemorative marginal inscription, and in the beginning, issued for a special event or occasion such as a philatelic exhibition. Stamps in souvenir sheets are valid for postage. Many prolific stamp-issuing countries now routinely issue souvenir sheets along with their commemoratives, a practice that has resulted in a diminution of significance and appeal that souvenir sheets once had.

space filler a damaged or otherwise normally uncollectible copy of a stamp good for no other purpose than filling an album space until a collectible copy comes along. The term implies that the stamp has little or no value.

special delivery stamp stamps intended for use on special delivery mail. Special delivery service is now obsolete in the United States, replaced by express mail service. When it was available in the United States, special delivery service paid for the immediate delivery of an item to the addressee once it had arrived at its destination post office.

special handling stamp a class of stamps, now obsolete, used to pay a fee that entitled parcel post items to be given the same preferential handling as first-class mail.

specialist one whose collection is narrowly focused on a specific country, issue, stamp, or collecting interest.

special printing   referring to the special circumstances under which an issue is released as much as the way in which it was produced; some are produced from original plates, others from new plates; some are valid for postage, others not valid.

special stamp   (or special-issue stamp) a stamp issued for a special occasion or purpose such as Love stamps and Christmas, Hanukkah, and Kwanzaa stamps. Special stamps are neither definitives or commemoratives. The Postal Service originated the term; however, it is not widely used in philatelic circles.

specimen stamp   a sample rendered postally invalid by the application of an overprint (e.g., "specimen" or "sample").

speedy bag   an informal postal term for a clear plastic sack used to identify and hold special delivery mail. The bag was then placed inside regular sacks of dispatched mail. It kept this mail separate from other mail in transit and expedited its delivery.

splice   the point at which two pieces of paper are joined. Early coil stamp rolls were spliced (glued) together from sheet stamp stock, and pairs containing such splices are known as *paste-up pairs*. Modern issues, especially coil stamps, sometimes contain splices where paper from two web rolls was taped together during printing. Modern stamps containing splices are usually removed from finished rolls of coil stamp production but sometimes escape and find their way into hands of collectors.

split grill   a misregistered grill impression yielding portions of two or more separate grills on one stamp.

spray-on marking   an ink-jet marking sprayed on by mail-processing machinery to confirm the time and place a piece of mail passed through the system, usually appearing at the upper right on a cover.

s/s abbreviation for **souvenir sheet**.

stamped card a card upon which postage has been printed. Formerly known as **postal cards**.

stamped envelope an envelope upon which postage has been printed. See also **postal stationery**.

stampless cover a cover sent through the mail without postage stamps, the payment of postage evidenced by handstamp or manuscript. Usually refers to covers prior to the advent of postage stamps.

star route an obsolete and informal designation for a highway contract route based on the former practice of marking contract routes with asterisks on dispatch schedules. See also **highway contract route**.

state revenue a revenue stamp issued by a state (e.g., cigarette stamps, bedding stamps, and hunting permit stamps).

straight edge a nonperforated edge. The term is usually used to refer to the naturally occurring, nonperforated edges of sheet or booklet stamps. Straight edges are usually created as a result of severing panes from press sheets and as a result do not contain perforations. Straight-edged sheet stamps are eschewed by collectors, who prefer to see perforations on all sides for aesthetic reasons. Because of this preference, straight-edged examples of expensive stamps, which are worth only a small fraction of their fully perforated counterparts, are often reperforated in an attempt to enhance their value and deceive the unwary.

strike the impression made by a canceling device and used in the sense of a "clean strike" or "poor strike," and so on.

strip three or more unseparated stamps arranged side to side or end to end.

subject a term used to refer to a single image, either on a sheet of stamps or on a stamp printing plate, such as a 160-subject plate.

substrate a technical term for the material upon which a stamp is printed, such as paper.

supplement an installment of album pages to bring a loose-leaf album up to date, usually published annually.

surcharge an overprint that changes the face value of a stamp or an item of postal stationery. See also **overprint**.

surface mail   in international mail, mail that is transported by any mode other than air (i.e., sea, rail, or highway).

surface tagged   paper coated with luminescent tagging, as opposed to being impregnated with it.

sweatbox   a box, usually small and usually made of plastic, containing a sponge situated beneath a perforated shelf and most often used in an attempt to salvage mint stamps stuck together or to paper and preserve as much original gum as possible. Humidity from the sponge acts to soften the adhesive and release the stamp from whatever it is stuck to. Results vary according to how firmly stamps are stuck down, and although original gum can often be retained, it will almost always show signs of being disturbed.

sweeper   an informal postal term for a clerk who removes the mail from the bins or stackers on mechanical and automated mail-processing equipment and then places it in the equipment for dispatch.

syncopated perforations   rows of perforations containing the occasional intentional omission of one or more holes at regular intervals. Stamps with syncopated perforations do not separate as readily as stamps with normal perforations. The Netherlands used syncopated perforations on vending machine stamps to prevent them from accidentally separating while they were being dispensed.

T   abbreviation for the French word *taxe*, and the international symbol for postage due.

tab   a piece of selvage attached to an individual stamp, and in some cases on foreign stamps, containing a printed inscription.

tagged   possessing luminescent tagging.

tagging   a luminescent coating applied to stamps during printing. Usually invisible to the naked eye, tagging can be observed under ultraviolet light. Tagging may cover all (*overall tagging*) or part of a stamp (*bar tagging* or *block tagging*). See also **luminescent ink**.

tagging ghost   see **ghosting**.

target cancel   a killer cancellation in the shape of a target.

teeth   see **perforation tooth**.

tercentenary   300th anniversary.

territorial cover   a cover used during the territorial (prestatehood) period of a state later within the United States.

test stamp   (or testing stamp) a dummy stamp, usually in coil form, used to set up or test postage vending machines. Testing stamps are also known in booklet form.

tête-bêche   (pronounced "tet-besh") two adjacent stamps, one of which is inverted in relation to the other. From the French, meaning "head to foot."

thematic   a synonym for a topical stamp, especially in Great Britain.

tied   indicates that a cancellation strike falls on both stamp and cover. Such a stamp is said to be "tied to cover."

toned   discolored by exposure to light or chemicals. Toned paper is often yellowish or brownish in color and usually darker than it was originally.

topical   a stamp related to a topic such as birds, flowers, medicine, sports, and so on. Topical collectors form collections of stamps relating to their chosen theme or subject.

town cancel   a postmark bearing the name of a town and usually a date.

transfer roller   a steel roller used to transfer an engraved design from the master die to printing plates. The image from a finished die is impressed onto the soft steel of a transfer roll, which is then hardened and used to impress, under great pressure, individual subjects on a printing plate.

transient   refers to a nonrepetitive anomaly, as opposed to a constant variety.

transition multiple   any multiple that contains one or more error stamps together with one or more normal and/or partially normal examples. Transition multiples are interesting because they show a progression from normal to error.

transit mark   a marking, usually in the form of a postmark, applied to a cover at a point along its journey.

treaty port   a port (and in some cases, a larger territory) in China or Japan operated by foreign powers under treaty forced upon the country. Great Britain, France, Germany, Russia, and the United States established postal operations and issued stamps for use in these territories. They did so because they could not rely on the native local service.

trial color proof   a proof in a color other than the issued color. Trial color proofs are made to assess the aesthetics of various colors and select the one most appropriate to the design.

true franking   postage affixed to a mailing piece that exactly pays the rate for the piece.

turned cover   a used cover that has been turned inside out and used again, a practice sometimes used during periods of paper shortage, such as in the South during the Civil War.

two-cent reds   a generic name applied to the 2¢ U.S. commemorative stamps issued during the 1920s and early 1930s, which were invariably red in color to conform to the UPU color standard for domestic first-class stamps.

type   in philately, a term used to denote versions of nearly identical stamps that vary in minor respects.

typeset   printed by letterpress. See **letterpress**.

typographed   printed by letterpress. See **letterpress**.

unaddressed   a first day cover that contains no address. Unaddressed covers are usually serviced in bulk and returned to cachet producers under separate cover; therefore, no address is necessary.

uncut press sheet   see **press sheet**.

underfranked   an item with less than the required amount of postage affixed.

unexploded   an intact booklet. A booklet dissembled into separate panes is said to have been exploded.

ungummed   without gum. Usually implying the stamp was issued without gum. See also **no gum**.

unique   only a single example known to exist.

unique ZIP code   a ZIP code assigned to a company, a government agency, or an entity with sufficient mail volume, and based on average daily volume of letter-size mail received, availability of ZIP code numbers in the postal area, and Postal Service cost-benefit analyses.

unissued   refers to stamps that were prepared but never put on sale.

Universal Postal Union   (abbreviated UPU) international postal governing body to which all recognized nations belong. The UPU administers postal treaties and the transmission of mail between member states. It was founded in 1863.

unlisted   not recognized by a catalogue publisher as being a postage stamp, either by virtue of having been issued by an entity not recognized as a legitimate government or not having been issued for postal purposes.

unmounted   [British] never hinged.

unofficial first day cover   a first day cover postmarked in any city other than one designated as "official." An official first day cover is one postmarked in the city (or one of the cities) where the stamp was officially first placed on sale. See also **first day cover**.

unsevered   attached. The term has been used in reference to postal reply cards that remain attached to the sender's card; also, to stamps or panes that have not been separated from larger pieces.

untagged   a stamp without tagging. In the early days of tagging, some stamps of certain issues were released with tagging and others without tagging. Those without tagging are said to be untagged. Later, when all issues were routinely tagged, some inadvertently escaped tagging and are known as *untagged errors*.

unused   a stamp that has not been used (canceled). Although the term can be applied to any uncanceled stamp, either with or without gum, it is frequently used—mostly in auction catalogs and advertising—to mean an uncanceled stamp lacking original gum, and in that sense has become nearly idiomatic. When using an auction catalogue or buying from an advertisement, be sure you understand the connotation of the term as it relates to the offering, because a stamp without original gum is worth considerably less than one with original gum. See also **mint**.

unwatermarked   not possessing a watermark. See **watermark**.

UPSS   abbreviation for United Postal Stationery Society.

used   a stamp that has been canceled. See also **postally used**.

used abroad   a stamp used or postmarked in a country other than that of its origin.

USIR   (United States Internal Revenue) the initials appear on paper watermarked for use on revenue stamps, and in a couple of cases by error on paper used to print postage stamps.

USPOD   (United States Post Office Department) the name of the post office before the official change in 1971 to United States Postal Service (USPS).

USPS   abbreviation for United States Postal Service.

valentine   an informal postal term for a test card that delivery supervisors leave in collection boxes to ensure that mail is pulled on schedule.

value   synonym for denomination, for example, dollar-value Columbians or a set containing all values.

vending and affixing machine perforations   (or private perforations) perforations applied by makers of vending machines and affixing machines in the early twentieth century. The firms purchased imperforate stock from the Postal Service and applied their own distinctive perforations, intended to work with their machines.

viewcard   a commercially produced card containing an illustration (often a landmark, landscape, or building, or sometimes with a humorous message or greeting) and usually sold or given as a souvenir. Also called a *postcard* or *picture postcard*.

vignette   (pronounced "vin-YET") the central portion of a stamp design appearing inside an outer frame or border, usually a portrait or scene, and often in a color different than that of the frame. See also **frame**.

walk sequence   the order in which a carrier delivers mail for a route. This order is required for most carrier route presort mail.

wallpaper   common, inexpensive, colorful stamps of the type sold in bulk and having little individual value.

want list   a list itemizing stamps one is interested in acquiring, often given to dealers or fellow collectors.

washed   (1) stamps whose cancellations have been chemically removed, usually in bulk and for the purpose of illicitly reusing them; (2) archaic term for soaked stamps.

water-activated gum   stamp gum made sticky by the application of moisture, such as saliva. Stamps possessing water-activated gum, as opposed to those with self-adhesive gum, are sometimes called *lick-and-stick stamps*.

watermark   a design impressed into paper during its manufacture, sometimes visible when held up to light, but most often visible when immersed in watermark fluid.

way letter   a letter presented to a post rider along his route, which is to be carried to and left at the next post office, a practice common before the twentieth century.

way pouch   a pouch containing mail for post offices along a particular route. It is opened at each office to remove local mail and add mail from that office to other destinations on the route.

web   a large roll of paper used on high-speed presses to print in a continuous fashion.

wet gum   gum that is shiny or glossy in appearance, as opposed to dry gum, which is flat in appearance. See also **dry gum**.

wet printing   intaglio printing utilizing paper dampened in order to make it receptive to ink. Paper used for wet printing usually has a moisture content of 15 to 35 percent; paper used for "dry" printing usually contains only 5 to 10 percent moisture content. Wet-printed stamps usually appear flat and lackluster when compared to dry-printed stamps. See also **dry printing**.

withdrawn   refers to an issue that has been officially removed from sale by a postal administration.

wove paper   a finely textured, smooth paper. The most common type of paper, both within and outside philately.

wrapper   a piece of postal stationery used to wrap periodicals for mailing, and in the philatelic sense, usually with postage preprinted on it.

ZIP   as in ZIP code, an acronym that stands for Zone Improvement Plan, which was introduced in 1963.

ZIP block   a block of stamps that contains an inscription promoting the use of ZIP codes.

ZIP+4   the nine-digit numeric code, established in 1981, composed of two parts: (a) the initial code: the first five digits that identify the sectional center facility and delivery area associated with the address, followed by a hyphen; and (b) the four-digit expanded code: the first two additional digits designate the sector (a geographic area) and the last two digits designate the segment (a building, floor, etc.).

WORLDWIDE PHILATELIC AGENCIES

THE FOLLOWING PHILATELIC agencies are listed together with their addresses. Telephone numbers are given where known. Numbers are listed as provided to us and without revision regarding dialing protocols. Be aware that many agencies do not answer in English nor do they have English-speaking staff on duty. Fax numbers and e-mail addresses are listed where known.

Web site addresses are listed where known. Philatelic Web sites are usually a subsite within the postal administration's regular Web site. Not all postal Web sites include a philatelic section. And of those that do, not all permit online ordering. Nevertheless, postal service Web sites are included where known because they often contain other information of interest, such as the history of the postal service, its stamps, current post offices and regular products, and local philatelic clubs and societies. Most sites that host a philatelic section usually identify it by a recognizable variant of the word "philately," such as "filatelie." Many sites are either in English or offer an English-language version. It is usually identified by the word "English" or by a symbol, most often the British flag.

Addresses of many foreign agencies appear in their native language. This is actually more efficient in delivery, since the only element of the address that needs to be comprehensible to U.S. Postal Service personnel is the last line, the nation of destination. Postal protocol dictates that a nation's name appear by itself on the last line of the address. In some cases, an additional modifier is used, such as "South Atlantic."

Information in this section was gathered either by visiting the nation's Web site or as furnished by the postal authority. Although accurate at press time, it is subject to change.

ÅLAND
Posten PÅ Åland
Filateli Servicen
PB 100
Mariehamn
FIN-22101, Åland
Finland
Web site: www.posten.aland.fi/start_en.asp

ALBANIA
Albanian Post
Reshit Collaku Str.
Tirana
Albania
Phone: +355 42 29696
Fax: +355 42 32133
E-mail: alpost@icc.al.eu.org

ALDERNEY
Alderney Post Office
55 Victoria Streeet
St. Anne
Alderney G79 3UF
Great Britain
Phone: 01481 822 644
Fax: 01481 823 790
E-mail: alderney.post@virgin.net

ALGERIA
Ministere des Postes et Tel.
Direction des Services Postaux
Service des Valeurs Postaux et Philatélie
4, BD Krim Belkacem
16 000 Alger
Algeria
Web site: www.postelecom.dz

ANGUILLA
General Post Office
The Valley
Anguilla, West Indies
Phone: (264) 497 2528
Fax: (264) 497 5455
Web site: http://gov.ai/angstamp/

ANTIGUA
Antigua Philatelic Bureau
General Post Office

High Street
St. John's, Antigua
Antigua
Phone: 1-268-462-0992
Fax: 1-268-460-9650

ARGENTINA
Correo Argentina
Departmento de Filatelia
Casilla de correo 4224
Correo Central
C1000WBQ Buenos Aires
Argentina
Phone: (54-11) 4316-3338
Fax: (54-11) 4316-3038
E-mail: filatelia@correoargentino.com.ar
Web site: www.correoargentino.com.ar

ARMENIA
Namakanish
22 Sarian Street
Yerevan 375002
Republic of Armenia
Phone: (374 1) 52 45 90
Fax: (374 1) 15 16 21
Web site: www.iatp.am/stamps

ARUBA
Philatelic Service
J.E. Irausquinplein 9
Oranjestad
Aruba, West Indies
Phone: 297-8-21900
Fax: 297-8-27930
Web site: www.geocities.com/
    TimesSquare/Corridor/1290/
    psamissn.html

ASCENSION ISLAND
Ascension Island Post Office
Georgetown ASCN 1ZZ
Ascension Island, South Atlantic Ocean
Phone: +247 6260
Fax: +247 6152
E-mail: PostOffice@atlantis.co.ac
Web site: www.ascension-island.gov.ac/
    postoffice.htm

AUSTRALIA
Australian Philatelic Bureau
Box 4000
Ferntree Gully, VIC 3156
Australia
Fax: 61 3 9887 0236
Web site: www.auspost.com.au/stamps

AUSTRIA
Oesterreichische Post AG
Sammler-Service
Steinheilgasse 1
A-1210 Wien
Austria
Phone: +43-(0)1-250 25-4040
Fax: +43-(0)1-250 25-4080
E-mail: sammler-service@post.at
E-mail: stamps@post.at
Web site: www.post.at/english/index1.shtml

BAHRAIN
Philatelic Bureau
P.O. Box 1212
Postal Directorate
Manama
State of Bahrain
Phone: 00973 523403
Fax: 00937 533455
E-mail: stamp@bahrain.gov.bh

BARBADOS
Barbados Postal Service
General Post Office
Cheapside, Saint Michael
Barbados, West Indies
Phone: 246-426-0381
Fax: 246-429-4118
E-mail: gpophilatelic@caribsurf.com
Web site: www.gpobarbados.com

BELARUS
Philatelic Department
Belarus Post
Publishing Centre "Marka"
10, F. Skaryna Avenue
220050, Minsk
Belarus
Phone: +375 17 206-59-32
Fax: +375 17 227-46-38 or 226-11-70

E-mail: marka@tut.by
Web site: www.belpost.by

BELGIUM
Postage Stamps
Philatelic Department
Egide Walschaertsstraat 1,
2800 Mechelen
Belgium
Phone: +32 (0) 15 285 821
Fax: +32 (0) 15 285 816
E-mail: philately@post.be
Web site: www.philately.post.be

BELIZE
Belize Philatelic Bureau
General Post Office
Belize City
Belize, Central America
Phone: 501 2 72201 or 72178
Fax: 501 2 30936
E-mail: postgenbze@btl.net

BERMUDA
Philatelic Department
General Post Office
56 Church Street
Hamilton HM PM
Bermuda
Phone: (441) 297-7797
E-mail: gpo@ibl.bm
Web site: www.bermudapostoffice.com

BHUTAN
Philatelic Bureau
Bhutan Post
GPO Building Thimphu
Bhutan
Phone: 00975-2-322296
Fax: 00975-2-323108
E-mail: phly@bhutanpost.com.bt
Web site: www.BhutanPost.com.bt

BOLIVIA
Empresa de Correos de Bolivia
Departamento de Filatelia
Nivel Plaza
Palacio de Communicaciones
Avenue Mariscal Santa Cruz
La Paz, Bolivia, S.A.

Phone: (591-2) 374 145
Fax: (591-2) 391 620
E-mail: filatelia_cen@correosbolivia.com

BRAZIL
Departamento de Filatelia/Defil
SBN Quadra 01, Bloco A
Edificio Sede da Ect
12 Andar
70002-900 Brasilia DF
Brazil
Phone: (+5561) 426 1800 or 1822
Fax: (+5521) 503 8638
E-mail: internationalmarket@
    correios.com.br
E-mail (orders): centralvendas@
    correios.com.br
Web site: www.correiosonline.com.br

BRITISH ANTARCTIC TERRITORY
British Antarctic Territory
Philatelic Bureau
Falkland Islands Post Office
Stanley
Falkland Islands, South Atlantic Ocean
E-mail: philatelic.fig@horizon.co.fk
Web site: www.falklands.gov.fk/pb/bat

BRUNEI
Controller of Posts
Philatelic Bureau
P.O. Box 3000
Bandar Seri Begawan 1930
Brunei Darussalam
Web site: www.brunet.bn/gov/post

BULGARIA
Bulgarska Philatelia & Numismatika
8, Haydushka poliana Str.
BG-1612 Sofia
Bulgaria
Phone: (+3592) 953 1752
Fax: (+3592) 953 1826
E-mail: irenabg@bgpost.bg

CANADA
Canada Post
National Philatelic Center

75 St. Ninian Street
Antigonish, NS B2G 2R8
Canada
Fax: (800) 732-0038
Web site: www.PostesCanada.ca or
    www.canadapost.ca

CAPE VERDE
Correios de Cabo Verde SARL
CP 92–Praia
Cape Verde
Phone: 61 1049
Fax: 61 1575; 61 3478
E-mail: correioscv@mail.cvtelecom.cv

CAYMAN ISLANDS
Philatelic Bureau
Main Post Office
Georgetown, Grand Cayman
Cayman Islands, West Indies

CHAD
Postmaster General
Office National des Postes et
Telecommunications (ONPT)
Service Philatelique
Ndhamena
Tchad

CHINA (PEOPLE'S REPUBLIC)
Beijing CPI NETECH Co., Ltd.
CNPC Building, 10th Floor
14 Taipinghudongli, Xicheng District
Beijing 100031
P.R. China
E-mail: cpi@cnpc.cpi.com.cn
Web site: www.cpi.com.cn/cpi-e/cpi-e.htm

CHINA (REPUBLIC OF)
Philatelic Department
Directorate General of Posts
55 Chin Shan South Road, Section 2
Taipei, Taiwan 10603
Republic of China
Phone: +886-2-235-69670
Fax: +886-2-239-69125
E-mail: phila@mail.post.gov.tw
Web site: www.post.gov.tw

COLOMBIA
Division de Filatelia
Administracion Postal Nacional
Edificio Murillo Toro, Of. 212
Cra 8 entre Calle 12A y 13
Bogota D.C.
Colombia
Phone: (51) (1) 243 81 62
Fax: (51) (1) 283 80 06
Web site: www.adpostal.gov.co

COOK ISLANDS
Post Office
Philatelic Bureau
P.O. Box 200
Rarotonga
Cook Islands, South Pacific Ocean
Phone: (682) 22428

CROATIA
HP–Hrvatska Posta d.d.
Jurisiceva 13
10000 Zagreb
Croatia
Phone: +385 1 4873-890
Fax: +385 1 4873-892
E-mail: hp-marketing@posta.tel.hr
Web site: www.posta.hr

CYPRUS
Department of Postal Services
Philatelic Service
CY-1900 Nicosia
Cyprus
Phone: +(357) 2 805726
Phone: +(357) 2 805731
Fax: +(357) 2 304154
E-mail: cyprus.gov@cytanet.com.cy
Web site: www.pio.gov.cy/dps

CZECH REPUBLIC
Czech Post
Philatelic Service
P.O. Box 111
360 02 Karlovy Vary 2
Czech Republic
Phone: +420 17 3540153
Fax: same as phone

E-mail: bulkova.zdenka@sfkv.cpost.cz
  or info@info.cpost.cz
Web site: www.cpost.cz

DENMARK
Post Denmark
Frimaerker
Telegrafvej 7
DK-2750 Ballerup
Denmark
Phone: (+45) 4473 0505
Fax: (+45) 4466 2575
E-mail: pdk.frm@post.dk
Web site: http://postdanmark.dk/stamps

ECUADOR
Ecuador Post Office
Av. Eloy Alfaro 354
& 9 de Octubre
Quito
Ecuador
E-mail: info@correosecuador.com
Web site: www.correosecuador.com

EGYPT
Arab Republic of Egypt
The National Postal Organization
Philatelic Office
Philatelic Museum Department
Cairo
Egypt
E-mail: npo@idsc.gov.eg
Web site: www.stamps.npo.gov.eg

EL SALVADOR
Departamento de Filatelia
Direccion General de Correos
Centro de Gobierno
San Salvador
El Salvador, Central America
Phone: 271-1922
Fax: 271-1965
E-mail: correos@telemovil.com

ESTONIA
EESTI Post
Pallasti 28
EE–19098 Tallinn
Estonia

E-mail: est.phil@online.ee
Web site: www.post.ee

ETHIOPIA
Philatelic Section
Ethiopian Postal Service
P.O. Box 1112
Addis Ababa
Ethiopia
Phone: (251-1) 15 90 38
Fax: (251-1) 51 29 99
E-mail: EMS@telecom.net.et

FALKLAND ISLANDS
Falkland Islands
Philatelic Bureau
Stanley
Falkland Islands, South Atlantic Ocean
E-mail: philatelic.fig@horizon.co.fk
Web site: www.falklands.gov.fk/pb

FAROE ISLANDS
Philatelic Service
Tradagota 38
FO–159 Torshavn
Faroe Islands
Phone: +298 315577
Fax: +298 310576
E-mail: filateli@postverk.fo
Web site: www.stamps.fo

FIJI
Post Fiji Philatelic Bureau
GPO Box 100
Suva
Fiji
Fax: +679 308 156
E-mail: orders@stampsfiji.com
Web site: www.stampsfiji.com

FINLAND
Finland Post
Philatelic Center
P.O. Box 2
FIN–00101 Posti
Finland
Phone: +358 20 451 5522
Fax: +358 20 451 5580
E-mail: postimerkkikeskus@posti.fi
Web site: www.pmk.posti.fi/eindex.html

FRANCE
Service Philatelique de la Poste
18 rue Francois-Bonvin
75758 Paris Cedex 15
France
Phone: 33 1 40 61 52 00
Fax: 33 1 43 06 24 62
E-mail: info.spp@sntp.laposte.teleposte.fr
Web site: www.laposte.fr

FRENCH POLYNESIA
Philatelic Center of French Polynesia
8 rue de la Reine Pomare IV
Papeete, Tahiti
French Polynesia
Phone: (689) 41 43 35
Fax: (689) 45 25 86
E-mail: info@tahiti-postoffice.com
Web site: www.tahiti-postoffice.com/english

GAMBIA
Philatelic Bureau
General Post Office
Liberation Avenue
Banjul
The Gambia
Phone: (220) 227 204
Fax: (220) 224 837
E-mail: gpo@gamtel.gm

GERMANY
Deutsche Post AG
Niederlassung Philatelie
Versandstelle fur Postwertzeichen
60281 Frankfurt
Germany
E-mail: servicecenter.philatelie@
    deutschepost.de
Web site: www.deutschepost.de

GHANA
Ghana Postal Services Corporation
Philatelic Bureau
General Post Office
Accra
Ghana
Fax: 233-21-668139
E-mail: philabru@gppo.africaonline.com.gh
Web site: www.ghanapost.com/philately.html

GIBRALTAR
Philatelic Bureau
P.O. Box 5662
Gibraltar
Phone: (350) 75662
Fax: (350) 42149
E-mail: stamps@gibnynex.gi
Web site: www.gibraltar-stamps.com

GREAT BRITAIN
British Philatelic Bureau
21 South Gyle Crescent
Edinburgh EH12 9PB
Scotland
Web site (postal): www.ukpo.com

GREECE
Hellenic Post
Philatelic Service
2, Vyssis & Eolou Str.
GR-101 88 Athens
Greece
Phone: 3310 732
Fax: 3310 110

GREENLAND
Filatelia
P.O. Box 121
DK–3913 Tasiilaq
Greenland
Phone: +299 98 11 55
Fax: +299 98 14 32
E-mail: stamps@tele.gl
Web site: www.stamps.gl

GUATEMALA
Direccion General de Correos de
Guatemala
Depto. Filatelico
7a. Ave 12-11 Zona 1
Guatemala Cuidad
Guatemala, Central America
Phone: (502) 232-2250;
    (502) 232-6101 ext. 5
Fax: (502) 232-3956
E-mail: filatelia@intco.com.gt
Web site: www.guatefilatelia.com

GUERNSEY
Guernsey Philatelic Bureau
Postal Headquarters
Guernsey, GY1 1AB
Channel Islands, U.K.
Phone: +44 (0) 1481 716486
Fax: +44 (0) 1481 712082
E-mail: philatelic@guernseypost.com
Web site: www.guernseypost.com

GUINEA (REPUBLIC OF)
Office de la Poste Guinéenne
B.P: 2984
Conakry
Republic of Guinée
Phone: (224) 41 14 22
Fax : (224) 41 40 50
E-mail: opg@eti-bull.net
Web site: www.eti-bull.net/opg/

GUYANA
Philatelic Services Department
Post Office Corporation
Robb Street
Georgetown
Guyana
Phone: 592 225 0211 or 226 9836
Fax: 592 226 4370 or 225 5405
E-mail: guypost@solution2000.net

HONG KONG
Post Office Headquarters
General Post Office
2 Connaught Place
Central
Hong Kong
E-mail: spd@hkpo.gcn.gov.hk
Web site: www.hongkongpost.com

HUNGARY
Magyar Posta Rt.
Filatéliai Központ Levelezési cím: 1570
Budapest
Hungary
Phone: 349-13-37
Fax: 329-42-75
E-mail: philately@posta.hu
Web site: www.posta.hu

ICELAND
Postphil Philatelic Service
Storhofdi 29
IS-110 Reykjavik
Iceland
Phone: + 354 580 1050
Fax: + 354-580 1059
E-mail: stamps@postur.is
Web site: www.stamps.is

INDONESIA
Philatelic Office
Pos Street No. 2
Jakarta 10710
Indonesia
Phone: 62-21-348 34738
Fax: 021-386 1787
E-mail: kdivfil@pos.wasantara.net.id
Web site: filateli.wasantara.net.id

IRAN
Philatelic Bureau
3rd Floor, Post Mechanized Building
Lashgar Cross Road
P.O. Box 13185-4149
Tehran
I.R. Iran
Phone: (+98 21) 646 6172
Fax: (+98 21) 646 0965

IRELAND
Philatelic Bureau
P.O. Box 1991
Dublin 1
Ireland
Fax: +353 1 872 2683
E-mail: philatelic.web@anpost.ie
Web site: www.anpost.ie

ISLE OF MAN
Isle of Man Post Office
Philatelic Bureau
P.O. Box IOM
Douglas IM99 1PB
Isle of Man, U.K.
Phone: +44 (0)1624 698430
Fax: +44 (0)1624 698434
E-mail: stamps@po.gov.im
Web site: www.gov.im/stamps

ISRAEL
The Israel Philatelic Service
12 Shderot Yerushalayim
68021 Tel Aviv–Yafo
Israel
E-mail: philserv@netvision.net.il
Web site: www.postil.com/postunit.nsf/
    def2/index

ITALY
Poste Italiane S.p.A.
Divisione Filatelia
Piazza Dante, 25-00185
Rome
Italy
E-mail: info@poste.it
Web site: www.poste.it

IVORY COAST (CÔTE D'IVOIRE)
Centre Philatelique d'Abidjan
Direction de la Production
01 BP 4056 Abidjan 01
Republique de Côte d'Ivoire
Phone: (225) 2032 99 13; 2033 18 96
Fax: (225) 2032 24 82

JERSEY
Jersey Philatelic Bureau
Postal Headquarters
Jersey JE1 1AB
Great Britain
Phone: + 44 (0)1534 616612
Fax: + 44 (0)1534 873690
E-mail: stamps@jerseypost.com
Web site: www.jerseypost.com/stamps

JORDAN
Philatelic Section
Ministry of Post & Communications
P.O. Box 9903
Amman 11191
Jordan
Phone: (9626) 658-58668
Fax: (9626) 658-58668
E-mail: info@stamps.gov.jo
Web site: www.stamps.gov.jo

KENYA
Kenya Stamp Bureau
Postal Corporation of Kenya

P.O. Box 30368
Nairobi
Kenya
Phone: 254-2-243434 ext. 2036
E-mail: customercare@posta.co.ke
Web site: www.posta.co.ke

KIRIBATI
Philatelic Bureau
P.O. Box 494
Betio, Tarawa
Kiribati, Central Pacific
Phone: (686) 26515
Fax: (686) 26193
E-mail: Kiribati.philatelic.bureau@
    tskl.net.ki
Web site: www.tskl.net.ki/kiribati/
    business/stamps/

KOREA (SOUTH)
Korean Philatelic Center
C.P.O. Box 5122
Seoul 100-651
Republic of Korea
Phone: (822) 779-0667 or
(822) 776-2559
Fax: (822) 773-4438
E-mail: phila@phila.or.kr

KUWAIT
Post Office Department
Philatelic Bureau
P.O. Box 888
Safat 13009
Kuwait
E-mail: trafic@netscape.net
Web site: http://members.spree.com/sip/
    salam49

KYRGYZSTAN
State Enterprise "Kyrghyzstamp"
227, Chuy Avenue
720001 Bichkek
Kyrghyzstan
Phone: (0-996 312) 217 932 or 211 664
Fax: (0-996 312) 219 224
E-mail: kp_main@infotel.kg
Web site: www.stamp.elcat.kg

LAOS
Philatelic Service
Enterprise des Postes Lao
Lane Xang Avenue
01000 Vientiane
PDR Laos
Fax: (+85621) 212 779

LATVIA
Latvia Post
Philatelic Department
Brivibas Bulvaris 21
Riga PDP, LV-1000
Latvia
Phone: + 371 701-8717
or + 371 701-8736
Fax: + 371 701-8747
E-mail: infofil@pasts.lv
Web site: www.riga.post.lv

LESOTHO
Lesotho Philatelic Bureau
P.O. Box 413
Maseru 100
Lesotho
Phone: 09266 323 812
Fax: 09266 310 476

LIECHTENSTEIN
Liechtenstein Post Office
Philatelic Bureau
Städtle 38, Postfach 1255
FL-9490 Vaduz
Liechtenstein
Phone: +423 236 66 44
Fax: +423 236 66 55
E-mail: briefmarken-fl@llv.li
Web site: www.news.li/stamps/go-e.htm

LITHUANIA
Stamp Department
Giedraiciu g. 60 A
LT-2042 Vilnius
Lithuania
Phone: (+370-2) 724-297 or 761-815
Fax: (+370-2) 779-911
E-mail: postage.stamps@post.lt
Web site: www.post.lt/eng/menu/
    fr_stamps.html

LUXEMBOURG
Office Des Timbres
4, rue d'Epernay
L-2992 Luxembourg
E-mail: ptofftim@pt.lu
Web site: www.philately.lu

MACAO
Macao Post
Philatelic Bureau
Largo do Senado
Macau
Peoples's Republic of China
Phone: (853) 574 491
Fax: (853) 336 603
E-mail: macpost@macau.ctm.net

MACEDONIA
Macedonia Post
Philatelic Department
Orce Nikolov bb.
91000 Skopje
Republic of Macedonia
Phone: (02) 164-040, 165-286
Fax: (02) 164-040, 165-286
E-mail: fila@mp.com.mk
Web site: www.mp.com.mk/eng

MALAWI
Malawi Posts Corporation
Philatelic Bureau
P.O. Box 30700
Chichiri BT3
Malawi
Phone: 670 778
Fax: 620 188
E-mail: mpcpmg@malawi.net

MALAYSIA
Philatelic Bureau Kuala Lumpur
Tingkat 1
Ibu Pejabat Pos Malaysia,
Kompleks Dayabumi
50670 Kuala Lumpur
Malaysia
Phone: (6)03-22741122 ext. 6715 or 6651
Fax: (6)03-2942139
E-mail: filateli@pos.com.my
Web site: www.pos.com.my

MALDIVE ISLANDS
Stamps and Philatelic Bureau
Maldive Post Limited
Boduthakurufaanu magu
Male' 20-05
Republic of Maldives
Phone: +960 321 558
Fax: +960 321 559
E-mail: philately@maldivespost.com
Web site: www.malidivespost.com

MAURITIUS
Mauritius Philatelic Bureau
General Post Office
Quay Street
Port Louis
Mauritius
Phone: (+230) 208 2851
Fax: (+230) 212 9640
Web site: ncb.intnet.mu/mitt/postal

MEXICO
Servicio Postal Mexicano
Departamento de Promocion Filatelica
Netzahualcoyotl No. 109-6° Piso
Col. Centro
C.P. 06082 Mexico D.F.
Mexico
Phone: (5) 722 96 74
Fax: (5) 722 96 72
E-mail: filasepomex.gob.mx
Web site: www.sepomex.gob.mx

MONACO
Office des Emissions de Timbres-Poste
23, Avenue Prince Héréditaire Albert
MC 98050 Monaco Cedex
Monaco
Phone: (+377) 93 14 4141
Fax: (+377) 93 14 4141
E-mail: oetp@gouv.mc

MONTSERRAT
Monserrat Philatelic Bureau
General Post Office
Brades
Montserrat, West Indies
Phone: 664 491 2996

Fax: 664 491 2042
E-mail: monphil@candw.ag

MOROCCO
Direction des Services Postaux
Service de la Philatelie
10000 Rabat
Complexe PTT
10 000 Rabat
Morocco
Phone: (07) 70.46.21
Web site: www.bam.net.ma/english.htm

MOZAMBIQUE
Empresa Filatelica e Numismatica
25 de Setembro Avenue No. 1509
P.O. Box 4444
Maputo
Mozambique
Phone: 002581-308705
Fax: 002581-426800

NAMIBIA
Namibia Stamp Centre
Namibia Post Ltd.
Private Bag 13336
Windhoek
Namibia
Phone: +264 61 201-3107
Fax: +264 61 25-9467
E-mail : philately@nampost.com.na
Web site: www.nampost.com.na

NETHERLANDS
PTT Post
Collectors Club
Postbus 30051
9700 RN Groningen
Netherlands
Phone: (050) 586 12 34
Fax: (050) 586 31 11
E-mail: filatelie@wxs.nl

NETHERLANDS ANTILLES
Philatelic Service
Waaigatplein 1
Willemstad
Curaçao
Netherlands Antilles

Phone: (599-9) 461-3023
Fax: (599-9) 465-1176
E-mail: stamps@philantilles.com
Web site: www.philantilles.com or
www.postna.com

NEVIS
Nevis Philatelic Bureau
Head Post Office
Charlestown
Nevis, West Indies
Fax: 869-469-0617
E-mail: philbur@caribsurf.com
Web site: www.nevisisland.com/
philatelic.htm

NEW ZEALAND
New Zealand Post Stamp Centre
Private Bag 3001
Level 2, 60 Ridgway Street
Wanganui
New Zealand
Phone: 64-6-349 1234
Fax: 64-6-345 7120
E-mail: enquiry@wgmsc.nzpost
Web site: www.stamps.co.nz

NORFOLK ISLAND
Postal Services
Philatelic Bureau
Post Office
Norfolk Island 2899
South Pacific Ocean
Phone: 6723 23344
Fax: 6723 23636
E-mail: info@stamps.gov.nf
Web site: www.stamps.gov.nf

OMAN
Ministry of Communications
Philatelic Service
P.O. Box 51
PC 112
Ruwi
Sultanate of Oman
Phone: 00-968 701374
Fax: 00-968 792276
E-mail: pttphil@gto.net.om
Web site: www.comm.gov.om

PAKISTAN
National Philatelic Bureau
F-7 Markaz
Islamabad
Pakistan
Phone: 92-51-9202577
Fax: 92-51-9221259
E-mail: gpo@isb.paknet.com.pk
Web site: www.pakpost.gov.pk/philately/
  purchase.html

PANAMA
Direccion General de Correos y
Telegrafos
Panama 0815
Republic of Panama
Phone: (507) 225-2803
Fax: (507) 225-2812
E-mail: filatelia@cwpanama.net

PARAGUAY
Direccion de Correos
Asesoria Filatelica
Alberdi 130
1029 Asuncion
Paraguay
Fax: 595 21 493 997
E-mail: surpostal@mopc.gov.py

PITCAIRN ISLAND
Pitcairn Island Philatelic Bureau
Office of the Governor of Pitcairn
Islands
Private Box 105 696
Auckland
New Zealand
E-mail: pitcairn.stamps@iconz.co.nz

POLAND
Poczta Polska
Centrum Handlu i Poligrafii
Trade and Printing Centre
ul. Grochowska 23/31
00-942 Warszawa
Poland
Phone: (48-22) 610-66-85
Fax: (0-22) 610-62-65
E-mail: chip@poczta-polska.pl
Web site: www.poczta-polska.pl

PORTUGAL
Filatelia
Av. Casal Ribeiro, 28-6°
1049-052 Lisboa
Portugal
Phone: +351 213 111 700
Fax: +351 213 111 848
E-mail: mercadointfil@ctt.pt
Web site: www.ctt.pt

ROMANIA
C.N. Posta Romana–Romfilatelia
Calea Grivitei 64-66
P.O. Box 12-201
Bucharest
Romania
Phone: (401) 314 6996
Fax: (401) 314 6006 or 6998

ROSS DEPENDENCY
Available through **New Zealand**.

RUSSIA
PTC Marka
str. B. Gruzinskaya
123242 Moscow
Russia
E-mail: stamp@aha.ru
Web site: www.aha.ru/~stamp/english.htm

SAMOA
Philatelic Bureau
Samoa Communications Limited
Private Bag
Apia
Samoa
Phone: 685 20720 or 67766
Fax: 685 24000
E-mail: arieta@samcom.com

SAN MARINO
Philatelic & Numismatic Department
Piazza Garibaldi 5
RSM-47890
Republic of San Marino
Phone: (+) 378 0549 882365
Fax: (+)378 0549 882363
E-mail: aasfn@omniway.sm
Web site: www.aasfn.sm

SAUDI ARABIA
Ministry of P.T.T.
Directorate General of Posts
Stamps Department
Philatelic Section
Riyadh
Saudi Arabia
E-mail: info@arabianstamps.com
Web site: www.arabianstamps.com

SENEGAL
Dakar Philatelie
Immeuble Direction Generale Poste
6, rue Abdoulaye Seck Marie Parsine
Dakar
Senegal
Phone: 00221 849 2135 or 849 2187
Fax: 00221 849 2185
Web site: www.laposte.sn

SERBIA
JUGOMARKA
Palmoticeva 2
665 Belgrade
Yugoslavia
Fax: (011) 34 41 118
Web site: http://posta.ptt.yu

SINGAPORE
Singapore Post
Philatelic Department
10 Eunos Road 8 #01-33
Singapore Post Centre
Singapore 408600
Fax: (65) 8413378
E-mail: sinstamp@singpost.com
Web site: www.singpost.com.sg

SLOVAKIA
Slovenská posta, s.p.
Technická ústredna pôst
POFIS
Mamateyova 16
850 05 Bratislava 55
Slovak Republic
Phone: 07 / 6231 7991
Fax: 07 / 6231 8311
E-mail: lanim@tup.slposta.sk
Web site: www.slposta.sk

SLOVENIA
Posta Slovenija, d.o.o.
Philatelic Service
SI-2500 Maribor
Slovenia
Phone: +386 2 449 2247
Fax: +386 2 449 2112
E-mail: info@posta.si
Web site: www.posta.si

SOLOMON ISLANDS
Philatelic Bureau
P.O. Box 1930
Honiara
Solomon Islands
Phone: (677) 22108
Fax: (677) 20440
Web site: www.commerce.gov.sb/
    Business_Directories/AdvHPages/
    Philatelic.htm

SOUTH AFRICA
South Africa Post Office
Philatelic Services
Private Bag X505
Pretoria 0001
South Africa
Phone: (012) 804 7735
Fax: (012) 804 6745
E-mail: sastamps@sapo.co.za
Web site: www.sapo.co.za/philately/
    index.htm

SOUTH GEORGIA AND
SANDWICH ISLANDS
South Georgia
Philatelic Bureau
Falkland Islands Post Office
Stanley
Falkland Islands, South Atlantic Ocean
E-mail: philatelic.fig@horizon.co.fk
Web site: www.falklands.gov.fk/pb/sg

SPAIN
Servicio Filatélico Internacional
Palacio de Comunicaciones
C/ Montalban S/N
28070 Madrid
Spain

Phone: 34 91 396 2050
Fax: 34 91 396 2885
E-mail: atcliente.filatelica@correos.es
Web site: www.correos.es

SRI LANKA
Philatelic Bureau
M.I.C.H. Building
Fort, Colombo 1
Sri Lanka
Phone: 94 -325588
E-mail: slpost@sri.lanka.net
Web site: www.lanka.net/slpost

ST. LUCIA
St. Lucia Philatelic Bureau
General Post Office
Bridge Street
Castries
St. Lucia, West Indies
Phone: 452 2671
Fax: 453 7702
E-mail: gpo@candw.lc
Web site: www.stampcafe.com

ST. PIERRE ET MIQUELON
Bureau Philatelique de l'Archipel
B.P. 4323
F-97500 Saint-Pierre
Saint-Pierre et Miquelon
Phone: (508) 41-36-07
Fax: (508) 41-22-97
E-mail: conseilg@cancom.net

ST. THOMAS AND PRINCE ISLANDS
Empresa de Correios
Departamento de Filatelia
Av. Marginal 12 de Julho
R/C–S.Tome
São Tomé e Príncipe–West Africa
Phone: (239 12) 22202 or 22421
Fax: (239 12) 21897
E-mail: correios@cstome.net

SURINAME
Suriname Post
Kerkplein 1
Paramaribo
Suriname

Phone: (597) 477524
Fax: (597) 410534
E-mail: surpost@sr.net
Web site: parbo.com/weekly/post.html

SWAZILAND
The Stamp Bureau
P.O. Box 55
Mbabane H100
Swaziland
Fax: (+268) 404 4500
E-mail: postmaster@swazi.net
Web site: www.sptc.co.sz/
    stamp_bureau.htm

SWEDEN
Sweden Post Stamps
Customer Service
SE-981 84 Kiruna
Sweden
Phone: + 46 8 781 4936
Fax: + 46 9 808 1490
E-mail: kundservice@pf.posten.se
Web site: www.posten.postnet.se/03/
    03a.htm

SWITZERLAND
Swiss Post
Stamps & Philately
Ostermundigenstrasse 91
CH-3030 Berne
Switzerland
Phone: ++41 (0)31 338 06 09
Fax: ++41 (0)31 338 73 08
E-mail: stamps@post.ch
Web site: www.post.ch

THAILAND
Philatelic Department
Communications Authority of Thailand
99 Chaeng Wattana Road
Thung Song Hong
Don Muang, Bangkok 10002
Thailand
Phone: (662) 506-3340 or 3263
Fax: (662) 573-4494
E-mail: stamp@cat.or.th
Web site: www.cat.or.th

TONGA
Tonga Post
Philatelic Bureau
P.O. Box 164
Post Office Headquarters
Nuku'alofa
Kingdom of Tonga, South Pacific
Web site: www.tongatapu.net.to/tonga/
   todo/stamps.html

TUNISIA
République Tunisienne
Ministère des Communications
Recette Principale de Tunis
1000 Tunis RP
Republic of Tunisia
Web site: www.pttnet.gov.tn/stamps

TURKEY
Philatelic Section
General Directorate of PTT
Financial Post Department
TR–06101 Ankara
Turkey
Phone: +90 (312) 309 53 35
Fax: +90 (312) 309 53 08
Web site: www.ptt.gov.tr

TURKISH REPUBLIC OF NORTHERN CYPRUS
Directorate of the Postal Department
Philatelic Branch, Lefkosa
Mersin–10
Turkey
Phone: +90 392 228 3646; 227 1278
Fax: +90 392 228 8618

TUVALU
Tuvalu Philatelic Bureau
P.O. Box 24
Funafuti
Tuvalu, Central Pacific
Fax: (688) 20 712
Web site: http://members.nbci.com/
   _XOOM/tuvaluonline/stamps-
   index.htm

UKRAINE
USEPC "Ukrposhta"
Publishing House "Marka Ukrainy"
Khreschatyk 22
01001 Kyiv 1
Ukraine
Phone: 229-59-30
Fax: 229-21-82
E-mail: philatel_markaua@ukr.net
Web site: www.stamp.kiev.ua

UNITED ARAB EMIRATES
Philatelic Bureau,
General Postal Authority
P.O. Box 8888
Dubai
United Arab Emirates
E-mail: philatelic@gpa.co.ae
Web site: www.gpa.gov.ae/english/stamps

UNITED NATIONS
United Nations Postal Administration
P.O. Box 5900, Grand Central Station
New York, NY 10163-9992
Phone: (212) 963-7684 or
   (800) 234-UNPA
Fax: (212) 963-9854
E-mail: unpa@un.org
Web site: www.un.org/Depts/UNPA

UNITED STATES
U.S. Postal Service
Stamp Fulfillment Center
P.O. Box 219424
Kansas City, MO 64121-9424
Phone: (800) 782-6724 or
   (816) 545-1000
Fax: (816) 545-1212
E-mail: icustomercare@usps.com or
   customer@email.usps.gov
Web site: www.stampsonline.com or
   www.usps.com

URUGUAY
Administración Nacional de Correos
División Filatelia
Casilla de Correos 1296
Montevideo
Uruguay
E-mail: Filatelia@correo.com.uy
Web site: www.correo.com.uy

UZBEKISTAN
"Uzbekistan Markasi" JSC
28-A Navoi Str.
Tashkent 700011
Republic of Uzbekistan
Phone: 99-871-133-7033
Fax: 99-871-133-3648

VANUATU
Vanuatu Post
Philatelic Bureau
Port Vila
Republic of Vanuatu
Phone: 678 + 22000
Fax: 678 + 23900

VATICAN CITY
Ufficio del Filatelico
Poste Vaticane
Vatican City
Phone: 0039 06 6988 3708
Fax: 0039 06 6988 3799
E-mail: ufn@scv.va
Web site: www.vatican.va/vatican_city_state/
  services

VIETNAM
Viet Nam Stamp Company (Cotevina)
14 Tran Hung Dao
Hanoi
Vietnam
Phone: (844) 825 3670 or 826 4288
Fax: (844) 826 9917
E-mail: cotevina@hn.vnn.vn
Web site: www.vietnamstamp.com.vn

WALLIS AND FUTUNA
Service des Postes et Telecommunications
B.P. 00
98600 Mata-Utu
Wallis & Futuna, South Pacific
Fax: (681) 72 25 00
E-mail: adminspt@wallis.co.nc
Web site: www.wallis.co.nc/philatelie

YEMEN
Main Philatelic Bureau
Stamps Department
Posts and Postal Savings Corp.

P.O. Box 1993
Sanaa
Yemen
Phone: (967 1) 331 449
Fax: (967 1) 331 433
E-mail: post@y.net.ye

ZAMBIA
Philatelic Bureau
Zambia Postal Services Corporation
P.O. Box 71857
Ndola
Zambia
Phone: 260 096 909933
Fax: 260 02 621186
E-mail: chellah@zamnet.zm

CHAPTER 31

PHILATELIC SOCIETIES AND CLUBS

PHILATELIC SOCIETIES ARE divided into groupings according to area of interest. The categories include general, state and regional, special interest, foreign, and topical. The societies are listed together with their addresses. E-mail and Web site addresses are listed where known. Although accurate at press time, information contained in this section is subject to change.

GENERAL

AMERICAN PHILATELIC SOCIETY
P.O. Box 8000
State College, PA 16803-8000
Web site: www.stamps.org

INTERNATIONAL SOCIETY OF WORLDWIDE STAMP COLLECTORS
Anthony Zollo MD
P.O. Box 150407
Lufkin, TX 75915-0407
Web site: www.iswsc.org

JUNIOR PHILATELISTS OF AMERICA
Jennifer Arnold, Executive Secretary
P.O. Box 2625
Albany, OR 97321-0643
E-mail: editor@jpastamps.org
Web site: www.jpastamps.org

PHILATELIC COMPUTING STUDY GROUP
Robert de Violini
P.O. Box 5025
Osnard, CA 93031-5025
E-mail: dviolini@west.net

Web site: www.pcsg.org
Aim is to assist stamp collectors who use computers.

ROYAL PHILATELIC SOCIETY OF CANADA
Charles J. G. Verge, FRPSC, President
P.O. Box 929, Station Q
Toronto, Ontario M4T 2P1
Canada
E-mail: info@rpsc.org
Web site: www.rspc.org

TRANS-MISSISSIPPI PHILATELIC SOCIETY
Alfred Mack
2571 Guthrie Avenue #210A
Des Moines, IA 50317-3019
E-mail: suealmack@home.com

UNITED STATES STAMP SOCIETY
Executive Secretary
P.O. Box 6634
Katy, TX 77491-6634
Web site: www.usstamps.org

STATE AND REGIONAL

ALASKA
Alaska Collectors Club
David Schwantes
8148 East 4th Avenue
Anchorage, AK 99504
E-mail: eknapp@gci.com

ARIZONA
*Arizona–New Mexico Postal
History Society*
J. L. Meyer
20112 Westpoint Drive
Riverside, CA 92507
E-mail: jlmeyer_2000@yahoo.com

COLORADO
Colorado Postal History Society
Roger Rydberg
354 South Nile Street
Aurora, CO 80012
E-mail: cphs@att.net

CONNECTICUT
Connecticut Postal History Society
Stephen W. Ekstrom, President
P.O. Box 207
Cromwell, CT 06416-0207
E-mail: sweckstrom@aol.com

DAKOTAS
Dakota Postal History Society
Gary Anderson
P.O. Box 600039
St. Paul, MN 55106
E-mail: garyndak@ix.netcom.com

FLORIDA
Florida Postal History Society
Deane R. Briggs MD, Secretary/Treasurer
160 East Lake Howard Drive
Winter Haven, FL 33881
E-mail: drb@gte.net

GEORGIA
Georgia Postal History Society
Mike O'Reilly
P.O. Box 1131
Huntsville, AL 35807
E-mail: mcoreilly@worldnet.att.net

HAWAII
Hawaiian Philatelic Society
Mr. Kay H. Hoke, Treasurer
P.O. Box 10115
Honolulu, HI 96816-0115

IDAHO
See **Pacific Northwest**.

ILLINOIS
Illinois Postal History Society
Dr. Harvey M. Karlen
1008 North Marion Street
Oak Park, IL 60302
E-mail: eachteacher@aol.com

IOWA
Iowa Postal History Society
Alfred Mack, Secretary/Treasurer
2571 Guthrie Avenue #210A
Des Moines, IA 50317-3019
E-mail: suealmack@home.com

MASSACHUSETTS
Massachusetts Postal Research Society
Hugh J. W. Daugherty
P.O. Box 1146
Eastham, MA 02642

MINNESOTA
Minnesota Postal History Society
John Grabowski
P.O. Box 536
Willernie, MN 55090
E-mail: minnjohn@alum.mit.edu

MONTANA
See **Pacific Northwest**.

NEW MEXICO
See **Arizona**.

NEW YORK
Empire State Postal History Society
John Lange, Secretary
373 Root Road
Ballston Spa, NY 12020-3277

OREGON
See **Pacific Northwest**.

PACIFIC NORTHWEST
Pacific Northwest Postal History Society
Bill Beith
P.O. Box 301263
Portland, OR 97294-90263
E-mail: wrbeith@home.com
Web site: http://members.dsl-only.net/
~simcoe
Covers postal history of Idaho, Montana, Oregon, and Washington.

PENNSYLVANIA
Pennsylvania Postal History Society
Norman Shachat
382 Tall Meadow Lane
Yardley, PA 19056
E-mail: nshachat@aol.com

TEXAS
Texas Postal History Society
Lyle Boardman
3916 Wyldwood Road
Austin, TX 78739-3005

VERMONT
Vermont Philatelic Society
Dr. Paul G. Abajian, Executive Director
P.O. Box 475
Essex Junction, VT 05453
E-mail: pga@surfglobal.net

WASHINGTON
See **Pacific Northwest**.

WISCONSIN
Wisconsin Postal History Society
James Maher
150 Terrace Lane
Hartland, WI 53029-2242
E-mail: westiejim@voyager.net

SPECIAL INTEREST

AIRMAIL
American Airmail Society
Stephen Reinhard
P.O. Box 110
Mineola, NY 11501
E-mail: sr1501@aol.com
Web site: http://ourworld.compuserve.
com/homepages/aams/

CANCELLATIONS
Machine Cancel Society
Gary M. Carlson
3097 Frobisher Avenue
Dublin, OH 43017
E-mail: gcarlson@columbus.rr.com
Web site: www.machinecancel.org

Universal Ship Cancellation Society
Steve Shay, Secretary
747 Shard Court
Fremont, CA 94539-7419
E-mail: shaymur@flash.net
Web site: www.uscs.org

U.S. Cancellation Club
Roger Rhoads, Secretary/Treasurer
3 Rothana Way
Hockessin, DE 19707
E-mail: rrrhoads@aol.com
Web site: http://geocities.com/athens/
2088/uscchome.htm

CENSORED MAIL
Civil Censorhip Study Group
Charles J. LaBlonde
15091 Ridgefield Lane
Colorado Springs, CO 80921-3554
E-mail: clablonde@aol.com

CEREMONY PROGRAMS
American Ceremony Program Society
John Peterson, Secretary/Treasurer
6987 Colehill Drive
San Diego, CA 92119-1953
E-mail: jkpete@pacbell.net
Web site: www.webacps.org

CINDERELLAS
Cinderella Stamp Club
Joseph E. Foley
P.O. Box 183
Riva, MD 21140
E-mail: jfoley4197@aol.com

COVERS
Cover Collectors Circuit Club
Thom Eggleston-Youssoupoff
10102 Oakleaf Avenue
Tampa, FL 33612
E-mail: stamptmf@frontiernet.net
Web site: www.geocities.com/coverccc/
   index.html

DISINFECTED MAIL
Disinfected Mail Study Circle
V. Denis Vandervelde
25 Sinclair Grove
London NW11 9JH
United Kingdom

DUCK STAMPS
National Duck Stamp Collectors Society
P.O. Box 43
Harleysville, PA 19438
E-mail: ndscs@hwcn.org
Web site: www.hwcn.org/link/ndscs

ERRORS
*Errors, Freaks, and Oddities
Collectors' Club*
Cwo Jim McDevitt
955 South Grove Boulevard, #65
Kingsland, GA 31548-5263
E-mail: cwouscg@aol.com

EXHIBITING
American Society of Philatelic Exhibitors
Tim Bartsche, Secretary
13955 West 30th Avenue
Golden, CO 80401-1503
E-mail: timbartsche@aol.com

FIRST DAY COVERS
American First Day Cover Society
Doug Kelsey, Exective Director
P.O. Box 65960
Tucson, AZ 85728

E-mail: afdcs@aol.com
Web site: www.afdcs.org

FIRST ISSUES
First Issues Collectors Club
Kurt Streepy
608 Whitethorn Way
Bloomington, IN 47403
E-mail: kstreepy@msn.com
Web site: http://clubs.yahoo.com/
   ficconweb

LOCAL POSTS
Local Post Collectors Society
Peter Pierce, President
7 Pratt Avenue
Oxford, MA 01540-2826
E-mail: p.oxbou@verizon.net

MAXIMAPHILY
North American Maximaphily
George Constantourakis
2115 Girouard Avenue
Montreal, Quebec H4A 3C4
Canada

MOBILE POST OFFICES
Mobile Post Office Society
Douglas N. Clark
P.O. Box 427
Martson Mills, MA 02684-0427
E-mail: dnc@math.uga.edu
Web site: www.eskimo.com/~rkunz/
   mposhome.html

PLATE NUMBER COILS
*Plate Number Coil Collectors Club
(PNC³)*
Gene Trinks
3603 Bellows Court
Troy, MI 48083
E-mail: gctrinks@sprynet.com
Web site: www.pnc3.org

PLATE NUMBER SINGLES
American Plate Number Single Society
Rick Burdsall, Secretary
608 South Bennett Avenue
Palatine, IL 60067-6706
E-mail: reb608@home.com

Web site: www.stamps.org/directories/
    affiliat.asp

POSTAGE METERS
Meter Stamp Society
R. Stampbaugh, Bulletin Editor
613 Old Corlies Avenue
Neptune, NJ 07753-3959
Web site: www.meterstampsociety.org

POSTAL HISTORY
Military Postal History Society
Robert T. Kinsley
5410 Fern Loop
West Richland, WA 99353-9512
E-mail: kinsley@owt.com
Web site: http://homepage.mac.com/
    mphs/index.html

Postal History Foundation
Elizabeth Towle
920 North First Avenue
Tucson, AZ 85719
E-mail: pht3@mindspring.com

Postal History Society, Inc.
Kalman V. Illyefalvi
8207 Daren Court
Pikesville, MD 21208-2211
E-mail: kalphyl@juno.com

POSTAL LABELS
Postal Label Study Group
Charles H. Smith
13910 B Rio Hondo Circle
La Mirada, CA 90638
E-mail: smithplsg@aol.com

POSTAL ORDERS
The Postal Order Society
Jack Harwood
P.O. Box 32015 Midtown Station
Sarasota, FL 34239
E-mail: jharwood@attglobal.net

POSTCARDS
*International Federation of
Postcard Dealers, Inc.*
John H. McClintock, President
P.O. Box 1765
Manassas, VA 20108

Postcard History Society
Jim Ward
1795 Kleinfeltersville Road
Stevens, PA 17578-9669
E-mail: midcreek@ptd.net

POSTMARKS
Mailer's Postmark Permit Club
Joseph Lo Preiato, President
165 Old Farm Drive
Newington, CT 06111-1819
E-mail: enotriaLP@aol.com
Web site: www.philatelic.com/mppc

Maritime Postmark Society
Tom Hirschinger
P.O. Box 497
Wadsworth, OH 44282

Postmark Collectors Club
David Proulx
7629 Homestead Drive
Baldwinsville, NY 13027
E-mail: stampdance@baldcom.net
Web site: www.postmark.org

PRECANCELS
Precancel Stamp Society
Arthur Damm
176 Bent Pine Hill
North Wales, PA 19454
E-mail: abentpine1@aol.com
Web site: www.precancels.com

REVENUE STAMPS
American Revenue Society
Eric Jackson, President
P.O. Box 728
Leesport, PA 19533
E-mail: eric@revenuer.com
Web site: www. revenuer.org

State Revenue Society
Kent Gray, Secretary
P.O. Box 9726
Dyess AFB, TX 79607
E-mail: staterevs@home.com
Web site: www.hillcity-mall.com/SRS

SOUVENIR PAGES AND PANELS
American Society for Philatelic Pages and Panels
Gerald Blankenship
P.O. Box 475
Crosby, TX 77532-0475
E-mail: gblank1941@aol.com

U.S. POSSESSIONS
Canal Zone Study Group
Richard H. Salz
60 Twenty-Seventh Avenue

San Francisco, CA 94121-1026

U.S. Possessions Philatelic Society
Robert C. Hoge, President
12138 Heathertree Court
Cincinnati, OH 45249

WESTERN COVERS
Western Covers Society
John Drew, Secretary
15370 Skyview Terrace
San Jose, CA 95132-3042
E-mail: jandndrew@aol.com

FOREIGN

AFRICA
Philatelic Society for Greater Southern Africa
Bob Hisey
7227 Sparta Road
Sebring, FL 33875
E-mail: bobhisey@strato.net
Web site: www.homestead.com/PSGSA

West Africa Study Circle (North America)
Dr. Peter Newroth
#33–520 Marsett Place
Victoria, BC V8Z 7J1
Canada
E-mail: prnew@shaw.com
Web site: http://members.xoom.com/wasc99

ALBANIA
Albania Study Circle
Norman Ames
Ashton House, Ashton Keynes
Swindon 5NG 6NX
United Kingdom
E-mail: ames@dircon.co.uk

AUSTRALASIA
Society of Australasian Specialists/Oceania
Hugh Wynn
7442 Spring Valley Drive, PV-107
Springfield, VA 22150

E-mail: hughwynn@juno.com
Web site: http://members.aol.com/stampsho/saso/html

AUSTRIA
Austria Philatelic Society (US)
Ralph Schneider
P.O. Box 23049
Belleville, IL 62223
E-mail: rsstamps@aol.com
Web site: www.ausps.esmartnet.com

BELGIUM
American Belgain Philatelic Society
Kenneth L. Costilow
621 Virginius Drive
Virginia Beach, VA 23452-4417
E-mail: kcos@home.com
Web site: http://groups.hamptonroads.com/ABPS/

BERMUDA
Bermuda Collectors Society
Thomas J. McMahon
P.O. Box 1949
Stuart, FL 34998
E-mail: tommcmahon@adelphia.net

BRAZIL
Brazil Philatelic Association
William V. Kriebel
1923 Manning Street
Philadelphia, PA 19103-5728
E-mail: kriebewv@drexel.edu

BRITISH NORTH AMERICA
British North America Philatelic Society
H. P. Jacobi, Secretary
5295 Moncton Street
Richmond, BC V7E 3B2
Canada
E-mail: beaver@telus.net
Web site: www.bnaps.org

BRITISH VIRGIN ISLANDS
British Virgin Islands Philatelic Society
P.O. Box 704
Road Town, Tortola
British Virgin Islands
E-mail: issun@candwbvi.net
Web site: www.islandsun.com

BRITISH WEST INDIES
British West Indies Study Circle
W. Clary Holt, FRPSL
P.O. Drawer 59
Burlington, NC 27216

BURMA
Burma Philatelic Study Circle
Alan Meech
7208–91 Avenue
Edmonton, AB T6B 0R8
Canada

CANADA
Canadiana Study Unit
John G. Peebles
P.O. Box 3262, Station A
London, Ontario N6A 4K3
Canada
E-mail: john.peebles@odyssey.on.ca

CHINA
China Stamp Society
Paul H. Gault, Secretary
P.O. Box 20711
Columbus, OH 43220
Web site: www.chinastampsociety.org

COLOMBIA
*Colombia/Panama Philatelic
Study Group*
James A. Cross

P.O. Box 2245
El Cajon, CA 92021
E-mail: jimacross@cts.com

COSTA RICA
Society for Costa Rica Collectors
Raul Hernandez
4204 Haring Road
Metairie, AL 70006
E-mail: rherna3870@aol.com
Web site: www.socorico.org

CROATIA
Croatian Philatelic Society
Eck Spahich
P.O. Box 696
Fritch, TX 79036
E-mail: ou812@arn.net
Web site: www.croatianmall.com/cps/

CZECHOSLOVAKIA
Society for Czechoslovak Philately
R. T. Cossaboom
P.O. Box 25332
Scott AFB, IL 62225
Web site: www.czechoslovakphilately.com

DANISH WEST INDIES
Scandinavian Collectors Club
Danish West Indies Study Group
John DuBois
c/o Thermalogic Corp.
22 Kane Industrial Drive
Hudson, MA 01749
E-mail: jld@thlogic.com
Web site: http://dwi.thlogic.com

ETHIOPIA
Ethiopian Philatelic Society
5710 Southeast Garnet Way
Milwaukie, OR 97267
E-mail: fbheiser@home.com
Web site: http://members.home.net/
    fbheiser/ethiopia5.htm

FALKLAND ISLANDS
Falkland Islands Philatelic Study Group
Carl J. Faulkner
c/o The Williams Inn on the Green
Williamstown, MA 01267

FRANCE
France & Colonies Philatelic Society
Ed Grabowski
P.O. Box 364
Garwood, NJ 07027
E-mail: edjjg@bellatlantic.com
Web site: www.fcpsonline.org

GERMAN COLONIES
German Colonies Collectors Group
John Miller
P.O. Box 27
Newton Upper Falls, MA 02464
E-mail: jmiller_ma@hotmail.com

GERMANY
*GDR (German Democratic Republic)
Study Group*
Ken Lawrence
P.O. Box 8040
State College, PA 16803-8040
E-mail: apsken@aol.com

Germany Philatelic Society
Christopher Deterding
P.O. Box 779
Arnold, MD 21012
E-mail: germanyphilatelic@starpower.net
Web site: www.gps.nu

GREAT BRITAIN
Great Britain Collector's Club
Parker A. Bailey Jr., Secretary/Treasurer
P.O. Box 773
Merrimack, NH 03054-0773
E-mail: pbaileyjr@worldnet.att.net
Web site: www.gbstamps.com/gbcc

GREECE
Hellenic Philatelic Society of America
Nicholas Asimakopulos MD, FRPSL
541 Cedar Hill Avenue
Wyckoff, NJ 07481
E-mail: nick1821@aol.com

GUATEMALA
*International Society of Guatemala
Collectors*
Mae Vignola
105 22nd Avenue
San Francisco, CA 94121-1216

HAITI
Haiti Philatelic Society
Ubaldo Del Toro, Secretary/Treasurer
5709 Marble Arch Way
Alexandria, VA 22315
E-mail: u007ubi@aol.com

HONG KONG
Hong Kong Stamp Society
Ming W. Tsang
P.O. Box 206
Glenside, PA 19038
E-mail: hkstampsoc@yahoo.com
Web site: www.hkss.org

HUNGARY
Society for Hungarian Philately
Robert B. Morgan, Secretary
2201 Roscomare Road
Los Angeles, CA 90077-2222
E-mail: rbmorgan@9iname.com
Web site: www.hungarianphilately.org

INDIA
India Study Circle
John Warren
P.O. Box 7326
Washington, DC 20044
E-mail: warrenjohn@epa.gov

INDOCHINA
Society of Indo-China Philatelists
Ron Bentley
2600 North 24th Street
Arlington, VA 22207
E-mail: ron.bentley@veridian.com
Web site: www.imnahstamps.com/sicp/
index.htm

IRAN
Iran Philatelic Study Circle
Darrell Hill
1410 Broadway
Bethlehem, PA 18015
E-mail: d.r.hill@att.net
Web site: www.iranphilatelic.org

IRELAND
Eire Philatelic Association
Myron Hill III, Secretary

P.O. Box 1210
College Park, MD 20741-1210
E-mail: mhill@radix.net
Web site: www.eirephilatelicassoc.org

ISRAEL
Society of Israel Philatelists
Gary Theodore, Membership
P.O. Box 3025
Long Branch, NJ 07740
Web site: www.israelstamps.com

ITALY
Italian-American Stamp Club
William Otto, President
2150 South 84th Street
West Allis, WI 53227

Italy & Colonies Study Circle
Richard Harlow
7 Duncombe House
8 Manor Road
Teddington TW11 8BG
United Kingdom
E-mail: L.R.Harlow@bkinternet.com
Web site: www.icsc.fsworld.co.uk

JAPAN
*International Society for
Japanese Philately*
Kenneth Kamholz
P.O. Box 1283
Haddonfield, NJ 08033
E-mail: isjp@home.com
Web site: www.isjp.org

KOREA
Korea Stamp Society
John E. Talmage, Secretary/Treasurer
P.O. Box 6889
Oak Ridge, TN 37830
E-mail: jtalmage@usit.net
Web site: www.pennfamily.org/KSS-USA/

LIBERIA
The Liberian Philatelic Society
William Thomas Lockard
P.O. Box 106
Wellston, OH 45692-0106
E-mail: tlockard@zoomnet.net

LIECHTENSTEIN
Liechtenstein Study Group
Ralph Schneider
P.O. Box 23049
Belleville, IL 62223
E-mail: rsstamps@aol.com
Web site: rschneiderstamps.com/
liechtenstudy.htm

LITHUANIA
Lithuania Philatelic Society
John Variakojis
3715 West 68th Street
Chicago, IL 60629
E-mail: variakojis@earthlink.net
Web site: www.filatelija.lt/lps/

LUXEMBOURG
Luxembourg Collectors Club
Gary Little
3304 Plateau Drive
Belmont, CA 94002-1312
E-mail: lcc@luxcentral.com
Web site: www.luxcentral.com/stamps/LCC

MEMEL AND SAAR
Plebiscite, Memel and Saar Study Group
Clay Wallace
100 Lark Court
Alamo, CA 94501
E-mail: wallacec@earthlink.net

NETHERLANDS
*American Society for Netherlands
Philately*
Jan Enthoven
221 Coachlite Court South
Oralaska, WI 54650
E-mail: jenthoven@centurytel.net
Web site: www.cs.cornell.edu/home/rvr/
NL/neth_philately.html

NICARAGUA
Nicaragua Study Group
Erick Rodriquez
11817 SW 11th Street
Miami, FL 33184-2501
E-mail: nsgsec@yahoo.com
Web site: http://clubs.yahoo.com/clubs/
nicaraguastudygroup

OCEANIA
Society of Australasian
Specialists/Oceania
Hugh Wynn
7442 Spring Valley Drive, PV-107
Springfield, VA 22150
E-mail: hughwynn@juno.com
Web site: http://members.aol.com/
    stampsho/saso/html

OTTOMAN EMPIRE
Ottoman and Near East
Philatelic Society
Robert Stuchell
193 Valley Stream Lane
Wayne, PA 19087
E-mail: rstuchell@msn.com
Web site: www.oneps.org

PAKISTAN
Pakphil–The Pakistan Philatelic
Study Circle
Jeff Siddiqui
P.O. Box 7002
Lynnwood, WA 98046
E-mail: jeffsiddiqui@msn.com

PAPUA NEW GUINEA
Papuan Philatelic Society
Steven Zirinsky
P.O. Box 230049, Ansonia Station
New York, NY 10023
E-mail: szirinsky@cs.com

PHILIPPINES
International Philippine
Philatelic Society
Bob Yacano
P.O. Box 100
Toast, NC 27030
E-mail: yacano@advt.net

PITCAIRN ISLANDS
Pitcairn Islands Study Group
Nelson A. L. Weller
2940 Wesleyan Lane
Winston-Salem, NC 27106
E-mail: nalweller@aol.com

PORTUGAL
International Society for
Portuguese Philately
Clyde J. Homen, Secretary/Treasurer
1491 Bonnie View Road
Hollister, CA 95023-5117
E-mail: cjh@hollinet.com
Web site: www.portugalstamps.com

RHODESIA
Rhodesian Study Circle
William R. Wallace
P.O. Box 16381
San Francisco, CA 94116
E-mail: bwall8rsr@earthlink.net
Web site: www.RhodesianStudyCircle.org

RUSSIA
Rossica Society of Russian Philately
Ged Seiflow, Secretary
27 North Wacker Drive, Suite 167
Chicago, IL 60606-3203
E-mail: ged.seiflow@rossica.org
Web site: www.rossica.org

RYUKYU ISLANDS
Ryukyu Philatelic Specialist Society, Ltd.
Carmine J. DiVincenzo
P.O. Box 381
Clayton, CA 94517-0381

SAINT HELENA
St. Helena and Dependencies
Philatelic Society
J. L. Havill
205 North Murray Boulevard, #221
Colorado Springs, CO 80916
E-mail: jhavill2@compuserve.com
Web site: www.atlanticislands.com

SAMOA
Fellowship of Samoa Specialists
Jack R. Hughes
124 Commonwealth
Boston, MA 02116
Web site: http://members.aol.com/
    tongajan/foss.html

SARAWAK
Sarawak Specialists Society
Stuart Leven
P.O. Box 24764
San Jose, CA 95154
E-mail: stulev@ix.netcom.com
Web site: http://britborneostamps.org.uk

SCANDINAVIA
Scandinavian Collectors Club
Don Brent, Executive Secretary
P.O. Box 13196
El Cajon, CA 92022
E-mail: dbrent47@sprynet.com
Web site: www.scc-online.com

SPAIN
Spanish Philatelic Society
Robert H. Penn
1108 Walnut Drive
Danielsville, PA 18038
E-mail: roberthpenn@aol.com

TANNU TUVA
Tannu Tuva Collectors Society
Ken Simon
513 6th Avenue South
Lake Worth, FL 33460
E-mail: bigelow9427@cs.com
Web site: www.seflin.org/tuva

THAILAND
Society for Thai Philately
H. R. Blakeney
P.O. Box 1
Thai Prakanchiwit Post Office
Bangkok, 10326
Thailand
E-mail: blakeney@mozart.inet.co.th
Web site: www.thaiphilately.org

UNITED NATIONS
United Nations Philatelists, Inc.
Blanton Clement Jr., Secretary
292 Springdale Terrace
Yardley, PA 19067-3421
E-mail: bcelmjr@aol.com
Web site: www.unpi.com

VATICAN CITY
Vatican Philatelic Society
Sal Quinonez, Membership Chairman
1 Aldergate, Apt. 1002
Riverhead, NY 11901
Web site: http://members.tripod.com/
~DCelani/index-VPS.html

YUGOSLAVIA
Yugosalvia Study Group
Mike Lenard
1514 North 3rd Avenue
Wausau, WI 54401-1903
E-mail: mjlenard@aol.com

TOPICAL

GENERAL
American Topical Association
Paul Tyler, Executive Director
P.O. Box 50820
Albuquerque, NM 87181-0820
E-mail: atastanos@juno.com
Web site: http://home.pren.org/~pauld/ata

AFRICAN-AMERICAN HERITAGE
ESPER (Ebony Society of Philatelic Events and Reflections)
Sanford L. Byrd
P.O. Box 8888
Corpus Christi, TX 78468-8888

E-mail: esper@stx.rr.com
Web site: www.slsabyrd.com (then click on ESPER)

AMERICANA
Americana Unit of the ATA
Dennis Dengel, Secretary
17 Peckham Road
Poughkeepsie, NY 12602-2018
E-mail: info@americanaunit.org
Web site: www.americanaunit.org

ARCHAEOLOGY
Mesoamerican Archaeology Study Unit
Chris L. Moser
P.O. Box 1442
Riverside, CA 92502

Old World Archaeological Study Group
Merle Farrington, President
10 Clark Street
Medway, MA 02053

ART
Fine and Performing Arts Philatelists
Ruth Richards
10393 Derby Drive
Laurel, MD 20723

ASTRONOMY
Astronomy Study Unit
George C. Young
P.O. Box 632
Tewksbury, MA 01876-0632
E-mail: george-young@msn.com

BIOLOGY
The Biology Unit of ATA
Christopher E. Dhale
1401 Linmar Drive
Cedar Rapids, IA 52402
E-mail: chris-dahle@uiowa.edu

CAPTAIN COOK
Captain Cook Study Unit
U.S. Agent, CCSU
173 Minuteman Drive
Concord, MA 01743-1923
E-mail: USAgent@CaptainCookStudy
  Unit.com
Web site: www.CaptainCookStudy
  Unit.com

CATS
Cats on Stamps
Mary Ann Brown, Secretary/Treasurer
3006 Wade Road
Durham, NC 27705

CHESS
Chess on Stamps Study Unit
Eugene Bedard

50 Sawyer Street
Gardner, MA 01440-3266
E-mail: gbedard7@hotmail.com

CHRISTMAS
Christmas Philatelic Club
Linda Lawrence, Secretary
312 Northwood Drive
Lexington, KY 40505-2104
E-mail: stamplinda@aol.com
Web site: www.hwcn.org/link/cpc

Christmas Seal & Charity Stamp Society
Florence Wright, Secretary
33 Northumberland Road
Rochester, NY 14618-2405
E-mail: FHW-33@worldnet.att.net
Web site: http://members.aol.com/
  betsychuck/cscss.htm

COLUMBUS
Christopher Columbus Philatelic Society
Donald R. Ager
P.O. Box 71
Hillsboro, NH 03244-0071
E-mail: don_ager@corknet.com

DOGS
Dogs on Stamps Study Unit
Morris Raskin, Secretary
202A Newport Road
Monroe Township, NJ 08831-3920
Web site: www.dossu.org

EARTH'S PHYSICAL FEATURES
Earth's Physical Features Study Group
Fred W. Klein
515 Magdalena Avenue
Los Altos, CA 94024

EUROPA
Europa Study Unit
Hank Klos
P.O. Box 611
Bensenville, IL 60106-0611
E-mail: eunity@aol.com

GEMS AND MINERALS
Gems, Minerals and Jewelry Study Unit
George C. Young

P.O. Box 632
Tewksbury, MA 01876-0632
E-mail: george-young@msn.com

GOLF
International Philatelic Golf Society
Ron Spiers
8025 Saddle Run
Powell, OH 43065
E-mail: rwspiers@aol.com
Web site: www.ipgsonline.org

GRAPHICS
Graphics Philately Association
Mark H. Winntegrad
1450 Parkchester Road
Bronx, NY 10462-7622

JOURNALISTS, AUTHORS, POETS
Journalists, Authors, Poets on Stamps
Sol P. Baltimore, Secretary/Treasurer
28742 Blackstone Drive
Lathrup Village, MI 48076

LIGHTHOUSES
Lighthouse Stamp Society
Dalene Thomas
8612 W. Warren Lane
Lakewood, CO 80227-2352
E-mail: dalene1@wideopenwest.com
Web site: www.LighthouseStampSociety.org

LIONS INTERNATIONAL
Lions International Stamp Club
John W. Bargus, Secretary
304–2777 Barry Road
RR2, Mill Bay BC V0R 2P0
Canada

MASKS
Mask Study Unit
Carolyn A. Weber
E-mail: kencar@venturalink.net

MASONIC
George Washington Mason Stamp Club
Stan Longenecker
930 Wood Street
Mount Joy, PA 17552-1926
E-mail: natsco@usa.net

Masonic Study Unit of ATA
Stan Longenecker, Chapter Rep.
930 Wood Street
Mount Joy, PA 17552-1926
E-mail: natsco@usa.net

MATHEMATICS
Mathematics Study Unit
Estelle A. Buccino, Secretary/Treasurer
5615 Glenwood Road
Bethesda, MD 20817-6727
Web site: www. math.ttu.edu/msu

MEDICAL
Medical Subjects Unit of the American Topical Association
Frederick C. Skvara MD,
    Secretary/Treasurer
P.O. Box 6228
Bridgewater, NJ 08807
E-mail: fcskvara@bellatlantic.net

MESOAMERICA
See **Archaeology**.

MUSIC
Philatelic Music Circle
Cathie Osborne
P.O. Box 1781
Sequim, WA 98382

NAPOLEONIC AGE
Napoleonic Age Philatelists
Ken Berry
7513 Clayton Drive
Oklahoma City, OK 73132
E-mail: krb2@earthlink.net

PARACHUTES
Parachute Study Group
Bill Wickert
3348 Clubhouse Road
Virginia Beach, VA 23452-5339
E-mail: bw47psg@worldnet.att.net

PERFORMING ARTS
See **Art**.

PHILATELIC/NUMISMATIC
Society of Philatelists and Numismatists
Joe R. Ramos, Secretary

1929 Millis Street
Montebello, CA 90640
E-mail: span@atsecure.net
Web site: http://span.atsecure.net

POLAR PHILATELY
American Society of Polar Philatelists
Allen Warren, Secretary
P.O. Box 39
Exton, PA 19341-0039
E-mail: alanwar@att.net
Web site: www.south-pole.com/aspp.htm

RELIGION
Collectors of Religion on Stamps
Verna Shackleton
425 North Linwood Avenue #110
Appleton, WI 54914-3476
E-mail: corosec@powernetonline.com
Web site: www.powernetonline.com/
~corosec/coros1.htm

ROTARY
Rotary on Stamps
Donald E. Fiery, Secretary
P.O. Box 333
Hanover, PA 17331

SCOUTS
Scouts on Stamps Society International
Kenneth A. Shuker
22 Cedar Lane
Cornwall, NY 12518-2100
Web site: www.sossi.org

SHIPS
Ships on Stamps Unit
Robert P. Stuckert
2750 Highway 21 East
Paint Lick, KY 40461-9075

SPACE
Space Unit of the American Topical Society
Terry Chamberlain
5901 Mark Lane
Rowlett, TX 75089
E-mail: tchamberlain@gdainet.com
Web site: http://stargate.1usa.com/
stamps/memforma.htm

SPORTS
Sports Philatelists International
M. A. Jones
5310 Lindenwood Avenue
Saint Louis, MO 63109-1758
E-mail: docj3@juno.com

STAMPS ON STAMPS
Stamps on Stamps Collectors Club
William E. Critzer
1360 Trinity Drive
Menlo Park, CA 94025
E-mail: wcritzer@avenidas.org
Web site: www.stampsonstamps.org

ZEPPELIN
Zeppelin Collectors Club
Cheryl Ganz
P.O. Box A3843
Chicago, IL 60690-3843

U.S. AND TOPICAL STAMP CATALOGUES

UNITED STATES AND U.S. AREA

Brookman Stamp Price Guide. Brookman Stamp Company, 10 Chestnut Drive, Bedford, NH 03110. *Stamp price guide. Published annually.*

Comprehensive Catalogue of United States Stamp Booklets. Robert Furman. Krause Publications, 700 East State Street, Iola, WI 54990. Web site: www.krause.com. *Comprehensive listings and values for all U.S. booklets and booklet panes from the first issue onward, including varieties. Profusely illustrated.*

Durland Standard Plate Number Catalog. United States Stamp Society, P.O. Box 23707, Belleville, IL 62223. *The most comprehensive listing of U.S. plate blocks. Lists every known plate block by number and position. Illustrated.*

Errors on U.S. Postage Stamps. Krause Publications, 700 East State Street, Iola, WI 54990. Web site: www.krause.com. *Comprehensive catalogue of U.S. major error stamps, fully illustrated, includes section on EFOs. Published annually.*

Harris US/BNA Postage Stamp Catalog. H. E. Harris & Co., P.O. Box 817, Florence, AL 35631. *Catalogue/price list for U.S. and British North America. Published annually.*

Krause-Minkus Stamps and Prices. Krause Publications, 700 East State Street, Iola, WI 54990. Web site: www.krause.com. *A concise catalogue of U.S. stamps. Published annually.*

Krause-Minkus Standard Catalog of U.S. Stamps. Krause Publications, 700 East State Street, Iola, WI 54990. Web site: www.krause.com. *Specialized catalogue of U.S. stamps featuring a wealth of information about each issue. Published annually.*

Mystic U.S. Stamp Catalogue. Mystic Stamp Company, 24 Mill Street, Camden, NY 13116-9111. *Catalogue of U.S. stamps featuring full-color illustrations.*

Planty Photo Encyclopedia of Cacheted First Day Covers. Earl Planty. Michael A. Mellone, P.O. Box 206, Stewartsville, NJ 08886. *Highly detailed multivolume catalogue devoted to cacheted FDCs of the classic period, 1901–1939.*

The Postal Service Guide to U.S. Stamps. United States Postal Service, Box 219424, Kansas City, MO 64121-0924. *Noteworthy for its full-color illustrations. Available by mail, but also available at many post offices and most philatelic windows.*

Sanabria Airmail Catalogue. Krause Publications, 700 East State Street, Iola, WI 54990. Web site: www.krause.com. *Catalogue of airmail stamps of the world.*

Scott Specialized Catalogue of U.S. Stamps and Covers. Scott Publishing Co., P.O. Box 828, Sidney, OH 45365. Web site: www.scottonline.com. *Detailed, comprehensive listing of all U.S. postage stamps, postal stationery, revenue stamps, and more. Published annually.*

Scott Standard Postage Stamp Catalogue. Scott Publishing Co., P.O. Box 828, Sidney, OH 45365. Web site: www.scottonline.com. *Multivolume set listing all postage stamps of the world. Published annually.*

Town & Type Catalogue. Precancel Stamp Society, PSS Catalogs, 108 Ashswamp Road, Scarborough, ME 04074. *Complete listing of all recognized U.S. precancels.*

U.S. First Day Cover Catalogue and Checklist. Mike Mellone. Scott Publishing Co., P.O. Box 828, Sidney, OH 45365. Web site: www.scottonline.com. *Detailed listings for U.S. first day covers. Published annually.*

U.S. Pocket Stamp Catalogue. Scott Publishing Co., P.O. Box 828, Sidney, OH 45365. *Full-color pocket catalogue of U.S. stamps. Published annually.*

TOPICAL

Brookman Black Heritage First Day Cover Catalog. Brookman Stamp Company, 10 Chestnut Drive, Bedford, NH 03110. *Comprehensive catalogue/price guide of first day covers relating to Black Heritage.*

Brookman Price Guide for Disney Stamps. Brookman Stamp Company, 10 Chestnut Drive, Bedford, NH 03110. *Complete catalogue/price guide of stamps featuring Disney characters and subjects.*

Domfil Topical Catalogues. Domfil (Grupo Afinsa), U.S. Office, 775 Passaic Avenue, West Caldwell, NJ 07006. Web site: www.domfil.com. *Publishes separate catalogues for a variety of topics including railroads, sports, dogs, cats, birds, chess, Disney, automobiles, scouting, mushrooms, marine life, butterflies and insects, and prehistoric reptiles.*

FOREIGN STAMP
CATALOGUES

FOREIGN STAMP CATALOGUES are especially useful for collectors specializing in an individual country. Foreign specialized catalogues go into greater detail than general catalogues.

Listings for catalogues are arranged by country. The publisher's name, address, Web site, and e-mail are given where known. Some publishers publish more than a single catalogue. Many foreign catalogues are available from U.S. supply dealers, and in many cases, it is more convenient to order from them. Most foreign catalogues are published in the language of their nation of origin. Some Web sites include an English-language version.

GENERAL

Scott Standard Postage Stamp Catalogues. Scott Publishing Co., P.O. Box 828, Sidney, OH 45365. Web site: www.scottonline.com. *Publishes a general multivolume catalogue of stamps of the world, also selected individual countries are available on CD-ROMs.*

BY COUNTRY

AUSTRALIA

Australian Commonwealth Specialists' Catalogue (ACSC). Brusden-White, 673 Bourke Street, Melbourne, VIC 3000, Australia. Web site: www.rap.com.au; e-mail: raperry@rie.net.au. *Specialized catalogue in three volumes covering seven issues: Kangaroos, King George V, King George VI, Queen Elizabeth II, Decimals 1966–1975, Booklets 1904–1973, and Postage Dues.*

Australia Stamp Catalogue. Seven Seas Stamps, Ltd., P.O. Box 321, Brookvale, NSW 2100, Australia. Web site: www.sevenseas.com.au; e-mail: stamps@sevenseas.com.au. *Catalogue of stamps of Australia and states.*

Standard Catalogue of Australia Stamps. Krause Publishing, 700 East State Street, Iola, WI 54990. Web site: www.krause.com. *Catalogue of stamps of Australia.*

AUSTRIA

Austria Netto Katalog. Verlag Austria Netto Katalog, Taborstrasse 47-49, 1020 Vienna, Austria. E-mail: office@active-intermedia.at. *Publishes a specialized catalogue of stamps of Austria.*

BELGIUM

Catalogue Officiel de Timbres-Poste Belgique. Chambre Professionnelle Belge des Negociants en Timbres-Poste, Galerie du Centre Bureau 343, rue des Fripiers 17, 1000 Bruxelles, Belgium.

BRAZIL

RHM Catalogue. RHM Philatelists, Al. dos Guaicanans, 712–Pl. Paulista, Sao Paulo, Brazil. Web site: www.rhm.br. *Specialized catalogue of stamps of Brazil.*

CANADA

Unitrade Catalogue. Unitrade, 99 Floral Parkway, Toronto, Ontario M6L 2C4, Canada. Web site: unitradeassoc.com; e-mail: unitrade@unitradeassoc.com. *Specialized catalogue of stamps of Canada, including British Columbia and Vancouver Island, New Brunswick, Newfoundland, Nova Scotia, and Prince Edward Island.*

DENMARK

AFA Danmark Frimaerke Katalog. Aarhus Frimaerkehandel, Bruunsgade 42, 8000 Aarhus, Denmark. Web site: www.afa.dk; e-mail: afa@afa.dk. *Publishes a specialized catalogue of stamps of Denmark, also a catalogue of stamps of Scandinavia.*

FINLAND

LAPE. Lauri Peltonen Ky, Pl 39 (Lasitehtaankatu 3), 10901 Hanko, Finland. Web site: www.lape.net; e-mail: lape@surfnet.fi. *Specialized catalogue of stamps of Finland.*

FRANCE

Cérès. Editions Philateliques de Paris, 23 rue du Louvre, 75001 Paris, France. *Specialized catalogue of stamps of France.*

Yvert & Tellier. Yvert & Tellier, 37 rue des Jacobins, 80036 Amiens Cedex 1, France. *Specialized catalogues for stamps of France and colonies.*

GERMANY

Michel. Schwaneberger Verlag GmbH, Muthmannstrasse 4, 80939 Munich, Germany. Web site: www.michel.de; e-mail: michel@michel.de. *Publishes a variety of catalogues covering specialized areas of Germany, German postal stationery.*

GREAT BRITAIN

Standard Catalogue of Great Britain Stamps. Krause Publishing, 700 East State Street, Iola, WI 54990. Web site: www.krause.com. *Catalogue of stamps of Great Britain.*

Stanley Gibbons. Stanley Gibbons Publications, 5 Parkside Christchurch Road, Ringwood, Hampshire, BH24 3SH, England. Web site: www.stanleygibbons.co.uk; e-mail: info@stanleygibbons.co.uk. *Publishes a set of worldwide catalogues as well as a number of specialized volumes devoted to a range of British issues.*

GREECE

Hermes. A. Karamitsos, 34 Tsimiski Street, 54623 Thesaloniki, Greece. Web site: www.karamitsos.com; e-mail: karamitsos@karamitso.gr. *A. Karamitsos distributes the Hermes specialized catalogue of stamps of Greece.*

Vlastos. Vlastos Philatelic Center, 40 Vassileos Georgiou Street, GR-15233 Halandri, Greece. Web site: www.vlastos.gr; e-mail: sales@vlastos.com. *Publishes a specialized catalogue of stamps of Greece.*

HUNGARY

Philatelica Hungarica. Philatelica Hungarica, P.O. Box 28, H-1675 Budapest, Hungary. Web site: www.philhun.hu; e-mail: philhun@mail.matav.hu. *Publishes a specialized catalogue of stamps of Hungary.*

INDIA

Phila India Colour Catalogue. Philatelia, One Moti Street, Calcutta 700 013, India. Web site: www.91-33.com/philatelia/stamps.html; e-mail: philatelia@91-33.com. *A comprehensive catalogue of stamps of India, including British Dominion, independence, officials, military stamps, rocket mail, and first day covers.*

ISRAEL

Bale. Chariot Global Marketing Ltd., P.O. Box 10824, Ramat Gan, Israel. Web site: www.bale-catalogue.com. *Publishes a specialized catalogue of stamps of Israel, also catalogues relating to the Turkish and British mandate periods.*

Stamps of Israel Encyclopedia & Catalogue. SweetChild Software, P.O. Box 4064, Jerusalem 91040, Israel. Web site: www.sweetchild.com; e-mail: orders@sweetchild.com. *A digital catalogue of stamps of Israel, including postal stationery, machine-vended stamps, and maximum cards.*

Standard Catalogue of Israel Stamps. Krause Publishing, 700 East State Street, Iola, WI 54990. Web site: www.krause.com. *Catalogue of stamps of Israel.*

ITALY

Sassone. Sassone srl, Via Benedetto Croce 68/116, 00142 Roma, Italy. Web site: www.interpress.it; e-mail: sassone@interpress.it. *Publishes a specialized catalogue of Italy and the Italian area.*

Unificato. C.I.F. Catalogo Unificato, Via Privata Maria Teresa 11, 20123 Milano, Italy. *Publishes a specialized catalogue of stamps of Italy.*

Vaccari Catalogues. Vaccari srl, Via M. Buonarroti 46, 41058 Vignola (MO), Italy. Web site: www.vaccari.it. *Publishes specialized catalogues and handbooks for periods and areas of Italian philately.*

JAPAN

Japanese Stamp Specialized Catalog (JSCA). Japan Philatelic Society Foundation, Mejiro 1-4-23, Tokyo 171-0031, Japan. Web site: http://yushi.or.jp/english/e_kaiin/jcat.htm; e-mail: info@yushi.or.jp. *Specialized catalogue of stamps and postal stationery of Japan, including quantities printed, cancellations, constant flaws, and so forth.*

Japan Postage Stamp Catalogue. Japan Stamp Dealers Association, Central P.O. Box 1003, Tokyo, Japan. *Specialized catalogue of stamps of Japan.*

Sakura Catalog of Japanese Stamps. Japan Philatelic Society Foundation, Mejiro 1-4-23, Tokyo 171-0031, Japan. Web site: http://yushi.or.jp/english/e_kaiin/jcat.htm; e-mail: info@yushi.or.jp. *Specialized color catalogue of stamps of Japan, including Ryukyu issues, Manchukuo issues, Japanese occupation issues, and postal stationery.*

KOREA

KPC Korean Postage Stamp Catalogue. Korean Philatelic Co. Ltd., C.P.O. Box 323, Seoul 100-603, Korea. *Specialized catalogue of stamps of Korea.*

LIECHTENSTEIN

VSBH Briefmarken-Katalog. Multipress Verlag AG, Romerstrasse 45, CH-4135 Reinach BL 1, Switzerland. E-mail: sbk.multipress@birki.ch. *Publishes a specialized catalogue that includes stamps of Switzerland, Liechtenstein, and UN offices in Switzerland.*

Zumstein Schweiz/Liechtenstein Katalog. Zumstein & Cie, Zeughausgasse 24, 3000 Bern 7, Switzerland. Web site: www.briefmarken.ch; e-mail: post_zumstein@briefmarken.ch. *Publishes a catalogue that includes stamps of both Liechtenstein and Switzerland.*

LUXEMBOURG

Prifix Catalogue. Banque du Timbre, 17 Boulevard Prince Henri, Luxembourg City, Luxembourg. Web site: www.bdt.lu; e-mail: info@bdt.lu. *Published annually, specialized catalogue of Luxembourg stamps including first day covers.*

MALAYSIA

Standard Catalogue of Malaysia-Singapore-Brunei Stamps and Postal History. International Stamp & Coin Sdn. Bhd., 2.4 & 2.5 Pertama Shopping Comples, 2ns Floor, Jalan Tuanku Abdul Rahman, 50100 Kuala Lumpur, Malaysia. *Catalogue of stamps of Malaysia, Singapore, and Brunei.*

MALTA

J.B. Catalogue of Malta Stamps and Postal History. Sliema Stamps, 91 Manwel Dimech Street, Sliema SLM14, Malta. Web site: www.sliemastampshop.com.mt; e-mail: sales@sliemastampshop.com.mt. *Specialized catalogue of stamps of Malta.*

NETHERLANDS

NVPH Netherlands Catalogue. Nederlandsche Vereniging van Postzegel Handelaren, Weteringkade 45, 2515 AL, Den Haag, Netherlands. Web site: e-mail: info@nvph.nl. *Specialized catalogue of stamps of the Netherlands.*

Zonnebloem. Uitgeverij Zonnebloem B.V., Haarlemmerstraat 74, 2181 HD Hillegom, Netherlands. *Publishes a catalogue of stamps of the Netherlands and colonies.*

NEWFOUNDLAND

Newfoundland Specialized Catalogue. Walsh's Philatelic Service, 9 Guy Street, Saint John's, Newfoundland A1B 1P4, Canada. Web site: www.nsscat.fn.ca; e-mail: nsscat@nf.sympatico.ca. *Specialized catalogue of stamps of Newfoundland, including postage stamps, inland revenue stamps, tobacco stamps, advertising covers and corner cards, picture postcards, and Newfoundland town post office cancellations.*

NEW ZEALAND

ACS Colour Catalogue of New Zealand Stamps. Auckland City Stamps Ltd., P.O. Box 3496, Auckland, New Zealand. Web site: www.nzstamps.com; e-mail: acs@nzstamps.com. *Specialized catalogue of stamps of New Zealand.*

Campbell Patterson Catalogue of New Zealand Stamps. Campbell Patterson Ltd., P.O. Box 5555, Auckland, New Zealand. Web site: cpnzstamps.co.nz; e-mail: service@cpnzstamps.co.nz. *Specialized catalogue of the stamps of New Zealand, published in color in loose-leaf form with permanent pages for essential information and temporary pages for prices and other updates.*

NORWAY

Norgeskatalogen. Oslo Filatelistklubb, Postboks 298 Sentrum, N-0103 Oslo, Norway. Web site: www.filatelist.no/klubber/oslo/ofk-nk2.htm. *Specialized catalogue of stamps of Norway, including first day covers.*

POLAND

Fischer Katalog. Fischer, Rynek 11, Bytom, Poland. Web site: www.fischer.pl; e-mail: fischer@fischer.pl. *Publishes specialized catalogues of stamps of Poland, including occupations issues, local issues, plebiscite issues, and fantasy issues.*

PORTUGAL

Afinsa/Portugal. Afinsa Portugal, Rua Dr. Ricardo Jorge 53, 4050-514, Porto, Portugal. Web site: www.afinsaportugal.com; e-mail: selos@afinsaportugal.com. *Specialized catalogue of stamps of Portugal.*

SAINT-PIERRE AND MIQUELON

St. Pierre and Miquelon Specialized Catalog. Penny Black Publishing, 2335 Paliswood Road, Calgary AB T2V 3P6, Canada. Web site: http://members. home.net/james-taylor/index.htm. *Specialized catalogue of stamps of Saint-Pierre and Miquelon, including overprints with illustrated varieties, first day covers, proofs, trial color proofs, and imperforates.*

SOUTH AFRICA

South African Stamp Colour Catalogue. International Philatelic Service, P.O. Box 567, 2000 Johannesburg, South Africa. *Specialized catalogue of stamps of South Africa and South African homelands.*

SPAIN

Afinsa. Afinsa, Lagasca 18, 28001 Madrid, Spain. *Specialized catalogue of stamps of Spain.*

Filabo. Filabo Sa, Vallespir 20, 8970 San Juan Despi, Barcelona, Spain. *Specialized catalogue of stamps of Spain and Andorra.*

SWEDEN

Facit. Facit Forlag AB, Box 321, S-72107 Vasteras, Sweden. *Catalogue of stamps of Sweden and certain other Scandinavian countries.*

SWITZERLAND

VSBH Briefmarken-Katalog. Multipress Verlag AG, Romerstrasse 45, CH-4135 Reinach BL 1, Switzerland. E-mail: sbk.multipress@birki.ch. *Specialized catalogue that includes stamps of Switzerland, Liechtenstein, and UN offices in Switzerland.*

Zumstein Spezialkatalog Schweiz. Zumstein & Cie, Zeughausgasse 24, 3000 Bern 7, Switzerland. Web site: www.briefmarken.ch; e-mail: post_zumstein@briefmarken.ch. *Publishes several specialized catalogues of stamps and postal stationery of Switzerland, as well as a combined Switzerland and Liechtenstein catalogue.*

PHILATELIC
REFERENCE BOOKS

PHILATELY IS BLESSED with a wealth of literature few other hobbies can match. During the past 150 years, thousands of knowledgeable collectors from all over the world have written books on just about every aspect of philately. No matter how esoteric or obscure your area of interest, you will almost certainly be able to find a philatelic reference specific to the subject.

Never hesitate to invest in books. An old maxim counsels, "Buy the book before buying the stamp." It's wise advice. A kernel of knowledge can mean the difference between buying or selling a stamp for pennies versus hundreds of dollars. Books are truly worth their weight in gold, not only in terms of knowledge, but as collectors' items. Philatelic specialty books are frequently labors of love printed in small press runs, typically 100 to 2,000 copies. They're often expensive new, but once out of print, they sell for a multiple of their original cover price.

Out-of-print books are available from philatelic literature dealers, or you can borrow them from philatelic libraries. Refer to Chapter 36, "Resources."

GENERAL READING

Basic Philately. Kenneth A. Wood. Krause Publications, 700 East State Street, Iola, WI 54990. Web site: www.krause.com.

Facts and Fantasy About Philately. John M. Hotchner. P.O. Box 1125, Falls Church, VA 22041. *Delightful book of stamp-collecting wit and wisdom by one of America's best-known philatelic columnists and writers. Especially recommended for beginners.*

Focus on Forgeries. Varro E. Tyler. Linn's Stamp News, P.O. Box 29, Sidney, OH 45365. Web site: www.linns.com. *A useful guide that enables collectors to easily recognize the difference between genuine and forged stamps.*

Franklin D. Roosevelt & the Stamps of the United States 1933–1945. Brian C. Baur. Linn's Stamp News, P.O. Box 29, Sidney, OH 45365. Web site: www.linns.com. *Rare, behind-the-scenes look at the origins of some of America's best-loved stamps and the stamp-collecting president's input into their creation.*

Franklin D. Roosevelt: The Stamp Collecting President. Brian C. Baur. Linn's Stamp News, P.O. Box 29, Sidney, OH 45365. Web site: www.linns.com. *An exciting and historic book about the philatelic life of one of our most beloved presidents and his dedication to the hobby of stamp collecting.*

Fun and Profit in Stamp Collecting. Herman Herst, Jr. Linn's Stamp News, P.O. Box 29, Sidney, OH 45365. Web site: www.linns.com. *Informative and thoroughly enjoyable look into the world of stamps and money by one of America's best-loved philatelic writers.*

Fundamentals of Philately. L. N. Williams. American Philatelic Society, P.O. Box 8000, State College, PA 16803. Web site: www.stamps.org. *An 880-page masterwork loaded with information of use to every philatelist from beginner to specialist. Hundreds of illustrations.*

Linn's U.S. Stamp Yearbook. Linn's Stamp News, P.O. Box 29, Sidney, OH 45365. Web site: www.linns.com. *Published annually since 1983, loaded with massive detail about design, alternate designs, varieties, stamp production, problems, and more, for each stamp issued each year.*

More of the World's Greatest Stamp Collectors. Stanley M. Bierman. Linn's Stamp News, P.O. Box 29, Sidney, OH 45365. Web site: www.linns.com. *Companion volume to Bierman's* World's Greatest Stamp Collectors.

More Who's Who on U.S. Stamps. Richard Louis Thomas. Linn's Stamp News, P.O. Box 29, Sidney, OH 45365. Web site: www.linns.com. *Capsule biographies and illustrations of individuals honored, but not pictured, on U.S. stamps.*

Nassau Street. Herman Herst, Jr. Linn's Stamp News, P.O. Box 29, Sidney, OH 45365. Web site: www.linns.com. *Enjoyable memoir of a stamp dealer active during the golden era of philately. Philately's all-time best-selling book is a must-read for anyone—beginner and advanced collector alike—who collects stamps.*

On the Road: The Quest for Stamps. Stephen R. Datz. General Philatelic Corporation, P.O. Box 402, Loveland, CO 80539. *A stamp dealer's entertaining true-life adventures while on the road buying stamp collections from the public all across America.*

Philatelic Forgers: Their Lives and Works. Varro E. Tyler. Linn's Stamp News, P.O. Box 29, Sidney, OH 45365. Web site: www.linns.com. *Intriguing narrative of some of the most famous and prolific philatelic forgers. The most comprehensive work on the men who faked stamps and the stamps they faked.*

Spurious Stamps: A History of U.S. Postal Counterfeits. H. K. Petschel. American Philatelic Society, P.O. Box 8000, State College, PA 16803. Web site: www.stamps.org. *Fascinating history of postal fraud from 1895 into the 1970s, written by a retired postal inspector. Includes color plates of fakes.*

Still More Stories to Collect Stamps By. Herman Herst, Jr. Mekeel's Stamp News, P.O. Box 5050, White Plains, NY 10602. Web site: www.linns.com. *More stories by the best-selling author of Nassau Street.*

Successful Stamp Dealing. Peter Mosiondz, Jr. Krause Publications, 700 East State Street, Iola, WI 54990. Web site: www.krause.com. *Practical advice on how to start and build a successful stamp dealership.*

Who's Who on U.S. Stamps. Richard Louis Thomas. Linn's Stamp News, P.O. Box 29, Sidney, OH 45365. Web site: www.linns.com. *Capsule biographies and illustrations of more than 400 people portrayed on U.S. stamps between 1847 and 1990. Thomas also authored the companion volume* More Who's Who on U.S. Stamps.

The Wild Side: Philatelic Mischief, Murder, and Intrigue. Stephen R. Datz. General Philatelic Corporation, P.O. Box 402, Loveland, CO 80539. *Veteran stamp dealer's real-life experiences with a rogues' gallery of scoundrels, eccentrics, and misfits from the side of philately the public seldom sees.*

The World's Greatest Stamp Collectors. Stanley M. Bierman. Linn's Stamp News, P.O. Box 29, Sidney, OH 45365. Web site: www.linns.com. *Highly readable biographies of the world's greatest stamp collectors. Bierman also authored the companion volume* More of the World's Greatest Stamp Collectors.

REFERENCE GUIDES

Affordable Foreign Errors. Paul S. Greenlaw, with Martin Sellinger. Krause Publications, 700 East State Street, Iola, WI 54990. Web site: www.krause.com. *Comprehensive guide to identifying and collecting foreign stamp errors, many of which are readily affordable.*

American Stamp Dealers Association Membership Guide. American Stamp Dealers Association, 3 School Street, Glen Cove, NY 11452-2548. Web site: www.asdaonline.com. *Guide to stamp dealers in America cross-referenced by specialty.*

The Buyer's Guide. Stephen R. Datz. General Philatelic Corporation, P.O. Box 402, Loveland, CO 80539. *Highly detailed, stamp-by-stamp analysis of quality U.S. stamps for the selective buyer, including premium characteristics, gum and hinging, fakes and problem stamps, when to expertise, etc. Completely illustrated.*

Classic United States Imperforate Stamps. Jon Rose. Linn's Stamp News, P.O. Box 29, Sidney, OH 45365. Web site: www.linns.com. *An in-depth handbook devoted to the very first U.S. issues, those in use prior to the invention of perforating equipment.*

The Duck Stamp Story. Eric Jay Dolin and Bob Dumaine. Krause Publications, 700 East State Street, Iola, WI 54990. Web site: www.krause.com. *Comprehensive coverage of the duck stamp story, including conservation program, artwork, production information, and figures, a fantastic book coauthored by Bob Dumaine, one of the nation's leading authorities on duck stamps.*

How to Detect Damaged, Altered, and Repaired Stamps. Paul W. Schmid. Krause Publications, 700 East State Street, Iola, WI 54990. Web site: www.krause.com. *The most authoritative and easy-to-use book on the subject of altered U.S. stamps. Well illustrated. Highly recommended.*

International Encyclopedic Dictionary of Philately. R. Scott Carlton. Krause Publications, 700 East State Street, Iola, WI 54990. Web site: www.krause.com. *Offers more than 1,000 sources for further research on stamp collecting terms including English translation of foreign terms.*

An Introduction to Revenue Stamps. Bill J. Castenholz. Krause Publications, 700 East State Street, Iola, WI 54990. Web site: www.krause.com. *A review of U.S. revenue stamps from the Civil War to the 1990s, with special attention to the first issues.*

Introduction to the Stamps of Mexico. Dale Pulver. Linn's Stamp News, P.O. Box 29, Sidney, OH 45365. Web site: www.linns.com. *Covers all aspects of Mexican philately, including prestamp postal history through the Exporta series.*

Introduction to U.S. Revenue Stamps. Richard Friedburg. Linn's Stamp News, P.O. Box 29, Sidney, OH 45365. Web site: www.linns.com. *Covers the earliest issues to the very latest. Everything you need to know about starting a revenue stamp collection.*

Linn's Plate Number Coil Handbook. Ken Lawrence. Linn's Stamp News, P.O. Box 29, Sidney, OH 45365. Web site: www.linns.com. *The definitive work on this popular specialty. Copiously illustrated.*

Mekeel's U.S. Reference Manual. Mekeel's Stamp News, P.O. Box 5050, White Plains, NY 10602. *In-depth look at selected U.S. special-interest stamps and covers, including rarities and difficult-to-identify items.*

Micarelli Identification Guide to U.S. Stamps. Charles Micarelli. Scott Publishing Co., P.O. Box 828, Sidney, OH 45365. Web site: www.scottonline.com. *Comprehensive identification guide to U.S. definitive stamps, fully illustrated, and especially useful for hard-to-identify nineteenth-century issues. Highly recommended.*

Post Dates. Kenneth A. Wood. Krause Publications, 700 East State Street, Iola, WI 54990. Web site: www.krause.com. *A 400-page chronology of more than 6,000 intriguing events in the mails and philately beginning with the year 4000 B.C.*

The Serrane Guide. American Philatelic Society, P.O. Box 8000, State College, PA 16803. Web site: www.stamps.org. *An illustrated identification guide to forged stamps up to the year 1926. A highly respected classic on the subject.*

StampFinders Stamp Selection Guides. USID, Inc., 6175 N.W. 153rd Street, Suite 201, Miami Lakes, FL 33014. *Investment-oriented stamp price performance guides. Volumes include the United States and Canada, British Commonwealth, Mexico and South America, Germany and German Colonies, and the Far East.*

Stamp Investing. Stephen R. Datz. General Philatelic Corporation, P.O. Box 402, Loveland, CO 80539. *Comprehensively covers all aspects of stamps as investments.*

This Is Philately: An Encyclopedia of Stamp Collecting. Kenneth A. Wood. Krause Publications, 700 East State Street, Iola, WI 54990. Web site: www.krause.com. *Superb three-volume reference covering every conceivable aspect of philately.*

Top Dollar Paid: The Complete Guide to Selling Your Stamps. Stephen R. Datz. General Philatelic Corporation, P.O. Box 402, Loveland, CO 80539. *Best-selling how-to guide loaded with practical information and entertaining narrative about the stamp business. Not only for sellers, but for all who buy or collect stamps.*

Triangular Philatelics. Charles Green. Krause Publications, 700 East State Street, Iola, WI 54990. Web site: www.krause.com. *Guide for collectors interested in this perennially popular topic, includes listings for every country that ever issued triangular stamps.*

The United States 1¢ Franklin 1861–1867. Don L. Evans. Linn's Stamp News, P.O. Box 29, Sidney, OH 45365. Web site: www.linns.com. *A comprehensive volume devoted to the classic 1¢ stamp of 1861–67.*

United States Postage Stamps of 1869. Jon Rose. Linn's Stamp News, P.O. Box 29, Sidney, OH 45365. Web site: www.linns.com. *The complete story of our nation's perennially popular first pictorial and first bicolored stamps.*

United States Postal History Sampler. Richard B. Graham. Linn's Stamp News, P.O. Box 29, Sidney, OH 45365. Web site: www.linns.com. *Fifteen fully illustrated chapters cover a broad range of topics around which cover collections can be built. Profusely illustrated.*

U.S. Stamp Facts, 19th Century. Linn's Stamp News, P.O. Box 29, Sidney, OH 45365. Web site: www.linns.com. *Detailed listings for important stamps of the nineteenth century. Devotes a page to each stamp and includes information on* *plate numbers, plate arrangement, quantity issued, earliest known use, number of surviving covers, and more. Fully illustrated. Recommended for any buyer of nineteenth-century U.S. stamps.*

Where in the World? Krause Publications, 700 East State Street, Iola, WI 54990. Web site: www.krause.com. *Comprehensive and useful atlas of stamp-issuing entities since 1840.*

ELECTRONIC MEDIA

AlbumGen. SoftPro 2010, 18 Leverhume Crescent, Toronto, Ontario M1E 1K4, Canada. Web site: www.stamptools.com. *Album page design software with stamp art import capability. SoftPro also manufactures other philatelic software.*

AlbumPro. The Well-Centered Publishing Company, P.O. Box 8459, Greenville, SC 29604. Web site: www.albumpro.com. *Album page design software with clip art and graphics import capability. Highly rated.*

Linn's Guide to Stamp Collecting Software. William F. Sharpe. Linn's Stamp News, P.O. Box 29, Sidney, OH 45365. Web site: www.linns.com. *Rates and evaluates software, includes chapters on hardware, CD-ROMs, stamp inventory programs, album page creation, plus stamp collecting sites on the Internet. Loaded with practical information.*

Scott U.S. Stamp Collector's Database. Scott Publishing Company, P.O. Box 828, Sidney, OH 45365. Web site: www.scottonline.com. *Basically a stamp catalogue CD-ROM with prices and full-color images of U.S. stamps, plus inventory feature and want-list feature.*

StampBase with StampPics. Changing Seasons Software, Ltd., 5881 Roanoke Drive, Madison, WI 53719. Web site: www.stampbase.com. *Database software, stamp inventory system for Windows featuring annual catalogue value updates, includes full-color stamp images and want-list features. Other products are available.*

Stamp Collector's Data Base. SCDB Software, Inc., 8505 River Rock Terrace, Suite B, Bethesda, MD 20817. Web site: www.scbdsoft.com. *Database software inventory system for Windows or DOS, featuring annual catalogue value updates, includes full-color stamp images and want-list features, accommodates yearly updates.*

Stamp Keeper. HobbySoft. Web site: www.compuquote.com. *Database software, stamp inventory system, including catalogue prices. Deluxe version includes U.S. stamp images. Yearly catalogue value updates available.*

StampTRAC. USID, Inc., 6175 N.W. 153rd Street, Suite 201, Miami Lakes, FL 33014. Web site: www.stampfinder.com. *Free downloadable database inventory software.*

PHILATELIC PERIODICALS

THE BEST WAY to stay current with the hobby is a periodical subscription. Philatelic newspapers feature news, calendars of forth coming issues, schedules of stamp shows across the country, and advertisements with current market prices. In addition, dozens of specialized societies publish monthly or quarterly journals. Foremost among them is the *American Philatelist*, the monthly magazine published by the American Philatelic Society. For information on contacting philatelic societies for information about their publications, refer to Chapter 31, "Philatelic Societies and Clubs."

MAGAZINES

American Philatelist. American Philatelic Society, P.O. Box 8000, State College, PA 16803. Web site: www.stamps.org. *Monthly journal of the American Philatelic Society.*

NEWSPAPERS

Global Stamp News. (monthly) Global Stamp News, P.O. Box 97, Sidney, OH 45365. Phone: (937) 492-3183; fax: (937) 492-6514. *Devoted to foreign stamps. This hefty monthly boasting a bargain-priced subscription rate, loads of articles, and lots of ads is a must for beginner, generalist, or advanced collector alike.*

Linn's Stamp News. (weekly) Linn's Stamp News, P.O. Box 29, Sidney, OH 45365. Phone: (937) 498-0801; Web site: www.linns.com. *General newspaper covering all aspects of philately.*

Mekeel's and Stamps Magazine. (weekly) Mekeel's and Stamps, P.O. Box 5050, White Plains, NY 10602. Phone: (800) 635-3351; fax: (914) 997-7261.

Scott Stamp Monthly. Scott Stamp Monthly, P.O. Box 828, Sidney, OH 45365. Phone: (937) 498-0802; fax: (937) 498-0807; Web site: www.scottonline.com. *Highly recommended, packed with excellent articles of interest to collectors of all levels, beginner to advanced.*

Stamp Collector. (every other week) Stamp Collector, 700 East State Street, Iola, WI 54990. Phone: (715) 445-2214; fax: (715) 445-4087; Web site: www.krause.com. *General newspaper covering all aspects of philately.*

RESOURCES

ALBUM, MOUNT, AND SUPPLY MANUFACTURERS

H. E. HARRIS & CO.
P.O. Box 817
Florence, AL 35631
Phone: (800) 528-3992
Fax: (205) 766-7058
Albums, mounts, supplies.

KRAUSE PUBLICATIONS
700 East State Street
Iola, WI 54990
Phone: (715) 445-2214
Fax: (715) 445-4087
Web site: www.krause.com
Albums and supplements.

LIGHTHOUSE PUBLICATIONS, INC.
P.O. Box 705
Hackensack, NJ 07602-0705
Phone: (201) 342-1513
Albums, mounts, supplies.

LINDNER PUBLICATIONS, INC.
P.O. Box 5056
Syracuse, NY 13220
Phone: (315) 437-0463
Fax: (315) 437-4832
Web site: www.lindner-usa.com
Albums, mounts, supplies.

SAFE PUBLICATIONS, INC.
P.O. Box 263
Southampton, PA 18966
Phone: (215) 357-9049
Fax: (215) 357-5202
Web site: www.safepub.com
Albums, mounts, supplies.

SCOTT PUBLISHING COMPANY
P.O. Box 828
Sidney, OH 45365
Phone: (937) 498-0802
Fax: (937) 498-0807
Web site: www.scottonline.com
Albums, mounts, supplies.

VIDIFORMS, INC.
115 North Route 9W
Congers, NY 10920
Phone: (914) 268-4005
Fax: (914) 268-5324
Albums, mounts, supplies.

WASHINGTON PRESS
2 Vreeland Road
Florham Park, NJ 07932
Web site: www.washpress.com
ArtCraft first day covers, White Ace album pages, Stampmounts.

CONSERVATION

ARTHUR SALM FOUNDATION
1029 North Dearborn Street
Chicago, IL 60610
*Nonprofit organization that issues reports
on the quality and durability of philatelic
materials, forgeries, bogus stamp issuing
entities. Include a self-addressed stamped
envelope when making inquiries.*

DEALER ORGANIZATIONS

**AMERICAN PHILATELIC SOCIETY
(APS)**
P.O. Box 8000
State College, PA 16803
Phone: (814) 237-3803
Web site: www.stamps.org
Dealer guide.

**AMERICAN STAMP DEALERS
ASSOCIATION (ASDA)**
3 School Street, Suite 205
Glen Cove, NY 11542-2548

Phone: (516) 759-7000
Fax: (516) 759-7014
Web site: www.amerstampdlrs.com
Dealer guide and dealer referral service.

**NATIONAL STAMP DEALERS
ASSOCIATION (NSDA)**
P.O. Box 7176
Redwood City, CA 94063
Web site: www.nsdainc.org

DIRECTORIES

**WHERE TO BUY IT GUIDE TO THE
STAMP WORLD**
Krause Publications
700 East State Street
Iola, WI 54990
Phone: (715) 445-2214
Fax: (715) 445-4087
Web site: www.krause.com

**YELLOW PAGES FOR STAMP
COLLECTORS**
Linn's Stamp News
P.O. Box 29
Sidney, OH 45365
Phone: (937) 498-0801
Web site: www.linns.com

EXPERTIZING

**AMERICAN PHILATELIC
EXPERTIZING SERVICE (APEX)**
P.O. Box 8000
State College, PA 16803
Phone: (814) 237-3803
Web site: www.stamps.org
*Send for submission forms before
submitting stamps.*

PHILATELIC FOUNDATION
501 Fifth Avenue, Room 1901
New York, NY 10017
Phone: (212) 867-3699
*Send for submission forms before
submitting stamps.*

GIFTING

STAMPS FOR THE WOUNDED
P.O. Box 1125
Falls Church, VA 22041

MUSEUMS

HALL OF STAMPS
United States Postal Service
475 L'Enfant Plaza
Washington, DC 20260

NATIONAL POSTAL MUSEUM
Smithsonian Institution
2 Massachusetts Avenue NE
Washington, DC 20560

SPELLMAN MUSEUM OF STAMPS AND POSTAL HISTORY
235 Wellesley Street
Weston, MA 02493
Phone: (781) 768-8367
Fax: (781) 768-7332
Web site: www.spellman.org

PHILATELIC LIBRARIES

AMERICAN PHILATELIC RESEARCH LIBRARY (APRL)
100 Oakwood Avenue
State College, PA 16803
Phone: (814) 237-3803
Fax: (814) 237-6128
Web site: www.stamps.org
One of the largest collections of philatelic books in the world. Open to the public; borrowing by members only.

BALTIMORE PHILATELIC SOCIETY LIBRARY
1224 North Calvert Street
Baltimore, MD 21202
Phone: (410) 226-8598

CALGARY PHILATELIC SOCIETY LIBRARY
6219 Dalton Drive, NW
Calgary, Alberta T3A 1E1
Canada

THE COLLECTORS CLUB LIBRARY
22 East 35th Street
New York, NY 10016-3806
Phone: (212) 683-0559

Fax: (212) 481-1269
Open to the public; borrowing by members only.

THE POSTAL HISTORY FOUNDATION
920 North First Avenue
P.O. Box 40724
Tucson, AZ 85717
Phone: (520) 623-6652

ROCKY MOUNTAIN PHILATELIC LIBRARY
2038 South Pontiac Way
Denver, CO 80224
Phone: (303) 759-9921

SAN DIEGO COUNTY PHILATELIC LIBRARY
4133 Poplar Street
San Diego, CA 92105

SMITHSONIAN INSTITUTION LIBRARIES
National Postal Museum Branch
Smithsonian Institution
Washington, DC 20560
Phone: (408) 733-0336

SPELLMAN MUSEUM PHILATELIC LIBRARY
235 Wellesley Street
Weston, MA 02493
Phone: (617) 768-8367
Fax: (781) 768-7332
Web site: www.spellman.org

VINCENT GRAVES GREENE PHILATELIC RESEARCH LIBRARY
First Canadian Place, Box 100
Toronto, Ontario M5X 1S2
Canada

WESTERN PHILATELIC LIBRARY
Room 6, Building 6
1500 Partridge Avenue
Sunnyvale, CA 94087
Phone: (408) 733-0336

WINEBURGH PHILATELIC RESEARCH LIBRARY
University of Texas at Dallas
P.O. Box 830643
Richardson, TX 75083-0643
Phone: (214) 883-2570
Fax: (214) 883-2473

PHILATELIC LITERATURE DEALERS

PHILIP T. BANSNER, INC.
P.O. Box 2529
West Lawn, PA 19609
Phone: (610) 678-5000
Fax: (610) 678-5400
Web site: www.philbansner.com
Inventory of 5,000 new and out-of-print titles.

REQUESTS TO ISSUE A STAMP

CITIZENS' STAMP ADVISORY COMMITTEE
c/o Stamp Development, U.S. Postal
   Service
475 L'Enfant Plaza, SW, Room 5670
Washington, D.C. 20260-2437
Requests must be in writing.

STAMP INSURANCE

AMERICAN PHILATELIC SOCIETY
Insurance Advisor
P.O. Box 8000
State College, PA 16803
Phone: (814) 237-3803
Fax: (814) 237-6128

COLLECTIBLES INSURANCE AGENCY
P.O. Box 1200
Westminster, MD 21158
Phone: (888) 837-9537
Fax: (410) 876-9233
Web site: www.collectinsure.com

STANDARD TWO-LETTER ABBREVIATIONS FOR STATES AND POSSESSIONS

STATES AND POSSESSIONS

AK	Alaska	MS	Mississippi
AL	Alabama	MT	Montana
AR	Arkansas	NC	North Carolina
AS	American Samoa	ND	North Dakota
AZ	Arizona	NE	Nebraska
CA	California	NH	New Hampshire
CO	Colorado	NJ	New Jersey
CT	Connecticut	NM	New Mexico
DC	District of Columbia	NV	Nevada
DE	Delaware	NY	New York
FL	Florida	OH	Ohio
FM	Federated States of Micronesia	OK	Oklahoma
GA	Georgia	OR	Oregon
GU	Guam	PA	Pennsylvania
HI	Hawaii	PR	Puerto Rico
IA	Iowa	PW	Palau
ID	Idaho	RI	Rhode Island
IL	Illinois	SC	South Carolina
IN	Indiana	SD	South Dakota
KS	Kansas	TN	Tennessee
KY	Kentucky	TX	Texas
LA	Louisiana	UT	Utah
MA	Massachusetts	VA	Virginia
MD	Maryland	VI	Virgin Islands
ME	Maine	VT	Vermont
MH	Marshall Islands	WA	Washington
MI	Michigan	WI	Wisconsin
MN	Minnesota	WV	West Virginia
MO	Missouri	WY	Wyoming
MP	Northern Mariana Islands		

ARMED FORCES

AA   Armed Forces America (except Canada)
AE   Armed Forces Europe, Middle East, Africa, and Canada
AP   Armed Forces Pacific

STANDARD INTERNATIONAL URL SUFFIXES

UNIFORM RESOURCE LOCATOR (URL) SUFFIXES FOR COUNTRIES OF THE WORLD

.ac	Ascension Island	.br	Brazil
.ad	Andorra	.bs	Bahamas
.ae	United Arab Emirates	.bt	Bhutan
.af	Afghanistan	.bv	Bouvet Island
.ag	Antigua and Barbuda	.bw	Botswana
.ai	Anguilla	.by	Belarus
.al	Albania	.bz	Belize
.am	Armenia	.ca	Canada
.an	Netherlands Antilles	.cc	Cocos (Keeling) Islands
.ao	Angola	.cf	Central African Republic
.aq	Antarctica	.cg	Congo
.ar	Argentina	.ch	Switzerland
.as	American Samoa	.ci	Ivory Coast (Côte d'Ivoire)
.at	Austria	.ck	Cook Islands
.au	Australia	.cl	Chile
.aw	Aruba	.cm	Cameroon
.az	Azerbaijan	.cn	China
.ba	Bosnia and Herzegovina	.co	Colombia
.bb	Barbados	.cr	Costa Rica
.bd	Bangladesh	.cs	Czechoslovakia (prior to division into Czech Republic and Slovakia)
.be	Belgium		
.bf	Burkina Faso		
.bg	Bulgaria	.cu	Cuba
.bh	Bahrain	.cv	Cape Verde
.bi	Burundi	.cx	Christmas Island
.bj	Benin	.cy	Cyprus
.bm	Bermuda	.cz	Czech Republic
.bn	Brunei Darussalam	.de	Germany
.bo	Bolivia	.dj	Djibouti

.dk	Denmark	.iq	Iraq
.dm	Dominica	.ir	Iran
.do	Dominican Republic	.is	Iceland
.dz	Algeria	.it	Italy
.ec	Ecuador	.jm	Jamaica
.ee	Estonia	.jo	Jordan
.eg	Egypt	.jp	Japan
.eh	Western Sahara	.ke	Kenya
.er	Eritrea	.kg	Kyrgyzstan
.es	Spain	.kh	Cambodia
.et	Ethiopia	.ki	Kiribati
.fi	Finland	.km	Comoros
.fj	Fiji	.kn	Saint Kitts and Nevis
.fk	Falkland Islands	.kp	North Korea
.fm	Micronesia	.kr	South Korea
.fo	Faroe Islands	.kw	Kuwait
.fr	France	.ky	Cayman Islands
.fx	France (metropolitan)	.kz	Kazakstan
.ga	Gabon	.la	Laos
.gb	Great Britain (United Kingdom)	.lb	Lebanon
.gd	Grenada	.lc	Saint Lucia
.ge	Georgia	.li	Liechtenstein
.gf	French Guiana	.lk	Sri Lanka
.gh	Ghana	.lr	Liberia
.gi	Gibraltar	.ls	Lesotho
.gl	Greenland	.lt	Lithuania
.gm	Gambia	.lu	Luxembourg
.gn	Guinea	.lv	Latvia
.gp	Guadeloupe	.ly	Libya
.gq	Equatorial Guinea	.ma	Morocco
.gr	Greece	.mc	Monaco
.gs	South Georgia and South Sandwich Islands	.md	Moldova
		.mg	Madagascar
.gt	Guatemala	.mh	Marshall Islands
.gu	Guam	.mk	Macedonia
.gw	Guinea-Bissau	.ml	Mali
.gy	Guyana	.mm	Myanmar
.hk	Hong Kong	.mn	Mongolia
.hm	Heard and McDonald Islands	.mo	Macau
.hn	Honduras	.mp	Northern Mariana Islands
.hr	Croatia	.mq	Martinique
.ht	Haiti	.mr	Mauritania
.hu	Hungary	.ms	Montserrat
.id	Indonesia	.mt	Malta
.ie	Ireland	.mu	Mauritius
.il	Israel	.mv	Maldives
.in	India	.mw	Malawi
.io	British Indian Ocean Territory	.mx	Mexico

.my	Malaysia	.sr	Suriname
.mz	Mozambique	.st	São Tomé and Príncipe (Saint Thomas and Prince Islands)
.na	Namibia		
.nc	New Caledonia	.su	Soviet Union (former U.S.S.R.)
.ne	Niger	.sv	El Salvador
.nf	Norfolk Island	.sy	Syria
.ng	Nigeria	.sz	Swaziland
.ni	Nicaragua	.tc	Turks and Caicos Islands
.nl	Netherlands	.td	Chad
.no	Norway	.tf	French Southern Territories
.np	Nepal	.tg	Togo
.nr	Nauru	.th	Thailand
.nt	Neutral Zone	.tj	Tajikistan
.nu	Niue	.tk	Tokelau
.nz	New Zealand	.tm	Turkmenistan
.om	Oman	.tn	Tunisia
.pa	Panama	.to	Tonga
.pe	Peru	.tp	East Timor
.pf	French Polynesia	.tr	Turkey
.pg	Papua New Guinea	.tt	Trinidad and Tobago
.ph	Philippines	.tv	Tuvalu
.pk	Pakistan	.tw	Taiwan
.pl	Poland	.tz	Tanzania
.pm	Saint-Pierre and Miquelon	.ua	Ukraine
.pn	Pitcairn	.ug	Uganda
.pr	Puerto Rico	.uk	United Kingdom
.pt	Portugal	.um	U.S. Minor Outlying Islands
.pw	Palau	.us	United States of America
.py	Paraguay	.uy	Uruguay
.qa	Qatar	.uz	Uzbekistan
.re	Reunion	.va	Vatican City
.ro	Romania	.vc	Saint Vincent and the Grenadines
.ru	Russia (Russian Federation)	.ve	Venezuela
.rw	Rwanda	.vg	Virgin Islands (British)
.sa	Saudi Arabia	.vi	Virgin Islands (U.S.)
.sb	Solomon Islands	.vn	Vietnam
.sc	Seychelles	.vu	Vanuatu
.sd	Sudan	.wf	Wallis and Futina Islands
.se	Sweden	.ws	Samoa
.sg	Singapore	.ye	Yemen
.sh	Saint Helena	.yt	Mayotte
.si	Slovenia	.yu	Yugoslavia
.sj	Svalbard and Jan Mayen Islands	.za	South Africa
.sk	Slovakia	.zm	Zambia
.sl	Sierra Leone	.zr	Zaire (now the Democratic Republic of the Congo)
.sm	San Marino		
.sn	Senegal	.zw	Zimbabwe
.so	Somalia		

OTHER SUFFIXES

.arpa	Advanced Research Projects Agency
.com	U.S. commercial
.edu	U.S. education
.gov	U.S. government
.int	international
.mil	U.S. military
.nato	NATO
.net	network
.org	U.S. organization

RECENT OR CONTEMPLATED ADDITIONS

.aero	services and companies dealing with air travel
.biz	businesses and corporations
.coop	cooperative organizations
.info	information-based services such as newspapers, libraries, etc.
.museum	museums, archival institutions, and exhibitions
.name	individuals' and personal Web sites
.pro	professions such as law, medicine, accounting, etc.

INDEX

A

Abbreviations used on foreign stamps, 365–399
Abrasives, 65
Accessories, 40–44
Acid-free paper, 41, 66, 67
Acidity in paper, 67
A (or Combination) press, 169
Add-ons, 28
Addressed covers, 29
Agencies, worldwide list of, 467–482
Agents, auction, 135–136
Airbills, 10
Airborne Co., 10
Airmail, first routes, 10–11
Albinos, 112–113
Albums, 40–41
  at auction, 131–132
  for covers, 41
  pages in, 40–41
  resources list, 515
  storage of, 63
  used albums, 40
Album weeds, 75
Altered cancels, 77
American Bank Note Company, 157, 158
American First Day Cover Society, 30
  expertizing services, 97–98
American Philatelic Expertizing Service (APEX), 50, 97
American Philatelic Research Library (APRL), 50

American Philatelic Society (APS), 50
  mail-order dealers in, 48
  The Serrane Guide, 73–74
American Philatelist, 44, 50
American Stamp Dealers Association (ASDA), 48
American Topical Association (ATA), 21
Ancillary markings, 78
Andreotti press, 168–169
Animal stamps, 13
Appendages, 117
Approvals, 48
A-press cylinders, 169
Arabic inscriptions, 208–210
Archival paper, 67
Archival plastics, 70
Archival tapes, 65–66
Armed forces abbreviations, 520
Armed services. *See* Military service
Armenian inscriptions, 210
Arthur Salm Foundation, 78
Asian inscriptions, 210–211
Aspect ratio, 183
Astronaut on a Space Walk stamp, 13
Auction agents, 135–136
Auctions, 127–150. *See also* Internet auctions
  absentee bids, 127
  bidding increments, 127
  buyer's premiums, 128
  buying at, 129–136
  cash advances to sellers, 137
  commissions from, 137

Great Britain. *See also* London
  albums for, 40
  British Commonwealth stamps,
    watermarking, 38
  Charles II, England, 5
  Hill, Sir Rowland, proposals of,
    6–8
  Penny Post, 5–6
  stamp identifiers for, 203
  Victoria, Queen, 8
Greek inscriptions, 204–205
Green cancels, 77
Grill errors, 110
Guarantees from investment firms, 98
Gum. *See also* Disturbed gum;
    Regumming
  both sides, gumming on, 112
  condition of, 55–58
  hinges and, 41
  on nineteenth century stamps, 56
  skips, 57
  symbols as to, 57
Gum-breaker ridges, 84
Gutter errors, 109–110
Gutter pairs, 109
Gutters, 109
Gutter snipes, 109

H

Hand-colored cachets, 28
Handling stamps, 65
Hand-painted first day covers (FDCs),
    27–28
Handstamping mail, 5
Harlequin Duck stamp, 13
Heat, exposure to, 64
Heavily hinged (HH) stamps, 56
Herodotus, 3
Hieroglyphs, 2
Hill, Sir Rowland, 6–8, 189
Himalayan Peaks and Glacier stamp, 14
Hindenburg, 11
Hinges, 41. *See also* Thins
  condition of, 55–58
  never-hinged stamps, 65
  peelable hinges, 55

  remnants, 56
  watermark detectors and, 38
Hitler, Adolf stamp, 15
Holy Roman Empire, 4
Horizontal perforations, gauge of, 36
House of Thurn and Taxis, 4
Huck press, 167
Humidity, exposure to, 63–64
Hungary, stamp identifiers for, 203

I

Identifying foreign stamps
  illustrated stamp identifier, 201–213
  list of countries, 215–359
Illegal stamps, 74
Illustrated stamp identifier, 201–213
Imperforate errors, 105–106
  fake imperforates, 76, 124
Imperforate margins, 114–115
Inclusions, 60, 92–93
Indian inscriptions, 210
India paper, proofs on, 95
Ink
  color-omitted errors and, 105
  irregularities, 119
  thins and, 87
  underinked stamps, 116
Inscriptions
  identifying, 216
  illustrated stamp identifier, 201–213
Insects
  damage to stamps, 65
  as inclusions, 93
Insurance, 70–71
  APS plan, 50
  on auction consignments, 140
  mail, insured, 186
  resources for, 518
Intaglio printing, 160–162
  A (or Combination) press, 169
  albinos, 112–113
  B press, 169–170
  color errors, 108
  color-omitted errors, 106–107
  Cottrell press, 166–167
  C press, 170

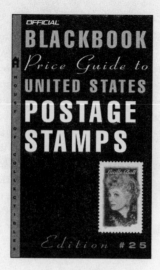

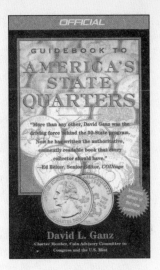

0-609-80770-6

AMERICA'S HOTTEST COLLECTING CRAZE

The Official® Guidebook to America's State Quarters shows you why collecting coins has never been more fun. This invaluable source is a must-read for anyone collecting state quarters.

- Detailed information for all the state quarters
- How to identify mint errors and value your collection
- Learn the design process and how to be a part of it in future issues
- Find out when your state's coin will be released
- Fully illustrated
- And much more!

BUY IT • USE IT • BECOME AN EXPERT™

**HOUSE OF
COLLECTIBLES**

www.houseofcollectibles.com

Available at bookstores everywhere!

ＯＵSE OF COLLECTIBLES SERIES

THE OFFICIAL PRICE GUIDES TO

	ISBN	Price	Author
...d.	0676601790	$21.95	Stuart Wells & Main Toys
..., 3rd ed.	0876375131	$12.00	Roy Erhardt
... & Collectibles, 18th ed.	0676601855	$16.00	Rinker Enterprises
...atles Records & Memorabilia, 2nd ed.	0676601812	$18.95	Perry Cox
Bottles, 13th ed.	0676601847	$17.95	Jim Megura
Civil War Collectibles, 2nd ed.	067660160X	$17.95	Richard Friz
Collecting Books	0609807692	$18.00	Marie Tedford & Pat Goudey
Collector Knives, 13th ed.	0676601898	$17.95	C. Houston Price
Collector Plates, 7th ed.	0676601545	$19.95	Rinker Enterprises
Costume Jewelry, 3rd ed.	0609806688	$17.95	Harrice Simmons Miller
Dinnerware of the 20th Century	0676600859	$29.95	Harry L. Rinker
Elvis Presley Records & Memorabilia, 2nd ed.	0676601413	$17.00	Jerry Osborne
Glassware, 3rd ed.	067660188X	$17.00	Mark Pickvet
Hake's Character Toys, 4th ed.	0609808222	$35.00	Ted Hake
Hislop's International Fine Art	0609808745	$20.00	Duncan Hislop
Military Collectibles, 6th ed.	0676600522	$20.00	Richard Austin
Mint Errors, 6th ed.	0609808559	$15.00	Alan Herbert
Overstreet Comic Books, 32nd ed.	0609808214	$22.00	Robert M. Overstreet
Overstreet Indian Arrowheads, 7th ed.	0609808699	$24.00	Robert M. Overstreet
Pottery & Porcelain, 8th ed.	0876378939	$18.00	Harvey Duke
Records 2001	0676601871	$25.95	Jerry Osborne
Rinker Collectibles, 4th ed.	0676601596	$19.95	Harry L. Rinker
R. L. Wilson Gun Collecting, 3rd ed.	0676601537	$24.95	R. L. Wilson
Silverware of the 20th Century	0676600867	$24.95	Harry L. Rinker
Star Wars Collectibles, 4th ed.	0876379951	$19.95	Sue Cornwell & Mike Kott
Stemware of the 20th Century	0676600840	$24.95	Harry L. Rinker

THE OFFICIAL GUIDES TO

Title	ISBN	Price	Author
America's State Quarters	0609807706	$5.99	David L. Ganz
Flea Market Prices	0609807722	$14.95	Harry L. Rinker
How to Make Money in Coins Right Now, 2nd ed.	0609807463	$14.95	Scott Travers
Official Directory to U.S. Flea Markets, 8th ed.	0609809229	$14.00	Kitty Werner
One-Minute Coin Expert, 4th ed.	0609807471	$7.99	Scott Travers

THE OFFICIAL BECKETT SPORTS CARDS PRICE GUIDES TO

Title	ISBN	Price	Author
Baseball Cards 2002-2003, 22nd ed.	0609809024	$7.99	Dr. James Beckett
Basketball Cards 2001, 10th ed.	0676601936	$6.99	Dr. James Beckett
Football Cards 2002, 21st ed.	0609808435	$7.99	Dr. James Beckett

THE OFFICIAL BLACKBOOK PRICE GUIDES TO

Title	ISBN	Price	Author
U.S. Coins 2003, 41st ed.	067660174X	$7.99	Marc & Tom Hudgeons
U.S. Paper Money 2003, 35th ed.	0609809482	$6.99	Marc & Tom Hudgeons
U.S. Postage Stamps 2003, 25th ed.	0609809490	$8.99	Marc & Tom Hudgeons
World Coins 2003, 6th ed.	0676601774	$7.99	Marc & Tom Hudgeons